Depth

# Depth

*An Account of Scientific Explanation*

Michael Strevens

Harvard University Press

Cambridge, Massachusetts

London, England

First Harvard University Press paperback edition, 2011

*Library of Congress Cataloging-in-Publication Data*
Strevens, Michael.
Depth : an account of scientific explanation / Michael Strevens.
p. cm.
Includes bibliographical references and index.
ISBN 978-0-674-03183-8 (cloth : alk. paper)
ISBN 978-0-674-06257-3 (pbk.)
1. Causation.   2. Explanation.   3. Science–Philosophy.   I. Title.
BD541.S77 2008
122—dc22
2008019211

*To my parents*

# Contents

## Part I.  The Causal Approach to Explanation

## Part II.  The Kairetic Account of Explanation

## Part IV.   Probabilistic Explanation

## Part V.  Valediction

# Figures and Table

## *Figures*

## Table

# Preface

*Depth* advances a theory of explanation, the kairetic account, on which explanatory relevance is primarily a matter of causal relevance. It is centered around a conception of causal difference-making (originally presented in Strevens (2004) and further developed in chapter three) that allows properties that are extremely abstract to be causally, and thus explanatorily, relevant to the phenomena that science seeks to explain. To this end, I formulate a recipe that extracts from any detailed description of a causal process a higher level, abstract description that specifies only difference-making properties of the process. The resulting causal-explanatory abstraction is, I contend, responsible for a number of striking features of our explanatory practice: the appearance of absences or omissions in causal explanation, the possibility of causal equilibrium explanations that are silent about the particular causal pathway taken to the event to be explained, the explanatory value of robustness, the utility of idealization in explanation, the importance of probabilistic explanation in deterministic systems, and more.

In later chapters, I introduce a noncausal variety of explanatory relevance that has at its core the notion of *entanglement*, a kind of local modal dependence between properties (section 7.3). A property becomes relevant to an explanandum in this second way not by being entangled with the explanandum but by having its instances entangled with instances of another property that plays a part in causing the explanandum. The explanatory relevance that issues from entanglement is, compared to causal relevance, subsidiary; yet it too helps to make sense of a range of features of scientific explanatory practice, such as the relevance constraints on properties that explain (and feature in) many high-level laws, and the nature of covering-law explanation. It also supplies missing parts of the answers to the above questions about equilibrium explanation, robustness, and the probabilistic explanation of deterministically produced events.

A property may figure in an explanation, then, by bearing either of the two kinds of explanatory relevance relations—the causal and the entanglement relations—to other relevant properties. There is in addition a third rationale for a property's appearance in an explanatory model, a rationale that does not require the property to be explanatorily relevant at all, indeed, one that neutralizes any relevance it has: the property may belong to, or it may be a placeholder for something that belongs to, the *explanatory framework*, a construct similar to Mackie's causal field (section 5.3). As entanglement is less important to scientific explanation than causal relevance, so the explanatory framework is much less important still. But it has a role to play, especially in understanding, first, the practical side of the organization of explanatory inquiry in science (section 5.4) and second, causal-explanatory claims in everyday discourse (of which I claim all causal claims of the form *c was a cause of e* are instances; see chapter six). The three criteria for entrance to explanatory models may be seen at work side by side in section 12.2.

No particular view of the metaphysics of causation is assumed in *Depth*. I do, however, make certain assumptions as to how the correct metaphysics will turn out. In particular, I claim that the raw metaphysical material from which the relation of causal-explanatory relevance is to be fashioned can be found entirely in the causal structure uncovered by fundamental physics. It is not especially controversial, outside perhaps of certain corners of the philosophy of physics, to hold that the right kind of causal material is to be found in physics—many, perhaps all, well-known accounts of the metaphysics of causation imply as much (section 1.4). It is far more controversial to claim that this physical-level causal influence will suffice for the purposes of causal explanation in biology, psychology, economics, and so on. In advancing this thesis, I do not assert that biological phenomena can be explained in the same way as physical phenomena. I assert only that the raw causal ingredient is the same in biology as in physics; when prepared according to the recipe provided here, explanations of different kinds of phenomena and at different levels may take quite different forms. My position does, nevertheless, commit me to a certain species of explanatory reductionism or physicalism: everything that can be explained, I hold, can be explained in terms that are reducible to physical terms.

That said, I accept the modern view that many terms put to explanatory use in the higher-level sciences cannot be translated into physical language; my position is that other, physically reducible terms are capable of reproducing their explanatory functions. The nonphysical properties, though convenient, are therefore explanatorily dispensable (section 12.4).

*Depth* does not discuss every major topic in the philosophy of explanation; I have in particular avoided, or treated only very briefly, issues for which the kairetic account has no especially novel consequences. Some of the omissions: there is no discussion of functional explanation in biology and the social sciences, that is, explanation in which the presence of a trait or practice is explained by the (typically beneficial) role that it plays in the system to which it belongs; I have nothing to say about how-possibly explanation; there is no treatment of the interesting, although recently virtually abandoned, question of explanation in history; I have not mentioned work, some of it my own, on the explanatory role of representations outside of belief/desire psychology, for example in developmental biology and cognitive ethology.

Further, there are a number of problems in explanation proper to the higher-level sciences—biology, psychology, sociology and anthropology, economics—that I would have liked to have discussed further, if my hard drive were not already sagging under the weight of the manuscript. You will find hints here and there as to how I would proceed, as well as a short chapter in which some initial moves are sketched (chapter twelve).

Chapter one of *Depth* lays some ground rules and selectively surveys approaches to understanding explanation. A minimalist causal account is constructed. Chapter two critiques this minimalism and launches the project of augmenting minimalism with a criterion for causal difference-making; various such criteria are considered and rejected.

Chapter three presents the kairetic criterion for difference-making. In chapter four, I show how to assemble from various facts about difference-making what I call a standalone explanation; for any given event, there are many such explanations, each taking up the causal story at a different point. All standalone explanations for an event are in their own way self-contained, but some are better than others; the respects in which standalone explanations can be ranked are discussed. The kairetic account of explanation is then extended in various ways in chapter five: among other things, I define a measure of explanatory weight, I give accounts of contrastive and what I call aggregative explanation, I introduce the notion of an explanatory framework, and I interpret explanation that makes use of "black boxes." Chapter six examines some particular problems concerning event explanation, such as cases of "preemption," familiar more from the literature on causation than the literature on explanation, and pursues a kairetic understanding of each.

In chapter seven, I turn to the question of the explanation of laws and other regularities. I approve of the general approach taken to such explanations in the literature on causal explanation, but I suggest that much more should be said about the explanatory role of basing generalizations, that is, statements of the matters of physically contingent fact—as opposed to the fundamental laws—on which so many scientifically important generalizations depend. One consequence is a sketch of a metaphysics of high-level deterministic laws, to be extended in chapter ten to the statistical case. Chapter eight focuses on the question of the explanatory value of idealization and other abstracting techniques in regularity explanation.

Chapters nine, ten, and eleven together provide an account of probabilistic explanation, principally in deterministic systems. Chapter nine surveys the major issues. Chapter ten tackles the question of the explanation of frequencies and other statistics, both by probabilities proper and by qualitative analogs that I call quasiprobabilities (as when an event is explained by pointing to the fact that it was "very likely"). Chapter eleven turns to the explanation of single outcomes.

Two short concluding chapters examine, first, the kairetic account's application to several topics in the higher-level sciences, and second, the role of the aesthetic sense in explanation.

I have tried to give *Depth* as modular a structure as possible. Let me briefly mention some of the principal interdependencies. Everything depends on the account of difference-making presented in chapter three. The account of probabilistic explanation depends also on the notion of a basing generalization developed in chapter seven; it relies much less heavily on the material in chapters four and five. The account of explanatory idealization, although focused on the explanation of regularities and laws, calls upon just the preliminary discussion of such explanation in sections 7.1 and 7.2 and of course on chapter three's criterion for difference-making. The discussion of preemption in chapter six also depends principally on chapter three only; the treatments of causal absences and transitivity, however, make considerable use of chapter five.

I thank the many philosophers who have helped me with this project, including among others: Brian Weatherson for examples from economics (including the suvs in section 5.4) and a great number of helpful comments, in particular concerning my treatment of the role of black boxes and functional kinds and properties in explanation; Ned Hall for his many perceptive comments on parts one and two; André Ariew for making me think harder about biological explanation, especially aggregative explanation invoking fitness (exemplified in section 5.5); Michael Friedman for pinpointing the weakness of an earlier attempt to understand probabilistic explanation in deterministic systems; J. D. Trout for pressing me to say more about reductionism; Jason Stanley for insisting that I clarify my views about the nature of the explanatory relation germane to explanation within a framework (sections 5.3 and 6.1); and all those colleagues, students, and friends who gave me comments on and asked questions about earlier versions of this work presented on paper and in talks.

Special thanks to Joy Connolly for her love and support.

Depth

# — I —

## The Causal Approach to Explanation

# — 1 —

# Approaches to Explanation

## 1.1 Causal Explanation and Explanatory Relevance

If science provides anything of intrinsic value, it is explanation. Prediction and control are useful, and success in any endeavor is gratifying, but when science is pursued as an end rather than as a means, it is for the sake of understanding—the moment when a small, temporary being reaches out to touch the universe and makes contact.

But what kind of contact? That is the problem of scientific explanation—or, equivalently, of scientific understanding, as I take scientific understanding to be that state produced, and only produced, by grasping a true explanation.

This book offers an account of explanation in the causal tradition. Explaining a phenomenon is, according to this tradition, a matter of understanding how the phenomenon was or is causally produced.

Rival causal accounts of scientific explanation differ on two questions. First is the essentially metaphysical question concerning the nature of the causal relation that provides the basis for explanation, that is, the question of what constitutes the raw causal material from which an explanation should be fashioned. Second is the question of what material to use for any particular explanatory task, that is, the question of how, given a phenomenon to explain and the causal network in which that phenomenon is embedded, to extract from the network the particular causal facts that are relevant to understanding the phenomenon.

In this characterization I have committed controversy already: among proponents of the causal approach to explanation, there is almost complete consensus that the second question is otiose; no selection principle—no additional criterion for explanatory relevance—is needed. Once the explanatory causal relation is identified, anything that bears that relation to the phenomenon to be explained is a part of the explanation. Every cause is explanatorily relevant. The result is a *one-factor*, as opposed to a *two-factor*, causal account of explanation.

To take the one-factor approach is, I believe, an error. It is an error that has gone to a great degree unnoticed, because it is possible to build a good part of the correct criterion for explanatory relevance into the notion of causation, producing a selective conception of what it is for one thing to be a cause of another that avoids the most straightforward embarrassments of the one-factor approach (chapter two tells the story).

What is lost, then, by building the complete criterion for explanatory relevance into the causal relation? Three things.

First, there are certain aspects of explanatory relevance that simply cannot be conceived of as part of the metaphysics of causation. For example, in part four I will argue that in some cases, the relevance criterion will choose from a deterministic causal basis so selectively that the best possible explanation of a deterministically produced phenomenon is given by a probabilistic model. Thus explanation in a deterministic world can be, and sometimes must be, indeterministic. But it is too much to accept that causation itself can be indeterministic in a deterministic world.

By restricting their attention to those parts of the relevance criterion that can be plausibly incorporated into a metaphysics of causation, proponents of the causal approach to explanation have missed the opportunity to give fruitful (or for the most part, any) theories of probabilistic explanation in deterministic systems and of other important explanatory phenomena, such as the pervasive use of idealized models in explanation (see chapter eight).

Second, folding the criterion for explanatory relevance into the metaphysics of causation renders the metaphysics answerable, in ways that it should not be, to explanatory concerns. As a result, debates that ought properly to concern explanatory practice in science are cast instead as debates about the nature of causation. The question of whether omissions can be causes, and if so, which omissions are causes, provides a good example (section 6.3).

The issue is further clouded by the widespread equation of the investigation of the metaphysics of causation with the investigation of the truth conditions for claims of the form *c was a cause of e*. I will later argue that such claims do not assert the existence of a raw metaphysical causal relation between two events $c$ and $e$; rather, they are causal-explanatory claims that assert that $c$ is a part of the causal explanation of $e$ (chapter six).

Third, the criterion for explanatory relevance—certainly, the relevance criterion developed in this book—looks to be applicable not only to causal explanation, but to other kinds of explanation as well, such as mathematical, moral, and aesthetic explanation (and possibly also noncausal explanation in science, if there is such a thing). I will tentatively propose that the complete philosophical theory of explanation is modular: it consists of two components, a criterion for explanatory relevance that is the same in every kind of explanation, and a domain-specific dependence relation. The relevance criterion selects from the given domain of dependence relations those that must be appreciated in order to understand the phenomenon to be explained. When the domain of dependence is causal, the result is a causal explanation. When it is mathematical, the result is a mathematical explanation. And so on. Although this book focuses solely on causal explanation, the existence of explanatory modularity is, I think, an important insight (section 5.7)—an insight that would be entirely obscured were a one-factor schema to be imposed on causal explanation.

The modular structure of our explanatory practice will, I might add, allow the development of a criterion for explanatory relevance that addresses many of the major problems about scientific explanation while assuming as little as possible about the metaphysics of causation. "As little as possible" is still something, but my project is predicated on the bet that it is the nature of explanatory relevance rather than the nature of causation itself that holds the key to the broad range of questions that I ask.

At the core of everything that follows, then, is a criterion for explanatory relevance. I call it the *kairetic criterion*; it is developed in chapters three, four, and five.[1] When the kairetic criterion is conjoined with a causal approach to scientific explanation—so that explanation in science is understood as a matter of finding, by way of the kairetic criterion, which of the causal influences on a phenomenon are relevant to its occurrence—you have what I call the kairetic account of scientific explanation. The kairetic criterion shares with other explanatory relevance criteria found in the literature the idea that the aspects of a causal process that are explanatorily relevant to a phenomenon are those aspects that *make a difference* to whether or not the phenomenon occurs. However, the account of difference-making that I propose is quite different from other well-known accounts such as the counterfactual and the probabilistic relevance accounts.

The remaining chapters apply the kairetic account to various kinds of explanation: chapter six to problems arising in the explanation of events, the chapters in part three to the explanation of laws and other regularities, and the chapters in part four to probabilistic explanation. Among the topics covered are the nature of causal claims of the form *c was a cause of e* (chapter six), the motivation for idealization in explanation (chapter eight), and the advantages of using probabilistic explanation to account for deterministically produced events (chapters ten and eleven). In this introductory chapter, I characterize the causal approach to explanation and contrast it with its rivals.

## 1.2   Preliminaries

### *1.21   Two Senses of Explanation*

Philosophers sometimes talk as if an explanation were something out in the world, a set of facts to be discovered, and sometimes as if it were a communicative act. In the first sense, explanations are or should be a part of the stock of scientific knowledge; in the second, they are a means of communicating scientific knowledge (Bromberger 1965).

Either sense may be given precedence. When the first is declared the more fundamental, explanation as a communicative act is understood as an attempt to convey some part of the stock of known explanatory facts. When the second sense is taken as fundamental, a fact counts as explanatory just in case it provides a suitable basis for the communicative act.

I follow the lead of most philosophers of explanation, and of most proponents of the causal approach in particular, in giving the first, ontological sense of explanation precedence. What explains a given phenomenon is a set of causal facts. It is an aim of science to discover these sets of facts, these explanations. The communicative acts that we call explanations are attempts to convey some part of this explanatory causal information (but not just any part; see section 4.1).

The communication of explanatory facts is subject to the same pragmatics as any act of communication (Hempel 1965a, §5.1; Lewis 1986a, §5). Violation of these communicative rules results in something that is rightly called a bad explanation, provided that *explanation* is understood in the second, communicative sense. It would be a mistake, however, to think that this kind of explanatory goodness and badness provides systematic clues about the nature of explanation itself, if *explanation* is understood in the first, ontological sense.

It does not follow that the pragmatics of communication are irrelevant to my inquiry: to discern the nature of explanation in the ontological sense, you must acquire the ability to see past the communicative conventions and strategies of scientists to the explanatory facts themselves. A philosopher of explanation will therefore occasionally discuss communicative conventions, just as an astronomer might study atmospheric distortion so as to more clearly see the stars.

From this point forward, I use *explanation* exclusively in the first, ontological sense. Most of the theories of explanation to be considered in this chapter clearly understand *explanation* in the same way. Less clear is whether Hempel's is account of probabilistic explanation and van Fraassen's "pragmatic" account are pursuing the ontological notion of explanation. Both accounts imply, for different reasons, that the explanatory facts depend in part on the conversational context, broadly construed. This provides some evidence that they give precedence to the second sense of explanation.

Peter Achinstein, by contrast, quite explicitly gives precedence to the second sense (Achinstein 1983, 4); he consequently contends that his account of explanation is, unlike van Fraassen's and Hempel's, genuinely "pragmatic" (Achinstein 1985).

An approach to explanation, such as Achinstein's, that is closely allied to the project of understanding explanatory communication, sees a theory of explanation as essentially an account of what constitutes an adequate answer to certain kinds of questions, principally *why*-questions, that is, questions of the form "Why is the sky blue?" and "Why does science care so much about priority in discovery?"[2] Because of my ontology-first approach to explanation, I will have little to say about *why* and other questions, but as far as I can see, the kairetic account is as suitable a basis as any for constructing a theory of explanatory answers to such inquiries.

### 1.22  The Objects of Explanation

What can be explained? Just about anything. The objects of explanation can be usefully divided, however, into two classes. In one class are singular events, such as a light's being switched on in a particular room at a particular time, and singular states of affairs, such as a light's being on in a particular room at a particular time. For my purposes, there is no need to distinguish between the two; I will call them both *events*.

As Hempel (1965b, 421–423) argued long ago, the kinds of events that are typically explained are not *concrete events*—events individuated by all the details of their happening, by all of their intrinsic properties—but what might be called *high-level events*. When you explain why Vesuvius erupted in 79 C.E., to use Hempel's example, you are not attempting to explain why it erupted in exactly the way it did, down to the trajectory of the last particle of ash; you are attempting to explain only why it erupted, as opposed to not erupting, around the given time. You are, in other words, attempting to explain what might variously be called a fact, a state of affairs, or as I have suggested, a high-level event. (For further discussion, see sections 2.22 and 3.3, and Bennett (1988).)

The other class of objects suitable for explanation consists of things that are, each in their own way, robust generalizations. They include:

1. Laws, such as Kepler's laws,

2. Theories, such as classical thermodynamics,

3. Dispositional properties, such as the magnetic properties of iron,

4. Ongoing phenomena, such as the aurora borealis, and

5. "Effects," such as the Hall effect.

These categories overlap considerably, of course, for which reason most writers on explanation group them together, as I will. For convenience, I call this the category of *laws*, hoping that the virtues of verbal economy will outweigh the vice of minor terminological abuse.

There are, then, two kinds of things that can be explained: events and laws—at least according to my rather coarse-grained and surely not entirely exhaustive classification. Explanations of the first kind of thing I call *event explanations*, explanations of the second, *regularity explanations*. (In classing explanations of laws as a kind of "regularity explanation," I do not mean to imply that laws are a kind of regularity—again, convenience trumps conceptual accuracy.)

Although event explanation and regularity explanation differ in various respects, it is useful to have a general term that encompasses all possible objects of explanation. I will use *phenomenon*. Another useful term, found everywhere in the literature, is *explanandum*, meaning simply the thing that is being explained.

### 1.23 The Explanatory Relation

Two elements can be distinguished in any philosophical account of explanation:

1. The relation between explanation and explanandum that the account claims gives an explanation its force, which I call the *explanatory relation*

2. The formal criteria that an explanation must, according to the account, satisfy in order to qualify as a good explanation, which I call the *formal requirement*

Formal requirements are not to be confused with what are sometimes called requirements of formal adequacy; in my use, the meaning of *form* is very broad.

An account of explanation need not both state a formal requirement and take a position on the explanatory relation, but if it does, the formal requirement is of course to be understood as picking out those things that stand in the explanatory relation to the explanandum. As it happens, all major accounts of explanation take a position on the explanatory relation and give at least somewhat formal criteria for picking out the explanatory relata. By distinguishing the two elements of an account, it is possible to separate the question whether the explanatory relation chosen is the right one and the question whether the formal requirement succeeds in picking out things that stand to one another in the chosen explanatory relation.

A sketch of Hempel's seminal deductive-nomological, or DN, account of event explanation will demonstrate the value of making the distinction between the explanatory relation and the formal requirement. The formal criteria for a DN event explanation are as follows (Hempel and Oppenheim 1948, 247–248):

1. The explanation must be a deductive argument that has as its conclusion the proposition that the explanandum occurred.

2. At least one of the premises of the argument must be a law of nature.

3. The premises of the argument must be true.

Hempel was prepared to count almost any scientifically significant generalization as a law—for example, *All robins' eggs are greenish-blue*—initiating, in the philosophy of explanation, a tradition of liberality in the use of the term *law* that I am happy to follow. Unlike Woodward (2003), for example, neither Hempel nor I require laws to have universal scope or to perform a fundamental organizing role in a theory. I also follow Hempel, however, in aiming eventually to lay down a strict criterion distinguishing those generalizations that can play the role of laws in explanation and those that cannot (section 7.6).

According to the DN account's formal requirement, the relation between an explanation and its explanandum is the relation between the premises of a sound, law-involving deductive argument and its conclusion. Is this logical relation itself the explanatory relation?

Hempel thought not: he gave two contrasting accounts of the explanatory relation. The theory that he turned to more often was an *expectability* account:

> [A DN explanation] shows that, given the particular circumstances and the laws in question, the occurrence of the phenomenon *was to be expected*; and it is in this sense that the explanation enables us to *understand why* the phenomenon occurred (Hempel 1965a, 337).

In this passage, then, Hempel holds that an event is explained when it is shown that it was to be expected. The force of a good explanation is just the force of a good (law-involving) argument.

When Hempel stepped back to summarize his approach to explanation, however, he characterized the explanatory relation as a kind of *pattern subsumption*:

> The understanding [explanation] conveys lies . . . in the insight that the explanandum fits into, or can be subsumed under, a system of uniformities represented by empirical laws or theoretical principles (Hempel 1965a, 488).

Hempel left us in no doubt as to the DN account's formal requirement. But he was ambivalent about the nature of the explanatory relation: is it an expectability-conferring relation or a pattern-subsumption relation that drives explanation? In the short term, his ambivalence was quite fruitful. It allowed philosophers to focus on the adequacy of the formal requirement, without the distraction of larger questions about the explanatory relation, and so allowed the study of explanation to become a respectable topic in technical philosophy of science. But in the longer term, it has become impossible to discuss explanation without discussing the explanatory relation—without taking a stand, for example, on whether the explanatory relation is a causal relation. For this reason, the discussion that follows classifies accounts of explanation according to their view of the explanatory relation. As it must, the DN account appears twice, once as an expectability account and once as a pattern-subsumption account.

Some readers will observe that the classification of approaches to explanation offered in the next section of this chapter differs in certain respects from Salmon's (1984) well-known classification. A short comment, then, on the relation between Salmon's system and mine.

Salmon distinguishes ontic, epistemic, and modal views about explanation. The ontic class includes the causal and the pattern-subsumption views. The epistemic class includes Hempel's nomic expectability view and some other approaches not discussed here. The modal class, unlike the other two, is defined not according to explanatory relation but according to formal requirement: what modal views have in common is the primacy their formal requirements accord the notion of necessity. Because necessity comes in many forms—metaphysical, causal, epistemic, and so on—the modal approach is compatible with almost any conception of the explanatory relation.

I have two reasons for not adopting Salmon's scheme. First, and more decisive, the scheme does not distinguish the two approaches that interest me most, the causal and the pattern-subsumption views. Second, I do not find the modal category useful, largely because of my preference for a classification based exclusively on the explanatory relation.

Finally, an advance apology: the treatment of accounts of the explanatory relation in the next section is far from being a neutral survey; it rather focuses on those aspects of the literature on explanation that will be most important to the development of the kairetic account. Strevens (2006) offers a more even-handed, if shallower, overview of the field.

## 1.3   Accounts of the Explanatory Relation

### 1.31  Nomic Expectability

On the nomic expectability view, to understand a phenomenon is to see that it was to be expected, given certain law-including facts. It follows that an explanation is a kind of retrospective prediction, and that the proper form for an explanation is an argument.

Hempel's DN account of explanation was described in section 1.23. A less ambiguous example of a nomic expectability theory is Hempel's later account of probabilistic event explanation, the inductive-statistical (IS) account, which I will sketch here (Hempel 1965a, §3). Whereas Hempel's comments on the significance of expectability in relation to the DN account might be seen as an afterthought, expectability plays a central role in the derivation of the formal requirement for the IS account. Thus, it can be said with some confidence that the IS account was intended from the very beginning as a nomic expectability account.

The DN account understands a deterministic event explanation as a deductive, law-involving argument for the occurrence of the explanandum. The IS account understands a probabilistic event explanation as an *inductive*, law-involving argument for the explanandum's occurrence. The requirement of inductive soundness imposes two conditions on IS explanations that have no parallel in the DN account:

1. Probabilistic explanations must satisfy a near-equivalent of the requirement of total evidence: they must mention (almost) every factor known to affect the probability of the explanandum. Hempel called this the *requirement of maximal specificity*.

2. The premises of a probabilistic explanation must confer a high probability on the explanandum. How high? Whatever probability is sufficient, according to the canons of inductive logic, for acceptance of a conclusion probabilified to that degree, but, at any rate, greater than one-half.

Both requirements are motivated by the expectability approach to explanation.

Two remarks. The first applies to the IS and DN accounts equally: it is quite unclear what reason there is for requiring expectability to be nomic. If understanding an event is a matter of seeing that it was to be expected— if it is a matter of experiencing that "oh, of course it was going to happen" feeling—why must laws be involved? Of course, it may be that, as a matter of fact, a law is always required in order to generate the feeling, but why rule out other possibilities? The pattern-subsumption and causal approaches to explanation are better able to account for the special explanatory role of laws.

Second, the maximal specificity requirement makes an essential reference to the explainer's knowledge situation. A good IS explanation must take into account every *known* probabilistically relevant factor, but it need not take into account either those that are unknown or those known to exist but not known to be relevant. What explains an event, then, depends on what you know, a consequence of the IS account that many have found objectionable (Coffa 1974). Epistemic relativity is, however, a natural consequence of the expectability approach: to explain an event is to show that it ought to have been expected, but what you ought to have expected depends on what you knew.

Why is there no epistemic relativity in the DN account, then? Why does the DN account allow that you can explain an event successfully using deterministic law statements that you have no reason to believe, provided that you happen to be lucky enough to choose statements that are true? Surely in such a case, you ought not to have expected the explanandum to occur, yet your putative explanation satisfies the DN account's formal criteria, which require only that the statements in the explanation are true, not that they are known to be true, or even suspected to be true?

In his original formulation of the DN account, Hempel remarks that it might "seem more appropriate" to require that the premises of a DN explanation be highly confirmed, as opposed to true (Hempel and Oppenheim 1948, 248). He rejects the confirmation criterion, however, precisely because it leads to observer dependence. Hempel seems, then, to have realized that the expectability view of the explanatory relation called for a reference to knowledge of, rather than the truth of, the premises of an explanation. But though he favored the expectability view, he favored explanatory objectivity more—until he returned to expectability, and embraced it more fully, in his approach to probabilistic event explanation.

### 1.32 Pattern Subsumption

According to the pattern-subsumption approach, a good explanation shows that the phenomenon to be explained is an instance of a more general pattern. To understand an event, then, is to see that it is an instance of a pattern of events. To understand a law is to see that it is an instance of a pattern of laws; in the Newtonian explanation of Kepler's laws, for example, the elliptical orbits of the planets are shown to be just one instance of the many kinds of motion generated by the inverse square law of gravitation.

Pattern-subsumption accounts of explanation have been offered by Hempel (in some moods), Cartwright (1983), and, under the rubric of the unification approach, by Friedman (1974) and Kitcher (1981, 1989). (The distinctive features of unification accounts are identified below.) Salmon's sr account of explanation (section 1.34) might also be interpreted as a pattern-subsumption view.

Not every pattern explains: seeing that a black object has its blackness in common with other black objects in no way explains the blackness. The paradigmatically explanatory pattern rather associates one property with another. Patterns of this sort are captured by universal generalizations with an if/then or *All Fs are G* structure: *All ravens are black*, for example, or *If an apple falls from a tree of height d at time t it will hit the ground at time* $t + \sqrt{2d/g}$ (where *g* is gravitational acceleration). That the consequent of such an if/then pattern obtains in some particular instance is explained by seeing that it is accompanied by the antecedent, and that there is a general pattern of such antecedents being accompanied by such consequents. In the simplest case, then, an object's *G*-ness is explained by pointing to, first, the object's *F*-ness, and second, a general pattern of *G*-ness in *F*s.

The formal requirements of the DN account provide a simple framework for representing subsumptions. The following DN explanation, for example, represents the "simplest case" from the end of the last paragraph:

$$All\ Fs\ are\ G$$
$$\underline{x\ is\ an\ F}$$
$$x\ is\ a\ G$$

As you can see, the "law" states the pattern and the deduction demonstrates that the explanandum, *x*'s *G*-ness, falls under the pattern. It is quite straightforward, then, to interpret the DN account of explanation as a pattern-subsumption account. (To do so, it must be argued that the DN form is capable of representing subsumption under any explanatory pattern; in what follows, however, I will for simplicity's sake confine my attention to patterns of the if/then variety typically found in event explanation.)

The pattern-subsumption interpretation illuminates two aspects of the DN account that on the nomic expectability interpretation remained obscure. First, it is quite clear on the pattern-subsumption interpretation why something like a law must figure in an explanation: an explanation must cite a pattern, and, on certain empiricist views of the nature of laws, including that advocated by Hempel and Oppenheim (1948), to state the existence of a pattern just is to state a law.

Second, the pattern-subsumption interpretation of DN explanation carries no implication of epistemic relativity. For an explanandum to be an instance of a pattern, the pattern must be real, but it need not be known to be real. Thus, on the pattern-subsumption interpretation, it is clear why the premises of a DN explanation must be true but need not be known to be true.

The DN account's formal requirements give a satisfactory account of which states of affairs instantiate which explanatory if/then patterns, but they say too little about which if/then patterns are explanatory. A genre of problem cases devised by Salmon, Kyburg, and others shows that not every if/then pattern—not even of the simplest, most straightforward, *All Fs are G* variety—is explanatory.

Consider, for example, the following scenario (Kyburg 1965). A sample of salt is "hexed" by intoning some magical-sounding words in its vicinity and then is placed in water. The salt dissolves. The dissolving is just one instance of a general pattern of dissolving: all salt that is hexed in this way dissolves. If no restrictions are placed on explanatory patterns, then, the dissolving can be explained by observing that the salt was hexed and placed in water. But this cannot be right. The dissolving is explained by the salt's being placed in water, but not by its being hexed. The unqualified DN account fails to distinguish between two elements in the pattern: an element that is genuinely explanatorily relevant, the placing in water, and an element that is not relevant, the hexing. Salmon calls this simply the problem of relevance.[3]

To solve the relevance problem, a pattern-subsumption account must put some restriction on the if/then patterns that are to qualify as explanatory. Nancy Cartwright's simulacrum account of explanation shows how this can be done (Cartwright 1983). Cartwright's account brings the additional benefit of exemplifying an approach on which nonlinguistic scientific constructions can function as explanations.

A simulacrum explanation begins with a scientific model, which may be understood as representing the sort of if/then pattern introduced above. (Note that *model* here is used in its informal, scientific sense.) Think of the model as having "inputs" and "outputs," where the inputs represent initial or other boundary conditions of the modeled system and the outputs represent the behavior of the system in the conditions represented by the inputs. A model for the apple generalization above, for example, will take the distance fallen as an input and produce the time taken as an output.

Almost any formal construct may serve as a model: a universally quantified sentence, such as the apple generalization or "All gases expand when heated"; a set of equations, such as the ideal gas law, $PV = nRT$; a full-blown theory, such as statistical mechanics; a computer simulation; or a mechanical representation such as an orrery, a working model of the solar system. Understood correctly (and this may require a certain hermeneutic finesse—or an instruction manual), any of these models will represent a pattern of input/output pairs, which I call the pattern *generated* by the model.

For the purpose of a simulacrum explanation, the internal workings of the model need not correspond to anything in the represented system: "A model is a work of fiction" (Cartwright 1983, 153). Thus, the explanatory power of a model is determined entirely by the pattern it generates; nothing else counts. Further, as you will see shortly, even this pattern need not precisely reflect what is found in the real world, though the more closely it resembles a real-world pattern, the better.

A model explains a particular output just in case it reproduces that output. For example, an apple's taking 1.4 seconds to fall 10 meters is explained by showing that, in or according to the model, an apple takes 1.4 seconds to fall 10 meters. I understand simulacrum explanations as proceeding by pattern subsumption: a model encapsulating the apple generalization—*If an apple falls from a tree of height d at time t it will hit the ground at time $t + \sqrt{2d/g}$*—represents a pattern of distances fallen and times taken in real apples, and explains particular distance/time pairs by subsuming them under the pattern.

The resources to deal with the relevance problem are provided by a ranking that Cartwright imposes on models, and therefore, on explanatory patterns: "The [explanatory] success of the model depends on how much and how precisely it can replicate what goes on" (also p. 153).

Cartwright's ranking rule has two parts, which I will call the criteria of accuracy and generality. The pattern generated by a model is *accurate* to the degree that it reflects a pattern in the real world, that is, to the degree to which the input/output pairs generated by the model match the relevant actual input/output pairs.[4] The pattern generated by a model is *general* in proportion to the number of actual input/output pairs it generates. To put it another way, a model is general in proportion to the frequency with which the inputs it accepts—the cases that satisfy the antecedent of the if/then—are realized in the actual world, and accurate to the degree to which the outputs generated by the model given these inputs match the real world outputs. The generality of the apple generalization, for example, depends on the number of actual apples that actually fall in our world—the more falling apples, the greater the generality. The generalization's accuracy depends on the accuracy with which it yields the actual time taken by these apples to fall. Factors such as air resistance, then, slightly diminish the generalization's accuracy.[5]

There are two ways to interpret the doctrine that a more accurate and general model is a more explanatory model. You might say that an accurate, general model has great explanatory power simply because it generates a pattern with many actual instances, that is, actual input/output pairs, thus because it explains a great number of phenomena. Or you might say that, in addition, an accurate and general model explains each one of those phenomena better—that is, all other things being equal, of two models both generating a given explanandum, the more accurate and general model provides the better explanation *of that very phenomenon*. It would follow that there is a certain holism to the explanatory enterprise: the success with which a pattern explains one particular phenomenon depends on its ability to successfully subsume many other phenomena. This second interpretation is by far the more interesting and fruitful, I think; I take it that it is what Cartwright intends.

Some versions of the pattern subsumption account mandate an even stronger claim. According to what Woodward (2003, §8.8) aptly calls the "winner-takes-all" approach, the pattern that maximizes generality and accuracy is not just the *best* explanation of the phenomena it subsumes, it is their *only* explanation.

Salmon's relevance problem can now be solved. The difficulty, recall, was that the pattern articulated by the universal generalization

1. All hexed salt dissolves when placed in water

is at best a flawed explanation of its instances. The simulacrum account shows why. Any instance of hexed salt's dissolving in water is not only an instance of (1) but also of (2) below:

2. All salt dissolves when placed in water.

Since (2) is considerably more general than (1)—it makes predictions about all salt, not just hexed salt—and equally accurate, it provides a better explanation than (1) of the dissolution of any particular sample of hexed salt. Further, on a winner-takes-all version of the simulacrum account, an explanation that cites hexing is not merely explanatorily dominated; it has no explanatory power at all—a preferable conclusion, I think.

The pattern-subsumption account is still, however, incomplete. Model (2) above—the "theory" that all salt dissolves in water—is general, but not as general as the theory obtained by conjoining it with another true but irrelevant generalization, say, *All ravens are black*. That is, the "theory" *All salt dissolves in water and all ravens are black* is more general, because generating more actual phenomena (dissolving salt *and* black ravens) than the dissolution law alone. But it hardly constitutes an irrelevancy-free explanation of an episode of dissolution.[6]

Why is the set of events generated by *All salt dissolves in water and all ravens are black* not an explanatory pattern? Prima facie, because it is not a pattern at all: there is little or nothing that dissolving salt and black ravens have in common, so there is no single pattern instantiated by all and only salt and ravens. It seems, then, that a further requirement should be added to the theory of explanatory patterns: the phenomena generated by a model do not constitute an explanatory pattern unless they resemble one another in some respect, or as I will say, unless the putative pattern is *cohesive*.[7]

What sort of resemblance is required? Intuitively, a pattern generated by a model is cohesive only if the output of each input/output pair is related to the input in the same or a similar way. That is, there should be a single rule, presumably embodied by the model itself, that determines the output for each input. There should also be a single rule that determines what counts as a possible input, that is, that determines the scope of the model; all systems to which the model applies should, in other words, have a single, shared nature. (It is in virtue of this second aspect of the cohesion requirement that a pattern such as that specified by *All ravens and lumps of coal are black* is considered insufficiently cohesive for explanatory duty.) In itself, this is hardly a substantive account of cohesion, without some further account of what constitutes a "single" rule. No doubt a standard for similarity, among other things, would be needed to fully characterize cohesion, bringing with it the usual problems (Goodman 1971). My aim here, however, is not to define a pattern subsumptionist notion of cohesion but simply to point to its importance. (I will have more to say about cohesion in sections 3.6 and 7.34.)

When the simulacrum account is augmented by adding a cohesion desideratum, the result is the following sophisticated pattern-subsumption account of explanation. A phenomenon is explained by showing that it is generated by a model that optimizes the following desiderata:

1. Generality: maximize the number of actual phenomena that qualify as inputs.

2. Accuracy: maximize the goodness of fit between generated outputs and actual outputs.

3. Cohesion: maximize the degree to which the phenomena generated by the model share a resemblance both in their inputs and in the way that their outputs are related to their inputs.

There is a point where the drive for cohesion and accuracy acts in opposition to the drive for further generality. This is the point at which accuracy, cohesion, and generality are jointly maximized; the optimally explanatory subsuming pattern is found here.

An additional desideratum is sometimes added to the three above:

4. Simplicity: maximize the simplicity of the model.

Unlike the other desiderata, this is, at least on the face of things, a condition on the model rather than on the generated pattern.

Observe that the simplicity desideratum duplicates some of the work done by the cohesion desideratum, because simpler models tend to generate more cohesive sets of phenomena. But neither desideratum renders the other redundant. Of two equally cohesive models, one may be simpler, and of two equally simple models, one may be more cohesive.

A pattern of great generality, accuracy, and cohesion is a pattern that has considerable unifying power: it brings together many perhaps disparate-seeming phenomena and shows that they fit a single template. If explanation is a matter of pattern subsumption, then, it is thereby also a matter of unification. For this reason I classify unification accounts of explanation (Friedman 1974; Kitcher 1981, 1989) as a species of the pattern-subsumption approach.

Two things set unification views apart from other sophisticated pattern-subsumption views. First, unification accounts tend to impose a simplicity desideratum. Second, and more importantly, unification accounts tend to require even more holism than is already inherent in the pattern-subsumption approach. On Kitcher's unificationism, for example, a model explains a phenomenon that it generates just in case it belongs to the set of models that best unifies (that is, optimizes accuracy, generality, cohesion, and simplicity over) *all* the phenomena. A lesser holism might require unification of phenomena only on a domain-by-domain basis. Kitcher has weakened his holism in this way in recent years.

### 1.33  Causality

The explanatory relation is a causal relation, according to the causal approach. On a two-factor causal view, such as the kairetic account advocated in this book, the explainers of a phenomenon must both bear the causal relation to the phenomenon and pass a test for explanatory relevance. On the prevalent one-factor approach, the explainers of the phenomenon must simply bear the causal relation to the phenomenon.

One-factor accounts differ in many ways in their conception of the nature of the causal relation. Most obviously, they differ in their selectivity. A completely nonselective causal view classifies as explainers of a phenomenon anything that, from the point of view of fundamental physics, exerts a causal influence on the phenomenon, up to and including the gravitational influence of the distant stars. Salmon's (1984) causal-mechanical theory of explanation is of this sort.

A selective causal view, while perhaps allowing that the ever-present influence of the distant stars constitutes a causal relation of a sort, holds that the kind of causal relation required for explanation is a far rarer thing. Of the myriad physical influences on a phenomenon, only a few will count as the phenomenon's *causes* and so qualify for admission to its explanation. Lewis (1986a) and Woodward (2003) offer relatively selective views of causal explanation.

Two-factor approaches can also have their selectivity assessed. The kairetic account begins with an extremely nonselective view of the causal relation but adds a highly selective criterion for explanatory relevance.

The motivation for the causal approach to explanation is the subject of section 1.4; the causal account's many flavors will then be explored in chapter two.

### 1.34  Other Accounts of Explanation

#### Statistical Relevance

Wesley Salmon's influential statistical relevance, or sr, view of explanation offers the following formal criterion for an explanation of an event $e$: what explains $e$ is a complete list of all factors statistically relevant, either positively or negatively, to $e$, to its alternatives, and to events that are similar to $e$, along with a statement of the statistical laws that determine the degrees of relevance in each case (Salmon 1970, 1984).

To explain a teenager's car theft, for example, Salmon requires a list of all the factors that made a difference to the probability that the particular teenager in question would steal a car, along with the factors that would make a difference to the probability of anyone's stealing a car. What is required is, in effect, a complete probabilistic sociology of car theft (Salmon 1984, 38–39).

What view of the explanatory relation drives the sr account? Salmon is, it seems, deliberately ecumenical: he believes that a formal criterion of statistical relevance can be motivated by expectability concerns (Salmon 1970, 78–81), but he later contrasts his view with epistemic conceptions of the explanatory relation, among which he counts the nomic expectability approach (Salmon 1984, chap. 4).

Putting aside exegesis of Salmon, two views of the explanatory relation seem most compatible with the sr account. On the one hand, the relation of statistical relevance itself might be identified as the explanatory relation (probably Salmon's preferred alternative to ecumenism). On the other hand, the sr account might be seen as a species of the pattern-subsumption approach to explanation. The relevant patterns are, of course, those implied by the statistical laws that underlie the relations of statistical relevance. Salmon's requirement that the probabilities proper to explanation be those characterizing *maximal homogeneous* reference classes fits well with the sophisticated pattern-subsumption view. The demand that reference classes be homogeneous corresponds, roughly, to the joint action of the desiderata of accuracy and cohesion, while the demand that the classes be maximal corresponds to the desideratum of generality.

The SR account's influence on recent work in explanation has been felt not so much in adherence to the account in the pure form proposed by Salmon but rather in the widespread perception that statistical relevance is an important component of, or is diagnostic of, the explanatory relation. Salmon himself, after rejecting the SR account and endorsing a causal approach to explanation, explored both views. He first suggested that statistical relevance relations provide evidence for the existence of the causal relations that are the basis of all explanation (Salmon 1984). Changing his mind over a decade later, he suggested a two-factor causal account of explanation on which only causal influences on an event that are also statistically relevant to that event participate in its explanation (Salmon 1997); this idea is discussed further in section 2.3 and part four. A third possible view, that statistical relevance is built into the causal-explanatory relation, is advocated by Woodward (2003).

### Van Fraassen's Relativism

On a relativist theory of explanation, the nature of the explanatory relation changes according to preferences, cultural traditions, knowledge, conversational context, or some other observer-dependent factor.[8]

Van Fraassen's "pragmatic" account of explanation (van Fraassen 1980, chap. 5) might be understood as a partly relativist view. The pragmatic account's explanatory relation has two parts: a statistical relevance relation—different, but not too different, from Salmon's—and another relation determined by the context of a particular request for explanation. Once this other relation is fixed, whether or not it holds may be an objective matter, as when, say, the explanatory context determines that the appropriate relation is one of causal relevance. But this does not make the identity of the explanatory relation itself an objective matter unless there is some very strong objective constraint on which relevance relations may be fixed by an explanatory context. If, as van Fraassen implies, there is no such constraint, then what counts as explanatorily relevant will, it seems, depend entirely on the person who makes the explanatory request—though it might also be understood, nonrelativistically, as a proper part of the request, like my explanatory frameworks (see page 184). For an extended discussion of this aspect of van Fraassen's account (which perhaps does not pay sufficient attention to the account's statistical relevance component), see Kitcher and Salmon (1987).

Hempel's IS account of probabilistic event explanation is not, note, a relativist account. This is because, although whether or not the nomic expectability relation holds is determined in part by observer-dependent facts—namely, the explanation's epistemic context—the nature of the relation is not itself determined by these facts.

### Metaphysical Necessity

To explain why there is no void, Descartes shows that the metaphysical nature of matter, as pure extension, necessitates that all of space is filled with stuff. The explanatory relation here is one of metaphysical necessity: the facts cited by the explanation metaphysically necessitate the explanandum. Contrast this with the kind of causal view on which the explanatory facts necessitate the explanandum not metaphysically but nomologically.

Overtly metaphysical explanation has of course fallen out of favor, and with it the metaphysical view of the explanatory relation. In late modern philosophy it is likely to be found, if at all, in the work of philosophers arguing against the possibility of explanation, such as Duhem (1954). The explanatory relation is one of metaphysical necessitation, the argument goes, but there are no relations of metaphysical necessitation—or at least, we do not have epistemic access to such relations—therefore the pursuit of explanation is pointless.

## 1.4   The Causal Element in Explanation

### 1.41   The Direction of Explanation and the Direction of Causation

Certain well-known counterexamples to the DN account provide strong reasons to prefer a causal approach to explanation over either an expectability or a pattern-subsumption approach.

Given the height of a flagpole, the position of the sun, and a simple physical law—light travels in straight lines—you can deduce the length of the shadow cast by the flagpole. Thus, according to the DN account, you can explain the length of the shadow by citing the flagpole's height, the position of the sun, and the rectilinear propagation of light.

In the same way, however, you can deduce the height of the flagpole from the law, the position of the sun, and the length of the shadow. Thus, according to the DN account, you can explain the height of the flagpole by citing, among other things, the length of its shadow. Contrary to the DN account, however, we do not consider the length of the shadow to explain the height of the flagpole. Therefore, the DN account is mistaken.[9]

How ought the DN account's troubles to be diagnosed? There is an asymmetry in explanatory power where there is no asymmetry in logical power. This suggests there is something more to explanation than mere argumentative force, and that this something is a relation that is asymmetric in the case at hand—a relation that holds between flagpole and shadow, but not between shadow and flagpole. The obvious candidate is the relation of causation. The flagpole causes the shadow to exist, but the shadow does not cause the flagpole to exist. Explanation, it seems, flows in the same direction as causation.

This conclusion is reinforced by another famous counterexample to the DN account. Suppose that, whenever the needle on a barometer dips, there is a storm. From this meteorological law and a particular needle dip, you can deduce that a storm will occur. Thus, according to the DN account, you can explain the storm by citing the law and the fact that the needle dipped. Contrary to the DN account, however, we do not consider the barometer reading to explain the ensuing storm. Therefore, the DN account is mistaken.

Again, it seems that the existence of a sound deductive argument is not sufficient for explanation. What is also required is, as in the case of the flagpole, a causal relation between the explanatory facts and the explanandum. What the barometer does not cause, it cannot explain.

### 1.42  Toward a Causal Basis for Explanatory Asymmetry

The counterexamples discussed in section 1.41 provide good reason to think that the explanatory relation has a causal element (for two alternative views, see section 1.47). Let me outline what I take to be more or less the minimal assumptions about causality necessary to handle explanatory asymmetry.

Take as a starting point a schematic causal constraint on explanation, which counts as the explainers of an event $e$ only entities satisfying one of the following three criteria:

1. An explainer can be an event or state of affairs that bears a certain causal relation to *e*. Without prejudice, call this the relation of *causal influence*. Thus, to qualify under this first criterion, a potential explainer should be a causal influence on *e*.

2. An explainer can be a causal law in virtue of which an event satisfies criterion (1), that is, a causal law in virtue of which an event causally influences *e*.

3. An explainer can be a background condition in virtue of which a causal law satisfies criterion (2), that is, a background condition, satisfaction of which is necessary for an event to causally influence *e* in virtue of a certain causal law.

Call any event, law, or set of background conditions that satisfies one of the criteria a causal influence on *e*. In this sense, the causal influences include not only the events connected to *e* by the causal influence relation but also the laws and background conditions in virtue of which such connections exist—a slight abuse of terminology, perhaps, but economical. You can then say that all explainers of *e* must be causal influences on *e*. In what follows, I will focus on potential explainers that qualify under clause (1).

In the above scheme, *causal influence* is a mere placeholder: it is an open question what kind of thing the influence relation might be. If the causal constraint on explanation is to deal with the flagpole/shadow problem and other similar cases, however, the influence relation must take a certain form. In particular, the influence relation must have the properties of *asymmetry* and *particularity*.

An influence relation is *asymmetric* if it is possible for causal influence to run in one direction only, that is, for *c* to causally influence *e* without *e*'s influencing *c*. (Mutual influence is possible, then, but not necessary.) It is the asymmetry of influence that allows us to distinguish, on causal grounds, between the nomological dependence of the length of the shadow on the height of the flagpole and the nomological dependence of the height of the flagpole on the length of the shadow, declaring one but not the other to be a relation of causal dependence, and so a potentially explanatory relation. Typically (though perhaps not always), the causal influence relation should run from past to future, providing the undergirding for the notion that states earlier in time causally explain, but are not explained by, states later in time.

Asymmetries in causal influence should be found everywhere, since in almost every process—evolutionary, ecological, economic—science distinguishes a causal order and holds that explanation must not run counter to that order. It is perhaps too much to say, yet, that every explanation must follow the direction of causal influence, but certainly in every domain there are explanations that must do so. This is true even of fundamental physics, since the intuitions of explanatory asymmetry summoned up by flagpole/shadow cases do not disappear at the fundamental level. The positions of Rutherford's scintillations—showing the final positions of alpha particles passing through gold foil—no more explain the structure of the gold atom than the shadow explains the dimensions of the flagpole. But the quantum scattering processes involved are just about as fundamental as you can get. Analogs to the barometer/storm case are equally easy to find. (Skepticism about the applicability of causal concepts to fundamental physics will be discussed in section 1.5.)

So much for asymmetry. An influence relation between events is *particular* to the degree to which it relates very finely individuated aspects of the world. An influence relation that is not particular at all might simply relate the complete state of the world at one time to its complete state at a later time (Maudlin 2007). Such a relation provides enough discriminatory power to deal with flagpole/shadow cases, because the length of the shadow at any moment depends on the height of the flagpole at a slightly earlier time, and so an attempt to explain the former in terms of the latter goes contrary to even this very coarse-grained causal relation. But it is less well able to deal with barometer/storm cases, since here the spurious explainer, the barometer reading, temporally precedes the event to be explained; it therefore belongs to a state of the world that causally influences the state of the world to which the explanandum belongs, so its explanatory status cannot, if influence is unparticular, be called into doubt on purely causal grounds.

A causal influence relation that is very particular runs, by contrast, between very fine-grained aspects of earlier and later states of the world; it therefore allows you to discriminate between those aspects of a world state that do and those that do not causally influence a later storm. (That said, the presence or absence of causal influence alone may not be enough to identify all barometer-like spurious explainers; see section 1.43.) Because the causal influence relations found in the literature are, Maudlin's excepted, all very particular, I will say no more about particularity in later sections; it will be there in the background but unacknowledged.

What next? A natural strategy is to find the best available account of causation that provides a causal influence relation satisfying the requirements of asymmetry and particularity. To study explanation, then—or causal explanation at least—is first to study the metaphysics of causation. Causal accounts of explanation in the literature have tended to take just this approach, running up their flags over some or other metaphysical theory of causation before exploring the terra incognita of explanation (Salmon 1984; Lewis 1986a; Woodward 2003).

I will do something different. There are several attractive accounts of causation that provide a relation of causal influence that is both asymmetric and particular. Why choose? I propose a provisional causal ecumenism. As the investigation proceeds, this ecumenism will go from provisional to provincial, but none of the accounts of causation I am about to describe will be declared entirely incompatible with the kairetic account of explanation.

Three views of causation well equipped to supply explanation with its particular asymmetry are Dowe's conserved quantity account, Lewis's various counterfactual accounts, and Woodward's manipulation view. Let me say something about each, focusing, for now, on the deterministic case. (I should note that, when I say that these accounts are well equipped to handle the explanatory asymmetry problem, I do not mean that they are free of problems, let alone that they are fundamentally correct in their approach to causation. I mean that the various kinds of causal relation they posit, *if they are correct*—and presumably at most one can be correct—are adequate to deal with the asymmetry problem.)

## 1.43  The Conserved Quantity Theory

Dowe (2000), building on the work of Reichenbach (1956) and the "process theories" of Fair (1979) and Salmon (1984), defines an asymmetric relation of *causal connection* based on the notion of a conserved quantity, that is, a quantity preserved by the physical laws, such as mass-energy or charge. Two objects-at-times are causally connected just in case a line can be drawn in space-time from one to the other that at every point either (a) follows the world line of a single object, or (b) switches from the world line of one object to the world line of another at a point where the lines intersect and where the two objects exchange a conserved quantity. Causal connection, then, is by any combination of *persistence* and *interaction*, where persistence is simply the relation between an object at one time and the same object at any other time, and interaction is the exchange of a conserved quantity by two objects in the same place at the same time.

An electron at time $t_1$ might be causally connected to an electron at time $t_2$, for example, because at some time after $t_1$ the first electron emits a photon (the bearer of electromagnetic force) that influences the second electron before time $t_2$. The causal connection goes from the first electron at $t_1$ to the same electron at the time of the emission by persistence, from the electron to the photon at the time of the emission by interaction, from the photon at that time to the time when the photon interacts with the second electron by persistence, and so on. This, according to Dowe, is the reason that what appears to us to be a repelling of one electron by the other (and vice versa, of course) is indeed a genuine causal connection.

The direction of causation, usually but not always forward in time, is not determined by the nature of either persistence or interaction but by a separate element of the account based on one of Reichenbach's ideas, which I will not describe here (Dowe 2000, chap. 8).

Dowe's account offers a definition of a symmetric causal connection relation between objects as well as a definition of the local direction of causation, but to solve the explanatory asymmetry problem, what is wanted is an asymmetric causal influence relation between events or states of affairs. No problem; count an event $c$ as causally influencing an event $e$ just in case $c$ and $e$ involve objects that are causally connected and, if they occur at different times, the connection from $c$ to $e$ at all times goes in the local direction of causation.

This gets you what you want with the flagpole and shadow: the direction of causal influence is never from the shadow to the flagpole. The case of the barometer is slightly more complicated. It is tempting to say that there is no causal influence between the barometer and the storm, ruling out the explanation of one by the other. But this is not quite correct: the parts of the barometer exert a minute gravitational influence on the parts of the atmospheric whole that is the storm. The simple reaction is to disregard the influence on the grounds that it is so small as to be negligible. To take this course, some way of quantifying causal influence is required. You might, for example, set the degree of influence equal to the amount of conserved quantity exchanged, relative to the whole. For reasons that will emerge in chapter two, I think that this simple reaction is not the last word on the explanatory significance of minute causal influences, but let it stand for now.

Note that on Dowe's account, the causal connection between any two objects or events, such as barometers and storms, will ultimately depend on the causal connections between their fundamental constituents—the fundamental particles that either make up the object or whose behavior realizes the event. In particular, two events are causally related just in case any two fundamental constituents of the events are causally related (and the direction of causation is right). In this sense, Dowe's account can be said to be a *fundamental level* account of causation: all causal relations go by way of the fundamental level. The other two views of causation considered in this chapter will provide a contrast.

### 1.44  The Counterfactual Theory

According to the simple counterfactual theory of causation, an event $c$ causes an event $e$ just in case, had $c$ not occurred, $e$ would not have occurred. An icy patch on the road is a cause of a car crash, then, because if the icy patch had not been there, the crash would not have happened. But it is not true that if the crash had not happened, the icy patch would not have been there. So the icy patch causes the crash, but the crash does not cause the presence of the icy patch. When the effect is an ongoing state of affairs, such as a shadow's being a certain length, you have to be more careful of your evaluation of the counterfactuals; in particular you have to be careful not to use "backtracking" counterfactuals (Field 2003, 448–450). When precautions are taken, you get the asymmetric relation you want: the shadow counterfactually depends on the flagpole, but not vice versa.

Lewis (1973a) offers an account of causation based on the simple counterfactual theory: $c$ causes $e$ just in case there is a chain of counterfactual dependence relations connecting $c$ and $e$. For my purposes in this chapter, there is no need to distinguish Lewis's from the simple account; for more on the difference, see section 2.4.

The counterfactual account has what is in one sense a far more selective conception of the causal relation than Dowe's account.[10] Events that are causally connected in Dowe's sense are often not causally connected in the counterfactual sense. Suppose I let out a whoop while you hurl a cannonball at a window. The window breaks. On Dowe's view, my whoop and your cannonball-hurling are both causally connected to the window's breaking—my whoop because the sound waves transfer energy to the window as it breaks, by causing it to vibrate. But had I not whooped, the window would still have broken, so the whoop is not a cause on the counterfactual account.

Nevertheless, the counterfactual account can make a certain kind of sense of Dowe's claim that there is a causal connection between the whooping and the breaking, as follows. Consider the concrete events that realize the events of the whooping and the breaking. A concrete event, recall from section 1.22, is an event individuated by all its intrinsic properties. Thus, the concrete realizer of the whooping is the event of the whooping's happening in exactly the way it did, down to the last ululatory waver, and the concrete realizer of the breaking is the event of the breaking's happening in exactly the way it did, down to the shape, size, and trajectory of the smallest shards of broken glass. The realizer of the breaking counterfactually depends on the realizer of the whooping: if I had not whooped, the breaking would not have happened in exactly the way it did, since the sound waves I generated did have some slight influence on the movement of the glass molecules. Say, then, that one event *causally influences* another if, had the concrete realizer of the first not occurred, the concrete realizer of the second would not have occurred.

This causal influence relation is not, note, a different kind of relation from the counterfactually defined *is a cause of* relations between high-level events: it is simply the subset of the *is a cause of* relation that has as its relata only concrete events. I have introduced a new name for some of the *is a cause of* relations admitted by the counterfactual account, rather than adding anything new to that account. Now, a charitable proponent of the counterfactual account of causation can interpret Dowe's claims as being about counterfactual dependences between concrete events, that is, as being about causal influence relations.[11]

I called Dowe's account of causal connection a fundamental-level account. The counterfactual account can be said to contain a fundamental-level account of a certain kind of causal connection—the influence relation—but much more besides, namely, the account of *is a cause of* relations between high-level events. For this reason, it might be called a *multilevel* account of causation, an account that posits distinct causal relations at all levels. Although the causal relations at one level—between biological events, say—will not be entirely independent of the causal influence relation at the fundamental level, since the fundamental laws of nature have a hand in determining both, the higher-level causal relations are not in any simple way made up of, let alone identical to, the influence relations.

Now to my main point: to solve the problem of explanatory asymmetry, only the relation of causal influence is required, or in other words, you only need look at *is a cause of* relations between concrete events. You could handle the asymmetry problem by looking at higher-level *is a cause of* relations, but you do not need to: that part of the counterfactual account that overlaps substantially with the Dowe account is sufficient for the job. Either Dowe's or the counterfactual theorist's version of causal influence will asymmetrically relate flagpoles to their shadows, cold fronts to storms, but not shadows to flagpoles or barometers to storms.[12]

## 1.45  The Manipulation Theory

Causal facts are equivalent to, or have as their basis, facts about in-principle manipulability, according to a manipulation account of causation (Gasking 1955; Menzies and Price 1993). For example, flipping a switch is a cause of a light bulb's illumination because you can manipulate the state of the light by manipulating the switch. Traditionally, such accounts have defined what it is to be a manipulation in terms of human agency, yielding a rather anthropocentric definition of causation. Woodward (2003) holds out the prospect of a more objectivist manipulation account, providing at least a formal structure on which a manipulationist metaphysics might be built. Let me suppose that such a project succeeds.[13] I will call the resulting theory of causation the Woodwardian account.

In the first instance, Woodwardian causal relations connect quantities, such as the height of a flagpole or the length of a shadow. To say that flagpole height causes shadow length is to say that the length of a shadow can be changed by manipulating the height of the corresponding flagpole. To say that shadow length causes flagpole height is to say that the height of a flagpole can be changed by manipulating the length of its shadow. The first claim is true; the second false. Thus, flagpole height causes shadow length, but not vice versa. (What constitutes a manipulation is a complex question for manipulationists; I am writing as though it has been, one way or another, definitively settled.)

A relation of singular causation between events is derived from the type relation between variables. The form of the derivation will be examined in somewhat greater detail in section 2.5; for now a counterfactual précis of Woodward's view will suffice. The manipulation account declares $c$ to be a cause of *e* just in case the following counterfactual is true for some putative causal path between *c* and *e*: if *because of an intervention c* had not occurred, *and had all variables not on the putative path been held constant*, *e* would not have occurred. It is in virtue of the italicized phrases that Woodward's counterfactuals differ from those invoked by Lewisian approaches to causation; as you will later see, it is the latter qualification that is by far the more important.

The manipulation account of causation is a multilevel account, in the sense defined in the previous section: it posits distinct causal relations at all levels, independently relating the variables of fundamental physics, biological variables, economic variables, and so on. I want to show that the causal relations the manipulation account posits between fundamental-level variables are sufficient on their own to solve the problem of explanatory asymmetry. As with Lewisian approaches, the key is to focus on the causal relations between the concrete realizers of high-level events.

Say that a high-level event *c* causally influences another high-level event *e* just in case the concrete realizer of one is a cause, in the manipulationist's sense, of the concrete realizer of the other, which is to say, just in case there is a causal pathway from one realizer to the other with respect to which the Woodwardian counterfactual holds—just in case, had a manipulation prevented the occurrence of *c*'s realizer, and had all variables not on the pathway in question been held to their actual values, *e*'s realizer would not have occurred. So defined, the manipulationist's causal influence relations are of a piece with the other causal relations between events posited by the manipulation account; they simply constitute a subset of the full complement of manipulationist singular causal relations. This subset is enough, I submit, to deal with the explanatory asymmetry problem: the influence relation will hold between flagpole and shadow but not vice versa, and so on. The close correspondence between Lewis and Woodward counterfactuals should be enough to convince you that this claim is at least roughly correct.

### 1.46 Causal Ecumenism

The conserved quantity account (and by extension, other process views of causation), the counterfactual account, and the manipulation account all agree, to a great extent, on the existence of a fundamental-level causal relation that I have called causal influence. Furthermore, they pretty much agree on what causal influence relations there are, that is, which concrete events causally influence which other concrete events, though of course they disagree on the metaphysical basis of the relations. If I am correct in holding that any of these variants of the causal influence relation provides enough fine-grained causal asymmetry between the right things to found a causal solution to the problem of explanatory asymmetry, then there is no need to endorse a particular metaphysics of causation in order to commit to a causal account of explanatory asymmetry (though you may have to reject certain other metaphysical theses about causation, as explained below).

I would like to carry over this causal ecumenism to the task of constructing a scientific account of explanation. That is, I would like to advocate a causal account of explanation that requires, from the metaphysics of causation, something that a broad range of theories of causation can provide and on which they are extensionally if not intensionally agreed. That something will be the causal influence relation.

The causal influence relation in the raw provides a rather unsophisticated account of causal explanation, for reasons examined in depth in chapter two. Thus, investigators of causal explanation have tended to appeal in their work to more elaborate metaphysical machinery, such as high-level counterfactual dependence or manipulability relations. In so doing, they lose the ecumenical advantage that I hope to retain, that is, the advantage of giving a causal account of explanation that is not held hostage to the details of some particular metaphysics of causation. They are in any case wrong to try to solve all of their explanatory problems metaphysically, for reasons adumbrated in section 1.1—but ecumenism will be my ostensible motivation for now.

Let me put the advantages of the ecumenical approach on display by pointing to some gnarly metaphysical questions about causation that are left happily unresolved by the minimal assumptions I propose to make about the causal influence relation.

First is the question whether causal relations exist only at the fundamental level or whether they exist at all levels, as multilevel accounts assert. My ecumenism entails ignoring, for explanatory purposes, the wealth of high-level causal relations offered by multilevel accounts of causation, but it need not mean denying the existence of these relations or their importance to endeavors other than explanation. (They clearly have heuristic use in explanation itself; see section 3.8.) It is quite consistent, then, to endorse (a) a causal approach to explanation, (b) a multilevel account of causation, and (c) the view that only the fundamental level causal relations play a part in explanation—though I suppose that few would choose to do so (see section 3.23).

Second is the question of whether the causal relation is reducible to noncausal facts. On Woodward's view, causal relations—and so, a fortiori, relations of causal influence—are irreducible. On Lewis's view, causal relations are ultimately reducible to a "Humean supervenience basis": facts about causal relations are nothing more than patterns of particular matters of fact (albeit global patterns). On Dowe's view, causal relations are reducible to noncausal matters of fact about persistence and the exchange of conserved quantities, but these physical matters of fact are not necessarily further reducible to Humean facts. My use of the causal influence relation is compatible with any of these positions.

Third is the question of the role of laws in causation. For some writers, following Davidson, two events are causally related only if they fall under a law: $c$ is a cause of $e$ only if there is a law *All Fs are Gs*, where $c$ is an $F$ and $e$ is a $G$. Others have imposed the even stronger requirement that there must be a law of the form *All Cs are Es*, that is, a law under which the events fall in virtue of the very properties by which they are specified in the causal claim, though this is now thought to be obviously unreasonable. Finally, it is sometimes said that there need be no law at all. What I assume concerning the causal influence relation is consistent with any of these views. (You will observe, however, that the three accounts of causation described above all envisage a close relation between the fundamental physical laws and the causal influence relation—Lewis's and Woodward's because of the central role played by laws in the evaluation of counterfactuals.)

Two further questions left open by my ecumenical assumptions concern the relation between causation, time, and locality. Can there be backward causation? Must all causation be local? I assume no particular answers to these questions, though the particular accounts of causation mentioned above in some cases do.

All religions, however ecumenical, need someone to burn. And there is, not surprisingly, a view of the nature of causation that is ruled out by even my ecumenism. I have in mind an emergent view of causation, on which there are no causal relations at the level of fundamental physics, only at higher levels—that is, no causal relations between fundamental events, only between higher level events.[14] To abandon this possibility is no loss for the proponent of the causal approach to explanation, however, since it is the one view of causation that clearly cannot solve the problem of explanatory asymmetry. The reason: there are explanatory asymmetries in many fundamental physical explanations, such as the case of Rutherford's gold foil (section 1.42). To explain these asymmetries causally, you need a fundamental-level causal relation. Causal emergentism has no place in the causal approach to explanation.

This last point serves to reiterate an underlying advantage of ecumenism: what I assume in the way of causal relations is not only something that causal metaphysicians can agree on; it is also just what is needed, and no more, to provide a causal resolution of the explanatory asymmetries.

### 1.47  Alternatives to the Causal Account

It seems only fair to consider two noncausal approaches to the problem of explanatory asymmetry. The first noncausal approach, due to Hempel (1965a, 374–375) and Salmon (1970), is to find some asymmetry in cases like that of the barometer and the storm that is not causal but which can be used, like the causal asymmetry, to impose a preferred direction on explanation. Both Hempel and Salmon appeal to the fact that the front that (intuitively) causes the storm will be more reliably correlated with the storm than will the barometer reading (Hempel using a different example). Salmon's more sophisticated approach uses Reichenbach's notion of *screening off*. Roughly, one potential explainer $c$ screens off another potential explainer $d$ from the explanandum $e$ just in case the correlation between $d$ and $e$ is entirely due, in a noncausal sense spelled out in the formal definition, to a correlation between $c$ and $e$, but not vice versa (Reichenbach 1956).

Reichenbach introduced the notion of screening off, however, to impart his empiricist account of the *causal relation* with the requisite asymmetry. Inevitably, I think, proposals like Hempel's and Salmon's have come to be regarded not as attempts to provide an asymmetric relation to stand as an alternative to the causal relation but rather as attempts to provide an empiricist version of the causal relation, in the manner of Reichenbach. When the proposal is regarded in this way, it becomes an attempt to provide an empiricist foundation for a causal account of explanation (as in Salmon 1984) rather than as a genuine alternative to the causal approach to explanatory asymmetry.

Taking a second noncausal approach to explanatory asymmetry, Kitcher argues that the unification account of explanation is well able to handle cases such as that of the flagpole and the shadow (Kitcher 1981). His treatment appeals to features of the unification approach present in any winner-takes-all pattern-subsumption view.

On such a view, a phenomenon is not explained by just any pattern under which it can be subsumed. Rather, one particular pattern is uniquely explanatory, namely, the subsuming pattern that maximizes generality, accuracy, and cohesion. (On Kitcher's account, simplicity is also a desideratum, and optimization is global.) Call this pattern the *optimal subsuming pattern* for an explanandum. Now, according to Kitcher, the optimal subsuming pattern for the shadow's length is the pattern described by the law relating flagpole height and shadow length. Thus, the flagpole's height explains the shadow's length.

This pattern is not, however, the optimal subsuming pattern for the flagpole's height. There is a pattern that attains a superior mix of accuracy, cohesion, and—in particular—of generality, namely, the pattern corresponding to what Kitcher calls an *origin and development* derivation, a kind of narrative in which the formation and subsequent modification of an object are recounted. All such stories, Kitcher suggests, have something in common, and thus they instantiate a single pattern of great generality. It is this origin and development pattern that explains the height of the flagpole.

At this point, Kitcher attempts a grand metaphysical inversion: our notion of causation is, he proposes, derivative of our notion of explanation. One thing is causally relevant to another just in case it is explanatorily relevant, with explanatory relevance being determined by the unification account. Thus, Kitcher endorses the thesis that explanatory asymmetry and causal asymmetry go together, but in an unconventional way: rather than relieving the burden on Kitcher's account of explanation by taking care of some potential counterexamples, the association of the two symmetries increases the burden by requiring that all features of the causal relation be derived from the acausal unification criteria for explanation.

By taking on such a heavy load, Kitcher has vastly increased the potential rewards of the unification account's success. But does it succeed? I am not convinced that the origin and development derivations form a real pattern. What do the stories of the building of a flagpole and the formation of the sun have in common? Nothing, except that they are processes of causal production, a feature to which Kitcher cannot appeal. To put the point more formally, any model that could generate both a flagpole and a class G star would, I think, be rather incohesive—so incohesive as to easily nullify its great generality.

## 1.5   The Pursuit of Explanation

The philosophical study of scientific explanation can be divided into two parts, a description of actual scientific explanatory practice and an evaluation of this practice. The evaluative project in turn has three parts. First, the internal consistency of the practice can be assessed. Second, the assumptions, both metaphysical and physical, implicit in the practice can be assessed. Under this heading you might ask, for example, whether the asymmetry in the causal influence relation is consistent with modern physics. Third, the value of the practice can be assessed. Under this heading you might ask whether there is anything worthwhile, intrinsically or otherwise, in the practice of enquiring into the causes of phenomena (Strevens 2007c). This book will be almost entirely concerned with the descriptive project; the second and third evaluative questions will be raised only in passing. (On the third, see sections 4.4 and 7.36.)

It is extremely valuable, I think, to treat the descriptive part of the study of explanation separately from the evaluative part. We should first ask: what do we regard as explanatory? And only then ask: how might we be mistaken? Mixing the descriptive and the prescriptive elements of the study can result in a certain abuse: prescriptive arguments are used to rationalize deficiencies in the description. That is, where an account of explanation fails to capture fully our actual explanatory practice, a normative argument is introduced to the effect that the part of the practice not captured is worthless. Of course, such normative arguments are not necessarily faulty; they ought, however, to be regarded with suspicion.

How, then, ought a purely descriptive study of explanation to proceed? The goal of the descriptive project is to say what kinds of explanations we give and why we give them. This is what I call our explanatory practice. The most important source of evidence concerning our explanatory practice is the sum total of the explanations regarded as scientifically adequate in their day, together with an understanding of the background against which they seemed adequate.

This immediately raises an exceptionally important question: has our explanatory practice changed over the centuries? Of course it has. But I will suppose that, although it has changed, there is an underlying set of principles that has always determined what does and does not count as a good explanation for us. Any change in explanatory practice is due to some change in the parameters of those principles.

For example, many philosophers and psychologists suspect that humans have for millennia sought causes as explanations. Insofar as our understanding of the mechanisms of causal influence has changed, the nature of cause-seeking has also changed. To take a particular case, we no longer believe in final causes, in the Aristotelian sense, and so we no longer deploy them in explanations. But underlying this change in practice is an unchanging principle—that explanations give causal information. It is principles of this sort that I hope to describe.

My approach to the descriptive project, then, is based on a gamble that there is a certain constancy in human explanatory practice, or at least—since my examples are all relatively modern—that there has been constancy since the seventeenth century. To put it another way, I am betting that relativism, in the sense defined in section 1.34, is false. (For a brief overview of the psychological evidence against explanatory relativism, see Keil (2006, 246–247).)

The second most important source of evidence concerning our explanatory practice is introspective reports on the principles used in assembling particular explanations. An example is our feeling that it is a causal principle that rules out the explanation of the height of the flagpole by the length of its shadow. Introspective reports are one step removed from the construction of explanations, and so they are to be trusted less as evidence than the body of explanations themselves. There exists the possibility that we are simply mistaken about some of the principles we are using to create explanations. Nevertheless, I will rely quite heavily on evidence of this sort.

A possible third source of evidence is psychological or neurobiological research on the nature of the mental machinery used to construct explanations. Studies of this sort are beginning to appear (Gelman and Kremer 1991; Atran 1995; Keil and Wilson 2000; Lombrozo and Carey 2006); see Lombrozo (2006) and Keil (2006) for recent reviews of the literature.

Finally, some information about our explanatory practice may be present in the sweeping generalizations about the nature of explanation invoked by certain philosophical arguments. One example is the thesis that explanation always proceeds in the direction of causation. Another is the often-asserted claim that probabilistic explanation is possible only when the explanandum is produced by a nondeterministic process (see section 9.6). The value of these generalizations depends very much on their provenance; in no case, however, do they count as evidence per se.

In some cases, a philosophical generalization about explanation is an extension of a principle intuited to be at work in some particular class of explanations, that is, an extrapolation of evidence of the second sort. The causal hypothesis about explanatory asymmetry falls into this category. These generalizations ought not to be regarded as evidence, however, but rather as hypotheses to be tested by the evidence. You do not directly observe that causal asymmetries underlie all explanatory asymmetries; you hypothesize as much, and then you confirm the hypothesis either directly, by finding particular cases where the causal asymmetry is introspected to be at work, or indirectly but more reliably, by showing that a theory of explanation that incorporates the thesis accounts for the body of explanations accepted by the scientific community.

In other cases, a philosophical generalization about explanation has been introduced in order to perpetrate the sort of abuse described earlier, namely, to argue, a priori, that a certain well-entrenched explanatory practice is mistaken just because it is inconveniently inconsistent with some philosopher's favored view of explanation. Such a generalization has *negative* value as evidence, since it has been deliberately constructed to clash with the embarrassing element of real explanatory practice. Anyone with a genuine interest in probabilistic explanation, for example, soon discovers that the majority of probabilistic explanations are applied to processes that are, or at least are thought to be, effectively deterministic.

A descriptive approach to explanation allows some kinds of information to be deliberately ignored. Information from physics about the actual structure of the nomological dependence relations, for example, will be put aside in favor of, say, psychological information about the structure that we humans attribute to the dependence relations. This is not, of course, to deny the philosophical importance of the argument from physics, but rather to put it in its proper place: not in the elucidation of our explanatory practice, but in the critique of that practice.

Consider a salient example. In order to use causal asymmetries to account for the flagpole/shadow and barometer/storm problems, you must assume that our explanatory practice posits a time-asymmetric causal relation. But fundamental physics provides some reason to think that fundamental-level nomological dependence relations are time-symmetric, in the sense that if a future property instance $G$ nomologically depends on a past property instance $F$, then $F$ also depends on $G$.

Suppose that this view of the symmetry of fundamental nomological dependence relations is correct. A purely descriptive account of our explanatory practice may happily ignore this fact, provided that it is a part of our explanatory practice to attribute time-asymmetric dependence relations to fundamental-level properties, as the case of Rutherford's gold foil suggests (section 1.42). It is an interesting question what would remain of our practice if we were forced to abandon the asymmetry assumption. Could we apply the kairetic criterion for difference-making to the symmetrical nomological dependence relations and extract something that is recognizably an explanation? Perhaps, but I will not attempt an answer here.

I will finish with a few words about empiricist metaphysics of causation. The kairetic account is quite compatible with Humeanism. You might wonder, however, whether on a Humean account of causal influence, a causal theory of explanation might not lose its special charm. To a realist, the causal approach is attractive because a causal explanation describes a process that makes the explanandum happen. On a Humean understanding of causation, nothing makes anything happen. Things just are.[15] But then what is the explanatory interest of a Humean relation of causation?

The question ought to be divided into three parts, the first two belonging to the descriptive side of an inquiry into explanation, the third belonging to the evaluative side:

1. Can a Humean account of causal influence capture all the properties of the influence relations needed to account for our explanatory practice?

2. First, is our notion of causal influence a realist one? A Humean one? A notion that does not presuppose either realism or Humeanism? Second, if (as I suspect) our notion has at least a realist tinge, would explanation lose its importance for us if we were to become convinced that realism concerning causal influence is mistaken?

3. If causal influence is given a Humean interpretation, does explanation still have intrinsic value? Or extrinsic value?

These are all excellent questions; none will be answered here.

# — 2 —

# Causal and Explanatory Relevance

## 2.1   The Minimal Causal Account of Event Explanation

The theories of causation described in chapter one all admit a causal influence relation, and agree to a great extent on which events causally influence which other events. Causal influence is just the sort of relation to which the usual causal accounts of explanatory asymmetry appeal. Does an account of explanation—or at least, of deterministic event explanation, which will be my focus in this chapter—need anything more? Perhaps not. Perhaps an event is explained by whatever other events causally influence it, together with the laws and background conditions in virtue of which they do so. This is the *minimal causal account* of explanation.

The minimal account is a one-factor account that is not at all selective: to include every causal influence in the explanation of an event *e* is to include anything that, for example, exerts a gravitational influence on the objects involved in *e*. (To see this, consider the counterfactual test for causal influence: if the gravitational influences had not been present, then although *e* itself would still have occurred, it would have been realized by a slightly different concrete event, thus its actual concrete realizer would not have occurred.) Even the distant stars win a place in the explanation. Furthermore, the influence relation extends back in time without limit: the initial conditions of the big bang itself are just as much causal influences on a present-day event *e* as the events in yesterday's news.[1]

The minimalist can censor much of this causal profusion by pointing to the negligible degree of influence exerted by most spatiotemporally distant events, a strategy discussed at the end of this section. But even then the minimalist account turns out to be insufficiently selective, as I will show in section 2.2. The remainder of the chapter explores various ways of supplementing the causal influence relation with a criterion for explanatory relevance so as to create a more selective explanatory relation, in the process moving from a one-factor to a two-factor account of causal explanation.

41

It is primarily as an expository device that I have introduced the minimal account, but I note that two well-known causal accounts of explanation are close in spirit to minimalism, those of Wesley Salmon and Peter Railton. Salmon calls his explanatory causal relation *causal relevance*:

> if we want to show why *e* occurred, we fill in the causally relevant processes and interactions that occupy the past light cone of *e*. (Salmon 1984, 275)

Salmon's causal relevance is more or less what I am calling causal influence: one event is causally relevant to another

> if there is a causal process connecting them, and if that causal process is responsible for the transmission of causal influence from one to the other. (p. 207)

It seems, then, that Salmon counts all causal influences on an event, and nothing else, as explainers of an event, and so that he is a genuine minimalist.

For Railton, not every explanation ought to be a causal explanation, but when a causal explanation is appropriate, it seems, no causal influence ought to be left out of the picture. Using the term *ideal text* to refer to the full explanation of an event, Railton writes that

> an ideal text for the explanation of the outcome of a causal process would look something like this: an inter-connected series of law-based accounts of all the nodes and links in the causal network culminating in the explanandum, complete with a fully detailed description of the causal mechanisms involved and theoretical derivations of all the covering laws involved. This full-blown causal account would extend, via various relations of reduction and supervenience, to all levels of analysis, i.e., the ideal text would be closed under relations of causal dependence, reduction, and supervenience. It would be the whole story concerning why the explanandum occurred, relative to a correct theory of the lawful dependencies of the world. Such an ideal causal . . . text would be infinite if time were without beginning or infinitely divisible, and plainly there is no question of ever setting such an ideal text down on paper. (Railton 1981, 247)

Whether Railton's notion of the explanatory causal relation is as liberal as my notion of causal influence is not clear, but Railtonian causal explanation certainly tends to inclusivity. Indeed, a Railtonian explanation will go beyond a minimal account in one respect: it will include information about "relations of reduction and supervenience" that I presume is not entailed by the facts about causal influence alone.

The most obvious difficulty facing the minimal causal account is the apparently unreasonable vastness of a complete minimal causal explanation. As I pointed out above, in a quasi-Newtonian world like our own, an event's minimal explanation ought in principle to mention anything that has ever exerted a gravitational force on the objects involved in the event, anything that had previously exerted a force on these exerters, and so on. But all scientific explanations, even the most well regarded, describe much less than the complete causal history of the explanandum. The minimalist must make sense of this fact. Here it is possible to appeal to Railton's work in defending his own causal account.

First, consider the "ontological" sense of explanation, the sense in which an event's explanation is a set of scientific facts, as opposed to a communicative act (section 1.21). According to Railton, what is meant by the claim that science has discovered such an explanation is not that the ideal explanatory text has actually been created—that is more or less impossible—but that science is in a position to create the text. That is, all the knowledge and techniques required to create the text are in place; only the time, money, and patience are lacking. Here is Railton again:

> The actual ideal is not to *produce* [ideal explanatory] texts, but to have the ability (in principle) to produce arbitrary parts of them. It is thus irrelevant whether individual scientists ever set out to fill in ideal texts as wholes, since within the division of labor among scientists it is possible to find someone (or, more precisely, some group) interested in developing the ability to fill in virtually any particular aspect of ideal texts—macro or micro, fundamental or "phenomenological," stretching over experimental or historical or geological or cosmological time. (Railton 1981, 247)

What if science lacks the knowledge to construct a complete ideal explanatory text, but can construct some of the text? Railton's position is that science's explanation is good roughly in proportion to the amount of the ideal text that can be constructed (Railton 1981, 240–246). Every little detail makes the explanation a little better, but if a large piece of the ideal text cannot be constructed, science's explanation falls some way short of perfection.

Second, consider the sense in which an explanation is an act of communication. Railton holds that the quality of such an explanation is roughly proportional to the amount of the ideal text that is transmitted to the audience. Since what is communicated is inevitably a vanishingly small fragment of the ideal text, an act of communication will always be, when considered on its intrinsic merits as a Railtonian explanation, a paltry thing, however useful it may be to its recipient. As the passage quoted above suggests, no one person ever comes close to understanding completely any phenomenon; if there is complete understanding, it is something possessed by the scientific community as a whole.

Pragmatics will, for Railton as much as anyone, play a role in the evaluation of explanations as acts of communication: an explainer ought not to be penalized for failing to mention an element of the ideal text that is common knowledge, for example, since you do not add to what is communicated by explicitly stating such things. But these pragmatic considerations are not proprietary to the study of explanation. Railton would, I suppose, like Lewis (1986a), deny that there is any distinctive pragmatics of explanation—correctly, I think.

In summary, then, according to the minimal causal account:

1. Every causal influence on an event is explanatorily relevant to its occurrence.

2. You do not fully understand a phenomenon until you are in a position (in principle) to articulate the role played in the production of the phenomenon by every one of these causal influences.

3. When you cannot construct the full history of causal influence, or you communicate less than the full history, the quality of the explanation increases with the proportion of the history you can construct, or that you do communicate.

As stated, the minimal account's requirements are demanding, but they can be used to defend the account against the charge that it mandates, absurdly, that the influence of the distant stars be included in the explanation of an everyday event such as a window's breaking. The defense has three steps.

First, a measure of *degree of causal influence* is introduced and the distant stars shown to have only a vanishingly small influence on the window's breaking. (I observed in section 1.43 that influence must in any case be quantified in order to deal with the barometer/storm asymmetry using facts about causal influence alone. See that discussion and note 12 of chapter one for two approaches to quantification.)

Second, the explanatory importance of a causal factor is equated with its degree of influence. It follows that the distant stars have almost no explanatory importance with respect to the window's breaking.

Finally, conversational pragmatics is invoked to argue that such unimportant factors will never appear in an explanation—in the communicative sense—of the window's breaking, as follows. Given the practical limits on the length of explanations, to mention the distant stars at all in an account of the breaking would be to implicitly ascribe to them a degree of importance far beyond their actual explanatory weight. Their relevance, though real, is simply so slight that in no imaginable context would it be conversationally correct even to allude to their presence. (Lewis (1986a) mentions some further pragmatic criteria that could plausibly be used to account for the stars' explanatory absence.)

None of this changes the fact that the stars are explanatorily relevant; what it does is to explain, rather well, the appearance of irrelevance. You may have lingering doubts: surely the stars are irrelevant not just in practice but in principle? I concur. But there are better places to take a stand.

## 2.2 The Problem of Relevance

### 2.21 Rasputin's Death

When a cabal of Russian nobles decided at last to do away with the mad Russian monk Rasputin, they took decisive action:

> Rasputin was invited to visit Yusupov's home and, once there, was given poisoned wine and tea cakes. When he did not die, the frantic Yusupov shot him. Rasputin collapsed but was able to run out into the courtyard, where Purishkevich shot him again. The conspirators then bound him and threw him through a hole in the ice into the Neva River, where he finally died by drowning. (Encyclopedia Britannica, CD 1998 standard edition, s.v. "Rasputin")

Rasputin's last stand makes a compelling story because, of all the death-promoting causal factors with which the conspirators assailed their victim—poison, shooting (twice), and drowning—the last alone explains Rasputin's demise. No human can escape drowning when tossed through a hole in an icy river with hands and feet bound. Only a truly infallible method of murder could finish off Rasputin (though he is said by some to have partially freed himself before succumbing to the icy Neva).

On the minimalist account, all causal influences on an event, or at least all non-negligible causal influences, participate in that event's explanation. Rasputin's being poisoned and shot are causal influences on his death, influences that are, in contrast to the gravitational effect of distant stars, quite substantial. Consider: Rasputin is convulsing from the poison and bleeding from the gunshot wounds even as he finally dies of asphyxiation, so the process of his dying is thoroughly interwoven with the process of his convulsing and bleeding. Consequently, the poisoning and the shooting have a considerable effect on the concrete realization of his dying, and so they count as major causal influences on the dying. The minimalist therefore has no choice but to accord them a large measure of explanatory importance.

According to the minimal account, in other words, poisoning and shooting are as much, or almost as much, a part of the explanation of Rasputin's death as his being bound up and thrown into the river. But this cannot be right. The poison and shooting failed to kill Rasputin, and so they are irrelevant to his death, or, at least, are vastly less relevant than his being thrown into the river.

Minimalism, it seems, is too minimal. What the enterprise of causal explanation requires is some criterion for distinguishing between the causal influences that explain Rasputin's death and those that do not. To find such a criterion is this chapter's *problem of explanatory relevance*. As you will recall from section 1.32, variants of the relevance problem have been noted many times. The seriousness of the problem, however, has often been underestimated, perhaps because the irrelevant factors appearing in the standard counterexamples have had so small a degree of causal influence—in many cases, such as the hexing of the salt, virtually none at all—that they are easily dealt with by the minimal account.

You may have noted a parallel between our explanatory and our causal commentary on Rasputin's death: just as we say that Rasputin's being thrown into the river, but not his being poisoned and shot, *explains* his death, so we say that his being thrown into the river, but not his being poisoned and shot, *caused* his death. The causation in question is the kind of high-level causal relation that the minimalist account deliberately ignores; the possibility of abandoning explanatory minimalism to appeal to high-level causation will be discussed in due course (section 2.23).

## 2.22  Three Defenses of Minimalism

The relevance problem cannot be solved by even the most creative use of the resources allowed by the minimal account, or so I will argue, considering three minimalist strategies for dealing with the case of Rasputin. The first argues that, on the minimal account, Rasputin's influviation—his being bound and thrown into a river (cf. defenestration)—is, after all, a better explanation of his death than poisoning or shooting. The second tries to explain away the whole phenomenon of relevance by appealing to pragmatics. The third contends that poisoning and shooting are, contrary to the explanatory intuitions exploited above, highly explanatorily relevant to Rasputin's death.

To the first defense, then. The hope is to establish that an explanation that cites Rasputin's influviation will contain more information about the causal network culminating in death than one that cites, say, poisoning. Clearly, the influviation and its consequences do not encompass a larger volume of the network than the poisoning; if anything, the reverse is true, since the poisoning occurs earlier and continues to exert its influence up until the moment of death. It would have to be, then, that the influviation has a greater degree of causal influence than the poisoning on the concrete realizer of the dying, and so that information about the influviation carries more explanatory weight.

It is plausible that this is so: more features of the dying's realizer depend on the influviation than depend on the poisoning. Thus, the influviation is relatively more important, explanatorily speaking, than the poisoning. But this is not enough in itself to solve the relevance problem. What is shown is that the poisoning is somewhat less explanatory than the influviation, but what needs to be shown is that the poisoning is not relevant at all, or at least that it has minimal relevance.

Second, you might hope that the pragmatics of explanation will offer a way out. Could it be that poisoning is in fact just as relevant to Rasputin's death as influviation, objectively speaking—just as the minimalist account would have it—but that influviation appears to be far more important because it is more practically relevant in the conversational contexts where Rasputin's death is typically explained? If this were true, there would be a conversational context (perhaps very seldom realized) in which poisoning would be highly relevant, and therefore in which poisoning would have to be mentioned in an explanation. But there is no such context. Poisoning had little or nothing to do with Rasputin's death, and so does not explain it; no context can alter this fact.

I do not deny that, in any particular act of explanation, context can make some factors more salient than others. But contextual salience—a pragmatic matter—is to be distinguished from explanatory relevance. Context can make salient or nonsalient a factor that is already explanatorily relevant, but as the case of Rasputin's death shows, it cannot confer explanatory relevance where it does not exist or remove it where it does exist. Poisoning is irrelevant to Rasputin's death and influviation is relevant, no matter what the context.

Of course, the conversational context can make poisoning relevant by altering the explanandum itself: if what is wanted is an answer to the question why Rasputin's assassins resorted to throwing him into the river, their unsuccessful attempt at poisoning may well figure in the explanation. But that is simply to change the subject.

The third defense of minimalism dissents from the prevailing view that the explananda of event explanations are normally high-level events (section 1.22), proposing instead that in scientific explanation, at least, they are usually or always concrete events, events individuated by every minute physical detail of their happening. The concrete event of Rasputin's death is an entity so fine-grained that it would have been a different event had the smallest detail of the death been different. The fact that Rasputin's body was full of poison or punctured by bullet holes is an essential, and not inconsiderable, part of the concrete event of Rasputin's death; hence it makes intuitive sense after all that poisoning and shooting should appear in the explanation of the fact that this event occurred—this *exact* event, in all its detail. In other words, if the explanation of Rasputin's death is an explanation of the death's concrete realizer, then poisoning and shooting are intuitively explanatorily relevant, just as the minimalist account implies.

As was pointed out long ago by Davidson (1967), following Hempel, this proposal does not sit well with our explanatory practice. Consider two propositions: that Rasputin died, and that Rasputin's body contained poison as he died. These two descriptions pick out the same concrete event, because the goings-on they name occupy the same spatiotemporal region. It follows that, if it is the concrete event that is the explanandum, then the two propositions, considered as descriptions of explananda, are equivalent and so ought to attract the same explanation. But this is not so: the explanation of the first is that Rasputin was tied up and thrown into the river (poison is irrelevant), while the explanation of the second is that Rasputin was poisoned shortly before his death (how he died, hence his being tied and thrown into the river, is irrelevant).

This last objection goes some way to exposing a fundamental flaw in the minimalist's way of thinking: according to minimalism, all explananda occurring or holding in the same pockets of space-time will have the same explanations. But as Rasputin's death and many other examples show, our explanatory practice is far more discriminating than the minimalist allows (see also Strevens 2003a, §4). We distinguish between explananda whose occurrence depends on the content of the same space-time region in different ways, that is, between different high-level events with the same concrete realizers, counting different causal influences as explanatorily relevant in each case. Treating explananda as high-level events is an important prerequisite for all the accounts of explanatory relevance considered in this and the next chapter (section 3.3).

## 2.23  Augmenting the Minimal Account

The problem of explanatory relevance is the problem of picking out, from among all the causal influences on an event, those that genuinely explain the event. The task, then, might be neutrally characterized as follows: find a selection principle able to make the appropriate relevance distinctions, and then add it under some guise to the minimal causal account of explanation.

Although the development of an apt selection principle is still many pages away, it is not possible to avoid a major decision as to the strategy for incorporating the selection principle, whatever it may be, into the theory of explanation. Let me lay out the decision and then show that it is not as final as it seems.

One way for an explanatory causalist to rein in the minimalist's judgments of explanatory relevance is to adopt a more selective conception of the causal relation. As I observed earlier, we are inclined to say that Rasputin's influviation, but not his being poisoned or shot, is a cause of his death. This would seem to indicate the existence of a high-level causal relation between the influviation and the death, and the nonexistence of a corresponding relation between the poisoning or the shooting and the death.

High-level causal relations of this sort are exactly what multilevel accounts of causation such as the counterfactual and manipulation accounts provide. In particular, the absence of a high-level causal relation between, say, the poisoning and the death is indicated by the negative outcome of the counterfactual test for causal dependence between those two high-level events: if Rasputin had not been poisoned, he would still have died.

The proper solution to the relevance problem for a causalist might seem clear, then. For the poisoning to explain Rasputin's death, it must not merely stand in the causal influence relation to the death; it must stand in a high-level causal relation to the death. On the assumption that there is a high-level causal relation between events $c$ and $e$ just in case the causal claim $c$ *was a cause of* $e$ is true, the solution gets you what you want: since we say that influviation was a cause of Rasputin's death whereas poisoning was not, the influviation but not the poisoning will qualify as a part of the explanation of the death. Whether Lewis's or Woodward's or some other view gives the correct truth conditions for causal claims does not matter; the idea is that whatever account of causal claims is correct also solves the problem of explanatory relevance.

An alternative approach to the relevance problem—my own—aims not to invoke more causal metaphysics than is already inherent in the relation of causal influence. The selection rule that distinguishes the relevant causal influences from the rest is conceived not as a proper part of the metaphysics of causation but as an independent element of a causal theory of explanation. I am proposing, then, what I called in section 1.1 a two-factor account of explanation. One factor is a causal relation, namely, causal influence. The other factor is a noncausal criterion of explanatory relevance that selects just those causal influences that are explanatorily relevant to a given explanandum.

The two-factor approach has the advantage of preserving metaphysical ecumenism: by committing itself to nothing more than the causal influence relation, it remains compatible with a broad range of views about the nature of causation. This advantage, and the other advantages of two-factorism mentioned in section 1.1, may however seem to pale in the light of the following objection. We humans have a well-established practice of making causal claims such as *The poisoning did not cause Rasputin's death*. Unless we are deeply mistaken, this indicates the existence of, and our everyday deployment of, a wealth of high-level causal relations eminently qualified to solve the relevance problem. Surely, even in the name of so high-minded a goal as ecumenism, it makes no sense to turn your back on such causal riches? Why not have it all: the high-level *is a cause of* relation, a set of truth conditions for all of our causal claims, and a solution to the problem of explanatory relevance?

On my two-factor approach, I promise, you will have it all, in just as neat a package as the one-factorites proffer. Begin with the proposition that claims of the form *c was a cause of e* assert that *c* is a part of the causal explanation of *e*. This is, of course, a view necessarily endorsed by the kind of one-factor theory under consideration. But a two-factor theorist can— and I will—hold the same view.

The two-factor interpretation gives the thesis a new cast. The causal claim *c was a cause of e* does not, it turns out, assert the existence of a high-level causal relation between *c* and *e*. Rather, it asserts the existence of an *explanatory relation* between the two events, the explanatory relation in question being a combination of a low-level causal influence relation and the high-level explanatory relevance relation.[2] Consequently, the correct account of explanatory relevance, when brought together with the relation of causal influence, gives you both the truth conditions for causal claims and an account of the high-level *is a cause of* relation, now understood not as a purely causal relation but as the causal-explanatory relation, the relation that an event must bear to another event in order to participate as a cause in its explanation.

The fundamental difference between the two-factor and the one-factor views is, then, that on the two-factor view the explanatory facts are prior to and account for our practice of making *is a cause of* claims, whereas on the one-factor view the relation expressed by *is a cause of* claims is a high-level causal relation that is prior to and forms the basis for our explanatory practice.

At this early stage, I do not expect you to assent to the two-factor over the one-factor approach. I do want you to see that the two-factor approach is not at an inherent disadvantage in giving a unified account of explanatory relevance, causal claims, and the appearance of a high-level causal relation. These phenomena go together as neatly on a two-factor as on a one-factor approach.

How to decide, then, between the one-factor and the two-factor strategies? There seem to be limited grounds on which to opt for one over the other, yet the decision will determine, fundamentally, the character of causal explanation.

As it happens, although to make a decision at this point is convenient, it need not have momentous consequences. I will proceed as though the two-factor view is correct, searching for a criterion for explanatory relevance with which to sift through the information about causal influence. But in so doing, I will not entirely spurn the one-factorites. Any of the relevance criteria I consider in this book can be folded into the metaphysics of causation to yield a high-level causal relation. That is, it is always possible to take a two-factor explanatory relation and to reinterpret it as a species of causal relation. This is true even for the explanatory relation I endorse, the kairetic difference-making relation. When $c$ makes a difference to $e$, and so helps to explain $e$, say that there is a high-level causal relation between $c$ and $e$, if you will. Although, as the difference-making criterion soars to the heights of abstraction in parts three and four, it will seem less and less plausible that it plays any part in the metaphysics of causation, I do not forbid a metaphysical construal.

Further, both the one-factor and the two-factor strategies suggest the same difference-making tests for causal-explanatory relevance, namely, the probabilistic, counterfactual, manipulationist, and kairetic criteria examined in this and the next chapter. With a minimum of reinterpretation, then, my comments on each are as pertinent to the one-factor as to the two-factor project. Though expository convenience calls for a schism, it need not go very deep.

## 2.3   The Probabilistic Solution

The criteria for explanatory relevance considered in what follows—the probabilistic, counterfactual, manipulation, and kairetic criteria—all pick out as explanatorily relevant those factors that, in some sense, *make a difference* to the fact that the explanandum obtains. But they offer quite different procedures for determining difference-makers.

The causal influences that make a difference to an explanandum, according to the probabilistic approach, are those that change the probability of the explanandum. (If the probability is decreased, an influence is negatively relevant. In what follows, I avoid the difficult question of the explanatory significance of negative relevance; however, I will take a stand in part four.)

Take the minimal causal account of explanation, or something like it, such as Salmon's account, and augment it with a probabilistic criterion for relevance. You then have the sort of probabilistic causal account of explanation advocated by Railton (1978), Humphreys (1981, 1989), and, in response to Hitchcock's (1995) criticisms, Salmon (1997) himself. (Railton's probabilistic causal account is intended for a different class of explananda than the causal account sketched in section 2.1.) The equivalent one-factor approach posits a probabilistic account of high-level causation, following such writers as Reichenbach (1956) and Suppes (1970).

Any probabilistic criterion for explanatory relevance that is applicable to Rasputin's death faces a striking prima facie problem: being poisoned generally increases your chance of dying. Thus, Rasputin's being poisoned appears to pass the probabilistic test for explanatory relevance. (The same goes, of course, for his being shot.)

The probabilist's natural response to this problem is to hold that, although being poisoned increases most people's chances of dying, it did not increase Rasputin's chance of dying. More exactly, being poisoned in this particular way and on this particular day did not affect his chance of dying, presumably because of some lucky combination of local factors—low-level facts about the poison, the preparation of the tea cakes, Rasputin's metabolism, and his earlier meals that day—that rendered the poison ineffective.[3]

I will examine three objections to this strategy. The first objection is that, for a certain class of poisonings, the strategy either fails or trivializes the probabilistic relevance account.

The kind of cases I have in mind are those in which we would say that Rasputin's surviving the poisoning was a fluke. By this I mean that he survived not because of the presence of some systematically countervailing causal factor, such as an antidote or a particular kind of metabolism, but for one of the following two reasons:

1. Indeterministic case: some step of the poisoning process was indeterministic, and Rasputin was fortunate enough that the step happened to fall through.

2. Deterministic case: some step of the poisoning process depended on certain low level physiological details and, as it happened, that day the details were not quite right. In other words, the initial conditions deviated slightly from what was required for a successful poisoning.

I consider these scenarios in turn.

First, the indeterministic case. If the success of the poisoning turns on an indeterministic step, then there is no way for the probabilistic relevance account to avoid the judgment that poisoning was relevant to death. For in such a case, poisoning *did* raise the probability of Rasputin's dying, but he was lucky, and so he did not die. (For similar counterexamples to probabilistic approaches to relevance, see Achinstein (1983, §5.5) and Gluck and Gimbel (1997).)

The situation is analogous to the following unhistorical case, which has the advantage that the causal pathway is far simpler than in a poisoning. Suppose that Rasputin's enemies placed a bomb under his chair controlled by a quantum trigger that gave it a 75% probability of exploding. As it happened, the bomb did not explode, so they drowned him. Clearly, the placing of the bomb increased Rasputin's chances of dying; equally clearly, the bomb made no difference to his actual death. (This case is treated successfully by the kairetic account in section 11.3.)

Second, the deterministic case. In order for the probabilist to say that poisoning did not increase the probability of Rasputin's death in a scenario where a few apparently insignificant details made the difference between death and survival, every detail must be taken into account in fixing the probability for the death. But if every minute detail that might make a difference is taken into account when calculating probabilities, then given the assumption of underlying determinism, the probabilities can only come out as zero or one. Those factors that raise the probability of an event from zero to one will count as difference-makers; the rest will not. The result is something that resembles the counterfactual account of difference-making, to be discussed in the next section, more than any probabilistic relevance account.

In summary, the process by which poisoning leads to death is either indeterministic or not. If indeterministic, the probabilistic relevance account fails. If deterministic, in order not to fail, the account must take so much detail into account when determining probabilities that they all go to zero or one, in which case it is transformed into a kind of counterfactual account.

A second and related problem with the probabilistic handling of the Rasputin case: we do not know whether the poisoning process in Rasputin's case was genuinely indeterministic or not, and if indeterministic, whether it was the kind of case where Rasputin's survival was due to brute good luck—

where the poisoning raised the probability of death but he lived anyway—or where, because of the presence of some factor, such as a cautionary advance dose of the antidote, the poisoning never raised the probability of death at all. That is, we do not know whether or not the poisoning raised the probability of Rasputin's death. But we confidently judge that the poisoning was irrelevant to death. Therefore, the poisoning's irrelevance cannot turn on the question of whether death's probability was raised. In this case, at least, there is more to our judgment of relevance than a difference in probabilities.

Now to the third objection, the nub of which is not so much that the probabilistic relevance account fails to handle a particular kind of case, but that it is missing an essential component.

Suppose that the problem raised above—that of which details are to play a role in fixing the value of a probability—is solved, so that for any specification of a scenario and an event there is a definite probability of the event's occurring in the given scenario. Then there is a fact of the matter about Rasputin's probability of dying after he is given the poison. This fact is not enough, however, to determine whether poisoning is probabilistically relevant to death. Also required is a fact about the probability of Rasputin's dying had he not been given the poison.

In order to settle on such a probability, you need a procedure for determining the relevant counterfactual, nonpoisoning scenario. In the Rasputin case, this is not so easy. Should your specification of the scenario mention the fact that Rasputin's assassins had him in their power and were determined to kill him? If so, it seems that no specific causal factor, not even influviation, will raise the probability of death, since that probability is already at its maximum value of one. The assassins' intentions, then, had better be left out. But what principle guides these decisions? The probabilistic relevance account of difference-making does not provide an answer.[4]

Let me put this in the form of a general observation about any "difference-making" criterion for explanatory relevance. All such accounts have a common form. To determine whether a causal influence $c$ makes a difference to an explanandum $e$, a comparison is made between two scenarios: the actual scenario, in which $c$ is present, and a nonactual scenario in which $c$ is not present. The facility with which $e$ occurs in each scenario is evaluated. If it varies, then $c$ is classified as a difference-maker. There are two steps, then, to the comparison:

1. The two scenarios to be compared are determined. The principal problem is to determine the details of the nonactual scenario, the scenario
   from which $c$ has in some sense been removed.

2. The facility with which $e$ occurs in each scenario is evaluated, and
   these "facilities" compared.

What counts as a scenario and what determines the "facility with which $e$
occurs" depends on the account of difference-making. In the probabilistic
account, a scenario might be a model in some probabilistic theory, and
the facility with which $e$ occurs the probability that the model ascribes to
$e$. In Lewis's counterfactual account, a scenario is a possible world, and
the facility with which $e$ occurs is the truth value, in the world, of the
proposition that $e$ occurred (no probabilities are involved in Lewis's basic
account).

A complete difference-making account of explanatory relevance will,
then, contain two parts: a removal procedure and a comparison procedure.
The probabilistic criterion provides a comparison procedure—a procedure
that will, once it is amended to deal with exploding chairs and the like, continue to be useful—but it lacks a removal procedure. The counterfactual
and manipulation criteria, to be considered next, fill this gap.

## 2.4   The Counterfactual Solution

According to what I will call the simple counterfactual approach to explanatory relevance, an event $c$ that causally influences another event $e$ is
explanatorily relevant to $e$ just in case, had $c$ not occurred, $e$ would not
have occurred. Adopting such a criterion is, of course, roughly equivalent to
taking the one-factor approach to causal explanation and adopting a simple counterfactual account of high-level causation. (It is not quite equivalent, because there is no causal influence requirement for the one-factor
approach's high-level causation.) Lewis (1986a) himself exploits the similarity by advocating a one-factor account of causal explanation on which
the explanatory high-level causal relation is given, as you would expect, by
his own version of the counterfactual account.

The great virtue of a counterfactual approach to relevance is that, when
conjoined with the Stalnaker/Lewis account of counterfactuals, it gives a
full account of removal, thus satisfying the demand made at the end of the
previous section. Let me elaborate this claim using the simple counterfac-

tual criterion for relevance and Lewis's original account of counterfactuals' truth conditions (Lewis 1973b). The effect of removing a factor, on this approach, is to be determined by finding the closest possible worlds—the possible worlds most similar to the actual world in both matters of actual fact and in laws of nature—in which the factor is not present. Whatever holds in all such worlds is what holds if the factor is removed. (I ignore here the possibility, allowed by Lewis, that there are no maximally close worlds but rather sets of worlds of increasing closeness.)

The heart of Lewis's removal procedure is the account of the relation of closeness between possible worlds. When the factor to be removed is a spatiotemporally discrete event, such as a shooting or an influviation, there is a relatively straightforward algorithm for determining the closest worlds. They are the worlds that best conform to the following description: (a) they are identical to ours up until shortly before $c$ actually occurred, (b) at which time a small divergence from actuality (perhaps a "small miracle") prevents, as conservatively as possible, the occurrence of $c$, after which (c) events unfold as prescribed by the laws of the actual world. (For a comprehensive discussion of the algorithm, and in particular of the nature of "conservative" divergences, see Bennett (2003).) As you will see shortly, the removal of other kinds of states of affairs may be more involved.

Let me raise two problems for the counterfactual account of difference-making, considered as an account of explanatory relevance. The first is the well-known problem of preemption.

Writing about probabilistic relevance in the previous section, I suggested that, given Rasputin's assassins' determination to end his life and the fact that they had him entirely within their power, they were sure to kill him one way or another. But if this is true, then it seems that if they had not thrown Rasputin into the river, he would have died anyway by some other nefarious means. Rasputin's being thrown into the river fails the counterfactual test for difference-making, then, and is therefore counted as explanatorily irrelevant. This conclusion is not in accord with our explanatory practice. The simple counterfactual account will, as explained in more detail in section 6.2, make the same mistake in any case of preemption, that is, in any case where there was a backup cause that would have brought about the explanandum if the actual cause had not.

Lewisians have tried to solve the preemption problem in a number of ways. Lewis's original reaction was to define causation as the ancestral of counterfactual dependence, so that $c$ is a cause of $e$ just in case there is a series of events $d_1, \ldots, d_n$, such that $d_1$ depends on $c$, each of the other $d$s depends on its predecessor, and $e$ depends on $d_n$. It is now accepted that this solution does not correctly treat cases of what is somewhat cryptically called *late preemption*, of which the Rasputin case is an example. Try to find an effect of influviation—a $d_i$—on which Rasputin's death counterfactually depends; you cannot, because for any promising $d$, Rasputin's assassins will react to the nonoccurrence of $d$ by finding some other way to kill him.

This is, of course, only the beginning of the debate between Lewis and his critics, which has involved two amendments to the counterfactual account, Lewis (1986c) and Lewis (2000), the second a radical reformulation that attempts to analyze causal claims using nothing more than the relation of causal influence. I argue against the radical reformulation in Strevens (2003a). But for my purposes here, what is important is not that the counterfactual account fails outright, but that it stalls. This is enough reason to consider a new alternative.

The preemption problem is essentially a problem with the counterfactual approach's removal procedure: it fails to remove or otherwise neutralize backup causes, so rendering actual causes irrelevant. My second objection to the counterfactual approach also arises from a problem with removal. Though Lewis's removal procedure generally yields a well-defined result when removing events, it is less satisfactory when removing ongoing states of affairs, background conditions, facts about objects' structure, and so on (cf. Field 2003, 448–450).

Suppose that you want to explain why a lump of sodium exploded when thrown into a pool of water. The correct explanation depends on sodium's having a loosely bound outer electron, which makes it susceptible to ionization. But in addition to sodium's loosely bound electron, many other facts about its atomic structure causally influence its behavior. Its number of neutrons, twelve in the only naturally occurring isotope, also counts as a causal influence on the explosion: the neutron number in part determines, for example, sodium's density, and so the rate with which it sinks. Neutron number does not, however, explain the explosion.

An account of explanatory relevance should make this distinction, counting the loosely bound electron as relevant, and neutron number irrelevant, to the explosion. The counterfactual criterion for relevance will do so by examining claims such as *If the sodium had not had twelve neutrons per atom, it would not have exploded*. On the Lewis approach, such a counterfactual is evaluated by finding a possible world (or set of worlds—this complication will not affect the argument) in which the exploding sodium has some number of neutrons other than twelve. If the sodium explodes in this world, the neutron number is irrelevant; if not, it is relevant.

A world in which the sodium sample has a different number of neutrons, or in which its outer electron is not loosely bound, is a world with a radically different physics from ours (at least in the vicinity of the sample). To determine whether sodium explodes in such a place, you must fix all the important details of this physics and reason about its consequences. This is a far more difficult task, I will suggest, than discerning the explanatory irrelevance of neutron number and the relevance of loose binding, so it cannot be, as the counterfactual account proposes, the means by which we arrive at knowledge about explanatory relevance.

Start with neutron number. In the actual world, the twelve-neutron isotope of sodium is, as noted above, the metal's only stable form. In the closest world where the neutron number is different, is the sodium stable? If not, its reaction with water will depend on its rate of decay and the chemistry of the decay products. If it is stable, what facts about the physics of atomic nuclei have been changed to ensure stability? Will these interfere with sodium's chemical properties, in particular its proclivity to react with water? Vexing questions.

Or take the relevance of the loosely bound outer electron. What is the physics of a sodium sample where the outer electron is bound more tightly? Are the rules of shell-filling changed, so that sodium's $p$ shell fits seven electrons rather than six? It would then be a nonreactive substance like neon. But perhaps this is the wrong change to make: it would require too fundamental a revision of quantum chemistry to allow an odd number of electrons to fill a shell. Make the $p$ shell accommodate eight electrons, then. Now the outer electrons are all tightly bound, but sodium is a reactive substance like fluorine.

Perhaps you should forget about shell-filling and instead make the electromagnetic force stronger, leaving sodium's eleventh electron alone in the outer shell but tying it more tightly to the nucleus. It will now take more energy to dislodge the electron—but there is more available, because the attraction between the hydrogen nuclei in the water and the electron is also stronger. Or could you tweak the physics of sodium while leaving unchanged the physics for the constituents of water? Who knows what would happen then?

Now, none of the foregoing considerations rule out the possibility that there is a determinate fact about the closest physics (or closest range of physics) in which sodium lacks various of its actual properties, nor that there is a determinate fact about whether or not sodium reacts explosively with water in worlds with such physics. Perhaps the counterfactual account does supply an answer to questions about the explanatory relevance of sodium's properties. But this could not possibly be the way that *we* answer such questions. I doubt that any expert on sodium's chemistry would venture a view on the issues raised above. By contrast, they are able to assert confidently that neutron number is irrelevant, and loose binding relevant, to sodium's reaction with water. Our scientific practice settles questions about relevance, then, without having to settle questions about the relative closeness of various physics to our own. The correct philosophical account of that practice will do likewise.

As I remarked above, the counterfactual account's difficulty with both questions discussed in this section arises, in different ways, from its removal procedure's requiring you to extrapolate entire possible worlds around the absences you posit. You may fiddle with the details of Rasputin's death, but you must evaluate the consequences of your fiddling in a world that contains the entire Russian court, malevolent and powerful conspirators included. Likewise, your tweaking of the sodium sample's properties must be made consistent with the complete underlying physics of the sample, with the dismaying result not that your question gets the wrong answer, but that it is rendered for practical purposes unanswerable.

The holism of Lewis's removal procedure is perhaps appropriate for elucidating the truth conditions of counterfactual claims, but it makes impossibly heavy going of picking out explanatorily relevant factors. The correct difference-making criterion for relevance will, I suggest, allow relevance to be deduced from isolated models of relatively small parts of the workings of the world. The manipulation account, to be considered next, and the kairetic criterion both satisfy this demand.

## 2.5   The Manipulationist Solution

Can another difference-making account with a counterfactual flavor, the manipulation view advocated by Woodward (2003) and others, improve on the simple counterfactual view and its Lewisian variants? I will answer this question with reference to the same two issues discussed in the previous section, preemption and the question of the explanatory relevance of structural properties such as neutron number.

As with the counterfactual account, I will be taking an account of high-level causation and converting it into a criterion for explanatory relevance suitable for a two-factor approach to causal explanation. What happens, then, if you count as explanatorily relevant to an event *e* only those causal influences that the Woodward account counts as the "actual causes" of *e*? Let me answer this question by explaining Woodward's handling of cases of preemption.[5]

Consider a simplified Rasputin case involving some very hands-off conspirators. The mad monk is invited to tea, but the conspirators depart before he arrives, leaving poisoned teacakes on the table. Worrying that Rasputin may have recently eaten, they construct a backup trap as well. If the teacakes remain untouched for a certain period, the floor of the room opens up, dropping Rasputin into the Neva.

The Woodward treatment begins, always, with a causal graph showing the relevant type-level causal relations between variables (figure 2.1A). All variables in the graph are binary, corresponding to a given event's occurrence or nonoccurrence. When an event occurs, it triggers the event indicated by the "+" arrow; when it does not occur, it triggers the event indicated by the "−" arrow. (Where there are no arrows, there are no consequences.)

The causal graph is capable of being instantiated in different ways. Suppose that, in the actual scenario, Rasputin eats the teacakes and dies. Then the instantiated graph is as shown in figure 2.1B (events that are crossed out fail to occur; uncrossed events occur).

Suppose that Rasputin did not eat the teacakes? What would have happened then? The graph can be used to represent the evaluation of this counterfactual, as follows.[6] Flip the variable representing the eating of the teacakes so that the eating event no longer occurs, and then stand back and let the consequences propagate through the graph. The result is as shown in figure 2.1C: the nonoccurrence of the eating causes the floor to open, so that Rasputin is influviated and subsequently dies. This corresponds to our intuitive answer to the counterfactual question: if Rasputin had not eaten the teacakes he would still have died. Because Rasputin dies either way, the simple counterfactual test for explanatory relevance does not count the teacake-eating that actually occurs as relevant to his death, a classic preemption counterexample to the simple counterfactual account of either relevance or causation. (This is the sort of case, incidentally, that Lewis's more sophisticated counterfactual criterion is easily able to handle.)

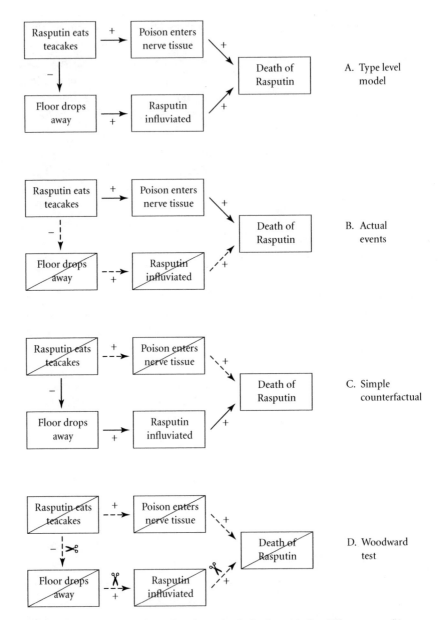

**Figure 2.1** The counterfactual and manipulationist tests for difference-making contrasted

Woodward's account does better than the simple counterfactual test. To determine the relevance of an event $c$ to another event $e$, a Woodwardian uses the following procedure:

1. Find a path in the (type level) causal graph leading from $c$ to $e$, that is, a path that begins with a "+" arrow emerging from $c$ and ends with a "+" arrow leading to $e$.

2. Assign all variables not on the path their actual values, then sever all the arrows pointing into these variables, in effect holding the variables constant no matter what (while maintaining any effects they may have on variables on the chosen path).

3. Flip the variable representing $c$ so that it represents $c$'s nonoccurrence, and let the effect propagate through the graph.

If this operation results in $e$'s not occurring for *any path* from $c$ to $e$, then $c$ is relevant to $e$ (and causes $e$, on Woodward's interpretation). The relevance is, of course, by way of the path in question.

Figure 2.1D shows the Woodward manipulation of the graph for the only path leading from teacake-eating to death. The scissors indicate the notional cutting of the causal links not on this path. (You can see that in this case just the first needs to be cut, but in principle they should all be cut.) When the eating is set not to occur, the floor remains in place, since the link between the non-eating and the floor's opening has been severed. Consequently, the death does not occur. For this reason, the death counterfactually depends in the Woodwardian sense on the eating, and so the eating is relevant to the death, as desired.

Note that the ability of the manipulation account to handle preemption has little or nothing to do with its manipulationist element: what works the magic is not the fact that the causal potency of the putative cause $c$ is assessed by manipulating $c$'s occurrence but a logically separate element of the test, namely, its holding the off-path elements to their actual values.

The Woodward account for the most part gives the right answers about relevance (for remaining problems, see sections 3.82, 6.25, and 11.4), but it relies heavily on the discriminating power of the type-level causal relations that connect the event variables. What are these relations? They cannot be relations of causal influence, for the following reason. The floor mechanism (so the story goes) is rather elaborate, and Rasputin studies it bemusedly as he dines on the teacakes. As a result, he eats fewer teacakes than he might have otherwise and dies a slower death. On this story, the floor mechanism is an important background condition influencing the way that the teacakes cause death—it makes a real difference to the way that death is realized. But then, if Woodward's arrows represent causal influence, the floor mechanism is on the putative causal path from teacake-eating to death (sitting down to eat the teacakes causes Rasputin to notice the mechanism, which in turn affects the manner of his eating), and so the link between teacakes and floor cannot be severed; as a consequence, when the model is manipulated so that the teacakes are no longer eaten, Rasputin will be deposited into the Neva.

It is crucial to the correct operation of the Woodward procedure, then, that irrelevant influences such as the floor mechanism are excluded at the type level. Intuitively, the causal generalizations represented in the graph with which the procedure begins must concern just those causal factors that can potentially make a difference to the event of interest, the explanandum.

What is the nature of these high-level difference-making relations between variables? What is the metaphysical basis for the type-level graph that tells all? Woodward sometimes appears to believe that the high-level causal relations are metaphysically irreducible; at other times, he appears to be agnostic on this question. But whether they are metaphysically reducible or not, there is something deeply unsatisfactory about the manipulationist's notion of relevance. On the one hand, if the high-level relations between event types are irreducible—if they are, for example, metaphysically basic high-level facts about manipulability—then the manipulationist relevance criterion is certainly well grounded, but at the cost of positing primitive facts about high-level explanatory (or for a one-factor theorist, causal) relevance, a disappointing outcome. If on the other hand the high-level relations are reducible—if they hold in virtue of lower-level causal relations and other noncausal facts—the manipulationist account of explanatory (or causal) relevance is incomplete. In order to see what is and is not relevant to Rasputin's death, we need to know what does and does not lie on each of the various type-level causal pathways to death. But Woodward and other manipulationists, whether out of a belief in irreducibility or otherwise, stop short of supplying a reductive theory of type-level causal relations. In short: the manipulationist may successfully account for high-level relevance between singular events in terms of high-level relevance between event types, but without any further theory about relevance between types, the story is only half told.

Similar remarks apply to any manipulationist attempt at a solution to the problem, presented in the previous section, of sodium's reactivity. Somehow, it must be shown that reactivity does not depend on neutron number. It is plausible enough that no high-level causal generalization exists relating reactivity to neutron number, whereas such a generalization does exist relating reactivity to the strength of sodium's outer electron's bond. Given these facts about what variables are related to what, the Woodward approach can account for the relevance of bond strength and the irrelevance of neutron number to a sodium-powered explosion. But as long as nothing is said as to why high-level causal relations hold between some variables and not others, this hardly constitutes a solution to the relevance problem.

# — II —

# The Kairetic Account of Explanation

# — 3 —

# The Kairetic Account of Difference-Making

## 3.1 Overview of the Kairetic Account

To understand a phenomenon is to see what made a difference to the causal production of the phenomenon and how it did so. At the heart of the kairetic account of explanation, then, is a criterion for difference-making. This chapter develops the criterion and puts it to work determining explanatory relevance. Chapter four uses the relevance criterion to construct an account of event explanation. Chapter five extends the account of explanation in several important ways, and chapter six applies it to several outstanding problems concerning event explanation. Let me give you a preview of what is to come.

The kairetic theory provides a method for determining the aspects of a causal process that made a difference to the occurrence of a particular event. The essence of the theory is a procedure that does the following: given as input a causal model $M$ for the production of an event $e$, the procedure yields as output another causal model for $e$ that contains only elements in $M$ that made a difference to the production of $e$. A model that contains explanatory irrelevancies is, then, "distilled" so that it contains only explanatorily relevant factors.

An application of the kairetic procedure to $M$ does not identify all the difference-makers for $e$, only difference-makers that appear in $M$. Further, the procedure may not identify all the difference-makers for $e$ that are in $M$. I claim, however, that if a causal influence (a law, event, or background condition) is a difference-maker for $e$, then there exists at least one causal model for $e$ that represents the influence and with respect to which the kairetic procedure identifies the influence as a difference-maker. In principle, then, the method has the power to identify all the difference-makers for a given event.

How to show that a causal factor is not a difference-maker for *e*? Show—this is easier than it sounds—that the factor will be eliminated by the kairetic procedure from any causal model for *e* in which it appears.

The kairetic procedure functions as follows. I assume, in this initial treatment, that all causal models are deterministic. (The probabilistic case is taken up in part four.) A deterministic causal model for an event *e* is, I will suppose, a set of statements that, first, entails the occurrence of *e* and, second, does so in such a way (to be explained below) that the derivation of *e* mirrors the causal production of *e*. The difference-making parts of a causal model are those parts that play an essential role in the entailment, meaning roughly that, if they were to be removed from the model, it would no longer entail *e*'s occurrence, or it would not do so in the right sort of way. This is what I call the *eliminative procedure*: remove as many pieces as you can from a model *M* for an event *e* without invalidating the entailment of *e*. Everything that remains in the model is a difference-maker for *e*. (Some precursors in the literature on explanation and high-level causation, in particular Mill and Mackie, are discussed in section 3.83.)

The eliminative procedure turns out to be too crude a measure of difference-making in several ways. Once it has served its expository function, it will therefore be set aside in favor of what I call the *optimizing procedure* for determining difference-making. It is the optimizing procedure that will serve as the basis for the kairetic account of explanation developed in chapter four.

Whereas the first phase of the account of explanation, namely, the purging of explanatorily irrelevant factors from causal models, is essentially a matter of reduction, the second phase is a matter of construction. A *standalone explanation* of an event *e* is a causal model for *e* containing only difference-makers for *e*. It is built from the models that have been stripped down by the eliminative or optimizing procedures. To understand the structure of standalone explanations is, I claim, the ultimate object of an inquiry into the nature of scientific explanation.

There are, I should note, many standalone explanations of any given event; these are all, in a sense, on a par, in that they are all complete and satisfactory scientific explanations of the event. But there are other senses in which one standalone explanation of an event may be better than another; these dimensions of explanatory goodness will be investigated in chapter four.

## 3.2  Causal Models

Explanatory information—that is, information about difference-making—is conveyed by a set of causal models that have been, first, stripped down by the kairetic procedure so as to contain only difference-makers and, then, sewn together to form a standalone explanation.

Before describing the kairetic procedure, I propose a canonical form for causal models, and I examine the way in which models of this form represent information both about the presence of causal influences—events, laws, and background conditions—and about the way in which these influences bear on a given event, hence about the causal production of that event.

A causal model for an event $e$ is a representation of the different chains of causal influence that come together with the net effect of causally producing $e$. Such chains may be extremely complex—hence the metaphor of the causal web—and a detailed model will therefore be similarly complex, perhaps extending outward to the distant stars and backward to the beginning of time. Of practical necessity, any of our causal models will represent only a small part of a complete causal process. I will begin by considering the structure of the simplest class of causal models, those that represent a single link in a causal chain. I call these *atomic models*. More complex causal models are, as the name suggests, constructed from atomic models.

### 3.21  Atomic Causal Models

A *veridical, deterministic, atomic causal model* for an event $e$ is, for the purposes of this book, a set of true statements about the world that entail $e$ (more precisely, the occurrence of $e$) in a certain way, to be specified shortly.

Such a model is veridical because the statements are true. It is deterministic because the statements entail that $e$ occurs, rather than merely entailing that it occurs with some particular probability, or entailing a range of possibilities only one of which is $e$. (Nondeterministic causal models are discussed in section 9.7.) It is atomic because no intermediate steps in the causal process are identified explicitly. There may well be intermediate steps; what matters is that the steps are not spelled out in the model itself. Finally, the model is causal because the statements in the model do not merely entail that *e* occurs; they *causally entail e*, meaning that the entailment of *e*, or more exactly the derivation of *e*, mirrors a part of the causal process by which *e* was produced. The nature of this mirroring is the subject of section 3.23.

An atomic causal model for an event will have the same form as a DN explanation of that event:

> I threw a cannonball at the window,
> It is a law that the throwing of a cannonball at a window will
>     cause the window to break, provided that nothing interferes
>     with the ball's flight,
> Nothing interfered with the cannonball's flight, thus,
> _____
> The window was broken.

Both the causal model and the DN explanation are law-involving deductive arguments that the event occurred (using the term *law* liberally); the difference between them is that a causal model purports to represent a chain of causal influence running from the states of affairs identified by the premises to the event identified by the conclusion.

I call the event *e* whose occurrence is causally entailed by an atomic causal model the *target* of the model. I call the set of statements that make up the premises of the entailment the model's *setup*, and I call the derivation in virtue of which the entailment is demonstrated the model's *follow-through*. (A follow-through is, then, what Hempel in his presentation of the DN view called an argument, and what logicians call a proof.) It is the follow-through that must mirror the causal production of *e*, if the model is to *causally* entail *e*. The two kinds of information that must be conveyed by a causal model, then—the identity of the causal influences, and the process or processes by which their combined influence causally produced the target—reside in, respectively, the setup and the follow-through.

The simple atomic model for window-breaking contains, you will observe, a negative condition, requiring that nothing interfere with the flight of the cannonball. It is in general true that a causal model, when it cites enough detail to entail the occurrence of its target, will contain one or more negative conditions, in addition to laws, events, and other background conditions. Metaphysically, a negative condition can be understood, like any state of affairs, as a high-level event (section 3.3). Thus, it can be said without distortion that a causal model specifies only laws and events causally entailing its target. But negative conditions have a rather different feel than "positive" events such as cannonball hurlings and baseball bat swingings; though I insist on calling them "causal influences" (section 1.42), I acknowledge that the terminology is strained.

An atomic model may be thought of as representing a link in a causal chain or, perhaps better, a strand in a causal web, but it ought not to be thought of as the shortest possible link. Many events come between my throwing the cannonball and the window's breaking, and all of these events are a part of the causal chain leading to the breaking. The "link" corresponding to the above model, then, can be broken into many shorter links. Calling the model *atomic* is not intended to suggest otherwise. After all, in a continuous causal process such as the breaking of the window, there is no shortest link. Conveniently, this frees up the term *atomic* for the use I put it to here.

A causal model is composed of statements, but in what language? Choose a natural language, and you limit the range of the model in whatever way that language is limited. It is crucial to the kairetic account of difference-making that the expressive power of the statements that make up a model be limited in no way whatsoever; I assume, then, an ideal language in which any state of affairs, law, or property can be represented. More or less equivalently, a model's setup might be taken to be composed of propositions rather than sentences.

### 3.22 Compound Causal Models

A compound causal model consists of two or more atomic models strung together to give a fuller description of the causal production of the target event. Take, for example, the model for window breaking above and add to it a model for my throwing the cannonball, say, the following derivation:

> I wanted to throw the cannonball at the window,
> Wanting to throw a thing invariably causes me to throw it, thus
> _____
> I threw the cannonball.

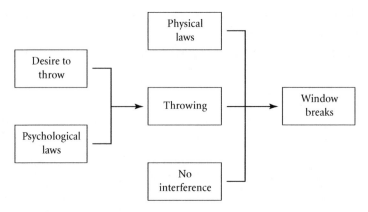

**Figure 3.1**  A compound causal model for a window's breaking

The result is a compound causal model for the window's breaking, in which the target of the new model, my throwing the cannonball, is a part of the setup for the original model, as shown in figure 3.1.

Like a veridical, deterministic, atomic causal model for *e*, a veridical, deterministic, compound causal model for *e* contains a set of true statements that causally entail *e*. In contrast to an atomic model, however, the compound model contains statements that are in effect intermediate steps in the derivation of *e*. My throwing the cannonball is, of course, the one such step in the window-breaking example. Intermediate steps in the derivation represent intermediate steps in the causal chain leading to *e*. I will call a statement corresponding to an intermediate step, or a set of such statements, an *intermediate setup*.

A compound model can always be converted to an atomic model by removing its intermediate setups; the result is an atomic model that entails the compound model's intermediate setups. Thus a compound model does not convey any more information than its corresponding atomic model; it merely spells out some of what is already implicit in the atomic model. All the same, compound models have a distinct role to play in explanation; some of their uses are discussed in section 4.32.

### 3.23  Causal Entailment

The purpose of a causal model's follow-through, that is, the purpose of the logical derivation of the model's target from its setup, is to represent a causal process, namely, the process by which the various causal influences—events, laws, and background conditions—specified in the model's setup work together to causally produce the event that is the model's target. To perform this function, the follow-through must have the structure of an argument or, to put it more technically, a proof. In principle, then, every causal model consists of a setup and a proof of the target using the setup. In practice, the intended proof is usually obvious and is therefore omitted; in what follows I will often talk of entailments without making explicit reference to the concomitant proofs.

When a model's follow-through is constructed so as to represent the causal production of its target, I say that its setup *causally entails* the target. An entailment's being causal is not a logical property, then, but rather a matter of its bearing a certain relation to the nonlogical facts about causality, namely, its representing by the lights of those facts a possible causal pathway. How, then, does a derivation represent a causal process? What is causal entailment?

The occurrence of an event can be entailed by many different things. The breaking of a window, for example, might be entailed, as in the causal model above, by

1. The fact of my throwing a cannonball, some laws governing projectile motion and the molecular structure of glass, and the relevant background conditions.

But it might equally well be entailed by any of the following:

2. The content of a newspaper report describing the breaking and a generalization about the trustworthiness of the press,

3. A description of a photograph of my throwing the cannonball, a generalization concerning the accuracy of the camera, and the laws governing projectile motion and the molecular structure of glass together with the relevant background conditions, or

4. The conjunctive claim that the window broke and that Rasputin is dead.

You recognize immediately that the first of these entailments mirrors a causal process leading from the causal influences on the breaking to the breaking itself, whereas the others do not. Entailments (2) and (3) mirror causal processes involving the breaking, but they run counter to the direction of causation at some point. Entailment (4) does not represent a causal process at all.

The same recognition underlies the causalist's solution to the problems of explanatory asymmetry: in the DN explanations of the flagpole's height in terms of the length of its shadow, and of the occurrence of the storm in terms of the barometer's dip, the direction of deduction runs either counter to the direction of causal influence or along a path where there is no nonnegligible causal influence at all.

For my purpose—to characterize the notion of causal entailment—it is almost enough to rely on these intuitive judgments as to which entailments mirror causal processes and which do not; if you are prepared to accept the judgments at least provisionally, you might move on to the next section. If you have a skeptical turn of mind, however, you may suspect that our judgments about causal entailment are based in part on judgments about high-level causal relations or, even worse, on judgments about causal-explanatory relevance. In what follows, I will show that an adequate notion of causal entailment can be built on the relation of causal influence alone.

Let me begin at the bottom, with the facts about causal entailment between concrete events. Consider a putative deterministic causal model for a concrete event $e$ that cites in its setup another concrete event $c$. I assume that $c$ is connected to $e$ by a causal influence relation, with $c$ as influencer. The question is whether the model's derivation of $e$ mirrors the causal influence of $c$ on $e$.

In the interests of clarity, I will make an assumption that is no doubt limiting in some respects: a causal influence relation between events $c$ and $e$ exists just in case there exists a causal law connecting a property $P$ of $c$ and a property $Q$ of $e$, a law having roughly the form *If $P(c)$ and $Z$ then $Q(e)$*, for some set of background conditions $Z$. (The formulation is clearly simplistic; a more realistic causal law will not refer directly to $c$, $e$, $P$, and $Q$; rather, it will be a universally quantified second-order expression relating values of determinables, for example, relating the quantity of mass at one place to the component gravitational force due to that mass at another.)

What is a causal law? For the purposes of this discussion, it is a logical consequence of the fundamental laws that satisfies a further condition whose content is dictated by the correct metaphysics of causal influence. On the conserved quantity view, a consequence of the fundamental laws of the form *If $P(c)$ and $Z$ then $Q(e)$* is a causal law just in case it holds because, in the presence of $Z$, there is a correctly oriented path of persistence and interaction running from the $P$-hood of $c$ to the $Q$-hood of $e$. On the manipulation view, the condition is rather that the law holds because, in the presence of $Z$, there is a relation of manipulability between the relevant properties of $c$ and $e$, in the sense that the $P$-hood of $c$ can be used, in principle, to manipulate the $Q$-hood of $e$. Finally, on the counterfactual view, the causal law must hold because, in the presence of $Z$, $e$'s $Q$-hood counterfactually depends on $c$'s $P$-hood.

More generally, *If $P(c)$ and $Z$ then $Q(e)$* is a causal law if the fundamental laws together with the metaphysics of causal influence jointly imply that if $c$ has $P$ and conditions $Z$ hold, then $e$ has $Q$ in virtue of the causal influence of $c$'s $P$-hood on $e$'s $Q$-hood. (Again this is rough: because it is typically determinables that are related, such as component force and mass, it must be that the one determinable has its determinate value because of the causal influence of the other's determinate value.) Note that, first, this is not a definition but a definition schema whose content is determined by the correct metaphysics of causal influence, and second, that a causal law in my sense is not a fundamental but a derived entity. I should add that in section 7.6, I will propose a theory of causal laws that supersedes the notion of a causal law defined here; indeed, the present notion will not figure anywhere but in the definition of causal entailment.

I now define causal entailment in the obvious way: the derivation of the $Q$-hood of $e$ from the $P$-hood of $c$ is a causal entailment just in case it goes by way of modus ponens applied to a causal law (or consists of a chain of such deductions).[1]

There is something more to add. Apply the characterization of causal entailment as it stands so far to a world of point mass particles in which the sole physics is Newtonian gravitation. Here, the gravitational force law appears to be the only causal law. (At least, it is a causal law once it is imbued with causal content by the correct metaphysics of causation, which will, I assume, identify each of two interacting particles as causally influencing the other in virtue of the gravitational force exerted.)

The force law is not enough in itself, however, to determine how a particle's state—that is, its position and velocity—will change with time. You can use the force law to calculate the causal influence exerted on a particle by every other particle in the universe. But to infer the effects of the sum total of these influences you require a principle of *causal composition*, which states the net effect of the influences. The Newtonian principle of causal composition is of course very simple: the net force on, hence acceleration of, a particle is the vector sum of the individual component forces/accelerations.

All such composition principles have, I will assume, the same if/then form as the laws of influence, with the facts about individual influences as antecedents and the resulting net influence as consequent. A derivation that goes by way of a principle of causal composition is a causal entailment if it applies modus ponens to the principle in the obvious way.

I classify the composition principles, like the influence principles, as causal laws. All the causal laws in the Newtonian world, then, have (or can be put into) a natural if/then form, and causal entailment is a matter of deriving effects from causes by way of the straightforward application of modus ponens. I suggest that this holds true for almost any choice of causal metaphysics and fundamental physics. As the *almost any* indicates, what I have said above is not intended as an exhaustive theory of causal entailment, that is, as an exhaustive theory of the way in which science might use logical relations to represent causal relations. But it is close enough to the way our current science represents causation with logic, I think, to provide the substrate for a theory of causal explanation.

I have provided a criterion for determining when the derivation of one fundamental-level-property instance from another is a causal entailment. What is wanted for a theory of causal models, however, is a criterion that applies to the derivation of events.

That a concrete event occurs, or a concrete state of affairs obtains, is a matter of certain fundamental-level properties being instantiated in a particular way—in particular places and times, that is. To derive the occurrence of a concrete event, then, is to derive the instantiation of some set of fundamental properties. Such a derivation is causal if the derivation of each of the property instances is causal. In other words, a derivation of the concrete event $e$ mirrors the causation of $e$ if it mirrors the causation of the property instantiations constitutive of $e$.

What, then, is a causal entailment of the occurrence of a high-level event? For a set of concrete premises—premises concerning the occurrence of concrete events and the causal laws in virtue of which they have their influence—to causally entail the occurrence of a high-level event $e$ is for the premises to causally entail the occurrence of a concrete event that realizes $e$. For a set of high-level premises—premises concerning the occurrence of high-level events and so on—to causally entail the occurrence of a high-level event $e$ is for every concretization of the premises to causally entail $e$ (where a concretization of a premise is a specification of some concrete realization of the premise).

Note that this talk of the concrete realizers of high-level events, and of concretizations of high-level premises, assumes the existence of correspondence rules linking higher- and lower-level vocabulary or properties. It is often said that correspondence rules will, or should, take the form of definitions, thus that they must give necessary and sufficient conditions for instantiating some high-level property in fundamental-level terms (Dupré 1993). You may doubt that necessary and sufficient conditions of this sort exist. I doubt it too; it is important to see, therefore, that the kairetic account requires for its causal entailments something much weaker than this, namely, locally necessary conditions and locally sufficient conditions for high-level property instantiation, of which there are more than enough. This liberal approach to correspondence will be defended and qualified in section 7.52; until then, I assume that the need for correspondence rules poses no problems.

Let me show how the characterization of causal entailment applies to the window-breaking model above. For the model's derivation of the window's breaking to constitute a causal entailment, every concrete realization of the model must causally entail its target. The facts about realization are determined by the relevant correspondence rules, that is, the rules determining which concrete events constitute throwings, breakings, and so on.

Consider any one of the concrete models that realize the higher-level model for window breaking. Such a model connects a concrete realization of the initial conditions specified in the setup with a concrete realization of the target. It represents, in other words, the way in which a maximally specific cannonball-throwing causes a maximally specific window-breaking.

The laws specified in the concrete model are, I will assume, the low-level physical laws that connect the realizers of throwings, breakings, and so on; the sense in which they constitute a realization of the high-level law cited in the high-level model will be discussed shortly. According to any of the metaphysical accounts of causation introduced in chapter one, these laws are causal: they have an if/then form that relates an antecedent cause to a consequent effect, and they hold in virtue of the influence of the antecedent on the consequent.

Further, the concrete model's entailment of the breaking goes by way of the application of modus ponens to the low-level if/then laws. For example, the deduction of the ball's trajectory from the fact of its being thrown will apply modus ponens to a causal law relating the force exerted on the ball by the thrower (on the "if" side) to its acceleration (on the "then" side).

Or perhaps it is better to understand the derivation as going by way of two applications of modus ponens to two laws: a law of influence relating the throwing to the component force, hence to the component acceleration, and a law of composition relating the component force and the absence of other significant forces to the net acceleration.

Three remarks on the example. First, in Newtonian and similar worlds, such as ours, an object's velocity at one time will count as a "causal influence" on its velocity at a later time. This is a straightforward consequence of the conserved quantity, manipulation, and counterfactual accounts of influence quite independently of the kairetic framework (because, for example, an object's position at one time typically depends counterfactually on its velocity at earlier times); it is, nevertheless, somewhat unintuitive. Perhaps a finer-grained account of our causal conceptual inventory would discriminate between "active" and "passive" causal dependence. For the sake of simplicity, however, I am happy to go along with contemporary causal metaphysics' eliding of the distinction.

Second, the no-interference or no-other-forces aspect of the model's setup ("Nothing interfered with the cannonball's flight") is introduced by the principle of causal composition. I conjecture that in worlds with a broadly Newtonian structure to their mathematical physics (again I include our own), negative conditions are usually or always introduced in this way: they are assumptions of "no forces other than those specified" that are made in the application of the composition principle, in order to make the transition from an enumeration of certain component forces to the existence of a net force equal to the sum of the enumerated forces. Sometimes a negative condition may have the form "no other objects," but the forbidden objects will be those that, if they existed, would be in a position to exert forbidden forces. (My Newtonian idiom notwithstanding, to have this quasi-Newtonian compositional structure fundamental-level causal influences need not take the form of "forces"—they might equally well be "potentials," for example—and they need not compose by vector summation.) The topic of "no-interference" conditions is further discussed in section 6.22.

Third, as noted earlier, the causal laws that connect the throwing and the breaking in the concrete realization of the high-level model must themselves be realizers, in some sense, of the causal laws cited in the high-level model, which is to say, the high-level law statements must be more abstract, less detailed characterizations of the same causal facts characterized by the low-level law statements (or of course, they might be identical to the low-level law statements). In the window-breaking case, it is easy to see, because of the physicality of the high-level laws, that this criterion is satisfied.

In biological or sociological explanation, the connection between high-level and low-level causal laws is far less clear. But the case that every high-level causal law has a fundamental-level realization will be made in section 7.6, where I argue that the nomological constituents of a high-level law are certain, perhaps abstract, properties of the fundamental laws (see also section 3.52). This means that a high-level law can be concretized as easily as a high-level event: just find the fundamental laws, certain of whose properties constitute the high-level law, or in other words, find the fundamental laws in virtue of which the high-level law exists. These (along with entities I call basing patterns, to be discussed in chapter seven) are the high-level law's concrete realization. The notion of the concretization of a high-level causal model does not founder, then, on the question of laws, and so my criterion for causal entailment in a high-level model, which makes essential use of the notion of concretization, is sound.

The characterization of causal entailment offered in this section tightly binds the causality of a high-level model to the causal facts at the fundamental level, as foreshadowed by my preference, expressed in chapter one, for invoking only fundamental-level, as opposed to a multilevel, causal relations to resolve problems in the philosophy of explanation (section 1.4). In chapter one, I portrayed my view as ecumenical, on the grounds that many different views of the nature of causality agree on the existence of fundamental-level causal influence. To use fundamental-level influence to resolve the explanatory asymmetries (the flagpole and the shadow; the gold foil and the scattering pattern) was therefore a conservative strategy. I am now proposing that the fundamental level provides sufficient metaphysical resources to understand any causal aspect of scientific explanation—that everything that can be explained causally can be explained in terms of fundamental-level causal influence, properly massaged.

This will strike many readers as strongly, perhaps radically, reductionist. It commits our explanatory practice to the thesis that all causality worth caring about for explanatory purposes has its sole origin in relations of fundamental-level causal influence. Why think that the world will cooperate in providing what is needed? There are two connected worries to be addressed. (Note that in what follows, the reductionism with which I am concerned posits the reduction of high-level causal facts to fundamental level causal facts; I will have nothing to say here or elsewhere on the question whether the fundamental level causal facts can be reduced to noncausal facts.)

First, some philosophers suspect that the thesis is in fact false: there are irreducible high-level causal relations that are quite capable of providing understanding of the phenomena that they relate. Given what we now know, these suspicions are, I believe, extravagant: there simply are no causal relations of which we are aware that cannot be attributed to lower-level interaction and, ultimately, to the causal influence of fundamental particle on fundamental particle. This is a matter of empirical fact, a great lesson about the nature of the world learned from centuries of scientific work, not the conclusion of some a priori argument; it is not apodictic, then, but it can hardly be ignored. (I should add that the fundamental-level causal story behind high-level causal claims is not always straightforward, as is shown, for example, by the discussion of the causal role of omissions in section 6.3.)

Second, even if it is acknowledged that our world has a fundamental level that is the source of all (or at least, all scientifically significant) causality, it seems clear that things need not have turned out this way. Is it not implausible that our explanatory practice should have all along built such a strong assumption of causal reducibility into its being, an assumption that would make many apparently sensible possible worlds literally incomprehensible—their every feature inexplicable—to us?

I might perhaps reply that many of our cognitive faculties are tailor-made for the actual world. But in truth, I believe that this objection to my explanatory reductionism is sound. In work published elsewhere, I have argued that our explanatory practice does not require the existence of a single fundamental causal level, but rather one or more domain-specific "basic levels" (Strevens 2007c). How does this work? For any particular domain, we pre-theoretically suppose that there is a locally fundamental level, causality at which is the raw material of all explanation within the domain (and which constrains causal entailment just as the ultimate fundamental level does in the characterization above). Thus, we may allow that there is a physically basic level, a biologically basic level, a psychologically basic level, and so on; the relations of causal influence that exist at these levels provide the metaphysical ingredients for explanations concerning the behavior of, respectively, physical objects, living things, and minds. The existence of multiple basic levels is quite compatible with antireductionism, as well as with the view that the world has no ultimately fundamental level at all. Thus, our explanatory practice can make sense, in principle, of profoundly irreducible phenomena.

In our actual world, however, it has turned out (so we believe) that there is a single basic level, the fundamental physical level. Our practice has thus taken the form sketched above: all explanatory causality is derived from fundamental physics. For simplicity's sake, I am treating this as an axiom of our practice, when in fact it is derived from a more liberal metaphysical framework along with an observation about the causal structure of the actual world. In principle, our explanatory thinking is not reductionist, but in practice—in this world we inhabit—it is. My focus will be on the practice.

### 3.24 Other Approaches to Causal Modeling

Any system of representation that is able to furnish a setup and a follow-through—any system that can represent the fact that certain laws and states of affairs obtained, and that can represent the structure of the causal dependence relations in virtue of which those laws and states of affairs causally produced an event—can be used, in principle, to construct a deterministic causal model with that event as its target. A diagram such as that shown in figure 3.1 above, for example, can be interpreted as a causal model in its own right, provided that the arrows are understood in the obvious way, that is, as relations of causal influence by which the states of affairs at one end jointly produce the event at the other end.

I use natural language sentences and entailment as my representational tools solely for convenience: natural language needs no further interpretation, and the entailment relation is familiar and well understood. But what is important, let me repeat, is not the means of representation but what is represented. What is represented are certain things in the world: states of affairs, laws, and the relations of causal influence between them. Any representation able to capture such facts can be used as a causal model, and indeed, there are a range of representational devices used in the scientific literature to communicate causal facts. By using a canonical form for my own causal models, I am in no way suggesting that this diversity of forms of causal representation is not to be desired.

## 3.3    States of Affairs

The explananda of event explanations are normally not concrete events but entities that I call states of affairs or high-level events, sometimes called facts. States of affairs are important to explanation in three ways in addition to their role as explananda: they, rather than concrete events, are usually the difference-makers in an explanation, they have a role to play in regularity explanation that is just as important as their role in event explanation, and finally, they are akin to the difference-making relation itself in an important way.

What kinds of things might they be? Let me ask instead what work a metaphysics for states of affairs has to do, as far as the theory of explanation is concerned.

Two things. First, on a difference-making approach to the explanatory relevance criterion, what is important above all is that the states of affairs that appear in explanations have individuation conditions clear enough to determine whether they obtain or not. If you accept the simple counterfactual account of explanatory relevance, for example, then in order to decide whether not an event $c$ is relevant to an event $e$, you look to the closest world in which $c$ does not occur to see whether or not $e$ occurs. The outcome of such a procedure depends on the criteria that determine whether or not $c$ and $e$ occur in a given scenario or possible world. So there had better be clean individuation criteria for both the things that are to be explained and the things that do the explaining. Precisely how these criteria are to be determined, and what underlying metaphysics is to prop them up, is less important.

Second, the metaphysics of states of affairs ought to encompass any particular that might, in principle, be explained. This requirement inclines me toward the broadest possible answer to the question about the nature of states of affairs, an answer that has as a consequence that almost any event-like entity discussed in the philosophical literature is a species of state of affairs in my intended sense: concrete events, facts when distinguished from events, events in Kim's (1973) sense, events in Quine's (1960) sense, events in Davidson's (1969) sense, negative states of affairs such as Zeus's not existing, and so on—since it would be bizarre to say that any of these entities is in principle inexplicable.

The desired range of states of affairs can be captured by a simple metaphysical schema (with obvious affinities to Kim (1973)). Let a state of affairs consist of two entities, standing in the instantiation relation. The first entity is some set of particulars: perhaps a region of space-time, or an object and an interval of time, or even the entire universe. The second entity is a property, perhaps relational. The state of affairs obtains, or equivalently, the high-level event occurs, if the particulars instantiate the property in the appropriate way. The event of Vesuvius erupting in 79 c.e., for example, might consist of a certain volcano and year (Vesuvius and the year 79), and the relational property of erupting in that year. The event occurred because the given particulars stand in the given relation: Vesuvius did erupt in 79.

Some remarks on this schema for states of affairs. First, an event is high level, rather than concrete, when the property whose instantiation is required for its occurrence is a relatively abstract property, a property that may be realized in a number of somewhat different ways. The event of Vesuvius's eruption is high level, for example, because the property of erupting in a given time span may be realized by eruptions that differ in many of their details. This event may be contrasted with the more concrete event of Vesuvius's having erupted in a very particular way, with the trajectory of the ash particles finely specified and so on, and at a very particular time. It is because of the high-level event's relatively robust individuation conditions that many aspects of the geological process leading up to the eruption were not difference-makers for the eruption itself: they affected the way the eruption occurred, not the fact that there was an eruption.

Second, insofar as there are negative properties, there are negative states of affairs. These play an important part in explanation, most of all because various negative states of affairs must be satisfied (at least in our universe) for any causal process to run to completion. For a certain cannonball to break a certain window, for example, it may be necessary that nothing interfere (too much) with the cannonball's flight except the force of gravity. This state of affairs obtains just in case, for a certain period of time, an object—the cannonball—instantiates the property of being unaffected by nonnegligible nongravitational forces. The negative state of affairs is composed, then, of the cannonball, the time frame, and the negative property just described.

Third, I use the terms *state of affairs* and *high-level event* interchangeably, choosing largely on the basis of whether it seems more appropriate to say that the thing *obtained* or *occurred*. I do not claim that these terms are synonymous, however; in fact, it seems likely that they are not. Arguably, for example, in everyday usage, the state of affairs of Rasputin's dying (in a certain time frame) and the event of his death—even conceived of as a high-level, rather than as a concrete event—are not the same thing. The state of affairs would have obtained had he died in absolutely any way you like; the event, however, perhaps has somewhat more fragile individuation conditions: had Rasputin been run down by a cart rather than murdered, the actual Rasputin death-event would not have occurred, though a different event, also a death of Rasputin, would have occurred in its place. (On these questions, and many more event-related subtleties, see Bennett (1988).) This kind of issue I would like to avoid. It is easy to do so, because in almost any circumstances, the state of affairs and the high-level event, even if technically distinct, will have the same explanation. Use the individuation criteria for the state of affairs, then, to determine the difference-makers for the death, and you will find the same difference-makers as had you used the individuation criteria for the event.

Fourth and finally, on the kairetic account, the difference-making relation itself turns out to fit the schema for a high-level state of affairs. In the same way that breaking is a high-level property of (some) windows, and a particular event of window-breaking is the instantiation of that property by a particular window, so the generic difference-making relation between a characteristic set of difference-makers for breaking and the generic breaking itself is a high-level property of generic causal influence relations, and the obtaining of such a difference-making relation in a particular case is the instantiation of *that* property by a particular bundle of causal influences on a particular window-breaking.

## 3.4    The Eliminative Procedure

### 3.41   The Eliminative Procedure Characterized

The kairetic account understands explanatory relevance as causal difference-making, and it understands causal difference-making in deterministic systems as follows. A causal influence makes a difference to an event $e$— it plays an essential role in bringing about $e$—if there exists a veridical, deterministic, atomic causal model for $e$ in which the influence plays an essential role in causally entailing $e$. Since the causal entailment represents the actual causal production of $e$, the thought goes, the factors essential for causal entailment are just those essential for causal production. Something like this proposal has been made in the context of theories of high-level causation by Mackie (1974), following Mill (1973), and in the context of theories of high-level explanation, though rather less explicitly, by Garfinkel (1981), following Putnam (1975). The primary challenge for difference-making accounts of this sort is to spell out what it is for a causal factor to play an essential role in a causal entailment. That task will occupy the remainder of the chapter.

Let me begin with a simple, rather obvious, response to the challenge: a member of a set of propositions jointly entailing $e$ is essential to the entailment just in case it cannot be removed from the set without the entailment's being destroyed. Never mind for now the complications that arise in certain cases, for example, if two propositions in the set are each sufficient in themselves to entail $e$; also ignore for now the sensitivity of such a criterion to the way in which information is packaged into propositions. These issues will be dealt with in due course.

When applied to the problem of determining difference-makers, the suggested criterion yields the following principle, a simple version of the kairetic criterion for difference-making:

> If a factor $c$ cannot be removed from a veridical, deterministic, atomic causal model for an event $e$ without invalidating the entailment of $e$, then $c$ is a difference-maker for $e$.

The converse does not hold: if $c$ can be removed from a model for $e$ without invalidating $e$'s entailment, $c$ might nevertheless be a difference-maker for $e$. In order to establish that $c$ is not among $e$'s difference-makers, it is necessary to show that $c$ can be safely removed from *every* veridical, deterministic model for $e$ in which it appears.

What does it mean to remove a causal factor $c$ from a model? The factor must, of course, be a part of the model's setup, in the sense that one of the sentences in the setup must assert that $c$ is present. To remove $c$ from the model is to remove this sentence from the setup. The result is a model that is silent as to whether or not $c$ was present—not, note, a model that asserts that $c$ was absent. Removing $c$ from a model is in this respect quite unlike moving to a possible world in which $c$ is absent (Lewis's removal), or performing a Woodward manipulation as a result of which $c$ no longer obtains (Woodward's removal). For Lewis and Woodward, a scenario with $c$ removed is one in which $c$ determinately fails to occur; on the kairetic account it is rather one in which there is no fact of the matter as to whether $c$ occurs.

It will be convenient to operate with a criterion for difference-making that, rather than defining what it is for a single factor to be a difference-maker, as does the principle articulated above, instead takes the form of a procedure to be applied to a causal model, the result of which is to pare down the model so that it contains only factors that are difference-makers for the target. The procedure, more exactly, takes a veridical, deterministic, atomic causal model for an event $e$, and produces another veridical, deterministic causal model for $e$ with a setup that is a subset of the original model's setup, and in which all factors are difference-makers for $e$. I call this new atomic model an *explanatory kernel* for $e$. A causal factor is a difference-maker for $e$, then, just in case it appears in at least one explanatory kernel for $e$.

As the name suggests, an explanatory kernel for $e$ is an explanation of $e$; furthermore, all atomic causal models that are explanations of $e$ are explanatory kernels for $e$. I will propose in section 4.1 that all compound causal models that are explanations of $e$ are composed of explanatory kernels, either for $e$ itself or for $e$'s difference-makers.

In what follows, I will describe several increasingly sophisticated procedures for extracting explanatory kernels from models. The first of these kernel-determination procedures, based straightforwardly on the principle above, I call the *eliminative procedure*. It is quite simple: remove from a given model every causal factor that you can without invalidating the setup's entailment of the target, then stop. Everything that is left in the model is a difference-maker for the target. Let me now show how the eliminative procedure is able to deal with the issues that caused problems for other difference-making criteria in chapter two.

### 3.42 The Influence of Mars

Let me warm up with a ridiculously simple case, one that causes few problems for any account of difference-making. Throughout the course of events leading to Rasputin's death, the planet Mars exerted a slight gravitational pull on the principal actors. This pull is a bone fide causal influence on the death, according to any of the theories of causal influence described in chapter one, since Mars did have some effect, however small, on the concrete realization of the death. There will therefore be veridical atomic causal models for the death that specify Mars' gravitational effect. What I need to show is that such specifications are invariably removed by the eliminative procedure.

It is easy to see that this is the case. The elements in a causal model that do the work of entailing the death all concern ropes, ice, and rivers. Discourse on Mars can therefore be dropped without invalidating the entailment. What will be left behind is a preexisting negative condition specifying that there were no significant gravitational influences on the scenario except for the earth's.[2] Mars' influence, then, made no difference to the death.

Now some fine print. It is quite permissible to say informally that Mars made no difference to the death; strictly speaking, however, it is not Mars that is removed from the model by the eliminative procedure but the proposition that Mars has a certain property. What fails to make a difference to Rasputin's death, then, is not Mars itself but the state of affairs of Mars' exerting such and such a causal influence. More generally, as foreshadowed above, difference-makers and non-difference-makers alike are, on the kairetic account, events or states of affairs—not objects or systems but the fact of objects or systems instantiating certain properties.

Further, it would be an error to think that the application of the eliminative procedure produces a model that has nothing whatsoever to say about Mars. The model, by specifying an upper limit on the total nonterrestrial gravitational influence, places an implicit limit on Mars' gravitational field in particular, and thus it implicitly attributes a property to Mars. This property, since it remains in the model after elimination, is a difference-maker: it makes a difference to Rasputin's death that Mars' gravitational pull was not enormously large, or to state the difference-making state of affairs more positively, that the pull fell into an interval with a certain upper bound. For more on this kind of negative difference-making, see section 6.3.

### 3.43  *The Influence of Poisoning*

Next consider Rasputin's poisoning. Although poison is a typical cause of death, in this particular case it does not explain the death; I need to show that the kairetic account concurs.

Take a veridical deterministic causal model for Rasputin's death that represents his being poisoned. Provided that the model also represents his being thrown into the river, the poisoning can be removed without invalidating the entailment of death. Poisoning, therefore, is not a difference-maker in virtue of such a model.

But what if Rasputin's influviation is not in the model? Can you construct a veridical model that causally entails Rasputin's death in a way that essentially involves his poisoning? If so, then because poisoning could not be removed from such a model, it would count as a difference-maker. It had better be that any model for Rasputin's death that hinges on his poisoning is either not veridical or does not genuinely entail his death.

What would be the structure of a model for Rasputin's death by poisoning? Very schematically, its setup would have two parts: initial conditions specifying that Rasputin was poisoned in such and such a way and that other important background conditions $Z$ held, and laws having a consequence of the following form:

> When a person is poisoned in such and such a way, and conditions $Z$ obtain, that person will die.

(This generalization connecting poisoning and death need not itself be a law; see section 3.46.)

In order to entail death, the poisoning model must specify that conditions $Z$ held. But conditions $Z$ could not have held, because Rasputin *was* poisoned in such and such a way, yet he did not succumb. Whatever conditions were necessary for a successful poisoning were not wholly present. If the poisoning model asserts that these success conditions held, it is not veridical; if it fails to assert that the conditions held, it does not causally entail death. Thus, there is no model in virtue of which poison counts as a difference-maker for Rasputin's death. (For the kairetic account's treatment of a modified Rasputin story in which the poison would have eventually killed him, had he not been drowned first, see the treatment of "late preemption" in section 6.23.)

### 3.44 The Influence of Influviation

Finally, consider Rasputin's influviation, that is, his being bound and thrown into a river. Influviation made a difference to Rasputin's death; I need to show that the kairetic criterion counts it as a difference-maker. To this end, consider a deterministic causal model for Rasputin's death by influviation constructed along the same lines as the model for death by poisoning described above. The model's setup states that Rasputin was bound and thrown into a river, that various other background conditions obtained, and that it is a consequence of various relevant laws that people bound and thrown into a river in the stated conditions die. If constructed correctly, the model is veridical and entails Rasputin's death; further, influviation cannot be removed from the model without invalidating the entailment. Influviation, then, is a difference-maker.

The simple counterfactual test for difference-making, you will recall, was prevented from declaring influviation a difference-maker because of the following fact: if Rasputin's attackers had not drowned him, they would certainly have killed him in some other way. The kairetic criterion has no such problems; for Rasputin's influviation to qualify as a kairetic difference-maker, it is sufficient that there exists a single veridical model for death from which the influviation cannot be removed. There is such a model, namely, a model that makes no mention of Rasputin's attackers' determination to kill him. Of course, there exist other veridical models for death that do cite the assassins' resolution, and from which influviation can therefore be removed without invalidating the entailment of death. But these models cannot compromise the status of influviation as difference-maker: one model is enough to confer difference-making power irrevocably. Alternative models, you will see, can never subtract from, but only add to, the list of difference-makers. In particular, Rasputin's attackers' murderous resolve will be counted as a difference-maker, but alongside, rather than in place of, his influviation.

The decisive difference in this case between the kairetic and the counterfactual accounts is, then, that whereas on the counterfactual account an event $c$'s making a difference to $e$ depends entirely on its playing an essential role in a certain uniquely significant veridical model for $e$ (roughly, a model specifying the complete state of the world up to the time that $c$ obtains), on the kairetic account $c$ is a difference-maker if it plays an essential role in any one of a wide range of veridical models. The kairetic criterion for difference-making is therefore rather weaker (though not strictly weaker) than the counterfactual criterion, which in the Rasputin case and others involving "backup causes" is just what is needed. Some more challenging scenarios involving backup causes will be examined in section 6.2.

## 3.45 A Disjunctive Twist

Let me defend the eliminative procedure, and more broadly, the entire kairetic approach, from a familiar objection. The eliminative procedure's appeal to facts about what does and does not play an essential role in an entailment calls to mind a similar appeal by Hempel's DN account of explanation, which requires that at least one law be essentially involved in the deduction of the explanandum, and various attempts to make the hypothetico-deductive account of confirmation more sophisticated, which hold that only those parts of a theory that play an essential role in making a particular prediction are confirmed by that prediction. There is a deep problem with all these appeals to facts about what is and is not essential to an entailment. In what follows, I pose the problem for the kairetic account of difference-making.[3]

Begin with a veridical, deterministic model for Rasputin's death that mentions the gravitational influence of Mars. Take some other element of the model that incontrovertibly plays a part in entailing death, say, the proposition $d$ that Rasputin was thrown into the river. Replace $d$ with the proposition $c \supset d$, where $c$ describes the influence of Mars. This does not affect the model's entailment of the death nor, apparently, the model's veridicality. Yet $c$ cannot be removed from this new model without destroying the entailment of death. Thus $c$—the influence of Mars—is after all a difference-maker.

This would be a telling objection if the kairetic account required only that, in order to qualify as a difference-maker, the influence of Mars should play an essential role in entailing Rasputin's death. But more is needed: the influence of Mars must play an essential role in *causally* entailing the death.

This requirement is not satisfied. The derivation of death from Mars' influence by way of $c \supset d$ (where $c$ is Mars and $d$ is influviation) does not correspond to a real causal process. In particular, the step in which $d$ is derived from $c$ by applying modus ponens to $c \supset d$ does not correspond to the actual causal process by which $c$, or Mars, had its causal influence on the death. The actual process involved the law of gravitation; $c \supset d$ does not pick out this or any other causal law. (You will recall from section 3.23 that it is a necessary condition on causal entailment that in every application of modus ponens, the conditional should be a causal law.) Thus, the entailment of death is not causal entailment, and the corresponding model not a causal model. It is therefore powerless to determine difference-makers.

I cannot emphasize strongly enough that the use of entailment in the kairetic account of explanation is quite different from its use in the DN account. The DN account, which of course epitomizes the logical empiricists' "syntactic" approach to philosophy, jettisons from the philosophy of explanation what are held to be unacceptably metaphysical notions, in particular, causal notions, substituting a logical relation, entailment, whose structure bears the entire burden of deciding what is and is not a potentially good explanation. The kairetic account, by contrast, uses entailment to represent causal relations. What is important in the kairetic account, then, is not so much the structure of the entailment relation as the causal structure of the world; above all, it is the world's causal structure that is principally responsible for determining the structure of what I am calling the causal entailment relation.

In dealing with this familiar recipe for the creation of counterexamples to syntactic philosophizing, note, I am doing something that should be utterly familiar and unobjectionable to anyone sympathetic to the causal approach to explanation: it is what all causalists do to handle the case of the flagpole and the shadow. The flagpole/shadow problem arises, recall, because the deductive argument by which the length of the shadow "explains" the height of the flagpole is identical in all relevant formal respects to the argument by which the height of the flagpole explains the length of the shadow (section 1.41). The causal approach to explanation breaks the tie by claiming that the second entailment, but not the first, represents a real causal process.

I have made the same move in this discussion: I have claimed that some entailments do, and some do not, represent causal processes, and that only the latter are suitable vehicles for causal explanation. Both the standard causal treatment of the flagpole/shadow problem and my treatment of the "disjunctive twist" assume, of course, that the facts about causal influence are rich enough to make distinctions between different entailments, but this is a sine qua non of the causal approach to explanation, not some additional demand imposed on the influence relation by my particular handling of the twist.

A different kind of attempt to deal with the disjunctive twist would blame not the course taken by the derivation of $d$ from $c$ in the model's follow-through but the presence of $c \supset d$ in the setup, on the grounds that such "disjunctive" states of affairs are for some reason inherently unfit for explanatory work. I can understand the appeal of the approach: given the form of this world's fundamental causal laws, it appears that there is simply no role for such a state of affairs to play in a causal process. So, it can be ruled out of a causal model's setup irrespective of the form of the model's follow-through. Yet I think that this line of thought overgeneralizes: in unusual circumstances, a disjunctive state of affairs might be a condition of application for a causal law, that is, it might be the $Z$ in *If F in conditions Z, then G*, for a mechanism that is set up in a very particular way. Thus, it might play a valid role in a causal entailment, genuinely representing the course of some causal process. For this reason, disjunctive states of affairs ought not to be excluded unconditionally from causal models; it is the form of the follow-through that should decide the question.

### 3.46  An Unhealthy Dependence on Laws?

The causal models invoked by the kairetic account appear to contain a wide range of subtle and powerful laws of nature. Consider, for example, the way that the kairetic account deals with Rasputin's poisoning (section 3.43). The poisoning is determined not to make a difference because one of the antecedent conditions in the deterministic causal law of the form

> When a person is poisoned in such and such a way, and conditions $Z$
> obtain, that person will die

is not satisfied by the actual events leading up to Rasputin's death.

Fully fleshed out, this is a remarkable law statement. It is framed in terms of high-level kinds such as persons, poisons, and death, yet it is not only strictly deterministic, it specifies precisely the circumstances under which poisoning is guaranteed to lead to death. Can there really be a law of nature corresponding to the statement?

Probably not. But the existence of such a law is not required for the kairetic account to do its work. A deterministic causal model for an event $e$ that cites an event $c$ in its setup need not cite a single law covering the entire transition from $c$ to $e$; what is needed is a group of laws that jointly ensure, in the circumstances, that the transition occurs. These may each cover a link in the chain from $c$ to $e$, but even that is not necessary. Many different laws may work in tandem to realize a single link. In the case of Rasputin's poisoning, then, though the statement above may not pick out a single law, it will follow from other, biologically more basic, laws.

But this claim, too, might sound tendentious: surely even the basic biological laws have exceptions and so fail to imply anything deterministic? Perhaps. In a deterministic world, however, something like the poisoning generalization must follow from the fundamental-level laws (and correspondence rules), if not from any set of higher-level laws. Thus, there is a basis at the fundamental level, for the assumed deterministic generalization—and this is all that the kairetic account requires in the way of laws. Indeed, if it turned out that the only genuine laws of nature were fundamental laws of nature, the kairetic account would function perfectly well, since the role of laws in the account is to determine what causally produces what, and, as explained in section 3.23, this is a wholly fundamental-level matter.[4]

Suppose, then, that the fundamental laws of nature, correspondence rules, and various background conditions entail the poisoning generalization stated schematically at the beginning of this section, and that it is in virtue of the generalization so entailed that Rasputin's poisoning made no difference to his death. A further problem: on the kairetic account, to know that poisoning is not a difference-maker, you must know something about the form of the "poisoning law," but how, if the generalization's provenance is some fantastically complicated entailment based in the fundamental laws, could we possibly know anything about such a law? The law is beyond us, yet the judgment that poison makes no difference, based according to the kairetic account on knowledge of the law, is easily made. Surely, then, the kairetic account, even if technically correct, cannot capture the psychology of our criterion for difference-making?

It is true that there is much about the "poisoning law" that we do not know, and perhaps will never know, if only for lack of interest. But we are quite capable of discerning the facts about the law that need to be known to make accurate difference-making judgments in many cases. Suppose that a certain poison, when it kills, does so within an hour. Rasputin is poisoned, but he lives on for two hours before suffering influviation. It follows that one of the conditions required for the operation of the poisoning law did not obtain. You have no idea, perhaps, which one, but you do not need this information to make the judgment that poisoning was not a difference-maker for death. This, I hardly need add, is exactly the situation we are in with respect to Rasputin's actual death: no one, as far as I know, can say what saved Rasputin from the poison, but his survival shows that something saved him. The observation generalizes: it is often possible to see that one of a law's antecedent conditions did not obtain, or, conversely, that all antecedent conditions did obtain, without having much idea what the antecedent conditions are.[5]

A related question: is our explanatory practice really so fixated on laws? Do we genuinely think of the process by which a certain poison has its effect as, in essence, a law-governed process?

Consider the following alternative. We think of the relevant processes as driven by underlying mechanisms. The operation of the mechanisms is based in fundamental physical processes. In a deterministic world, every mechanism has a set of enabling conditions: when the enabling conditions obtain, a mechanism runs to completion; otherwise not. In Rasputin's poisoning and like cases, what we recognize, without understanding every detail of the mechanism's operation, is that some of the enabling conditions did not obtain.

This alternative picture is, I suggest, merely a different way of expressing the same facts as the law-based picture; the equivalence is due to the extremely close relationship between fundamental laws and mechanisms, discussed in section 7.6.

## 3.5    Abstraction and Optimizing

### 3.51   Elimination Is All or Nothing

The principal weakness of the eliminative procedure lies in its offering only two choices in dealing with a causal factor: either the factor is completely removed from the model in question, or it is retained in its entirety. Frequently, what is wanted is something between these two extremes, as the following example shows.

I throw a cannonball at a window, and the window breaks. Does the fact that the cannonball weighs exactly 10 kg make a difference to the window's breaking? The natural answer to this question is no. The fact the cannonball is rather heavy made a difference, but the fact that it weighed in at exactly 10 kg did not. You would like to say, then, that a certain fact about the ball's mass—that it was rather heavy—made a difference, but that finer details about the mass did not.

The eliminative procedure does not allow such delicate distinctions. Take a model for the window's breaking that includes in its setup only one proposition concerning the cannonball's mass, namely, a proposition stating that the mass was 10 kg. If the proposition is removed from the model, there is no longer any constraint on the ball's mass at all. The new setup, then, is compatible with the ball's having the mass of a grain of sand; consequently, the setup will no longer entail the window's breaking. Because the fact of the ball's exact mass cannot be removed from the model, the exact mass is counted by the eliminative procedure as a difference-maker for the breaking, an unwanted conclusion.[6]

### 3.52 Abstraction

The problem is solved by introducing a way of removing detail from a causal model's setup that stops short of completely excising a proposition. You would like to take a proposition such as *The ball's mass was 10 kg* and make it less exact, so that it says, say, *The ball's mass was greater than 1 kg*. I will call the suggested operation *abstraction*.

Say that one model $M$ is an abstraction of another model $M'$ just in case (a) all causal influences described by $M$ are also described by $M'$, and (b) $M'$ says at least as much as $M$, or, a little more formally, every proposition in $M$ is entailed by the propositions in $M'$. Intuitively, if $M$ is an abstraction of $M'$, then $M'$ may be obtained by "fleshing out" $M$, that is, by adding some additional causal details to $M$'s description of a causal process.[7] The abstraction ordering is a partial order in the technical sense.

Let me construct a replacement for the eliminative procedure that substitutes abstraction for removal. Whereas the eliminative procedure transforms a causal model $M$ for an event $e$ into a kernel for $e$ by removing elements of $M$ until no further elements can be removed without invalidating $M$'s entailment of $e$, the new procedure transforms $M$ into a kernel by performing abstraction operations on $M$'s setup until no further abstraction is possible without invalidating $M$'s entailment of $e$.

As an illustration, apply this abstraction procedure to the case of the cannonball's breaking the window. Suppose you begin with a causal model for the breaking that contains a statement of the cannonball's exact mass. The eliminative procedure could not touch this statement; its removal would invalidate the entailment of the breaking. The new procedure can, by contrast, make the claim more abstract, that is, less detailed, resulting in a setup that, rather than stating an exact mass for the ball, states a range of possible masses. The setup contains, in other words, a statement of the form *The ball's mass was between a and b kg*. (The range must include the actual mass, of course, or the statement would be false and the setup nonveridical. Because any abstraction of a veridical model is itself veridical, this requirement need not be made explicit.)

Suppose that any mass for the ball greater than 1 kg is sufficient, in conjunction with the other states of affairs stipulated by the setup, to entail that the window breaks. Then the maximum abstraction possible without invalidating the entailment of the breaking would result in the setup's saying *The ball's mass was greater than 1 kg*. Consequently, a model for the breaking that involves the ball's mass will, upon application of the abstraction procedure, end up making just this statement about the mass. Thus, you have the conclusion you want: the one and only fact about the mass that is a difference-maker for the breaking is the fact of the mass's being greater than 1 kg. You can say that it mattered that the ball was heavy, but it did not matter *how* heavy it was.

A cannonball's breaking a window is not an event of great scientific interest, but the ability to abstract rather than merely to remove the elements of a causal model in the search for explanations is important to science as well as to common sense. I will argue in later chapters that abstraction underlies the many important explanatory phenomena already mentioned in the preface: explanatory omissions, equilibrium explanations, robustness, idealization, the use of probabilistic explanation in deterministic systems, and so on.

The move from elimination to abstraction clarifies, by the way, an earlier claim about the kairetic account's treatment of causal factors such as Mars' gravitational influence on Rasputin's death. When treating this case in section 3.42, I asserted that the eliminative procedure deleted from a model for Rasputin's death any part of the setup stating the magnitude of Mars' gravitational pull, while "leaving behind" a condition specifying that there were no significant gravitational influences on the process except for the earth's. If such a negative condition were already present in the model's setup, then things would work as stated; you can now see that even if the condition were not present, it would be created by abstraction from the specifications of various gravitational fields of nonterrestrial origin. The model, in other words, would summarize the explanatorily relevant information about these fields simply by saying that they were not very large.

All elements of a causal model are subject to abstraction: not just its events and other singular states of affairs, but also its laws. Consider, for example, window breaking. A causal model for a cannonball's breaking a window might contain many details about the laws of physics, such as the complete theory of gravity, the physics of air resistance, and the laws governing the molecular structure of the window. Much of this detail can be removed. The laws pertaining to the cannonball's trajectory can be abstracted to the simple theory developed by Galileo governing the motion of terrestrial projectiles. The laws concerning molecular detail can be abstracted to a simple law specifying only what is relevant to the brittleness of ordinary glass. An explanatory kernel, then, will cite only these expurgated versions of the underlying laws.

Or take Rasputin's death. A causal model for Rasputin's death by drowning might contain many complex physiological generalizations about the precise effects of oxygen deprivation, among other things. If the explanandum is simply death, however, the precise effects are irrelevant, provided that they result in Rasputin's dying. They may be abstracted away, then, leaving behind the simple relation between oxygen deprivation and death. There are limits to this abstraction, but I will not dwell on them here; they will be explored in sections 3.6 and 5.4.

With some of their details removed by explanatory abstraction, is it right to say that the original laws are nevertheless difference-makers for the explanandum? They are not difference-makers in their entirety; rather, certain of their aspects or high-level properties are difference-makers. These aspects take the form of more abstract versions of the original laws; they are themselves law-like. The process of kernel determination thus takes the raw nomological material present in the source model and produces its own high-level laws, each with a level of abstraction customized for the explanatory task at hand, so as to specify only properties and processes that are relevant to the explanandum.

This is the case even when the source model describes a causal process entirely at the level of fundamental physics. The high-level laws in the resulting kernel should be regarded as nothing new, then, but merely as a more abstract description of the same fundamental-level causal process, or, in other words, as a high-level description of the fundamental-level laws (and perhaps other fundamental-level states of affairs) obtained by omitting all non-difference-making details in the fundamental-level model. In chapter seven, I will propose that all high-level causal laws, not just those produced by kernel determination, have what I call "underlying mechanisms" that are simply the kairetic procedure's distillations of the fundamental laws. In this way, the kairetic procedure is in a certain sense responsible for the structure of the high-level sciences.[8]

### 3.53 Path Dependence and the Optimizing Procedure

The procedure for determining an explanatory kernel by abstraction requires some further tuning, as a slightly more complex cannonball/window example will show. Suppose that in order to break the window, the cannonball must have a momentum of at least 20 kg m s$^{-1}$. (The momentum of the cannonball is its mass multiplied by its velocity.)

The actual cannonball had, say, a mass of 10 kg and a velocity of 5 m s$^{-1}$. You would like to know what facts about the ball's mass and velocity were difference-makers for the breaking. You ought to be able to answer this question by taking a causal model for the breaking that states the exact mass and velocity, and then abstracting until you can abstract no further without invalidating the entailment of the breaking. Whatever claim about mass and velocity remains spells out the difference-making facts.

In implementing this procedure, a problem arises: the kernel determined by the procedure, and in particular the claims about the mass and velocity of the ball that appear in the kernel's setup, will vary depending on the order in which the abstractions are performed. The procedure, then, does not provide a well-defined set of difference-makers.

Suppose, for example, you begin with a model that states an exact mass and velocity for the ball, namely, 10 kg and 5 m s$^{-1}$, and you decide to abstract velocity, that is, to substitute for the specification of the exact velocity a specification of a range of velocities. The widest, hence most abstract, range you can specify without invalidating the entailment of the window's breaking is that the velocity is 2 m s$^{-1}$ or more. If the lower bound on the velocity is reduced any further, the momentum of the ball will, given that its mass is specified to be 10 kg, fall below 20 kg m s$^{-1}$, and so will no longer be sufficient to entail that the window breaks. Now abstract the mass. Because the lower bound on velocity is 2 m s$^{-1}$, the mass cannot be reduced at all; you are therefore left with a specification that the mass is 10 kg or greater. In summary, the difference-making facts about mass and velocity turn out to be that the mass was equal to or greater than 10 kg, and that the velocity was equal to or greater than 2 m s$^{-1}$.

But now suppose that you had abstracted the mass first. With the velocity fixed at this initial stage at its actual value of 5 m s$^{-1}$, you can specify a range for the mass of 4 kg and up. When you come to abstract the velocity, you are left with a range of 5 m s$^{-1}$ and up. Thus, in this case, the difference-making facts about mass and velocity turn out to be that the mass was equal to or greater than 4 kg, and that the velocity was equal to or greater than 5 m s$^{-1}$, in conflict with the conclusion of the previous paragraph. You will see that there are other possible end points of the abstraction process, too: for example, you might conclude that the difference-making facts were that the mass was equal to or greater than 5 kg and that the velocity was equal to or greater than 4 m s$^{-1}$.

The conflict is resolved by specifying a unique end point for the abstraction operation, as follows. Given a model $M$ for an event $e$, the corresponding kernel for $e$ is the maximal abstraction of $M$ that causally entails $e$. Because the abstraction relation is only a partial ordering, it is not guaranteed that $M$ will have a maximal abstraction, that is, an abstraction that is more abstract than any other abstraction. But in the case of the cannonball, there is such a model. It specifies the following constraint on the mass $m$ and velocity $v$ of the ball:

$$mv \geq 20.$$

You will see that a kernel built around this specification is at least as abstract as any of the possible end points considered above. It is also clearly the most abstract such specification: a more abstract specification would have to allow a momentum for the ball less than 20 kg m s$^{-1}$, and in so doing, could no longer guarantee the breaking of the window.

What if there is no unique maximally abstract model? I could say that in such cases there are no determinate facts about difference-making, or rather, no determinate facts save those on which all the most abstract models agree. Or I could break the tie by appealing to a richer notion of generality, such as that introduced in section 4.35. Nothing crucial, I think, turns on the choice.

Whereas the earlier procedures for kernel determination specified a process, the new procedure specifies a goal, the maximally abstract model. I call this new procedure the *optimizing procedure*—or at least I will do so once the problem of cohesion is addressed.

## 3.6   Cohesion

### 3.61   A Disjunction Problem

A disjunction always says less than its disjuncts. Thus, it is always possible to make a causal model more abstract by forming a disjunction of the model's setup and the setup for some other causal model with the same target, resulting in a set of uselessly disjunctive difference-makers. This spells trouble for the optimizing procedure. Let me give an example.

Consider two causal models that represent Rasputin's dying in two quite different ways, say, a death by drowning due to his being thrown into a river, and a death by poisoning due to his being fed toxic teacakes. Suppose that the influviation model contains the real difference-makers for Rasputin's death; the poisoning model is therefore not veridical.

Now take the disjunction of the setups of the two models and form a new model that has the disjunction as its setup: it states that *either* Rasputin was thrown in a river etc. *or* he was fed poison teacakes etc. The disjunctive model is veridical, since one of these chains of events did occur, as claimed, and it entails Rasputin's death, since both chains of events lead to death. Worse, it is more abstract than the influviation model, because its setup is entailed by the influviation model's setup but not vice versa.

It would appear, then, that the optimizing criterion for difference-making will favor the disjunctive model over the influviation model. As a consequence, Rasputin's being thrown into the river will not qualify as a difference-maker for his death; the difference-maker is rather the more abstract event of his being either thrown into the river or poisoned. (More exactly, the difference-maker is the state of affairs picked out by the disjunction of the descriptions of the two causal chains in their entirety.) This is not a tolerable conclusion. Even if the disjunction can be said in some extenuated sense to be a difference-maker, the disjunct—the influviation—ought to be a difference-maker too.

### 3.62  The Cohesion Requirement and Its Foundations

The disjunctive model is defective, but in what way? It is tempting to say that a model with a single premise that lumps together events, laws, and background conditions in an inextricable way is not a genuine causal model, perhaps because its entailment of its target is not causal entailment. There may well be something to this, but I am unwilling to put too much more weight on the notion of causal entailment, and in any case, there is an opportunity here to pursue a deeper issue.

Rather than the form of the disjunctive model, focus on the different kinds of scenarios that can realize the model. These fall into two classes: the poisonings of Rasputin, and the influviations of Rasputin. There is something wrong, I suggest, with a causal model that is realized by, and only by, two quite different kinds of causal processes. I say—alluding to the property of the same name employed by the pattern-subsumption approach to explanation (section 1.32)—that such a model lacks *cohesion*. Even after application of the kairetic criterion has eliminated such a model's non-difference-makers, it is unable to function as an explanation because it models not one but two distinct difference-making processes. To use such a model to pick out the difference-makers in a causal process cannot succeed, because to say that the process realizes the model leaves it indeterminate which difference-making process is at work. This accounts for the unsatisfying indeterminacy of the states of affairs deemed difference-makers by a disjunctive kernel. I therefore make the following amendment to the optimizing procedure for kernel determination: an explanatory kernel must be cohesive. The cohesion requirement acts as a brake on abstraction, halting it before it crosses the line into disjunction. In so doing, the requirement not only prevents technical philosophical trickery such as the disjunction problem, but it also determines how abstract a description of the workings of the world can be while still giving explanatorily useful information about fundamental-level causation.

I have given only the loosest and most intuitive characterization of cohesion. What is it for a model to be realized by two different causal processes? In Strevens (2004), I defined cohesion as follows. The disjunctive model for Rasputin's death mentions a number of causal elements: teacakes, toxins, ropes, rivers, and so on. These can be divided into two sets—the sets on opposite sides of the disjunction—corresponding to the two ways that the model can be realized. Some systems realize the model by possessing the elements in one set, some systems by possessing the elements in the other. Call a model incohesive, then, to the extent that its different realizers appeal to different sets of the causal elements mentioned in the model, or, in other words, call a model cohesive only if all of its realizers possess the same causal elements.

This way of defining cohesion in effect explains what it is for a model to describe two different causal processes by appealing to a distinction between different causal elements: causal processes are individuated by their elements. But how are causal elements to be individuated?

Let me consider two possibilities. First, there is perhaps some metaphysical or psychological criterion for individuating causal elements that lies entirely outside the sphere of explanation and to which philosophers of explanation may appeal without further justification. Suspecting as I do that high-level causal talk is in part explanatory talk, I do not regard this as a secure option.

Second, differences between causal elements are perhaps to be discerned at the level of fundamental physics. Certainly, fundamental physics is capable of recognizing any difference you like, but there may be too much discernment and so too many differences: every concrete realization of Rasputin's death looks somewhat different from every other.

There is something of a dilemma in the making, then. If the causal difference between a poisoning and a drowning is something that emerges only at the high level, then like all high-level causal facts, on my view, it is in part an explanatory fact and so should be given a basis in a theory of explanation, rather than forming a part of the basis for a theory of explanation. This suggests a fundamental-level basis for the distinction I need. But from a fundamental-level perspective, every causal process is unique. To forbid causal models that can be realized by different causal processes would be to forbid abstract models altogether.

What to do?

### 3.63 Cohesion as Causal Contiguity

My solution is to opt for a fundamental-level basis and to invoke a notion of contiguity. Suppose that fundamental-level causal processes can be rated as more or less similar to one another on a continuous scale of similarity, so that all such processes form a similarity space. Any particular realization of a causal model will correspond to a point in this similarity space. A model is cohesive, I propose, if its realizers constitute a contiguous set in causal similarity space, or, as I will say, when its realizers are *causally contiguous*. Thus, two realizers of a causal model may be quite dissimilar without disrupting its cohesion, provided that it is possible to trace a path through causal similarity space from one realizer to the other without passing through any nonrealizers.

In its broad outlines, this definition of cohesion solves the problems outlined in the previous section: it gives cohesion a fundamental-level basis, but admits models with realizers that are from a fundamental-level point of view (or even a high-level point of view) extremely diverse.

To posit a similarity space subsuming every kind of causal process may seem rather optimistic, however. Let me remind you what is at issue here. The ultimate goal is to characterize our practice of scientific explanation. To base cohesion on causal contiguity, then, is to assume that our practice in-cludes procedures for making similarity judgments about causal processes and that these judgments, if they exist, play a certain role in evaluating explanatory models. I take it that it is the existence of the judgments them-selves that is more likely to raise doubts.

Two remarks. First, it is not necessary to show that the similarity judg-ments are based on some objectively real property of resemblance. If the similarity relation in question is a part of our explanatory practice, then it belongs in an account of scientific explanation, even if it is a mere arti-fact of human cognition. Second, it is not necessary to show that, given any two causal processes, a scientific practitioner can assess their degree of sim-ilarity. What is needed is that, given a causal process, the practitioner can identify its close neighbors in the similarity space, that is, that the practi-tioner can identify small "similarity neighborhoods."[9]

Nevertheless, the obstacles to finding an account of similarity judgments are considerable. Even if a cognitive basis for the judgments does exist, it may be a complex psychological matter that is for the most part beyond the means of contemporary philosophy to discover. How even to begin creating a formal system capable of representing all possible causal processes, espe-cially when *possible* means, as you will see, not just physically possible but metaphysically possible?

For the purposes of this book, I propose a proxy for causal contiguity that I call *dynamic contiguity*. Dynamic contiguity is a necessary condition for causal contiguity, I will suggest, and in certain circumstances, a sufficient condition. Thus, it can be used to flesh out the notion of cohesion—and as a necessary condition, to provide decisive judgments about incohesion—without my having to investigate further the nature of the similarity of causal processes.

Every causal process—if you like, every concrete realization of a causal model—corresponds to a trajectory in the state space of fundamental phys-ics. (State space contains a point for every possible state of a given system. A trajectory in state space therefore traces the way in which the system's properties change as a causal process unfolds.) Take the trajectories corre-sponding to every one of a model's concrete realizers, each a thread in state space. If this set of state space threads is contiguous, the model is *dynami-cally contiguous*.

Were it the case that a trajectory in state space represented all the facts about the corresponding causal process, then causal contiguity might be defined as dynamic contiguity. But a trajectory contains information about causation only indirectly; it reveals the overt effects of the causal influences at work in a system, but it does not reveal the nature of the influences themselves. The same trajectory in state space might be caused in two quite different ways, corresponding to two different sets of possible fundamental physical laws. (If the fundamental laws are fixed, then there is, given determinism, just one causal process per trajectory, since "the system" in a fundamental-level causal model by definition comprehends all causal influences. But as you will see, it is important to the kaireatic account that cohesion be defined for models that have realizers with fundamental laws different from the actual fundamental laws.)

I propose that dynamic contiguity is necessary for causal contiguity, at least when working with the kinds of physical theories that seem to characterize our universe. A model with dynamically noncontiguous realizers, then, is not cohesive. Dynamic contiguity conjoined with a certain additional factor is sufficient for causal contiguity. What is the extra ingredient? I have only a sketch of an answer: the dynamic contiguity of a model guarantees its causal contiguity provided that either (a) the model allows only one fundamental physics, that is, all concrete realizations of the model agree on the fundamental laws, or (b) the different, competing sets of fundamental laws allowed by the model themselves form a contiguous set in some appropriate similarity space for fundamental physical theories. In this way, the problem of finding a causal similarity space is reduced to the problem of finding a dynamic similarity space along with a similarity space for fundamental theories. I would like to think that this constitutes progress.

In any case, although dynamic contiguity alone is not sufficient for causal contiguity, hence not sufficient for cohesion, I propose nevertheless that, within the framework of the kaireatic criterion for difference-making, the dynamic contiguity test can for the most part be safely used in place of the causal contiguity test. The shortcomings of dynamic contiguity as a mark of cohesion will, I suggest, be covered up in almost all cases by the kaireatic criterion's generality desideratum: models that are wrongly judged cohesive by the dynamic contiguity test will be rejected anyway for being insufficiently general. Why? When the sets of fundamental laws cited in the various concrete realizations of a model are not contiguous, there will exist, I am guessing, a more abstract model that fills in the gaps, and so (given dynamic contiguity) passes the test for cohesion. But I will not try to justify this claim here. Let me simply take dynamic contiguity as a proxy for cohesion and let the results speak for themselves.

An example: consider the trajectories corresponding to the concrete realizations of a causal model in which Rasputin dies by influviation. These, I submit, form a contiguous region in the state space of fundamental physics. That is, you can get from one realizer to any other by making (speaking roughly here) a perhaps very long series of very small changes in the realization, adjusting incrementally the place where Rasputin hits the water, the temperature of the water, the weight and composition of his clothes, and so on, in such a way that every intermediate stage is itself a realizer of the model. The influviation model therefore passes the dynamic contiguity test for cohesion. The trajectories corresponding to the realizers of the disjunctive model do not, by contrast, form a contiguous set.[10] Thus, the disjunctive model is, as desired, judged incohesive.

Three remarks. First, how to compare realizers with different numbers of particles? The corresponding trajectories occupy differently dimensioned state spaces, the smaller of which cannot be meaningfully embedded in the larger. A similarity metric that reaches beyond any particular state space is required, then, to determine which $n$ particle systems are more, which less, similar to a given $n + 1$ particle system.

Second, as I have already observed, the test for cohesion must deliver judgments about models that have physically impossible systems among their realizers, that is, models that are consistent with sets of fundamental laws other than the actual laws of fundamental physics. In chapter eight, for example, I will consider a model that can be realized by both classical and quantum systems. Classical and quantum physics have rather different state spaces. If the dynamic-contiguity approach is to succeed in evaluating the cohesion of such models, there must be some way of projecting trajectories in these different spaces onto some common space where their contiguity can be evaluated. In particular, there must be some way of deciding whether a classical and a quantum theory are making almost the same or quite different predictions about the time evolution of a given system.

To find a basis for such judgments is a difficult problem. Yet it is clear, I think, that we are in fact capable of comparing predictions in this way, at least in some cases. We can, for example, compare the predictions of classical and quantum theories in situations where, on the quantum side, well-defined wave packets are involved. (For another example, see section 8.24.)

Third, it is quite possible that, on top of connectedness in the technical sense, a set of trajectories should satisfy some further geometrical constraints if it is to qualify as cohesive. I have already suggested (in note 10) that all parts of the set ought to be of the same dimension, and in particular, that the contiguity of the set ought not to be due to low-dimensional "bridges" between its parts. Even trajectory sets that satisfy this additional requirement may, if their geometry is too extreme, fail to measure up to our intuitive standards for cohesion in some other way.

The notion of dynamic contiguity needs further work, then. I am in any case not entirely confident that causal contiguity is the key to understanding what is explanatorily unsatisfying about disjunctive models. A contiguity criterion for cohesion does have certain advantages, however: it is a fundamental-level criterion, so does not lean on a metaphysics of the higher level, and it is a strong principle, whose consequences for the nature of explanation will be interesting and controversial. Let me proceed, then, on the understanding that some fundamental-level account of cohesion is required and that the contiguity account is as good a placeholder for the correct account as any.

An aside: In endorsing the contiguity conception of cohesion, I am claiming that our explanatory practice is committed, in principle, to giving explanations by way of models that are realized contiguously at the fundamental level. It does not follow that every explanation is explicitly vetted for this property, or even that human explainers have much idea what the fundamental level looks like. Cohesion may turn in principle on the nature of the fundamental level, but in practice, the cohesiveness of an explanatory model is likely to be tested by high-level heuristics. Explanatory claims, like all other scientific conclusions, are forever—well, almost forever—provisional.

Let me examine, briefly, two controversial consequences of the contiguity conception of cohesion. Consider the cohesion of a model that attributes Rasputin's death to poisoned teacakes. Different poisons act in different ways. It seems likely, then, that the various realizations of poisoning will not form a contiguous set at the fundamental level. The poisoning model is therefore incohesive: it should be broken down into cohesive models each representing the effect of a certain kind of poison on Rasputin's system. Strictly speaking, if Rasputin had (contrary to the facts) died from poisoning, it would not have been poisoning per se that made a difference to his death but a certain kind of poisoning.

Is this consequence tolerable? I think it is not only tolerable but has the ring of truth. What makes something a poison is (in part) that it causes death. But to say that Rasputin was killed by ingesting something that causes death is to give an incomplete explanation of the death; a model that cites poison without saying more is therefore explanatorily defective, just as the kairetic criterion would have it. The kairetic account's treatment of multiply-realizable kinds is discussed further in section 5.4; on functionally defined kinds in particular, see section 4.33.

Next consider the model that attributes Rasputin's death to influviation. Suppose that, as a matter of definition, influviation involves the victim's being bound hand and foot. Being bound is surely a multiply-realizable property: it can involve rope, wire, duct tape, and so on. Do influviations performed using these various kinds of binding form a dynamically contiguous set? It is hard to say. There are discontinuities between different molecular structures, but the points of configuration space between the structures do not represent equilibrium states. However, it is implausible that the explanatory power of the influviation model depends, or depends that much, on the resolution of such questions. (Compare my second criticism of the counterfactual criterion for difference-making in section 2.4.)

Two responses. First, it may be that the answer to the question about binding makes little or no difference to most explanatory questions because, even if there were a separate explanatory model for every mode of binding, these models would, for the most part, identify the same difference-makers for death: the water, the sinking, and so on. Thus, you can extract determinate facts about difference-making even if you do not know enough about the physics of binding to determine the correct kernel: all plausible candidates for the kernel concur in almost all their judgments of difference-making.

Second, if cohesion is made a desideratum rather than a requirement, then the influviation model can be seen as one that trades a relatively small amount of cohesion for a big increase in abstractness. It does not maximize cohesion, but it maximizes combined cohesion and abstractness. Such tradeoffs are discussed further in section 5.43.

## 3.7   The Optimizing Procedure

According to the optimizing procedure for kernel determination, the explanatory kernel corresponding to a veridical deterministic causal model

$M$ with target $e$ is the causal model $K$ for $e$ that satisfies the following conditions:

1. $K$ is an abstraction of $M$,
2. $K$ causally entails $e$,

and that, within these constraints, maximizes the following desiderata:

3. $K$ is as abstract as can be (generality), and
4. The fundamental-level realizers of $K$ form a causally contiguous set (cohesion).

I have made cohesion a desideratum rather than a requirement, as suggested at the end of section 3.63; you might also treat cohesion as nonnegotiable.

Three remarks. First, condition (2) is strictly speaking redundant, as it merely reiterates the specification that $K$ be a causal model for $e$.

Second, the optimizing procedure's desideratum of generality is subtly different from the pattern-subsumption account's desideratum of the same name: whereas the pattern-subsumption account's generality requirement counts only actual phenomena subsumed, the kairetic account's generality requirement in effect counts possible but non-actual systems. (Weisberg (2003) provides an extended discussion of the significance of these two kinds of generality.)

Third, generality and cohesion should not be regarded as distinct explanatory virtues. They have no value in themselves (though see section 4.35); their sole role is the determination of difference-makers.

## 3.8   Rival Accounts of Difference-Making Reconsidered

One way to establish the kairetic difference-making criterion's superiority over its rivals is to display the rivals' difficulties and shortcomings, as I did in chapter two. Another, perhaps better, way is to explain the rivals' successes—to show, given the truth of the kairetic account, why they work when they do.

### 3.81  The Counterfactual Criterion

In singular event explanation at least, the simple counterfactual criterion is almost never wrong when it rules that an event is a difference-maker for another event. It is also usually right when it rules that an event is not a difference-maker for another event, the main exceptions being cases of preemption. Let me explain why the simple counterfactual account succeeds when it does, and why it fails when it does, taking as my premise the correctness of the kairetic criterion. (I leave the corresponding explanation for more sophisticated variants of the counterfactual account as an exercise for the reader.)

First, the counterfactual criterion's positive rulings about difference-making. According to the kairetic criterion (at first I will employ the eliminative version), a necessary and sufficient condition for an event $c$'s making a difference to the occurrence of an event $e$ is that

> There exists a model, obtained by removing $c$ from a veridical deterministic causal model for $e$, that does not causally entail $e$.

The counterfactual criterion for difference-making tests whether an event $c$ is a difference-maker for an event $e$ by looking to the closest possible world $w$ where $c$ does not occur (in what follows, I assume for simplicity's sake that there is always a determinately closest world). If $e$ does not occur in $w$, then $c$ is a difference-maker; if $e$ occurs in $w$, then $c$ is not a difference-maker.

Suppose the counterfactual criterion declares that $c$ is a difference-maker for $e$ in virtue of such a $w$. This judgment is vindicated by the kairetic criterion, provided that $w$ realizes a model $M$ obtained by removing $c$ from a veridical deterministic model for $e$, since if $e$ does not obtain in $w$, the setup of $M$ cannot causally entail $e$. (In effect, $w$ is simply one way of filling out the incomplete causal story told by $M$.)

The question, then, is whether the setup of some relevant $M$ is true in $w$. When $c$ is a particular event or local state of affairs, as I have been assuming, this is likely to be the case for any such $M$. Why? The closest world is one that differs as little as possible from the actual world before the occurrence of $c$, typically the result of a "small miracle" that prevents the occurrence of $c$ while changing little else (section 2.4). Whatever states of affairs are specified in $M$'s setup are therefore very likely present in $w$. The counterfactual criterion's positive difference-making judgments are for this reason generally correct (though I will qualify this claim shortly).

Next, the counterfactual criterion's negative difference-making rulings. According to the kairetic account, an event $c$ fails to make a difference to an event $e$ just in case every model $M$, obtained as above by removing $c$ from a veridical deterministic model for $e$, causally entails $e$. The counterfactual criterion for difference-making holds that $c$ is not a difference-maker just in case $e$ occurs in the closest possible world in which $c$ does not occur. Suppose that $c$ fails the counterfactual test: in the closest world $w$ in which $c$ does not occur, $e$ still occurs. Since $c$ is a local event or state of affairs, the miracle that ensures that $c$ does not obtain in $w$ is very likely small enough that all aspects of the actual world that were causal influences on $e$, apart from $c$ and its causal consequences, are present in $w$. Thus, as before, the elements in the setup of any relevant $c$-less model $M$ for $e$ hold in $w$.

Assume that $e$ holds in $w$ because it is causally entailed by certain facts in $w$ (as best I can tell, this is usually true). It follows that for every relevant $M$, there is a set of causal factors and laws consistent with the setup of $M$ that causally entails $e$, namely, the facts in $w$ that causally entail $e$. But this does not imply that such an $M$ itself causally entails $e$, since the causal entailers of $e$ in $w$ need not be represented in the setup of $M$: $e$'s obtaining in $w$ may be due to some causal process other than the one represented by $M$. This is just the situation found in cases of preemption (sections 2.4 and 6.2); the kairetic account predicts, then, that the counterfactual account's negative rulings are unreliable in the presence of a backup cause.

Now, a complication: I assumed above that the correct answers about difference-making are given by the kairetic account's eliminative procedure. Thus, I have established only that the counterfactual criterion's judgments of difference-making are as reliable as the eliminative procedure's judgments. It should come as no surprise, then, that when the eliminative procedure fails, the counterfactual criterion also fails.

Consider the case of the cannonball and the window from section 3.53. You will recall that a cannonball of mass 10 kg hurled at 5 m s$^{-1}$ breaks a window, a momentum of 20 kg m s$^{-1}$ being sufficient to cause the breaking. The kairetic kernel for the breaking specifies of the mass and velocity only that their product is greater than or equal to 20.

Put the following question to the counterfactual criterion: did it make a difference that the velocity of the ball was at least 2 m s$^{-1}$? To answer the question, find the nearest possible world where the velocity is less than

2 m s$^{-1}$. Because this world is chosen to be maximally similar to our own up until the time of the throw, I assume that the ball will have a velocity barely under 2 m s$^{-1}$ and that the mass will be the same, 10 kg. The ball's momentum in this world is just under 20 kg m s$^{-1}$, so the window is not broken. The ball's having a velocity of at least 2 m s$^{-1}$ is therefore declared a difference-maker.

If the kairetic criterion is correct, this claim is false. There are realizations of the optimal model for the window's breaking in which the velocity of the ball is less than 2 m s$^{-1}$, for example, a realization in which the velocity is 1.5 m s$^{-1}$ and the mass is 15 kg. The counterfactual account fails to capture this subtlety in our reasoning about difference-making.

In summary, the kairetic account of explanatory relevance is able to account for the major strengths and weaknesses of the simple counterfactual account: the account works badly in cases of preemption, but it works well in other cases of event explanation, provided that the putative difference-maker is itself a singular event and so can be removed using a small miracle, and that the case is not one in which abstraction, rather than removal, is appropriate. When the putative difference-maker is not an event and the removal miracle is not so small, the counterfactual account may fail to give a clear answer, as shown in section 2.4.

## 3.82 The Manipulation Criterion

The manipulation criterion for explanatory relevance succeeds for more or less the same reasons as the counterfactual criterion. Like the counterfactual and kairetic criteria, to test whether an event $c$ makes a difference to an event $e$, the manipulation criterion asks whether $e$ occurs in a scenario from which $c$ has been "removed." Like the counterfactual criterion, the manipulation criterion considers a scenario in which $c$ determinately does not occur; like the kairetic criterion, it conceives of the scenario abstractly, by way of a less than complete description of the relevant goings-on.

When the manipulation criterion makes a positive relevance judgment (with respect to a given causal pathway), it does so because $e$ does not occur in a certain causal model in which $c$ does not occur. Given the manipulationist's rules for determining the nature of the model, it is more or less guaranteed that the model is a fleshing out of a veridical deterministic model for $e$ from which $c$ has been removed in the kairetic sense—again, call it $M$. Since a fleshing out of $M$ is consistent with the nonoccurrence of

$e$, it follows that $M$ itself cannot entail $e$ and so that $c$ is a difference-maker. The manipulation criterion's positive judgments of difference-making are, therefore, accurate. (However, the manipulation criterion shares with the counterfactual criterion an inability to deliver subtle judgments about difference-making in cases where the optimizing procedure yields a different model than the eliminative procedure, as explained in the previous section.)

The negative judgments made by the criterion are more accurate than the simple counterfactual criterion's negative judgments, which fall through in cases of preemption, you will recall, because the counterfactual criterion's $c$-less scenario—the scenario it examines to ascertain the consequences of removing $c$—includes too much. The manipulation criterion's $c$-less model will contain much less than is contained in a possible world. In this respect, it is already ahead of the counterfactual criterion. But as the example discussed in section 2.5 and pictured in figure 2.1 shows, the manipulationist model may nevertheless contain backup causes.

The reliability of the manipulation criterion in preemption cases is due, then, to something else—namely, what it does with the backup causes when creating its $c$-less model, which is to assign every causal variable not on the putative causal path from $c$ to $e$ its actual value. Schematically, a typical backup cause has two states, active and passive. It starts out in its passive state and assumes its active state, in which it is able to cause $e$, only if called on to do so by the failure of the main cause. In a standard preemption scenario, the backup cause does not lie on the causal path from $c$ to $e$, and it remains in its passive state at all relevant times, since the main cause is successful in bringing about $e$. The manipulation criterion, then, holds the backup cause in its actual state—the passive state—even in a $c$-less model, and so $e$ does not occur in such a model. The criterion in effect removes not only $c$ but also the consequences of the triggering mechanism by which the nonoccurrence of $c$ would activate the backup cause.

From a kairetic perspective, then, in cases of preemption the manipulation criterion does something wrong, but it also does something else that neutralizes its wrong-doing. When removing $c$, it retains the backup mechanism. (The kairetic account, by contrast, attributes difference-making power to a preempting cause $c$ in virtue of a model that does not mention the backup mechanism; see section 6.2.) But it disables the mechanism, achieving much the same result as if it had entirely removed it.

Is the manipulation criterion infallible in its negative judgments of relevance? Only if it always succeeds, in cases of preemption, in neutralizing the backup mechanism. From the justification of its success above, one potential weak point is clear: since only mechanisms not on the putative causal path from $c$ to $e$ are disabled, the manipulation criterion will run into a certain amount of difficulty when the variables that constitute the backup mechanism themselves lie on the path from $c$ to $e$—in which case the same variables play a dual role as both backup mechanism and assistant to the main mechanism, the mechanism by which $c$ actually did cause $e$. Such cases are discussed in Strevens (2007a, 2008a); I give an additional argument against the manipulation criterion in section 6.25.

### 3.83  The Mill/Mackie Criterion

I neglected in chapter two the influential criterion that, following J. S. Mill, looks for necessary and/or sufficient conditions for the explanandum. This approach is best captured by Mackie's (1974) notion of an INUS condition. As with most other philosophical attempts to articulate a notion of difference-making, Mackie's criterion was presented as the core element of an account of high-level causation. (For an account of explanation with hints of Mackie, see Garfinkel (1981), especially pp. 62–66.) I reinterpret Mackie's theory as a criterion for difference-making, as follows.

According to Mackie, $c$ is a difference-maker for $e$ if $c$ is an insufficient but nonredundant part of an unnecessary but sufficient condition for the occurrence of $e$. That is, to find a cause of $e$, find some bundle of conditions that is sufficient for $e$—such as the conditions asserted by a deterministic causal model for $e$—and pick out a nonredundant part of the bundle. What is a nonredundant part? It is a part of the bundle that cannot be removed without making the bundle no longer sufficient for $e$.

You will see that the Mackie account of difference-making is similar to the kairetic criterion, and in particular, to the preliminary version of the kairetic criterion that I call the eliminative procedure. The main differences are, first, that the kairetic criterion's optimizing procedure represents a more sophisticated characterization of what makes a condition nonredundant, and, second, that for Mackie, a set of conditions is sufficient for $e$ if the conditions logically entail $e$, while on the kairetic account, they must causally entail $e$.

The most famous weakness of the unadorned INUS account—its apparent inability to deal with barometer/storm cases, such as Mackie's example of the Manchester factory hooters—is due to its putting no further constraint on the entailment. Mackie attempted to deal with the problem by requiring something a little like causal entailment (Mackie 1974, chap. 7). The INUS account is therefore in many ways a precursor of the kairetic account (Strevens 2004; Strevens 2007b).

# — 4 —

# The Kairetic Account of Explanation

## 4.1 Standalone Explanation

The centerpiece of a theory of explanation should be an account of what I will call *standalone explanation*, by which I mean an explanation that is complete, that is not missing any of its parts. Or you might consider the following precept to be an implicit definition of standalone explanation: science understands a phenomenon just in case it can provide a standalone explanation of the phenomenon.

Neither characterization should be taken to imply that there is only one standalone explanation per explanandum; on the contrary, the kairetic account implies that every event has infinitely many standalone explanations. Any one of these explanations is complete in the relevant sense, and knowledge of any is sufficient for scientific understanding of the event's occurrence.

A standalone explanation is always a causal model, either atomic or compound. (A compound model, recall, describes one or more intermediate steps in the causal chain leading to the explanandum, called intermediate setups.)

An atomic causal model is a standalone explanation of an event just in case it is a (veridical) explanatory kernel for that event. In other words, for an atomic causal model to be a standalone explanation for its target, it must be optimal in the kairetic sense: the application of the optimizing procedure must leave it unchanged. The optimizing procedure is not only a device for determining difference-makers, then: it constructs standalone explanations.

It would be convenient if the optimizing procedure, or something like it, could convert a compound causal model into a standalone explanation that was itself compound. This is not possible, however; the optimizing procedure always (given determinism) produces kernels that are atomic.

An example should show why this is in general true. Consider a causal process in which an event $c$ causes an event $d$, which in turn causes the explanandum event $e$. To keep things simple, assume that $c$ is sufficient for the occurrence of $d$, and that $d$ is sufficient for the occurrence of $e$. Thus, $c$ causally entails $d$, and $d$ causally entails $e$. (This is, of course, not at all realistic, ignoring as it does the essential role played by laws in causal entailment.)

Take a compound model for $e$ with an initial setup including $c$ and an intermediate setup including $d$. You might hope that after applying the optimizing procedure, you would get a stripped-down compound model having $c$ alone as its initial setup and $d$ alone as its intermediate setup. But the optimizing procedure will not oblige. Either $c$ or $d$ can be removed from the stripped-down model without invalidating its entailment of $e$. One of the two must be discarded, then, leaving an atomic model for $e$. A compound model represents the way things are at several points along a causal chain; the example shows that (given a deterministic starting point) a product of the optimizing machinery will only ever represent the way things are at one point on the chain.

I propose that compound standalone explanations are built from atomic standalone explanations, that is, from explanatory kernels. More exactly, a compound explanatory model is a chain, or a number of converging chains, of explanatory kernels.

Let me put this more formally. A standalone explanation for an event $e$ is a causal model constructed using a set of kernels consisting of

1. an explanatory kernel for $e$, and

2. standalone explanations for zero or more singular events or states of affairs in the kernel's setup.

Equivalently, a standalone explanation for $e$ is a causal model built according to the following procedure:

1. Start with a kernel for $e$. Call it the current explanation of $e$.

2. Either stop, or do the following: Choose a singular event or state of affairs in the current explanation that has not been chosen before. Add to the current explanation a kernel for this event or state of affairs. The

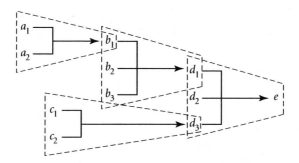

**Figure 4.1** Compound standalone explanation for $e$ composed of four kernels, indicated by dashed lines. Arrows represent difference-making causal entailments.

chosen event thereby becomes an intermediate setup in a compound causal model.

3. Repeat (2) as often as you like.

A compound explanation is created and enlarged, then, by adding to a kernel explaining $e$ explanations of events in the kernel's setup. As many or as few of these events may be explained as you like. You cannot enlarge a standalone explanation by explaining a law in the kernel's setup, unless your explaining is really a *deepening*, in a sense to be discussed in section 4.33. The structure of a typical standalone explanation is shown in figure 4.1.

An event has many standalone explanations. The event of the window's breaking, for example, has a standalone explanation that mentions just my throwing the cannonball and the absence of interfering factors, and another standalone explanation that mentions not only these things but also my motives for throwing the cannonball. Are some of an event's standalone explanations better than others? The answer is rich and complex; it will form the greater part of this chapter (section 4.3).

A standalone explanation is by definition self-contained—it has no internal gaps or missing parts. The account of standalone explanation presented above is, then, an account of explanatory integrity. Let me contrast my view of integrity with two other positions in the literature (positions that are more or less independent of their proponents' views on the nature of explanatory relevance).

One conception of integrity, and thus of the nature of standalone explanation, is suggested by Railton's account of causal explanation: any event has just one self-contained explanation, namely, an explanation that specifies, at least implicitly, every explanatorily relevant fact (Railton 1981). At the other end of the spectrum is an extremely permissive view suggested by some aspects of Lewis's account of causal explanation (Lewis 1986a, 219–220): the presentation of any piece at all of explanatorily relevant information, even a single difference-making event, constitutes a self-contained explanation.

My view is intermediate in its liberality. Unlike the view I associate with Railton, I hold that there are many standalone explanations for a given phenomenon, each of which omits some explanatorily relevant factors but includes others. In particular, it is not necessary, in order to fully understand an event, to trace the event's causal history back to the big bang. A full understanding of the extinction of the dinosaurs, for example, can be achieved by taking into account the occurrence of a catastrophic meteor strike or a sudden onset of widespread volcanism, together with various climatological mechanisms, aspects of dinosaur physiology, and the workings of Cretaceous ecosystems. The addition of an explanation of the existence of the meteor or the physiology of the dinosaurs, while illuminating, is not compulsory—though science may lack this information, it may nevertheless regard the occurrence of the extinction itself as understood.

Unlike the view I associate with Lewis, I hold that not every piece of relevant information stands alone. If the dinosaurs died out because of the unhappy coincidence of meteor strike and volcanism—if either one or the other on its own would not have led to the extinction—then science does not understand the extinction if it knows about the meteor strike only, even though the meteor strike is by anyone's lights a difference-maker.

Let me conclude with a remark about the sense in which a causal model not meeting the specifications above—a model missing some of its parts or containing explanatorily irrelevant parts—is defective.

When a causal model that fails to satisfy the kairetic specification is proffered as an explanation of its target, on the face of things everything that is said is true. A causal story is told about the way that the target is causally produced, and this causal story is accurate as far as it goes.

In what sense has something gone wrong? To state that a causal model is an explanation, I propose, is to state that it is a standalone explanation, and thus to claim, first, that the model is not missing parts, and second, that every aspect of the causal story represented by the model makes a difference to the causal production of the explanandum. When a causal model that is not self-contained, or that mentions non-difference-makers, is presented as an explanation, then, a false claim is made. It is not merely that not enough, or too much, information has been communicated. Though the claims of the causal model itself are true, to make these claims in an explanatory context is to say something false.

## 4.2   Difference-Making and Transitivity in Compound Explanations

Every element in a standalone explanation of an event $e$ is, I will show, a difference-maker for $e$. It follows that the difference-making relation is transitive: if $c$ makes a difference to $d$, and $d$ makes a difference to $e$, then $c$ makes a difference to $e$.

To demonstrate that every factor in a compound explanation is a difference-maker for the explanandum, it is sufficient to establish that every factor in the explanation appears in some explanatory kernel for the explanandum. In order to do so, I show how to construct such a kernel from the compound explanation, as follows.

First some terminology. Say that a causal factor $d$ is *explanatorily downstream* of another factor $c$, relative to a compound explanation of which they are both a part, if you can get from $c$ to $d$ by following the difference-making arrows in the sort of graphical representation of the model shown in figure 4.1, or more formally, if the model contains a standalone explanation of $d$ of which $c$ is an element.

Now to the argument. Suppose that a causal factor $c$ is part of a compound explanation for an event $e$. The goal is to show that $c$ is a difference-maker for $e$, by constructing a kernel for $e$ containing $c$. Take the setup of the kernel for $e$ in the compound explanation and perform the following operation on this set repeatedly until the result is a set that contains $c$:

> For each element $d$ in the setup that is explanatorily downstream of $c$ in the original compound explanation, replace $d$ with the setup of the kernel for $d$ in the original explanation.

The resulting set is veridical, causally entails $e$, and has no removable or abstractable factors (since, if a factor were abstractable, this would imply that some kernel in the compound model was not maximally abstract). Thus, it is the setup of a kernel for $e$. Since it contains $c$, it follows that $c$ is a difference-maker for $e$.

For example, beginning with the compound model shown in figure 4.1, to construct a kernel with $a_1$ in the setup proceed as follows. Begin with the elements in the setup of $e$, namely, the $d_i$s. Of these, $d_1$ is downstream from $a_1$, so replace it with the elements in its kernel's setup, namely, the $b_i$s. Repeat the operation: since $b_1$ is downstream from $a_i$, replace it with its kernel's setup, namely the $a_i$s. You now have a kernel for $e$ containing the following elements: $a_1, a_2, b_2, b_3, d_2, d_3$. All are therefore difference-makers for $e$.

From the fact that every element in a standalone explanation of an event $e$ is a difference-maker for $e$, the transitivity of difference-making follows immediately: if $c$ is a difference-maker for $d$ and $d$ is a difference-maker for $e$, then there is a kernel for $d$ containing $c$ and a kernel for $e$ containing $d$. These kernels may be put together to make a compound standalone explanation for $e$. The explanation includes $c$, so $c$ is a difference-maker for $e$.

The transitivity of difference-making may not come as a great surprise, but it creates a potential problem for the kairetic account. There are examples in the literature on causation that are supposed to show that causal claims of the form *c was a cause of e* are not transitive. Because I interpret such claims as asserting that $c$ was a difference-maker for $e$, these cases would seem to show that difference-making is not transitive. Section 6.5 will defuse these apparent counterexamples.

The claim that difference-making is transitive can, in any case, be detached from the rest of the kairetic account. If you are a partisan of transitivity failure, you will assume that the above argument is faulty in some respect. (Or you might worry that when generality can be traded off for other properties, the argument does not go through so smoothly.) Suppose, then, that the difference-making relation is not transitive. In order to ensure that all causal factors mentioned in a standalone explanation are difference-makers for the explanandum, simply add an explicit difference-making requirement to the definition of standalone explanation: every causal factor in a standalone explanation of $e$ must make a difference to $e$. It is not pretty, but it works.

## 4.3   Comparing Standalone Explanations

An event typically has many standalone explanations. Some of these explanations contain, or appear to contain, more information about difference-makers than others. Does the additional information make for a better explanation? If so, how?

There are three strategies for explanatory enlargement. First, the causal history of the explanandum can be traced back further in time, by adding to a model standalone explanations for (nonintermediate) events or states of affairs in its setup. Call this *elongation*. Second, aspects of the causal history of an explanandum already implicitly covered by a model can be made explicit, by adding to the model intermediate setups where there were none. Call this *intensification*. Third, the laws and other theoretical generalizations that appear in an explanation may be themselves explained as manifestations of lower-level laws (and if necessary, background conditions). This might seem like a kind of theoretical elongation, but as I will argue in section 4.33, it is in fact a rather different operation; I call it *deepening*. Let me say something more about the nature and virtues of elongation, intensification, and deepening.

### 4.31   Elongation

Take an unexplained event in a standalone explanation's setup and add a standalone explanation for that event. You have elongated the explanation. As a result, the model describes an explanatorily relevant part of the causal process that it did not describe before—it recounts further relevant aspects of the explanandum's causal history, thus telling you more about the things that made a difference to the occurrence of the explanandum.

Is elongation always a good thing? We do not always seem to want the additional information provided by an elongation. Perhaps this is in part because we are unable to cope with the large amounts of information added by the elongation of already sizeable models. Perhaps it is in part because of our nonexplanatory interests—the glazier may want to know that it was a brick that broke the window, but they may not much care who threw it. Neither of these possibilities is incompatible with the view that we are somehow, in virtue of our explanatory practice, committed to finding the information interesting in principle.

Elongation does, I propose, invariably improve an explanation, by adding to the stock of difference-makers—of explanatorily relevant factors—comprising the explanation. But let me reaffirm the elementary virtues of standalone explanation, the virtues to which even an unelongated explanation can lay claim: any standalone explanation is in a certain sense complete, and any standalone explanation is sufficient for scientific understanding.

Two grades of goodness of explanation might therefore be distinguished. A standalone explanation is complete in its own way and sufficient for scientific understanding. But an *exhaustive* standalone explanation mentions everything that makes a difference to the explanandum. An exhaustive explanation is a standalone explanation so long that further elongation is impossible. In a world without beginning, then, an exhaustive explanation is infinitely long. With Railton, I point to exhaustive explanation as an ideal to which we may aspire; unlike Railton, I hold that the principal aim of explanation, full scientific understanding, can be achieved without realizing the ideal.

## 4.32 Intensification

Our practice of enlarging an explanation by adding intermediate setups is prima facie perplexing. On the one hand, it can easily be shown that, in the deterministic case, intensification adds nothing to the information contained in a standalone explanation. On the other hand, certain intensifications do seem to bring explanatory improvements. Let me explain these claims, and then attempt to resolve the conflict.

For simplicity's sake, begin with an atomic explanation, that is, a kernel, for some event $e$. To intensify the explanation is to add an intermediate setup that specifies the occurrence of some events—in this case, say, just one event $d$—downstream from the explanation's original setup. The result is a compound explanation composed of two kernels (see figure 4.2):

1. a kernel for $d$ that has as its setup part or all of the setup for the original atomic explanation, and

2. a kernel for $e$ that has as its setup $d$ and (most likely) parts of the setup for the original atomic explanation.

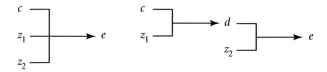

**Figure 4.2** Intensification. On the left is an atomic model for an event $e$; on the right is the model intensified by the addition of an intermediate setup containing a single event $d$.

What does the new intensified explanation tell us about the causal process that the old atomic explanation did not? Nothing. The intensification makes it explicit that $d$ occurred. But the setup of the original atomic explanation already entailed that $d$ occurred, since the new kernel for $d$ has a setup that entails $d$ and that is composed only of elements that appeared in the setup of the original model. To intensify a deterministic explanation is, in short, to make explicit what is already implicit in the explanation. No new information is added.

Let me give a more picturesque example. Suppose that I throw a cannonball at a window. My aim is off, and the ball heads away from the window, but it hits a nearby mailbox and rebounds toward the window, breaking it. A veridical kernel for the breaking that includes in its setup my throw will also have to include, if it is to entail the breaking, some information about the position of the mailbox. This information is sufficient to entail that the ball hits the mailbox. It is possible to intensify the model by adding an intermediate setup stating that the ball hits the mailbox, but such a setup contains no new causal information.

What, then, is the point of intensification?

First, and most obviously, the specification of intermediate setups may perform a purely practical function. It may alert an explanation's recipient to entailments they would otherwise perhaps not have noticed, or it may help them to keep track of entailments regardless of whether they would have noticed them otherwise. It is especially helpful for a causal model that contains converging causal chains to identify explicitly the points of convergence, such as collisions between one object and another. The causal facts about the convergence are, as I have said, implicit in the relevant setups, but spelling them out makes the structure of the causal process explicit in a most helpful way.

Similarly, intermediate setups might be employed to structure a model's follow-through so as to demonstrate that the model's entailment of its target is a causal entailment—breaking down the steps in the derivation, then, to show that it follows an appropriate modus ponens pattern (section 3.23). I am inclined to regard this use, too, as more practically helpful than explanatorily profound.

The second function of intermediate setups is potentially more significant. Consider again the abstract case above (figure 4.2), in which the question is whether to add to an atomic explanation for the event $e$ an intermediate setup stating that the event $d$ occurred. The fact of $d$'s inclusion in a standalone explanation of $e$ would tell us two things about $d$: first, that $d$ occurred and was a part of the causal process leading to $e$, and second, that $d$ was a difference-maker for $e$. The information in the original atomic model's setup entails the first of these pieces of information, but does it entail the second? If not, then $d$'s inclusion conveys an explanatorily important piece of information not otherwise present in the model.

There are many factors that are causally entailed by the setup of a kernel, and that causally influence the kernel's target, but that are not difference-makers for the target. Think, for example, of any side effect of the process set in motion by the events in the setup that has some gravitational influence on the target. Yet it cannot be that the inclusion of an intermediate setup containing a factor $d$ is necessary to prevent $d$'s being mistaken for a mere side effect, for the following reason.

When an intermediate event $d$ can be added to an atomic standalone explanation to make a compound standalone explanation, there must be elements of the original explanation's setup that, in combination with $d$, form a kernel for the explanandum. It is in virtue of the existence of this kernel (perhaps among others) that $d$ is a difference-maker. But this means that the resources are there in the original explanation to see that $d$ is a difference-maker. To make $d$ an intermediate setup does not convey any information about difference-making that was not already available in the original explanation. Thus, however useful intermediate setups may be in making salient various difference-making facts, the benefit is merely practical: it makes information about difference-making more accessible to limited cognizers.

Let me illustrate the third function of intermediate setups with another example. The store owner is now defending his window with a baseball bat. I throw my cannonball, and he swipes at it with the bat. He misses; the ball goes on to break the window.

In such a case, it would be natural, if not compulsory, to add to the usual cannonball-breaks-window model a statement that the store owner failed to connect with the ball. What is the explanatory status of this statement?

It is not an intermediate setup in the usual sense. The causal process by which the ball breaks the window is identical with the store owner present, but missing the ball, and with the store owner absent. The missing of the ball changes nothing. Why is it mentioned at all?

One of the difference-makers for the ball's breaking the window is the negative state of affairs of nothing's interfering with the ball's flight. If the store owner had swatted away the ball, this difference-making condition would have failed to hold. The store owner's missing the ball, then, is a difference-maker for the negative condition, and thus a difference-maker for the breaking. Mentioning the miss is not intensification but elongation: rather than simply stating the fact of the negative condition's holding, a partial explanation is given for the condition's holding.

(The explanation is only partial because for the negative condition to hold, many other potential, if unlikely, deflectors of the ball must be ruled out: errant birds, stray meteors, and so on. In the section 6.3 discussion of causation by omission, you will see that in everyday discourse these factors need not be mentioned for the explanation to count as complete.)

Of the three apparent virtues of intensification discussed so far, two are practical and the last is a result of the intensification's being a covert elongation, and thus not a virtue of intensification at all. Let me finish with an example of an intermediate setup that, unlike those considered above, does real explanatory work.

One of the explanatory models for Rasputin's death, already encountered in earlier discussions, cites in its setup that Rasputin's assassins were determined to kill him and had him utterly in their power. You might think that this sort of model entails no particular mode for Rasputin's death—but this cannot be right, as such a model would lack cohesion. A cohesive model must state or otherwise entail the mode of death, then, perhaps in the form of a compound explanation according to which Rasputin's murderers, determined to kill him and having him completely within their power, tied him up and threw him into a river.

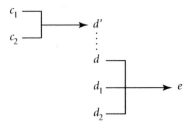

**Figure 4.3** The structure of a hybrid causal model. The dashed line represents the token abstraction relation between a more abstract state of affairs $d'$ and a less abstract state of affairs $d$ with the same concrete realizer.

Consider the composition of such a model. Its intermediate setup is the setup of the influviation model for death, while its initial setup specifies the psychology and power of the conspirators. In section 3.22, I claimed that a compound model's initial setup entails its intermediate setups. But the fact that Rasputin's assassins wanted to kill him does not entail that they went about the murder in any particular way. How, then, is the model structured?

There are two possible answers. First, the compound model could be brought into line with the entailment doctrine by adding to its setup further information about the assassins' state of mind, say, the fact that they believed that drowning was the best way to kill him.

Second, the entailment doctrine might be loosened to accommodate cases such as these. What I have in mind is the structure shown in figure 4.3, where the arrows represent causal entailment, as usual, and the dashed line represents the abstraction relation, that is, the relation that holds between two states of affairs, one an abstraction of the other, that share the same concrete realizer.

Here, the more abstract state of affairs $d'$ is the assassins' doing *something* to bring about Rasputin's death, and the less abstract $d$ specifies the nature of that something.

Although the hybrid explanation shown in figure 4.3 does not conform to the specifications for a standalone explanation, its deviance does not seem very serious. It is perhaps worth making an exception, then, for explanations of this sort, at least in cases where cohesion demands at a certain point in the narrative an abrupt increase in the level of specificity with which the story is told. (For further comments on the awkwardness of hybrid explanation, see section 5.43.)

If hybrid explanation is permitted, then hybrid models constitute the only case I know of in which the intermediate setups of a deterministic compound causal model convey information that is not implicitly contained in the original setup. Probabilistic explanation, you will see in section 11.3, introduces an entirely new, and far more important, role for intermediate setups to play, namely, specifying whether or not an event to which the initial setup assigns only a probability actually occurs.

## 4.33 Deepening

A causal model is *deepened*, I will say, by giving a lower-level account of some causal process represented by the model. The paradigm of deepening is taking a higher-level law cited by the model and giving it a lower-level explanation—for example, providing a physical explanation for one of a model's biological laws.[1]

Physical explanations of higher-level laws are the subject of chapter seven. For the purpose of the present discussion, it will be enough to stipulate that such explanations describe the patterns of fundamental-level causal influence in virtue of which the higher-level laws hold. (The stipulation entirely ignores the role of contingent patterns of initial or background conditions in explaining many high-level laws; see section 7.3.)

Does deepening a model enhance its explanatory power? If so, is deepening optional or obligatory? As you would expect, deepening constitutes an explanatory improvement; less expectedly, it is on the kairetic account not merely recommended but compulsory. Why so? In principle the kairetic procedure always takes as its raw material a model spelling out the facts about causal influence, which are fundamental-level facts (section 3.23). The procedure then removes some information about those influences, but in so doing it does not change the subject: its descriptions remain descriptions, however abstract, of fundamental-level causal processes. The result is an abstract model, but not an unphysical model. It may cite very high-level properties, but they are high-level properties of the fundamental laws of physics. A properly constructed explanatory kernel cannot but be deep, then. Whenever a shallow explanation is given, aspects of the kernel have been censored: some physics that ought to have stayed in the model has been excised.

That a kairetic explanation is always at bottom a physical explanation does not imply, I remind you, that kairetic explanatory models must describe the trajectories of individual fundamental-level particles. This book contains a number of examples to illustrate this point, notably the case of the explanation of gas behaviors using kinetic theory (chapter eight), in which a physical explanation describes not individual trajectories but a statistical profile of trajectories, and certain kinds of equilibrium explanation, in which a physical explanation does not represent trajectories at all (section 7.41). The case of gas behavior illustrates another dimension of physical abstraction: a kinetic theory model can be realized by a range of different possible sets of fundamental physical laws (section 8.24). In these and many other cases, the depth-seeking descent to the fundamental level is quite consistent with a high degree of abstraction.

Although depth is mandatory, there are a wide range of apparently explanatory models that are quite empty of physics. Are these models in some way shallow, and therefore explanatorily deficient? They can be divided into two classes: the models that cite high-level causal covering laws, and the models that deploy what I will call black boxes. The latter, but not the former, I will argue, are insufficiently deep.

I begin with causal covering laws. Many explanations in biology or chemistry are driven entirely by biological or chemical laws or other generalizations: they do not cite the fundamental physical underpinnings of these (relatively) high-level laws. Yet in some sense they seem quite satisfactory; they are not in need of repair by the physics department. Why is it possible for explanatory purposes to cite, say, a chemical law without citing the physical mechanism that underlies the operation of the law?

In section 7.6, I will argue that a chemical causal law is identical to the components of the causal model that explain it, which is to say that the law is identical to its underlying fundamental physical mechanism (or perhaps to the mechanism conjoined with some background conditions; see section 7.3). To cite the law, then, is to cite the mechanism. Of course, in a typical chemical explanation the details of the mechanism are not spelled out, which is to say, the nature of the thing that is being cited is not made fully explicit. But it is cited nonetheless, and since it is the law, and not the description of the law, that does the explaining, the shallowness of the chemical explanation is therefore merely an apparent shallowness.

In saying this, I am not retracting my claim that, in order to understand a phenomenon fully, you must grasp the workings of the relevant causal mechanism in fundamental physical terms. An explanation that cites only high-level laws will, unless supplemented, fail to engender such understanding, because it fails to describe completely what it cites. This is a communicative shortcoming, however, not an explanatory shortcoming.

To clarify this remark, recall from section 1.21 that there are two senses of explanation: an ontological sense, in which an explanation is composed of the causal facts—aspects of the initial conditions and the physical laws—picked out by an explanatory model, and a communicative sense, in which an explanation is an attempt to transmit those facts to an audience, real or imagined.[2] Now consider two rival explanations of some chemical phenomenon: a covering-law explanation that cites a chemical law and initial conditions, and a detailed mechanistic explanation that, in place of the chemical law, cites the aspects of the fundamental laws of physics in virtue of which the law holds. Given the identity of the law and the fundamental physical facts, the two "rivals" turn out to cite precisely the same explanatory facts, and they are thus in the ontological sense one and the same explanation. But they are not, of course, the same explanation in the communicative sense: they convey the explanatory facts in two different ways. Because the kairetic theory aims to give a theory of explanation in the ontological sense, it does not distinguish the two explanations; at the same time, there is a legitimate sense in which they are distinct. There is no inconsistency here, merely ambiguity in the term *explanation*.

A causal covering-law explanation, I have proposed, is only apparently shallow. What does it take, then, for a causal model to be genuinely shallow? The model must substitute for a law or mechanism a *black box*, that is, a functional specification of what gets done that makes no reference, explicit or implicit, to the patterns of causal influence in virtue of which it is done.

A familiar example will illustrate the notion. A Romanov princess drinks a potion and falls into a deep sleep. There is a long chemical and biological story specifying the potion's pernicious ingredients and the way they caused the princess to lose consciousness, but for maximal generality, why not simply say that the princess's sleep is explained by the fact that something about the potion causes humans to sleep? This is the notorious *dormitive virtue* explanation, which explains $c$'s causing $e$ by citing only the fact that $c$ has the property of being $e$-producing.[3]

The kairetic account does not allow "dormitive virtues" to explain sleep, on the grounds that they lack depth: they do not in any way capture the causal influences that are responsible for sleep. This deficit is manifest in the logical connection that the dormitive-virtue model makes between the explaining property, that of being dormitive, and the explanandum, sleep. The connection is too close to be causal, in the following sense. The potion has the dormitive virtue—the property of being sleep-producing—in virtue of some causal laws, initial conditions, and so on, which are responsible for a certain kind of sleep-producing causal process. A causal model for this process must mention the laws and initial conditions, and demonstrate the role they play in causally connecting the potion to the sleep. If a model for the sleep fails to do this, its setup's entailment of the sleep is not a causal entailment, thus the model is not a causal model and cannot be deployed in explanation. By characterizing the cause in terms of its effect, the dormitivity explanation allows the entailment relation to circumvent the causal laws. This generalizes: a model that is not deep is not genuinely causal, in the sense that its entailment of its target is not a causal entailment.

Now let me take something back. The previous paragraph dismisses the explanatory use of black-boxing models altogether, on the grounds that they are not sufficiently deep and therefore not causal. But in fact, science has a number of explanatory uses for black-boxing models, to be discussed at length in sections 5.3 and 5.4. Although a black-boxing model cannot stand on its own, because of the causal deficiency noted above (and also because it will tend to lack cohesion), when propped up by what I will call an explanatory framework, it may find a place in legitimate explanatory inquiry. This elaboration of the kairetic account in no way weakens, you will see, the claims I have made about the explanatory importance of depth.

A deep explanation attributes a property, often rather abstract, to the fundamental laws of physics and then shows that in virtue of that property, the combined causal influence of the states of affairs cited in the explanation's setup brought about the model's target, the explanandum. Two parting remarks.

First, it is not sufficient for depth that a model mentions the fundamental laws; even the dormitive-virtue model might, for example, be understood as saying "the potion has, given the nature of the fundamental laws, the property of being sleep-producing." Depth demands that the property attributed to the laws must participate in a causal entailment; it must play a role in the model's representation of a pattern of causal influence.

Second, although a kairetic model attributes a property to the fundamental laws, it does not demonstrate that the fundamental laws indeed possess the cited property. This is as it should be: there is no scientific explanation of the fact that the fundamental laws have the properties that they do; it is just the way they are. An explainer may, nevertheless, want to show that the laws do have the property; for communicative purposes, they will then append to an explanation a derivation, from premises about the fundamental laws, of the high-level property in question. (The derivation will presumably be a mathematical explanation, which might account for the sense that it does explanatory work.) Because the derivation cites the fundamental laws in the form that we are used to seeing them and derives a high-level conclusion, it is tempting to suppose that it is a proper part of the explanation, or even that it is the only part of the explanation where the fundamental laws figure. This I encourage you not to do: the fundamental laws enter into a causal explanation in virtue of those of their high-level properties that are difference-makers for the explanandum. Everything else about them is irrelevant.

### 4.34 An Overview of Explanatory Augmentation

To summarize the story so far, there are three ways to augment a standalone explanation: elongation, intensification, and deepening. A fourth lies in the offing.

1. *Elongation* is optional, because an unelongated standalone explanation is both internally complete and is sufficient for scientific understanding. However, it improves a standalone explanation by providing additional information explanatorily relevant to the explanandum, that is, by telling more of the relevant causal story.

2. *Intensification* is both optional and, in a deterministic model, unnecessary, since it provides no new explanatorily relevant information. It may nevertheless serve an important practical role by making explicit information that is otherwise difficult to discern. (In a probabilistic model, intensification does add relevant information; see section 11.3.)

3. *Deepening* is compulsory: a causal model that is not as deep as possible is not a standalone explanation.

4. *Basing* is an explanatory augmentation of causal models that will be introduced in chapter seven. Like elongation, it is desirable but optional; unlike elongation, it does not add to a model's causal content.

## 4.35 Comparative Generality

So far, I have considered the possibility that one standalone explanation might be better than another because the one contains, in various ways, more information than the other. But weight of information is not the sole possible source of explanatory superiority.

I propose that, all other things being equal, of two explanatory models for the same explanandum, one is a better explanation than the other if it is more general, that is, more abstract. More broadly, it might be argued, one explanatory model is better than another if it provides a better combination of generality, cohesion, and accuracy (for accuracy, see sections 5.1 and 5.2); however, I will focus in what follows on generality.

This invocation of generality is distinct from its use in the optimizing procedure itself. The optimizing procedure uses generality comparisons to determine a unique explanatory model, or kernel, for a given atomic causal model. Models of inferior quality are not lesser explanations; they are not explanatory at all. What I am suggesting here is a comparison between two models that are both end products of the optimizing procedure, hence each optimal in its own way—locally optimal, as it were.

The generality of two such models cannot be compared using the abstraction hierarchy, since one cannot be strictly more abstract than the other, or the other would not be even locally optimal. But when models are sufficiently similar, judgments of relative abstractness can be made. Let me give an example, which will also provide some intuitive basis for the idea that more general is better.

In what is called a spin-echo experiment, a magnetic field is applied to a crystal lattice, aligning the spins of the nuclei and so creating a highly ordered state. Because of imperfections in the crystal, the nuclei gradually drift out of alignment. Eventually they become quite disordered. After a certain interval of time, an electromagnetic pulse is used to flip the spins, an operation that has the same effect (for the purposes of this discussion) as exactly reversing the direction of their motion, so that they drift toward alignment at precisely the speed that they were previously drifting away from alignment. As a result, after a further time interval of the same length has elapsed, they have become exactly aligned once more. (For a less metaphorical description of the experiment, see Sklar (1993, 219–222).)

Suppose you want to explain the fact that the spins are aligned at the experiment's end. You might choose either of two causal models. Model *A* tells the story as I have above, starting with the original alignment of the spins using the magnetic field. Model *B* takes up the story halfway through the procedure, immediately after the spins are flipped. This second model will have to give the facts about each individual nucleus's spin if it is to deduce the exact alignment of the spins at the end of the experiment. It contains, then, a vast amount of microlevel detail. Model *A*, by contrast, need cite only the few macrolevel facts described in the previous paragraph. Thus, model *A* is far more general, more abstract, than model *B*. As a result, I suggest, model *A* is also a much more satisfying—a much better— explanation of the alignment than model *B*.

Two caveats. First, model *B* is a legitimate standalone explanation of the alignment. It is capable of no further abstraction. If science possesses only this model of the causal process leading to alignment, it understands the alignment. But it understands it less well than it would if it had access to model *A*.

Second, model *A*, being loosely speaking (though not technically) an elongation of model *B*, contains more explanatorily relevant information than model *B*, because it traces the causal history of the alignment farther back into the past. But this is not the principal source of *A*'s superiority, I suggest. What is far more important is the quality of the explanatory information conveyed by *A*, as revealed by its much higher generality.

Of two explanations of a phenomenon, why prefer the more general? Why prefer difference-makers that are higher-level states of affairs, all other things being equal? Why look to the macro over the micro?

The answer is surely related to generality's role in the optimizing procedure. In the spin-echo experiment, the precise initial conditions halfway through the experiment are, because they appear in a kernel—namely, model *B*—genuine difference-makers for the final alignment and therefore genuinely explanatorily relevant. But suppose that these same microlevel details were specified in model *A*, that is, that model *A* included an intermediate setup specifying the state of the individual nuclear spins immediately after they were flipped. The details would have to be removed; within the context of model *A*, they are irrelevant.

You might draw the following conclusion: the nuclear microstate is, in the greater scheme of things, effectively irrelevant. Once you appreciate the facts laid out in model *A*, you can no longer regard the nuclear microstate as explanatorily important, though it is all the same technically a difference-maker.

I propose that our preference for more general explanatory models is connected to this phenomenon of effective irrelevance. Where there are rival explanatory models of differing generality, there are effectively irrelevant difference-makers in the less general model; we prefer to avoid citing effectively irrelevant difference-makers, hence whenever possible we cite the more general model. The next section will further pursue the question of the value of generality.

## 4.36  The Second Axis of Depth

My eponym *depth* plays three roles in theoretical discourse about explanation. Most obviously, it is the distinctive attribute of the explanatory enterprise in science—science is said to be deep just when it provides understanding—and it is of course principally in this capacity that it provides my title.

There are, in addition to the depth that by definition accompanies any successful explanatory effort, two kinds of depth that explanations possess in varying amounts, and thus with respect to which it is possible to discriminate between explanations, preferring one to another because the one is "deeper." These are the two dimensions, or axes, of depth. In one dimension, an explanation is deep when it drills down to the explanatorily foundational level, to the ultimate explanatory basis. I have given a traditional account of this foundation: it is the web of relations of causal influence orchestrated by the fundamental physical laws. Further, I have put physical depth at the center of the kairetic account, claiming that no explanation can stand alone unless it articulates the properties of the fundamental physical relations in virtue of which the phenomenon to be explained occurs. A full explanation must, in other words, be deep along the physical axis.

Now to the second axis of depth.

Some explanations are quotidian: step by patient step, they recount the causal history of a singular event or the workings of a causal mechanism, all in perfect accordance with the kairetic account, remarking on no details that do not make a difference to the explanatory target, acquitting themselves in a manner that is, explanatorily speaking, exemplary—yet uninspiring.

Other explanations light up our minds with a bolt of insight. We are at the same time illuminated and astonished. Such explanations have over their mundane counterparts the advantage of depth along a second axis.

Their characteristic property is, I think, an unusual degree of generality, the same generality that was held up, in the previous section, as an explanatory virtue.

Explanations having depth along the second axis strip away vast quantities of apparently relevant, large-scale causal detail, showing thereby that the phenomenon to be explained depends on only a kind of "deep causal structure" of the system in question, a structure that is deep now not because it is so physical (though it is that) but because it is so abstract. The salient but irrelevant causal details are the shallows, then, and the more abstract—that is, more general—properties of the system are its depths, fleshed out by the details but inconsequentially so.[4]

The explanations that are deep along the second axis are, in short, explanations that account for phenomena in terms of a small number of abstract properties of the generating systems' causal dynamics. One example is provided by the spin-echo explanation described in the previous section. Equilibrium explanations of regularities in complex systems, such as Fisher's explanation of the one-to-one sex ratio or Boltzmann's explanation of the second law of thermodynamics, are perhaps the paradigms of depth along the second axis, combining as they do two monumental abstractions: first, the abstraction of a high-level dynamics from the physical underpinnings, as when kinetic theory extracts a simple, probabilistic description of molecules' movements from the physics of molecular collision, and second, in the equilibrium stage, the abstraction of a certain even higher-level property of the dynamics—the universality of a particular end point—from the high-level dynamics obtained in the first step.

Depth along the second axis may be obtained at the expense of depth along the first axis—generality obtained at the expense of physicality— by black-boxing. But the two axes of depth do not run contrariwise; they need not be in tension. In the explanatory enterprise, quite the reverse: our greatest explanatory achievements lie precisely where the two kinds of depth intersect, in models that account for a phenomenon by picking out a causal structure that is at the same time very abstract and very physical.

The title of this book is apposite three times over, then. First, it announces the subject matter: scientific explanation. Second, it gestures at the raw material of all explanation: physical causal influence. Third, it looks to the end point of the supreme and sublime explanatory maneuver that transforms the raw material into something providing understanding: abstraction.

## 4.4   Laplacean Blindness

Daniel Dennett and Elliott Sober ask, "What is Laplace's demon missing?" (Sober 1984, §4.3; Dennett 1987, 25). Laplace's demon, I remind you, is a creature capable of knowing the complete state of the world at any particular time and of using this knowledge, together with the fundamental laws of physics (assumed to be deterministic), to predict any later event in any amount of detail. For the purposes of the discussion, imagine a species of demon that never thinks about the world in any other way, so that it represents the world entirely in terms of fundamental laws and concrete events—entirely by way of fundamental-level models, if you like. Such a creature would be a perfect prediction machine, Dennett and Sober surmise, but it would be missing a certain kind of understanding of the world. Does Laplace's demon suffer from a selective scientific blindness?

Before answering the question, let me comment on a feature of our own understanding of the world that the fable of the demon serves to bring to light. Our science provides us with two, quite distinct, pictures of the world. On the one hand, there is a picture provided by our fundamental physics that corresponds, more or less, to the contents of the demon's head. On the other hand, there is the picture—or better, the set of pictures—provided by sciences at a higher level than fundamental physics: biology, psychology, history, and also much of physics itself.

In the fundamental-level picture, the universe is made up of instantiations of irreducible physical properties, such as values of various fields at space-time points. These quantities depend on one another in ways spelled out by the fundamental laws of physics. Because they tend to influence one another indiscriminately—as in Newtonian physics, where every massive particle simultaneously influences every other massive particle—the web of dependency is a dense and tangled thing. Call this the low-level picture of the world. In some sense, fundamental physics asserts, the low-level picture represents all there is to the world. That, at least, is the maxim in accordance with which Laplace's demon and its sympathizers conduct their intellectual lives.

The picture provided by the higher-level sciences differs from the low-level picture in two ways. First, the two perspectives differ as to what things there are: rather than a single layer of properties or tropes, the high-level perspective posits a hierarchy of properties bearing various ontological dependence relations to one another and, ultimately, to the basic physical properties. Economic properties depend on psychological properties, which depend on biological properties, which depend on chemical properties, and so on. For this reason, call the high-level perspective the hierarchical picture.

Second, the two pictures differ as to the nature and the structure of the nomological dependence relations between properties. On the hierarchical picture, there are dependence relations at every level, and sometimes between levels, including but perhaps not limited to those specified by high-level laws. These relations do not form the intricate, convoluted webs that the fundamental-level relations do, but, rather, the relatively spare networks that we call causal chains. Although the hierarchical picture proliferates properties, and thereby proliferates dependence relations between properties, it simplifies the structure of dependence, at least at every level other than the fundamental (Elga 2007).

The high-level dependence relations in the hierarchical picture are, in my view, none other than the explanatory relations. It follows that it is one of the purposes of the descriptive study of explanation to understand how we think about the high-level relations. If this is correct, then the philosophy of explanation constitutes an important part of the theory of our representation of the world. The theory of explanation is, I assert, able to play a part of the philosophical role played by transcendental psychology for Kant (on one interpretation) and by logic for the Vienna Circle.

According to the kairetic account of explanation, the explanatory relations, and hence the high-level dependence relations, are difference-making relations: to represent the relations is to represent which high-level events make a difference to which other high-level events. The account of difference-making presented in this and the previous chapter, and elaborated throughout the rest of the book, can be understood, then, as providing the set of rules by which we grasp (if you are a realist) or constitute (if you are a projectivist) the high-level causal structure of the world.

What use is the hierarchical picture? If you are not a demon, and your knowledge of the world is gained and then deployed slowly and painfully rather than by infernal agency, then the hierarchical picture is more accessible and easier to exploit than the low-level picture. Of course, to master the entirety of the hierarchical picture is more difficult than to master the entirety of the low-level picture, since the hierarchical picture represents everything that the low-level picture does and more. But unlike the low-level picture, the hierarchical picture can be divided, because of the relatively simple structure of the dependence relations at higher levels of the hierarchy, into many parts independently useful to limited creatures such as ourselves.

The original question, though, concerned the significance of the hierarchical picture to a demon that already has the low-level picture at its claw-tips. What more could the demon need?

To the question whether the demon ought to avail itself of the layers of properties provided by the hierarchical picture, I have little to say. If the demon were human, however, it certainly would want to represent the world hierarchically, for there are many interests proper to humans that are high-level interests, in the sense that we care that some high-level event or state of affairs obtains but we do not care about the concrete details of its realization:

Thou shalt love thy neighbour as thyself.

True philosophers make dying their profession.

To sleep late, have fun, get wild, drink whiskey, and drive fast on empty streets with nothing in mind except falling in love and not getting arrested . . .

But what does it matter which neighbor you love, or which molecules of whiskey, or hemlock, exactly, pass through your lips? To represent our values and goals, our conception of the good life, then, we must represent high-level events, and so we require the representational resources provided by the hierarchical picture.[5]

Now, given that we care whether or not high-level events occur, it is natural that we should care why they occur. To understand why concrete events occur requires only an appreciation of fundamental-level dependence relations, that is, of relations of causal influence. But to understand why high-level events occur is, if the kairetic account is correct, to appreciate the difference-making relations that hold between such events—in other words, to appreciate the high-level dependence relations present in the hierarchical, but not the low-level, picture of the world. (You may have noticed that information about difference-makers is useful to would-be predictors and controllers, as well as to would-be explainers.)

The question can now be answered: Laplace's demon understands concrete events but neither high-level events nor high-level laws. What the demon does not see is the high-level structure of the world.

Fallen philosophers will perhaps retort that the demon has no reason to understand the high-level structure of the world, since it has no reason to care about high-level events. Maybe so. But whether it cares or not, whether or not the high level has any intrinsic worth for omniscient immortals, high-level understanding is, all the same, what the demon lacks.

# — 5 —

# Extending the Kairetic Account

## 5.1  Quantifying Explanatory Relevance

One of the apparent advantages that the probabilistic relevance criterion for difference-making has over the other criteria reviewed in chapter two is its ability to quantify explanatory relevance, that is, to provide a foundation for the intuition that some relevant causal factors play a more important role than others in producing a given explanandum.[1] I will show that the kairetic criterion, too, has the resources to quantify explanatory relevance, even for explananda that are deterministically produced.

Call a factor's degree of explanatory relevance its *explanatory weight*. I propose that a difference-making factor has only a low explanatory weight—equivalently, that it makes only a small difference—just in case it can be removed from kernels for the explanandum in which it appears at only a small cost in the kernels' accuracy. More generally:

> the explanatory weight of a causal factor $c$, relative to an explanandum $e$, is proportional to the decrease in accuracy that results from removing $c$ from any $c$-involving kernel for $e$.

You will see that the definition of weight implicitly assumes that whatever $c$-involving kernel is chosen, the decrease in accuracy resulting from the removal of $c$ will be the same.[2] You will also see that the proponents of any of chapter two's relevance criteria might define a similar notion of weight.

What is accuracy? An explanatory model's accuracy is a measure of the similarity between its target and the explanandum. A deterministic model for an explanandum by definition has maximal accuracy, thus any deterministic kernel or other standalone explanation is fully accurate.

Removing or abstracting a factor from a deterministic kernel will invalidate the model's causal entailment of the explanandum. Some modicum of accuracy may remain, however: although it no longer causally entails the explanandum, the model may causally entail that one of a range of possibilities occurs, all similar to the explanandum. (Given the nature of removal, the explanandum itself will be one of the possibilities.) Quantify the accuracy of such a model as follows. Take the member of the range of possibilities that is most dissimilar to the explanandum. The similarity between this possibility and the explanandum is the accuracy of the model. If the least similar possibility is still very similar to the explanandum, then, the model is very accurate.

Consider as an explanandum, for example, the exact orbit of the planet Mars over the course of a year.[3] A completely accurate model of Mars' orbit will take into account both the gravitational attraction between Mars and the Sun and the attraction between Mars and the other planets. (Ignore comets, distant stars, and so on.) The model can be simplified in certain ways, at a cost in accuracy. Suppose that the gravitational influence of the other planets is abstracted away, producing a model that is consistent with, but that does not spell out, the existence and orbits of the planets. The kind of model I have in mind will put an upper limit on the number and mass of the planets and a lower limit on any planet's distance from Mars, but it will otherwise leave open a wide range of possibilities: what it says in its setup will be true of the actual solar system, of any solar system broadly similar the actual system, and of a solar system with Mars as its only planet.

Such a model cannot causally entail Mars' exact orbit. But it will causally entail that Mars' orbit is one of a range of possible orbits, all of which are close to (or identical to) the exact orbit. The accuracy of the model is equal to the accuracy of the least accurate of these possible orbits.

The model for Mars' orbit obtained by abstracting away the effects of the other planets is not as accurate as it could be. Yet it is not inaccurate. Therefore, according to the definition of explanatory weight presented above, interplanetary pull has low explanatory weight; it does not make much of a difference to the orbit of Mars.

Abstract away the Sun, by contrast, and the model will no longer be at all accurate: since it is consistent with both the Sun's presence and its absence, the model causally entails an enormous range of possible dynamics (more exactly, the disjunction of the possibilities in this range). The actual dynamics belongs to the entailed range, since the model is veridical, but so do other dynamics that are not like the actual dynamics at all. Because the accuracy of the model is determined by the least accurate dynamics it allows, it must be declared hopelessly inaccurate. It follows that, while the gravitational effects of both the other planets and the Sun are explanatorily relevant to the Martian orbit, the influence of the Sun has far greater explanatory weight than the influence of the planets.

Note that the explanatory weights of the causal factors in a kernel do not necessarily, or even usually, sum to one. If a kernel contains two factors, both necessary for the entailment of anything remotely resembling the explanandum, then both factors have 100% weight, since removing either results in a model of 0% accuracy.

Note also that accuracy is relative to the explanandum, thus that the accuracy-determining comparison is always with the high-level event that is the explanandum, not the concrete event that realizes the explanandum. A model that entails that Mars' orbit is elliptical is a fully accurate explainer of the orbit's elliptical nature, though it may not come anywhere close to entailing the exact orbit.

I will later have use for a probabilistic measure of accuracy, in addition to the measure characterized above. The probabilistic measure assumes the notion of a probabilistic causal model, which is not discussed formally until part four; however, for the purpose of defining accuracy, all that need be said about probabilistic causal models is that—no surprises—they assign a certain probability to their targets. A difference-maker has low explanatory weight, on the probabilistic measure of accuracy, if its removal from an explanatory model makes only a small difference to the probability assigned to the explanandum. (On removals that raise the probability of the explanandum, see sections 10.42 and 11.5.)

There is one further source of inaccuracy in models: a model's high-level descriptive apparatus may be vague, or in other words, the correspondence rules connecting the high-level vocabulary to the fundamental level may not make determinate judgments in all cases. In particular, the correspondence rule for some event $e$ might treat a certain set of concrete events as "borderline cases," withholding its judgment as to whether or not the occurrence of one of these events constitutes an occurrence of $e$. Suppose that a causal model causally entails that one of a large set of concrete events occur, all of which are either clear cases of $e$ or lie in the borderline set for $e$. The accuracy of such a model can be quantified in various ways. If there is a probability distribution over the concrete events produced by the model, the accuracy might be set to the probability of obtaining a definite $e$ realizer plus one-half (or some other coefficient) of the probability of obtaining a borderline $e$ realizer. If there is no probability distribution, the standard (uniform) measure over the set of entailed possibilities might be used. And so on.

There are, then, three ways that a model for an event $e$ may have less than perfect accuracy:

1. It may causally entail the occurrence of one of a range of events, including but not limited to $e$. The accuracy of the model is high if all of the events are similar to $e$.

2. It may assign to $e$ a probability of less than one. The accuracy of the model is high if the probability is near one.

3. It may causally entail the occurrence of one of a set of concrete events, some of which are borderline cases of $e$, the rest clear cases of $e$. The accuracy of the model is high if most of the realizers (perhaps probabilistically weighted) are clear cases of $e$.

Insofar as the removal of a causal factor from a model results in any of these kinds of inaccuracy, the factor's explanatory weight may be quantified accordingly.

A measure of explanatory weight can be used to rank incomplete explanations in the obvious way: an explanation that leaves out a factor of low explanatory weight is better, everything else being equal, than an explanation that leaves out a factor of high weight.

## 5.2 Trading Off Accuracy for Generality

A perfectly accurate causal model for an event entails that the event occurred. An imperfectly accurate causal model entails at best either that something like the event occurred, or that the event occurred with a certain probability. I have so far required that explanatory kernels, hence standalone explanations, have perfect accuracy. What if this requirement were relaxed?

If accuracy is negotiable, then what would have counted as a maximally abstract model under the strict accuracy regime may be further abstracted. To use the example from the previous section, a model for Mars' exact orbit may leave out the effect of the planets at a small cost in accuracy. The payoff is a large gain in generality. In an experimental vein, let me make the following proposal: when large amounts of generality can be obtained with a small sacrifice in accuracy, the tradeoff should be made. The best standalone explanation, in other words, will reflect the tradeoff, by omitting where appropriate difference-makers with low explanatory weight. For example, the ideal explanation of Mars' orbit will leave out the effects of the planets.

In the rest of this section, I will investigate, in a preliminary way, the consequences of and rationale for trading off accuracy for generality, or as I will say, making accuracy tradeoffs. The investigation is preliminary because I do not present a fully fleshed-out argument for allowing accuracy tradeoffs. Though I do believe that such an argument can be made, it is long and complex; because I will not make any essential appeals to accuracy tradeoffs in later parts of this book, I leave the details to another time.

An accuracy tradeoff allows a factor to be dropped from a deterministic model at some cost in accuracy in order to obtain a greater increase in generality. The resulting model will not causally entail the explanandum (or else there would have been no cost in accuracy). Thus, according to the definition of difference-making proposed in chapter three—which I will not amend—the dropped factor is a difference-maker for the explanandum. Since tradeoffs will be made only when the cost in accuracy is low, factors that are dropped will tend to have low explanatory weight, which is to say, they will not make much of a difference to the explanandum (section 5.1). But they will make some difference. They are, nevertheless, because removed from the model by the optimizing procedure, explanatorily irrelevant.

Allowing accuracy tradeoffs therefore breaks the connection between difference-making and explanatory relevance that has served as a foundation of the earlier discussion, or rather it breaks it in one direction: a causal factor cannot be explanatorily relevant unless it is a difference-maker, but it can be a difference-maker yet count as explanatorily irrelevant. The difference-makers dropped in the course of an accuracy tradeoff, then, literally make no contribution to our understanding of the explanandum. It is not that they are explanatory but that other concerns motivate their omission from the optimal explanatory model; they are omitted because they are unexplanatory.

How can this be? What is gained by leaving small difference-makers out of an explanation, apart from convenience and economy? In the most interesting cases, the generality gained is not simply a matter of removing clutter, but of moving to a new and more abstract scheme of description that better captures the high-level difference-making structure of the causal processes that produced the explanandum.

Consider as an example a complex mechanism whose operation can be modeled using rigid body mechanics. (I will discuss the explanatory workings of such idealized models in chapter eight.) The model is, I assume, an imprecise representation of causal reality: it captures the behavior of the system up to a certain level of detail, and no more. Take some behavior of the system. Specify it using an abstract description, thereby picking out a high-level event realized by the behavior. Suppose that this event is to be explained, and that thanks to its liberal individuation conditions, the rigid body model entails that the event occurs. The rigid body model, then, is a completely accurate explanatory model for the event.

Now adjust the grain of the explanandum description so as to specify more details of the behavior in question, thus picking out a somewhat more concrete event as the explanatory object. Once a certain amount of detail is added to the description, the explanandum will have become sufficiently concrete that its occurrence is no longer entailed by the rigid body model. At this point, the model goes from being completely accurate to just less than completely accurate.

Suppose that accuracy tradeoffs are disallowed. Then at the same point that the model goes from complete to less than complete accuracy, it yields its status as optimal model to another model that more closely tracks the causal goings-on in the system in question. In the rigid body case, the new optimal model will abandon the assumption of complete rigidity to allow the parts of the system to flex, stretch, and so on; by representing these aspects of the system, it will be able to reproduce the behavior at a much finer level of detail.

If accuracy tradeoffs are allowed, by contrast, the rigid body model will not lose its optimal status right away, because the greater generality achieved by ignoring flexing, stretching, and so on, will more than compensate for the infinitesimal loss of accuracy. Only for an explanandum specified at a considerably more concrete level will the loss of accuracy nullify the generality advantage and the more complex model take over as the best explanation.

To allow accuracy tradeoffs, then, is to endorse the following doctrine: it is not worth relinquishing a very abstract, high-level explanation of the workings of a system in order to prevent only a very small loss of accuracy.

The simple representational system of rigid body mechanics, for example, ought not to be abandoned as an explanatory ideal until its margin of error reaches a certain threshold.

Three remarks on the consequences of allowing accuracy tradeoffs.

First, although the small difference-makers excluded from a model are explanatorily irrelevant to the explanandum itself, they are not explanatorily irrelevant to certain closely connected states of affairs, such as the fact that the explanandum was realized in a certain way.

Second, accuracy tradeoffs will not always remove difference-makers of low explanatory weight. No such difference-makers will be removed when, for example, the explanandum is the cumulative effect of large numbers of small difference-makers acting in concert.

Third, allowing accuracy tradeoffs deals elegantly with the vagueness of high-level language discussed in the previous section. When the realization conditions for a high-level event are vague, you will recall, some concrete events are borderline realizers for the high-level event: it is indeterminate whether they realize the event or not. A causal model specifying such events in its setup, or having such an event as its intended explanandum, may for this reason not determinately entail the occurrence of the explanandum, in which case it must have less than maximal accuracy. The use of such models is questionable if maximal accuracy is an inviolable requirement for explanatory kernels, but it poses no qualitative problems if accuracy is merely one of several desiderata. It is conceivable that in some circumstances, an accuracy tradeoff will result in a precise model's being made vague, if the decrease in accuracy due to vagueness is outweighed by a concomitant increase in generality. To explore this possibility would, however, require an exploration of the connection between vagueness and generality that would take me too far from my principal topics.

## 5.3   The Explanatory Framework

You are asked to explain the fact that Rasputin survived his being poisoned. According to the kairetic account, you should proceed as follows. Take a model that represents the poisoning process and that has Rasputin's survival as its target. Remove whatever causal factors can be removed without invalidating the entailment of survival. The factors that remain are difference-makers for survival; they may be cited as explaining Rasputin's survival.

Suppose that the poison was neutralized thanks to rasputinase, an enzyme peculiar to Rasputin's metabolism. Take a causal model of the poisoning that specifies the presence of rasputinase. Because of the enzyme, the model will entail survival. Many details can be removed from the model without jeopardizing this entailment: what Rasputin had for breakfast, his rude good health, his religious beliefs. If rasputinase is removed, however, the model will no longer entail survival. Thus, rasputinase will count as a difference-maker for survival, as desired.

Wrong. Suppose that you have pared the model down to the point where it mentions only the fact of the poisoning and the presence of rasputinase (as well as, necessarily, a few background biological processes). Remove the fact of the poisoning. The model still entails survival, so this move is legitimate. But now there is no work for rasputinase to do. It, too, can be removed. All you have left are the background biological processes that keep anyone alive. Rasputinase is not a difference-maker.

What has gone wrong with the optimizing procedure? The procedure would have functioned as desired if you had somehow been forbidden to remove poisoning from the model, but what would be the grounds for such a prohibition? The answer is that the fact of Rasputin's being poisoned is in a certain sense a presupposition of or a background assumption built into the explanandum, or at any rate, built into the explanatory request. The original request for explanation might well have been phrased as follows: *given that Rasputin was poisoned*, why did he survive? When an explanatory request can be framed in this way, the fact following the *given* is treated as a fixed part of the explanatory framework against which difference-making is evaluated.

The notion of a framework is not novel. It draws in particular on Mackie's notion of a causal field (section 6.1). But although it may be a familiar idea, it is much underused, I think, in philosophical work on both explanation and causal claims. As I hope to show in this and the next chapter, many otherwise obscure elements of our explanatory practice are accounted for by the presence of frameworks.

Let me present, then, a theory of explanatory frameworks.

Although difference-making is canonically a relation between two states of affairs—a difference-maker and an event to which the difference is made—

some difference-making relations are relativized to a background or framework, a third and distinct state of affairs. (You may think of the framework as a part of the explanandum or as a third relatum in the explanatory relation—it does not matter.)

If an explanatory request specifies an explanatory framework consisting of or containing a state of affairs $c$, then kernel determination, and thus the determination of difference-makers, proceeds as normal but with these modifications:

1. Only causal models containing $c$ are considered. Thus, all kernels must contain $c$.

2. $c$ may not be removed or abstracted.

3. Though it necessarily remains in the model, $c$ is not a difference-maker.

4. Yet it is incorrect to say that $c$ does *not* make a difference. A causal factor that resides in the framework is neither a difference-maker nor a non-difference-maker relative to that framework. All questions as to its difference-making status are, in effect, suspended.

Note that $c$'s special status does not affect its role within a causal model: as a causal entailer, it operates just like any other causal factor. Note also that $c$ must actually obtain; an explanation with a fictional framework is an explanation with a fictional causal model, and is thus a bad explanation.

Now as I have said, when you ask why Rasputin survived his poisoning, you are not merely asking why he continued to live in the time frame shortly after the poisoning. You are asking why he continued to live given that he was poisoned—this much is implied by the use of the term *survival*. The explanatory request therefore specifies a framework containing a single event, the poisoning itself.

To determine the difference-makers for Rasputin's surviving his poisoning, then, you must consider only causal models for Rasputin's continued existence that specify the fact of poisoning, and you must never remove the poisoning in the course of abstraction. The optimizing procedure will then deliver the correct judgment: rasputinase was a difference-maker for survival. And poisoning, although it appears in the explanatory model, is of course not a difference-maker.

A framework may be introduced into explanatory discourse in any number of ways. Sometimes the phrasing of the explanandum itself introduces an implicit *given that* by way of presupposition or some other kind of implicature, as when a term such as *survival* is used. Sometimes the framework is established by the nature and goals of a particular conversation: if we have just been talking about the fact that the switch is on, and you ask me to explain why the light is shining, it is natural for me to understand you as asking for an explanation of the shining given that the switch is on—if I say "because the switch is on," I am not just being obnoxious; I am failing even to satisfy partially your explanatory request. Sometimes the framework is determined by a convention governing a certain class of discourse, as in an explanation of the behavior of a fuel pump that takes the supply of electricity as given, or as in almost any textbook explanation of the workings of a functional part of a more complex whole. And, of course, sometimes the framework is introduced explicitly: *given that* the baseball was headed straight for your head, what explains your concussion is your failure to dodge the throw in a timely manner, and not the malicious intentions of the pitcher.

The specification of an explanatory framework is, as I have said, optional: many explanatory claims are not made relative to a framework, and so they specify absolute rather than relative relations of difference-making. The practice of explaining phenomena within a framework is, I think, a derivative practice; a tribe of scientists who construct only framework-independent explanations is not in any important sense lacking understanding of the nature of things. Thus, although it is formally feasible to think of every explanation as relative to a framework, with the "framework-independent" explanations taking as their frameworks an empty set of background events, it is a distortion of the true order of understanding. (Likewise, it is a mistake to think that all explanation is contrastive; see section 5.6.)

Note that the inclusion of $c$ in a framework not only renders $c$ itself ineligible as a difference-maker, but also any events that are difference-makers for $c$; an explanation that frameworks $c$, then, cannot be elongated through $c$.[4] Because the poison does not explain Rasputin's survival, neither do the actions that led to the ingestion of the poison: the plotting, the invitation to tea, the sprinkling of the poison on the teacakes, and so on. This is a straightforward consequence of the irremovability of $c$, since with $c$ held constant any difference-maker for $c$ can be removed.

An explanatory framework may include, in addition to events, causal mechanisms—either the workings of lower-level processes, as when atomic structure is taken for granted in valence-based explanations of chemical reactions, or the workings of same-level processes whose behavior is necessary for the explanation, as in an explanation of some behavior of the immune system that takes for granted a working circulatory system. When a mechanism is bracketed within the framework, its place in the explanatory model may be taken by a *black box*, a description of the consequences of a causal mechanism that does not specify anything about the mechanism's implementation, but only what "outputs" it gives for what "inputs." If I say that a certain element in a computing device is an integrator, for example, I am black-boxing that element: I am telling you that it integrates (i.e., sums in a certain sense) its inputs, but I am not describing the causal pathways by way of which the integration is done. (Black boxes were introduced in section 4.33; there they were distinguished from covering laws, which require no framework.)

A mechanism may be consigned to the explanatory framework under two epistemically quite different circumstances. On the one hand, the nature of the frameworked mechanism may be known, and it may be bracketed merely for convenience. On the other hand, the mechanism may be unknown, in which case it is frameworked more from necessity. In the former case, black-boxing is possible but not compulsory; in the latter case, black-boxing is the only option.

Either way, when a frameworked mechanism is black-boxed, the black box itself stands in for the mechanism, which is to say, it functions as a placeholder for a certain, determinate mechanism, either known or unknown. (In the case where the mechanism is unknown, it must of course be placed in the framework by a phrase or intention that picks it out indirectly, for example, "the mechanism that is actually responsible for such and such a behavior of such and such a component of the system.") What is explained when a mechanism is black-boxed, then, is how the explanandum was produced given the existence of *that very mechanism*, not given the existence of some mechanism fulfilling such and such a functional specification. For example, if in explaining the workings of the human immune system you black-box the circulatory system, you are explaining immune reactions not given that there is some circulatory system or other, but given the actual human circulatory system.

This doctrine has an immediate and important consequence. Outside the context of a framework, a causal model containing a black box is explanatorily deficient for two reasons: because it is causally empty, it does not causally entail its target (section 4.33), and because it is multiply realizable, it is (typically) incohesive (section 5.41). Within a framework, by contrast, a black box stands in for a particular frameworked mechanism. It is the causality and the cohesion of that mechanism, not of the black box, that matter for determining the causality and cohesion of the model as a whole.

Accordingly, a view advanced in section 4.33, that a model containing a black box does not provide a legitimate standalone explanation, must be moderated. When a black box is a placeholder for a mechanism in the framework—when what is being explained is not the fact that some event occurred simpliciter but rather the fact that some event occurred *given that* such and such a mechanism was in place to perform such and such a role— then if everything else is in order, the explanation containing the box may stand alone: it will be causal, cohesive, complete.

This does not constitute a genuine weakening of the standards for standalone explanation, however. A black-boxing model "stands alone" only because it enjoys the tacit support of the framework. To put it another way, a framework-relative explanation's "given thats" limit the explanatory power of the model: to explain a phenomenon *given* a set of circumstances is a lesser achievement than explaining the phenomenon in an unqualified way. The ultimate aim of science is unqualified understanding, which can be achieved only by framework-independent explanatory models, thus, only once the interiors of all explanatory black boxes are illuminated and their blackness thereby dispelled.

Two levels of standalone explanation should therefore be distinguished. There is first the sense in which an explanation stands alone if it is technically complete. A model with black boxes is complete in this first sense if the black boxes are standing in for mechanisms in the explanatory framework. Second, there is the kind of standalone explanation that provides a full understanding of the explanandum in an unqualified, that is, framework-independent, sense, and that therefore contains no black boxes; I call this *deep standalone explanation.*

I have now distinguished three grades of explanation and three grades of understanding that they confer:

1. An explanation with black boxes requires the support of a mechanism-containing framework to stand alone; though technically complete, such an explanation confers, you might say, only a partial or qualified understanding of the explanandum.

2. A deep standalone explanation confers full understanding of the explanandum.

3. What I called in section 4.31 an exhaustive standalone explanation—a maximally elongated, possibly infinite, explanation—confers what you might call exhaustive understanding, a state no doubt as tiring as the name suggests.

Exhaustive understanding is a kind of ideal, but an ideal to which those interested only in full understanding need not take the trouble to aspire.

Two further remarks on the view that a framework-relative black box is an explanatory proxy for a real mechanism. First, let me reiterate that a black box can perform this placeholder role even if the nature of the underlying mechanism is not known. That said, to black-box an unknown mechanism is to offer an explanatory hostage to fortune: your explanatory model is successful only if there turns out to be a single, cohesive causal mechanism standing behind the black box. In explaining a single, singular event, this can hardly fail to be the case; in aggregative and regularity explanation, by contrast, there is a real risk.

Second, as a placeholder, a black box itself is not attributed any causal relevance. This resolves the longstanding problem as to how a property defined partly in terms of its ability to cause a particular event can usefully appear in a causal explanation of that event. It does so not in virtue of its own dubious causal powers but as a surrogate for something with real causal-explanatory oomph. Section 12.2 applies this view to the interpretation of explanations in belief/desire psychology.

## 5.4   Black Boxes, Functional Properties, and Multiple Realizability

### 5.41  *Multiply Realizable Explanatory Models*

The kairetic account of explanation thrives on the deliberate neglect of causal detail; at the same time, it puts a strict upper limit on causal abstraction by way of the cohesion constraint, which requires a certain kind of causal homogeneity among an explanatory model's realizers. Some explanations, however, appear to take explanatory abstraction far outside the bounds imposed by the need for cohesion: they cite explanatory models that are inhomogeneous, or in other words, radically multiply realizable.

An explanation why the supply of SUVs in Western economies increased during the 1990s might, for example, cite the contemporaneous decrease in the price of oil: as the oil price dropped, and the cost of SUV ownership dropped along with it, demand for SUVs increased; the supply then increased to match the demand. Such a model deliberately fails to specify any properties of the relevant underlying causal mechanisms, such as the means by which the increased demand of the consumers is communicated to the producers. Yet it might seem to give a completely satisfactory explanation for the proliferation of SUVs.

On the kairetic account, the explanation cannot, apparently, stand alone. Consider the different ways that SUV manufacturers might learn of the increasing demand for their product: they might be notified by their dealers, or the upswing in demand might be forecast by the management in Detroit, or it might become apparent in rising auction prices (if hard-to-find models are put up for sale on eBay, say). Any one of these mechanisms, or (more likely) a combination of several, could have been responsible for the suppliers' sensitivity to increased demand. A model that does not specify the actual communication channels can therefore be realized in one of several quite different ways, and so it appears to violate the kairetic account's cohesion constraint. Yet just such a model is found at the center of orthodox economic explanations. How to understand this facet of our explanatory practice?

Let me begin with a brief overview of the sources of multiple realizability. An explanatory model may be multiply realizable for any number of reasons, but the principal causes of multiple realizability are three: either the model contains black boxes, or it engages in functional analysis, or it cites functional properties. A few words on each of these explanatory strategies.

A black box is a causal model that says nothing about the workings of the systems that it describes, except in one way: it specifies, for any set of inputs (within a certain range), the system's output, or in other words, for any set of initial conditions, the system's ultimate behavior (sections 4.33 and 5.3).[5] It consists entirely, then, of a functional specification, a generalization linking its output to its input. The functionally characterized boxes encountered in real science are perhaps more often gray than black: their workings are not entirely opaque, but important parts of the causal story are missing. I might tell you that an integrator has a clockwork mechanism, that it is implemented in brain tissue, or perhaps something more specific, but not enough to entail that it will produce its outputs from its inputs; you will always need the accompanying functional specification.

What Cummins (1975, 1983) calls functional analysis is a kind of wall-to-wall black-boxing, in which no causal mechanisms are specified below a certain level. Simple examples are the usual explanations of the ways in which a computer's CPU or an internal combustion engine's ignition system work. Typically, the explanandum is some capacity of the system, such as the ignition system's capacity to emit a series of sparks synchronized with the movement of the engine's pistons or the CPU's capacity to execute a series of machine language instructions. The explanation is a description of the causal mechanism whose effects constitute the exercise of the capacity (for more on such explanations, see section 7.42). In the sort of functional analysis I have in mind, this description breaks down the mechanism into a number of interconnected gray or black boxes identified chiefly by function, such as spark plugs (mechanisms that emit a spark when fed an electrical pulse) or electronic logic gates (circuits that maintain a voltage on their outputs that depends in a certain way on the voltage on their inputs).

A kind or property is functionally defined if it is defined partly in virtue of certain of its causal powers (a sufficient condition only). *Poison* is a functional kind, because it is delineated partly by the power of causing death, when ingested, for humans or other organisms. Like most functional kinds, it is not purely functional: death must come a certain way. *Currency* is another, more complex functional kind, delineated—as far as I can see—by a certain economic role. The most famous functional kinds in philosophy are perhaps the propositional attitudes, often thought to be characterized in terms of their causal role alone. The atoms of a functional analysis, such as *spark plugs* and *logic gates*, are also typically, perhaps always, functional kinds. Even *bonds*—the sort that are used to suppress an influviation victim's movement—are in some sense functionally characterized; certainly, they are multiply realizable, as noted in section 3.63.

The explanatory uses of black boxes, functional analysis, and functional properties differ, I think, more in form than in substance. To appeal to poisoning in explaining death, for example, is to construct a black box connecting the ingestion of a substance and the death (though appeals to functional properties may often be more gray than black; see section 5.43).[6] Certainly, black boxes and other functional strategies raise the same two problems for the kairetic account of explanation for the same reason: because they contain no specification of a causal implementation, (a) they cannot participate in causal entailment (section 4.33) and (b) they are realized by a range of causal mechanisms so diverse as to be incohesive.

For the purposes of this section, let me focus exclusively on the problem of multiple realizability and incohesion, which has not been adequately discussed as yet here and which has generated a richer literature. Despite this simplification of the subject matter, my treatment will have as many implications for the problem of causality as for the problem of cohesion.

Begin with a restatement of the problem. Many explanations—perhaps most explanations in the higher-level sciences, such as biology, psychology, and sociology—make liberal use of black boxes, either explicitly or by deploying functionally defined properties. The resulting explanatory models are radically multiply realizable, because many quite different kinds of physical properties are capable of filling out the boxes in question. Such multiple realizability poses a challenge for any causal account of explanation: is a black-boxing model too generalized to serve as a representation of the particular causal process responsible for a particular explanandum? Is a black-boxing model too incohesive to be causally explanatory?

For the kairetic account, which individuates causal processes according to the criterion of causal contiguity, the question is whether the radically different realizers of a black-boxing model form a causal continuum or whether, by contrast, there are gaps in "causal similarity space" between different kinds of realizers (section 3.63).

Causal contiguity is consistent with radical multiple realizability: the distance in similarity space from one end to the other of a contiguous set may be very large. Let me distinguish, then, two varieties of multiple realizability. A black box or functional kind is *discretely* multiply realizable if its realizers form a noncontiguous fundamental-level set. If a kind's realizers form a contiguous fundamental-level set that is nevertheless heterogeneous in some striking way, it might reasonably be said to be multiply realizable; however, it is not discretely but *smoothly* multiply realizable. It is, of course, the discretely multiply realizable black boxes and functional kinds that pose a threat to the kairetic account of explanation.

### 5.42 A Pragmatic Approach to Black-Boxing

Our explanatory practice's many black boxes always—or almost always (see section 5.43)—stand in for a mechanism in the relevant explanatory framework, or so I will argue. As such, they do not undermine the cohesion of the models to which they are attached. What determines that a black box represents a part of the explanatory framework, rather than standing only for itself? Practical considerations; hence what I have to offer is a "pragmatic approach" to black-boxing. Let me illustrate this approach with the help of an example.

Consider an abstract model of predator/prey interaction in population ecology, say, the sort of model that explains patterns of stability or instability in predator/prey ecosystems by exhibiting the behaviors that arise when different ranges of values are assigned to the model's parameters (Volterra 1926). The predators and prey in the model are not assumed to be any particular kind of animal: they might be dueling microorganisms, or algorithms in a system of artificial life implemented on a computer, or the predators might be parasitic worms that infest a much larger prey.

The model therefore entirely omits any nonfunctional characterization of the nature of the predator and prey, indeed, any characterization of their relation to the world aside from their relation to one another. As such, it does not give a lower level account of predator/prey dynamics—no account of why the parameters have the ranges that they do or why they induce the population dynamics that they do. All lower-level biological processes are black-boxed, as you might expect given that *predator* and *prey* are themselves prime examples of functional kinds in science.

The investigation of the properties of the predator/prey model resembles a kind of applied mathematics. Certain assumptions are made about the behavior of the abstract kinds *predator* and *prey* and formalized as differential equations. The mathematical properties of the equations, and thus of the behavior, are then explored.

What happens when such a model is applied to explain, say, the stability of a particular predator/prey ecosystem? The black boxes stand in for the corresponding mechanisms in the system, which are relegated to the explanatory framework. Three consequences of the mechanisms' frameworking, drawn from the account of frameworks presented in section 5.3, are as follows:

1. The black-boxing model does not explain the stability of the ecosystem simpliciter. Rather, it explains the stability *given that* the organisms in question, because of the presence of the frameworked mechanisms, satisfy the functional definitions of predator and prey, and thus interact in a certain way.

2. The black boxes' contribution to the model's cohesion is not the cohesion of the multiply realizable boxes themselves but rather the cohesion of the particular frameworked mechanisms for which they function as placeholders. Provided that the frameworked mechanisms are cohesive—provided that the mechanisms driving the behavior of the particular organisms whose behavior is to be explained are not discretely multiply realizable—the black-boxing model is cohesive.

3. Because a model that secretes some mechanisms in its explanatory framework does not confer what I called in section 5.3 "deep" or "full" understanding of the phenomenon that constitutes its target, the black-boxing model is limited in its explanatory power. A deep explanation of the ecosystem's stability must flesh out the model's black boxes rather than leaving the causal details in the framework.

The same is true, I propose, of the explanation of the increase in supply of suvs and for the black-boxing explanation of any other singular event. In each case, black boxes stand in for frameworked mechanisms and so avoid undermining their models' cohesion, at the price of a shortfall in explanatory depth.[7]

So much for the use of the predator/prey model to explain some aspect of a particular ecosystem. How to understand the use of the model to explain a property of ecosystems in general? What does it mean, for example, to cite the model as explaining the fact that all predator/prey ecosystems having a certain configuration of parameters are stable, regardless of the nature of the predators and prey?

Since *predator* and *prey* are discretely multiply realizable kinds, the kairetic account is committed to the view that the stability in question is to be explained slightly differently in each ecosystem, the explanatory difference corresponding, obviously, to the difference in the implementation of the black boxes. It follows that there is no single explanation of stability across the ecosystems in question, although the explanations of stability in each system do share a single high level structure, captured by the black-boxing model. You might say that this model functions as an explanatory template, to be filled out in different ways to obtain deep explanations of stability in different ecosystems. The sense in which the black-boxing model explains the stability of a wide range of ecosystems is at best partial, then: the model does not itself explain stability in each such system; it rather provides the schema for the individual, case-by-case explanations.

Why all this black-boxing in population ecology? Most ecologists would, I think, agree with the kairetic account that predator/prey models are explanatorily incomplete: in order to understand the population dynamics of some particular ecosystem, it is not enough to understand the mathematics of the relevant differential equations; you must understand why it is these differential equations that capture predator/prey interaction in the ecosystem. The black-boxing, then, does not mark a line below which the population ecologist has nothing relevant to learn.

The black boxes' borders are drawn where they are, rather, on practical grounds: it is convenient to separate the behavior of the population from the behavior of the individual for three reasons. First, black-boxing makes ecological models more modular and therefore easier to handle. Second, in the longer term, black-boxing enables economy through specialization: rather than every ecologist having to know something about everything, different scientists can focus on different levels of description. Third, distinct explanations may have common parts. If the explanation of predator/prey dynamics among foxes and rabbits, among humans and tapeworms, and among denizens of a system of artificial life, though different in some ways, have something mathematically in common at the higher level, it makes sense to capture the similarity using an appropriately abstract representation of predator/prey ecosystems. A black-boxing model is a natural choice for this explanatory template.

As in ecology, so in the rest of science. Systematic black-boxing enables the stratification, and more generally, the modularization of explanatory knowledge, much as the division of the university into departments enables the stratification and modularization of scientific knowledge. The evolutionary biologists can explain selection events using models that black-box genetic and ecological processes; the geneticists can explain inheritance phenomena using models that black-box molecular processes; and so on. A full or deep explanation requires that this knowledge be brought together into a single whole, an explanation that black-boxes nothing; the pursuit of explanatory knowledge is, however, far more efficiently divided between the disciplines.

The black boxes of scientific explanation are, then, the microcosmic manifestations of a macrocosm of institutionalized epistemic frameworks that exist for reasons that are ultimately practical. (Should the different scientific disciplines and subdisciplines be defined in part in terms of the frameworks against which their characteristic research endeavors typically take place? No; although economists normally black-box psychological processes, an inquiry into the economically relevant aspects of these processes—the discipline of experimental economics—is not misnamed; it is, for all its psychologizing, a branch of economics.)

Let me take stock. The pragmatic approach to black-boxing endorsed in this section yields the following conclusions:

1. Black-boxing explanations are in a certain sense shallow (even though, given the right explanatory framework, they may technically stand alone).

2. To obtain a deep standalone explanation of a phenomenon for which you have a black-boxing model, you must fill out the black boxes, by specifying (perhaps quite abstract) properties of the fundamental level processes that link the boxes' inputs to their outputs. You may have to visit many other university departments, finishing of course with the physics department, to accomplish this end.

3. A black-boxing model cannot constitute a standalone explanation of a pattern of behavior across an incohesively diverse range of systems; for example, the predator/prey model cannot be considered a complete explanation of stability in all predator/prey systems sharing merely a certain range of parameters. It may, however, function as an explanatory template.

4. The decision to black-box, and where to do so, is a practical matter; it is not dictated by the nature of explanatory relation.

What might the alternative be? Go back to the explanation of the increase in suv supply. On the pragmatic approach, such an explanation is not as deep as it could be: it would be improved, for example, if it were supplemented by a model of the mechanism by which the suv producers learn of the increased demand for their products. A contrary, attractive view that I hinted at when I first introduced the example, one that is especially popular in the philosophy of psychology (Putnam 1975), is that this information is explanatorily quite irrelevant. Once you grasp the relationship between the decreasing price of oil and the increasing demand for suvs, on the one hand, and the relationship between the increasing demand for suvs and the increasing supply of the same, on the other, you see as fully as can be the reasons for the increase in supply. Information about the communication mechanisms is nothing more than explanatory detritus, distracting clutter.

At the core of such a treatment must be an account of the explanatory relation that declares the nature of the communication mechanisms to be irrelevant. It might be a difference-making account, on which the details of the communication mechanisms turn out not to make a difference to the increased production of suvs. It might even be an account much like the kairetic account, but with a more lenient standard for cohesion that admits causal models realized by a range of communication mechanisms. If such a model were declared cohesive, then the optimizing procedure would not merely allow, it would require that the details of the communication mechanisms be omitted from the model, so creating a bona fide black box in the center of the relevant kernel, standing alone unassisted by any framework.

The principal appeal of the kairetic account is the place it makes for abstraction in the explanatory enterprise. Anyone drawn to the account for this reason, including its author, will find the possibility of further abstraction, by way of the principled black-boxing of lower-level mechanisms, intriguing. Yet I do not see how to formulate a cohesion constraint that is able both to disbar disjunctive models from explanation yet also to allow black-boxing in a deep—that is, framework-independent—explanation.

The best hope is, perhaps, to adopt a standard for individuating causal processes whose grain varies with the level of explanation, a standard on which a given black box would be acceptable with respect to some explananda or explanations but not with respect to others. On such a view, it might be, for example, that when explaining Rasputin's death at the sociopolitical level, all murder methods may be classed together as a single kind of causal process, effectively forming a black box, while when explaining the death at the level of individual action, the very same classification would be counted as criminally disjunctive. It is clear, I hope, that the kairetic machinery, excepting the causal contiguity conception of cohesion, is capable of accommodating such a level-relative standard—but of course I have no such standard to offer here, nor even a hint of how it might be formulated. I therefore stand by the account of cohesion as causal contiguity, outlawing as it does the explanatory use of any black box not connected to the explanatory framework (with a few exceptions to be discussed in the next section).

In this defensive spirit, let me show you how the kairetic account addresses in its pragmatic way several concerns about the view that deep explanation can make no use of black boxes.

First, going back to the suv case, it might seem obvious that the details of the mechanism by which increased demand is communicated are explanatorily irrelevant: an economics paper, class, or textbook that concerned itself with these details, when attempting to explain the increased demand for suvs in the 1990s, would be wrong to do so.

And they are wrong. The paper, the class, and the textbook are formulated in the usual economic context, which supplies an explanatory framework in which the existence of appropriate communicative channels is taken as given. It is always a mistake to attempt to explain elements of the framework (section 5.3); thus, relative to the economic framework, it is indeed forbidden to describe the communicative mechanism. You might say, then, that the details are *economically* irrelevant, meaning that they are irrelevant relative to the usual economic framework (though as I remarked above, there is no single framework for all of economics, and, further, those frameworks that are, for now, customary in economics departments are subject to change).

Second, it may seem clear that, given the existence of some appropriate communicative channel or other, the facts about the low-level workings of the channel do not make a difference to the demand for suvs. This insight, too, is reproduced by the kairetic account as it stands. It is not necessary, here, to appeal to the usual economic framework: the *given the existence of* formulation explicitly places the communicative channel into the explanatory framework. More generally, it is possible to say of any black box in any explanatory context: provided that the box is implemented somehow, the details of the implementation are not explanatorily important, because the *provided that* notionally shifts the actual implementation to the explanatory framework, removing the need to—indeed, disallowing any attempt to—cite its workings for explanatory purposes.

Third, for related reasons, it is tempting to say that the explanation for the increase in SUV production would have been the same however the communication channels were implemented. (Compare the thought above that a purely mathematical model can single-handedly explain the stability of a wide range of predator/prey ecosystems.) The kairetic account can lend this temptation a certain degree of legitimacy: in the case where it is not a deep explanation but rather a framework-relative black-boxing explanation that is on offer, exactly the same explanatory model figures in the explanation of the increase in production however communication is implemented (albeit with respect to a different explanatory framework, or at least a different part of the explanatory framework, in each case).

Fourth, it is perhaps disappointing to have to accept a purely pragmatic answer to the question of what an explainer should black-box. Is it really just convenience or shared professional interest that motivates population ecologists to black-box, say, a predator's digestive processes but not (typically) the availability of its prey?

There is, in fact, something more that I, as a proponent of the pragmatic approach, can say about the question of what to black-box. I cannot, of course, dictate that the boundaries of black boxes should trace natural explanatory joints, since I hold that there are no such joints between levels. But I do not have to say that black-boxing is entirely a matter of convention. The pragmatic rationale for black-boxing prescribes a certain degree of modularity in the explanatory enterprise, to be achieved by judicious black-boxing, but it does not dictate any particular partition. I suggest that the question of how to divide up the disciplines and subdisciplines for these purposes is largely determined by the nature of the causal processes in question.

Why? The fruitful use of black boxes requires a certain articulation in the subject matter that cannot be imposed on nature from without. Modularity is possible in the ecological case, for example, because the individual and population levels come apart mathematically in an especially simple way, in spite of their intimate metaphysical and causal relationship (Strevens 2003b, 24, §5.5). You cannot black-box wherever you like, then, with equally rewarding results; there are certain joints at which it is, for quite objective reasons, in your interests to carve. There is, then, a theory of where to black-box and where not to black-box—but it is not a proper part of the theory of explanation.

### 5.43  Causal-Explanatory Black Boxes

For all that I have said in previous sections, the kairetic account under some circumstances allows black-boxing even when there is no corresponding mechanism in the explanatory framework.

### Causal Covering Laws as Black Boxes

First and very briefly, let me present a case in which there is the misleading appearance of an explanatory black box. In the course of describing the workings of some component of an explanatory mechanism, a model may cite a high-level causal covering law that relates the inputs and outputs of the component in a form that does not make explicit the mechanism that underpins the law. The specification of a functional relation between inputs and outputs unaccompanied by any details of implementation has the hallmarks of a black box. But it is no such thing, for the reason given in section 4.33: to cite a causal law is implicitly to cite the law's underlying mechanism.

### Smooth Multiple Realizability

Kinds that are multiply realizable in some intuitively interesting sense may be, nevertheless, smoothly rather than discretely multiply realizable; hence, they may not bring incohesion to an explanatory model. Certain apparent counterexamples to the kairetic cohesion desideratum—functional kinds appearing in deep standalone explanations—involve smoothly multiply realizable kinds of this sort, and so they do not constitute counterexamples after all.

A favorite example of Jerry Fodor's is *airfoil* (Fodor 1989). An airfoil is defined by its aerodynamic properties, which may be realized in a number of ways. Most strikingly, airfoils include not only naturally rigid wing-shaped objects but sails whose temporary rigidity is due to airflow itself. Because the kind of airflow that creates the necessary temporary rigidity is the same airflow that characterizes an airfoil, it is plausible that *airfoil* is smoothly multiply realizable. Make a naturally rigid airfoil more and more flexible, and the airflow does more and more of the work of conferring temporary rigidity. Thus, between the wing and the sail there exists a smooth continuum of airfoils of varying flexibility. An explanatory model can cite the property of being an airfoil, then, without compromising its cohesion.

The case for the smooth multiple realizability of airfoils is easiest to make, I think, when airfoils appear in the context of some fairly well-specified laws of physics. What you have, then, is not a black box but a gray box: the physics of air flow is specified with the necessary degree of causal detail, but the composition of the central object, the airfoil, is only functionally specified.

Not only objects, however, are smoothly multiply realizable; some causal processes have the property too. Consider, for example, the process of molecular scattering that plays an important role in explaining various behaviors of gases (chapter eight). A process counts as an intermolecular scattering if it consists in a certain characteristic pattern of molecular movement's being caused by powerful but short-range repulsive interactions. Many possible physics give rise to such interactions between particles. But it is plausible that these different dynamical realizations of scattering form a causally contiguous kind, and hence that scattering is smoothly multiply realizable.[8]

Finally, consider kinds defined in terms of functional roles that require for their implementation only the most basic intrinsic causal powers. One such kind, also an example of Fodor's, is *mountain*; another more interesting example is *currency*: just about any reasonably persistent physical stuff can be currency, so it is plausible that the varieties of currency will form a contiguous fundamental-level set, indeed, a nearly exhaustive fundamental-level set.

## Cohesion/Generality Tradeoffs

If cohesion is, as I proposed adventurously at the very end of section 3.63, a desideratum rather than a requirement, the best explanatory model for a phenomenon may not be maximally cohesive. When the explanatory deployment of a discretely multiply-realizable kind introduces relatively little incohesion for a relatively great increase in generality, the kairetic account will not only allow, but will require, that the kind be used in place of a smoothly realizable subkind.

I suggested in section 3.63 that the bonds used in Rasputin's influviation (the devices by which Rasputin is bound hand and foot) are discretely multiply realizable, but that a cohesion/generality tradeoff might account for the optimality of a model that cites the property of bondhood. Let me return to this example.

Suppose that you have a causal model for Rasputin's death by influviation that specifies his being bound hand and foot with three-ply hemp rope. Remove the description of the rope, leaving only the implication that he was bound with *something*. The result is a considerably more general model, one that covers all influviations rather than merely all influviations in which the victim was bound with a certain kind of rope.

The cost is incohesion: the realizers of the bonds form discrete sets in fundamental-level physical space (or so I will assume). It can be argued that the degree of incohesion is not that great, however, for two reasons. First, because all bonds have various physical similarities, the different realizers form a cluster in physical space, and the gaps between them are likely not that great. Second, the bonds play a relatively small, though important— because difference-making—role in the story. Why relatively small? Suppose that Rasputin would probably have drowned even without the bonds. Then the bonds have relatively low explanatory weight: they make a difference, but only a small difference. Incohesion in factors of low weight, I tentatively suggest, counts for less. If the cost in incohesion is small for either of these reasons, and cohesion/generality tradeoffs are allowed, then abstracting from the particular composition of the rope to the functional kind *bond* is mandated by the kairetic account.

There are many more cases in which the possibility of cohesion/generality tradeoffs ameliorates worries about possible gaps in the space of realizers. Take, for example, the case of *airfoil* again. Are airfoils composed of some strange new alloy contiguous in their causal behavior with aluminum airfoils? It does not matter much, because the gap between the sets of realizers is small, and so the incohesion, if any, is easily compensated for by increased generality.

It is possible, I suppose, that the discontinuities in the realizers of kinds like *predator* and *prey* also have their negative effect on cohesion outweighed by their positive effect on generality. But this is murky territory.

A number of parameters come into play: the way that cohesion and generality are weighted, the question of the standards—relative or absolute?—according to which the size of the gap between sets of realizers is measured, and of course the question of the standards according to which the size of the role played by a causal element in an explanatory model is measured. Let me travel no further in this direction.

### Effectively Irrelevant Difference-Makers

Consider again a sociopolitical explanation of Rasputin's death. As noted above, such an explanation typically specifies no particular details of the death; after a story of intrigue at the Russian court, it runs out of causal steam with the conspirators' decision to assassinate Rasputin, noting simply that they succeeded. The entire assassination process is, then, black-boxed. It is vitally important that the black box be counted by the kairetic account as thoroughly incohesive—for the reasons given in section 3.6, lack of cohesion is all that prevents the box itself from being a standalone explanation of death. How, then, can a sociopolitical explanation that black-boxes death be a good explanation?

Consider the alternative, a compound causal model containing two parts. The first is the sociopolitical component, a causal model culminating in the conspirators' decision. The second is the murder model, which specifies how the dirty deed is done. One element in the murder model's setup, the conspirators' decision, is the target of the sociopolitical model; the rest are the various initial conditions that determined the events of that fateful day. To keep things simple, suppose that the murderers successfully poisoned Rasputin. (The hybrid model discussed in section 4.32 is one way of constructing a representation of this process.)

The murder model is a perfectly good explanatory model. Conjoining it with the sociopolitical model in the manner prescribed by the recipe for standalone explanation (section 4.1), then, should produce a compound model that is also a perfectly good explanation. But the compound model has a peculiar property. In the context of the sociopolitical model with which the poisoning model is now conjoined, the poisoning itself no longer looks like a difference-maker. The by-now familiar reason: given the conspirators' resolve and (I am assuming that this is in there somewhere, or is a part of the explanatory framework) their relative power, Rasputin cannot but have died somehow. That he died by poisoning, in particular, has the look of an unnecessary detail. What you have is a case of effective irrelevance, discussed in section 4.35 in connection with the spin-echo experiment.

I stand by the definition of standalone explanation from section 4.1, insisting that the compound explanation is a good one. You have effective irrelevance, but not the real thing, not genuine irrelevance. Still, effective irrelevance is sufficient to create a pressure to black-box death. First, there is some reason to think that explainers have a primitive aversion to citing effectively irrelevant difference-makers such as the means of death in their explanations (section 4.35). Second, and less presumptuously, mentioning an effectively irrelevant difference-maker has at the very least the appearance of being unnecessary. To go ahead and mention it, then, is to insist on mentioning what appears to be unnecessary. This insistence suggests—by the usual pragmatics of communication—that special importance is being attached to the means of death. Sociopolitical explainers do not want to create such an impression, so they black-box death. Technically, they err; from a more practical viewpoint, they do the right thing.

More generally, whenever an upstream event has the potential to cause the explanandum in one of several fundamentally noncontiguous ways, and it is certain or almost certain that it will in fact do so, the downstream details will be effectively irrelevant, and so there will exist a pressure to black-box the details.

## 5.5   Aggregative Explanation

The core kairetic account of explanation assumes that an explanandum event is produced by a single causal process. This is not always so: some singular states of affairs, quite susceptible of explanation, are aggregate or relational properties of a set of events, each independently produced by a distinct causal process. The core must therefore be extended.

Two examples of aggregative explanation. First, suppose that you want to explain why there were more than ten Atlantic hurricanes during the 2005 season. Your explanandum is a fact about the set of all Atlantic hurricanes—or perhaps better, all Atlantic weather events—namely, that it contained more than ten hurricanes. Each of the events is caused by a different (if in some cases, overlapping) process, thus your explanatory model must represent aspects of a number of distinct processes.

Second, you drop a cannonball and a tennis ball from the top of the leaning tower of Pisa. The cannonball hits before the tennis ball. How to explain this fact? Again, there is no single causal model that can do the job, since the cannonball's relatively early arrival at ground level is a fact about a relation between two independently produced outcomes.

The simplest way to apply the kairetic account to aggregative cases is as follows. An aggregative explanandum has the following form: it is the state of affairs of a certain set of events having a certain property in the aggregate. The explanation of such a state of affairs has two parts. One part offers a separate kairetic explanation for each event in the set. The other part shows that the set as a whole has the aggregative property to be explained. The first part, then, is causal; the second part is a logical deduction.

On this view, the explanation of there being more than ten Atlantic hurricanes in the 2005 season consists of a causal explanation of every weather event in the season, along with a simple count demonstrating that at least eleven of the events were hurricanes. The explanation of the cannonball's faster fall likewise consists of two models, one for the cannonball's flight time and the other for the tennis ball's flight time, along with a comparison of the two showing that the latter was longer.

There is something about these explanations that is not quite right. If I ask you why the cannonball hit first, you will tell me that it encountered proportionally far less air resistance than the tennis ball. You do not explain the falling time of each ball in detail; indeed, factors that would be explanatorily relevant to explaining even approximate falling times, such as the strength of the gravitational field in Pisa, seem irrelevant to explaining why the cannonball fell faster. Likewise, it seems that you might have a satisfactory explanation for the abundance of 2005 hurricanes without being able to explain why any particular hurricane developed as and when it did.

What to do? I have been assuming that the optimizing procedure is separately applied to each of the individual causal models in an aggregative explanation, removing factors that make no difference to the models' targets taken one by one. I now propose that the scope of the abstraction process be broadened, so that whatever can be removed from the set of models as a whole without invalidating the entailment of the aggregative explanandum be removed. Then, for example, the magnitude of the gravitational acceleration specified by the explanation of the cannonball's faster fall can be abstracted to the point where all that is said is that the acceleration was the same for both balls and large enough for air resistance to have a marked effect. Any further information about the size of the gravitational field is declared irrelevant, as desired. Likewise, causal factors that made a difference to where and when certain hurricanes formed but that made no difference to their overall number are irrelevant to the explanation of the abundance of 2005 storms.

You might wonder if this is enough. When asked to explain the cannon-ball's faster fall, is it not sufficient to point to air resistance? Or, asked to explain the large number of 2005 hurricanes, might you not simply re-ply that (according to some theorists) global warming is responsible? What you are doing in such a case is, I suggest, not giving a standalone expla-nation, but simply citing a difference-maker of special interest—much as when, asked for the explanation of a car accident, you might cite the driver's exhaustion, even though exhaustion is not enough in itself to explain the crash.

A more interesting phenomenon is as follows. Suppose you are asked to explain why the U.S. presidents between 1893 and 1921 were elected in alphabetical order: Cleveland, McKinley, Roosevelt, Taft, Wilson. The ordering is a paradigm of an aggregative fact. Apply the kairetic account, and you will get an explanation that models the election of each of the five presidents and then simply notes that their order of election is alphabetic. But we would not offer such a model as an explanation for the fact of the alphabetical election. We would surely say that it has no explanation: things just happened to turn out that way.

This shows, I think, that a request for an aggregative explanation is typ-ically asking for some difference-making similarity or difference between the individual causal processes in question. What I want in the presiden-tial case is a force at work in each election ensuring alphabeticality. Because there is no such force, I conclude that the explanatory request cannot be fulfilled. Likewise, what I want in the hurricane case is a storm-promoting force at work in sufficiently many of the Atlantic weather events in question. In a comparative case such as the falling balls, what I am after is a difference: something present in one case and not the other. Thus, I am more likely to cite the variation in air resistance than the fact that, for both balls, the grav-itational acceleration was large enough to make air resistance a significant factor.

I am disinclined, however, to build this concern for similarities or dif-ferences into the theory of explanation itself, for the following reason. Although it is appropriate to say that there is "no explanation" of the alphabetic election of U.S. presidents between 1893 and 1921, it would be wrong to say that there is something about this well-ordered state of affairs that we do not understand. My reply to you, then, means that there is no explanation of the sort that you are seeking, not that there is no explanation at all. I conclude that the importance of similarities and differences in aggregative explanation is due to the interests of typical explanatory inquirers, rather than to the nature of aggregative explanation itself.

An aggregative explanatory model should not be confused with the kind of incohesive causal model that can be realized by causally noncontiguous processes, such as the disjunctive model for Rasputin's death that has both death by influviation and death by poisoning as realizers (section 3.61). The disjunctive model purports to represent a single causal process, namely, the process actually leading to Rasputin's death. An aggregative model, by contrast, represents two or more numerically different processes (even in the case, discussed in detail in sections 10.2 and 10.3, where it consists of a single, unified, abstract description picking out features shared by the relevant processes).

The scientific importance of aggregative explanation can be seen in the following generic example from evolutionary biology. Suppose that you have two strains of bacteria living in a petri dish. There is some source of nutrition, and they are reproducing steadily. One strain's metabolism is better attuned to the ambient temperature in the lab; these bacteria make more efficient use of their food and as a consequence reproduce faster. Every night a certain fixed proportion of the bacteria in each strain are culled. There is no interaction between the strains (perhaps not even between individuals of the same strain, though I will put no weight on this). Over time, one strain comes to dominate and eventually take over the population; it goes to fixation while the other strain goes extinct. What explains the fact that the proportion of the one strain in the population increases over time?

The explanandum is aggregative twice over. First, a strain's rate of population change is a property of the entire population taken as a whole, in the same way that the fact of there being more than ten Atlantic hurricanes in 2005 is a property of the 2005 Atlantic weather events taken as whole. Second, the fact that one rate of population change is greater than the other is a relational fact, in the same way that the fact that one Pisan ball hits the ground before the other is a relational fact.

The explanation for one strain's increasing at the expense of the other, and eventually going to fixation, is therefore constructed according to the rules for aggregative explanation. It is a causal model for bacterial feeding and reproduction that picks out just those causal factors sufficient to entail that one strain will reproduce faster than the other. Such a model can be divided into two parts: a causal background common to both strains, and a list of differences between the strains. In the case at hand, the differences will be whatever biological facts are responsible for one strain's superior metabolism. Such causal elements will, of course, be the focus of the explanation. (I note in passing, though it is not important here, that this is a case of equilibrium explanation, to be treated in section 7.41.)

You might wonder whether aggregative explanation, as I have characterized it, is a genuine variety of causal explanation. Consider the bacteria, for example. The state of affairs to be explained is that one variant outdoes the other and eventually comes to dominate the population completely. Can such a state of affairs be explained causally? Intuitively, there is a sense in which nothing causes the state of affairs to come into being: there is no master cause that makes one trait replace the other. After all, by assumption, there is no causal interaction between the two subpopulations: the victorious variant does not eat the vanquished variant, does not steal its food, does not in any way exist at its expense. Rather, the dynamics of each population constitute two (or more) distinct, independent causal processes, one of which has as its end point population zero.

Causally, the situation is no different from a case in which the two populations occupy separate dishes. One variant, because of its low reproduction rate, is unable to overcome the nightly cull. Thus, it eventually goes extinct. The explanation for the extinction, then, is a causal process that is quite independent of the ups and downs of the other variant's population change. Likewise, the explanation of the victorious variant's bountiful increase is a causal process quite independent of the vanquished variant's decline. The explanation for the victorious variant's taking over the combined population of the two dishes, then, seems not to be a single cause of the state of affairs to be explained, but two causes for two independently produced events that together logically add up to the explanandum. The same is true for the single dish case, in which the relevant causal processes are no less independent.

This characterization of the explanation cannot be disputed. Nevertheless, it seems quite acceptable to us to say that the cause of the explanandum's coming to hold—the cause of one strain's going to fixation at the expense of the other—is the difference in metabolic efficiency. Metaphysically, this difference is incapable of supplying causal oomph in the case at hand, being as it is an abstract relation between two states of affairs that act independently. We call it a cause all the same, assigning it the starring role in the explanation of fixation (the supporting role being played, of course, by the common causal background). Jackson and Pettit (1988, 392–393) make more or less the same point.

I do not propose to justify this behavior of ours; it is a feature of our explanatory practice, and is thus, given the goals of this book, to be characterized rather than questioned. For all the foregoing, we count aggregative explanation as a species of causal explanation, and thus we count a state of affairs such as the difference in metabolic rates as a causal-explanatory factor, calling it, like all other such factors, a cause—despite its metaphysically dubious causal status. I consider this to be a part of the case that our causal claims, our assertions of the form *c was a cause of e*, concern not raw metaphysical causal relations but rather causal-explanatory relations (section 2.23). A similar argument based on our willingness to attribute causal status to omissions is made in section 6.3.

## 5.6   Contrastive Explanation

The term *contrastive explanation* is used of two different kinds of explanation, with correspondingly different kinds of explananda. Some contrastive explanations account for the fact that one thing happened rather than another—why did Truman rather than Dewey win the election? In these explanations, there is some causal process that could have turned out in (at least) two ways; the question is why the process unfolded in one particular way rather than another particular way. Other contrastive explanations account for the fact that one thing happened but another independently did not. Why did Eliot win the Nobel Prize while Pound did not? Here there are two separate causal processes: both things could have happened, but only one did. The question is why.

What these two kinds of explanation have in common is the form of their explananda: why $e$ and not $f$? In one case, $e$ occurs in place of $f$; in the other case, $e$ and $f$ might have both occurred. The latter kind of explanation is, I propose, a form of aggregative explanation, involving as it does the comparison, characteristic of that endeavor, of different causal processes. (As an example, consider the explanation, in section 5.5, of why one bacterial strain can overcome the nightly cull while the other cannot.) The former is sui generis; for it alone I reserve the term *contrastive explanation*. What follows is an account of this pure kind of contrastive explanation.[9]

You are asked to explain why Rasputin's murderers decided to kill him by throwing him into a river rather than into a volcanic crater. What is wanted is a contrastive explanation in the pure sense.

To illustrate how a contrastive explanation differs from a regular explanation, suppose that three facts motivated Rasputin's assassins' choice to throw him into the river:

1. The method of murder (i.e., influviation) would be certain to succeed.

2. A suitable apparatus (i.e., the river) was at hand.

3. By killing him this way, they avoided exposure to his unholy blood.

All three would have to be cited as difference-makers if the explanatory request were simply: why did the assassins decide on the river? For the contrastive explanation, however, only (2) should be cited. Facts (1) and (3) do not explain the choice of river over crater, because the crater, too, would have ensured a certain and bloodless death.

Let me sketch an account of contrastive explanation within the kairetic framework. Your task is to explain why $e$ rather than $f$ occurred, or for short, why $e$-not-$f$. You proceed by constructing separate explanatory causal models for $e$ and $f$ that satisfy the following conditions:

1. The model for $e$ is veridical; it is a (noncontrastive) standalone explanation for why $e$ occurred.

2. The model for $f$ is veridical except for one or more states of affairs that you might call the *switching events*. The model falsely represents the switching events as not having occurred.

3. Each of the switching events appears in the model for $e$. They are therefore difference-makers for $e$.

4. The model for $f$ is in some sense the most plausible story as to how $f$ might have occurred. (Perhaps it is the model instantiated in the closest possible world in which $f$ occurs.) I will have no more to say in the main text about this requirement, but see note 10.

The result is a pair of causal models redolent of the tales of the legendary trolley car: the modeled process may go down one of two tracks; the question is as to which. It is the switching events that determine that it will be the process leading to $e$, rather than the process leading to $f$, that is actualized.

The switching events, then, are difference-makers responsible for the fact that $e$ rather than $f$ occurred. (They may not be the only such difference-makers, if there are other pairs of causal models for the contrasted events that satisfy the above requirements.)

In the Rasputin case, for example, it is possible to build two causal models of the course of events leading to Rasputin's death, one for Rasputin's being thrown into the river and one for the contrasting event of his being thrown into a volcanic crater, that agree on (and thus are veridical with respect to) facts (1) and (3) above, but disagree on (2), that is, on whether a river was at hand (and that otherwise satisfy the requirements on contrastive explanation enumerated above). The availability of the river was therefore a switching event, and so it counts as a difference-maker responsible for Rasputin's being influviated rather than incinerated. There is in addition a second event on which the models disagree, namely, whether there was a volcanic crater at hand: the model for incineration says yes, while the model for influviation says no. (I assume that the influviation model must take a stand on this issue—the unavailability of otherwise satisfactory alternative murder methods—if it is to causally entail the influviation.) There being no nearby crater is also a switching event, then. Conjoining the two switches, what made the difference between Rasputin's being thrown into the river and his being thrown into a crater was the fact that a river but not a crater was available. By contrast, there exist no such pairs of models that disagree on facts (1) or (3)—or at least no pairs in which the model for incineration is as plausible as that considered above—so these states of affairs are not switching events for influviation-not-incineration.[10]

A contrast's switching events in a loose sense constitute its explanation. Thus, we might say that Rasputin's being thrown into a river rather than a crater is explained by the fact that a river, but not a volcano, was available. This does not quite amount to a standalone explanation, however; full understanding comes only by comprehending the models in the context of which the switching events do their switching. The full explanation of influviation-not-incineration, then, consists of both models, with the switching events highlighted to illustrate their role as explanatory pivot.

Sometimes the difference-maker for a contrast (the explanation of the contrast, in the informal sense) is another contrast. For example, what explains the fact that I ordered the meat pie rather than the *frisée aux lardons* is the fact that I grew up in New Zealand rather than France—it is not simply the fact that I grew up in New Zealand, which at best explains only why I ordered the meat pie rather than something else. In cases such as these, the model for the contrast event (ordering the *frisée*) does not merely specify that the switching event (my early antipodean experience) does not occur; it specifies a particular way that it fails to occur—my growing up in France. To generalize: suppose you have a standalone explanation for $e$'s rather than $f$'s occurring—that is, a pair of causal models, one for $e$ and one for $f$—that satisfies the conditions specified above with (for simplicity's sake) a single switching event $c$. The model for $f$ either explicitly states that $c$ does not occur or states that some alternative $d$ to $c$ occurred (and thereby entails that $c$ did not occur). In the first case, it is $c$ simpliciter that is the switch for, and thus the informal explanation of, $e$-not-$f$; in the second case, it is $c$-not-$d$ that is the switch for and informal explanation of $e$-not-$f$.[11]

Some writers assert that all explanation is contrastive.[12] True? If so, an apparently noncontrastive scientific explanation of an event $e$ would have to be interpreted as an explanation why $e$ rather than $\neg e$ occurred. If you construct a contrastive explanation of $e$-not-$\neg e$ using the recipe outlined in this section, you will find yourself with a pair of causal models, one for $e$'s occurring and one for $e$'s not occurring. (Causal explanations of nonevents are covered in section 6.4.) It is pretty clear that our usual scientific explanations do not have this dyadic structure; in particular, explaining why an event occurs does not require the construction of a model for its *nonoccurrence*. I conclude that a standalone explanation of $e$-not-$\neg e$ is not the same thing as a standalone explanation of $e$. In section 9.54, I will review a more specific reason to reject the thesis that all explanation is contrastive.

Is there ever any reason to construct a contrastive explanation for $e$-not-$\neg e$? Yes; you might do so to answer a question about a contrastive difference-maker, as illustrated in section 6.53.

## 5.7   Beyond Causal Explanation

Is all scientific explanation causal explanation? A good case can be made that the answer is *yes*, but even so, it is not hard to imagine a world similar to ours where the answer would be *no*. Perhaps, then, our explanatory reach is wider than our causal reach.

Let me give an example of Peter Railton's (reported by Lewis 1986a, §3). A star undergoes gravitational collapse, contracting to a much smaller size.

What explains the fact that the collapse stopped at this very point? According to Railton, the answer in some cases is that the Pauli exclusion principle makes further contraction impossible: for the star to get any smaller, it would have to enter a state declared impossible by the exclusion principle.

Suppose that the exclusion principle is an independent fundamental law of nature (something quite likely not true in our world, I will suggest in section 7.51). Then the collapse's halting is not due to any features of the causal law that governs the earlier dynamics of the collapse. Rather, an independent law, the exclusion principle, steps in and simply rules that the collapse can go no further.

It seems quite acceptable to say that the exclusion principle explains the collapse's sudden arrest. Is the relation between the principle and the arrest in any way causal? This is a question to be answered by the metaphysics of causation, and in particular, by the metaphysics of causal influence. Most accounts of causal influence require the influence relation to hold between particulars, thus entailing that for causal influence to be present there must be an object, property instance, or event to occupy the role of influencer. There appears to be no such particular in the exclusion case—nothing but the exclusion principle itself can be considered a cause of the arrest—thus there is no relation of causal influence, or so I will assume for the sake of the argument.

What relation holds between the law and the arrest, then, in virtue of which the one explains the other? Let me give a partial answer: the relation is, like causal influence, some kind of metaphysical dependence relation. I no more have an account of this relation than I have an account of the influence relation, but I suggest that it is the sort of relation that we say "makes things happen." For example, because this (asymmetric) dependence relation holds between the exclusion principle and the arrest, we are apt to say that the exclusion principle makes the arrest happen. It is in virtue of such dependence that the principle explains the arrest. (Note that the claims in this paragraph are consistent with a rather weak, even deflationary, account of what we mean by "making things happen.")

Now, it should occur to you immediately that, despite the absence of causal influence, the language of difference-making is entirely appropriate here. The exclusion principle is a difference-maker, indeed the only difference-maker, for the arrest. I suggest that while the causal influence relation is one kind of raw metaphysical dependence relation that can serve as the basis of the difference-making relation, there are others as well, and that any of the difference-making relations so based is explanatory.

On this view, the kairetic account of explanation has several independent parts. The first part is the causal influence relation itself, concerning which I have remained ecumenical. Second is the optimizing procedure, the kairetic criterion for difference-making. Third is the kairetic account of standalone explanation, that is, the set of rules according to which difference-makers are assembled to form explanations of both events (chapter four) and laws (chapter seven). Each of these parts provides the raw material for the next: the account of causal influence provides facts about influence to the optimizing procedure, and the optimizing procedure provides facts about difference-making to the account of explanation proper.

So far I have talked as though *only* these parts can supply appropriate raw material for the later parts. I now suggest a partial revision of this implied doctrine: the difference-making criterion takes as its raw material any dependence relation of the "making it so" variety, including but not limited to causal influence. Given a relation by which a state of affairs depends on some other entities, the kairetic criterion will tell you what facts about those entities are essential to the dependence relation's making it so.

To explain the stellar collapse's sudden arrest, for example, take a model representing the dependence relation between the exclusion principle and the arrest, and then apply the optimizing procedure. What remains is a model containing just those aspects of the exclusion principle that made a difference to the arrest (which in this case perhaps almost exhaust the content of the principle).

Our explanatory practice has, according to this proposal, a modular structure. The part of the practice that determines difference-making relations, and that uses them to construct explanatory relations, is distinct and detachable from the part of the practice that determines the raw dependence relations, such as causal influence.

In my causal ecumenism, I have already taken advantage of this modularity: because the kairetic account does not presuppose much about raw causal dependence, it is compatible with a broad range of accounts of the causal influence relation. I am now suggesting that the kairetic account does not even presume that raw dependence is causal.

So what does it presume? First, in order for the things a state of affairs depends on to count as prima facie explainers of that state of affairs, the dependence relation must have, as I have already said, the "making it so" aspect (the elucidation of the nature of which I leave as an exercise to the reader). Second, in order for the kairetic machinery as developed in this study to be applied, it must be possible to represent the dependence relation using the entailment relation, or some extension thereof (as I will extend the entailment relation in section 9.7, for example, to encompass what I called probabilistic causal entailment for the purpose of modeling probabilistic processes).

Clearly, dependence relations other than the causal can satisfy these requirements. Besides noncausal physical dependences such as the exclusion dependence envisaged by Railton, the candidate of most interest to philosophers of science is mathematical dependence. If there is a dependence relation in mathematics that goes beyond mere entailment, and that determines in some sense which mathematical structures and properties are the basis of which other mathematical structures and properties, then a satisfactory account of mathematical explanation, I speculate, will be obtained by feeding models of this dependence relation to the kairetic accounts of difference-making and standalone explanation. (See also section 7.44.)

Peering further into the philosophical distance, I can see dimly that the kairetic account of difference-making might play a role in understanding moral explanation. Given facts about the dependence of derivative moral facts on fundamental moral facts, and a system for representing this dependence using relations of logical entailment, the kairetic account can tell which aspects of the fundamental facts support which derivative facts, thereby explaining, say, the moral badness of an act by pointing to certain properties of the fundamental moral precepts. Something similar can be said, perhaps, of epistemological explanation, aesthetic explanation, literary explanation, and any other sphere of human intellection in which understanding a phenomenon or state of affairs is a matter of appreciating the structure of the relations of dependence between the matter to be explained and some set of facts taken to be fundamental.

# — 6 —

# Event Explanation and Causal Claims

A causal claim is an assertion of the form *c was a cause of e*, where *c* and *e* are singular events. I have suggested (section 2.23) that causal claims state explanatory facts: if *c* and *e* are singular events, then *c was a cause of e* is true just in case *c* is a causal difference-maker for *e*.[1]

My aim in this chapter is to demonstrate that the kairetic account of explanation provides the resources for solving many well-known problems concerning causal claims, once they are interpreted as problems about causal-explanatory relevance. In a single chapter, I cannot hope to provide the kind of intensive treatment of the issues that will convince you that the kairetic account's solutions are better than others found in this fast-expanding literature, or even to give the other accounts the attention they deserve. I will settle, then, for persuading you that the kairetic account has something illuminating to say about a wide range of issues, traditionally the preserve of philosophers of causation, involving claims of the form *c was a cause of e*, which is enough, I hope, to provoke you to take seriously the view that causal claims should be understood as causal-explanatory claims.

The contents of this chapter will do double duty, because the same problems about causal claims, when recast as problems concerning the explanation of events, are of independent interest to philosophers of explanation. Some other issues concerning event explanation, however, will not be discussed until later chapters: covering law explanation of events (section 7.35); equilibrium explanation of events (section 7.41), event explanation involving idealization (section 8.3), the explanatory value of robustness (section 11.2), and the probabilistic explanation of events (chapters ten and eleven).

A cautionary note: I will make full use of the idiom of causal claims: when an event *c* makes a difference to another event *e*, and so the causal claim *c was a cause of e* is true, I will call *c* a cause of *e*. Please bear in mind at all times that to call *c* a cause of *e* in this context is not to claim the existence of a metaphysically pristine high-level causal relation between

181

$c$ and $e$, but rather to say that $c$ is a difference-maker for—is explanatorily relevant to—$e$.

## 6.1   Background Conditions versus Causes

I drop a lit match into the magazine rack, which bursts into flames. We say that the dropped match explains the fire, and is a cause of the fire. But we are less inclined to say that the presence of oxygen explains or is a cause of the fire; we prefer to say that it is a "background condition" or some such thing. Why the discrimination?

Clearly, any deterministic causal model for the fire must mention the oxygen. Failing to mention the oxygen leaves open the possibility that there was no oxygen present, and a model that allows this possibility cannot entail the occurrence of the fire. The kairetic account, then, puts the presence of oxygen on a par with the dropped match as a difference-maker, hence as an explainer and a cause, of the fire. Most accounts of causal claims do the same. How, then, to make sense of our disinclination to count oxygen as a cause?

A popular approach to this problem (Mill 1973; Lewis 1973a) locates the difference between causes and background conditions outside the ambit of the metaphysics of cause, and therefore (if causal claims are explanatory claims) outside the ambit of the theory of explanation. The difference is held to be a matter of mere practical concerns. The oxygen is just as much a cause of, and a difference-maker for, the fire as the dropped match, on this view, but for practical reasons it is less likely than the match to be cited as such. Perhaps inquirers about the fire are more interested in causes such as the match than in causes such as the oxygen; in answer to their inquiries, then, you mention the match but not the oxygen. Or perhaps it is clear to everyone that oxygen was present and was a cause of the fire; by not saying as much, you are merely refraining from pointing out what is already obvious.

I think that it is correct to look to conversational context for the answer to the oxygen problem. But context and explanatory practice interact: there is a conduit by which contextual suppositions make their way into explanations proper, namely, the explanatory framework. According to the treatment of frameworks offered in section 5.3, if a causal factor $c$ is a part of the explanatory framework—if the request for explanation takes as given $c$'s presence—then $c$ must appear in any explanatory model for the explanandum, but it is never itself considered a difference-maker for the explanandum. It is not a cause, then, but neither is it a non-cause (the latter in the sense that it would be wrong to claim that a frameworked factor *failed* to make a difference to the explanandum). The presence of oxygen is, I propose, typically part of the framework for a request to explain a fire; for this reason, the answer to the request will not cite oxygen as a cause of the fire. It is a part of every explanatory model for the fire—hence in a certain sense a "background condition"—but not, in the context of the framework, a difference-maker.

To take another popular example, a framework introduced by presupposition accounts for my birth's not counting as a cause of my death. To call an event a death is to presuppose a birth (or more broadly, a coming-to-be); to ask for an explanation of an individual's death is not merely to ask for an explanation of their nonexistence—the bare fact of nonexistence, I would say, requires no explanation, certainly no *causal* explanation—but is rather to ask for an explanation of the individual's non-existence *given* their existence at some earlier time. This earlier existence is a part of the explanatory framework, then, and so neither it nor the events that explain it can be causes of the death. The birth, in particular, does not qualify as a cause of the death. The reluctance to classify birth as a cause is far more robust than the reluctance to classify oxygen as a cause, note, because the very specification of the explanandum creates the presupposition of an earlier existence, thereby placing it in the explanatory framework.

I suggest that, in general, the causal factors that we are inclined to call background conditions as opposed to causes are those factors that tend to sit in the framework of typical explanatory requests. In making this suggestion, I take myself to be endorsing something close to Mackie's treatment of the issue (Mackie 1974, 34–37). Mackie—talking, of course, about high-level causal relations rather than explanation—holds that causal claims are normally made within what he calls a *causal field* (a suggestion made originally by Anderson (1962)). The causal field is a set of facts that are treated, for the purpose of assessing difference-making, just as I treat the facts in the explanatory framework: they are assumed to be present, but they are disqualified as causes themselves.

Mackie builds the causal field into the high-level causal relation, writing that "what is said to be caused . . . is not just an event, but an event-in-a-certain-field" (35). This sounds rather strained in a metaphysics of high-level causal relations; most philosophers are uncomfortable, I think, with either the notion that it is events-in-fields that are caused rather than events, or the notion that events cause other events relative to fields that can consist of any set of further events you like. To put the matter in a traditional (though somewhat misleading) way, causation is not a "three-place relation".

My proposal that causal claims do not take raw metaphysical relations as their subject matter, but rather causal-explanatory relations, allows us to hold on both to our "two-place" conception of causal metaphysics and to Mackie's insight that canonical causal claims are often evaluated relative to a set of conditions that acts like a causal field or (equivalently) an explanatory framework, since there is no objection, I take it, to an explanatory practice that allows relative as well as absolute explanations. This constitutes an argument for the causal-explanatory over the metaphysical interpretation of causal claims.

More generally, as the later discussions of explanation by omission, transitivity, and so on show, the truth values of causal claims have a sensitivity to the conversational context that would be mysterious, even alarming, if it reflected a corresponding sensitivity in the raw causal facts that are, on the prevailing view, the subject matter of such claims. Some of this sensitivity can, perhaps, be accounted for by communicative pragmatics; however, many philosophers have found these treatments unsatisfactory (see, for example, Lewis on omissions in section 6.32). The view that causal claims are in fact causal-explanatory claims offers an attractive alternative: while the facts about raw causation are never relativized, some facts about difference-making are relative to an explanatory framework. When a causal claim leaves its framework implicit, the details are typically filled in by the conversational context. The identity of the relation asserted by such a claim will consequently be determined in part by context; thus, the truth value of the utterance may change as the context changes.

Two clarifications. First, this is a "contextualist" rather than a "relativist" account of contextual relativity: the fact that one thing makes a difference to another relative to a framework holds true quite independently of conversational context; what changes with context is the identity of the framework, and thus the identity of the difference-making facts asserted by a causal claim. More formally, the proposition expressed by a causal claim spells out the explanatory framework; what changes with the context is the framework, and thus the proposition expressed, rather than the truth value of some unchanging proposition. Second, let me remind you that there are some nonrelativized or framework-independent difference-making facts, and these are the fundamental explanatory facts. While explanatory frameworks play an important role in my treatment of the practical, hands-on, everyday world of causal claims, they will barely figure at all in parts three and four.

What determines the explanatory framework relative to which a typical causal claim is made? I wrote in section 5.3 that there is no limit to the ways in which the content of an explanatory framework can be fixed. In what follows I want to say something about the role of conversational context, in particular, in filling out a framework that has not been explicitly circumscribed.

Suppose that a state of affairs $c$ has been explicitly acknowledged by all parties to a conversation to hold true, so that $c$'s obtaining has been added to the conversation's "common ground" or to the "conversational score." Does $c$ thereby become a part of the explanatory framework? Certainly not; no element of the framework can be cited as a difference-maker, and thus as explanatorily relevant, but our agreement that $c$ holds hardly precludes one of us from using it to explain some event of interest to the other.

Start again, then. Suppose that a state of affairs $c$ has been explicitly acknowledged by all parties to a conversation not only to obtain but also to have made a difference to an event $e$, so that $c$'s being a difference-maker for $e$ has been added to the conversational score. Does $c$ thereby become a part of the explanatory framework? Yes it does: if we are agreed that $c$ was a difference-maker for $e$, and I persist in asking for an explanation of $e$, I am asking why $e$ occurred given that $c$ occurred. To tell me that $e$ occurred because of $c$ would be a conversational error.

The same goes for difference-makers for $e$ that are not explicitly acknowledged but that are anyway part of the common ground. These are what we typically refer to as background conditions. To be a background condition for a causal scenario producing an event type $e$, then, is first, to be present and a difference-maker for $e$ in all such scenarios, and second, for this to be common knowledge. Oxygen is a background condition for household fires; gravity is a background condition for fatal falls; gasoline in the tank is a background condition for automotive events, and so on.

How are facts about difference-making added to and removed from the conversational score? In just the same way as any other facts—there is no distinctive pragmatics of explanation. Such matters may therefore be left to philosophers of language and linguists.

In theoretical scientific discourse, explanatory frameworks are much sparer than in everyday conversation, or even than in laboratory lunch-room talk. In a chemistry text, oxygen is as much a part of the explanation of fire as anything, while in a ballistics text, the accuracy of a weapon is in part explained by that most imperturbable of background conditions, the force of gravity. Where frameworks do exist, they are normally found when a researcher aims to understand the role of one part of a larger mechanism; the rest of the mechanism then forms a framework against which the explanatory investigation takes place.

## 6.2  Preemption

### 6.21  The Preemption Problem

The essential ingredient of a "preemption scenario" is a backup cause, an event that would have brought about the effect of interest if the actual cause had not. One famous example is the case of the backup assassin, in which a reserve shooter is standing by to gun down the victim if the principal assassin fails; another is the variation on Russian history described in section 2.5, in which Rasputin's failure to eat the teacakes will trigger a device that sends him plummeting into the Neva.

Colorful though these cases may be, in the interest of sober and exact discussion I will use as my principal source of examples another popular genre of preemption stories concerning the physics of which we have a surer grip:

> The malevolent fairy children Sylvie and Bruno are throwing cannonballs at a peerless Ming period vase. Bruno throws first. He is easily distracted, however, and not unlikely to miss. Therefore Sylvie, animated by an implacable hatred of fine ceramics and skilled in the projectile-flinging arts as only a fairy child can be, stands by. If Bruno's cannonball does not shatter the vase, she will throw her own, breaking it for sure. Bruno hurls his cannonball; he is on target for once, and the vase is shattered.

Bruno's throw is the actual cause of the shattering; Sylvie's hypothetical throw is its backup cause. The actual cause explains the effect, while the backup cause does not (unless it is also an actual cause in a different guise; see below). Is there a problem here for event explanation?

Yes, if you take the difference-making approach to explanation. On this view, one event $c$ explains another event $e$ only if the occurrence of $c$ makes a difference to whether or not $e$ occurred. When a backup cause is present, there is a certain sense in which $c$ does not make a difference to $e$, a sense captured succinctly by the counterfactual: had *c* not occurred, *e* would have occurred nonetheless. Despite this reduction in difference-making power, the actual cause's explanatory status appears to be undiminished by the presence of a backup cause.

The simple counterfactual account of difference-making is famously unable to do justice to this aspect of our explanatory practice. I have already shown that the kairetic account does better, at least in some cases. The purpose of the following treatment is to convince you that the kairetic account gives the correct answer to questions about explanatory relevance, causal claims, and the high level *is a cause of* relation in any preemption scenario.[2]

### 6.22 Preemption: Discounting the Actual Cause?

Preemption scenarios are typically used to show that difference-making accounts of causal claims are too conservative in their attribution of causehood: in the example above, the argument goes, Bruno's throw, the actual cause of the Ming vase's breaking, is not counted as a cause when it should be.

Consider a causal model for the breaking of the vase that contains in its setup the following propositions, stating the presence of both the actual cause of the breaking, Bruno's throwing, and the backup cause, ever-vigilant Sylvie:

1. Bruno threw his cannonball at time *t* from such and such a point with such and such a velocity.
2. Nothing interfered with the flight of the ball.
3. The vase was in such and such a position at time *t* + 1.
4. A statement of the aspects of the laws of physics in virtue of which a ball thrown in this fashion at time *t* will strike a vase in this position at time *t* + 1 hard enough to break the vase, provided that nothing interferes with its flight.
5. Sylvie was standing by, ready to throw if Bruno missed—and Sylvie never misses.

The propositions entail that the vase breaks. If (1) is removed, they continue to do so. It is for this reason that Bruno's throw does not, in a certain sense, make a difference to the breaking.

The kairetic account develops a notion of difference-making on which Bruno's throw counts as a cause: as I have already explained, as long as there is *some* causal model for the breaking from which (1) cannot be removed, the throw is a difference-maker. To find such a model, simply remove (5) from the setup above. (1) cannot be removed from the pared-down model without invalidating its entailment of the breaking, thus Bruno's throw gets to make its difference and so to stand in the *is a cause of* relation to the breaking.

More generally, for any preemption case there will always be a model from which the actual cause cannot be removed without invalidating the entailment of the explanandum, namely, a model that omits any description of the backup cause. Thus, the facts in virtue of which Bruno's throw is a difference-maker when Sylvie is standing by are identical to the facts in virtue of which Bruno's throw is a difference-maker when he is alone. The backup cause simply does not enter into the calculation.

There is a lacuna in this treatment of preemption, however. I assume that there is always a model for the actual cause's causing that omits any mention of the backup cause. This is correct provided that the backup cause plays no role in actually causing the explanandum, but there are cases of preemption in which the same event functions as both backup cause and actual cause.

Consider, for example, the following case. Bruno and Sylvie simultaneously throw their cannonballs at the vase. Sylvie's throw is, as always, on target. Bruno's throw is, as so often, wildly off course. The balls collide in mid-air, however, and Bruno's ball is deflected toward the vase, Sylvie's ball away from the vase. Bruno's ball hits the vase and breaks it (figure 6.1).

Bruno's throw is, as before, an actual cause of the vase's breaking, but Sylvie's throw is both an actual and a backup cause: actual, because it

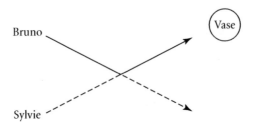

**Figure 6.1** Sylvie's throw (dashed line) is a both a backup cause and an actual cause of the vase's breaking.

deflects Bruno's ball toward the vase; backup, because if Bruno had not thrown, Sylvie's ball would have carried on undeflected and broken the vase itself.

The (somewhat abbreviated) setup of the model for the breaking will look like this:

1. Bruno threw his cannonball at time $t$ from such and such a point with such and such a velocity,

2. Sylvie threw her cannonball at time $t$ from such and such a point with such and such a velocity,

3. the vase was in such and such a position at time $t + 1$,

as well as propositions stating the causal laws governing the cannonballs' trajectories, their collision, and the eventual shattering of the vase.

Without (2), the entailment of the breaking does not go through, since Bruno's ball would have missed the vase had Sylvie not thrown. The kairetic criterion therefore counts Sylvie's throw as an actual cause of the breaking, just as it should. But without (1), the entailment does still go through, thus the kairetic criterion does not count Bruno's throw as a difference-maker.

In short, because Bruno's throw broke the vase only because it was accompanied by Sylvie's throw, Sylvie's throw must be mentioned in any explanation of the breaking that mentions Bruno's throw. But then, since Sylvie's throw is a backup cause of the breaking, Bruno's throw can be removed from such a model without invalidating the entailment of the breaking. The kairetic criterion, then, incorrectly discounts Bruno's throw as a difference-maker for the breaking in this devilish preemption scenario.

Or so it would seem. A closer inspection of the model for the breaking shows, however, that the above reasoning is faulty. If Bruno's throw is removed from a veridical model for the breaking, the model no longer entails the breaking, even though Sylvie's throw remains.

How can this be? For the Bruno-less model to entail breaking, it must have the following form (copied over from the beginning of this section):

1. Sylvie threw her cannonball at time $t$ from such and such a point with such and such a velocity.

2. Nothing interfered with the trajectory of Sylvie's ball.

3. The vase was in such and such a position at time $t + 1$.

4. A statement of the causal laws in virtue of which a ball thrown in this fashion at time $t$ will strike a vase in this position at time $t + 1$ hard enough to break the vase, provided that nothing interferes with its flight.

In the case at hand, no such model can be veridical, because premise (2) is false: something did, in fact, interfere with the trajectory of Sylvie's ball, namely, Bruno's ball. Or to put it another way, no veridical model for the breaking can contain premise (2), therefore no veridical model that mentions only Sylvie's throw can entail the breaking. Bruno's throw is, according to the kairetic criterion, a difference-maker after all.

You might wonder whether there is not some other, even more devilish, preemption scenario for which this defense of the kairetic criterion is unavailable. There could not be such a case, as you will see if you take a step back to consider the constraints on its logical structure. To say that an event is both an actual and a backup cause is to say that the event belongs to two causal chains. The first of these chains was actualized and led to the occurrence of the explanandum. The second of these chains is subjunctive—it was not realized—but it would also have led to the occurrence of the explanandum, had it been actualized. A fatally devilish preemption case would have the following property: every veridical model $M$ for the explanandum that describes the actual causal chain would have to contain a submodel (a model whose setup is a subset of $M$'s setup) that entails that the subjunctive causal chain was realized. Because the subjunctive causal chain was, by definition, not realized, some proposition in the submodel's setup is false. But then some proposition—the same proposition, of course—in $M$'s setup is false, thus $M$ cannot be veridical after all. There is no fatally devilish counterexample, then, to the kairetic criterion.

Devilish preemption cases do cause problems for every other difference-making approach to explanatory relevance or high-level causation that I know of. The difficulties faced by some of Lewis's accounts of causation in the light of Sylvie and Bruno's colliding balls are laid out in Strevens (2003a). At the end of section 3.82, I suggested that devilish preemption will also cause trouble for the manipulation account of difference-making; a particularly simple counterexample is sketched in Strevens (2008a).

A word on the no-interference clause (2) in the causal model above for the vase's breaking. This should not be understood as a kind of all-purpose ceteris paribus crypto-teleological stand-in that any causal model can (and perhaps must) invoke. It is rather a specification of the precise physical conditions that must hold for a particular causal entailment to go through; in this case, they are the conditions required to make the transition from the specification of certain component forces in the model, in particular the force that gives the cannonball its initial velocity, to a conclusion about the net force impressed on the cannonball at each point in time along its trajectory, that is, between $t$ and $t + 1$.

As I remarked in section 3.23, in a broadly Newtonian world like ours, this is the most common way, perhaps the only way, for negative conditions to find their way into a causal entailment. That is, conditions of the "no-interference" variety find a place in causal models because, in order to make the transition from the fact that forces $x$, $y$, and $z$ acted on some object at some time to the fact that the total force on the object at that time was $x + y + z$, you must assume that $x$, $y$, and $z$ were the only relevant forces—that there were no other forces acting on the object at the time.

What about explanations that are less overtly physical? Assuming that the underlying causal process producing some high-level explanandum is deterministic, there must be a deterministic causal model for the production of the explanandum that characterizes the process at the physical level. Some of the facts specified by this model will be, for the reasons given in the last paragraph, negative states of affairs. Apply the kairetic optimizing procedure to the model. The specifications of these negative states of affairs may become quite abstract. But however abstract, or however detailed, they turn out to be, they are the explanatorily relevant absences, hence the "no-interference" conditions for the explanation in question. No further, shady "ceteris paribus" condition is required.

Nevertheless, the appearance of negative conditions in causal models may bring to mind some of the well known problems in specifying the content of a law statement's "ceteris paribus hedge." First, what if the negative conditions (or for that matter, some positive conditions) must be specified in a much lower-level, more physical language than the rest of the explanatory model? Answer: mixing levels might be intolerable in a law statement, but it is unobjectionable in a causal model. Second, what if the "no-interference" condition turns out to be infinitely long, as you might imagine it would have to be to rule out every kind of factor that might derail the process in question? Given the way that "no-interference" conditions arise in our world, I think that the chances of this are slight. A single, compact "no-other-forces" prohibition is quite capable of ruling out an infinitude of interfering factors. But it is possible, I suppose, to imagine a strange world in which the innumerably many possible interferers for some class of processes had nothing in common, and so whose absence had to be specified individually and therefore *ad infinitum*. The kairetic account implies that in such a world, certain standalone causal explanations would be infinitely long. But this is, I think, though inconvenient, intuitively quite correct.

### 6.23  Preemption: Counting the Backup Cause?

The classic problem raised by cases of preemption is the disempowerment of the actual cause: since the explanandum would have happened anyway, the actual cause looks not to make a difference. The kairetic criterion, and other similar tests such as Mackie's INUS criterion (section 3.83), face a different sort of problem as well: in cases of what Lewis called *late preemption*, the backup cause looks to count, incorrectly, as an actual cause.

Begin, then, with the paradigm of late preemption. Sylvie and Bruno both launch their cannonballs at the vase, Sylvie a little later than Bruno. Both are on target; because Bruno threw first, his ball reaches the vase first and breaks it, but had he not thrown, Sylvie's ball would have broken the vase instead.

The kairetic criterion counts the actual cause, Bruno's throw, as a difference-maker for the usual reason: there is a model for the breaking from which the throw cannot be removed without invalidating the entailment of the breaking, namely, the model that does not mention Sylvie and her cannonball at all.

But you might well think that the kairetic criterion counts Sylvie's throw, too, as a difference-maker: take the model in virtue of which Bruno's throw makes a difference, substitute *Sylvie* for *Bruno* in the premises, amend the times specified in the model to reflect the slightly later occurrence of Sylvie's throw, and you have a model that also entails the vase's breaking but lays the blame at Sylvie's dainty feet.

This reasoning goes through, however, only if the premises of the Bruno model remain true under the substitution. They do not. Among those premises, recall, is the following:

The vase was in such and such a position at time $t + 1$,

where $t$ is the time that the relevant ball was thrown and $t + 1$ is the time of the ball's arrival at the vase's position. (You should satisfy yourself that such a premise is required for the entailment of the breaking to go through.) The premise is true when $t$ is the time of Bruno's throw, but false when $t$ is the slightly later time of Sylvie's throw, since on the latter interpretation, at time $t + 1$ Bruno's ball has just broken the vase, so the vase is no longer in the appropriate (or any) place.

There is no veridical model, then, in which Sylvie's throw breaks the vase. It could not be otherwise: if there were such a model, then it would follow that the subjunctive causal pathway in virtue of which Sylvie's throw is a backup cause was actualized. But it was not actualized, therefore there is no such model.[3]

The same considerations apply to a problem raised in the discussion of Rasputin's poisoning back in section 3.43. Suppose that the Rasputin story is changed somewhat, so that he would eventually have succumbed to the poison in the teacakes. His killers are unsure that the poison will have the intended effect, so they throw him into the Neva, and he drowns. Here, influviation is the actual cause, poison a backup cause that would have killed Rasputin if the influviation had been somehow frustrated. Poison is not an actual cause because a causal model for poisoning must assert, in its setup, that the victim is still alive at the moment before the poison exerts its lethal effect. This premise of the poisoning model is, of course, false in the imagined Rasputin case.

Perhaps Sylvie's throw is a difference-maker in virtue of another model, however. I have in mind a model that contains, in place of the premise stating

The vase was in such and such a position at time $t + 1$,

(where $t$ is the time of Sylvie's throw) a premise stating

Either the vase broke at some time before $t + 1$, or the vase was in such and such a position at time $t + 1$.

This new premise is true, since Bruno's ball broke the vase before time $t + 1$, and in conjunction with the other premises from the model for Sylvie's throwing it entails what I take to be the explanandum: that the vase broke at or before time $t + 1$ (nothing hangs on the particular choice of time interval). Removing the premise describing Sylvie's throw will invalidate the entailment. Therefore, Sylvie's throw is, after all, counted as a difference-maker for the breaking, when it is in fact a backup cause.[4]

If the model above is a veridical causal model, then the kairetic criterion for difference-making is in trouble. It is, as I have said, veridical, but it is not causal: its entailment of its target, the vase's breaking at or before time $t + 1$, is not a causal entailment. To see this informally, observe that the entailment does not in any way represent, or even mention, the actual causal process by which the vase was broken—Bruno's throw, you will recall.

To see the same more formally, go back to the definition of causal entailment in section 3.23. On that definition, a high-level deterministic model causally entails its target just in case every concretization of that model causally entails its target. Consider a particular subset of concretizations, those that describe a situation where the vase is broken, somehow, at time $t$, and so where Sylvie's ball arrives too late to break the vase. In these models, the explanandum—the fact that the vase is broken at or before time $t + 1$—is entailed by the fact of the vase's being broken at precisely time $t$. It is this entailment that must be causal if the concretizations are to causally entail their targets. Obviously, however, the entailment is not causal at all, but purely mathematical; more exactly, the derivation of the explanandum does not go by way of modus ponens applied to a causal law.

You might tweak the example so as to involve a causal law, as follows. Let the explanandum be the vase's lying on the floor in pieces at time $t + 1$. Then the vase's being broken at some previous time does not on its own entail the explanandum; something would have to be added to the effect that vases do not spontaneously reassemble themselves (together with a negative condition specifying that no itinerant vase repairman came by before $t + 1$, or the equivalent). A case might be made that the principle excluding spontaneous reassembly is a causal law, perhaps because it is true in part in virtue of the gravitational force pinning the individual vase shards to the floor. But then you have a concrete causal model whichever way the vase is broken: if Bruno's throw (or some other process) breaks the vase before time $t$, the causal entailment goes by way of the anti-reassembly law, whereas if the vase is intact at $t + 1$, so that it is broken by Sylvie's throw, the causal entailment goes by way of the usual laws of breaking.

What is wrong with a disjunctive model that can be realized by either of these two different processes? It is a causal model, in that it represents a causal process—or rather, two or more causal processes. But there lies the problem: it is not a cohesive causal model. It is unexplanatory for the same reason that the model for Rasputin's death that cites his being either poisoned or influviated is unexplanatory: it fails to specify determinately the causal process that led to the occurrence of the explanandum (section 3.6).

The factors it cites as difference-makers—Sylvie's throw in particular—therefore do not in virtue of their citation qualify as causes, any more than poisoning counts as a difference-maker for Rasputin's demise because it is mentioned in the poisoning-or-influviation description of his death by drowning.[5]

### 6.24  Overdetermination

Related to cases of preemption are cases of overdetermination. When Bruno's and Sylvie's cannonballs strike the vase simultaneously, they over-determine its breaking: either ball on its own would be enough to break the vase, and neither seems to have causal precedence over the other. (Lewis (1986c) called this symmetric overdetermination.)

Notoriously, our judgments about causehood are insecure when effects are overdetermined. Should we say that Bruno's throw, Sylvie's throw, both, or neither are difference-makers, hence causes, for the breaking? There is no reason to favor one throw over the other, and to say that neither throw is a cause of the breaking leaves it uncaused; most writers have settled, then, on the view that each overdetermining event is a cause in its own right (Schaffer 2003). There is something not quite intuitively right about this answer, however; we feel that the presence of Sylvie's throw, while not entirely undermining the status of Bruno's throw as difference-maker and cause, does weaken it, and vice versa. Is there any way to explain this sense of causal compromise?

At first blush, the kairetic criterion for difference-making reproduces the majority view about overdeterminers: all are difference-makers, so all are causes. In the case at hand there exists a model for the breaking from which Bruno's throw cannot be removed without invalidating the entailment of the target—namely, the model that says nothing about Sylvie's throw at all—and a parallel model for which the same is true of Sylvie's throw. Both throws, then, count as difference-makers.

But there is more to be said. Begin with the model containing Bruno's throw, and apply the optimizing procedure. As explained in section 3.5, the model's specification of exact values for various parameters will be replaced by specifications of a range of values. These ranges will be calculated so that they are just sufficient to guarantee that Bruno's cannonball hits the vase hard enough to break it. Applying the optimizing procedure to a model for Sylvie's throw will produce a similar model, saying just enough about Sylvie's ball to entail that it hits and breaks the vase.

The two optimized models are, I suggest, indistinguishable. They state that a thrown cannonball, with such and such physical parameters, hit and broke the vase. Both the process of Bruno's ball's hitting the vase and the process of Sylvie's ball's hitting the vase satisfy the description of either model. What such a model identifies as a difference-maker, then, is not the fact that some particular ball, say Bruno's, hit the vase, but rather the fact that some ball satisfying a certain description hit the vase, where both Bruno's and Sylvie's balls satisfy the description. Thus, neither model determinately identifies one of the throws in particular as a difference-maker—they are agreed that there was a throw that was a difference-maker, but they do not say enough to decide which throw.

This, I propose, accounts for the unsteady phenomenology of overdetermination. There is no optimal model in virtue of which Bruno's throw is determinately a difference-maker for the breaking, nor is there an optimal model in virtue of which Sylvie's throw is determinately a difference-maker. There is a model in virtue of which a certain kind of throw was determinately a difference-maker—but that throw is not determinately Bruno's nor determinately Sylvie's.[6]

Let me remind you that the difference-makers for a high-level event are always, on the kairetic approach, other high-level events or states of affairs, not particular objects or concrete events. It is in some sense misleading, even in the most straightforward cases, to say that it is Bruno's ball that made a difference to the breaking, since it is not the ball or some concrete thing that the ball does, but rather a high-level property of the ball-involving causal web, that is the difference-maker. Normally, the web has the relevant high-level property in virtue of some particular thing or concrete process, and it is safe to call that thing or process the difference-maker. Occasionally, however, as in cases of overdetermination, this is not true: the web determinately has the property—containing a certain sort of throw, for example—but there is no determinate single thing or process in virtue of which it has the property.[7]

A breaking overdetermined by simultaneous throws is a relatively rare occurrence, but look beyond acts of destruction and you will see that overdetermination is commonplace. The particles that make up the earth jointly determine the approximate orbit of the moon, for example, but there are many (large) subsets of these particles that would be sufficient in themselves to determine the same approximate orbit. We do not say, however, that each such subset separately makes a difference to the orbit's being approximately what it is. Rather, what makes a difference is a single fact about the earth, its having a certain approximate mass and geometry.

### 6.25  Ceteris Similibus Difference-Making

I am in the habit of leaving my cannonball on a small glass table in the foyer. The table can only take so much weight: a cannonball weighing 5 kg or more will cause it to crack and break. Fortunately, my cannonball has a hollow center and weighs only 4 kg, so the table is able to support it.

One day you fill my cannonball's hollow center with 1 kg of sand. I put it on the table, and the table breaks. Clearly, your filling the hollow with sand is a difference-maker for the breaking, in virtue of a model containing the following specifications, among others, in its setup:

1. My cannonball weighed at least $x$ kg.
2. You filled the cannonball with at least $y$ kg of sand.
3. $x + y \geq 5$.
4. I placed the cannonball on the table, which will break if the ball's total weight $x + y$ is 5 kg or more.

The filling with sand is a difference-maker because premise (2) cannot be removed without invalidating the entailment of the breaking.

You should immediately see, however, that the same model is realized by cases in which my cannonball already weighed 5 kg but you filled it with sand nevertheless. In such a case, we are inclined to say that your filling the ball with sand made no difference to the breaking, yet there is a model for the breaking—the model in the last paragraph—from which the filling cannot be removed. The kairetic criterion for difference-making apparently pronounces, contrary to our inclinations, that the filling made a difference after all.

How to resolve this apparent counterexample to the kairetic criterion? Is there some abstraction of the above model for the breaking that does not contain the filling? Such a model would have to put a 5 kg lower limit on the ball's unfilled weight. But in so doing, it would be in one respect less general than the model above. Thus, there is no such abstraction. The above model is optimal, and in virtue of its optimality, the filling with sand is a difference-maker for the breaking.

Let me argue that this is not nearly so unintuitive as you might think. A ball made up of 5 kg of iron and 1 kg of sand sits on a table. The table cannot take 5 kg or more of weight; thus, it cracks and breaks. Is the sand a difference-maker for the breaking? It is surely as much a difference-maker as any other 1 kg chunk of the ball. From a purely scientific viewpoint, it would be invidious to pick out the sand as a non-difference-maker rather than, say, the outermost 1 kg of iron. The sand is a difference-maker for the breaking, then, thus it is not so strange to say that the process that is responsible for the sand's being in a position to make a difference—its being placed in the ball—is also a difference-maker.

(Because the breaking is to some degree overdetermined, it is not quite correct to insist that the sand is determinately a difference-maker, for the reasons given in section 6.24 above. The true difference-maker is the ball's weighing at least 5 kg; the actual world contains many realizers of this state of affairs—every proper part of the ball weighing at least 5 kg—one of which does not include any sand. Thus, while it is certainly wrong to say that the sand is determinately a non-difference-maker, it is also wrong to say that it determinately makes a difference. The status of the filling of the ball as a difference-maker inherits this nebulosity—a complication that I will ignore.)

The problem is not entirely solved, however. On the one hand, given the transitivity of difference-making and the fact that filling the ball with sand made a difference to the presence of the sand, the filling should be a difference-maker for the table's breaking regardless of the weight of the cannonball, but on the other hand, it seems clearly correct to say that your filling my 5 kg cannonball with sand made no difference to the breaking. How can this be?

The latter difference-making claim—that the filling of the 5 kg ball was not a difference-maker—belongs, I propose, to a genre of claims made within a certain kind of explanatory framework, namely, a framework in which everything except the state of affairs whose difference-making status is under examination has its actual value (with the exception of some or all of the causal consequences of this state of affairs). In evaluating a difference-making claim relative to this framework, then, the precise actual states of all elements of the world not causally downstream from the state of affairs in question figure in the model as an unchangeable causal backdrop. When all of the causal consequences of the focal state of affairs are left unfixed, the effect is much like that of the counterfactual criterion for evaluating causal claims. When only the downstream consequences on a particular causal pathway are left unfixed, the effect is more like that of the Woodward criterion (sections 2.5 and 3.82). More on this shortly.

Relative to a framework in which most things have their exact actual value—I call it a *ceteris similibus* framework—the exact weight of the cannonball is specified in any model for the table's breaking. If this weight is enough on its own to entail the breaking, the ball's being filled with sand can be removed from such a model. In the ceteris similibus framework, then, filling a ball of 5 kg or more is not a difference-maker. When we say that filling the 5 kg cannonball with sand made no difference to the breaking, we make a ceteris similibus claim. The same claim made independently of a framework is false.

When are facts about ceteris similibus difference-making useful? In cases where a particular effect is sought and all factors but one are outside of human control, or where blame is to be attributed and all factors but one are in place at the time of the putatively blameworthy action. In both cases, the question is one of predicting the effect of an action in a causal context that is for practical purposes almost entirely fixed.

A proponent of the counterfactual or manipulation criterion for difference-making might complain that I am rejecting their ideas with one hand only to appropriate them with the other. That is, I advance my own criterion of difference-making to handle some cases, but to handle others I defer to the counterfactual or manipulation criteria because they give a better answer.

Such an interpretation of my dual strategy misses the fact that there is a genuine duality in the cannonball case: on the one hand, in everyday discourse we say that filling the cannonball with sand makes no difference to the table's breaking, while on the other hand, in a more scientific frame of mind we agree that there is no sense in which the sand is less of a difference-maker than the rest of the ball. To propose that two different difference-making relations are at work is hardly ad hoc. (In any case, the ceteris similibus relation introduces nothing genuinely new; it simply draws attention to a particular kind of explanatory framework.)

Indeed, precisely because the counterfactual and manipulation accounts confer difference-making status on the filling, they give the wrong answer about the difference-making status of the sand itself. More generally, these rival accounts deny that the overdetermining causes are difference-makers. They therefore endorse the conclusion that in the case of a 6 kg cannonball, each kilogram of ball considered on its own makes no difference to the table's breaking (since in considering a kilogram's causal role, they hold constant the effect of the other 5 kg). Yet the 6 kg of matter considered as a whole does turn out to make a difference, despite the fact that its (smaller) parts do not, and that the causal power of the whole is a simple aggregate of the causal power of the parts. The province of overdetermination is not a good place for the counterfactualist or the manipulationist to make a stand.

An application: in an election, does your bothering to vote make a difference? If your candidate wins by a majority of two votes or more, then your vote was not a ceteris similibus difference-maker. But it was still causally relevant, in the same somewhat ghostly way that the individual kilograms of a 6 kg cannonball, or any individual overdeterminers, are relevant to the event that they overdetermine.

### 6.3   Nonevents as Difference-Makers

We are happy to say *c was a cause of e* in many cases where *c* is the absence of some state of affairs or the nonoccurrence of some event. (*Absence* is the more general term, but the causation literature has fixed on *omission*, so I follow suit here, designating by that word not only certain behaviors of intentional agents but any causal absence at all.) Our frequent practice of citing omissions as causes, or equivalently, as difference-makers, raises two questions. First, you might wonder how there could be such a thing as causation by omission, given that an absence cannot exert a causal influence. Second, if causation by omission is allowed, there will—so it seems—be an ugly explosion of causes. To deploy the paradigm case, if my failing to water my flowers caused them to die, why not say that your failing to water my flowers also caused them to die, and so on for every living human, so that there are six billion or so separate failures that cause the flowers' death?

### 6.31   The Possibility of Explanatory Omissions

On the causal approach to event explanation, to explain an event is to give some of its causes, along with the laws and background conditions in virtue of which they are causes. What role, then, can an absence play in a causal explanation?

The answer should be clear from the treatment of the Rasputin case in section 3.4 and the treatment of preemption in section 6.2. The background conditions that need to be satisfied in order for a causal process to run to completion always, or at the very least almost always, require certain absences. In order for poisoning to count as a cause of Rasputin's death, it had to be the case that—among other things—he had not taken an antidote. In order for Sylvie's cannonball to count as a cause of the Ming vase's breaking, it had to be the case that nothing diverted the ball from its trajectory. These absences are a necessary part of the explanatory kernels for the explananda in question; if they were not specified in the setups, the kernels would not entail their targets. I have even gone so far as to designate the negative conditions' holding as a "causal influence," in an admittedly extenuated sense (section 1.42).

Consider a particular example of absences as explainers. A traffic signal fails to function. As a result, a freight train does not stop at a crossing and collides with a passenger train. A causal model for the crash that describes the railway traffic in the few minutes before the crash will specify the positions and speeds of the two trains and the layout of the tracks. In order to entail the occurrence of the collision, the model will have to specify that nothing, in particular no signal, slowed or stopped the freight train. This absence of a signal will therefore be a part of the explanation of the collision, and so it will be correct to say that the failure of the signal was a cause of the collision.

In this way, an absence $c$ can be a difference-maker for, hence a cause of, an event $e$ (cf. Thomson 2003). Many other events may come to be causes of $e$ because they are causes of the absence of $c$. A short-circuit may have caused the signal to fail; the short-circuit thereby becomes a cause of the collision. A failure to inspect the signal may have caused the short-circuit; a medical emergency may have caused the inspection to have been delayed; an absence of antibodies may have caused the emergency. All are causes of the collision by way of a nonevent, the lack of a signal. (Schaffer (1999) argues that absences play an important role in many more causal chains than you might expect.)

Some writers complain that attributing a role in a causal process to an absence is "spooky." I am tempted to respond that it seems less spooky when causal claims are understood as explanatory claims, and absences as explainers rather than as raw metaphysical causers. But I believe that in most imaginable physics, including both Newtonian physics and the physics of our own universe, even the raw metaphysics of causation must make space for absences, typically in the metaphysics of causal composition (see sections 3.23 and 7.43).

## 6.32  The Proliferation of Explanatory Omissions

The failure of the railway signal to operate is a necessary condition for the trains to collide. But so, it would seem, is the failure of a nearby goat to wander onto the tracks, since the goat would have been just as effective as the signal in causing the train to slow; thus, any model that neglects to rule out the possibility of a wandering goat fails to entail the collision. Why are we so much more inclined to cite the absence of the signal than the absence of the goat as a difference-maker for, or a cause of, the collision?

Call a nonevent, such as the goat's not wandering onto the tracks, that both (a) seems necessary for an event *e* to occur yet (b) is not normally counted as a cause of *e*, an *irrelevant omission* (because we count such omissions as causally or explanatorily irrelevant).

Irrelevant omissions are just as much of a problem for counterfactual and other difference-making accounts of causal claims as for the kairetic account. Two solutions to—or rather ameliorations of—the problem are typically canvassed:

1. Omissions, relevant or otherwise, are never genuine causes. There may be thousands of irrelevant omissions that are, in some sense, necessary for an event *e* to occur and so make a difference to *e*'s occurrence, but precisely because they are absences, they cannot be real causes of *e*. Thus, our reluctance to cite them as such (Dowe 2000, chap. 6).

2. Irrelevant omissions are genuine causes. If we do not cite them, it is for practical reasons: they are generally of no interest to our interlocutors (Lewis 2000, 196).

On the first of these views, our causal claims about omissions mean something radically different from our other causal claims. Yet there is nothing in our practice of making the claims to indicate this sort of duality.

The second answer is also an uncomfortable one. The world is full, on this view, of negative causes, but provided you do not ask about them, I will not mention them, and we can conduct ourselves as though the causal web is agreeably sparse. This does not sit well, in any case, with a tendency to deny the causal power of irrelevant omissions, to be illustrated below.

I will endorse a third, superior approach to the problem of irrelevant omissions, broadly similar to the account developed by McGrath (2005). Suppose that there were a number of farm animals in the vicinity of the railway tracks at the time of the collision. Had any of these animals wandered onto the tracks at the right place and the right time, the freight train would have slowed and the collision would not have occurred. The absence of each animal, then, is a necessary condition for the collision. If there are one hundred animals, are there one hundred negative causes of the collision?

The kairetic account says not. In pursuit of the most abstract possible model entailing the collision, the kairetic account will cite, not the absence of each farm animal, one by one, but simply the fact that no animal or other obstacle blocked the tracks. Rather than one hundred distinct negative causes, then, the kairetic account finds a single negative cause.

This observation is, however, not sufficient to account for all aspects of our omissions-citing practice. Consider again the paradigm case. My flowers have died; I did not water them. Had I watered them, they would have lived. But equally, had you watered them they would have lived; for that matter, had the provost watered them, they would have lived. The flowers' death, then, depends in the right way on many omissions: mine, yours, the provost's. The kairetic account tidies up this proliferation of absences by producing a kernel that cites only a single negative fact: no one watered the flowers.

The attribution of the flowers' death to a single vast act of collective negligence does not, however, reflect the causal claims we make in such a case. It is true, we would usually say, that my failure to water the flowers caused their death. It is not true that the provost's failure to water the flowers caused their death. As for you, it depends on your relationship to me and to the flowers. If we live together in a state of mutual horticultural responsibility, it is probably correct to say that your not watering the flowers was a cause of their death; if you are an anonymous reader of this book whom I have never met, then you no more caused the flowers' death than the provost. The question of responsibility seems important here: if I am away on vacation and I have arranged that you water my flowers, then your not watering them is a cause of their death but my not watering them is irrelevant.

How to make sense of this? Surely practical concerns must be invoked. Yet it is not right to say, with Lewis, that all of these absences are causes but only some are contextually salient. If you are asked, "Was the provost's failure to water the pansies a cause of their death?" you do not reply, "Yes, but I would not normally think to mention it"; you reply, "Not really," or simply "No." This fact must be explained.

I appeal, as I did in the case of background conditions (section 6.1), to the presence of an explanatory framework containing certain facts that are to be "taken as given" for the purposes of the explanation. Some absences do not qualify as causes in virtue of their being taken as given by the explanatory request; as explained in section 5.3, such states of affairs, though they are represented as holding in every explanatory model, are never themselves part of an explanation. We take it as given that the provost did not water the flowers; perhaps we take it as given that only I might have watered the flowers. If so, then the sole nonwatering that can count as a cause is my nonwatering. Similarly, we take it as given that no animal happened to wander onto the railway tracks at exactly the right time to forestall an accident; we do not take it as given that the signal was faulty. Thus, the signal's failure to slow the train, but not sundry goats', is a cause of the collision.

In everyday explanatory contexts, then, the framework will tend to carve a causal model's "one big negative condition" into two parts, one part explanatorily live and one part inert. The fact of no one's watering the flowers, for example, is divided into my not watering the flowers—unframeworked and therefore live—and everyone else's not watering the flowers, frameworked and thus, despite its presence in the causal model, explanatorily dormant.

How are the relevant explanatory frameworks constructed? As I suggested in my treatment of background conditions, statistically normal conditions known by all interlocutors to make a difference are usually placed in the framework. This is especially true for statistically normal absences: for explanatory purposes, we take it as given that the provost did not wander onto the railway tracks at just the right time, and that the goat did not water the flowers, because these events are so unlikely, and thus because their absence, or rather the negative state of affairs for which their absence is a necessary condition—nothing serendipitously on the tracks, no unexpected waterings—is in every relevant scenario acknowledged as a difference-maker, hence denied framework-relative causal status, by all parties to the explanatory inquiry. (There is, I should add, an obvious practical justification for our interest in difference-making relative to framework that "hides" normal absences.)

Since the role of the framework in determining what omissions count as causes is far more dramatic than its role in determining what difference-makers count as background conditions, let me urge again the argument advanced in section 6.1, that the impact of the conversational agenda on the acceptability of causal claims provides strong evidence that the relation asserted by such claims is not a purely metaphysical two-place relation between cause and effect, but rather a three-place causal-explanatory relation that makes room for a framework.

In section 6.1, I proposed that explanation in a theoretical context is typically framework independent. Does it follow that in a textbook explanation all absences necessary for the causal production of an event *e* are causes of *e*? Yes. The *scientific explanation* of the flowers' death does not, I suggest, distinguish the explanatory importance of the provost's and my non-waterings. What is important is that the plants were not watered. Everyone's failure to water contributes equally to our scientific understanding of that sadly barren outcome.

## 6.4 Nonevents as Explananda

Claims can be made about the difference-makers for or causes of negative events; for example, a leak might have caused the fuel tank to be empty this morning. But a negative event such as *there being no fuel in the tank this morning* cannot be causally connected to anything; how then, can it be the target of a causal model? There are two somewhat different classes of negative explananda to distinguish. In the first, a state of affairs used to hold but is *caused no longer to hold*, as in the case of the fuel tank that went from full to empty. In the second, the state of affairs is *prevented* from holding. (Some writers call both prevention.) I will discuss these two kinds of explananda separately, with the treatment of prevention invoking the prior treatment of causing-no-longer-to-hold. I use the high-level causal idiom throughout, but, of course, I take my conclusions to be in the first instance about difference-making and explanation.

## 6.41 Causing-No-Longer-to-Hold

Begin with the suggestion that to cause a state of affairs $e$ not to hold is to cause some other state of affairs $f$ that entails that $e$ does not hold. This account is far from adequate. Suppose that I caused there to be no fuel in the tank this morning by siphoning it out last night. I then put the fuel in a jar in the refrigerator. You come along this morning and, feeling thirsty, look in the refrigerator; you see the jar of fuel. Your thirst causes an event, seeing the fuel in the refrigerator this morning, that entails that the fuel is not in the tank. But your thirst is not responsible for the tank's emptiness.

The suggested account requires two amendments. First, as you have seen, it is wrong to require of a cause of $e$'s no longer holding only that it helps produce an event that entails the negation of $e$. That would implicate all witnesses to the deed, however innocent. Rather, I suggest, a cause must produce an event that entails the negation of $e$ in a very particular—a causal—way. Let $e$ be the event of the object $x$ having property $F$ at $t$. Then what must be causally entailed is that $x$ has the property $G$ at $t$, for some $G$ chosen so that it is not physically possible for an object to have $F$ and $G$ at the same time. (It might be better to say: where $F$ and $G$ are different determinates of the same determinable.) The account of causing-no-longer-to-hold becomes: $c$ causes $x$ not to have $F$ at $t$ just in case $c$ causes $x$ to have an incompatible property $G$ at $t$. In the case of the fuel, the property in question is one of position. My siphoning causes the fuel to move to a new position; your seeing the fuel does not. Thus, my siphoning, but not your seeing, is a cause of the fuel's not being located in the tank.

But this is not quite right either; a second amendment is needed. Suppose you drink the fuel in the refrigerator. Then you have changed the position of the fuel, but you still have nothing to do with the fuel not being in the tank. Your fuel-quaffing makes no difference to whether or not the fuel is in the tank, because the difference has already been made. The second amendment requires that a cause $c$ be part of a causal process over the duration of which $x$ goes from having $F$ to having $G$. One further clause—this must be the last time before $t$ that $x$ goes from having $F$ to having $G$—takes care of cases where the fuel is removed from the tank then replaced. Only the final removal counts.

In summary, then, $c$ causes $e$ no longer to hold, where $e$ is the event of $x$ having a property $F$ at time $t$, just in case $c$ is a difference-making part of a causal process that produces the event of $x$ going from having $F$ to having some physically incompatible property $G$ for the last time before $t$. An explanatory model for a causing-no-longer-to-hold, then, is a standard kairetic model with a very particular kind of target event.

### 6.42 Prevention

Bruno hurls a cannonball through a doorway at a Ming vase. Sylvie slams the door as the cannonball flies toward it. The cannonball bounces off the door and the vase is saved. Sylvie has prevented the vase from being broken. You might think that prevention is a causal notion: to prevent the vase's breaking is to cause the vase not to be broken. But the apparent effect here—the vase's integrity—though capable enough of being causally produced, is not something that Sylvie is in a position to cause, for all her pixie powers: the vase's integrity was produced, as it were, long ago at the vase factory.

What kind of causal process, then, is prevention? I propose the following account (similar in spirit to a number of treatments in the literature, e.g., Dowe 2000, §6.4, though it differs in the details):

> $c$ prevents $e$ just in case (a) $c$ obstructs a causal process that would otherwise have led to $e$ and (b) $e$ did not occur.

Clause (b) is needed only because *prevent* is a success term: no matter how hard you try, you cannot be said to have prevented $e$ if $e$ occurred. The discussion in the rest of this section will focus on clause (a).

An event $c$ obstructs a causal process that would otherwise have led to $e$, I propose, under the following conditions. First, there must be a causal model for $e$ that is veridical except for one element $d$ of its setup—in other words, a model that represents a causal process that would have led to $e$ if only that one element $d$ were present (and nothing else was changed). Second, $c$ must either have prevented $d$ from occurring or must have caused it no longer to hold. The appearance of the notion of prevention in the second condition makes the definition recursive. Because the recursion must end, I am committed to the claim that all preventions are eventually grounded in causings-no-longer-to-hold.

What is the structure, then, of a prevention explanation, that is, of the sort of explanation of an event $e$'s nonoccurrence that licences claims about preventers of $e$? There are two aspects of such explanations that merit comment. First, a prevention explanation of $e$'s nonoccurrence will have two parts: a standalone explanation of *e* that is veridical except for one state of affairs *d*, and a standalone explanation either for the prevention of *d* or for *d*'s coming no longer to hold. (If *d* is prevented then this second explanation will itself have two parts, and so on; see below.) Like a contrastive explanation, a prevention explanation has a nonstandard structure: it contains standalone explanations for two different targets.

Second, the parts of the standalone explanation of *e*, though they occur in the prevention explanation of *e*'s nonoccurrence, are not regarded as difference-makers for the nonoccurrence. Sylvie's slamming the door so as to deflect the cannonball helps to explain why the vase was not broken, but Bruno's throwing the cannonball in the first place does not. The difference-makers in a prevention explanation, then, are drawn exclusively from just one of its two parts, namely, the model for *d*'s coming no longer to hold (for the case where *d* is prevented, see below). This is true, I suggest, because in prevention explanation, the forestalled *e*-producing process is frameworked. An explanation of the nonoccurrence of *e* that cites a preventer *c* is always an explanation of the fact that *e* failed to occur *given that* an *e*-producing process was—nearly—operational. (In general, a frameworked element can be omitted from an explanatory model, being replaced by a black box; in a prevention explanation, I think, this option is not allowed, or at least is heavily circumscribed.)

If *d*, the element that would have secured *e*'s production, is prevented rather than caused-no-longer-to-hold, then the comments above continue to apply in an appropriately nested way. The model for *d*'s prevention will itself have two parts; one of these may in turn have two parts, and so on down to the point where the prevention is ultimately grounded in a model for a causing-no-longer-to-hold. Everything other than this model is frameworked, thus, only the elements of the explanation that participate in the causing-no-longer-to-hold count as difference-makers for *e*'s nonoccurrence.

## 6.5   Transitivity

The difference-making relation is transitive (section 4.2) and causal claims assert relations of difference-making (this chapter). Therefore, *is a cause of* is transitive: if *c* is a cause of *d* and *d* is a cause of *e*, then *c* is a cause of *e*. A number of philosophers have presented putative counterexamples to the transitivity of causal claims. Let me attempt to defuse them.

## 6.51  Misconnection

A *misconnection* counterexample to transitivity (Dowe's term (2000)) is one in which the event $d$ that is caused by $c$ turns out, on closer examination, not to be the same as the event $d$ that causes $e$. That $c$ does not cause $e$, then, does not constitute a violation of transitivity.

McDermott (1995, 531) gives the following example. A goat bites off the provost's right index finger. When he later hurls a cannonball at the chair of philosophy, the provost must use his left hand. The goat bite is a cause of the provost's hurling the cannonball using his left hand, and his hurling the cannonball using his left hand causes the chair to duck, but the goat bite is not a cause of the chair's ducking.

Or so the argument goes. It is true that the provost's hurling the ball with his left hand was caused by the goat bite. But the slightly more abstract event of hurling the ball (with some body part or other) was not caused by the bite. It is the latter event, however, that causes the chair to duck. In kairetic terms, the fact that the cannonball-hurling was effected with the *left hand* would be removed from any causal model for the chair's ducking, and so declared irrelevant to the entailment of the ducking. Thus, the goat bite did not cause the event that caused the chair to duck, so transitivity does not demand that the goat bite caused the chair to duck.[8]

## 6.52  Forestalled Threats

An event $c$ sets in motion a chain of events that threatens either to prevent $e$ or to cause $e$ no longer to hold. However, $c$ also causes an event $d$ that forestalls this chain of events, and $e$ occurs after all. Such "forestalled threat" scenarios invite us to say that $c$ causes $d$ and $d$ causes $e$, but that contrary to the kairetic account's claim of transitivity, $c$ is not a cause of $e$. A philosophically popular example (Hitchcock 2001a, 276): the provost hurls a cannonball at the chair of philosophy, who ducks. The cannonball misses the chair; had it hit, he would have been struck dead. The cannonball is a cause of the chair's ducking, and his ducking is a cause of his survival, yet the cannonball is not a cause of the chair's survival—intransitively so.

In what follows I show that the three causal claims in question are made with respect to different explanatory frameworks. Most importantly, the claim that the ducking caused (or better, explained) the survival is made relative to a framework that includes the cannonball's being hurled, whereas the claim that the cannonball caused the ducking is made relative to a framework that excludes the hurling. The kairetic account implies only intra-framework transitivity—that is, transitivity relative to a fixed explanatory background. Thus, forestalled threat scenarios do not counterexemplify the kind of transitivity to which the kairetic account is committed.

Let me go through all of that more slowly. First, to show that the framework for the ducking's explaining the survival contains the hurling: To say that the ducking causes or explains the chair's survival strikes us as equivalent to saying that the ducking causes or explains the chair's survival *given that* a cannonball was flying toward his head. This reveals that we understand the causal claim as being made within an explanatory framework containing the cannonball-hurling. It is easy to see why: the very term *survival* presupposes a threat to the chair's life—in the case at hand, the flying cannonball—and so inserts that threat into the explanatory framework. (In the absence of a threat, it is unnatural to talk about the causes of survival; if necessary, we talk rather about the mechanisms that sustain life.) You might equally well make the point as follows. The claim that the chair's ducking caused his survival is nothing but an awkward formulation of the claim that the chair's ducking prevented his death. In an explanation of the prevention of $e$, the would-be causers of $e$—in this case, the events that threaten death, above all the hurling of the cannonball—are frameworked (section 6.42). Thus, the claim that ducking causes death is relative to a framework containing the hurling.

Second, to show that the cannonball-hurling cannot appear in the framework for the hurling's causing the ducking: Nothing can be a difference-maker, and thus a cause, if it is itself frameworked. Any claim about the causal status of the cannonball-hurling, then, must be made relative to a hurling-free framework. (This is true even of negative claims: relative to a framework containing $c$, you can neither affirm nor deny that $c$ is a cause of $e$. Questions about its explanatory standing are simply off limits.)

Third, to show that the transitivity of difference-making holds only within a fixed framework: Suppose that $c$ causes $d$, which causes $e$, relative to some framework or other. Then it is easy to find a different framework with respect to which $c$ does not cause $e$, namely, a framework containing $c$. This trivial construction violates none of the precepts of kairetic explanation; therefore, the kairetic account cannot require transitivity across frameworks. Or to take a different approach: The transitivity of difference-making followed originally from an argument that any element in a standalone explanation for *e* is a difference-maker for *e*. The argument implies transitivity across frameworks only if standalone explanations can mix and match frameworks, that is, if they can comprise some kernels relative to one framework and some relative to another (or none at all). But such an explanation would be incoherent, as it would pronounce inconsistently about any element that appears in one framework but not others, saying that its explanatory status is both on and off the table. A single standalone explanation can have at most one explanatory framework; the kairetic account is therefore committed only to intra-framework transitivity, as claimed.

In the cannonball case, then, transitivity does not mandate that the cannonball explains the chair's survival. More generally, in any case of forestalled threat, I propose that when we credit the forestaller with making a difference to the explanandum, we do so in a framework containing the threat—we say that the forestaller made its difference *given that* the threat was present—while when we say that the threat-initiator caused the forestalling action, we do so in a different framework that does not contain the threat. The two causal claims do not, then, by transitivity falsely imply that the threat-initiator caused the explanandum.

You might well wonder how things come out when the causal roles of the cannonball-hurling, the ducking, and the chair's survival are assessed independently of any framework.

The hurling is, as I have said already, a framework-independent cause of the chair's ducking. The open question, then, is whether either or both the cannonball-hurling and the ducking are framework-independent causes of the chair's survival. But that is the wrong way to pose the problem, since, as I have remarked, the very term *survival* presupposes and thus frameworks a threat. Perhaps I should ask whether the hurling and ducking cause the chair to go on living? More awkwardness. It is best, perhaps, to return to the explanatory idiom. Do the hurling or the ducking help to explain the chair's continuing to live?

To see that something about the cannonball is indeed explanatorily relevant to the chair's continued existence, consider a causal model that has this event as its target. It will consist for the most part of an enumeration of the various essential bodily processes: respiration, circulation, and so on. It will also include a negative condition, ruling out serious bodily trauma. By implication, this condition will place constraints on the trajectories of various large objects—boulders, meteorites, SUVs—relative to the chair's more vulnerable parts. The chair's ongoing good health can therefore be explained in part by a model that has as its target some particular object's conforming to these constraints—for example, it can be partially explained by an explanatory model having as its target the fact of the cannonball's trajectory falling into the allowed class.

The same is true for the ducking, which by altering the chair's position makes a difference to the class into which the trajectories of the cannonball and other large objects must fall if the negative condition for the chair's continued existence is to be satisfied. The trajectories of both the cannonball and the chair himself are explanatorily relevant to the chair's continued existence, then, and the fact about them that makes the difference is their not intersecting. The hurling and the ducking contribute to the explanation insofar as they make a difference to the trajectories' having this property of nonintersection. It is unlikely that, when the process of abstraction is completed, they will be mentioned by name, but because the nonintersection condition puts constraints on their behaviors, they are in some sense explanatorily relevant.

Would we say, in a framework-independent state of mind, that the hurling or the ducking caused the chair's continued existence? For the purposes of capturing relations of explanatory relevance at this level of abstraction, causal claims are a crude tool (as the case of overdetermination shows). But it should be clear that the two cases are relevantly similar, and thus that they should be treated the same way: if the ducking is classed as a cause, the hurling should be too—a fact that forecloses any possibility of finding in framework-independent causation a counterexample to transitivity.[9]

You might find yourself asking again how anything about the hurling could be a cause of the chair's not dying. Let me try a less abstract answer. You can imagine a situation in which the provost fakes out the chair: the chair ducks but the provost launches the cannonball toward his new location, killing him regardless. The fact that the actual hurling did not impart *that* sort of trajectory to the ball is clearly relevant to the chair's continued existence—and this is, of course, precisely the fact about the hurling that I claim is explanatorily relevant.

### 6.53 Switching

An event $e$ might occur by one of two causal pathways. A crucial step partway along the first pathway is an event $d$. The event $c$—the switch—determines which pathway is taken: if $c$ occurs, the first pathway is taken (and $d$ occurs); if a certain alternative to $c$ occurs, the second pathway is taken (and $d$ does not occur). The occurrence of $c$, it seems, causes $d$, which in turn causes $e$. But we are not inclined to say that $c$ causes $e$, since whether $c$ occurred or not, $e$ would have occurred.[10]

To construct an example, I will need to call on all our little friends. Suppose that Sylvie and Bruno have kidnapped the provost. They toss a coin to determine their next move: heads they feed him to the goat, tails they throw him into the Neva with his hands and feet bound. It does not matter how the coin lands; neither method can fail to kill him. The coin lands tails, they throw him into the river, and he drowns. It seems that the coin's landing tails caused the provost to be thrown into the river, and that his being thrown into the river caused his death. But it seems wrong to say that the coin's landing tails caused his death (though Hall 2000 would disagree), since the provost would have died whether the coin showed heads or tails.

What to do? In this scenario, as in the case of the provost's cannonball-hurling, one of the causal claims is not as simple as it seems. The claim that the coin's landing tails caused the provost's death is, in our mouths, identical to the claim that the coin's landing tails rather than heads caused the provost's death. That is to say, it is a claim of contrastive causation or explanation, to be evaluated according to the procedure sketched in section 5.6. The claim is true, then, if there are two causal models, one for the provost's death and one for his continued existence, the first veridical and the second "plausible," that disagree only on the outcome of the coin toss. There is no such pair, so the claim is false: the coin's landing tails rather than heads is not a cause of death. (This is a case, note, in which there is a contrast in the putative cause but not in the effect—the one sort of case in which it makes sense to compare a causal model for an event with a model for the nonoccurrence of that event, rather than with a model for some other, more specific event.)

I hope it is intuitively clear to you that in order to evaluate the claim about tails causing death, you do indeed compare the two causal processes initiated by heads and tails, respectively; this is enough to confirm that the claim is implicitly contrastive. Another test: consider how you would go about testing the noncontrastive claim that the coin's landing tails caused the death. You should, according to the kairetic account, begin with a model that contains as an initial condition the coin's landing tails, and then abstract away from this event, checking to see whether the entailment of death is invalidated. The normal kairetic abstraction or removal of the toss would leave open the possibility that the coin lands heads, but it would also leave open other possibilities, for example, that for some reason the coin was never tossed. The fact that we do not consider these options at all when assessing the consequences of the toss shows that we are thinking contrastively.

What does all this have to do with switching and transitivity? The claim that the coin's landing tails caused the provost's death is a contrastive claim. But both the claim that the coin's landing tails caused the provost to be thrown into the river and the claim that the provost's being thrown into the river caused his death are noncontrastive. A genuine counterexample to transitivity would require either that the first of these three remain true when uttered, as it were, noncontrastively, or that the other two remain true when uttered contrastively.

Neither route to counterexemplification is viable. Asserted in a noncontrastive context, it is not true that the coin's landing tails made no difference to the provost's death: there are causal models for death in which removing the fact about the toss's outcome invalidates the causal entailment of death. Consider in particular a model that elucidates the kidnappers' plan given tails but says nothing about what they will do if the coin lands heads. Tails is a noncontrastive cause of death, then, as transitivity demands.

Is there a way to set up the counterexample using contrastive causation at every step? You might consider the following contrastive claims:

1. The coin's landing tails-not-heads was not a cause of the provost's death.
2. The coin's landing tails-not-heads was a cause of the provost's being influviated-not-eaten.
3. The provost's being influviated-not-eaten was a cause of the provost's death.

Claims (1) and (2) come out true, but (3) is false, since the provost, facing the Scylla and Charybdis of goat or river, would have died either way. There is no counterexample to transitivity here.

A final query: if tails is a noncontrastive cause of death, why do we never say so? Why do we insist, in other words, on understanding the claim that tails was not a cause of death, and similar claims about other switching events, contrastively? The switching events used in putative counterexamples to transitivity—tossed coins, railway junction boxes, and so on—are always parts of a larger mechanism. A question about their causal role, then, is naturally interpreted as a question about their role within the mechanism. Alternatives to the putative cause are considered only if they are compatible with the mechanism's normal functioning; this has the effect of rendering the ensuing questions and answers implicitly contrastive.

## 6.6   Three Kinds of Causation

If the picture of causal claims sketched in this book is correct, there are three kinds of causal relations that serve as the subject matter of our causal discourse.

First is the relation of causal influence, introduced in section 1.4 and concerning which I am a passionate ecumenist. This is a pure, raw metaphysical relation—if anything is the cement of the universe, the hidden wheels and strings, the connective tissue of all creation, it is causal influence.

Second is the relation of difference-making simpliciter, that is, difference-making unrelativized to an explanatory framework, introduced in chapter three. The facts about difference-making simpliciter depend only on the facts about causal influence and the standards for generality, accuracy, and cohesion invoked by the kairetic account's optimizing criterion for difference-making. They are observer-independent, then (or at least, as observer-independent as the facts about causal cohesion), but "cooked"—causal influence being the principal raw ingredient, and the optimizing criterion the recipe.[11]

Third is the relation of difference-making relative to an explanatory framework. It is with this third kind of claim that we can aspire to some of the more advanced acrobatics of causal discourse: ignoring background difference-makers, singling out some and rejecting other omissions as causes, and talking about prevention. The relativized difference-making facts are as observer-independent as the facts about difference-making simpliciter, but causal discourse about such facts may be in its significance as protean as the conversation itself, with type-identical causal sentences having varying (or perhaps no) truth values in different framework-determining contexts of utterance.[12]

Our everyday causal claims almost always concern the second and third kinds of relations, more often than not the third. As such, they provide rather distorted windows into the metaphysics of causation. Hall (2007) argues, for example, that a set of truth conditions for causal claims must draw on facts as to what constitutes a system or mechanism's *default state*. Suppose that he is right. It would be a mistake, I suggest, to infer from this observation that the fundamental stuff of causation somehow also depends on facts about defaulthood. The role of these facts is to determine appropriate explanatory frameworks for the third type of causal claim; they play no role, I assert, in the first or second type of claim, and so the facts about the metaphysics of causality (or for that matter, difference-making simpliciter) in no way depend on what is and is not a default state.

Or consider the evidence surveyed in section 6.32 that the conversational context plays a large role in determining which omissions have the status of causes. Again, it would be a mistake to conclude from this striking observation that the metaphysics of causality is sensitive in any way to practical concerns. What is sensitive to practical concerns is rather the process determining the salient explanatory framework.

It follows that many of the most complex and puzzling aspects of our causal claims have nothing at all to do with causality. The study of causal relations, either raw or cooked, is complete once the truth conditions for relativized and other causal claims are specified, and before any discussion of the semantic and pragmatic procedures for the contextual specification of explanatory frameworks commences. Much valuable recent work on causal claims should be understood as a proper part of the latter endeavor.

# — III —

## Explanation of Laws
## and Regularities

# — 7 —

# Regularity Explanation

## 7.1 Approaches to Regularity Explanation

The most profound scientific explanations are the regularity explanations: explanations of laws, generalizations, "effects," ongoing states of affairs, and so on. Yet the literature on regularity explanation is remarkably thin; with the exception of the unificationists, philosophers have for the most part provided only programmatic comments on the explanation of laws.

### The Expectability Approach

In his most expansive treatment of explanation, Hempel (1965a) advocates an approach to the explanation of laws that mirrors his DN treatment of event explanation: to explain a law is to deduce it from other true laws. When the explanandum is a deterministic law, Hempel calls the explanation a deductive-nomological explanation (pp. 343–44); when it is a probabilistic law, he calls it a deductive-statistical explanation (pp. 380–81). Although he does not say as much, it seems safe to presume that Hempel sees the explanatory relation involved in the DN and deductive-statistical explanations of laws as the same nomic expectability relation at work in DN and IS explanations of events. A law is explained, then, by showing that its truth was, given certain other laws, to be expected.

Twenty years earlier, however, Hempel and Oppenheim (1948) were not so sanguine in applying the nomic expectability approach to the explanation of laws. In fact, they declined to give a DN theory of regularity explanation at all, for reasons explained in what Wesley Salmon (1990b) calls their "notorious footnote 33." The notorious footnote gives the following counterexample to a DN account of regularity explanation. Let $k$ designate Kepler's laws and $b$ Boyle's law. Then Kepler's laws would, on the DN account, be explained by deducing them from the conjunction of $k$ and $b$. As section 7.43 will show, this problem of conjunction is closely related to the explanatory relevance problem discussed in chapter two.

219

Hempel never provided a solution to the conjunction problem. Nevertheless, the deductive account of the explanation of laws inherent in Hempel's nomic expectability approach became a de facto standard. Besides Hempel's own endorsement of the account in *Aspects of Scientific Explanation*, the equation of explanation and deduction is the motor of the classical account of theory reduction (Nagel 1979, chap. 11).

Indeed, Salmon (1990b, 94) writes that the conjunction problem was not "seriously attacked" in the literature after Hempel and Oppenheim until it was taken up by Friedman (1974), who rejected the DN account and advocated a unification approach.[1]

## The Pattern-Subsumption Approach

Of the three major approaches to explanation, the pattern-subsumption approach, and in particular the approach's unificationist variant, has been the friendliest to regularity explanation. Friedman (1974) launched the unification approach with a promise to provide an account of the explanation of laws, and Kitcher (1989), who has become the chief proponent of unificationism, holds the treatment of regularity explanation to be among the unification account's greatest advantages.

According to the pattern-subsumption approach, a law or other generalization is explained by showing that it is an instance of a more general pattern of laws or generalizations. To use a familiar example, the dynamics characterized by Kepler's laws are explained when they are seen to be instances of the more general class of dynamics characterized by Newtonian gravitational theory. The form of the rules for determining a suitable subsuming pattern are appropriate adaptations of the generality, accuracy, and cohesion rules described in section 1.32.

## The Metaphysical Approach

To explain an event, on the causal approach, is to give the causes of the event. Laws and other lawlike explananda do not have causes in the usual sense; what, then, should a causalist say about regularity explanation? There are two ways of answering this question.

First, you might broaden the scope of causalist thinking. To explain something is to show how it metaphysically depends on other things. In the case of events, the explanatory dependence relations are causal, and so to explain an event, you exhibit relations of causal dependence between that event, its causes, and the aspects of the fundamental laws in virtue of which they are causes. Laws are not caused, but if they are not fundamental, they do metaphysically depend on other things; in particular, they depend on other, lower-level laws. To explain a high-level law, then, is to exhibit a rich and suitably objective relation of metaphysical dependence between that law and the fundamental laws. Lewis (1986a, 223) suggests, for example, that a disposition (a person's immunity to smallpox) can be explained by giving its supervenience basis; the supervenience relation is, he argues, noncausal but explanatory.[2]

Second, and by contrast, a causalist may refuse to relinquish the idea that all scientific explanation is causal, holding that to explain a law is to have a kind of generalized understanding of the causes of instances of the law, what causalists often call an understanding of a mechanism.

I call these the *metaphysical* and *causal-mechanical* approaches, respectively, to regularity explanation. I will take the causal-mechanical approach in this study.

Why? The prospects of the metaphysical approach hinge on the availability of an appropriate relation of metaphysical dependence between laws. To me, the great appeal of the causal influence relation is that the facts about causal influence are more or less fundamental physical facts, or so I suppose, and thus are suitable stopping points for understanding.

By contrast, there is no relation of dependence between laws that can be read off the physics in the same way.[3] Indeed, by definition, the laws of fundamental physics do not stand in any kind of support relation to one another—they are fundamental. If, as I believe, all fundamental entities and relations are to be found in physical theory, then interlevel dependence relations are not fundamental. I conclude that, though they may play an intermediary role in explanation, they cannot be the end point of the search for explanatory facts.

For this reason (hardly conclusive, I concede), I favor the mechanistic approach to causal explanation, according to which the end point for regularity explanation is, as for event explanation, a causal model representing—however abstractly—facts about fundamental-level causal influence.

## The Causal-Mechanical Approach

The intuition behind the mechanistic approach to regularity explanation is succinctly described by Peter Lipton:

> To explain [a causal regularity] is to give information about the mechanism linking cause and effect. If we explain why smoking causes cancer,

we do not give a cause of this causal connection, but we do give information about the causal mechanism that makes it (Lipton 2004, 32).

Salmon (1984, 268–270) interprets a causal explanation of the law that
airfoils are less efficient in humid air than in dry air along similar lines,
holding that the explanation establishes a "causal connection" between the
humidity of air and the efficiency of airfoils.

What is a causal mechanism? What is the nature of this relation of "causal
connection" that holds not between particular events, as does the causal relation that powers event explanation, but between properties, dispositions,
types of events? Can all laws be explained by mechanisms? What about force
laws? Or laws that depend in part on physically contingent facts?

There is little or no discussion of these questions in the literature on
causal explanation. An investigation of the causal-mechanical explanation
of laws has as its starting point, then, little more than a slogan about mechanisms and a few paradigm explanations.

## 7.2   Explaining Laws with Mechanisms

Consider a law of the form *If F, then G*; assume that it is causal in the
sense that it is understood to assert or assume the existence of a causal
connection running from $F$-ness to $G$-ness. The mechanistic approach
to regularity explanation proposes to explain such a law by exhibiting the
causal mechanism in virtue of which the connection exists. Let me develop
this proposal with the help of a particular causal if/then law; later sections
will expand the treatment in several significant ways.

Here, then, is a simple if/then causal generalization:

> The apple law: If at time $t$, an apple falls from a tree on the surface
> of a planet with mass $M$ and radius $r$, it will hit the ground at time
> $t + r\sqrt{2d/GM}$,

where $d$ is the distance between the apple and the ground and $G$ is the
gravitational constant. You should understand this generalization as having
a few riders left implicit for simplicity's sake: the planet is approximately
spherical and is symmetrical in the way required in order to treat it as a
point mass for gravitational purposes, the planet's atmosphere is thin or
nonexistent, and the distance $d$ is relatively small. You should also understand the law as stating an *approximate* time for the apple's landing (otherwise the law would be false if there were any atmosphere at all, if the planet

were not exactly spherical, and so on). Finally, the entire discussion assumes a Newtonian, not an Einsteinian, conception of gravity.

An aside: you might well complain that a generalization so artificially restricted—to apples and trees, that is—cannot possibly qualify as a genuine *law*. Although I am a liberal in my use of *law*, I must concede that the complaint has substance: the metaphysics of lawlike generalizations sketched in section 7.6 ascribes to generalizations like the apple law a low position in the great chain of nomological being. That said, an account of regularity explanation ought to handle any true generalization, no matter how contrived: whether a generalization is a law or not does not affect its explicability. A gravitational generalization about apples may not be an exemplary law, but it is a legitimate object for regularity explanation. The question what to call it is of little consequence, then; I have chosen a name that is simple and short.

On the causal-mechanical approach, in order to explain the apple law, you must describe the causal mechanism—more specifically, the gravitational mechanism—in virtue of which any apple detached from its tree under the assumed circumstances in fact falls in the stated time. This mechanism is of course the same causal mechanism that forms the core of the event explanation of a particular apple's falling to the ground in the stated time, under the stated circumstances. The causal-mechanical approach to regularity explanation, then, takes the mechanism that explains any instance of the law and uses it to explain, in addition, the law itself. Consequently, a mechanism that has a role to play in regularity explanation always also finds a place in event explanation. You thus obtain the following defining tenet of the causal-mechanical approach to regularity explanation:

> *First Fundamental Theorem of Explanation:* The explanation of a causal generalization and the explanation of any instance of the generalization invoke the same causal mechanism.

A second fundamental theorem will be proposed in section 7.35.

This goes some way toward explaining why proponents of the causal approach to explanation are not often observed writing about regularity explanation: by providing an explicit account of event explanation, they take themselves to have thereby quietly provided an account of the mechanisms required for regularity explanation.

How does the causal-mechanical approach turn out within the kairetic framework? Take some instance of the apple law, in which a particular apple hanging at a particular height $d$ on a particular planet of mass $M$ and radius $r$ fell at time $t$ and hit the ground at approximately $t + r\sqrt{2d/GM}$. A standalone explanation of this event is provided, according to the kairetic account, by a causal model consisting of the deductive argument with the following premises:

1. The apple becomes detached at time $t$.

2. The distance of the apple from the ground is $d$.

3. A causal law, that a point of mass $M$ exerts a gravitational force of magnitude $GMm/r^2$ on an object of mass $m$ at distance $r$, causing a constant rate of downward acceleration equal to $GM/r^2$.

4. Some observations about the mathematics of gravitational dynamics bringing the causal law to bear on the situation: a planet with a certain symmetry acts gravitationally like a point mass; for small $d$, the gravitational acceleration on the apple is approximately constant, and so on.

5. A mathematical fact: an object experiencing a constant acceleration $a$ will cover a distance $d$ in time $\sqrt{2d/a}$.

The conclusion of the argument is, of course, what was to be explained: that the apple reaches the ground at time $t + r\sqrt{2d/GM}$.

Understood as a model of the causal production of a singular event, the argument's symbols $t$, $d$, $M$, and $r$ are constants taking the particular values historically responsible for the episode in question. They might be reinterpreted, however, as free variables, ranging over all physically realistic values for the mass of a planet, the distance of an apple from the ground, and so on. The argument would then constitute a schema for the causal explanation of any instance of the apple law, a description of the type of mechanism that is instantiated whenever the law itself is instantiated. It is this mechanism type that is responsible, and solely responsible, for the law's holding; I will take the mechanism type as the explanation of the law. To explain the apple law, then, you must provide a causal model of the mechanism type; this model will have the form of the schematic deductive argument above.

A little thought shows that the argument schema is what I have been calling the follow-through of the corresponding event explanation. An explanation of an instance of the apple law, then, has as its follow-through a mechanism schema realized by any instance of the apple law and as its setup a specification of the particular facts in virtue of which the process in question realizes the schema, including particular values for all the variables in the schema. In other words, the explanation of an instance comprises the explanation of the law together with the specifics of the instantiation. An explanation of an event instantiating a law is in this sense bigger than the corresponding law explanation: it contains the schema that explains the law and more besides. This is the kairetic account's particular version of the first fundamental theorem stated above.

In section 3.23, I understood the facts in virtue of which a follow-through exists as high-level properties of the fundamental laws. What I am calling a mechanism type, then, should be understood, metaphysically, as identical to a facet or facets of the fundamental laws. If a high-level law is explained by a mechanism schema, it follows that it is explained by certain, perhaps rather abstract, properties of the fundamental laws, that is, by the fact that the fundamental laws are a certain way. Let me emphasize that by calling the causal process types picked out by explanatory kernels *mechanisms*, I am not imputing to them either frequency or organic unity. The history of Rasputin's chaotic last day, once purged of non-difference-makers, is the mechanism for his death, despite its being a diffuse and improbable assemblage of difference-makers. In my idiolect (standard for a proponent of the causal-mechanical account, but contrast Machamer et al. (2000)), any difference-making causal process is a mechanism.

Both laws and the mechanisms that explain them have a certain domain of application, or scope. The apple law, for example, applies only when the distance $d$ between the apple and the planetary surface is small. The mechanism is limited in the same way: it is instantiated only by apples falling relatively short distances. (Where is this limit expressed? The mechanism's causal entailment of the falling time goes through only when $d$ is small; thus, somewhere in the follow-through $d$'s small size must be either explicitly or implicitly assumed.) Clearly, the scope of the mechanism that explains a law or other generalization must be at least as wide as the scope of the explanandum itself.

The scope of laws has a modal as well as an actual dimension. The apple law, for example, applies not just to actual apple falls but to certain possible yet non-actual fallings as well—or at least, this is how we typically understand such laws. To explain the law, it seems, you need to explain not only why it holds for actual apples that actually fall, but for actual apples that might have fallen but did not (that is, that counterfactually fall), and for apples that might have existed and fallen but did not (that is, counterfactual apples that counterfactually fall). The explaining mechanism should therefore have modal extent.

This requirement is easily satisfied by the apple-falling mechanism: because it is a high-level property (or properties) of the fundamental laws, the mechanism is to be found wherever the fundamental laws hold. The scope of the mechanism extends, then, to all physically possible apple fallings (in which $d$ is small, and so on). It is therefore well able to explain the modal sweep of the physically necessary apple law.

Some further remarks about mechanism schemas and their explanatory role. First, whereas the target of an event-explaining model is the event to be explained, the target of a law-explaining model is not the law to be explained—and could not be, since a law cannot be the target of a causal model. Rather, a law-explaining model has as its target a property that completes the instantiation of the law. In a law of the *All Fs are G* variety, for example, the target is typically *G*-ness. Thus, in an explanatory model for an event, the explanandum and the target are identical, whereas in an explanatory model for a law, they are entirely different kinds of entity. When, in what follows, I talk of a regularity explanation's *explanatory target*, I mean the target of the explanatory model, not the law that is to be explained.

Second, the causal-mechanical approach to explanation does not distinguish between the explanation of laws and the explanation of other generalizations. A modally and spatiotemporally narrow generalization such as *All actual apples that fall, in the year 2008, to the surface of the earth . . .* is explained in just the same way as the wider-ranging apple law, or as a bona fide law of nature such as Coulomb's law.

Third, the causal-mechanical account of regularity explanation does not assume that the antecedent and consequent of the law to be explained are, in any instance, distinct events the one of which occurs before the other. The "antecedent" property may persist and be active causally as long as the "consequent" property is manifested, as when the period of a pendulum over a certain length of time is explained by its length, or the seriousness of a recession is explained by a lack of consumer confidence, or the pressure exerted by a gas over a certain length of time is explained by its temperature and volume. Each of these causal event explanations provides the basis for a corresponding law explanation, namely, the explanations of the causal generalizations relating pendulum period and length, recession depth and consumer confidence, and Boyle's law. Thus, causal models may be used to explain what Hempel called laws of coexistence as well as what he called laws of succession (Hempel 1965a, 352).

Fourth, the optimizing procedure is applied to explanatory models for laws in exactly the same way that it is applied to explanatory models for events, with the same purpose: to purge explanations of causal irrelevancies.

You might apply the kairetic difference-making test to a causal model for sodium's reactivity, for example, by attempting to abstract away from the physiochemical details of the sodium atom in two ways. On the one hand, you might make the number of neutrons in the atoms indeterminate, so that the model describes not only the behavior of sodium-23, the single naturally occurring isotope of sodium, but the behavior of sodium's other isotopes as well. All are reactive, thus you have determined that there being exactly twelve neutrons does not make a difference to reactivity.[4]

On the other hand, you might make the strength with which the atom's outer electron is bonded indeterminate, perhaps by specifying a range rather than an exact value for the electromagnetic potential inside the atom, so that the model allows that the outer electron is bound with any of a wide range of different strengths. A model in which bonds have indeterminate strength is satisfied both by atoms that have tightly bound outer electrons and by atoms that have loosely bound outer electrons; since the atoms with tightly bound outer electrons will be nonreactive, abstracting away from bonding strength invalidates the entailment of the relevant explanatory target. You have determined that the looseness of the bonding makes a difference to sodium's reactivity. (Observe that when applying the kairetic criterion for relevance, by contrast with the counterfactual criterion (section 2.4), you do not have to rank different bond-tightening methods in order of the similarity between the chemistry they engender and the chemistry of the actual world, because the kairetic test does not have to fix on some "most conservative" way of tightening the bond.)

One consequence of the removal of irrelevancies is that the mechanism explaining a narrowed version of the apple law, such as a version that limits itself to apples falling in the year 2008, is the same mechanism that explains the full law: although a model that requires the year to be 2008 would have sufficient scope to explain the time-limited law, it attributes to the causal process an irrelevant property, the property of occurring during a certain time period. Remove this specification, as the optimizing procedure says you must, and you have a model describing the mechanism for the full, unlimited apple law. (A number of other irrelevancies will be removed in the process, for example, the specification of the fact that the falling object is an apple.)

Let me take stock. The causal-mechanical approach to regularity explanation has the advantage, it seems, of finding every regularity explanation already embedded in an event explanation, and thus—an adequate theory of event explanation in hand—of obviating the need to say anything special or particular about regularity explanation at all.

Such a picture is misleading, and the remainder of the chapter necessary, for two reasons. First, finding the appropriate mechanism for a law or generalization is not always straightforward; in some cases it raises substantive philosophical questions, to be investigated in sections 7.4 and 7.5. Second, many laws and other generalizations cannot be explained by mechanisms alone. They require for their explanation both a mechanism and what I will call a *basing generalization*.

## 7.3    Basing Generalizations

### 7.31  *The Need for Basing Generalizations*

Suppose that you want to explain why all ravens are black, or more exactly, why all normal ravens are black in natural conditions (though references to naturalness and normality will be suppressed whenever convenient in what follows). You are after a physiological explanation, not an evolutionary explanation, I will suppose. Thus, your principal concern will be to provide an account of the developmental mechanisms responsible for the growth and maintenance of black plumage in maturing ravens.

The core of your explanation is a causal model detailing the processes by which ravens' melanosomes, organelles within specialist cells called melanocytes, first synthesize the pigment melanin from the amino acid tyrosine and then migrate from the melanocytes to color the keratin from which feathers are made. (Perhaps the explanation will take up the story earlier, with the melanocytes' development in the neural crest area of raven embryos; the starting point does not matter.) To put things rather more schematically, the raven coloration mechanism will be described by a causal model in which certain aspects of raven physiology and other initial conditions (some environmental) causally entail, by way of the relevant biological and chemical laws, blackness. Let *P* denote the physiological properties, and assume that the other relevant initial and background conditions are identical to the "natural conditions" specified by the law itself. Thus, natural conditions, *P*, and the biochemical laws together causally entail blackness.

Is this causal model sufficient to explain raven blackness? No. It is sufficient to explain why, in natural conditions, anything with *P* is black, but in order to explain the blackness of ravens, it must be supplemented with a statement of the form *All normal ravens have P*. This is what I call a *basing generalization*.

The explanation of the blackness of normal ravens, then, has the following two parts:

1. A basing generalization: *All normal ravens have P*
2. A derivation of blackness from *P*, the relevant laws, and other initial conditions (the "natural conditions"), modeling the raven coloration mechanism

As you can see, the basing generalization plays the same formal role in this regularity explanation as a statement of initial conditions does in event explanation.

The explanation of the apple law shows that a basing generalization is not always necessary for regularity explanation. A large number of laws and other generalizations, however—perhaps the vast majority—cannot be understood in terms of mechanisms alone; a basing generalization stating structural facts or a pattern of initial conditions is required to complete the explanation.

The science of genetics, for example, began by asking the question why certain patterns of inheritance were observed in people, peas, and so on. These patterns take the form that they do in virtue of the particular, contingent structure of the mechanisms of reproduction found in sexually reproducing life on earth. This structure cannot be derived from the fundamental laws of physics (thus its contingency); any explanation of the inheritance patterns, then, must not only cite the fundamental laws but also describe the structure. Such a description takes the form of a basing generalization: *All sexually reproducing life on earth has reproductive mechanisms with property P*.

Likewise, the patterns that psychologists attempt to understand depend on the characteristic structure of the human brain, and the patterns that geologists attempt to understand depend on the structure of the planet earth. Even in physics, what appear to be contingent patterns of initial conditions play a role in determining the shape of a large class of explananda, namely, the entropic processes; more on this in the next section.

Let me go further. Many of the high-level sciences can be understood as having as their primary goal the exploration of the causal consequences of particular, pervasive structural patterns: physiology, the physical structure of different classes of organisms; genetics, the structure of their reproductive mechanisms; psychology, the structure of the higher nervous system in humans and perhaps other animals; sociology and some branches of anthropology, the structure of human societies and cultural systems; and so on. In each case, the structures are physically contingent, thus not explicable by the fundamental laws alone (as philosophers of biology, in particular have appreciated (Beatty 1995; Waters 1998)). The high-level sciences cannot make sense of their subject matter, then, without basing generalizations.

A qualification: Some writers have argued that economics is the study of the logical and mathematical consequences of certain definitions, rather than of the causal consequences of certain physical structures (Rosenberg 1992). The same might be said of any science whose subject matter is characterized in wholly functional terms, as for example belief/desire psychology is widely thought to be. The sweeping claim of the last paragraph must make an exception for such cases—though I myself doubt that there are any sciences that are entirely, or even mostly, functional in this sense.

In the remainder of this section, I ask a number of questions about the explanatory function of basing generalizations. What generalizations are capable of playing the basing role? What, exactly, does a basing generalization contribute to an explanation? Does something like the optimizing procedure apply to a basing generalization? The answers turn out to constitute a new wing of the kairetic account—a conspicuously noncausal wing. They also play a key role in understanding the nature of probabilistic explanation in deterministic systems, to be investigated in part four.

## 7.32 The Nature of Basing Generalizations

Define a basing generalization as any generalization implying the existence of a pattern of facts, which pattern must be added to a mechanism schema to create a causal model capable of explaining some law or other regularity. This is a broad characterization: arguably, it includes the initial conditions stated in at least some event explanations. Once the explanatory role of basing generalizations is better understood, it will become clear that all generalizations fitting the characterization do indeed share a fundamental explanatory function, and so that the basing generalizations form, from an explanatory perspective, a unified class.

Some examples of basing generalizations, along with explanations in which they might appear:

1. All water is $H_2O$—explaining the high surface tension of water in terms of hydrogen bonding.

2. The temperature of a simple gas is its mean molecular kinetic energy—explaining the ideal gas law.

3. Electrons have a charge of $1.602 \times 10^{-19}$ coulombs—explaining, say, the results obtained in the Millikan oil drop experiment.

4. Sexual reproduction in plants and animals on earth is implemented by such and such a mechanism—explaining (the approximate truth of) Mendel's laws.

5. Ford Pintos from the early 1970s have a differential housing with four sharp, protruding bolts facing the fuel tank—explaining why Pintos made before 1977 are prone to explode in rear-end collisions.

6. The velocities of the molecules in a gas at equilibrium are distributed in accordance with the Maxwell-Boltzmann law—explaining any result in kinetic theory, for example, Fick's law of diffusion.

7. The universe is currently in an "entropic" period, a period during which almost any system, at any particular time, is in the sort of microstate that will evolve, as time passes, to a state of increased entropy—explaining, say, (the approximate truth of) Newton's law of cooling.

The last of these is of such broad importance—because almost every interesting scientific generalization outside of fundamental physics assumes that we are in an entropic period—that it deserves to be explained more carefully.

Newton's law of cooling states that the rate with which a relatively warm body cools is directly proportional to the difference between the body's temperature and that of the surrounding environment. The law is true only within the scope of the second law of thermodynamics, or more generally, only within the scope of nonequilibrium thermodynamics, which is to say (at least on some interpretations of statistical mechanics, assumed here for the sake of the argument) that it is true only for systems that have initial conditions of a certain sort—call them entropic.

The initial conditions in our part of space and time are typically—indeed, close enough to invariably—entropic. However, it is an intriguing consequence of fundamental physics (on some understandings) that if the universe is allowed to exist for long enough, it will contain space-time regions in which entropic conditions are rare. In some such regions, relatively hot objects will not merely fail to cool as prescribed by Newton's law; they will grow hotter. Indeed, in the long run, decreases in entropy will be just as common as increases in entropy. Thus, regions of space-time that conform to Newton's law will by no means predominate.

You would not want to say, for all this, that Newton's law is false. A more natural way to understand the law is as applying only to those parts of the universe in which entropic initial conditions are the rule. It is not important to decide how, exactly, to characterize the scope of Newton's law. (Never mind, for example, whether the law is supposed to apply to systems in which there is no initial temperature differential, forbidding the spontaneous appearance of such a thing.) What is important is that, once the scope is characterized, the explanation of the law will have to contain a basing generalization asserting that all or almost all systems within the scope have entropic initial conditions, or that they have entropic initial conditions with very high probability.[5]

A diverse array of basing generalizations is now on the table. What can be learned about the prerequisites for playing the basing role in scientific explanation? A number of prima facie plausible constraints on the explanatory use of basing generalizations can be ruled out.

First, basing generalizations need not be scientific laws. The fact that pre-1977 Ford Pintos have protruding bolts on their differential housing, for example, is not a law—or better, a lawhood requirement so liberal as to embrace such a fact does not provide an interesting constraint on basing generalizations.

Second, basing generalizations might be physically contingent, physically necessary, or even metaphysically necessary. I emphasized the importance of physically contingent basing generalizations in the previous section, focusing in particular on the contingent physiology of life on earth, but necessity is no impediment to playing the basing role, as the generalizations concerning electron charge and (according to the Kripkean consensus) water and temperature show.

Third, basing generalizations need not be causal generalizations. Neither the water nor electron charge generalizations seem to be causal in any sense, and on some approaches, the appropriate statement about entropic conditions used to explain Newton's law is not causal either, being wholly concerned with the uncaused initial conditions of the universe.

Fourth, a basing generalization need not even be particularly robust, in the sense of holding under a wide range of counterfactual suppositions or of supporting a wide range of counterfactual conditionals. Presumably, had the engineers at Ford seen the consequences of the notorious protruding bolts, they would have redesigned the Pinto without them. Yet this in no way undercuts the importance of the bolts in explaining Pintos' explosive tendencies. A basing generalization must be as robust as the generalization that it is to explain (I elaborate on this point below), but there is no degree of robustness inherently necessary to perform the basing function.

Fifth, a basing generalization can contribute to our understanding of a law without itself being understood at all. We can, that is, construct a stand-alone explanation that provides a clear understanding of a generalization despite its calling on a basing generalization that is for us inexplicable. To deploy a basing generalization effectively, we should know that it is true, but we need not have any idea why it is true. Every one of the basing generalizations described above might serve as an example. You can understand why Pintos explode without knowing why the differential housing was designed so badly. You can understand the Mendelian patterns of inheritance without knowing the origins of the mechanisms of sexual reproduction, or why there is such a thing as sexual reproduction at all (arguably our present state of knowledge). And you can understand the chemistry of water and the behavior of gases without answering the deep philosophical questions as to why water is constituted of $H_2O$ or what kinds of things the probabilities invoked by statistical mechanics might be. In this respect, basing generalizations in regularity explanation are just like initial conditions in event explanation: you do not have to understand how a set of initial conditions was produced to use the conditions to explain an event, or else we would not yet have succeeded in explaining anything.

You might now think that I have run myself aground. I claim that the class of basing generalizations is unified by the nature of the generalizations' contribution to the explanations in which they appear, but given the almost complete absence of constraints on generalizations that would perform the basing function, it is hard to see what explanatory purpose they might have in common.

What every basing generalization does do is to assert the existence of certain patterns of phenomena. *Water is $H_2O$*, for example, implies that every possible sample of water is made up of $H_2O$, while *All ravens have a gene for tyrosinase* implies that all ravens have the tyrosinase gene (all normal ravens, at any rate). I call the pattern of phenomena corresponding to a basing generalization a *basing pattern*, and I propose that what a basing generalization contributes to an explanation is nothing over and above the fact of the existence of its corresponding basing pattern. (I should warn you that the notion of a basing pattern will be augmented in section 7.34, though not in a way that will require any of what follows to be retracted.)

Basing generalizations may, and often do, entail much more than the existence of a basing pattern. If they are causal laws, for example, they will assert or imply the existence of an underlying causal mechanism responsible for the pattern. Such assertions do not stand in the way of a generalization's playing the basing role, but nor do they contribute to that role. A basing generalization, though it may amount to much more than an existence claim for a basing pattern, nevertheless functions as such a claim in its explanatory context.

For this reason, a basing generalization functions, as I have already suggested, in much the same way as the specification of an initial condition in an event explanation. No story is given about why an initial condition holds, even though there may be such a story; the role of an initial condition specification in a causal model's setup is simply to establish the presence of a state of affairs that served as raw material for the causal process described by the model. Likewise, no story is given as to why a basing pattern holds; for explanatory purposes, nothing matters over and above the simple fact of its existence.

There is one significant difference between the explanatory contribution of a basing pattern to the typical regularity explanation and that of a set of initial conditions to an event explanation: because the paradigmatic object of regularity explanation, a law or other lawlike generalization, has a modal extent—it has something to say about counterfactual systems falling within its scope as well as actual systems—it requires for its explanation a basing pattern of equal or greater extent. Basing patterns, then, are normally not merely patterns of actual states of affairs, but also of counterfactual states of affairs.

As an illustration, consider the raven generalization, *All ravens are black*. Though many, perhaps most, philosophers would be reluctant to elevate it to the status of a law, the raven generalization has implications that go beyond the actual. It is true of a range of counterfactual ravens and actual ravens in counterfactual circumstances. Normally, for example, it is true of any two healthy ravens, male and female and of breeding age, that if they were to breed, their offspring would be black. In the case where the raven pair do not actually breed, this offspring is nonactual, yet the raven generalization as usually understood has implications for its color.[6] Or it is true of any healthy actual raven, that if it had hatched a day later, or been raised on a slightly different diet, it would still have been black. Here the raven is actual, but the complete system—raven plus relevant environmental and other background conditions—is counterfactual. Again, the raven generalization has something to say about the counterfactual system.

I take it that an explanation of the raven generalization is not complete unless some account is given of the reasons for blackness in nonactual ravens and in actual ravens in nonactual circumstances. Or to put the point more positively, I take it that our current scientific explanation of the raven generalization explains not only actual blackness, but also certain kinds of counterfactual blackness.

How do we manage this modal feat? Let $P$ be the set of properties that constitute the raven coloration mechanism, as above, and ignore for simplicity's sake the role of "natural environmental conditions" in the production of blackness. The explanation of the raven generalization attains modal extent by citing, alongside the causal mechanism by which $P$ causes blackness and the $P$-hood of all actual ravens in actual circumstances, the $P$-hood of certain nonactual ravens and of actual ravens in certain non-actual circumstances. In short, it cites a pattern of $P$-hood in ravens that extends beyond the actual. I should add immediately that the pattern does not extend that far beyond the actual: many possible ravens do not have $P$, since it was presumably at one time possible (and is perhaps still possible) that ravens would evolve to have a coloration scheme other than universal blackness. The basing pattern extends just as far as it needs to in order to explain the raven generalization's modal implications.

To a metaphysical minimalist, this may sound like madness. In order to explain the counterfactual implications of the raven generalization, is it necessary to be a modal realist, and in particular, to posit the literal exis-tence of nonactual ravens whose $P$-hood constitutes a part of the relevant basing pattern? Not at all. You are entitled to have precisely as shallow and deflationary conception of basing patterns, where they extend beyond the actual patterns, as you have of the facts about possible worlds that (on the Stalnaker/Lewis approach that I adopt here) underwrite the truth of coun-terfactual conditionals.

To see this, consider the way in which a counterfactual conditional con-cerning raven color is evaluated. (The topic is treated more thoroughly in Strevens 2008b.) Take for example the following claim: *If these two ravens had, contrary to the facts, bred last year, their offspring would have been black.* When asserted in normal circumstances, the conditional is true because, in the closest possible worlds where the ravens do breed last year, their off-spring is black. Let me explain why this closest offspring is black. As related in section 2.4, the relevant closest worlds are those that conform to the fol-lowing description: (a) they are identical to ours up until shortly before the ravens are counterfactually supposed to have bred, (b) at which time a small divergence from actuality brings about, as conservatively as possi-ble, the breeding in question, after which (c) events unfold as prescribed by the laws of the actual world. Why are the offspring in these worlds black, then? The answer, like the criteria for closeness, has three parts. Because the relevant closest possible worlds are identical to the actual world until shortly before breeding, the parents in these worlds have an identical phys-iology to the actual parents. Because the process leading to the breeding is conservative, it does not affect this physiology in any significant respect.

And because the causal laws in the closest possible worlds are identical to the laws in the actual world (after the breeding, at least), the physiology has the same effects as it has in the actual world: it passes the parents' $P$-hood on to the offspring, which $P$-hood then causes the offspring to develop a black color.

The raven generalization has its modal robustness in virtue of the truth of such counterfactual conditionals as this. What makes the raven generalization robust, then, is whatever makes the conditionals true. As you saw, the conditional is true for two reasons: first, in a certain possible world, a particular nonactual raven, the counterfactual offspring, has $P$, and second, in that world just as in ours, $P$ causes blackness. The truth of the conditional therefore depends (in part) on the $P$-hood of a nonactual raven, or in other words, on the same facts in virtue of which the explanatorily relevant basing pattern holds. There is no greater difficulty in talking about patterns of $P$-hood in nonactual ravens than there is in reasoning about the counterfactual color of nonactual ravens.

It is generally, if not universally, acknowledged that counterfactual conditionals can have well-defined truth values even if modal realism is false, and thus even if nonactual ravens do not literally exist, let alone literally have properties such as $P$. What gives the conditionals substance is not, in the first instance, facts about nonactual things, but facts about actual things, namely, those facts that determine that the "closest worlds" in which two ravens mate are worlds in which their offspring has $P$: (a) the state of the actual world shortly before the mating, (b) the actual constraints on "conservative divergences," and (c) the actual laws. The same facts about the actual world therefore also determine that certain nonactual ravens have $P$, and thus that the pattern of $P$-hood in ravens extends beyond the actual. In short, the fact that a certain basing pattern has modal extent is (on this approach to counterfactual conditionals) a fact that holds entirely because of the way things are in the actual world. It is this rather complex actual fact that explains the robustness of the raven generalization. For simplicity's sake, I continue to talk in modal terms; I take it that this talk is quite compatible with a lightweight metaphysics.

Let me return to the principal thesis of this section, that a basing generalization's contribution to a causal explanation is nothing over and above the basing pattern whose existence it entails, albeit a pattern that may have modal extent.

This is surely a controversial claim. On the one hand, the pattern-only view has its attractions. Along with the view that a standalone event explanation can cite initial conditions without explaining them, it has the advantage of ensuring a considerable degree of modularity in our understanding: you can construct a self-contained explanation of a phenomenon without knowing its complete provenance. Thus, you can understand the death of Rasputin without tracing its causal antecedents back to the days of Kievan Rus' a millennium before, and you can understand why ravens are black, from a physiological perspective, without knowing the full evolutionary history of the species.

On the other hand, proponents of the causal approach to explanation, in particular, may find it impossible to resist the thought that, where possible, a basing generalization contributes information about causal processes to the explanatory models in which it appears.

Consider, for example, what you might call the raven basing generalization: *All ravens have P*. The generalization is true in virtue of the causal mechanism by which $P$ is passed down from generation to generation of ravens (a mechanism that presumably overlaps with, but is not identical to, the mechanism by which $P$ causes blackness). Why not understand the basing generalization as contributing information about this mechanism to the explanation of raven blackness in which it appears—if not the details of the mechanism's operation, then at least the fact that it exists? Is our understanding of raven blackness not enhanced by our knowledge that the blackness-inducing property $P$ is omnipresent among ravens because of the mechanics of reproduction, as opposed to being, say, a complete coincidence?

My view that the raven basing generalization's explanatory contribution is nothing over and above a basing pattern is compatible with the most irresistible of these intuitions about explanation. First, a regularity explanation can be elongated by prefixing its causal model with an explanation—an additional causal model—of one or more of the explanation's basing patterns, in the same way that an event explanation can be elongated by adding an explanation of one or more of its initial conditions (section 4.31). As in the case of event explanation, the additional explanatory information improves our understanding of the original explanandum. So it is correct to hold that understanding the causal mechanism responsible for the promulgation of $P$ augments our understanding of raven blackness—a position that is quite consistent with the view that the raven basing generalization does not itself contribute this additional understanding.

Second, the question whether a basing pattern is accidental or not has ramifications for its modal extent. If all ravens have $P$ because of an inheritance mechanism, then possible but nonactual ravens that are the product of possible but nonactual matings will also tend to have $P$. By contrast, if it is a cosmic fluke that all actual ravens have $P$, then there is presumably a good chance that nonactual offspring will not have $P$. Thus, the fact that the raven basing generalization is nonaccidental increases its corresponding basing pattern's modal extent, and so increases its explanatory potential. It follows that our impression that the robustness of the basing generalization is explanatorily relevant even in an unelongated explanation is consistent with, indeed entailed by, the thesis that a basing generalization contributes only a basing pattern to the explanation. I conclude that the pattern-only view is not as radical as it may first seem.

Because almost any generalization entails the existence of some pattern of events or other, almost any generalization can play the basing role in explanation. There are several restrictions on explanatory basing generalizations, however.

1. They must be true.
2. They must entail basing patterns that match or exceed in scope the generalization to be explained.
3. Basing generalizations may specify only intrinsic properties of the systems falling within their scope. Further, these properties must be causally relevant; they must be conditions required for the operation of the explanatory mechanism. This accords with basing generalizations' role as specifiers of the systems' initial or background conditions.[7]
4. Basing generalizations must have a very particular form, simply attributing to a set of systems a set of properties. The entire content of a basing generalization, then, can be captured by an ordered pair of sets. Again, this accords with the generalizations' role as specifiers of patterns of initial conditions.

There is one further constraint on basing generalizations. It will be the subject of most of the rest of this section.

## 7.33 Basing Generalizations and Explanatory Relevance

Is there a relevance constraint on the properties cited in a basing generalization? For a generalization of the form *All Fs have P* to play the basing role, must a system's *F*-ness make a difference to its *P*-hood? Or can a basing generalization cite any property you like, as long as it entails the existence of a basing pattern of adequate scope?

There is a relevance constraint on basing generalizations, I will argue. It shows some formal similarities to the difference-making constraint, but it must be understood as serving a rather different purpose—to be an explanatorily relevant part of a basing generalization is to do work that is quite unlike the kairetic account's causal difference-making.

Suppose that you want to explain why all hexed ravens are black (see section 1.32 for instructions on how to hex salt, ravens, or any other object). You construct a causal model representing the mechanism by which some complex of physiological properties *P* causes blackness, and then you complete the explanation by adding a basing generalization: *All hexed ravens have P*. Is this a virtuous explanation? Does it provide as good an explanation as a causal model that cites the more familiar and wider raven basing generalization *All ravens have P*?

The answers are, I suggest, no and no. Suppose I say the following of a subset of ravens: they are black because they are hexed ravens, all hexed ravens have *P*, and *P* causes blackness. In doing so, I have committed an explanatory faux pas. I should have said: they are black because they are ravens, all ravens have *P*, and so on. As Kyburg, Salmon, and others have maintained (see section 1.32), the former explanation is defective because it attributes the ravens' blackness in part to an explanatorily irrelevant property, their being hexed. Of course, there is no difficulty in touching on the ravens' being hexed at some point in the explanation, given that the explanandum itself refers to hexing. Indeed, you may mention it as often as you like, provided that no explanatory role is imputed to the hexing. But mentioning it in the basing generalization turns out, perhaps surprisingly, to constitute just such an imputation.

What kind of relevance, then, does a causal explanation attribute to the properties specified in the antecedents of its basing generalizations? It cannot be causal relevance, because the raven basing generalization, *All ravens have P*, is a perfectly good basing generalization for the explanation of blackness, either in hexed ravens or in ravens generally, yet it mentions a property that is causally irrelevant to blackness: ravenhood. Why is ravenhood causally irrelevant? Because it does not exert any causal influence on blackness. Rather, it is certain features that go along with ravenhood—the elements of $P$, such as possession of the tyrosinase gene— that do so.

You might balk at this suggestion; a few paragraphs, then, on arguments that ravenhood is, after all, causally relevant. Might ravenhood have causal heft because possession of the tyrosinase gene and other elements of $P$ are constitutive of ravenhood? If a part of being a raven was to have $P$, then it would be metaphysically impossible for ravens not to be black. Yet there are nonblack ravens, such as albinos. Nor can $P$ be constitutive of being a *normal* raven since, had raven evolution gone slightly differently, ravens might have been some other color—which is to say, a normal raven without $P$ is metaphysically possible.

Further, even if ravenhood did consist in part of $P$-hood, it would consist of other things as well, since possession of the raven coloration mechanism is not sufficient for ravenhood. (Carrion crows might possess the same mechanism.) But then ravenhood would consist in part of properties that do not make a difference to blackness, and so would not itself be a difference-maker for blackness, and hence would not be causally relevant to blackness in the kairetic sense.

Another possibility: might ravenhood be a difference-maker for blackness by being a difference-maker for—by being essentially involved in the causal production of—some aspect of $P$, say, possession of the tyrosinase gene? The same arguments suggest not: ravenhood is compatible with the absence of whatever transmits the tyrosinase gene, and it is, in any case, a particular aspect of the physiology of ravens, not ravenhood as a whole, that is causally responsible for transmission. Besides which, some basing generalizations are not causal at all; whatever explanatory role is played by the antecedent properties in these generalizations clearly cannot be causal.

How, then, if not causally, is ravenhood explanatorily relevant but hexing irrelevant to blackness? And what kind of constraint ought therefore to be imposed on basing generalizations to ensure that they mention only relevant properties? I propose to approach the first question by way of the second question, that is, to find a plausible relevance constraint, and then to look for a conception of relevance that vindicates the constraint.

Suppose a certain hexed raven were not hexed. What then? It would still have $P$, and so be black. But suppose it were not a raven. Then it would not necessarily have $P$. (This is so even if, say, all carrion crows have $P$, since if the bird were not a raven, it would not necessarily be a carrion crow.) There is a sense, then, in which a hexed raven's $P$-hood, and thus its blackness, counterfactually depends on its ravenhood but not on its being hexed. I suggest that this is the test in virtue of which ravenhood is judged relevant, and hexing irrelevant, to blackness.

The proposal, then, is that a basing pattern must be picked out using a property that passes the following counterfactual test. If the pattern is the $P$-hood of the objects in a certain set, then the property $F$ used to pick out the set, by way of the basing generalization *All Fs have P*, must *not* render the following sort of counterfactual conditional true: if such and such an object with $F$ had not had $F$, it would still have had $P$.

Three remarks on the test. First, its unwieldy negative phrasing allows a property to pass the test in those cases where there is something indeterminate or flawed about the counterfactual. For example, if the counterfactual *If raven x were not a raven, it would still have had P* is not false but rather is indeterminate, ill defined, or otherwise defective, ravenhood still passes the test, because the counterfactual is not determinately true. However, in what follows I will for simplicity's sake assume that all such counterfactuals are either true or false. Thus, I will assume that when a property $F$ passes the counterfactual test with respect to property $P$, then counterfactuals such as *If x (an F) were not F, it might not have had P* are determinately true.

Second, as I have framed the official test, the putative basing generalization *All hexed ravens have P* fails the test because $P$ does not depend on the portmanteau property of hexed ravenhood, rather than—as you might have expected from the preliminary discussion—because $P$ does not depend on hexing per se. However, in the case of the ravens, the reason $P$ does not depend on hexed ravenhood is that the closest possible worlds in which an actual hexed raven lacks the property of hexed ravenhood are those in which it is an unhexed raven, and $P$ does not depend on hexing. It is therefore not at all misleading to say that the hexed raven basing generalization fails the counterfactual test because $P$-hood does not depend on hexing, Indeed, for simplicity's sake I will continue to write as though what matters is $P$'s dependence on hexing, not hexed ravenhood. (This makes for a clearer exposition because the natural interpretation of the counterfactual antecedent *If x had not been a hexed raven . . .* is *If x had been neither hexed nor a raven* . . . , rather than, as the counterfactual test requires, *If x had been either not hexed or not a raven* . . . .)[8]

Third, the test does not necessarily anoint a single basing generalization, or even a single basing pattern, as the unique legitimate choice for a given explanandum. To explain the blackness of hexed ravens, for example, you may cite either *All ravens have P* or *All ravens and carrion crows have P* (the latter since, if a given bird had not been a raven or carrion crow, it might not have had *P*). Thus, you may cite either of two distinct basing patterns: the *P*-hood of all ravens, or the *P*-hood of all ravens and carrion crows.

Suppose the counterfactual test is correct; what kind of relevance does it diagnose? Philosophers have for so long associated counterfactual dependence with causal dependence that it is tempting to suppose that, if a basing generalization *All Fs have P* passes the test, there must be some strong metaphysical dependence relation between *F* and *P* that is much like causation (Lepore and Loewer 1987). A close examination of the reasons that counterfactual dependence exists between, for example, ravenhood and possession of the tyrosinase gene shows that this line of thought is mistaken: there can be a relation of counterfactual dependence between properties in virtue of facts that do not constitute anything remotely like a metaphysical dependence relation.

If this raven had, contrary to the facts, been hexed on its first birthday, it would have had the tyrosinase gene. Why? To evaluate the counterfactual we look to the closest possible worlds in which the raven is hexed at the stated time, which are, as explained above, worlds in which a conservative deviation from actuality shortly before the bird's birthday results in its being hexed. Such evaluation worlds are identical to the actual world up until the moment of the deviation, thus in the evaluation worlds, the raven has the tyrosinase gene up until that moment. The deviation, being conservative, then causes as small a divergence as possible from actuality; since whether or not the raven is hexed is easily manipulated independently of its genetic makeup, the most conservative counterfactual hexings do not affect the gene.

If this raven had not been a raven, by contrast, it might not have had the tyrosinase gene. Why not? It is extremely difficult to manipulate an organism's species without manipulating its genetic makeup. (You should acknowledge this even if you believe that the essence of species membership has nothing to do with genes, or if you believe that species membership has no essence at all.) Thus, even (some of) the most conservative deviations that remove an organism's ravenhood will affect its makeup, perhaps deleting the tyrosinase gene.[9]

The reason that having the gene depends on ravenhood but not on hexing, then, is that it is easy to manipulate hexing but hard to manipulate ravenhood without affecting the gene. Manipulating ravenhood sometimes or always affects the gene for one of two reasons. Either the features that go into determining whether something is a raven are physically intermingled with the gene—you might say that their supervenience bases overlap—or the features that go into determining whether something is a raven are physically intermingled with properties that have an effect on the gene. Neither possibility entails a dependence relation between ravenhood and having the gene. At most, they entail that ravenhood and possession of the gene depend, causally or metaphysically, on some of the same things.

The variety of explanatory relevance diagnosed by the counterfactual test, then, is not a dependence relation of the sort characteristically championed by the proponent of the causal approach to explanation. What might it be? Perhaps it is an axiom of our explanatory practice that, wherever there is counterfactual relevance, there is explanatory relevance. For most of the next section, however, I want to explore the possibility that counterfactual relevance is diagnostic of some other property of more basic explanatory interest.

## 7.34  From Counterfactuals to Pattern Subsumption

### Beyond the Counterfactual Criterion

While the counterfactual criterion for basing generalization relevance is illuminating, it cannot, I think, supply the complete story about constraints on explanatory basing patterns, for two reasons. First, some basing generalizations pass the test but seem to specify explanatorily irrelevant facts. Suppose, for example, that the mechanism for raven coloration $P$ is harnessed by genetic engineers in the textile industry to produce a certain kind of black silk. Then not only all ravens, but also all the engineered silkworms, have $P$. In explaining the blackness of ravens, however, it seems incorrect to employ the basing generalization *All ravens and engineered silkworms have P*. The $P$-hood of silkworms strikes us as explanatorily irrelevant to the blackness of ravens. Yet the raven/silkworm basing generalization passes the counterfactual test—if a given raven were not a raven or an engineered silk-worm, it would possibly not have $P$.

Contrast with another case, the explanation of sodium's high reactivity. I take it that this explanation features a basing generalization implying that sodium atoms have loosely bound outer electrons. The generalization *All sodium atoms have loosely bound outer electrons* would do the job, as would *All alkali metal atoms have loosely bound outer electrons*. (The alkali metals make up group one in the periodic table.) The latter generalization is at least roughly equivalent to *Lithium, sodium, potassium . . . have loosely bound outer electrons*. Why is this basing generalization legitimate, while the basing generalization ascribing $P$-hood to ravens and engineered silk-worms is not? It surely has something to do with a unity or cohesion in the class of alkali metals that is absent in a class composed solely of ravens and silkworms. The counterfactual criterion for relevance fails to capture this something.

The second consideration suggesting the need to supplement the counterfactual criterion arises from the following question. In cases where two or more basing generalizations are equally legitimate, might one nevertheless be explanatorily superior to the others, just as an elongation of a standalone explanation is superior to the original (section 4.31)? So that, while any of the generalizations may be featured in an adequate standalone explanation, some of these explanations are in some sense better than others? The answer, I think, is yes. It is fine to explain sodium's reactivity by pointing to the fact that all sodium atoms have loosely bound outer electrons. But it is even better to point to the fact that sodium is one of the alkali metals, and that all the alkali metals have loosely bound outer electrons. The basing pattern with wider scope, then—the more general basing pattern—is to be preferred. The counterfactual test does not account for the explanatory importance of generality.

To summarize, satisfaction of the counterfactual criterion appears to be something less than the full story about explanatory virtue in basing generalizations: the cohesion and generality of a basing generalization are important, too. What, then, is the essence of relevance in basing generalizations, an essence that apparently embraces not only counterfactual relevance but also desiderata of generality and unity or cohesion? The request for generality and cohesion brings to mind the two great accounts of explanatory relevance introduced in chapter one: the causal and the pattern-subsumption accounts. I have dismissed the possibility that the variety of relevance germane to basing generalizations is causal; could it be a matter of pattern subsumption? That is the option I will explore in what follows.

## Entanglement

Because the role of a basing generalization is to state a basing pattern, you might think that a pattern subsumption–driven relevance constraint would simply require that the stated basing pattern provide the best mix of cohesion and generality (and accuracy, which will become important when considering probabilistic explanation in part four). The true constraint is not quite so simple. I will develop an understanding of the relevance-determining pattern from the bottom up, by inquiring into two conditions imposed on basing generalizations in previous sections: first, that they pass the counterfactual test, and second, that they have a scope at least as wide as the generalization that they are called upon to explain. My conclusion is that the pattern is one of what I call entanglement; the next few pages will concern entanglement without any mention of pattern subsumption.

The counterfactual test diagnoses what you might think of as a certain resistance to separation. *All ravens have P* passes the test because it is hard to detach ravenhood from an object without also disturbing its *P*-hood. By contrast, it is easy to detach hexing from an object while leaving its *P*-hood intact; this is why *All hexed ravens have P* fails the test.

That a basing generalization has a scope at least as wide as the scope of its explanandum usually, if not always, means that it has a modal scope. For example, because the blackness of ravens is robust under a range of counterfactual suppositions, the basing pattern invoked to explain blackness, the *P*-hood of ravens, must be counterfactually resilient in a similar way. Thus, *All ravens have P* must be true of some nonactual ravens and of some actual ravens in nonactual circumstances.[10]

A basing generalization of form *All Fs have P* that is true, has sufficient scope, and passes the counterfactual test therefore posits a connection between *F* and *P* that is a kind of two-way robustness. On the one hand, where you find *F* you will find *P*, and small manipulations of the system will tend not to undermine its *P*-hood. Further, small manipulations that create new *F*s tend to bring *P* along with them. On the other hand, there is one exception to the rule that manipulating an *F* does not affect its *P*-hood: manipulations that remove a system's *F*-ness tend to remove its *P*-hood, or, at least, do so often enough that you do not expect to find

$P$ in a case where $F$ has been removed. I will say that two properties that stand in this relation of two-way robustness are *entangled*; more precisely, $F$ is entangled with $P$.

Some remarks on entanglement. First, as the talk of "tendencies" connotes, the connection between an entangled $F$ and $P$ tolerates exceptions: not every $F$ need have $P$. It is, for example, possible for a small manipulation to undermine a raven's $P$-hood without undermining its ravenhood, perhaps by damaging its tyrosinase genes (the cause of albinism). There is no need for a basing generalization to hold in these circumstances, since the regularity to be explained will not hold either (unless accidentally).

Second, entanglement is an asymmetric relation: to say that $F$ is entangled with $P$ is not to say that $P$ is entangled with $F$. Where necessary, I rely on context to establish the direction of the entanglement; there should be no confusion.

Third, entanglement is promiscuous: that $F$ is entangled with $P$ does not preclude other properties also being entangled with $P$ (or $F$'s being entangled with other properties). On the contrary, polytropic entanglement is the rule rather than the exception.

Fourth, that $F$ is entangled with $P$ does not imply that $F$ causes $P$, that $P$ is metaphysically dependent on $F$, or that $F$ is responsible for the presence of $P$ in any other way. (The case of ravenhood and the tyrosinase gene, discussed above, shows this clearly enough.) Entanglement does not even imply an overlap in supervenience bases. Further, entanglement is a modally local matter: ravenhood and $P$ are entangled in the actual world, but in a world not too different from our own where ravens evolved a brown coloration, ravenhood is entangled with some alternative to $P$ that causes brownness. What is actually entangled with what may, then, depend on highly contingent physical events. I conclude that the interest of entanglement lies not in some underlying metaphysical connection that lurks wherever entanglement is found, but in its implications concerning the coinstantiation of the entangled properties under typical counterfactual suppositions. Entanglement is, in short, a state defined not so much in terms of its underpinnings as in terms of its ramifications.

Fifth, entanglement admits of degrees. The greater the range of $F$-preserving or $F$-creating counterfactual manipulations under which a typical $F$ has $P$, the greater the degree of entanglement. Similarly, the greater the range of $F$-destroying manipulations under which a typical $F$ loses its $P$-hood, the greater the degree of entanglement.

Sixth, any basing generalization that passes the counterfactual test picks out an entanglement of some degree. Its passing the test of course guarantees that there is some range of $F$-destroying manipulations that also destroy $P$. But why think that there is some range of $F$-preserving manipulations that also preserve $P$?[11] The answer is that any actual fact, no matter how contingent, has a certain degree of inertia under counterfactual suppositions, because the truth conditions for counterfactuals have an intrinsic conservatism: in determining the worlds relevant to the evaluation of a counterfactual, they preserve as much of the actual world's history as possible (section 7.32). Even if some particular $F$'s $P$-hood is a complete accident, then, it will be left unmolested by (contemporaneous) counterfactual manipulations if at all possible. There is sure to be some range of manipulations that preserve a given $F$'s $P$-hood, even if the coinstantiation of $F$ and $P$ is mere happenstance.[12] It is therefore possible to understand all explanatorily legitimate basing patterns, even those employed to explain accidental generalizations, as being patterns of entanglement to some degree, without any loss of generality. I will do so.

Let me conclude by comparing entanglement to some neighbors in the literature on explanation. To know that $F$ is entangled with $P$ is to know something about the effects of a range of manipulations: it is to know which manipulations of a system with $F$ will tend to leave its $P$-hood unchanged, and which will not. This is reminiscent of Woodward's manipulationist account of explanation, on which explanatory knowledge about the production of an event is knowledge as to how to manipulate whether or not that event occurs. There are a number of differences between Woodward's conception of explanatory information and the kind of manipulative knowledge that a basing generalization supplies, but the parallel is worth noting.

Entanglement may also be compared with Jackson and Pettit's (1990) relation of programming. A property $F$ programs for a property $P$ if the instantiation of $F$ entails the instantiation of $P$. Facts about programming look to be able to play a basing role. The blackness of ravens can be derived, for example, from the claim that ravenhood programs for $P$-hood together with a description of the process in virtue of which $P$ causes blackness.[13]

Is it reasonable to require a basing generalization to state facts about programming rather than facts about entanglement, in effect replacing my story about explanatory relevance in basing generalizations with Jackson and Pettit's rival story? No; the requirement that basing generalizations state programming relations is too weak in one way and too strong in another. It is too weak because if ravenhood programs for $P$ then hexed ravenhood also programs for $P$—yet hexing cannot be cited in the explanation of blackness. It is too strong because although *All ravens have P* can play the basing role, ravenhood does not in fact program for $P$. Why not? If raven evolutionary history had gone differently, ravens might have been brown, in which case they would not have had $P$. Thus, the instantiation of ravenhood cannot entail the presence of $P$. More generally, the relation between ravenhood and $P$ that plays the basing role in the explanation of raven blackness must be sensitive to biological contingencies: it must hold in the actual world, where ravens are black, but not in possible worlds where they are not black. Programming does not satisfy this requirement: if one property programs for another, the one is found with the other necessarily.

### Patterns of Entanglement

Now to put entanglement to work. I propose that relevance in basing generalizations is a matter of entanglement: in a basing generalization of the form *All Fs have P*, the requirement that $F$-ness be relevant to $P$-hood is nothing more or less than the requirement that $F$ be entangled with $P$. Further, the explanatory role of a basing generalization is to cite a systematic pattern of entanglement. The more general, cohesive, and accurate the pattern, the more explanatorily virtuous the generalization.

To understand what a pattern of entanglement might be, it is necessary to scrutinize more carefully the nature of facts about entanglement. So far, I have treated entanglement as a relation between properties. There is nothing catastrophically wrong with this way of talking, but it is potentially misleading: it fails to reflect the fact that entanglement is a modally local relation. As explained above, ravenhood and $P$-hood may be entangled in the actual world but not in worlds very similar to the actual world in which ravens evolve a different coloration. Let me propose an alternative way of thinking about entanglement, in which facts about entanglement are in the first instance facts about particular objects or systems.

Consider, for example, a particular raven in its particular ecological context, calling the whole thing a system. To say that ravenhood is entangled with $P$-hood *in this particular system* is to say, of this raven, that a certain class of manipulations will tend to preserve its $P$-hood, while a certain other class of manipulations will at least sometimes fail to do so. More specifically, manipulations that preserve ravenhood in the system will tend to preserve $P$, while manipulations that fail to preserve ravenhood will, in a substantial number of cases, not preserve $P$. The facts that matter here, then, are counterfactual facts about a particular system, although they do depend on the nature of the properties of ravenhood and $P$-hood more generally. Now the more general claim, not indexed to any particular system, that the properties of ravenhood and $P$-hood are entangled can be understood as asserting that ravenhood and $P$-hood are entangled in all relevant actual and counterfactual systems, that is, in all actual ravens, along with all counterfactual ravens that come into being as a result of small deviations from actuality.

I want to understand the basing pattern cited by a basing generalization as a pattern of entanglement in individual systems. The instances of the pattern, then, are systems—such as particular ravens (in context)—with respect to which two properties are entangled. A pattern of entanglement exists when a broad range of systems are entangled with respect to the same two properties, as ravens are with respect to ravenhood and $P$-hood.

Require an explanatory basing generalization, then, to cite such a pattern of entanglement, and request that the pattern be as systematic as possible, that is, that it exhibit the greatest possible degree of combined generality, cohesion, and accuracy. These properties should of course be understood along pattern subsumptionist (section 1.32), not difference-making (section 3.7), lines.[14] I will have relatively little to say about the technicalities of the pattern-subsumption aspect of the explanatory constraints on basing generalizations, with the exception of a discussion at the end of this section on cohesion. I think it is enough, for now, to sketch the way in which the constraint might function; the details can be investigated if the sketch turns out to be on the right track.

The explanatory contribution of a basing generalization is a pattern of entanglement; from this, it follows that there are two rather different ways that a basing generalization can fail to realize the explanatory ideal. First, it may cite properties that are not entangled, such as hexed ravenhood and $P$-hood. The purpose of a basing generalization is to state a fact about entanglement; thus, a basing generalization implies that whatever properties it mentions are entangled. If they are not in fact entangled, the generalization is false, or is as misleading as if it were false. Falsehood is a prime explanatory transgression; thus, this defect of a basing generalization is serious. An explanation that contains such a generalization is deeply flawed.

Second, a basing generalization may cite properties that are entangled, but it may not cite the most cohesive, general, and accurate pattern of entanglement available. Suppose, for example, that *All sodium atoms have loosely bound outer electrons* is used to explain sodium's reactivity. A more general, and equally accurate and cohesive, basing generalization is available: *All alkali metal atoms have loosely bound outer electrons*. It is preferable to cite this latter generalization, but to cite the former is not to commit an explanatory distortion of the same order as citing an irrelevant property such as hexing.

In short, to cite a pattern of entanglement that is not as general as it could be is to cite a property that is explanatory but not as explanatory as it could be, whereas to cite a pattern that is not one of entanglement is to cite a property that is unexplanatory. It is therefore forbidden to cite properties, such as hexed ravenhood, that are not entangled with underlying causes, but it is allowable to cite properties, such as sodium-hood, that are entangled with underlying causes but that unnecessarily restrict the basing pattern's generality. With respect to the latter kind of explanatory optimality, the situation is much as it is with elongation, the process in which an event explanation is enhanced by providing an explanation for its initial conditions (section 4.31): any basing generalization that cites a relevant pattern of entanglement explains, but more general basing generalizations explain better.


To test the versatility of my treatment of relevance in basing generalizations, consider a case that is quite different from the explanation of raven blackness, namely, the explanation of Newton's law of cooling (introduced in section 7.32 above). The explanatory model takes as its basing generalization the statement that all relevant sets of initial conditions are entropic, where the notion of an entropic initial condition has a definition in molecular terms that I need not go into here. Can such a generalization be understood as stating a pattern of entanglement?

If the basing generalization is to have the form *All Fs have P*, it is clear what $P$ must be: the property of being entropic. But what is $F$? It must be a predicate satisfied by the initial conditions of all systems concerning which Newton's law has something to say. There is room for disagreement as to which systems, precisely, these are; let me choose a particular answer, that $F$ is the property of being a *normal branch system* in the *early part of our universe.* Let me define the italicized terms. A "normal branch system" is one that is detached from a larger system that is in equilibrium in the relevant sense (for Newton's law, this is thermal equilibrium) by a macroscopic operation and allowed to evolve in a new, relatively isolated system—as when an ice cube is removed from the freezer. (A discussion of branch systems may be found in Reichenbach (1956).) A system's being a normal branch system does not entail that it has entropic initial conditions, then; nor does its not being such a system entail that its initial conditions are not entropic. The "early part of the universe" is the part in which the universe's entropy is increasing from its initial low state and has not yet reached its maximum value. We are living in this early part (so we believe), and will be for a long time.

Ignore for simplicity's sake the temporal part of the basing generalization. Then the generalization states that the property of being a normal branch system and the property of having entropic initial conditions are entangled. This amounts to two claims. First, (almost) all normal branch systems have entropic initial conditions, and under a range of manipulations and other counterfactual circumstances, they would still be entropic. For example, not only actual ice cubes but also counterfactual ice cubes— such as those that I could make but choose not to—are, on removal from the freezer, in an entropic state, in the sense that counterfactuals such as *If I made a batch of ice right now, its initial conditions, after its removal from the freezer, would be entropic* are true. Second, the range of circumstances under which such counterfactuals are true is nevertheless limited: if such a system were not a normal branch system—if the ice cube had been prepared in a special way, like a crystal in a spin-echo experiment or a plaything of Maxwell's demon (Sklar 1993, 219–221)—then it might well not have entropic initial conditions.

## The Nature of Basing Patterns

In section 7.32, I favored the view that a basing generalization contributes to an explanatory model nothing over and above a pattern of initial conditions. How must this claim be amended in the light of the revised view that basing generalizations' explanatory contribution is a pattern of entanglement?

On the original conception, the basing pattern contributed by a basing generalization of form *All F s have P* can be represented as an ordered pair consisting of a set of objects—the *F*s in the actual and relevant nearby possible worlds—and a property, namely *P*. The explanatory role of the antecedent property $F$, then, is to pick out the set of "nearby" $F$s, or in other words, to contribute to the basing pattern its extension in the actual and (certain parts of) certain counterfactual worlds. The property $P$, by contrast, does more than pick out a set of things; it must appear explicitly in the pattern, since it is called upon "by name," as it were, in the causal model that takes the basing pattern as its initial conditions.

On the new conception, the same basing generalization contributes a fact about entanglement, namely, that the connection between $F$ and $P$ is robust in two directions. The robustness in the first direction is constituted by the $P$-hood of certain nonactual $F$s, and of actual $F$s in nonactual circumstances; this sort of fact was already captured by a basing pattern on the original conception. The robustness in the second direction consists in the non-$P$-hood of some or many ex-$F$s, that is, of formerly $F$ things that have lost their $F$-ness, either counterfactually or actually (and perhaps also of the non-$P$-hood of some other nonactual non-$F$ counterparts of actual $F$s). This is also a fact about the pattern of $P$-hood in actual and nearby counterfactual worlds, and one that can equally well be captured if the property $P$ and the extensions of $F$ in the actual and nearby possible worlds are specified.

In short, on the new conception as on the old, a basing pattern can be thought of as determined by a set of actual and counterfactual objects, the actual and nearby counterfactual $F$s, and the property $P$. Whereas on the original conception of basing patternhood, such an ordered pair was interpreted as asserting simply the $P$-hood of everything in the set, on the new conception, it asserts in addition a falling off of the pattern of $P$-hood outside the set.

On both conceptions, the explanatory relevance of the antecedent property $F$ is exhausted by its actual and nearby counterfactual extension. The explanatory role of the property of ravenhood to raven blackness, for example, is to pick out both the actual ravens and the ravens in (certain parts of) nearby possible worlds—in other words, to pick out a certain set of actual and counterfactual objects. Any other property that picked out the same objects could play the same role, and thus would be explanatorily relevant in the same way—a fact that will play a role in the next subsection.

### Is This Really Relevance?

You might wonder whether the relation that ravenhood bears to blackness deserves to be called a relevance relation. My standard for explanatory relevance is straightforward: a property (or property instance, or thing, or state of affairs) is explanatorily relevant to a phenomenon if it makes a positive contribution to the phenomenon's explanation. Ravenhood satisfies this criterion: it plays a role in picking out a basing pattern, and this pattern is a substantive addition to the explanation of raven blackness.

Nevertheless, the way in which ravenhood is relevant to blackness strikes us as less substantial than the way that the causal property complex $P$ is relevant to blackness. Causal relevance is somehow more explanatory than "basing relevance," the relevance that has its foundation in patterns of entanglement. You might put this down to asymmetric dependence: a property can have basing relevance only by way of a preexisting relation of causal relevance, but the reverse does not hold; in other words, you can have explanations without basing generalizations but not without mechanisms.

I suggest that there is more to the intuition of relative insubstantiality than this. Although the property of ravenhood makes a real contribution to the explanation of blackness, it is a contribution that, as I pointed out in the previous subsection, can equally well be made by other properties that have the same extension in the actual and relevant nearby possible worlds (see section 12.4 for further details). Thus, ravenhood, though relevant, is not explanatorily indispensable. By contrast, the property complex $P$ makes a causal contribution to the explanation of raven blackness that no other property can make.

Perhaps there are other reasons, too, to conceive of basing relevance as less explanatorily central than causal relevance. In any case, I endorse the intuition of relative importance; basing relevance ought not to be put on a par with causal relevance. But it is, all the same, a genuine variety of explanatory relevance. Remove the parts of an explanation that are relevant in this secondary, basing way, and you have weakened the explanation. Some readers may not want to use the term *relevance* at all in connection with basing generalizations. I do not object; what is important is to acknowledge the role that basing patterns play in explanation.

## Cohesion in Basing Generalizations

I asked earlier why the subsumption of ravens' $P$-hood under the basing generalization *All ravens and engineered silkworms have P* is unexplanatory. The answer, I suggested, has something to do with cohesion; you can now see what that something is. The raven/silkworm generalization brings together two patterns of entanglement that together form an incohesive whole; the requirement that explanatory basing patterns be cohesive thus disqualifies the pattern from the explanatory enterprise. What is the nature of cohesion? I have a—rather exploratory—suggestion to make.

Clearly, the kind of cohesion involved cannot be the causal cohesion so central to the kairetic account of difference-making (section 3.6), since the connection between ravenhood and $P$-hood is, as in so many basing patterns, noncausal.

The pattern-subsumption approach to explanation has its own conception of cohesion, on which a pattern of $G$-ness among $F$s is cohesive to the degree that $F$s have a shared nature or similarity (section 1.32). The raven/silkworm generalization does appear to lack this kind of cohesion. You might reasonably ask, though, whether the notion of a "shared nature or similarity" can be given a secure philosophical foundation. Indeed, although all sophisticated accounts of scientific explanation make an appeal to a notion of cohesion, it might be seen as a considerable advantage of the causal approach that it has the hope of providing an objective basis for cohesion in the causal facts, whereas a pattern subsumptionist's cohesion will have no better grip on reality than is allowed by the slippery quality of similarity.

Might the cohesion of a basing generalization be evaluated using some narrower and better founded standard? A basing pattern is a pattern of property entanglement. To cite such a pattern is explanatorily illuminating, apparently, because knowledge of entanglement is illuminating. The virtues of an explanatory basing generalization ought therefore to be understood, as far as possible, as virtues of such knowledge. How, then, is our recognition of which basing patterns are and are not cohesive a valuable element of our knowledge of patterns of entanglement?

When two properties are entangled, there is typically a single reason for their entanglement (rather than a different reason for each coinstantiation). Ravenhood and $P$-hood are entangled, for example, in large part because of a causal process by which $P$-hood is transmitted from generation to generation of ravens. (This is not the complete story, I should add; it does not in itself explain why ravenhood satisfies the counterfactual relevance test with respect to $P$-hood.) The reason for entanglement is not always causal, however, as in the case of the entanglement of waterhood and $H_2O$-hood.

I propose that a pattern of property entanglement is cohesive to the degree that there is a single reason for the entanglement. The entanglement of ravenhood and $P$-hood is cohesive, then, because actual instances of raven-hood and $P$-hood are entangled for the same reason in (almost) every case. The entanglement of raven-or-worm-hood with $P$-hood is by contrast in-cohesive, because the raven/$P$ instantiations are entangled for a rather different reason than the silkworm/$P$ instantiations.

To make good on this definition of cohesion, I would need to provide a taxonomy, or at least the means for creating a taxonomy, of reasons for entanglement, along with a criterion for individuating such reasons. This is something I will not attempt here (though I have already offered what I imagine will be a significant component of the individuation criterion, namely, chapter three's account of cohesion in causal processes). Thus, the suggested definition must remain at a rather programmatic stage.

Though perfect cohesion in a basing pattern is possible, it ought not to be expected: for any two entangled properties, it is always possible to cook up a particular case where they are instantiated and entangled, but not for the usual reason. (An example is given in the next section.) This is unsurprising, given that entanglement is, from a metaphysical point of view, a rather weak relation, depending as it does on particular matters of local, contingent fact rather than on timeless, metaphysically necessary interproperty relations.

The suggested interpretation of cohesion also casts some light on the explanatory role of generality: we search for the most general, cohesive basing pattern in order to put the entanglements involving causally relevant property instances in the context of all other entanglements that exist for the same reason. What we do, then, is tantamount to citing the reason for entanglement, and therefore making the reason a part of the explanation. Yet I insist that the reason is not a part of the explanation. It can, if causal, be made a part, by adding to the explanation a causal model for the basing generalization, so executing an elongation. But in the absence of such an elongation, the reason is not in the model and so is not in the explanation. A basing generalization citing a general and cohesive basing pattern is, as it were, "explanation-ready"—it is formulated in the right way to serve as an explanandum—but in the unelongated model, it is not yet explained. I make some further relevant comments in section 7.36.

## 7.35 Basing Generalizations in Event Explanation

The best explanation of sodium's reactivity, I have suggested, cites as a basing generalization the loosely bonded electron found in all the alkali metals, of which sodium is just one example. The explanation therefore not only invokes the conditions that cause reactivity in sodium itself but also puts these conditions in a wider context. I want to investigate the possibility that event explanations do the same, that is, that they cite for explanatory purposes a wider pattern that subsumes the particular initial conditions required by their causal models.

Consider, for example, the explanation of blackness in a particular raven $x$. On the account of event explanation developed in part two, $x$'s blackness is to be explained by a model that cites certain of $x$'s properties $P$ together with the aspects of the fundamental laws in virtue of which $P$ causes blackness. (For simplicity's sake, ignore as before the causal role of environmental conditions.) The first part of the explanation can be replaced, I suggest, by a basing generalization citing the entanglement of ravenhood and $P$, along with the assertion that $x$ is a raven. Schematically, then, the new explanation will have the form of a deductive argument for $x$'s blackness having the following premises:

1. $x$ is a raven.
2. All ravens have $P$.
3. The fundamental laws have such and such properties (i.e., the properties in virtue of which $P$ causes blackness).

Such an explanation obviously cites factors that are causally irrelevant to $x$'s blackness: first and most notably, the $P$-hood of other birds whose blackness is not being explained, and second, $x$'s own ravenhood (causally irrelevant for reasons given in section 7.33). Factors of this sort are, I have argued, permissible in regularity explanation, in which there are species of explanatory relevance besides the causal. But what reason is there to think that basing generalizations, and the code of relevance to which they are subject, appear also in event explanation?

The legitimacy of what is often called covering-law explanation shows, I think, that there is a place for basing generalizations in event explanation. A covering law explanation of a particular raven $x$'s blackness has the form of a deductive argument for $x$'s blackness with the following premises:

1. $x$ is a raven.
2. The "raven law": all ravens are black.

Not everyone regards such an explanation as entirely satisfactory, but few would deny that the raven law is relevant to explaining why a particular (normal) raven is black—whatever the deficiencies of covering law explanation, they do not include irrelevance. Now, I proposed in section 4.33 that to cite a covering law is to cite the constituents of the law, which are, I will argue in section 7.6, the elements picked out by the causal model that is its explanation. To cite the raven law in an explanation, then, is just to cite the basing pattern and mechanism that explain it, namely, the $P$-hood of ravens and the aspects of the fundamental laws in virtue of which $P$ causes blackness. If the raven law is not irrelevant to $x$'s blackness, then a fortiori the raven basing pattern is not irrelevant. Apparently, to subsume causally relevant initial conditions under a broader pattern of entanglement is as explanatorily effective in event explanation as it is in regularity explanation.

This thesis amounts to two separate, substantive claims. First, a property of $x$ that is not causally relevant to its blackness, such as its ravenhood, is explanatorily relevant to its blackness if it is entangled with a causally relevant property. (Recall that entanglement is at bottom a relationship between property instances.) An event explanation can always be legitimately augmented, then, by citing a property that is entangled with a legitimate causal model's initial conditions. (I will later use this facet of event explanation to find an explanatory role for semantic properties in psychology (section 12.2).) Second, an event explanation can be further augmented by subsuming the entanglement of these local property instances under a more general pattern of entanglement. (The role of such patterns in event explanation will turn out to be especially important in the treatment of probabilistic event explanation, in part four.) Thus, a causal model for $x$'s blackness that cites its $P$-hood can be augmented, first, by citing $x$'s ravenhood, since it is entangled with its $P$-hood, and second, by citing the more general pattern of entanglement between ravenhood and $P$-hood.

I would like to go further, suggesting that both augmentations not only enlarge but also improve the explanatory model: an event explanation that cites a basing pattern is better than one that does not. It is explanatorily more illuminating, for example, to note that $x$ is a raven and that ravenhood is entangled with the blackness-producing property $P$ than simply to note that $x$ has $P$. Why should information about entanglement, both local and global, improve an explanation? I have argued already that such information is explanatorily relevant, and I take it that it is better to have more rather than less explanatorily relevant information about an explanandum. QED.

This is precisely the same argument, you will recall, that I offered for the explanatory benefit of elongation, the process in which a causal model is augmented by the addition of a further causal model for some or all of its initial conditions, thus extending the model's reach further back along the causal chain. Causal history is explanatorily relevant; more relevant information is better; therefore, elongating a causal model enhances its explanatory power (section 4.31). As with elongation, so with the inclusion of information about entanglement: it is desirable, but not compulsory.

There is some psychological evidence, as it happens, that the perceived quality of an event explanation increases as the frequency with which the explanatory model is instantiated becomes greater (Lombrozo and Carey 2006). It is not clear whether the experimental subjects are responding to the breadth of the relevant basing patterns in particular or to the frequency with which the entire mechanism is instantiated; however, these are of course closely connected, and a response to one might serve as a heuristic for the detection of the other.

From here on, then, I assume that event explanations should appeal to basing generalizations wherever possible, and that these generalizations should maximize combined generality, accuracy, and cohesion. It follows that you should prefer to account for raven $x$'s blackness using the three-part explanation above, that is, by citing the following facts:

1. $x$'s ravenhood

2. The pattern of entanglement between ravenhood and $P$-hood

3. The aspects of the fundamental laws in virtue of which $P$ causes blackness

To cite (2) and (3) is equivalent to citing the raven law; this explanation is therefore equivalent to the covering law explanation of $x$'s blackness, though it has a more perspicuous form, in that it makes the constituents of the explanatory model explicit. (The two explanations are equivalent in the ontological sense, then, but not the communicative sense; see sections 1.21 and 4.33.)

Since the raven law is explained by its own constituents, it follows that the best explanation of $x$'s blackness contains the constituents not only of the raven law but also of the complete *explanation* of the raven law. More generally you have the following theorem:

> *Second Fundamental Theorem of Explanation:* The optimal explanation of an instance of a causal generalization contains all components (mechanism and basing generalizations) of the explanation of the generalization itself.

The second fundamental theorem subsumes the first fundamental theorem, articulated in section 7.2.

As implied earlier, a basing generalization may not be cited in the absence of a corresponding local entanglement. Why not? An event explanation that cites a basing generalization implicitly claims that its actual initial conditions instantiate the corresponding basing pattern; since that pattern is one of entanglement, it follows that the relevant actual conditions must be entangled. For example, an explanation of raven $x$'s blackness may cite the raven basing pattern only if $x$'s ravenhood is entangled with its $P$-hood. Because entanglement depends on local circumstances, this condition may not be satisfied, even though the entanglement of ravenhood and $P$-hood is the rule.

Suppose, for example, that raven $x$ is a product of Dr. Moreau's lab; the doctor was determined to create an organism with $P$, but he was indifferent as to whether it was a raven, an octopus, or a leopard man. In this case, had $x$ not been a raven, it would still have had $P$. Thus, $x$'s ravenhood fails the counterfactual test; it is not entangled with $x$'s $P$-hood. It is therefore incorrect in the Moreau case to cite either the raven basing generalization or $x$'s ravenhood in the explanation of its blackness. You must cite either some other basing pattern or the simple fact of $x$'s $P$-hood alone.[15]

A related matter: given that entanglement comes in degrees (section 7.34), does a greater degree of entanglement make for a better explanation? For example, is an explanation of $x$'s blackness that cites its ravenhood a better explanation, the more robust the connection (in either direction) between ravenhood and the blackness-causing property $P$? I will not attempt to answer this interesting question here, since I have developed the theory of entanglement and basing patterns to a level sufficient for my purposes in this and later chapters. I do not doubt, however, that some important issues concerning entanglement have yet to be settled.

Note that, when a property is explanatorily relevant to an event by way of a basing generalization, we do not say that the property is a cause of the event; the relation asserted by a causal claim must be one of causal difference-making (see note 1 of chapter 6).

Note also that a causal model that cites a basing generalization in its explanation of an event uses deductive entailment to represent three distinct explanatory relations: a relation of pattern subsumption, a relation of entanglement, and a relation of difference-making. Consider, for example, the explanation of raven $x$'s blackness above. Given $x$'s ravenhood, the model's basing generalization and mechanism (its parts (2) and (3)) together entail $x$'s blackness. This entailment is best understood as having three distinct steps: first, a step in which the generalization entails that if $x$ is a raven, it has $P$; second, a step in which this conditional together with $x$'s ravenhood entail that $x$ has $P$; and third, a step in which $x$'s $P$-hood and the mechanism together entail blackness. The second step, the entailment of $x$'s $P$-hood by its ravenhood, represents the entanglement of $x$'s ravenhood and $P$-hood. The first step represents the subsumption of this entanglement under the relevant basing pattern, the $P$-hood of all ravens. The third step of course represents a causal difference-making relation. Only this third step is, and ought to be, a causal entailment.

The same observation applies to certain regularity explanations. Consider, for example, what I take to be the optimal explanation of sodium's reactivity:

1. Sodium is an alkali metal.
2. All alkali metals have loosely bound outer electrons.
3. The fundamental laws have such and such properties (i.e., the properties in virtue of which atoms with loosely bound electrons react easily),

These properties can be understood provisionally as constituting the "mechanism for reactivity." (For the official story about the explanation of dispositions such as reactivity, see section 7.42.)

The model's entailment of sodium's reactivity should be broken down into three stages. In the first stage, the basing generalization (2) entails that any particular alkali metal has loosely bound outer electrons. In the second stage, this fact and premise (1) together entail that sodium has loosely bound outer electrons. In the third stage, this and the mechanism (3) causally entail reactivity. The second entailment represents the entanglement relation between sodium's being an alkali metal and its having loosely bound electrons. The first entailment represents the pattern-subsumption relation between this entanglement and the broader pattern of entanglement between any substance's being an alkali metal and its having loosely bound electrons. The third entailment represents a kind of causal process.

### 7.36  The Significance of Explanatory Relevance in Basing Generalizations

Basing generalizations have introduced to the kairetic account of both regularity and event explanation a kind of explanatory relevance that is not causal; rather, it is one that draws on elements of the pattern-subsumption approach to explanation and in its notion of entanglement, to some extent—and in an acausal way—on a manipulationist approach. (It might also be compared to Jackson and Pettit's programming, discussed in section 7.34 above.) The kairetic account thus becomes something of a hybrid, more so than I had envisaged when I wrote a paper called "The Causal and Unification Accounts of Explanation Unified—Causally" (Strevens 2004).

The justification I have offered for this aspect of the account is simply that it captures our explanatory practice: I observe that science allows basing generalizations that are not causal, and that are not lawlike in any other way, to play a role in causal explanation, yet it does not allow just any generalization to play the basing role. Basing generalizations must cite patterns of entanglement, patterns that preferably maximize generality, cohesion, and accuracy. The kairetic account puts this aspect of our explanatory behavior in writing.

So far, so good—but what greater explanatory good is there in using the optimal, rather than any other, basing generalization? Why are basing generalizations that imply entanglement, and that offer generality, cohesion, and so on, to be preferred to the rest? A part of the answer is that the generalizations that are to be explained have a certain robustness, and so require for their explanation patterns of initial conditions with a similar robustness. But this leaves two elements of explanatory relevance in basing generalizations unaccounted for: the kind of robustness—the aspect of entanglement—for which the counterfactual criterion is a test, and the desideratum that a pattern of entanglement maximize generality, cohesion, and accuracy. Why should these particular properties of a basing pattern bring explanatory heft?

You might well ask the same question about the nature of relevance in the properly causal part of an explanatory model: why should causal information be explanatory, and information about difference-makers in particular? The standards for explanatory relevance imposed by the kairetic account on both basing patterns and mechanisms are, I think, explanatorily primitive, in the sense that our explanatory practice treats them not as a means to an end but as the end itself. There is no overarching explanatory goal toward which we aim, and which is achieved variously by the citation of difference-making factors and patterns of entanglement. The different elements of a causal model rather aim for different goals—mechanism descriptions for a specification of a standalone set of difference-makers, basing generalizations for broad, cohesive patterns of entanglement.

Within our explanatory practice, then, there is no unified conception of explanatory goodness. But given a wider perspective, such a unification might become apparent: whatever factors account for the existence of our explanatory practice might jointly account for each component of the practice in turn.

You might, for example, advance the following sort of thesis: while scientists regard explanation as an end in itself, perhaps even as the highest of scientific ends, they are engineered to see things this way not because of the intrinsic merit of scientific understanding but because to focus on explanatory facts is also to focus on facts that are ends for their designer. Typically, the designer in these stories is apotheosized natural selection, and the end is success in science's more practically oriented endeavors, prediction and control. Gopnik (2000) suggests, for example, that the explanatory pleasure we derive from uncovering an effect's causes exists to motivate us to acquire more knowledge of causal mechanisms, not so as to explain, but so as to be able to predict and control the characteristic effects of these mechanisms, with large numbers of ever healthier babies presumably constituting the payoff somewhere down the line. Woodward's (2003) manipulationist theory of explanation is conducive to a similar train of thought.

In section 4.4, I laid the foundation for such an account of the explanatory virtues of knowledge of causal difference-making, by pointing out that the question we need to answer about the mechanism producing some particular high-level effect, in order to predict or control the production of the effect, is what aspects of the mechanism are difference-makers for the effect.

You might therefore think that our explanatory tastes have been shaped by the invisible Darwinian *arbiter elegantiae* to motivate us, or rather to motivate us even more, to focus on knowledge of difference-making.

Likewise, you might think that knowledge of entanglement is equally, or almost equally, useful to the would-be predictor and controller, a property $F$'s entanglement with $P$ telling you as it does what you may and may not do, or see done, to a particular $F$ without having to relinquish your belief in its underlying causally relevant property of $P$-hood. Further, the more general and the more accurate the patterns of entanglement to which you are party, the more potent your knowledge of the connection between instances of the properties in question (the cohesion of the pattern guaranteeing that it is correct to talk of *the* connection).

Let me now suggest another, less practically oriented, approach to understanding the elements of our explanatory practice. Suppose that our practice is constructed so as to direct our attention to the world's causal patterns—never mind whether for pragmatic or other reasons. Then you might understand the various canons of explanatory relevance as purging our explanatory models of factors that distract us from seeing the true patterns. Factors that do not make a difference are obvious distractions: they are superfluous to any causal patterns having as endpoints the phenomena to which a difference fails to be made. But what do causal patterns have to do with basing patterns?

Suppose you observe a connection between ravenhood and blackness. You suspect the existence of an underlying causal pattern. That is, you suspect that there is something about ravens that causes blackness. To discern the causal pattern clearly, you must understand what this "something about ravens" is, which is to say you must appreciate the basing pattern. Now suppose that the basing pattern that attracts your attention is the $P$-hood of hexed ravens. If you focus exclusively on such a basing pattern, you will limit yourself to the causal pattern by which blackness is caused in hexed ravens, and so you will fail to appreciate the wider causal pattern. Hexedness is therefore a distraction; a good account of explanatory relevance will remove it from an explanatory model.

Push this line of thought to the extreme, and you will conclude that the basing generalization that is freest of distraction is (putting aside concerns of accuracy) the widest possible pattern. A criterion for explanatory relevance based on this conclusion will therefore consider *All ravens and engineered silkworms have P* to be explanatorily superior to *All ravens have P* (the silkworm case is discussed in section 7.34). Our criterion for relevance in basing generalizations, though it places a high value on generality, stops short of endorsing such a pattern, because of the pattern's lack of cohesion. Why?

I suggest, tentatively, that the untempered preference for generality that is a result of an exclusive concern with outgoing patterns is not so helpful if you have a taste also for incoming patterns. If you desire to carve up the possessors of $P$ purely for the purposes of delineating the production of blackness by $P$, then you will do no carving at all. But if you would also like to apprehend patterns in the causal production of $P$, you will want to partition $P$ possessors according to the ways in which their $P$-hood is produced.

Perhaps our criteria for explanatory relevance in basing generalizations are, among other things, heuristics that attempt such a partition. One such heuristic posits a probable difference in the manner of $P$ production when two properties are entangled with $P$ for different reasons, as in the case of the silkworms and ravens. The power of this rule of thumb explains our preference for cohesion in an explanatory basing pattern. Another heuristic posits that when a property $F$ fails the counterfactual test with respect to $P$, it is likely that $P$ is produced in the same way in a class of systems of which the $F$s are only a proper subset. The power of this rule explains our preference for basing patterns that pass the test. These are, I must emphasize, *mere* heuristics: their satisfaction is neither necessary nor sufficient for sameness in $P$'s mode of causal production. But they are powerful enough that it is worth our while to organize an aspect of our explanatory inquiry around them. Or so I speculate.

If this story is correct, then the explanatory constraints on basing generalizations display an interest in causal mechanisms at one remove. Our explanatory practice is constructed to illuminate patterns of causation. Careful individuation of basing generalizations matters because it helps us to perceive such patterns.

## 7.4 Property Laws

How widely can the causal-mechanical approach to regularity explanation be applied? The next two sections show how a number of different kinds of laws or generalizations can be explained by citing a causal mechanism. My aim is not to give a comprehensive account of regularity explanation, but rather to investigate some especially central, interesting, and challenging classes of explananda.[16]

The present section focuses on laws of the form *All Fs have property G*, which I call *property laws*. Some property laws—the property-generation laws, such as *All ravens are black*, which are true in virtue of a causal process by which $F$s become $G$—have uncontroversially causal explanations). They present no special difficulties for the kairetic account (once it is acknowledged that the $F$-ness itself does not have to do the causing). Some—notably, constitution laws such as *Water is $H_2O$*—seem clearly not to have causal explanations. Between these two extremes lie several important cases that I will attempt to assimilate to the account of regularity explanation given in section 7.2:

1. Property laws that are given equilibrium explanations, which I will interpret as a species of property generation law

2. Laws that ascribe dispositions, such as *Leaded crystal is quite fragile* or *Sodium is highly reactive*

3. Force laws, such as Coulomb's law or Archimedes' principle

I will also discuss laws of instantiation, such as *Temperature in a simple gas is mean molecular kinetic energy*, and, briefly, laws of constitution.

Note that property laws in my sense may state a functional relationship between determinables, as when the apple law in section 7.2 relates an apple's time of impact to its initial height and time of detachment. The *All Fs are G* schema obscures this possibility; it might be replaced by a schema containing one or more free variables, such as *If $R(x)$ then $S(x)$*. For the most part, however, the simplicity of the $F/G$ schema is welcome.

### 7.41 Property Generation through Equilibration

Consider the following laws:

1. Soap bubbles tend to have a spherical shape.

2. The Hardy-Weinberg law, which gives the proportions of different genotypes at a locus when natural selection is not operating on the locus.

3. A free market always clears, that is, all commodities on offer are sold.

4. Humans have a sex ratio of about one-to-one.


Each is explained by showing that the property attributed by the law is characteristic of the relevant system's equilibrium state. The causal process that underlies each law, then, is the process by which the kind of system in question reaches its equilibrium state.

For explanatory purposes, an equilibrium process is the same regardless of a system's starting point: it takes a system having whatever initial conditions you like and guides it to the equilibrium state by some trajectory or other, the details of which depend on the initial conditions. Particular facts about initial conditions and the subsequent trajectory are therefore not difference-makers in an equilibrium process; for this reason, all equilibrium processes of a given type ought to be represented by a single explanatory model.

For example, the explanation of soap bubbles' shapes shows that whatever its initial state, a bubble will (in the absence of external forces) pull itself into a sphere. The explanation of market clearing shows that a change in supply, whatever its magnitude and direction, will impact the price of a commodity so as to manipulate the number of buyers in just the right way. The sex ratio explanation shows how a population with any sex ratio other than one-to-one will (with high probability) be pushed by natural selection in the direction of a one-to-one ratio—and so on.

To better understand the form of equilibrium explanation, let me consider two worries as to its workings. Both are directed at the equilibrium explanation of particular events—the spherical shape of particular soap bubbles, or the clearing of particular markets at particular times—but since explanations of a law's instances contain all elements of the explanation of the law itself (by the second fundamental theorem of explanation, stated in section 7.35), a resolution of problems about instance explanation has direct implications for the explanation of the instantiated regularity.

Sober (1983) argues that an equilibrium explanation of an event is not a causal explanation, because it does not cite the "actual cause" of the event that it explains, the actual cause being the precise initial state of the system. To illustrate his claim, Sober gives the following simple example of an equilibrium explanation. Consider a ball released at the inside lip of a basin. The ball rolls down into, then back and forth inside, the basin, eventually coming to rest at its lowest point. This will happen no matter what the ball's release point. The reason is that first, the motion of the ball dissipates (through friction and other effects), so that in the long run, in the absence of a net force it will come to rest; second, wherever in the basin the ball goes, there is a net force pulling it in the direction of the lowest point of the basin; and third, at the lowest point itself, the forces acting on the ball are in equilibrium, so that it experiences no net force. Sober claims, quite rightly, that this equilibrium explanation—an explanation that neither specifies the ball's initial position on the lip nor traces the path that it takes to the bottom of the basin—is the best explanation of the ball's final resting place.

If you suppose that a causal event explanation must cite the initial conditions and the ensuing causal trajectory that led to the event's occurrence, then the equilibrium explanation is indeed acausal, as Sober claims. But it is not true that the explanation says nothing at all about the ball's starting point and trajectory. It identifies the starting point as one of a large class, namely, all starting points at the basin's lip, and likewise identifies the trajectory as one of an equally large class. Further, it shows how any member of the class of the starting points leads to the explanandum by way of a member of the class of trajectories, in virtue of certain causal influences at work in the system. On the kairetic conception of causal explanation, this is sufficient to qualify the equilibrium model as causal (given that the different trajectories form a cohesive set). Indeed, any further causal detail in the model would, according to the kairetic account, be antiexplanatory: the model gives you just enough causal information about the process that led to the explanandum, and no more.

To put it another way, while a casual inspection of the equilibrium model might give the impression that it says nothing about the particular causal process leading to the explanandum event, in fact the model is exclusively concerned to describe this very token process, but at an extremely abstract level, so abstract that the description is satisfied by every process by which the ball might have reached the bottom of the basin. Thus, although the mechanism in the event explanation is a description of the causal production of the particular event that is to be explained, when detached from this course of events it may also serve as a description of the kind of causal process in virtue of which any ball released at the lip of the basin makes its way to the lowest point—and thus as a description of the mechanism underlying the truth of the law according to which the ball always ends up at the bottom of the basin (as the first fundamental theorem of explanation would lead you to expect).

Let me move on to a different problem. Consider again the event of a particular ball's coming to rest at the lowest point of a basin, having been released shortly before at the lip. The mechanism of the equilibrium model discussed above would appear to have three principal components: the fact of the ball's release, some properties of the basin, and the relevant physics. It is the inclusion of the second component that ought to concern you. On its way to the bottom, the ball touches only a part of the surface of the basin, the part being determined of course by its exact trajectory. This part is not itself basin shaped, but is rather a kind of filigree—what you would get if you cut away all parts of the basin that did not come into direct contact with the ball at some point on the way to its final resting place.

Now observe that any part of the surface of the basin that does not belong to the filigree is not a causal influence on the ball's trajectory from basin lip to bottom.[17] By citing the existence of the basin as a whole, rather than just the filigreed part, the equilibrium model's mechanism therefore transgresses the rules of kairetic explanation. It cites elements of the system that would have had an effect on the event to be explained, if the initial conditions of the ball's release had been different, but that in fact had no such influence. It is important to see that this is not a matter of abstraction. The equilibrium explanation's description of the complete basin is not a high-level characterization of the filigreed surface. For abstraction, the facts about the filigree would have to entail the facts about the basin as a whole, but the entailment in fact goes in the reverse direction.

It seems, then, that the explanation of the ball's resting place should cite the existence only of the filigree, not of the entire basin. If this is so, however, then the explanation of each ball's journey to the bottom of the basin has a distinct causal mechanism, citing as it does a distinct basin filigree. Consequently, there is no single underlying mechanism for all such journeys, hence no unified causal explanation of the ball/basin law. You will see that this problem is liable to generalize to most or all cases in which we practice equilibrium explanation, undermining the kairetic account's treatment of the practice.

One solution to this problem is to allow a causal mechanism to mention potential but nonactual causal influences (Jackson and Pettit 1992a, 1992b). I will advocate a more conservative approach, in two stages. The first stage establishes that the causal mechanism for any particular ball's journey to the bottom of the basin is the same, and thus rescues the kairetic account of equilibrium explanation. The second stage establishes that the explanatory model for a particular ball's coming to rest at the basin's bottom does in fact cite the presence of the entire basin, despite the causal irrelevance of most of its parts—in a basing generalization.

Stage one. The mechanism of the equilibrium model for the ball's finding its final resting place invokes the following facts:

1. The ball was released at the basin's lip.

2. At each point on its trajectory after its initial release was a basin-like surface, that is, the kind of surface with the kind of orientation you would get if a complete basin were present.

3. The relevant physics: the constant dissipation of the ball's energy as it rolled, the gravitational force pulling the ball down, and the solidity of the basin-like surface.

(Also required, as usual, is a negative background condition, in this case asserting among other things the physical neutrality of any part of the system not on the filigreed surface.)

What the facts cited by the mechanism imply is the existence not of an entire basin but of whatever filigree is necessary to support the trajectory of the ball, given the exact initial conditions of its release. Since the initial conditions themselves are not specified, the model does not imply the existence of any particular filigreed surface; rather, it specifies for any precisification of the initial conditions which filigreed surface must exist. (Since the physics, too, will be left inexact by an optimal explanatory model, a precisification of the physics is also needed to determine a particular filigree.) The model asserts, then, not that some particular set of initial conditions held or that some particular filigreed surface existed but that a certain functional relation held between the initial conditions and the surface, just as the optimal model for the cannonball's breaking the window specifies not separate ranges for the ball's mass and velocity but a range for a function of mass and velocity (section 3.53; some limits on "functionalization" are discussed in section 10.24).

The same functional relation holds for any particular ball, release point, and filigree traced out by that ball as it realizes its gravitational destiny.

Thus, the description of the causal process recommended by the kairetic account for any particular ball's journey to the bottom of the bowl is satisfied by every ball's journey. It is this description that picks out the aspect of the initial conditions and the fundamental laws—the mechanism—that underlies and therefore explains the ball/basin law.

Note that the presence of the mechanism in question, when cited in an event explanation, never implies more than the existence of a particular filigree. (To see which filigree, you would need to go beyond the explanatory model and look at the details of the relevant initial conditions.) It follows that the same mechanism would be invoked to explain the ball's final position in a system in which only the filigree exists: if you cut away all other parts of the basin, and contrive to release a ball so that it never leaves the filigree that remains, you may explain your ball's ending up at the lowest point of the filigree by using the equilibrium mechanics.

It would be patently wrong to say, in this latter scenario, that you can give an equilibrium explanation of the ball's behavior. Yet did I not just say that the same mechanism figures in both the equilibrium explanation and the case in which only the filigree exists? Yes, but the equilibrium explanation and the equilibrium mechanism are not necessarily the same thing: the explanation may supplement the mechanism with one or more basing generalizations. And so it does, I will argue in the second stage of my treatment of the ball and basin: the equilibrium explanation cites a basing generalization that cannot be cited in the filigree-only case; thus, an equilibrium explanation cannot be given in such a case.

What the equilibrium model contains above and beyond the mechanism, I suggest, is a basing generalization that guarantees the existence of the appropriate filigreed surface for any given release point, and thus implies the existence of the entire basin. More exactly, the generalization cites a pattern of entanglement between basinhood, as it were, and the existence of an appropriate surface. (That this is a genuine entanglement follows from its bidirectional robustness. First, under the relevant counterfactual perturbations—whether of the release point or of the exact shape of the basin—the necessary filigreed surface continues to exist. Second, perturbations that remove the basinhood—for example, that cut holes in the vessel in which the ball is released or give it a nonconcave shape—will undercut the guarantee of the existence of the filigreed surface: after such an operation, the surface required given the actual release point may well no longer exist.)

The case where a ball ends up at the bottom of a basin, then, is not to be given the same explanation as the case where the ball ends up at the bottom of the filigreed structure. The explanations cite the same mechanisms, but they differ as to a basing generalization: whereas the first cites the existence of the basin as a whole and then connects it to the existence of the causally relevant filigreed surface by way of a pattern of entanglement, the second does not, asserting only the existence of the filigreed surface.

It follows that the equilibrium explanation cites elements of the system that do not causally influence the ball, namely, the parts of the basin's surface not on the ball's trajectory. It does not cite them in its mechanism, however, but in its basing generalization. Thus, though they are not causally relevant to the ball's final position, they are explanatorily relevant all the same, in just the way that the properties cited in the antecedent of any explanatory basing generalization are relevant to the explanatory target, and thus to the explanandum (section 7.33).

The second fundamental theorem of explanation, you will see, is vindicated. The explanation of any particular ball's final position cites a mechanism and a basing generalization that, taken together, explain any ball's ending up in the same position, and thus explain the ball/basin law. The explanation of the instance therefore contains the explanation of the entire law.

### 7.42 Dispositions

I endorse what I take to be the standard causal-mechanical line on the explanation of dispositions: To explain $F$'s disposition to $G$ in conditions $Z$ is to explain the fact that, when conditions $Z$ hold, $F$s tend to $G$.[18] The explanation of a disposition is thereby assimilated to the explanation of a causal generalization of the if/then form discussed in section 7.2. To explain sodium's reactivity, for example, is to explain why sodium reacts enthusiastically with a wide range of substances—as I tacitly assumed when discussing reactivity above. To explain a material's superconductivity is to explain why, in appropriate conditions, a current flows in the material without resistance; to explain moths' phototropism is to explain why they head toward nearby light sources; to explain the extreme virulence of the Ebola virus is to explain why most people infected with Ebola die.

Let me defend this position against an objection, that it inverts the explanatory order. A natural and appealing picture of the explanatory role of dispositions is as follows. If $x$ has a disposition to $G$, then its actual $G$-ing is (normally) to be explained by its disposition. On this view, the explanation of a disposition is logically prior to the explanation of the behavior that manifests the disposition: the behavior is explained by the disposition; the disposition is in turn explained by some theoretical consideration. Cummins (1983, 21–22) appears to endorse this view.

The causal-mechanical approach to dispositions is at odds with this way of seeing things: it implies that, in order to explain the disposition, you must explain the behavior. Thus, the explanation of the behavior is prior to (or at least, not posterior to) the explanation of the disposition.

On the former view, for example, the decanter broke because it was fragile, and it was fragile because of some facts about its material structure. On the latter view, what explains the decanter's breaking is also what explains the decanter's fragility.

The clash between these two ways of thinking about the place of dispositions in explanation appears to be intimately related to the debate about the metaphysics of dispositions, and in particular, to the question of the relation between a disposition and its categorical basis. I believe that the explanatory problem can be resolved, however, without taking any stand on the nature of dispositions.

Consider the kairetic (or any causal-mechanical) explanation of a property-generation law of the form *In conditions Z, all Fs are G*. The law is explained by providing a schematic causal explanation of its instances, that is, by a causal model of the mechanism by which, in conditions $Z$, something about $F$s causes $G$-ness. Thus, in order to explain the law, you explain the law's "empirical signature," the $G$-ness of $F$s in conditions $Z$ (including, I remind you, the $G$-ness of some counterfactual $F$s or $F$s in conditions that are counterfactually $Z$). At the same time, the law can be cited, in the role of covering law, to explain the $G$-ness of any particular $F$ (section 7.35). Thus, on the one hand, the law is explained by explaining its empirical signature—that is, the overt behavior to which it gives rise—but on the other hand, that behavior is explained by citing the law. This precisely parallels the apparent explanatory inversion engendered by the causal-mechanical account of disposition explanation: dispositions are explained by explaining the behavior to which they give rise, yet they are also supposed to explain that behavior.

The inversion phenomenon is not unique to dispositions, then; it is a generic feature of the causal-mechanical approach to regularity explanation. If you are prepared to allow that the causal-mechanical approach is plausible—that is, that causal laws are to be explained by exhibiting their underlying mechanisms—then you should have no additional qualms about the causal-mechanical approach to disposition explanation.

Still, there remains an interesting question as to how a proponent of the causal-mechanical approach should think about the apparent inversion. I will return to this issue in section 7.6.

### 7.43  Force Laws and Causal Composition

Some laws of the form *If F then G* are force laws, that is, laws in which *G* is not the occurrence of a certain kind of event but the existence of a certain kind of causal influence. Some examples of nonfundamental force laws:

1. Archimedes' law: liquids exert an upward force on a submerged object equal to the weight of the displaced liquid.

2. An ideal gas exerts a pressure *P* on the walls of its container equal to $kT/V$ (a force law because pressure is force per unit area).

3. Water has greater surface tension than pentane. (Surface tension is a measure of the inwardly directed force that a liquid exerts on the molecules at its surface.)

4. The earth exerts a gravitational force on objects outside its radius identical to the force that would be exerted by an equally massive point particle positioned at the earth's center.

The causal influence in question need not be a force in the Newtonian sense; however, for simplicity's sake I confine the discussion to laws of this sort.[19]

Can force laws be treated along the same lines as disposition laws? You might think they can, since any object experiencing a force is thereby disposed to move in a certain way. The suggestion is at odds, however, with our explanatory practice. If forces were to be explained as dispositions to movement, then the explanation of a force law would be a causal model for the movement of objects. But explanations of force laws do not have this form—they do not mention the movements of objects on which the force is exerted, and they may not mention objects at all.

Let me try a slightly different approach. A physical explanation of an object's movement will normally include an account of the forces acting on the object; I propose that this account, if extracted from the movement explanation, will stand alone as an explanation of the net force. Consider as an example an explanation of the path of a satellite's orbit around the earth. The explanatory model's follow-through—the derivation of the orbit—will proceed in several steps. The first of these might well be a demonstration that the earth's gravitational field is identical to the field of an equivalent point mass situated at the earth's center. This derivation constitutes, I claim, a standalone explanation of the corresponding force law (4) above.

What, then, is the structure of the embedded force law explanation? Prima facie, it is a simple mathematical derivation. The premises are the law of gravitation, giving the gravitational force exerted by a point mass, the facts about the distribution of mass within the earth, and the relevant principles of the integral calculus, used to find the cumulative effect of such a distribution of point masses. These entail that the earth's field is identical to the field of an equally massive, appropriately centered, point mass, which is to say, they entail the force law. Can you therefore give a kind of DN account of force law explanation?

A DN account is inadequate for the reason given in section 7.1: if any derivation of the force law is an explanation of the law, then a derivation of the law from the conjunction of Boyle's law and itself will count as an explanation. The kairetic account solved the corresponding problem for event explanation by insisting that explanatory derivations represent an explanatory relation, the relation of causal influence. Is there an explanatory relation that could play this role in the explanatory derivation of force laws? Causal influence, a relation between events or property instances, is not appropriate. But there is a relation of *causal composition*, introduced in section 3.23, that is precisely what is required.

Let me remind you about causal composition. In the case of the explanation of the satellite's orbital path, I asserted above, the relevant initial conditions, the structure of the earth, and the Newtonian law of gravitation for point masses together entail the total force on the satellite. This is not quite true. What is missing is some principle stating the way in which the individual forces due to each point mass combine to exert a single net force on the satellite. It is easy to overlook this principle because it is so straightforward in Newtonian mechanics: the net force is just the vector sum of the individual forces. But the composition principle is a necessary part of the derivation all the same, and it is a necessary part of the derivation because it is a necessary part of the causal story.

More generally, a critical part of any causal story—of any account of the way in which one event causes another—will be a description of the way that the relevant causal influences compose (assuming that more than one influence is active). As well as causal influences, then, a causal universe contains causal composings, that is, facts about the way in which individual causal influences combine to exert the aggregate causal influence that they do.

The facts about causal composition look promising as raw material for force law explanations. First, since the facts about the way that causal influences compose are spelled out in fundamental physics, causal composition is a fundamental physical relation, of a piece with causal influence and suited to an account of causal explanation, such as the kairetic account, that draws only on fundamental-level causality. Second, it is by anyone's lights an essential part of the causal web, and so on any version of the causal approach to explanation, a bona fide explanatory relation.

I propose that the derivation of the gravitational force law in the orbital path explanation should be regarded as a representation of a real explanatory relation, the relation of causal composition, in the same way that I have taken other derivations in causal models to represent relations of causal influence. The derivation of net force is explanatory, then, only if it mirrors a causal composition relation. Deriving a gravitational force law $g$ from the premises $b$ and $b \supset g$, where $b$ is, say, Boyle's law, does not conform to this requirement. Although the premises entail the force law, there is no corresponding principle of causal composition according to which the net causal influence due to $b$ and $b \supset g$ is that prescribed by $g$. This is not a new doctrine; the constraint has been a part of the kairetic account all along, since causal entailment was explicitly required in section 3.23 to reflect the aggregation of individual causal influences.

It should now be clear what account I wish to give of the explanation of force laws. A force law explanation describes the way in which causal influences compose to exert the net causal influence specified by the explanandum. With the notion of causal entailment understood to encompass derivations that model relations of causal composition as well as relations of causal influence, no amendment need be made to the account of regularity explanation. A force law of the form *All Fs exert a force G*, then, is explained by a model containing the following:

1. A basing generalization of form *All Fs have P* (if necessary)

2. A demonstration that possession of $P$ (or $F$) causally entails the exertion of force $G$

An explanation of a force law differs from an explanation of, say, a disposition in just two respects: its target is the state of affairs of a certain force being exerted, rather than the occurrence of a certain kind of event, and its causal entailment models only causal composition relations, not causal influence relations.

A few remarks. First, the kairetic apparatus for determining difference-makers applies just as much to models of causal composition as it does to models of causal influence. An explanation ought to cite only those properties of a group of causal influences that make a difference to that aspect of their net influence described by the force law to be explained. In explaining the earth's gravitational equivalence to a point mass, for example, the details of the earth's composition ought not to be cited; only certain symmetries are relevant (in particular, that the earth is composed of concentric spherical shells, each of uniform density).

Second, there is no need to reify the notion of force in order to understand the explanation of force laws. What is required is that causes compose in some principled way; the net causal influence need not be a thing in itself.

Third, the account extends to the explanation of any generalization that states facts about causal composition. It is not limited to Newtonian force; in a universe where causal influences did not have the aspect of forces, the principles of causal composition would be explained using the same rules for the construction of explanatory models laid out above. To get a sense of how such explanations might look, consider causal composition in a field theory or in analytical mechanics.

Fourth, the account of force law explanation introduces no elements to the explanatory schema that were not already required for event explanation. The kairetic account of the explanation of events, property generation laws, dispositions, and force laws is a unified whole. The explananda differ, but the notion of causal entailment and the optimizing criteria for mechanisms and basing generalizations are deployed in the same way in each explanation.

### 7.44 Instantiation and Constitution

*Water is $H_2O$* is a law of constitution; *Temperature in a simple gas is mean molecular kinetic energy* is a law of instantiation (section 7.32). How ought such laws to be explained?

I had perhaps first better ask *whether* they ought to be explained. Are they merely definitions, therefore empty of empirical content and as such not fit for scientific explanation? There are statements of the same form for which this is surely true, for example, *Pressure is force per unit area*.

The cases of water and temperature are, however, more complex. Begin with the instantiation law concerning temperature. This law has a genuine explanation, which is as follows (with certain complications suppressed). According to thermodynamics, temperature is that intensive heat-related quantity that equilibrates—that approaches the same value everywhere—as a system approaches thermal equilibrium. In different kinds of matter, the property that equilibrates is somewhat different. Temperature in a single gas is mean molecular kinetic energy because (for example) when two simple gases are in thermal equilibrium, it is the mean kinetic energy of their molecules—as opposed to, say, the mean velocity of their molecules—that is the same throughout each gas. The first part of this explanation, the definition of temperature, is semantic. The second part is empirical, and indeed causal, since the explanation of the equilibration of mean molecular kinetic energy is a causal explanation, an explanation that adverts to the mechanics of the process by which equilibrium is reached.

A plausible, though no doubt overly simple,[20] sketch of the form of an instantiation law explanation may be extracted from this case. To every property that may be the subject of an instantiation law, such as the property of temperature, there is a definition. In the case of temperature, it might be, as the "zeroth law of thermodynamics" has it, *intensive, heat-related quantity that is everywhere the same in a system in thermodynamic equilibrium*. An instantiation law is true in virtue of two kinds of facts: the semantic facts as to how the instantiated property is defined, and the empirical facts in virtue of which, in a given kind of system, such as a simple gas, a certain low-level property satisfies the definition. An instantiation law is explained by exhibiting these facts and the fact of satisfaction itself. It therefore has the form of a deduction.

Often the empirical facts are causal facts, as in the case of temperature, and so the explanation of the instantiation law is partially causal. Indeed, it is difficult to think of an interesting instantiation law whose explanation does not have a causal component. Nevertheless, such laws are surely possible, and in any case, the role played by definitions in the explanation of instantiation laws cannot be accounted for by a theory of causal explanation.

Is there a sense in which there might be a kairetic account of the non-causal explanation of instantiation laws? A fruitful starting point is the observation that, typically, some aspects of the semantic dependence relations brought into being by a scientific vocabulary make a difference to a low-level property's satisfying a given definition and some do not (compare with my remarks about mathematical explanation in section 5.7). But I will leave the examination of this noncausal species of difference-making to another time.

What about constitution laws? These too can be understood as arising from the interaction of semantic dependence relations, such as the facts about reference-fixing that determine the extension of *water*, and empirical facts, such as those that determine that the reference of *water* is fixed so that it is identical to, or constituted by, $H_2O$. It is perhaps far less common in the case of constitution laws for the empirical facts to be causal facts, and so far less common for the explanation of a law of constitution to be, even in part, a scientific explanation.

## 7.5  Other Laws

### 7.51  Negative Laws

Laws that involve negative states of affairs provide an especially interesting challenge to any account of explanation. Some examples of negative laws:

1. The Pauli exclusion principle, which forbids certain states of affairs that are otherwise easily represented in the quantum formalism.

2. All noble gases are inert, that is, nonreactive (Kitcher 1989).

3. The principle of competitive exclusion, according to which two different species in the same ecosystem cannot occupy the same ecological niche.

4. The fact that the smallpox vaccine confers immunity to smallpox (an adaptation of Railton's example; see Lewis (1986a, §3)).

The explanation of negative laws has been little discussed (not at all, as far as I know, although my examples have been put to work in discussions of other issues in the philosophy of explanation). By contrast, explanations involving negative events have received much attention in the literature on causal claims, under the headings of causation by omission and prevention. The kairetic account claims, first, to give a full account of causal claims, including cases of omission and prevention, by assimilating causal claims to event explanation (chapter six), and second, that many or all event explanations contain corresponding regularity explanations (the fundamental theorems of explanation; sections 7.2 and 7.35). If both claims are correct, and the laws corresponding to event explanations involving causation by omission and prevention are negative laws, then the kairetic account ought to be able to handle the explanation of negative laws.

And it can, as I will show by applying the accounts of causing-no-longer-to-hold and prevention (section 6.4) to the examples above, in reverse order. (Causation by omission is not invoked.)

To explain immunity is to explain a certain kind of prevention: a person is immune to smallpox because they instantiate some property that tends to prevent the smallpox virus taking hold. Consider the explanation of a particular immune person's resisting smallpox in virtue of their immunity. The explanation will assume, as a part of the explanatory framework, the presence of a smallpox infection, and it will recount the causal story as to how the virus was eliminated. In particular, it will describe how a condition required for viral survival and reproduction—the continued functioning of infected cells—is caused-no-longer-to-hold by the immune system's destruction of the cells. The same causal model (assuming that it cites the optimal basing patterns) explains the immune system's prevention of smallpox in any person with immunity, and therefore explains the disposition, immunity, itself.

To explain the competitive exclusion principle, you explain why, if two species did occupy the same niche, natural selection would drive one to extinction (unless it evolved to occupy a different niche). The explanation thus describes the causal process by which the system goes from having two species in the niche to having just one; it is a causing-no-longer-to-hold, where the property that is caused-no-longer-to-hold is the joint ecological tenancy of two species. There is much more to say about such an explanation. It is an equilibrium explanation (the derivation of the explanandum proceeds by showing that the equilibrium state for the system contains only one species). It is an aggregative explanation, for reasons explained in section 5.5. It is a black-boxing explanation, since the ecological situations to which it applies are discretely multiply realizable (section 5.4). But none of this pertains in particular to its negativity.

The explanation of inertness is a kind of prevention. Noble gas molecules, like the molecules of any substance, have many of the properties necessary to participate in chemical reactions (and they do participate in a few). But there are certain facts about the inert gases that prevent these properties, usually, from leading to a reaction. In other words, certain pre-conditions for reaction are not satisfied by the inert gases: the outer electrons of the atoms are not easily detached, and there are no empty slots in the atoms' outer shells. Many explanations of a pattern of some event type's nonoccurrence will have this preventative form: there is a certain mechanism that normally leads to the relevant type of event, but it is blocked in the systems to which the law applies.

The Pauli exclusion principle is an interesting case. It is often regarded as a fundamental law itself, in which case, it has no explanation, but there does exist a somewhat informal explanation of one part of the principle in quantum field theory (Weinberg 1995, 170–172, 223–224).[21] How does it work? Infamously, the art of applying quantum field theory to real systems involves the judicious invocation of rules with the form "such and such a quantity must disappear at large distances"; call them vanishing rules. I will interpret the vanishing rules as a proper part of quantum field theory. (The alternative, I suppose, is to regard them as signs of the theory's immaturity.) They are, then, fundamental truths about the world that are not themselves susceptible of explanation. The explanation of the exclusion principle (or rather, a part thereof) is a demonstration that if it were not true, then a vanishing rule would be violated. In other words, a part of the exclusion principle is deduced from the vanishing rules and other laws of quantum field theory. This sort of derivation is not a causal explanation per se; there is nothing causing particles to avoid getting themselves into states prohibited by the exclusion principle. It is rather a mathematical fact that, provided particles comport themselves in accordance with the precepts of quantum field theory, including all but not only those parts of the theory that describe causal relations, they will abjure the prohibited states. In this respect, the explanation of the exclusion principle is much like the explanation of more positive physical principles such as the conservation of energy or momentum: it is in essence a mathematical explanation, showing that trajectories that conform to the fundamental laws will have certain mathematical properties. Another interesting negative claim that perhaps stands to fundamental physics in this way is the prohibition on faster-than-light communication (Maudlin 1994).

### 7.52 Interlevel Explanation

In an interlevel explanation, elements of lower-level theory, such as laws of physics, are used to explain elements of higher-level theory, such as laws of biology. On the kairetic conception of explanation, all regularity explanations are interlevel explanations: to explain a law is always to specify the law's underlying mechanism, so to explanatorily invoke the lower-level laws that govern the operation of the mechanism. While it is often possible to say something useful about a law's mechanism without descending to a lower level, what is said without descent cannot stand alone as an explanation—or at least, cannot constitute a deep standalone explanation, a standalone explanation without black boxes (section 5.3). Why? You will recall that a deep standalone explanation must trace the operation of the explanatory mechanism to properties (perhaps quite abstract) of the laws of fundamental physics, this because a causal model is nothing more than a high-level description of the fundamental physical facts that constitute the mechanism and thus drive the causal production of the regularity in question (section 4.33).

Interlevel explanation—and thus all kairetic explanation that aspires to depth—requires correspondence rules relating higher- and lower-level vocabulary or properties. When making this observation for the first time in section 3.23, I claimed that contrary to the prevailing view (Dupré 1993), correspondence rules need not give conditions for instantiating high-level properties that are necessary and sufficient: rules with much weaker properties suffice to establish the required connections between high and low. Since the importance of correspondence rules is even more salient in regularity explanation, let me now briefly justify this assertion.

You are asked to explain why all $F$s are $G$ by relating the high-level properties $F$ and $G$ to two fundamental-level properties $P$ and $Q$, where $P$ causes $Q$. Your explanatory task, then, is to fill out the familiar bridge diagram shown in figure 7.1. The connection between $P$ and $Q$ is provided by the appropriate fundamental-level causal model; the role of correspondence rules is of course to allow the transitions represented by the dashed arrows: from $F$ to $P$ and then from $Q$ to $G$.

If you suppose that the sole constraint on the correspondence rules is that they allow the deduction of the law relating $F$ and $G$ from the law relating $P$ and $Q$, then it is clear that the rules need not go so far as to provide necessary and sufficient conditions for $F$ and $G$, for four reasons.

First, the rules need hold only locally, by which I mean within the scope of the regularity to be explained. When explaining the short-term dynamics of a particular population of rabbits, for example, you may assume that any descendant of rabbits is a rabbit. This is not true in general, as rabbits

**Figure 7.1**  The bridge diagram giving a schematic explanation of the $G$-ness of $F$s

are presumably capable of spawning a new species, but it is true within the limits assumed by the population law to be explained, and it is therefore quite adequate for the purposes of the explanation.

Second, in transitioning up to and down from a high level of description, though you may need necessary conditions and sufficient conditions, you never need conditions that are both necessary and sufficient. To infer that a rabbit eaten by a fox is dead, for example, you do not need a definition of *death*; all you need is to know that being eaten is sufficient for death. (The distinction between brain death and cessation of heartbeat is irrelevant when neither organ any longer exists.) Likewise, to infer that a rabbit can be eaten by a fox, you do not need a definition of *rabbit*; you need only know that rabbits are small, unprotected morsels of meat, a necessary condition for rabbithood, in the technical sense, but obviously not a sufficient condition.

Third, if your "necessary" and "sufficient" conditions have exceptions, it is no great tragedy: provided your explanandum is coarse-grained—a trend or pattern in population dynamics, say, rather than an exact, day-by-day bunny count—and the exceptions remain under control (a complicated issue, but an important part of scientific modeling by anyone's lights), you will have the causal entailment you need. Even when you do not have entailment, thus perfect accuracy, a model of near-perfect accuracy will in many cases be well within reach.

Finally, it is, for similar reasons, unlikely to be a problem if the correspondence rules are vague, in the sense that they allow borderline cases, that is, complexes of low-level properties that neither determinately instantiate nor determinately fail to instantiate a given high-level property. At worst, your causal model will be a little less than completely accurate; almost-complete accuracy is quite good enough for explanatory purposes, indeed mandatory if the vagueness allows for greater generality (section 5.2).

So far, I have assumed that the sole condition of adequacy to which the correspondence rules must answer is that they allow the deduction of the high-level explanandum from a low-level mechanism. Though all of what I have said above in the light of this assumption will stand—correspondence rules need only be locally reliable, they need not be necessary and sufficient conditions, they may have exceptions or allow borderline cases—I now abandon the assumption itself. The correspondence rules must, I think, not only establish the local coinstantiation of high- and low-level properties that will serve as adequate ground for the relevant deduction, they must also establish in addition a close metaphysical relation between the coinstantiated properties.

You might think that the appropriate metaphysical relation is one of realization. To explain the blackness of ravens, for example, you might think that it is not enough to describe a causal mechanism that produces a property that is always accompanied by blackness; the mechanism must produce blackness itself. By parallel reasoning, it is not enough to describe a mechanism by which something about ravens causes blackness; the ravenhood itself, or some aspect of the ravenhood, must do the producing. More schematically, you might think that the correspondence rules should entail, within the scope of the generalization to be explained, the following:

1. $Q$-hood realizes $G$-ness, that is, every $Q$ is, in virtue of its $Q$-hood, a $G$.

2. $P$-hood realizes $F$-ness, that is, every $P$ is, in virtue of its $P$-hood, an $F$.

The first of these constraints is, I think, genuine: when giving a causal explanation for the $G$-ness of $F$s, you must model the causal production of some set of realizers of $G$-ness. But the second is not. For the purposes of causal explanation (involving, as here, a single one-way mechanism) it is allowable for $P$ to be an intrinsic property of $F$s that does not in itself realize $F$-ness; it is possible, therefore, that an intrinsic property of $F$s rather than their $F$-ness itself does the causing of $G$.

This weakening of condition (2) is of course mandated by the theory of basing generalizations developed in section 7.3. If what I have said about basing generalizations is correct, then in order to explain why all $F$s are $G$, it is enough to find a pattern of entanglement between $F$-ness and some property $P$ that does the actual causing of $G$. A correspondence rule governing a downward explanatory transition, then—the "left-hand side" rule in figure 7.1—can be a basing generalization. Indeed, it *will* be a basing generalization of some sort, and so the constraints on downward correspondence rules are simply the constraints on explanatory basing generalizations. A downward correspondence rule must, in other words, cite as general, cohesive, and accurate a pattern of entanglement as possible between $F$ and an intrinsic property of $F$s.

And an upward or a right-hand side correspondence rule? Here, I suggest, the sole constraint is of realization: the correspondence rule must imply that within the scope of the generalization to be explained, $Q$-hood realizes $G$-ness.

Because a basing generalization can serve as a downward correspondence rule, but nothing like a basing generalization can be an upward correspondence rule, a tighter connection is required between the low-level and high-level property in the upward case than in the downward case. To explain the blackness of ravens, for example, you must show that some intrinsic property $P$ of ravens plays a part in causing a realizer $Q$ of blackness. Your downward correspondence rule need only point to an intrinsic property $P$ of ravens that is entangled with ravenhood, while your upward correspondence rule must single out a property $Q$ that itself realizes blackness. Why the asymmetry?

That an intrinsic property is required on the downward path and a realizer on the upward path in part reflects the directions of the paths themselves: as pointed out above, even on a simple deductive conception of interlevel explanation, what is required in the downward transition is a necessary condition (for ravenhood), while what is required on the upward transition is a sufficient condition (for blackness).

This observation does not exhaust the asymmetry, however. The connection posited by a downward rule may apparently be metaphysically looser than the connection posited by an upward rule. The blackness-causing property $P$ must be something that all ravens have, but it need not be a part of their ravenhood—that is, it need not overlap with the complex of properties that, metaphysically, make a bird a raven. Take a raven's $P$-hood (and nothing else) away, and it will still be a raven. By contrast, the ravens' blackness consists in their having $Q$. Take their $Q$-hood away, and they will no longer be black.

Why the explanatory need for a closer metaphysical connection at one end of the causal difference-making relation than the other? I conjecture that the asymmetry is due to a feature of the kinds of causal patterns that, for us, constitute explanatory knowledge (section 7.36). These patterns are themselves asymmetric: they are captured by a template of the form *Something about F causes G*. On the left-hand side you have something about *F*; on the right-hand side you have *G* itself. An explanatory pattern may therefore be looser on the left than on the right. The asymmetry in our template for causal knowledge might be attributed in turn to an asymmetry in patterns of causal inquiry: we tend to look for hidden causes of observable effects. But here I have stepped outside the investigative boundaries drawn in section 1.5; I will say no more.

A final remark on interlevel explanation. Some writers have claimed that higher-level laws can help to explain lower-level laws (Kitcher 1984, §5). In all such cases, I believe, the higher-level law in question functions as a basing generalization. This poses no problem for my claim that within the purely causal part of an explanatory model, higher-level regularities are understood in terms of the properties of the fundamental physical laws.

## 7.53 Multimechanism Explanation

Jade, as all philosophers know, is a name for either of two distinct substances, jadeite and nephrite. All jade is hard. But the hardness of jadeite and the hardness of nephrite are due to somewhat different molecular facts. An explanation of why all jade is hard will therefore cite two distinct causal mechanisms—it is, in effect, a bundle consisting of two causal models. The pastiche quality of the explanation reflects a similar quality in the jade generalization itself; it is, you might say, a "multimechanism generalization."

Although multimechanism generalizations can of course be explained, their explanation is piecemeal. In effect, a regularity such as the jade-hardness law is explained by disassembling it into its constituent parts and then separately explaining the parts. (Compare with aggregative explanation; section 5.5.)

It follows that the explanation of an instance of the jade generalization—of the hardness of either a sample of jadeite or a sample of nephrite—will contain only a subset of the ingredients for an explanation of the generalization itself: it will cite only one of the two required mechanisms, whichever is applicable to the sample in question.

Two consequences of this observation: First, either the scope of the fundamental theorems of explanation must be limited to generalizations with a single underlying mechanism, or the notion of an instance must be rethought so that the jade generalization has no genuine instances. For simplicity's sake, let me take the former route.

Second, the jade generalization itself cannot be said to explain its instances. When those instances are samples of nephrite, they are explained by the "nephrite law" (consisting of the mechanism for hardness in nephrite), and when they are samples of jadeite, by the corresponding "jadeite law." A law about jade per se cannot, in short, function as an explanatory covering law (Kim 1992).

The same is true for any generalization about a discretely multiply-realizable kind. I remind you, however, that the scientific appearance of multiply-realizable kinds might in some cases be understood as a kind of black-boxing, in which the kinds stand in for lower-level or exogenous mechanisms relegated to the explanatory framework (section 5.42); the consequences for the understanding of belief/desire explanation are investigated in section 12.2.

One other, quite different, class of generalizations ought also to be given explanations that cite multiple mechanisms, namely, generalizations that assert a correlation between effects of a common cause, such as *Barometer needle dips are followed by storms* and *Substances with high thermal conductivity also tend to have high electrical conductivity*. The explanatory model for a causal correlation of the form *All Fs are G* will, I suggest, have three parts: a model for the causal production of $F$, a model for the causal production of $G$, and a generalization linking, where necessary, the conditions required for the operation of the $F$-producing mechanism to the conditions required for the operation of the $G$-producing mechanism.

A few words on this third part. When $F$ and $G$ are effects of a common cause, there will be considerable overlap between the setup of the $F$-producing mechanism and the setup of the $G$-producing mechanism. If the overlap were complete—if $F$ and $G$ were causal consequences of precisely the same initial conditions—then no further link would need to be established between the mechanisms; the explanation of the causal correlation would have just two parts, a model for $F$ and a model for $G$, with identical setups.

Complete overlap of this sort is extremely rare, however. The barometer dip and the storm may have a common cause—a certain kind of weather event—but they also have many causes that are not shared; after all, the conditions required for the functioning of a barometer are not entirely meteorological. In order for $F$ and $G$ to be found together, these unshared causes must be found together. Or more asymmetrically, in order for $G$ to be found wherever $F$ is found, the unshared causes of $G$ must be found wherever the unshared causes of $F$ are found.

At the very least, an explanation of the correlation between effects must state this correlation of unshared causes. I tentatively propose that it should go further and state a relevant pattern of entanglement—either between the unshared causes themselves or between some further set of explainers and both sets of unshared causes. As an illustration of this latter possibility, consider a generalization stating a correlation between certain symptoms of measles: the appearance of Koplik's spots is usually followed by a high fever. The physiological conditions required for the manifestation of the spots will differ to some extent from those required for the development of the fever, but a condition of application implicit in the generalization—that we are dealing with a human body—will be entangled with both. This entanglement will, along with the (measles-involving) mechanisms for spots and fever, explain why the one is typically followed by the other.

## 7.6   The Metaphysics of High and Low

### 7.61   The Constituents of a Causal Law

Laws loom large in explanation, both as explainers and as explananda. Yet I have avoided taking a stand on two important questions about laws: the question of demarcation, that is, of what generalizations count as laws, and the closely related question of constituency, that is, of what kind of thing a law is. This is a tactical agnosticism: my aim is to show that the kairetic account does not hinge in a critical way on how these questions are answered. The order of inquiry if anything goes the other way: the kairetic conception of explanation suggests attractive answers to questions about both constituency (this section) and demarcation (section 7.63).

Concerning constituency, I propose the following causal-mechanical thesis, already foreshadowed in many places above: high level causal laws— that is, all non-fundamental causal laws—are identical to the sum of the facts cited in their explanatory models, that is, to the mechanisms and basing patterns (if any) that explain them.[22] Although the causal-mechanical thesis provides a metaphysics for a certain kind of law, it will not seem much like other well-known accounts of laws of nature, because these other accounts primarily concern fundamental laws. (Lewis's (1973b) best-system account, for example, is a theory of fundamental laws alone.) Indeed, since the thesis takes the fundamental laws as its raw material without saying anything substantive about their nature, it is quite consistent with a range of views about the essence of fundamental lawhood.

Let me spell out the consequences of the causal-mechanical thesis for an uncomplicated causal law of the form *In conditions Z, all Fs are G*, understood (as above) as assuming or asserting a causal connection running from $F$ to $G$. If the law's explanatory model contains no basing generalizations, then the law's sole constituent is the mechanism in virtue of which the properties specified by the law's conditions of application $Z$ and antecedent $F$ causally produce the explanatory target, that is, the instantiation of $G$. Such a mechanism is, in effect, a high-level property of the fundamental laws—you might say that it is nothing over and above those aspects of the fundamental laws that are essential to establishing the connection from $Z$ and $F$ to $G$.

If the high-level law's explanatory model contains basing generalizations, then the law has two or more constituents: the basing patterns—the patterns of entanglement—whose existence is asserted by the basing generalizations, and the mechanism connecting the properties specified by the basing generalizations (and any causes specified explicitly by the law) to the explanatory target.

Three remarks. First, the causal-mechanical thesis entails that every law has a distinct explanatory model, that is, that there is a one-to-one mapping—an injection—from laws to explanatory models. Is this a plausible commitment? In section 7.63, I investigate the consequences of transforming it from a commitment to a stipulation, so creating one part of a demarcation criterion for laws.

Second, the thesis that laws are identical to their explainers, together with what I characterized in section 3.23 as the reductionist thesis that the causal ingredient in all explanation is derived from the fundamental laws, adds up to the reductionist metaphysics of causal laws that I have championed throughout this study, on which the laws are in their causal aspect (that is, aside from their basing patterns) not ontologically distinct from, but merely high-level properties of, the fundamental physical laws. The impact of basing generalizations on this explanatory physicalism will be discussed in section 12.4.

Third, in arguing for the causal-mechanical thesis as a metaphysics of high-level laws, I intend nothing more than the claim that the scientific role of high-level causal laws is played by mechanism/basing pattern bundles (and nothing else). In determining metaphysical correctness, then, I do not give any weight to intuitions about lawhood, or to coherence with other metaphysical doctrines. The question whether the causal-mechanical thesis offers the best metaphysics of lawhood outside of scientific practice is therefore left open.

In the remainder of this section, I explore the causal-mechanical thesis in two ways, first by pitting it against a plausible rival view of high-level lawhood, the modal regularity thesis, and then by using it to create a scheme for demarcating laws and, more generally, a scheme for carving up the space of causal generalizations in a useful way.

### 7.62  The Modal-Regularity Thesis

What could a high-level causal law be if not a mechanism or a mechanism/basing pattern bundle? A worthy alternative is what I will call the modal-regularity thesis, according to which a high-level law, causal or otherwise, is simply a regularity extending to certain possible as well as actual worlds. On this view, the raven law, for example, is identical to the fact that all actual and "nearby" possible ravens are black. (On the question how to understand "nearby," see section 7.32.) The sole difference between a mere empirical regularity and a law, then, is one of scope: the latter, but not the former, includes some possible as well as actual systems.

There are two considerations appearing to favor the modal-regularity view. First, you might consider it strange that, on the causal-mechanical thesis, a law is explained by its own constituents, so that it in effect explains itself. The modal-regularity view does not have this consequence, since the explainers of a modal regularity—that is, the relevant mechanism and basing patterns—are distinct from the regularity itself.

Second, the modal-regularity view respects the surface form of law statements: they appear to be mere, if modal, universally quantified claims. (Of course, I am far from being the only philosopher to consider the surface form misleading in this respect.)

On the other side, there are several powerful reasons to reject the modal-regularity thesis in favor of the causal-mechanical thesis. First, the causal-mechanical view preserves the idea that laws explain their instances. On the kairetic view, at least, only a mechanism (that is, a difference-making process) can explain an event, thus high-level laws can explain only if they are at least part mechanism. The same argument might be thought, if tentatively, to apply on any causal approach to explanation.

Second, and in a similar vein, the causal-mechanical view of laws preserves the idea that laws explain the generalizations that constitute the surface form of law statements. The raven law, for example, explains why all actual ravens are black and, indeed, why all "nearby" possible ravens are black. On the modal-regularity view, the raven law could do neither.

A third reason to prefer the causal-mechanical thesis to the modal-regularity thesis rests on the psychology and semantics of law statements, which when properly understood imply that law statements do not after all have the form of generalizations, but something else. Here I will report on, rather than argue for, a thesis about the content or meaning of law statements that I have proposed elsewhere.

Strevens (2000b) advances the thesis that the law statement *All ravens are black* has roughly the same cognitive significance as the claim *There is something about ravens that causes them to be black*.[23] Such a claim, then, states the existence of a property or property complex $P$ shared by all ravens, and claims that there is a high-level causal relation—a difference-making relation, I would now say—between $P$ and blackness. At least approximately, then, the law statement claims the existence of a basing pattern and a mechanism. For the law statement to be true—for the corresponding law to obtain—is just for an appropriate basing pattern and mechanism to exist. On this view, to assert a law statement of the form *All F s are G* is to assert, in the first instance, not the existence of a modal regularity—the $G$-ness of all actual and nearby $F$s—but rather the existence of a basing generalization and a mechanism that in turn entail and explain the regularity.

For these reasons, I endorse the causal-mechanical over the modal-regularity metaphysics of laws. Still, a question remains: how can it be that a law is explained by a causal model that is nothing more than a description of the law's constituents? If the causal-mechanical account is correct, then it seems that you explain a law by, as it were, uncovering its essential nature. A typical law statement does not spell out the nature of a law; it rather limits itself to articulating the consequences of that unspoken nature, attributing a pattern of behavior to an underlying mechanism while saying little or nothing about the mechanism's workings. (It is precisely this convenient silence that makes causal hypotheses an apt starting point for causal inquiry.)

Explaining the law, then, is a matter of abandoning this coyness, this indirection: it is an act of metaphysical revelation, in which the basing patterns and aspects of the fundamental laws that constitute the explanandum are made plain.

A further consequence of the causal-mechanical thesis is that the contrast between the metaphysical and the causal-mechanical approach to the explanation of laws (section 7.1) is more apparent than real. To cite a behavior-explaining causal mechanism is to display the explanandum law's metaphysical foundations in the fundamental laws; it is therefore to unveil the relations of dependence—in this case, the simplest of such relations, identity or constitution—between a law and the world. In other words, to show how the law causes behavior is to show how it is rooted in the world's fundamental ontology.

### 7.63  Demarcating the Laws

The causal-mechanical thesis tells you what kind of thing a high-level causal law is, but it does not entail any particular demarcation criterion, that is, it does not tell you which generalizations are laws and which are not—although it does entail, as you will see shortly, a necessary condition for lawhood. In this section, I will advocate and explore the consequences of a demarcation criterion that is based entirely on explanatory concerns and that dovetails neatly with the causal-mechanical thesis: the class of causal laws consists of all and only those causal generalizations that, deployed as covering laws, optimally explain their instances.[24]

Some philosophers have argued that there is no sharp boundary between laws and nonlaws (Mitchell 2002), others that lawhood is so strong a notion that it excludes most of the generalizations that do the scientific work usually attributed to laws (Woodward 2003). Each of these views is perhaps too extreme in its own way, but the demarcation of lawlike regularities is surely a complex matter. There are a number of classes of causal generalizations, any one of which might perhaps be deemed *the* causal laws. The task of a demarcator is more to map out the structure of these classes than to draw a single boundary line across the territory. For this reason, the instancehood definition of law should be understood as an attempt to pick out an especially interesting class of lawlike generalizations rather than the last word on lawhood.

Let me begin by determining what commitments concerning demarcation are inherent in the causal-mechanical thesis. I continue to focus on simple generalizations of the form *In conditions Z, all Fs are G* that hold in virtue of a causal connection running from *F*, or something about *F*, to *G*. According to the causal-mechanical thesis, a law is constituted by the elements of reality specified in its own explanatory model. It follows that a generalization that is constituted by something other than the components of its own explanatory model cannot be a law.

This necessary condition on causal lawhood rules out as laws generalizations that specify explanatory irrelevancies. Consider, for example, *All hexed ravens are black*. This is a bona fide causal generalization—it is true because of a causal connection running from something about hexed ravens to blackness. Further, it is what Woodward (2003) calls an invariant generalization, meaning that it is robust under various counterfactual suppositions, or more perspicuously, that it offers a considerable degree of counterfactual support. (Had this hexed raven been born a day later, it would still have been black, and so on.) Yet in the light of the causal-mechanical thesis, it is not a causal law.

Why not? I am going to assume, in the spirit of the causal-mechanical thesis, that any causal generalization, not just a law, picks out—or even better, is constituted by—the mechanism and patterns of initial conditions that intuitively make the generalization true. In particular, the hexed-raven generalization picks out a bundle consisting of the mechanism for raven blackness together with the pattern of $P$-hood in hexed ravens. Now, you will observe that this is not the bundle that explains the hexed-raven generalization—that bundle contains instead the pattern of entanglement between ravenhood and $P$-hood. (The relation between $P$ and hexed ravenhood is not one of entanglement at all.) Thus, the hexed raven generalization picks out a bundle that involves an explanatory irrelevancy, namely hexed ravenhood, but it is explained by a bundle that—of course—omits the irrelevancy. The observation generalizes: it is a consequence of the causal-mechanical thesis that no generalization, however invariant, that contains in its specification an explanatory irrelevancy (whether in basing pattern or mechanism) can be a causal law.

It is natural to ask whether this necessary condition can be transformed into a complete criterion for lawhood, to the effect that a causal generalization is a causal law just in case it picks out the mechanism/basing pattern bundle by which it is explained. You might call this the causal-mechanical demarcation criterion. If the causal-mechanical criterion is applied only to causal generalizations that are true in virtue of a single mechanism—the kind of *All Fs are G* mechanisms that have been my almost exclusive concern in this chapter—then it is equivalent to the instancehood criterion. That is, if a (single-mechanism) causal generalization picks out the elements of its own explanatory model, then it optimally explains its instances, and vice versa. This follows directly from the second fundamental theorem of explanation, which states that the mechanism and basing pattern that explain a (single-mechanism) causal generalization and the mechanism and basing pattern that explain any instance of the generalization are one and the same (section 7.35).

The causal-mechanical criterion comes apart from the instancehood demarcation criterion, however, in the case of multimechanism causal generalizations, that is, causal generalizations that are true in virtue of multiple mechanisms. Consider, for example, a multimechanism generalization whose explanatory properties were discussed in section 7.53: *All jade is hard*. It seems that the jade generalization picks out its own explanatory model, namely, a bundle consisting of the mechanisms for hardness in jadeite and nephrite. But the jade generalization does not explain its instances. The hardness of nephrite samples is explained by the mechanism for nephrite hardness, not a bundle consisting of both nephrite and jadeite mechanisms. It is the instancehood criterion for lawhood that should prevail, I suggest. The jade generalization is not a law, and the causal-mechanical criterion for lawhood is good only for single-mechanism generalizations.

I should add that the instancehood criterion does not deny lawhood to every multimechanism generalization. Consider another example from section 7.53: *Most sudden drops in barometer readings are followed by storms*. It can be argued that this generalization does explain its instances—the co-occurrence of barometer drops and storms—on the grounds that the explanatory model for the law, consisting of two overlapping mechanisms (one for storms and one for barometer drops), together with some basing patterns, explains any particular storm/barometer drop incident. Thus, the barometer generalization is perhaps a causal law.[25]

To summarize the conclusions drawn in this discussion about the demarcation of causal laws:

1. A causal generalization is a law just in case, when deployed as a covering law, it (or equivalently, its explanatory model) provides an optimal explanation of its instances—the instancehood criterion for lawhood.

2. The causal-mechanical criterion for lawhood—a causal generalization is a law just in case it picks out the elements of its own explanatory model—is equivalent to the instancehood criterion, and so is correct, for single-mechanism (but not multimechanism) generalizations. Put any single explanatorily optimized mechanism together with zero or more explanatorily optimal basing patterns, then, and you have a causal law.

More work is required to precisify the instancehood criterion, but the above conclusions are sufficient in themselves to yield some interesting consequences about lawhood.

First, every kind of causal process is a law in waiting. If there is a Rube Goldberg machine connecting $F$ and $G$ in conditions $Z$, then it is a law, on my account, that in conditions $Z$, all $F$s are $G$—the law being identical to the mechanism itself. Because $Z$ will specify an extremely intricate and (loosely speaking) improbable setup—the careful positioning and maintenance of ropes, pulleys, fires, kites, bugs, birds, and banana peel—the law will seldom if ever be instantiated. On these grounds, you might not want to call it a law at all. I will not fight you, but I will point out that a Goldberg generalization's explanatory credentials are as good as any law's: it explains its instances just as surely as its more frequently seen cousins in the nomological family, and so there is no explanatory ground to distinguish it from other generalizations that are less choosy about how and when they are instantiated.

Second, some writers have insisted that all properties specified in the antecedent of an if/then causal law must be causally relevant to its consequent (Davidson 1967; Fodor 1989). I suspect that the view is motivated, at least in part, by a commitment to the instancehood criterion for lawhood. Davidson and Fodor correctly hold that causal laws must explain their instances, I surmise, and so bar from lawhood generalizations, such as *Hexed ravens are black*, that mention irrelevancies. However, they mistakenly believe that explanatory relevance must be causal relevance, and so they require the causal relevance of antecedent properties. The instancehood criterion does put an explanatory-relevance constraint on the antecedent properties of a causal law, as the discussion of the causal-mechanical criterion above made clear. But some causally irrelevant properties, such as ravenhood, satisfy the constraint, in virtue of their involvement in an optimal pattern of entanglement with causally relevant properties, and so merit a place in the nomological antecedent.

I might add that the notion of high-level causal lawhood would be for practical purposes almost vacuous were causal irrelevancies not permitted in antecedents, since, arguably, almost no high-level laws are true in virtue of mechanisms—that is, in virtue of the fundamental laws—alone.

Third, as the jade generalization shows, the instancehood criterion has the following consequence: a generalization that relates two properties $F$ and $G$ in virtue of a causal connection running from $F$ to $G$ qualifies as a causal law only if there is a single, cohesive mechanism responsible in every instance for the connection. To put it another way, the connection between $F$ and $G$ must exist for a single, systematic reason, rather than because there are a number of quite distinct (i.e., causally noncontiguous) causal processes each connecting a different kind of $F$ to $G$.

This is at odds with the picture of high-level lawhood painted by Fodor (1974), which does not require fundamental-level systematicity, and thus allows the existence of laws with multiple underlying $F$-to-$G$ mechanisms. I will not try to undermine the Fodorian picture here—after all, as I stated earlier, there is a certain amount of slippage in the term *law*—however, I will make the bet that all interesting high-level causal generalizations will turn out to be causal laws in my sense (Strevens 2003b, §5.1).

# — 8 —

# Abstraction in Regularity Explanation

## 8.1 Problems of Abstraction in Regularity Explanation

Why *problems*? Because the three modes of abstraction that I discuss here—idealization, what I call preidealization, and the mathematical explanation of physical phenomena—seem to be at odds with a causal approach to explanation. This introductory section will be concerned to emphasize the difficulties.

Although these difficulties are discussed in the context of regularity explanation, they arise just as often in event explanation, because of the parallel between the explanation of events and the explanation of laws made explicit in the fundamental theorems of explanation (sections 7.2 and 7.35). Abstraction is less salient in event than in regularity explanation, however, because of the particularity inherent in the enterprise of explaining how a token causal process produces a singular event.

### 8.11 Idealization

An idealized explanatory causal model misrepresents elements of the causal mechanism that produces the explanatory target, either by omission, that is, by assuming the elements' absence, or by distortion, that is, by misdescribing their nature. No causal account of explanation—certainly not the kairetic account—allows nonveridical models to explain. It will be difficult, then, for the causalist to explain why idealization is so common.[1]

Some idealizations omit or distort what are, intuitively, only minor aspects of the relevant mechanism. To ignore the gravitational effect of the sun when computing the trajectory of an earthbound cannonball is a minor omission of this sort, since physics tells us that the causal influence of the sun on the cannonball is slight. Everyone has a story justifying these minor omissions: the expectability theorist (Hempel 1965a, 344–345), the causal minimalist (section 2.1), and of course the practitioner of kairetics

297

(though the kairetic account demands that factors be omitted in a way that does not compromise the veridicality of the model).

But other idealizations distort what are from the physical perspective important, perhaps pervasive, aspects of the causal story. The explanation of Boyle's law using the ideal gas model, to be examined at length in this chapter, assumes that the molecules in a gas never collide with one another. In fact, any given molecule will experience many collisions over even very short time intervals; consequently, the behavior of a molecule is almost entirely determined by the collisions it undergoes. The causal history of a gas consists, then, of almost nothing but collisions—yet for explanatory purposes, it seems, collisions can be profitably ignored.

### The Pragmatic Approach

Almost every justification of explanatory idealization belongs to a class of apologia that I call the *pragmatic justifications*. The defining characteristic of a pragmatic justification is the view that idealizations are a compromise. What is compromised is scientific understanding: an idealizing explanation is never as good as its nonidealizing counterpart. The reasons for the compromise may be many, but as the term *pragmatic* suggests, they are most likely to cite science's limited resources. Our grants are not large enough, our journals not fat enough, our minds are not good enough, that we can grasp fully the optimal, nonidealized models of the phenomena we wish to understand. Would that they were! But in a nonideal world we turn to nonideal explanations that simplify and distort the facts required for complete understanding.

Though on the pragmatic view, idealization is invariably deleterious to your understanding, even some of idealization's most prominent friends are pragmatists. For example, the leader of the Poznań school, Leszek Nowak, maintains that idealized models are mere way stations on the journey to explanatory fulfillment: science eventually removes, or ought to remove, every "counter-actual" idealization (Nowak 1992). An idealized model provides an "approximate explanation," on Nowak's view; only a model free of all idealization can produce a "perfect explanation."[2]

Pragmatists are not, of course, committed to the view that idealizing explanations are in principle misleading; a good idealized model, they will hold, clearly indicates which of its claims are intended literally and which are not (Railton 1981, 243). They do believe that such a model, however clearly it identifies its idealizations, is explanatorily only second best.

## The Empiricist Approach

According to the kind of empiricist view on which the aim of science is to save the phenomena, making up stories about the behind-the-scenes production of the phenomena will not in itself count against an idealized explanatory model. Further, insofar as an idealization allows the model to save the phenomena more economically or more elegantly, it may be counted a good thing. This is true above all on a unificationist approach to explanation, according to which elegance and economy are themselves explanatory virtues.

How would a unificationist make sense of the idealizations that appear in the standard explanation of Boyle's law? Simple: they would argue that correcting the causal idealizations in the ideal gas model would increase its complexity without any commensurate increase in the number of phenomena modeled, making for a decrease in overall unifying power. For the purpose of explaining Boyle's law, then, the ideal gas model is explanatorily superior to a more accurate representation of the inner workings of a real gas. Idealization, in this case, increases explanatory power; it is compulsory.

My aim here is not to argue against unificationism, but I should pause to note that there is a deep difficulty with this suggested unificationist treatment of the Boyle's law case. The ideal gas model correctly predicts certain behaviors of gases: their adherence, approximately, to Boyle's law, Gay-Lussac's law, Avogadro's law, and so on. But it fails to predict a number of other behaviors, for example, the relatively slow speed of gaseous diffusion, which is due to intermolecular collisions. A causally more realistic model of a gas is able to account for all the former phenomena and the latter as well. The claim that moving to a more realistic model results in a decrease in unifying power is therefore called into question: certainly, the move decreases the model's simplicity; but at the same time, it increases the number of phenomena unified. It is unclear which model is the more unifying, then. (According to Friedman (1974), it is the more realistic, unidealized model that unifies better.) Thus, the unificationist account of idealization appears to fall through: our best idealizations seem sometimes not to result in the greatest degree of unification. That said, I imagine that a committed unificationist or other empiricist might find a way around this problem and so preserve a distinctive empiricist approach to idealization, perhaps by opting for a less holism in the determination of explanatory models (section 1.32).

## The Kairetic Approach

Idealization makes an explanation better, I will argue, by conveying explanatorily essential information, that is, information that must be grasped in order to understand perfectly the phenomena to be explained. Once this is appreciated, two virtues of idealization will become clear:

1. An idealizing explanation (done right) is always better than its veridical counterpart (by which I mean the explanation that corrects the idealizing explanation's distortions).
2. An idealizing explanation is in one important respect explanatorily optimal: it cannot be further improved.

Omissions and distortions in scientific theorizing are not always ideal, of course; some will degrade an explanation so much as to make it worthless. I define an idealization as any misrepresentation of the causal process that improves the explanatory power of a model by comparison with its veridical counterpart; the genuine idealizations, then, should be distinguished from the everyday omissions or distortions that are mere errors or at best stepping stones to the truth.

### 8.12  Preidealization

A preidealization is a distortion of a causal model that decreases the power of the corresponding explanation, but one that does so by much less than the degree to which it distorts the causal story.

Consider, for example, Newton's gravitational explanation of the orbits of the planets. The explanatory model attributes the orbits to a force—gravity—that according to the general theory of relativity simply does not exist. You might well expect the Newtonian explanation to count as completely worthless—as worthless as the explanations tendered by other theories that do all their explaining by way of nonexistent entities, such as the phlogiston theory of combustion or Descartes' vortex theory of planetary motion. Yet for some reason the Newtonian theory is thought to retain considerable explanatory power. Newton's unwitting distortion of the causal facts about gravitation was a preidealization. The philosophical problem raised by preidealizations is to explain why they are so much less ruinous than other omissions and distortions of comparable size.

Strategies for making sense of preidealization will, naturally enough, parallel strategies for making sense of idealization. The pragmatic approach acknowledges no difference between idealizations and preidealizations: both sap explanatory power, and both are made because the alternative is even worse. My strategy will attribute to preidealizations some, but not all, of the qualities of idealizations, in a way that I will spell out in section 8.34.

## 8.13  Mathematical Explanation of Physical Phenomena

The explanations of some phenomena appear to be more mathematical than causal (Sober 1983; Kitcher 1989, 426–428). I have discussed one reason for this in chapter five: if an explanatory model black-boxes on a grand scale, the explicit content of the model may be entirely mathematical, as is perhaps true of some ecological and economic models (section 5.42). That is not my topic here, however; what I am interested in is rather a kind of explanation that contains no black boxes but that conveys an understanding that turns on the appreciation of a central fact that is a matter of mathematics alone. It would be going too far to say that such explanations have no causal component at all, but the mathematical element dominates. Let me give two examples.

### Marangoni-Bénard Convection

A thin layer of fluid is sandwiched between two plates; the lower plate is heated. Once the difference in temperature between the plates is great enough, convection begins: distinct upward currents form in some parts of the fluid, balanced by distinct downward currents in neighboring parts. The fluid then moves in a rolling motion, with hot fluid rising from below, cooling, descending, and warming again. Because the surface tension of the fluid changes with its temperature, the pattern of convection changes as the fluid warms. At a certain point a hexagonal pattern of convection cells forms, and the fluid takes on the aspect of an irregular honeycomb. Within each cell, the fluid wells up in the center and descends around the edges.

The explanation for the occurrence of the convection is a causal one. But the explanation for the hexagonal pattern of the convection cells is mathematical, that the closest packing of circles in a plane is hexagonal. Let me reiterate that this mathematical fact does not explain the pattern independently of causal information. It is important, in particular, that the causal process underlying Marangoni-Bénard convection creates cells with approximately radial symmetry. But in explaining the hexagonality, the mathematical fact dominates.

### Homozygosity in Elephant Seals

Northern elephant seals are homozygous at every gene locus that has been examined. (Homozygosity in two sentences: Because elephant seals, like humans, have paired chromosomes, at each gene locus there are two slots. When these slots are filled by copies of the same genetic variant, or allele, the locus is said to be homozygous; when filled by copies of different alleles, heterozygous. Since genes usually have more than one allele, heterozygosity is common. But in northern elephant seals it is unknown.)

Why? Hunting of the seals reduced their population, by 1900, to only 20 individuals. Their numbers have since recovered (to 100,000), but the near extinction of the seal resulted in a population bottleneck leading to the disappearance of much genetic diversity: most of the genes in the elephant seal gene pool now have just one allele. At the corresponding loci, homozygosity, of necessity, predominates.

The key premise in the explanation of homozygosity is that in very small populations, many alleles are over time likely to be lost. This conclusion follows from the more general theory of genetic drift, and in particular, the aspect of that theory according to which the smaller a population, the more likely an allele that is at no selective disadvantage is to disappear anyway, in effect by sheer bad luck. (Because drift operates independently of natural selection, in the smallest populations even alleles that are on balance advantageous can easily be lost.)

The following mathematical considerations account for the relation between population size and allele extinction rate. Genetic drift can be seen as a kind of random walk in gene frequencies imposed on top of whatever changes occur as a result of natural selection. Allele extinction occurs if this walk (or rather, the net effect of the walk and natural selection) crosses a certain boundary. The distance that must be traversed to reach the boundary is a function of, among other things, population size: the smaller the population, the closer the boundary, and hence the higher the probability of extinction. For reasonably sized populations, the extinction probability is low, but for very small populations, it is relatively large.

Putting it all together: how does elephant seals' being hunted nearly to extinction explain their homozygosity? Hunting decimated the species, upon which most of the remaining alleles went extinct because of *the very small size of the population*. Thus, a mathematical fact—the population's small size—plays the leading explanatory part.

### Beyond Derivation

The role usually accorded mathematics in explanation is that of derivation. Hempel's DN account is a paradigm: to explain something is to deduce it from laws and boundary conditions. The laws are frequently mathematical laws. Thus, mathematics is necessary for the deduction, and so necessary for the explanation.

Perhaps more surprisingly, no account of explanation since Hempel's has envisaged a role for mathematics beyond derivation. Mathematics goes more or less unmentioned in the causal account. Kitcher makes room for mathematical explanation of mathematical facts in the unification account, and he implies that there is space also for mathematical explanation of physical facts (Kitcher 1989, 426–428). But in the presentation of the account, mathematics seems to be serving the same role that it plays in Hempel's theory: it is a derivation tool, a means for showing that the explanandum (or explanatory target) can be derived using a certain kind of argument (from which it follows that the explanandum or target is subsumed under a certain unifying pattern).

The derivational conception of mathematics entirely fails to capture the illumination that mathematical facts bring in the explanations of Marangoni-Bénard convection, elephant seal homozygosity, and many other phenomena. It is not enough to be told that these phenomena follow mathematically from the relevant laws and boundary conditions. Somehow, in grasping the *way* that they follow—in understanding the mathematics as well as the physics of the scientific treatment of the explanandum—you come to understand the phenomena better. It is almost as though, by looking into the mathematical structure of the derivation, you can see the forces at work in nature itself.

Galileo famously remarked in *The Assayer* that "the Book of Nature is written in mathematical characters," suggesting a Pythagorean or Platonic view of the world as an inherently mathematical entity. To understand the workings of nature is to understand the workings of something mathematical; this is why, on the Platonic view, mathematics plays so important a role in explanation.

Hempel's philosophy has its origins, of course, in the logical empiricist tradition that attempts to avoid mathematical Platonism at all costs. It is not nature itself that is written in mathematics, for the empiricist; it is our representation of nature. Mathematics is the tool we use to encode our knowledge of observed fact. Thus, mathematics does not constrain nature, it constrains our representations—but only because our representations are constructed in accordance with these constraints. The use of mathematics in science, then, is like the use of a code. Because science is written mathematically, to find out what science has to say about a particular phenomenon, you must derive the desired statement using mathematics. In this way, the logical empiricist picture casts mathematics as a derivation tool, a tool for translating scientific theories, which are intrinsically mathematical, into statements about the intrinsically nonmathematical world.[3] Empiricism and mathematical derivationalism go hand in hand.

The prospect for making sense of mathematics' explanatory role as something more than derivational, then, might seem to turn on foundational questions about the nature of mathematics and its relation to the world. But it is possible to see how the derivational view of mathematics' role in explanation falls short without indulging in any of this excitement, or so I will argue later in this chapter (section 8.4). Mathematical reasoning in explanation is supplying something more than deductive glue, but you need no metaphysical assumptions to spell out its additional contribution to explanatory goodness.

## 8.2   Explaining Boyle's Law

### 8.21   Boyle's Law

I will find a theory of idealization and preidealization in the microcosm that is the explanation of Boyle's law. The law states that, when kept at a constant temperature, the pressure of a fixed amount of gas varies inversely with its volume. Increase the volume, and the pressure drops; decrease the volume, and the pressure rises accordingly. In symbols,

$$PV = k$$

where $P$ is pressure, $V$ is volume, and the constant $k$'s value is determined by the amount of gas and its temperature.

Three qualifications. First, attached to the law are some conditions of application, both explicit and tacit. The explicit conditions are, of course, the requirements that the temperature and amount of gas remain fixed, and that the gas is at thermal equilibrium. The tacit conditions codify modern discoveries about the limits of the law; for example, the law is stipulated to apply only to relatively dilute gases. These conditions will remain tacit in what follows; I will for the most part write as though the law simply says $PV = k$.

Second, largely because Boyle's law does not take into account the size of gas molecules and the forces between them, it does not hold exactly for any gas. To explain Boyle's law, then, is to explain a coarse-grained explanandum: why $PV = k$ is approximately true.

Third, the explanation of Boyle's law is, strictly speaking, probabilistic; it shows that gases have an extremely high probability of conforming to the law. For the purposes of my discussion, I will not distinguish between models that causally entail a behavior and models that confer a high probability on the behavior. The resources for making the distinction will be developed in part four.

### 8.22  The Textbook Explanation

There are many demonstrations of Boyle's law. Let me begin with the simple variety that appears in an introductory text such as Ebbing (1987) and then show how to augment it to obtain a more sophisticated explanation.

The simple explanation has two parts. First, there is kinetic theory's physical picture of a gas as a collection of very small, very fast-moving molecules. Second, there is a set of assumptions about the behavior of the molecules from which the law is derived, which are as follows:

A–1. The pressure that a gas exerts on a container is proportional to the frequency of collisions between the gas's molecules and the container's walls per unit area of wall. (It also depends on the force exerted by the colliding molecules.)

A–2. The frequency of molecule/wall collisions per unit area of a container's walls is proportional to the density of the gas. (It also depends on the velocity of the local molecules.)

A–3. The density of a gas is inversely proportional to its volume. (It also depends on the number of molecules in the gas.)

If pressure is proportional to collision frequency, collision frequency is proportional to density, and density is inversely proportional to volume, then pressure is inversely proportional to volume, just as Boyle's law would have it.

The explanation is less than fully satisfying for two reasons. First, the assumptions A–1, A–2, and A–3 are not themselves accounted for. Assumption A–2, in particular, is not obviously true and is thus itself in need of explanation. Second, the assumptions include parenthetical complications that are ignored without any justification. More sophisticated explanations of Boyle's law, such as that offered by McQuarrie and Simon (1997, §25–4), fill both gaps. In what follows, I show how the gaps are filled, and I spell out some of the idealizations that the sophisticated textbook explanation makes along the way.[4]

Begin with the parenthetical complications. The explicit conditions attached to Boyle's law, namely, the fact that the temperature and the quantity of the gas remain fixed, provide some justification for ignoring these qualifications. If the quantity of gas is fixed, then the number of molecules in the gas remains constant, so A–3's assertion of the dependence of density on volume *and* molecule number can be collapsed to an assertion of the inverse proportionality of density to volume alone, as required for the derivation of the law.

If the temperature is fixed, then the overall mean velocity of the molecules in the gas remains constant. This falls just short of supplying sufficient reason to conclude that the velocity of the molecules near the container's walls remains constant as the gas's volume changes, and so does not quite warrant your ignoring the parenthetical complications in A–1 and A–2—the problem being that the distribution of velocities within a container may change without affecting the overall mean velocity.

Of course the distribution does not change in this way:

D–1. The velocities of the gas molecules near a container's walls have the same statistical profile as in the gas as a whole.

Add D–1 to your set of posits about gases, then, and you can infer that the mean molecular velocity near a container's walls will not change if the temperature does not change. It then follows that the force and frequency of molecule/wall collisions remains the same under a change in volume, so that the ensuing change in pressure is determined solely by the change in volume. (D–1 and the other statistical posits laid out below have the status of basing generalizations, I will argue in part four.)

The statistical posit D–1 is not obviously true. (In fact it is not true at all, because long-range attractive forces between gas molecules exert an inhibitory effect on molecules heading away from the rest of the gas, as a result of which molecules on the edge of the gas—molecules, that is, near the container walls—will tend to hit the walls with an average velocity that is lower than the average velocity of the molecules in the gas as a whole. D–1 is, however, approximately true, which is good enough for what follows.)

Since it is nonobvious, more sophisticated derivations of Boyle's law justify, rather than merely stating, D–1. This justification invokes further assumptions about the distribution of the properties of gas molecules. All such assumptions are consequences of the Maxwell-Boltzmann probability distribution over the properties of the molecules of a gas in thermal equilibrium, a distribution that yields the probability that a molecule will be found in a specified region, or traveling in a given direction or at a given speed when there are no complicating factors (e.g., gravitational fields).

The property of the Maxwell-Boltzmann distribution that founds D–1 is

D–2. The speeds, directions of travel, and positions of a gas's molecules are stochastically independent; they are not correlated.

From D–2 it follows immediately that a molecule close to a container wall is just as likely to have a given speed or direction of travel as a molecule anywhere else, and so that D–1 is true; likewise, D–1's approximate truth follows from D–2's approximate truth. This concludes the justification for ignoring the parenthetical complications in A–1, A–2, and A–3.

The other improvement made by sophisticated explanations of Boyle's law is, you will recall, the justification of A–2. This is achieved by showing that A–2 follows from D–2 and two further properties of the Maxwell-Boltzmann distribution:

D–3. A gas's molecules are (with high probability) at all times evenly distributed throughout its container.

D–4. The directions of travel of a gas's molecules are (with high probability) evenly distributed among all the possibilities; that is, all directions are equally probable.

The demonstration proceeds by calculating the number of molecules that will collide with a small portion of the container wall over a short period of time, given the distribution assumptions and some assumptions about molecular dynamics. One major idealization is made in the course of the calculation, that nothing interferes with the molecules as they travel around the container, and in particular, that molecules do not collide with one another.

Call the explanation presented above the textbook explanation of Boyle's law. Let me summarize the idealizations made by the textbook explanation, that is, the respects in which its ideal gas model differs from reality. First, there is the assumption that there are no long-range forces between gas molecules, implicit as already noted in D–1 and therefore in the other distribution assumptions from which D–1 is derived. Second, there is the assumption that there are no intermolecular collisions, invoked as already noted in the derivation of A–2. A third idealization is that the combined volume of the gas molecules themselves is zero, that is, that molecules take up no space in the container. This is, strictly speaking, redundant: it is not required if it is already assumed that there are no collisions. I include it because it is well known that correcting for this idealization—given that there are intermolecular collisions—leads to a more accurate version of Boyle's law. (I am referring of course to van der Waals' law, which also corrects for the effect of long-range forces.) Fourth, the justification of A–1 assumes that molecule/wall collisions are perfectly elastic. A fifth and final idealization is the assumption of classical, rather than quantum, mechanics throughout.

The five idealizations, then, are as follows (reordered for later reference):

I–1. The volume occupied by the gas molecules is vanishingly small compared to the volume of the container.

I–2. The molecules exert no long range forces on one another.

I–3. Collisions between the molecules and the walls are perfectly elastic.

I–4. The molecules do not collide with one another (or interact in any other way at short range).

I–5. The behavior of the gas is as described by classical mechanics.

(This list is not intended to be exhaustive.)

When the density of a gas is low enough, I–1 and I–2 are approximately true, in the sense that the volume occupied by the molecules is almost vanishingly small and the long range intermolecular forces are almost zero. In this sense, they are "minor" idealizations.

I–3, however, is a more significant idealization, and I–4 is nowhere near true. I–5 is also a major idealization, because the quantum behavior of molecules is quite different in many respects from their classical behavior. It is worth noting that in other explanations using kinetic theory, where collisions are taken into account, the physics used is not only nonquantum, it is not even classical, in that molecules are assumed to bounce off one another as billiard balls appear to do, rather than, as they actually do, repel one another at very short distances.

### 8.23 Bernoulli's Explanation

The first correct explanation of Boyle's law is credited to Daniel Bernoulli, writing in 1738. Previously, Boyle himself had tried to explain the law as a consequence of what he supposed was the "spring-like" nature of molecules, and Newton had tried to explain it as a consequence of supposed short- to medium-range repulsive forces between molecules. Neither explanation attributed any significance to the motion of the molecules. Bernoulli's principal innovation was to hypothesize that pressure is the force exerted per unit area of the container wall by fast-moving molecules colliding with the wall.[5]

Bernoulli follows the A–1/A–2/A–3 schema in the previous section and includes a mathematical derivation of the relation between the frequency of collisions per unit area and the density of a gas. He makes the textbook assumptions about the distributions of the positions and directions of travel of the molecules, that is, D–2, D–3, and D–4 (or at least the closest such assumptions that are compatible with his molecules' cellular confinement, discussed below). However, he assumes that all molecules travel at the same speed.[6] He also makes two of the textbook idealizations, zero long-range intermolecular force (I–2) and classical behavior (I–5), the latter, of course, without thinking of it as such. Interestingly, he does not make I–1: his derivation allows for the volume taken up by the molecules, but he then goes on to show that for small values, molecular volume does not much affect the relationship between pressure and volume. Finally, in contrast to the textbook explanation's I–4, Bernoulli does not ignore collisions. His molecules collide, but in an odd way.

What Bernoulli assumes about collisions is not entirely clear from the text, but on one interpretation he thinks of each gas molecule as bouncing back and forth in its own tiny cell. The molecule is confined to its cell by its neighbors: when it reaches the border of its cell, it collides with one of its neighbors, also fortuitously at the corresponding position at the border of its own cell, and bounces back safely inside the boundary. The same collision sends the neighbor back inside its cell, as well. This is not an accurate picture of gas dynamics; although physically possible in a real gas, it would require a great deal of pre-established harmony.

In any case, from Bernoulli's assumption it follows that the volume of each of the cells will be the total volume of the container divided by the number of molecules in the gas. Thus, if the number of molecules is fixed, cell volume varies in proportion to the volume of the entire container. Bernoulli goes on to show, in effect, that the pressure exerted by the gas is inversely proportional to the volume of the cells, hence to the volume of the container.[7]

There are two false assumptions, then, that Bernoulli makes but that modern explanations do not:

B–1. All molecules travel at the same speed.

B–2. Molecules collide in such a way as to confine each other to small cells.

Despite these differences, we regard Bernoulli's explanation as imperfect but essentially correct.

I will later extract a treatment of what I call preidealization from the case of Bernoulli's explanation, arguing that the inaccuracies in the explanation, because they are preidealizations, count against the explanation far less than the scale of the causal misrepresentation would suggest.

### 8.24 The Canonical Explanation

I will contrast the textbook explanation of Boyle's law with what I call the canonical explanation of the law, by which I mean the explanation recommended by the kairetic account. Whereas the textbook explanation contains idealizations, the canonical explanation contains none. A comparison of the two explanations will reveal the explanatory role of idealization.

One conclusion that will be possible at the end of the presentation of the canonical explanation, before any particular thesis about the nature of idealization is formulated, is the following: if the distortion of the causal details perpetrated by the ideal gas explanation of Boyle's law were corrected—that is, if the distorted description were replaced by a true description of the same details—there would be no improvement in the quality of the explanation. In other words, the ideal gas explanation is in no way inferior to its veridical counterpart.

Suppose, then, that your task is to construct the canonical explanation of the approximate truth of Boyle's law. Following the account of regularity explanation developed in chapter seven, you should create a causal model that has as its explanatory target a gas's pressure. More exactly, the target will be a certain aspect of the pressure, namely, its having a magnitude related to the gas's volume by Boyle's law, that is, a magnitude of $k/V$. Call a gas's pressure's conforming to this constraint *Boylean behavior*.

A model for any aspect of a gas's pressure represents the causal process by which a given volume of gas in a given container exerts a given force on the container walls—the steady bombardment of the walls by the gas's molecules. A complete description of this process for a particular gas would have to document the trajectory of every molecule in the gas. The kinetic theory of gases allows you to give a statistical description of the process using the Maxwell-Boltzmann distribution that is, for all practical purposes, just as good. Take this statistical description of the bombardment mechanism as your starting point. (I will show in part four why the statistical description is in fact explanatorily superior to the more complete deterministic description; I will also provide some formal apparatus for constructing explicitly probabilistic models.)

Having found and described the underlying process or mechanism, the next step is to prune the mechanism description so that it mentions only aspects of the mechanism that make a difference to the explanatory target, that is, to Boylean behavior. This is where the kairetic criterion comes into its own.

A full description of a gas in modern kinetic theory accommodates all of the causal complications omitted in the ideal gas model: long-range forces, collisions, and so on. Include all of these factors in the initial causal model, then, along with whatever probabilistic assumptions are required to determine pressure given volume. The result is a description of a causal mechanism from which you can derive not just Boyle's law, but much else besides, such as the more sophisticated and more accurate law relating a gas's pressure and volume (and other properties) formulated by van der Waals.

Your job is to remove from this description everything that makes no difference to the inverse proportionality of pressure to volume, that is, everything that is not essential to the causal entailment of Boylean behavior. It does not matter that the stripped down model will be a far less rich theory of gases; your aim is not a theory of gases—you have one already—but the explanation of a very particular behavior of gases.

Without invalidating your model's causal entailment of Boylean behavior, you can discard the following elements. First, you can remove the specification of the gas molecules' volume and of the long-range intermolecular forces between them, substituting just the statement that the molecules are very small and the forces very weak. You are replacing the exact values for the volumes and the forces, then, with the specification that they fall into certain ranges, beginning at zero and ending at some value that is not too high. In so doing, you reveal that the exact values of these parameters make no difference to Boylean behavior; all that makes a difference is their not being too great.

Second, you can remove certain aspects of the Maxwell-Boltzmann probability distribution over the various properties of gas molecules. For example, kinetic theory ascribes a certain probability distribution over the speeds, or velocity magnitudes, of the gas molecules. The shape of this distribution makes no difference to Boyle's law. As you can see from the discussion in section 8.22, what is important are the properties required for D–1 to hold, namely, D–2, D–3, and D–4. Everything else should be stripped away.

Third, the details of intermolecular collisions make no difference to the derivation. Or almost no difference: it must be specified that, say, a collision between two molecules cannot double the speed of both, but the necessary limitations, such as the conservation of energy, are already spelled out elsewhere in the model, for example, in the physics of molecule/wall collisions. All the physics that is particular to the collisions, then, can be removed: whether collisions are billiard ball–style bounces (as in "hard-sphere" models of gases) or are really short-range repulsions (as in real gases); if repulsions, the way that they fall off with distance, and much more. As so often in applications of the kairetic account's optimizing procedure, particular parameters will be replaced by ranges of parameters, but in the case of collisions, these parameters can take on just about any values at all compatible with kinetic theory's "big picture" of gases as composed of large numbers of small, fast-moving molecules. Some of these values will imply that there are no collisions at all (short-range forces of zero strength in a repulsion physics, or molecules with zero size in a hard-sphere physics). The abstracted model will not even require, then, that collisions occur.[8] (I sketched an argument for a bolder claim, that a model for the scattering process characteristically caused by collisions might be abstracted to the point where it is radically multiply realizable without losing causal cohesion, in section 5.43.)

Fourth, you can remove various details of the physics of molecule/wall interactions. For example, in a real gas, there will be transfers of energy from molecules to walls, and from walls to molecules. These will balance out (since the walls are made up of molecules at the same temperature as the gas). The rates of transfer back and forth can be ignored; all that need be specified is that the transfers have no cumulative effect.

Fifth, many properties of a gas's container can be left unspecified. Most interestingly, the container can be any shape you like. That shape does not matter is already implicit in the very statement of Boyle's law, so it comes as no revelation, but it is worth remarking on. I will return to this point in section 8.4.

Sixth and finally, any other elements of physical theory not needed to derive A–1 and A–2 can and should be left unspecified in the model. As a result, the model may well encompass both classical and quantum physics, and many other possible, but nonactual, physics of the world.

The need for cohesion limits this radical physical indeterminacy. You might well wonder whether a model that tells a causal story consistent with both classical and quantum underpinnings could possibly be cohesive. In section 3.63, I proposed that the cohesion of a model that allows quite different fundamental-level physics in its realizers should be evaluated with respect to the trajectories in state space induced by the physics, by testing for what I called dynamic contiguity. The classical and quantum physical substrates can exist together in a cohesive model only if they induce similar patterns of motion in the gas molecules they describe.

You might begin to evaluate cohesion by comparing what the quantum model says about wave packets with what the classical model says about particles. In those quantum realizations where molecules are allowed to collide, however, wave packets will tend to be broken up by scattering interactions.

Even in an ideal gas model where there are no intermolecular collisions, it is not obvious how the classical and quantum trajectories of a molecule colliding with a wall ought to be compared. This problem of incommensurability, though difficult, is nevertheless not insurmountable. A quantum trajectory can be regarded as a superposition of trajectories in classical state space; simply run the contiguity test individually on these trajectories. Because the quantum physics of our world results in trajectories (and rates of collision, local densities, and so on) that conform to the predictions of the classical theory, when a suitable probability distribution is put over the initial conditions of the classical theory, I take it that the quantum and classical models for any phenomenon that can be modeled both ways will generate dynamically contiguous trajectories.

Dynamic contiguity is, however, a necessary condition for cohesion only. To complete the argument that a model with both classical and quantum realizations is cohesive, it would be necessary to show that the causal structures of the classical, quantum, and other physics allowed by the model form, in some sense, a contiguous set, or at least that the aspects of those structures relevant to Boylean behavior do so. I have not proposed any formal criterion for evaluating this sort of contiguity, but I think it is possible to make an informal case that the causal structures envisaged by the classical and quantum theories of a gas are nearly identical. To be sure, a quantum gas is in some respects quite different from a classical gas: its particles exist in superpositions and exhibit nonclassical statistics. But causation in a quantum gas is much like causation in a classical gas, with particles repelling one another at short range to create a scattering effect (albeit in superposition).

I conclude that a model that abstracts away from both uniquely classical and uniquely quantum aspects of a gas's physics would be, if the abstraction were performed in the right way, cohesive. But I have not specified what form such a union of the classical and quantum would take, and not just for lack of space. My conclusion must, then, be regarded as tentative. There will be much more to say about cohesion and abstraction before the philosophy of explanation is finished.

To return to the canonical explanation of Boyle's law: once all the factors listed above have been abstracted away, what remains in the model are just those high-level properties of the mechanics of kinetic theory that make a difference to gases' Boylean behavior. It is by appreciating that these and only these properties are the difference-makers that you understand Boyle's law.

A suggestive conclusion about idealization follows immediately. The setup of a model that makes the textbook idealizations enumerated in the previous section—each of I–1 to I–5—entails all the propositions in the setup of the canonical causal model for Boylean behavior and thus constitutes a fleshing out of the canonical model: it says everything that the canonical model does, and more besides. Though nonveridical, then, it contains every element of the best explanation of the law.

In this respect, it is no worse than the veridical, overly detailed model to which you applied the optimizing procedure. Both models state or entail all the explanatorily relevant properties of gases, but they then go on to state further irrelevant properties as well. It does not matter, for the purposes of explanatory power, whether the irrelevant details specified by a model are veridical or nonveridical. Either way, they contribute nothing positive to understanding, and they detract from understanding in the same way, by falsely claiming relevance for irrelevancies. The kairetic account explains, then, why the idealized model does not suffer for its falsehoods.

What is not explained is why the idealized model does not suffer for its irrelevancies. That will require a novel proposal about the meaning and purpose of idealization that is independent of the kairetic account itself.

## 8.3  A Theory of Idealization

The first half of the theory of idealization is in place. I have shown (for the case of Boyle's law, but the lessons are of course supposed to generalize) that the causal factors distorted by idealized models are details that do not matter to the explanatory target—they are explanatory irrelevancies. The distortions of the idealized model are thus mitigated. But how, if at all, do they make a positive contribution to the explanation?

### 8.31  Idealization in the Textbook Explanation

I suggest that the idealizations in the textbook explanation of Boyle's law are not to be taken at face value. This is in part because the explainers, the textbook writers, know they are not true, but also in part because they know they are irrelevant.

Immediately after deriving Boyle's law, the authors of one textbook write

> We . . . assumed that the molecules of the gas do not collide with each
> other . . . But if the gas is in equilibrium, on the average, any collision

that deflects the path of a molecule from [the path assumed in the deriva-
tion] will be balanced by a collision that replaces the molecule. (McQuarrie and Simon 1997, 1015)

The no-collision assumption is justified, then, by the fact that collisions or
not, the demonstration of Boyle's law goes through.

This is, I suggest, advice on how to interpret the idealizing explanation.
McQuarrie and Simon are not merely warning their readers not to take the
no-collisions assumption literally. If that were their aim, then they would be
using a proposition (no collisions) to do some work, then adding that the
proposition is false and cannot do the work but that fortunately another
proposition (collisions balance out) is true and can do the work instead.
Such a strategy would increase the complexity of the exposition without
reducing the ultimate cognitive load on the reader.

The authors must have something different in mind. My proposal: the
assumption that there are no intermolecular collisions is intended to communicate to the reader that collisions have no net effect on the relationship
between volume and pressure. One way to say that collisions have no net effect is to say that it is *as if* there are no collisions; this is how the idealizing
explanation is to be understood. If I am right, then on the subject of collisions, the canonical model and the idealized model say precisely the same
thing: collisions make no difference to Boylean behavior and thus are irrelevant to the explanation of Boyle's law. The idealized model, then, adopts
the optimal explanatory policy on collisions.

All idealizations, I suggest, work in the same way: an idealization does
not assert, as it appears to, that some nonactual factor is relevant to the explanandum; rather, it asserts that some actual factor is irrelevant. The best
idealized models will be equivalent in one explanatorily central sense to the
corresponding canonical models: when understood correctly, both kinds
of models cite the same relevant factors and no irrelevant factors. However,
they represent these explanatory facts using two different conventions: the
fact that certain pervasive causal influences play no role in bringing about
the explanatory target is left implicit in a canonical model—what is irrelevant is passed over silently—whereas it is made explicit in an idealizing
explanation's flagrant introduction of fictional physical factors.

To bolster this interpretation of idealization, let me examine the other
idealizations in the explanation of Boyle's law, showing that they are con-

structed to assert—as the corresponding canonical model does in its own way—that certain factors make no explanatory difference to the target.

Consider first I–1 and I–2, the assumptions that the gas molecules have no volume and that there are no long-range intermolecular forces. To set the volume and the forces to zero is to say that neither the volume nor the forces play a role in producing Boylean behavior: in respect to such behavior, it is as if they were not present at all.

Second, consider I–3, the assumption that molecule/wall collisions are perfectly elastic, which implies that during a collision, none of a molecule's kinetic energy is transferred to the walls as heat energy. Setting the energy transfer to zero indicates that energy transfer is not a difference-maker for Boylean behavior. (Elasticity also implies that a molecule's angle of reflection will equal exactly its angle of incidence, but for simplicity's sake, let me pass over this aspect of the idealization.)

Compare the following textbook justification of the elasticity assumption:

Since pressure is a property averaged over many wall collisions, we assume that in any one wall collision, there is no change in the molecule's translational kinetic energy. Although this assumption is false, it is "true" averaged over all the molecules, and hence gives the correct result for pressure. (Levine 2002, 458)

The point is that only the average energy transfer affects the pressure, so that individual transfers make no difference to the pressure provided that they cancel out. For the purpose of explaining pressure, the idealization implies, it is *as if* there is no energy transfer at all.

Third, what about I–5, the use of classical mechanics? Again the intent of the idealization is to state that much of the underlying physics makes no difference to Boylean behavior, and in particular, that the quantum aspects of our world's physics make no such difference. Classical mechanics is selected for the idealized model not because it sets some "quantum parameter" to zero but because it epitomizes for us the nonquantum—it is the natural way for physics to be nonquantum. That this is so is in part a matter of historical contingency, of course, but what is important for the idealization to play its role are not its detailed workings but the simple fact that it is the nonquantum default.

## 8.32  The Nature and Purpose of Idealization

To generalize the discussion of Boyle's law: the role of an idealization is to assert the explanatory irrelevance, that is, the failure to make a difference, of a salient causal factor. The three characteristics of an idealization are as follows:

1. It is evidently false. Blatant falsehood signals that an idealization's function is to make a claim about what does not make a difference, rather than about what does make a difference.

2. The false claim fills out certain details left unspecified by the canonical explanatory model. Thus, the claim is explanatorily irrelevant and so cannot stand in the way of the causal entailment of the explanatory target.

3. The details are filled out in a certain way: the relevant parameters are assigned a zero, an infinite, or some other extreme or default value. This is the idealization's way of asserting that the actual details do not matter. (More exactly, the details either do not matter at all or they do not matter provided that they lie in the vicinity of the default value. I will return to this equivocation shortly.)

The content of an idealized model, then, can be divided into two parts. The first part contains the difference-makers for the explanatory target and, if the model is perfect, is identical to the canonical model. The second part is all idealization; its overt claims are false but its role is to point to parts of the actual world that do not make a difference to the explanatory target. The overlap between an idealized model and reality, then—the properties that the fictional system described by the model shares with the system actually producing the explanatory target—is a standalone set of difference-makers for the target.

At the beginning of this paper, I promised to single out two respects in which idealization could be said to be explanatorily virtuous:

1. An idealizing explanation is always better than its veridical counterpart.

2. An idealizing explanation is as good in one important sense as the corresponding canonical explanation.

I will establish these two claims in turn.

First, the comparison with the veridical counterpart. An idealized model's veridical counterpart is the model that corrects the idealized model's causal distortions. Where the idealized model sets a parameter, such as the strength of long-range intermolecular forces, to zero, the veridical counterpart states the correct value for the parameter. All falsified causal details in an idealizing explanation are explanatorily irrelevant: they are non-difference-makers. The veridical counterpart, by correctly describing these details, falsely implies that they are difference-makers. It is therefore explanatorily inferior to the idealized model, which, properly interpreted, correctly identifies them as non-difference-makers.

Second, the comparison with the canonical model. I have already shown that an idealized model in one sense does the same explanatory work as the corresponding canonical model: both models correctly specify all the difference-makers and all the non-difference-makers. In chapter one, I discussed a well-known distinction between two senses of explanation, ontological and communicative (section 1.21). An explanation in the ontological sense is a collection of explanatory facts, namely, the causal and other facts picked out by an explanatory model, whereas an explanation in the communicative sense is a representation of such facts. One way to individuate explanations in the ontological sense is by the difference-makers they cite: two explanatory models for the same target are identical explanations of that target if they cite precisely the same difference-makers. On this view, it would appear that an idealized model represents exactly the same explanation of its target as the corresponding canonical model. If objective explanatoriness is your sole concern, there is consequently nothing to choose from between the idealizing explanation and the corresponding canonical explanation of a phenomenon.

Although this position is consonant with my greater goal of finding explanatory virtue in idealization, it must be resisted, I think, for two reasons. First, the proposed individuation criterion for ontological explanations attends only to an explanatory model's setup. But a causal model has two parts, a setup and a follow-through. The setup, a list of causal factors, specifies the difference-makers. The follow-through, a deduction of the explanatory target from the setup, represents the way in which they make a difference. This second part of the model surely ought to contribute to explanation individuation. If the follow-through is taken into account, however, it can be argued that an idealizing explanation is different from, and inferior to, a canonical explanation for the following reason. Although idealized models specify, and often highlight in a useful way, what does not make a difference, they are much less clear—quite often, completely silent—about why it does not make a difference. For example, although McQuarrie and Simon add a parenthetical comment on the balancing out of intermolecular collisions to their explanation of Boyle's law (quoted above), they do not provide enough information to see for sure that balancing out will occur. Contrast this with the canonical model, which, by demonstrating that Boylean behavior can be derived without making any specific assumptions about the nature of collisions, shows why the physics of collisions makes no difference to the behavior and thus why it is irrelevant to the explanation of Boyle's law. The canonical model in this way provides more objectively explanatory information than the idealized model.

Second, notwithstanding what I have said above, an idealized model is sometimes less clear than the corresponding canonical model when it comes to indicating what makes a difference. Suppose that a parameter in the idealized model is falsely assigned a value of zero. It follows that the exact value of the parameter makes no difference. But does this mean that the value of the parameter makes no difference at all—that it can take any value without affecting the occurrence of the explanatory target—or that, while its exact value makes no difference, it makes a difference that the parameter falls into a certain range? If the latter, what is the extent of the range? The idealized model on its own answers neither question (except to say that the range includes zero).

These are important differences between an idealized model and the corresponding canonical model. When an idealized model is presented in an informative context, however, they may disappear: appropriate annotations, or the reader's knowledge of the subject matter or of the writer's intentions, may supply the explanatory information that is missing from the idealized model considered in isolation. In other words, in context the canonical and idealizing explanations may well communicate precisely the same objectively explanatory information, namely, the information made explicit in the setup and follow-through of the canonical model. There is a sense, then, in which the two explanations are identical. There is also a sense—the communicative sense, in which an explanation's means of representation are taken into account—in which they are rather different, since the canonical model identifies non-difference-makers by failing to mention them, whereas an idealized model identifies non-difference-makers by conspicuously distorting their properties. Finally, there is a sense in which the two explanations are similar but not quite identical, namely, the sense that attends to the objective explanatory facts communicated by the models when isolated from their context.

Why idealize, rather than giving a canonical explanation? Here, at last, I will invoke considerations that are not intrinsic to the explanatory enterprise. There are three reasons to construct idealized models.

First, there are some causally salient factors that are, for all their salience, irrelevant to the explanation of certain phenomena. It is important to appreciate their irrelevance. If the factors are idealized, their irrelevance is underlined in a dramatic way—more dramatic, certainly, than a canonical explanation's knowing silence.

The second reason to idealize is also a practical one, familiar from the pragmatic approach to idealization (section 8.11), but unlike the first, it has nothing to do with communication. Because idealizations assign extreme or default values to their idealized parameters, an idealized model is simpler than a model that fills out the same details veridically; because it replaces ranges with definite values, it is also often simpler than the canonical model. As a consequence, the derivation of the explanatory target using an idealized model is typically more straightforward than the derivation using a veridical causal model. The explanation of Boyle's law is a good example: it is easier to derive Boyle's law from an assumption of zero long-range forces and no collisions than to derive it from the assumption that the parameters governing long-range forces and collisions fall into certain ranges.

Third, because an idealized model distorts only non-difference-makers, it is as effective an instrument of prediction as the canonical model, provided that the predictive target is not too different from the explanatory target (the ideal gas model is good for predicting changes in pressure due to changes in volume, but it is bad for predicting diffusion behavior, since collisions make a difference to diffusion behavior). Given that idealizations often, as just explained, make a model simpler to work with, idealized models are valuable scientific all-rounders: they make for excellent explanations, and they have in addition virtues that are more important to the predictive enterprise, such as simplicity and tractability. A certain economy is gained by using the same model for both explanatory and predictive work; this helps to account for the prevalence of idealizing explanatory models.

In summary, then, though an idealizing explanation is in certain ways inferior to a canonical kairetic explanation, there are considerations of communicative effectiveness, descriptive and computational simplicity, and scientific economy that motivate the widespread use of idealization in explanation. None of these considerations would count for much, however, unless idealizing explanations were intrinsically good explanations. It is in this respect that my view of idealization differs from the pragmatist's view (section 8.11). Let me conclude this section of the discussion, then, by reminding you of how excellent an idealizing explanation can be: it is vastly superior to its veridical counterpart—and as good, in one important sense, as the best possible explanation.

To test the view of idealization presented here, consider some other well-known idealizations in science. First, to explain the approximately parabolic trajectory of a cannonball, air resistance is set to zero. This indicates that air resistance, provided it is low, makes no difference to the trajectory's approximate shape.

Second, in explaining the appearance of a rainbow, it is assumed that raindrops are perfect spheres (Batterman 2002). In fact, local forces will tend to deform the drops slightly. By assuming zero deformation, the model asserts that deformations within the normal range make no difference to the existence of rainbows.

Third, in explanatory models in evolutionary biology, infinite populations are assumed. The effect of this assumption is to set the expected rate of genetic drift to zero. What such a model says is that drift, though present, made no difference to the feature of the gene pool to be explained, say, the extinction of an inferior trait. (The presence of drift is not neutral—it lowers the probability of the explanandum—but probability-lowerers are, on the kairetic account, irrelevant.) More precisely, the only property of drift that made a difference was its not being too large. Idealized biological infinitude is discussed further in section 12.1; you might also compare this case with the use of the deterministic apparatus of classical thermodynamics to explain phenomena that are, according to statistical mechanics, more accurately modeled probabilistically.

Fourth, when a genetic explanation assumes Mendel's law of independent assortment, it asserts that the correlation between any two alleles' being passed on to the same offspring is zero. Translation: the correlation, whatever it was, made no difference to the explanatory target.

Fifth, and perhaps most notoriously, much explanation in economics assumes that people are maximally rational in certain respects, for example, that they have a strictly transitive ordering of preferences. The influence of aspects of normal human psychology that may in various respects falsify this assumption is, in other words, effectively set to zero. What is asserted, I claim, is not that economic actors are inhuman, but that the aspects of human behavior that depart from the robotic utility maximization of *Homo economicus* make no difference to whatever phenomenon is in the course of being explained. I pursue this suggestion in section 12.3.

## 8.33 Structural Idealization

An act of idealization, I have suggested, sets one of the canonical explanatory model's parameters to zero, infinity, or some other extreme or default value. This characterization should, I now argue, be expanded in the light of a case from biological modeling.

In a typical model in population ecology or evolutionary biology, individuals are represented only in the aggregate: the model consists of mathematical rules describing the dynamics of populations or subpopulations as a whole. Some modelers, however, aspire to represent elements of individual behavior; they build computer programs, called agent-based models, that keep track of the state of every organism in a system.

The explanatory power of such models has been contested; on the kairetic approach, in particular, they are optimally explanatory only when the phenomenon to be explained depends on features of the dynamics of individuals that cannot be captured by population-level models, and thus for the most part, only for rather fine-grained explananda, something of a rarity on the ecological and evolutionary side of the biological sciences.

Still, such explananda exist, and their province may be rather wider than I have suggested. Suppose, then, that you have an agent-based model that captures the difference-makers for some biological event or phenomenon. What idealizations might legitimately be made? One simplification found in agent-based models is the discrete representation of a real-valued variable, as when, say, an organism's level of nutrition is allowed to take only whole-numbered values between one and ten, or its position is represented on a grid in which all creatures occupying the same patch of ground are assigned exactly the same coordinates. (Discrete representations are of course more or less unavoidable in models built on digital computers.)

Such idealizations are allowed, I propose, when the exact value of the variable in question makes no difference to the explanatory target, that is, when the canonical explanatory model specifies ranges of values rather than exact values for the variables. Provided that the ranges are wide enough that they each include at least one of a granular model's discrete values, that model will constitute a fleshing out of the canonical model. It is not perspicuous to think of a granular model as having been derived from the corresponding canonical model by setting certain parameters to extreme or default values. Better to think of the model as formed by way of a structural simplification of the canonical model, and more particularly, by a kind of concretization of certain of its abstract aspects, achieved by the substitution of particular values for specified ranges. (Note that when idealizing by setting parameters to extreme or default values, there may be a uniquely natural choice of idealized model. This is not so for granular models, since there are usually, perhaps always, many equally good choices of sets of discrete values.)

I place structural simplification alongside the setting of parameters to extreme or default values as a device for idealization. Other examples of structural idealization include the use of biological models assuming asexual reproduction to explain the dynamics of sexually reproducing populations, the use of the Ising model in statistical physics to explain certain properties of phase transitions (the material substrate in the Ising model has a simpler physical structure than that of the materials whose behavior it is invoked to explain), and perhaps the utility-maximizing psychology of *Homo economicus* in economic models.

In these cases, it is the idealized model that is discrete and reality continuous; sometimes, however, it is the model that is continuous where reality is discrete. The best known example is the representational apparatus of fluid mechanics, in which fluids are assumed to have the structure of a continuum rather than their true atomic structure. So which is it: is a discrete model a structural simplification of a continuous model, or is a continuous model a structural simplification of a discrete model?

It may well be that what constitutes an appropriate idealizing simplification varies from model to model. Even given a particular model, the standards of appropriateness may vary with the scientific practice or the cognitive and social constitution of the explainers. There is no need for a single objective standard in determining this element of idealization.

The criteria for judging an idealization may therefore be divided into two parts, one objective and one perhaps not so objective. The objective standard is straightforward: the setup of an idealized explanatory model for a phenomenon must entail the setup of the canonical explanatory model for that explanatory target, so guaranteeing that the elements of reality falsely represented by the model are non-difference-makers. The idealized model can therefore be understood as the conjunction of the canonical model and certain further, false claims about reality. The less objective standard concerns the choice of these false claims: they should set parameters of the canonical model to extreme or default values, or they should amount to a structural simplification of the canonical model. It is the terms *default* and *simplification* that introduce the subjectivity into the standard.

In short, as to the accuracy of its representation of the facts about difference-making, an explanatory model answers to the facts themselves, which are observer-independent (or at least, as observer-independent as the standards for cohesion and the other properties that figure in the kairetic account of difference-making). But as to the efficiency with which it communicates those facts, and in particular, the efficiency with which it distinguishes the true claims that single out difference-makers from the false claims that single out non-difference-makers, an idealized explanatory model answers to everything relevant to communicative effectiveness, which will surely include standards that vary from locale to locale.

### 8.34  A Theory of Preidealization

A preidealization is a falsehood in a model's causal story that impairs its explanatory power, but by less than the scale of the causal distortion would suggest. I will show that preidealizations are qualitatively different from both idealizations and ordinary explanatory errors.

Begin with Bernoulli's explanation of Boyle's law, which distorts the causal mechanism underlying Boylean behavior in two ways that the textbook explanation does not: it assumes that all molecules travel at the same speed (B–1) and that collisions confine each molecule to a small cell (B–2).

Some contemporary explanations also make the constant-speed assumption, as does what might be considered the first modern explanation of

Boyle's law, that given by Clausius (1857). Clausius and his successors explicitly note that the assumption is not a difference-maker for Boylean behavior; what is important is that D–1 holds, that is, that the distribution of speeds is the same everywhere in a gas's container (as explained in section 8.24). Thus in these modern explanations, B–1 may be regarded as a genuine idealization.

There is no indication as to whether or not Bernoulli was thinking along these lines. Assume for the sake of the argument that he regarded the constant speed assumption as essential to his explanation. What then? B–1 cannot be regarded as an idealization, since its inclusion in the explanatory model is intended to be taken literally, as asserting a difference-making role for constant speed. Consequently, Bernoulli's model cites too much, and this saps the quality of his explanation. Note that it makes no difference that the constant speed assumption is false; were it true, it would because of its irrelevance have the same anti-explanatory effect.

Nevertheless, Bernoulli's explanatory model, although imperfect, correctly cites all the difference-makers for Boyle's law. Compare this to the previous attempts to explain the law, such as Boyle's or Newton's stories, in which air molecules are "springy" or repel one another. Both explanations get the difference-makers wrong: they leave out the true difference-makers and include as difference-makers causal factors whose would-be difference-making is inconsistent with the action of the true difference-makers. This is an explanatory error of a different order of magnitude than Bernoulli's error. Boyle and Newton got the difference-making story wrong, whereas Bernoulli merely cluttered the story with unnecessary—and as it happens, fictional—detail.

An error of Bernoulli's sort is what I call a *preidealization*. A preidealization, then, is any filling-out of the details left unspecified by the canonical model that is intended to be taken literally. The damage done by a model's distortion of the explanatory mechanism depends to a great extent on whether the distortion is a preidealization or something worse. If a preidealization, the degree of distortion is immaterial, since only explanatorily irrelevant details are distorted. By contrast, if difference-making factors are misrepresented, the distortion undermines the explanation in proportion to its deformation of the mechanism. Preidealizations therefore damage explanations much less than the scale of their distortions might lead you to expect.

If a theorist is lucky, their preidealization might have the form of a genuine idealization, that is, it might set to an extreme or default value the irrelevant parameter whose value it specifies. Then the very same model containing the preidealization can be reinterpreted as an idealized model, as in the modern explanation of Boyle's law—Clausius's model—that recapitulates Bernoulli's preidealization B–1 as an idealization. The only difference between the preidealized and the idealized model in this case is the intended interpretation of the explanatory falsehood.

Bernoulli's assumption B–2 about the nature of collisions in a gas—that they confine each gas molecule to its own small cell—is also a preidealization. This is a rather serious misrepresentation of the dynamics of molecules inside a gas. But perhaps surprisingly, it is compatible with the canonical model for Boylean behavior: in a Bernoulli gas, every one of the canonical model's assumptions about the distribution of molecular position and speed is satisfied.[9] Boyle's law may therefore be derived from the model in the modern way. This is not quite how Bernoulli proceeds, yet his derivation succeeds for essentially the same reason that the modern derivation succeeds.

Thus, we count Bernoulli's explanation as basically correct. The canonical explanation of Boyle's law is in place, marred only by a few irrelevant details. Bernoulli's second preidealization is not an idealization that we would choose to make today, because it fails to announce the unimportance of collisions in an appropriate way, that is, by setting relevant parameters to extreme or default values. But because his errors were preidealizations, Bernoulli—not Boyle or Newton—gets the credit for being the first to explain Boyle's law.

What of the example I gave when I introduced preidealization in section 8.12, the Newtonian explanation of Kepler's laws? This is a case that is rather different from Bernoulli's explanation of Boyle's law.

You might think that the distortions in a Newtonian model go far beyond mere preidealization, misrepresenting as they do the very essence of gravitational acceleration, which is the single species of nonnegligible difference-making in the explanation of orbits and the rest. But you would be wrong.

To understand Kepler's laws, what is important above all is, first, to appreciate that all planetary acceleration, that is, all change in planetary motion, is caused by masses and their arrangement; second, to appreciate that the dependence between the acceleration $a$ of any particular body due to another body of mass $M$ at distance $r$ takes the approximate form $a = GM/r^2$; and third, to appreciate that the accelerations due to different bodies compose through simple vector addition. These claims are true on both the Newtonian theory and on the general theory of relativity.[10] Thus, although Newtonian theory has false things to say about the underpinnings of the dependence—implicating as it does a force acting directly between objects rather than by way of mass's effect on the curvature of space-time— what it says about the form of the dependence relation and the properties so related is correct. It is wrong about the fundamental laws, then, but it is right about the aspects of the fundamental laws responsible for Kepleresque behavior. (There is a lesson here for pessimistic meta-inducers.)

Consider a post-Newtonian model that simply spells out the properties of the fundamental laws stated in the previous paragraph, without committing itself in any way to the underlying details. If this model were cohesive, it would be the canonical explanation of Kepler's laws, and the Newtonian explanation would have only one defect by comparison, that it specifies that the inverse-square dependence is a fundamental law, rather than leaving open the question of the dependence's fundamental-level implementation. (Newton himself may have been more open-minded on this matter than what we call the Newtonian theory.)

I suspect, however, that the post-Newtonian model is not cohesive. By specifying only the form of the causal relationship between mass and planetary acceleration, the model black-boxes the relationship. Different implementations of this inverse-square black box may be causally quite different from one another, yet very similar to certain implementations of, say, inverse-cube dependency, which suggests that the implementations are not causally contiguous and therefore that the model containing the black box is incohesive. (In such a case, by the way, dynamic contiguity is surely not reliable as a sufficient condition for cohesion.)

Explanatory models that black-box may stand alone as explanations, however, if their black boxes stand in for mechanisms in the explanatory framework, in which case the black-boxing model advertises its incompleteness—its lack of causal information concerning the implementation of the box—rather than falsely implying that the information is not explanatorily relevant. As explained in section 5.3, such an explanation is not optimal, lacking as it does the required depth, but it is explanatorily substantive and has more than a few scientific uses (section 5.42). The post-Newtonian model is especially useful.

I suggest that the Newtonian explanation of Kepler's laws retains much of its explanatory status in the wake of Einstein because it is almost identical to the black-boxing post-Newtonian model. The Newtonian model, in other words, is—almost—the canonical explanation of why, *given an inverse-square dependence,* the planets exhibit Kepleresque behavior. But only *almost*: by positing fundamental laws where it ought to have a black box, the Newtonian model does not quite qualify for the explanatory canon.

What does this have to do with preidealization? Although Newton's explanation makes a false claim about the fundamental laws of nature where it ought to draw a black box, if the mechanism represented by that box is placed in the explanatory framework, as it is in the explanatory use of the post-Newtonian model, then the false claim is by fiat explanatorily irrelevant. Further, the Newtonian's false claim is the simplest possible way to flesh out the black box.

Thus, I suggest, the justification of the post-Einstein explanatory status of Newton's explanation of Kepler's laws has something important in common with the justification of the post-Clausius explanatory status of Bernoulli's explanation of Boyle's law. In both cases, the false content of the explanation, first, concerns something explanatorily irrelevant and, second, represents a relatively simple or default assumption about that irrelevant factor.

True, in the Newton case unlike the Bernoulli case, the false claim's irrelevance is a contextual matter—the claim is rendered irrelevant by an explanatory framework. But it is a scientifically fruitful, thus very salient, framework. Because the post-Newtonian model is still called on constantly to do explanatory work in celestial mechanics, the error in Newton's model strikes us as a mere preidealization.

## 8.4   Mathematically Driven Explanation

Mathematics plays a far more important part in explanation than its humble role as a derivational tool would suggest. This is, I suggest, for two reasons. First, the mathematical structure of an explanatory derivation must reflect the corresponding relations of causal production in the world. Only by grasping the mathematical structure do you follow the process of production from beginning to end. Second, the mathematics of the derivation tells you implicitly, and sometimes explicitly, what makes a difference to the causal production and what does not, and why it does or does not. In other words, it is by gaining insight into the mathematics of a derivation that you grasp, first, the causal processes by which the factors mentioned in the setup of a model produce the explanatory target and, second, the foundations of the difference-making relations inherent in these causal processes. No philosophy of mathematics, note, is invoked. I assume only that mathematics is somehow able to serve as a representer of things in the world; this is consistent both with the view that the world is inherently mathematical and with the contrary view.

I will have no more to add here about the importance of the structure of a derivation in representing relations of causal production. The explanatory role of the derivation—of a model's follow-through—has been asserted from the opening pages of part two.

Let me concentrate, then, on the importance of appreciating mathematical facts in order to understand facts about difference-making. In the most striking cases, the role of mathematics is to show that certain properties that you might expect to be relevant to your explanandum in fact make no difference at all. A few examples will illustrate this claim.

In understanding Boyle's law, it is important to see that changing the shape of a container will affect a gas's pressure only insofar as it affects the gas's volume. At first, this may seem surprising, since pressure is a force exerted on a container's walls, and the area of the walls can vary independently of the volume: changes in container shape that result in the same volume may result in radically different surface areas. When the surface area is considerably greater, there is, as it were, less gas to go around. Yet, Boyle's law implies, the pounding on any unit area of the wall is the same provided that the volume is the same, regardless of the ratio of surface area to volume.

The key to understanding the irrelevance of container shape is the fact that the statistical profile of a gas near a container wall is representative of the gas as a whole. The density will be the same, and the distribution of velocity will be the same, as elsewhere in the gas. From this it is easy to show, by a short mathematical argument, that the rate of pounding per unit area will be the same for all containers of equal volume, whatever their surface area. In containers with more surface area, then, though there is less gas to go around, gas molecules spend more time on average near walls, so as to compensate exactly.

It is mathematics that you use to see what features of a gas causally depend on what. By appreciating the relevant mathematical reasoning, you see why the dependences and independences exist—and this is the core of scientific understanding.

The same is true of both examples of mathematical explanation described in section 8.13. The hexagonality of Marangoni-Bénard cells is due to the fact that tightly packed but deformable circles will take on a honeycomb pattern, and that the convection cells have a circular but deformable shape. The role of the geometrical claim about circle packing is not just to serve as a premise for deriving hexagonality but to show what the hexagonal shapes do not depend on: anything that is not essential to the formation of circular convection cells.

The homozygosity of elephant seals is due to the high probability of extinction by drift in very small populations. The derivation of the high probability from the fact of low population number alone shows that almost nothing about the individual life histories of the individual seals makes any difference to the high rate of allele extinction. (High-level probabilistic explanations' principled neglect of individual trajectories is the subject of part four; for the mathematics relevant to ecological cases such as the elephant seals, see Strevens (2003b), or for a simpler presentation, Strevens (2005).)

Finally, consider the examples of equilibrium explanation discussed in section 7.41: the ball's ending up at the lowest point of its basin, the spherical shape of soap bubbles, humans' one-to-one sex ratio, market-clearing, and the rest. In each case, a large part of understanding the equilibrium phenomenon is to appreciate how many aspects of the boundary conditions for the relevant causal processes make no difference to the explanatory target. Such insights are almost always arrived at with the help of mathematics—the mathematics of energy minimization, of population genetics, of equilibrium economics.

In summary, it is by grasping mathematical dependences and independences that you grasp causal dependences and independences. The ability of mathematics to represent relations of causal dependence—wherever it comes from—is what qualifies it as an explanatory tool. That tool is most effective when mathematical reasoning is able to deliver high-level facts about dependences, and most spectacular when those facts are about *independence*.

# — IV —

# Probabilistic Explanation

# — 9 —

# Approaches to Probabilistic Explanation

## 9.1  Explanatory Questions

Some of the kairetic account's more striking consequences for probabilistic explanation will be investigated in the following chapters. I will not give a complete theory of probabilistic explanation, though the outlines of such are sketched in section 9.7. Why not? Because many elements of the kairetic account of probabilistic explanation depend on the variety of probability involved, and the kairetic account has much more to say—and in particular, much more to say that is new and interesting—when the probabilities involved are of the sort, or rather of the sorts, that science ascribes to the outcomes of processes that are at root deterministic. Chapters ten and eleven focus on these new and interesting consequences, thus on probabilistic explanation in deterministic systems.

Many of the kairetic account's contributions are novel solutions to long-standing problems; the purpose of the present chapter is to set up the problems and to review solutions previously given. The literature concerns the explanation of events almost exclusively, but because the kairetic account understands regularity explanation as being of a piece with event explanation (sections 7.2 and 10.51), this will not be the narrowing of horizons that it first appears.

Approaches to probabilistic explanation, like approaches to explanation generally (section 1.23), may be classified by noting their answers to two questions:

1. What is the explanatory relation? That is, in virtue of what relation between the explanation and the explanandum does an explanation confer scientific understanding?
2. What are the formal criteria for an adequate probabilistic explanation?

A few words about each.

The choices of explanatory relation for probabilistic explanation are more or less the same as for deterministic explanation: expectability, pattern subsumption, and causal accounts figure prominently in the literature. You will naturally ask whether the explanatory relation in probabilistic explanation is the same as in deterministic explanation. The answer is usually *yes*—Hempel, for example, gives an expectability account of both deterministic and probabilistic explanation, and Fetzer, by equating probabilities with causal dispositions, gives a causal account of both (references in section 9.4)—but not always. Railton, for one, denies that probabilistic explanations are causal explanations, which suggests that the explanatory relation in a probabilistic explanation is of a different kind than in a deterministic causal explanation (Railton 1981).[1] My approach to probabilistic explanation is of the monistic variety: the aim of a probabilistic explanation is to isolate the causal difference-makers, where the causal difference-making relation is the same high-level causal relation as in deterministic explanation—the relation, then, explored in this study's part two.

The main questions about the formal criteria for probabilistic explanation revolve around event explanation and concern probabilistic magnitude. Can a low probability explain an event? Do higher probabilities explain events better than low probabilities? Can a factor that decreased the probability of an event explain that event? I will classify all such questions as aspects of a larger debate between what I call *elitism* and *egalitarianism* (section 9.5).

There are two ways these issues might be settled. A top-down approach decides matters using the explanatory relation. If the relation is one of expectability, for example, then a low-probability event cannot be explained by its low probability, because that probability does not give you reason to expect the event. Not only Hempel, the author of this particular argument, but almost every other writer on probabilistic explanation—Salmon, Railton, Humphreys, and so on—has taken the top-down approach.

A bottom-up approach begins with the stock of scientific explanations, and searches for instances of low probability explanation, of probability decreasers cited as explainers, and so on. Formal criteria for explanation are found that encompass all actual explanations and no nonexplanations. If necessary, the explanatory relation is reconceived so as to generate the right formal criteria. Some of the explanation literature's best-known creators of counterexamples operate in this mode, for example, Scriven (1959) and Bromberger (1966).

I am of course a purveyor of overarching theory, besides which I have invested many pages in the presentation of my particular conception of the explanatory relation. On questions concerning the formal criteria for explanation, then, I will be taking the top-down approach. Indeed, perhaps the principal charm of my treatment of probabilistic explanation is its ability to answer questions proper to probabilistic explanation using an apparatus developed in earlier chapters that was explicitly limited to deterministic explanation. That will be the subject of chapters ten and eleven.

My intentions declared, however, I will pause to examine the enormous variety of probabilistic explanations to be found in science. You will see, I hope, why a number of recent writers (including myself (Strevens 2000a)) have advocated pluralism about the formal criteria for explanation, and often enough about the explanatory relation itself, in the face of such awesome diversity. Later, I hope even more fervently, you will be impressed with the kairetic account's provision of a single underlying principle to account for this explanatory array.

## 9.2   Varieties of Probabilistic Explanation: Examples

### Quantum Mechanics: Half-Life

The half-life of radium-226 is 1,620 years, meaning that about one-half of any given sample of this isotope of radium will have decayed by the end of a 1,620-year period. Why? Some sophisticated quantum mechanics both determines a certain probability that any particular atom of radium-226 decays in a given time period, and entails that the decays are stochastically independent. The probability that a particular atom decays in a 1,620-year time period is almost exactly one-half; given independence, then, and the law of large numbers, there is an extremely high probability—in a sample visible to the eye, only negligibly less than one—that about one-half of the atoms in a given sample will have decayed when 1,620 years have elapsed.[2]

### Quantum Mechanics: Tunneling

Radium-226 decays by emitting (along with some electromagnetic radiation) an alpha particle, a bundle of two neutrons and two protons. Classical models of the atom cannot explain alpha decay, as the emitted alpha particle must jump a potential barrier—a wall of force, if you like—so high that it would have negative kinetic energy at the apex of its leap. But radium atoms emit alpha particles all the same.

Quantum mechanics explains alpha decay by showing that over a given time interval there is a probability—a very small probability, but a probability nevertheless—that an alpha particle will jump the wall, or rather, in the preferred metaphor of quantum physicists, that it will tunnel through the wall. (These are, of course, the same probabilities that, taken en masse using the law of large numbers, explain the half-life of radium. They are small, then, only when the specified interval of time is small, say, one hour.) It is the existence of this small probability that is taken to explain a given atom's alpha decay, when it occurs.

### Sociology: Crime and the Family

African American teenagers are more likely than their peers to commit violent crimes. Many sociologists cite, as a partial explanation of this fact, the relatively higher rate of young, single parents in African American homes. Having a young, single parent is said to increase the probability of a teenager's engaging in violent crime; single parenthood of this sort therefore explains, in part, the higher rate of violent crime among African American teenagers (Wilson and Petersilia 2002).

### Medical Science: John Jones Recovers Swiftly

John Jones has a streptococcus infection. He is given penicillin and recovers within a week. The probability of such a swift recovery without penicillin is 10%; the probability with penicillin is 90% (Hempel 1965a, §3). It seems that the administration of the penicillin, then, explains the speed of Jones's recovery.

### Statistical Mechanics: Nature's Abhorrence of a Vacuum

Remove the air from a bell jar, wait a beat, and then open the jar. The surrounding air rushes to fill the vacuum. Statistical mechanics, in conjunction with the kinetic theory of gases, explains this behavior as follows.

The vacuum is empty space. The surrounding area is filled with gas particles. These gas particles move around the space available to them at random. (A more precise probabilistic characterization of their movements is unnecessary here.) A mathematical argument shows that randomly moving particles will tend, over time, to distribute themselves evenly in the space available, if that space is bounded. When the bell jar's valve is opened, the empty space inside the jar becomes available: the gas particles are no longer prevented from entering the jar. Thus, over time, the gas particles will distribute themselves inside the jar with a density equal to the density of the particles outside the jar. To the human observer, this redistribution takes the form of a rush of air into the jar.

To better understand the role of probability in this explanation, let me spell out the three main steps of the mathematical argument establishing a tendency to even distribution.

1. The probabilistic premise of the argument is that gas particles are engaged in a random walk through the space available to them.

2. A mathematical theorem shows that a particle engaged in a random walk through a bounded space will, after a time, be found anywhere in the space with equal likelihood. That is, after a certain amount of time has elapsed (determined by the pace of the walk and the shape and size of the space), the probability distribution over the particle's position will be uniform, meaning that the particle is equally likely to be found anywhere in the space available.

3. Because there are so many particles in a gas, and each is equally likely to be found anywhere in the space available, the law of large numbers can be applied to deduce an extremely high probability that the gas will be distributed evenly through space.

The tendency for gas to occupy an evacuated space, then, is a probabilistic tendency: there is a high probability that the space will be filled, but some chance that it will remain empty.[3]

### Evolutionary Genetics: Homozygosity in Elephant Seals

The explanation of elephant seal homozygosity was presented in section 8.13 as an example of an explanation that places great importance on a mathematical fact. I will use it here as a paradigm of an explanation that places great importance on a probabilistic fact. That fact, the cornerstone of the theory of drift, is that extinction through drift is more likely the smaller the relevant population. Because elephant seals were hunted to near extinction, their population was very small for long enough that most alleles that survived the hunting nevertheless drifted to extinction. For this reason, every known locus in the elephant seal genome is homozygous. Homozygosity in elephant seals is explained, then, by the relatively high probability of allele extinction during the period in which the elephant seal population was low.

### Evolutionary Ecology: Finch Sex and Famine

On the Galápagos islands, the ratio of male to female finches of the species *Geospiza fortis* after a drought year is much higher than the one-to-one ratio found in normal years (Grant 1986). This is explained as follows:

1. As a drought goes on, a higher and higher proportion of the edible seeds remaining on the islands are large and difficult to crack.
2. Larger-bodied, deeper-beaked birds have an easier time with large, hard seeds.
3. The probability of a finch's surviving a drought therefore increases with the size of its body and the depth of its beak.
4. *G. fortis* males are on average 5% larger than females, thus males are on average more likely to survive a drought than females.

Premise (3) is probabilistic because some small finches survive a drought and some large finches do not.

This is the sort of ecological explanation that provides the foundation for much Darwinian explanation in evolutionary biology. Ecological considerations are cited to show that, in a given environment, organisms with a certain trait—in this case, large body size and beak depth—have greater fitness, that is, roughly, a higher probability of survival or reproduction. The law of large numbers is then invoked to conclude that the representation of that trait in the population will increase as long as the environment persists. In most such explanations—in contrast to the case of *G. fortis*—the environment changes slowly, if at all, and the advantageous trait is fixed: it completely replaces all other competing traits in the population.

### 9.3   Varieties of Probabilistic Explanation: Commentary

*9.31   The Uses of Probabilistic Explanation*

There are at least three different reasons for the explanatory invocation of probability.

First, in the half-life and tunneling explanations, the quantum probabilities involved are, as far as we know, irreducible; as a consequence, the probabilistic explanations are the only possible explanations.

Second, in the crime and swift-recovery explanations, the use of probability is due in part to our ignorance of many of the relevant processes and much of the relevant information. Suppose, for example, that there are two equally common strains of streptococcus, one of which responds to penicillin 80% of the time, the other 100% of the time. If you knew that John Jones's infection were of the latter variety, you would give it a deterministic explanation. It is only because of your ignorance about the strain that you turn to probability.

Or suppose that the more susceptible strain is eradicated swiftly by penicillin 99% of the time. More knowledge, in this case, does not lead to a deterministic explanation, but to a different probabilistic explanation (or at least, an explanation that cites a different probability). Here, perhaps, probabilistic explanation is unavoidable, but we give the particular probabilistic explanation we do out of ignorance.

The same is often true when the explanandum is a regularity, as the crime case shows. Some kinds of single parenting may not increase children's tendency to violent crime at all, some may increase it only a little, and for some the increase, if any, may depend on other environmental factors. It is ignorance alone that leads scientists to cite a single probability, and not a complex statistical or deterministic relationship, in the explanation of the crime rate.

The third and final reason for using probabilistic explanation is illustrated by the examples from statistical mechanics and evolutionary biology. In complex systems such as gases and ecosystems, probabilistic reasoning constitutes a technique for ignoring the causal intricacies of the interactions between the systems' many parts while nevertheless deriving a near-one probability for the phenomenon of interest (Strevens 2003b, 2005). Probability here is not papering over an epistemic gap—

with respect to the macroscopic behavior of gases and the evolution of finches, we regard the details, accessible or not, as surplus to our explanatory requirements. Best to remove them entirely from our causal models so as to see more clearly the explanatory big picture. It is this use of probability in explanation that interests me most.

### 9.32  The Varieties of Explanatory Probability

Roughly paralleling the three uses of probabilistic explanation sketched in the previous section are three different kinds of probability, which I call simple probability, quasiprobability, and complex probability.

A *simple probability* is a metaphysically irreducible probability. The leading candidates in the world as we know it are the probabilities of quantum mechanics. If the quantum mechanical probabilities are genuinely irreducible—if there is no deterministic process underlying the processes that quantum mechanics declares probabilistic—then the probabilities appearing in the half-life and tunneling explanations above are simple. Simple probabilities are sometimes called single-case probabilities. The term *single-case* is not entirely univocal, I think; in any case, I have a use for it in section 10.5 that allows for the existence of single-case probabilities that are not simple.

A *complex probability* is a metaphysically reducible probability. Complex probabilities are found wherever a true scientific theory describes a process in exact probabilistic terms that is deep down deterministic. (If the probabilistic terms are inexact, the theory may be quasiprobabilistic.) A simple example is the one-half probability that a tossed coin lands heads. More sophisticated, interesting, and controversial examples are the probabilities of statistical mechanics and of evolutionary ecology.

The controversy comes from two quarters: first, the metaphysical view that irreducible probabilities alone are real, and second, the possibility that the probabilities of statistical mechanics are higher-level manifestations of irreducible quantum mechanical probabilities.

The first consideration—the reality of complex probabilities—is, for my purposes, beside the point: what is important is whether complex probabilities are explanatory, and science clearly treats them as such (section 9.6).

What if the probabilities of statistical mechanics and evolutionary biology are just simple probabilities differently expressed? Observe that these probabilities were treated as explanatory even in the great age of determinism, the nineteenth century,[4] and continue to be treated as explanatory today despite our uncertainty as to their quantum provenance. This is enough to show, at least provisionally, that their explanatory power is independent of their metaphysical roots.

A more substantive response to these worries will be found in the demonstration, in chapters ten and eleven, that the kairetic account of explanation demands that complex probabilities be posited and used to explain certain behaviors of certain deterministic systems. Not only can complex probabilities be used to explain; in some circumstances, they *must* be used to explain.

My third kind of probability is *quasiprobability*. Quasiprobabilities are explanatorily potent and are sometimes featured in the optimal explanation of an explanandum, but they do not have exact values. They may be thought of as imperfectly formed complex probabilities, in a sense that will be elucidated when they are discussed at length in section 10.3. A quasiprobability is a kind of statistical amalgam, like the probabilities cited in the violent-crime and swift-recovery explanations above; however, not every such amalgam is a quasiprobability. I will propose in chapter ten that it is explanatory concerns that distinguish the quasiprobabilities from lesser amalgams: it is in those special circumstances where an amalgam provides the best explanation of the explanandum that the amalgam can be counted as a genuine quasiprobability, a permanent part of the scientific picture of the world rather than a placeholder to be discarded as soon as more information comes in.

There may be probabilities that are more than mere quasiprobabilities but that are neither simple nor complex. They will depend in complicated ways on both metaphysically irreducible probabilities and on the kinds of deterministic processes that underlie complex probability. I called these *simplex probabilities* in an earlier work (Strevens 2003b), where they are more carefully characterized and further discussed. The treatment of simplex probability is convoluted, but it brings no new insights about the nature of probabilistic explanation, so simplex probability will be ignored, except parenthetically, in what follows.

I said above that there is a rough parallel between the three applications of probabilistic explanation described in the previous subsection and the three kinds of explanatory probability. Let me explain. When we turn to probabilistic explanation because no deterministic explanation is available, we cite simple (or simplex) probabilities. When we resort to probabilistic explanation out of ignorance, we use probabilities that are amalgams of simple or complex probabilities. If we are lucky, these probabilities are quasiprobabilities, and our explanations will endure. When we use probabilistic causal models to bypass complex interactions that ultimately make little or no difference to the explanandum, we typically cite complex probabilities (Strevens 2003b). (Possibly, however, we use simplex probabilities or even quasiprobabilities—the parallel of method and metaphysics is not perfect.)

### 9.33  The Forms of Probabilistic Explanation

There will be much more to say on this topic later (sections 9.5 and 9.7). Let me simply note that there are almost as many probabilistic relations between an explainer and an explanandum in this small sample of scientific explanations as have been suggested in the entirety of the explanation literature.

In some cases, an event or regularity is explained by citing its high probability: the half-life and vacuum cases are examples. In some cases, citing a low probability does the explaining: tunneling is a paradigm. In still other cases, the explanation proceeds by citing a factor that greatly increases the probability of the explanandum, as in the case of the swift recovery, or that merely increases the probability to some degree, as in the case of violent crime.

The one probabilistic relation sometimes claimed to be explanatory that is not represented in the examples I have chosen is the probability-decreasing relation; its conspicuous absence will be discussed in section 9.5.

### 9.4   Accounts of Probabilistic Explanation

Having tabled some evidence, let me return to the top-down approach to explanation, next surveying some theories of probabilistic event explanation influential over the last forty years. What I present here are the briefest sketches. The details of these views, where relevant, will be, or have been, discussed elsewhere in this book. (See also Strevens (forthcoming).)

## Nomic Expectability

On Hempel's nomic expectability account of explanation, an explanation is a law-involving argument that provides good reason to believe that the explanandum occurred. In the DN account, the argument is deductive; in Hempel's IS account of probabilistic explanation, it is inductive (Hempel 1965a, §3). According to Hempel, then, a probabilistic explanation is a sound law-involving inductive argument with the conclusion that the explanandum occurred. The IS account was described in section 1.31; I will not recapitulate the view here.

## Dispositional Accounts

Probabilities, some philosophers have argued, are a kind of disposition, like fragility and solubility, and ought to feature in explanations in just the way that dispositions do (Coffa 1974; Fetzer 1974). As such, probabilities ought to be thought of as causal properties responsible for bringing about the outcomes to which they are attached. Dispositional accounts belong, then, to the causal tradition in explanation and derive much of their substance from causal doctrines about deterministic explanation.

## Probabilistic Relevance

A probabilistic-relevance account, such as Salmon's SR account, holds that an event is explained by those factors that change its probability, either positively or negatively (Salmon 1970; Railton 1978; Humphreys 1989). A variant holds that only probability-increasing factors are explainers (van Fraassen 1980; Sober 1984).

As remarked in section 1.34, a variety of views on the nature of the explanatory relation are compatible with a probabilistic-relevance approach, notably the pattern-subsumption view and the view that probabilistic relevance itself is the explanatory relation.

In the literature concerned exclusively with probabilistic explanation, a causal version of the probabilistic-relevance approach is also important. On this kind of theory, the probabilistically relevant factors are held to be causally related to the explanandum in virtue of their contribution to the probability. Opinion varies as to whether or not the probability itself is a causal property. Salmon (1990a) holds that it is indeed causal: it is a kind of disposition. Humphreys (1989, 65) disagrees, stating somewhat enigmatically that "chance is literally nothing," though what Humphreys regards as the true explainers—the probabilistically relevant factors—owe their explanatory status to their effect on this "nothing."

### Railton's Deductive-Nomological-Probabilistic Account

A probabilistic explanation, according to the DNP account (Railton 1978), is a complete statement of all the facts and laws relevant to the probability of the explanandum, a deductive derivation of the probability from those facts and laws, and a note to the effect that the explanandum occurred. These formal requirements are compatible with any major view about the explanatory relation; Railton adds, however, two further elements to his account. First, he specifies that the size of the probability attached to the explanandum is irrelevant to the force of the explanation. This rules out an expectability interpretation of the DNP account. Second, as noted above, he makes a distinction between probabilistic explanation and explanation in deterministic systems, referring to the latter alone as causal explanation. This rules out, perhaps, a dispositional or other causal interpretation of the DNP account (but see note 1).

### Two Auxiliary Debates

The battle between the different accounts of the probabilistic explanatory relation has for the most part been fought by proxy, that is, by disputing certain adjoining territory in which the major views of the explanatory relation have strategic interests.

The next part of this chapter (sections 9.5 and 9.6) addresses two such auxiliary debates in the probabilistic explanation literature. Both debates can be joined in the top-down fashion, by taking a thesis about the explanatory relation as the major premise. But I will, at this stage, take the bottom-up approach, commenting on the debates in the light of the examples of probabilistic explanation described in section 9.2. A top-down resolution of many aspects of the debates, founded on the kairetic account's explanatory relation, will follow in chapters ten and eleven.

The debates, in the order of discussion, concern the following questions. First, does the size of a probability or the size and direction of a change in probability make a difference to the quality of the explanation? (This is what I refer to as the elitism/egalitarianism debate.) Second, can there be a probabilistic explanation of a deterministically produced event?

## 9.5 Elitism versus Egalitarianism

### 9.51 Varieties of Elitism and Egalitarianism

Elitism and egalitarianism are opposing views on the significance of probabilistic magnitude for explanatory power. Roughly speaking, elitists think that magnitude is significant, egalitarians that it is not. The debate is limited to event explanation.

If there is to be a probabilistic explanation of an event, then there must be a probability (or quasiprobability) for the event. A causal factor that enters into an explanation does so because it affects the value of this probability. There are two substantively different ways of framing the elitism/ egalitarianism debate. The first concerns the significance of the absolute size of the explanandum's probability, while the second concerns the significance of the change in this probability induced by various causal factors. Call these the *size debate* and the *change debate*; I will treat them separately. The various positions described in the course of the discussion are summarized in table 9.1.

**Table 9.1** Positions in the elitism/egalitarianism debate

|  |  | Size Debate | Change Debate |
| --- | --- | --- | --- |
| Elitism | Extreme | Only high probabilities explain. | ? |
|  | Moderate | High probabilities explain better. | Larger probability increases explain better; probability decreases do not explain. |
| Egalitarianism | Moderate | ? | All probability increases explain equally well; probability decreases do not explain. |
|  | Extreme | All probabilities explain equally well. | All probability changes, even decreases, explain equally well. |

## Size of Probability

Regarded as a debate about the significance of the size of the probability attached to the explanandum, the spectrum from elitism to egalitarianism is bounded by two extreme positions. *Extreme elitism* holds that an explanandum can be explained only if it has a high probability of occurring (where any probability greater than one-half may be counted as "high"). *Extreme egalitarianism* holds that the size of the probability attached to the explanandum makes no difference to the quality of the explanation. One event may occur with probability .99, another with probability .01, but if they both occur, we understand the occurrence of the one no better than the other.

A more moderate elitism holds that low-probability events can be explained, but that events with high probabilities are better explained than events with low probabilities—that we understand better why high probability explananda occurred.

Perhaps the best known argument for extreme size elitism is Hempel's, a consequence of his conception of the explanatory relation as one of expectability: to explain an event is to show that it was to be expected, but only events with high probability are to be expected, thus only high probability events can be explained.

Extreme size egalitarianism was advocated early and influentially by Jeffrey (1969); his arguments will be discussed in section 9.54. Railton's DNP account, too, is explicitly egalitarian.

Neither elitism nor egalitarianism is forced on the dispositional account. However the following argument is likely to incline proponents of that account to deny at least extreme elitism: when a low-probability event occurs, such as the decay of a given radium atom within a certain short time period, the explanation must be the atom's disposition to decay, which is identical, according to dispositionalists, to the low probability of decay.

Probabilistic-relevance accounts have little to say about the size debate; their focus is, naturally, on the change debate.

To the best of my knowledge, the only extended defense of moderate size elitism—and even this defense is restricted to the case of probabilistic explanation in complex systems, as in the examples above from statistical mechanics and biology—is Strevens (2000a).

## Size of Probability Change

When the elitism/egalitarianism debate is regarded as concerning the significance of the size of probability changes, the spectrum of positions looks rather different. There is no equivalent in the literature to the extreme elitism described above, but there is an *extreme egalitarianism* holding that any change in probability is equally explanatorily important, including negative changes. On this view, then, a factor $c$ explains an event $e$ equally well whether

1. $c$ increases the probability of $e$ by a great amount,
2. $c$ increases the probability of $e$ by very little, or
3. $c$ decreases the probability of $e$.

A *moderate egalitarianism* holds that probability decreasers do not contribute to understanding, but that among increasers, the size of the increase is irrelevant. Thus, $c$ explains $e$ equally well in cases (1) and (2) above, but it does not explain $e$ at all in case (3). A *moderate elitism* agrees that probability decreasers convey no understanding but denies the egalitarian doctrine on increases: the more a factor $c$ increases the probability of the explanandum $e$, according to the moderate elitist, the more $c$ contributes to the explanation of $e$.

Proponents of change egalitarianism, in both the extreme and the moderate versions, include Salmon (1970), Railton (1981), and Humphreys (1989). Among egalitarians, perhaps Salmon has struggled most with the question whether probability decreasers explain (Salmon 1984, 46); Humphreys' influential contribution to this debate will be discussed in section 9.53.

Proponents of elitist probabilistic-relevance views include, as noted earlier, van Fraassen (1980, chap. 5) and Sober (1984, 146).

### Remarks

First, it is a consequence of elitism that some explananda will not be explicable, or at least will be explicable only to a small degree. A common example is a particular atom's alpha decay: according to extreme size elitism, the decay is inexplicable, while according to moderate size elitism, the decay is explicable but the level of understanding conveyed by the explanation is low. This is true only of cases involving simple probability, however; even on the extreme view, an event that has a low complex probability or quasiprobability may have an explanation—a deterministic explanation.

Second, an issue that arises in connection with these positions is the question of how to measure size. Suppose a factor increases the probability of the explanandum from .01 to .1. Is this a small increase (merely .09) or a large increase (ten-fold)? This question is not much discussed in the literature. (The kairetic account will, it turns out, imply a scheme of measurement on which this is a small probability increase.)

Third, some positions in the size and change debates go together more naturally than others. It is, for example, difficult to be both an extreme size elitist and a moderate change elitist: if $c$ increases the probability of $e$ from almost nothing to not very much, and no other factors probabilify $e$ further, then an extreme size elitist says that $e$ is inexplicable, while a moderate change elitist says that $c$ explains $e$ to some degree. Even these two views can be combined by brute force, however; you might say that factors responsible for small probability increases are explainers only if the final probability is sufficiently high.

Fourth, advance notice of my own position in the elitism/egalitarianism debates: I hold that (a) for the reason given in section 9.73, the default position for a kaireticist is moderate elitism, but that (b) moderate elitism may be qualified somewhat in the light of the underlying structure of causal entailment in the explanatory model in question, which depends on the kind of probability involved in the explanation, simple, complex, or quasi (sections 10.4 and 11.5).

## 9.52  The Size Debate in Science

How do the various positions in the size debate fare as characterizations of the actual explanations offered in science?

It has long been known that extreme elitism does rather badly. Many low-probability events are given scientific explanations. An atom's alpha decay is explained by the low but nonzero probability of an alpha particle's tunneling through the potential barrier. A person's paresis is explained by their untreated syphilis, though the probability of paresis in untreated syphilitics is small (Scriven 1959).

These two examples both have the special feature that the probability without the cited factor (tunneling and syphilis respectively) is zero. This is not an essential feature of anti-elitist examples; an explanation may cite a factor that modestly increases a probability that is already nonzero. Suppose, for example, that penicillin increases the probability of John Jones' swift recovery from .03 to .3. That he does recover swiftly would normally be explained by citing the penicillin.

In response, the extreme elitist either may deny that these purported counterexamples are explanations at all, or may deny that they are probabilistic explanations. (Hempel, for example, holds that the paresis explanation is an incomplete deterministic explanation.)

To find evidence that decides between moderate elitism and extreme egalitarianism is more difficult, since both positions admit the same explanations, disagreeing only as to how powerful these explanations are.

To cast doubt on extreme egalitarianism, I point to a case where a scientific discovery whose main effect is to show that the probability of various phenomena is much higher than was previously thought is considered an explanatory advance. I have in mind Maxwell's and Boltzmann's development of statistical mechanics to explain the behavior of gases. The behavior in question, such as the regularities captured by the ideal gas law, was for the most part already known, and the molecular mechanics of that behavior had been well developed, by Clausius in particular. What Maxwell and Boltzmann added to the molecular picture was a probabilistic theory that showed not only that a gas made of fast-moving particles was capable of exhibiting the phenomena but also that it had a very high probability of doing so. That is, certain phenomena that were previously assigned a nonzero probability were shown to have a high probability. This was regarded as a major advance in explaining the behavior of gases. Egalitarianism cannot account for this fact. (The argument is developed at length in Strevens (2000a).)

If both extreme egalitarianism and extreme elitism are false, then something like moderate elitism must be true: low probabilities explain but higher probabilities explain better. I will later show that the kairetic account endorses this conclusion.

### 9.53  The Change Debate in Science

Extreme change egalitarians claim that factors that decrease the probability of an event nevertheless help to explain its occurrence. Is there any evidence for this claim?

No scientific explanation that I know of attributes the occurrence of an event to a factor that decreased its probability. Egalitarians have rallied around Humphreys (1989) to deflect this criticism. When an explanation of an event $e$ mentions a probability-increasing factor $c$ and a probability-decreasing factor $d$, it may do so in the following terms:

> $e$ occurred because of $c$'s holding, despite $d$'s holding.

There is no problem finding statements of this form in science, where $d$ is a probability decreaser. Humphreys' bold thesis is that such statements do not only cite $c$ but also $d$ as an explainer of $e$. The *despite*, on Humphreys' theory, in no way compromises the explanatory status of the factors it precedes; it merely indicates that their explanatory relevance is due to their decreasing, rather than increasing, the probability of the explanandum.

The question, then, is not whether *despite* clauses are found in explanatory contexts; they surely are. It is whether the factors that follow the *despite* are a proper part of the explanation, or whether they convey some other sort of information.

I will not attempt to settle this question here, but I will express skepticism. When I give my reasons for choosing to fly through Chicago, I may say, "I flew through Chicago *because* it was cheaper *despite* the fact that the flight takes longer." But the factor following the *despite* is not one of my reasons for choosing the flight I did. The linguistic construct is the very same one found in Humphreys' explanations (and quite likely, giving reasons is a kind of explanation, but I do not assume that here); for the same reason that the *despite* factors are not reasons, I suspect that they are not explanatory factors.

Evidence that might decide between the moderate versions of change elitism and egalitarianism is hard to come by for a reason familiar from the previous section: in the change debate, moderate elitism and moderate egalitarianism agree on the identity of the explanatory factors, disagreeing only on their explanatory weight, that is, on the size of their impact on our understanding of the explanandum.

Explanatory intuition militates against moderate change egalitarianism, I think. If the elephant seal population had gone through a population "bottleneck" of 20,000 (down from 100,000, recall), rather than 20, we would have a less clear grasp of the reasons for elephant seal homozygosity, though both bottlenecks increase the probability of homozygosity. But a moderate egalitarian will perhaps simply deny this intuition. Some progress toward refuting moderate change egalitarianism is made in Strevens (2000a), but I will put the argument to one side for now.

### 9.54  A Priori Arguments in the Elitism/Egalitarianism Debate

I have suggested that examination of actual explanations in science points to a moderate elitism in both the size and change debates. This conclusion will, I hope, work to the kairetic account's advantage when I show, in later chapters, that it entails a qualified moderate elitism.

However, there exist in the literature a priori arguments for positions entirely at odds with moderate elitism, arguments that therefore militate against the kairetic account (the more so because they do not depend on any particular conception of the explanatory relation). Naturally, I want to draw their sting.

I will focus on a priori arguments for the extreme theses in the size debate: extreme size elitism and extreme size egalitarianism. There are modifications of these arguments that support extreme positions in the change debate, or that support moderate versions of the extreme positions in both the size and change debates, but for the sake of brevity, these variants are ignored here.

### An Argument for Extreme Size Elitism

Extreme size elitism holds that only events with a high probability can be explained. Consider an event type $e$ and the event type of $e$'s not occurring, which I will write $\neg e$. Suppose type $e$ events have a high probability and so that $\neg e$ events have a low probability. Assume that when an $e$ event occurs, its occurrence can be explained by its probability. Now invoke the following reasonable-sounding principle about explanation, which Salmon (in a nonelitist context) calls *Principle I* (Salmon 1990b, 178–179):

> The same physical facts cannot explain both why an event of type $e$ occurs (on one occasion) and why an event of type $\neg e$ occurs (on another occasion).

It follows immediately from Principle I that one of the following must be false:

1. A type $e$ event can be explained by its probability.
2. A type $\neg e$ event can be explained by its probability.

If both are true, the same fact is explaining both $e$ and $\neg e$ events, in contravention of Principle I; here I assume that the probability of $e$ and the probability of $\neg e$ are just alternative descriptions of the same physical fact. It is less painful to reject (2) than (1), so you must conclude that low-probability events cannot be explained by their low probabilities (where a low probability is one-half or less).

Why believe Principle I? One possible route to the principle is by way of the following assumptions:

1. To explain $e$ is to explain why $e$ rather than $\neg e$ occurred.

2. An explanation of why $e$ rather than $\neg e$ occurred must identify some all-things-considered advantage that $e$ has over $\neg e$.

3. The same factor cannot imply that $e$ is both all-things-considered advantaged and all-things-considered disadvantaged relative to $\neg e$.

It is easy, however, for an opponent of extreme elitism to deny (1). I gave a high-level argument against the view that all explanation is contrastive in section 5.6. Here is a matching low-level argument: the explanation of alpha decay by way of quantum tunneling may explain a particular alpha decay (within a given time period), but it sounds peculiar or just plain wrong to say that it explains why the atom decayed *rather than* failed to decay. Indeed, it seems that this is precisely what is not explained. These issues, and contrastive explanation generally, are further discussed in van Fraassen (1980), Hitchcock (1999), and Lipton (2004).

### An Argument for Extreme Size Egalitarianism

Extreme size egalitarianism holds that an event is equally well explained whatever its probability. The following argument for extreme egalitarianism is inspired by (though not spelled out in) Jeffrey (1969). Consider a wheel of fortune divided into 100 segments, 99 red and 1 black. Suppose that it is a quantum wheel: when it is spun, the section on which the pointer comes to rest is determined by some quantum probabilistic process that chooses each section with a probability of 1/100. Elitism implies that the event of obtaining a red section is explicable, whereas the event of obtaining the black section is not (or in its moderate form, that *red* is better explained than *black*). But this cannot be correct. When the wheel comes to rest with the pointer indicating the black section, you understand the event just as well as when it comes to rest with the pointer indicating a red section. The two events are relevantly the same in every respect; understanding either is a matter of understanding the workings of the wheel's mechanism. Thus, in the wheel-of-fortune scenario at least, not only can low-probability events be explained, they can be explained just as well—in fact, identically to— high-probability events.

The argument is attractive, but flawed. Its crucial premises are these:

1. Once you understand the mechanism that produces outcomes on the wheel, a red outcome and a black outcome are equally explicable.
2. The probability of a red outcome is higher than the probability of a black outcome.

The argument equivocates, I suggest; it turns on an ambiguity in what is meant by "a red outcome," in particular, whether what is meant is the event that the section indicated is one of the red ones (call this event *red*), or the event that some particular red section was indicated (call this event *s*). The easiest way to distinguish these two events is by their probabilities. The probability of *red* is 99/100; the probability of *s* is 1/100, the same as it is for any other section, red or black. Now I claim that premise (1) is true only when "a red outcome" is understood as *s*, and premise (2) is true only when it is understood as *red*. Hence, the premises do not, after all, entail that events with different probabilities are equally well understood.

That premise (2) is true of *red* but not *s* is obvious, but why think that premise (1) is only true of *s*? There are two sets of facts that combine to produce the outcome *red*: the facts about the mechanism that determine that some particular section is indicated, and the facts about the color scheme on the wheel that determine that the particular section indicated is red. The first set of facts alone determines the probability of *s*. The second set needs to be added to determine the probability of *red*. But the argument for premise (1) insists that an understanding of the mechanism alone is enough to explain the occurrence of "a red outcome." The ratio of red to black in the paint scheme, in particular, is not mentioned. Therefore, what is meant is an event such as *s*.

## 9.6   Probability and Determinism

Probabilistic explanation in a deterministic system must invoke either complex probabilities or quasiprobabilities. For the purposes of this section, it is unnecessary to distinguish the two: call an explanation using either a non-simple probabilistic explanation.

The prevailing view of nonsimple probabilistic explanation is that it is either completely illegitimate or, at best, a sign of weakness. In the following brief survey of the literature, I will sketch three theses concerning non-simple probabilistic explanation, each increasingly less negative, and add a fourth, positive thesis of my own.

The three negative theses:

1. There is no such thing as nonsimple probabilistic explanation. Neither complex probabilities nor quasiprobabilities can be used in explanation.

2. Nonsimple probabilistic explanation is legitimate only if the explainer is ignorant of the underlying deterministic explanation. If the explainer is not ignorant, nonsimple probabilities have no explanatory value.

3. Nonsimple probabilities have some explanatory value even when the underlying deterministic processes are known. However, they can never have as much explanatory value as the deterministic explanation of the same phenomenon. Given a choice between the two, you ought always to prefer the deterministic explanation. (Practical considerations, such as a shortage of time or paper, might account for the occasions on which nonsimple probabilistic explanations are offered despite the availability of deterministic explanations.)

And the fourth thesis:

4. Often the objectively best explanation of a phenomenon is a nonsimple probabilistic explanation. In particular, a complex probabilistic explanation is often better than a deterministic explanation, regardless of the epistemic, practical, and other circumstances.

I will sketch some arguments for theses (1), (2), and (3); the case for my own thesis (4) will be made in the following chapters.

The first thesis states that nonsimple probabilistic explanation is impossible. This view is given succinct expression by Railton (1978, 223):

What must be given up is the idea that explanations can be based on probabilities that . . . serve only to describe deterministic phenomena . . . If something does not happen by chance, it cannot be explained by chance.

(Railton's second thoughts on this matter are discussed below.) An argument for the view is formulated by Fetzer (1971), using three premises:

1. Which probability explains a given event must be an objective matter.
2. Which complex probability appears in the explanation of a given event depends on the level at which the system that produced the event is described, that is, on the level of abstraction.
3. There is no objective method for deciding which level of description is appropriate for a given explanation.

I will later show that the kairetic criterion provides just the objective method that Fetzer seeks.

The view that nonsimple probabilities cannot explain is in any case at odds with explanatory practice. Scientists offer many probabilistic explanations of phenomena produced by deterministic processes. Examples given in section 9.2 include the explanations of violent crime, swift recovery, vacuum abhorrence, elephant seal homozygosity, and finch sex ratio. The view would appear to imply, then, that many of the explanatory achievements of physics, biology, physiology, and the social sciences are empty.

What of the thesis that nonsimple probabilistic explanation is possible only under conditions of ignorance? Such a view is entailed by Hempel's is theory, according to which probabilistic explanation must take into account all relevant information available to the explainer, so that if a deterministic explanation is available, the explainer must cite the elements of that explanation, rendering the explanation nonprobabilistic.

According to the third and mildest negative thesis, nonsimple probabilistic explanation is possible in any circumstances but is always inferior to deterministic explanation. Railton (1981), conceding that his earlier denial of the possibility of nonsimple probabilistic explanation was too extreme, argues that such explanation is often possible, but as a kind of approximation to the ideal of deterministic explanation, since understanding a phenomenon is a matter of knowing every detail that participated in the causal production of the phenomenon. Nonsimple probabilistic explanation elucidates, in its own way, some of this detail—certain facts about robustness in particular—but suppresses the rest, and so it is always less than perfect.

More generally, any account of probabilistic explanation on which the explanatory relation is something that approaches perfection in a deterministic explanation will discriminate against probabilistic explanation. The expectability approach is one example, since nothing confers expectation like a deductive argument; the minimal causal account is another.

## 9.7    Formal Elements of the Kairetic Approach

The kairetic treatment of probabilistic explanation varies with the nature of the probability involved—simple, complex, or quasiprobabilistic. When developing the kairetic account in chapters ten and eleven, I therefore take on explanation using complex probabilities and explanation using quasiprobabilities separately. Explanation using simple probabilities is barely discussed at all. This is because, as noted above, I do not think that the kairetic account has much that is novel to say about simple probabilistic explanation; for the most part, it follows the broad outlines of the DNP and similar accounts. The major exception is discussed in section 11.3.

The kairetic account's sensitivity to the probabilistic varietal notwithstanding, there are certain formal aspects of a kairetic probabilistic model that are universal. I present here a brief overview of these aspects, focusing on event explanation (for regularity explanation, see section 10.51).

### 9.71    The Kairetic Procedure

An attempt at a deterministic kairetic explanation of an event $e$ begins with a veridical, deterministic atomic causal model for $e$. That the model is deterministic and causal means that (a) the setup of the model entails the target $e$, and (b) this entailment mirrors a real-world relation of causal production. Such a model is subjected to the optimizing procedure; the result is an explanatory kernel, a model containing only factors relevant to the explanandum. A standalone explanation is built from explanatory kernels.

An attempt at a probabilistic kairetic explanation of $e$ may begin with a veridical, *probabilistic* atomic causal model for $e$. (Or, as shown in chapters ten and eleven, it may begin with a deterministic model, a possibility I overlook for now.) That the atomic model is probabilistic and causal means that (a) the setup of the model entails the target $e$ with a certain probability, and

(b) this entailment mirrors a real-world relation by which the factors in the model play a part in the causal production of *e*. I call an entailment that satisfies condition (b) a probabilistic causal entailment. (As in the deterministic case, condition (b) does not apply to that aspect of the entailment that represents the relations of pattern subsumption and entanglement that are the explanatory territory of basing patterns.)

The stipulation that the model entail the target with a certain probability is deliberately equivocal. It could mean that the model entails a certain physical probability for the target, or it could mean that the model entails, by way of a probabilistic or inductive logic, the target itself, with a certain inductive probability (as in Hempel's IS event explanation)—the entailment being not standard deductive entailment, then, but some sort of probabilistic entailment. Either logical relation is capable of representing the causal-explanatory facts; thus, either may be used as the basis for a probabilistic causal model. In this section, I focus on the former interpretation, since deductive logic is simpler and more familiar (though I will keep the latter interpretation in play). In chapters ten and eleven, however, I use the latter interpretation, appealing to a notion of probabilistic or inductive entailment, which provides a more perspicuous representation of the apposite explanatory relations.

For explanatory purposes, a probabilistic causal model is subjected to the same optimizing procedure as in the deterministic case. What remains is an explanatory kernel, a model containing only factors that are relevant to the explanandum. A standalone explanation is built from explanatory kernels.

Let me give three simple examples of the form of standalone probabilistic explanations.

First, suppose that a subatomic particle is confined within a potential well (meaning that forces prevent the particle leaving a particular region). Tunneling through the walls of the well is possible, but the probability of tunneling, over some given short interval of time, is very low. I then twist a knob that lowers the size of the potential, so that the probability of the particle's escape within the specified interval is quite high, say, 70%. The particle escapes. What is the explanation?

Call the event of the particle's escape *e*. Consider first an atomic model for *e* that does not mention my twisting the knob, but only the consequence of the twisting—the new value for the potential in the well. The setup for this model, I will suppose, specifies two factors: the background conditions *z* and the (new) value of the potential *d*. These factors entail the 70%

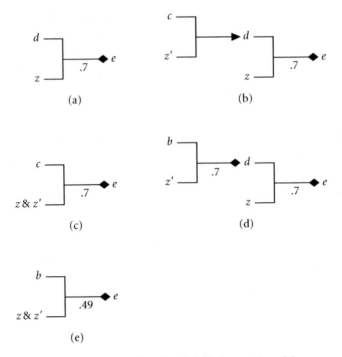

**Figure 9.1**  Examples of probabilistic causal models

probability for the explanandum $e$; the corresponding deduction is the model's follow-through. A graphical representation of the model is shown in figure 9.1(a).

Observe that the line in the diagram connecting the factors specified in the setup, $d$ and $z$, to the explanandum $e$, plays a more complicated role than in the deterministic case. In the deterministic case, the line represents two relations: first, the follow-through, a deduction relation that connects the model's setup to the explanandum; and second, a causal relation that connects the states of affairs represented by the setup to the explanandum.

In the probabilistic case, the line also represents both the model's follow-through and a causal process by which the factors specified in the setup produce the explanandum. How it does so depends on the sense in which the model "entails the explanandum with a certain probability"—on whether this directive is given a deductive implementation, on which a causal model should entail a certain physical probability for its target, or an inductive implementation, on which a causal model should entail its target with a certain inductive probability.

On the deductive implementation, the follow-through and the relevant causal process have relata different from those they have in the deterministic case. The causal relation connects, as before, the states of affairs specified by the setup to the explanandum. But the entailment relation connects the representation of the setup and the *probability* of the explanandum. In the diagram, the line is shown connecting the setup and the explanandum; the line, then, should be identified with the causal relation rather than the entailment. To remind you that there is a parallel entailment of the probability of the explanandum, I use an arrowhead that differs from the arrowhead used in deterministic models, and the probability value itself is noted under the line. (On the inductive implementation, the relata of the follow-through and the difference-making process are the same, but since the logic of the follow-through is inductive, the diagram's using a differently shaped arrow and an annotation showing the probability value are just as apt as on the deductive implementation.) The question as to how to understand *probabilistic causal entailment*—the kind of entailment required in a probabilistic explanation, on either the deductive or the inductive implementation—will be discussed shortly.

Now suppose that you want to integrate the event of my twisting the knob—call it $c$—into the explanation. There are two ways to do this. First, and more obviously, you can construct a deterministic atomic model for the low potential $d$ that cites as an explanatory factor the twist $c$ and then combine this model with the previous model to form a compound model for $e$, part deterministic and part probabilistic, as shown in figure 9.1(b). Note that an additional background condition $z'$ is added to represent the circumstances under which a twist of the knob lowers the potential.

Second, you can construct a model that has $c$ in its setup in place of $d$. Provided that the additional background condition $z'$ is included, the setup will entail $d$ and so will entail the 70% probability, as required. The new model is atomic, as shown in figure 9.1(c). Note that, although the models in figure 9.1(a) and (c) have the same graphical structure, there is a difference in the nature of the causal relationship between, on the one hand, $d$ and $e$, and on the other hand, $c$ and $e$, to be characterized in section 9.72.

For the sake of one last example, alter the scenario a little. Originally, my twisting the knob deterministically lowered the potential. Suppose now that, instead of twisting the knob, I push a button. The button push $b$

triggers a quantum process that has one of two possible outcomes. With a probability of 70%, the process will lower the potential as before. Otherwise, with a probability of 30%, it will raise the potential.

Assume that my pressing the button in fact lowers the potential and that the particle escapes. One way to explain the escape is with a compound model that combines two atomic probabilistic models, a model of the lowering of the potential $d$, and the original atomic model for the escape, as shown in figure 9.1(d).

Can there be an atomic model for the escape that explicitly cites the button-pushing but not the low potential? Yes: in this case, the probability ascribed to $e$ is 49% (the probability of $e$ is negligible if the potential is not lowered). The model is shown in figure 9.1(e).

Let me conclude with a remark on explanatory depth, an addendum to the discussion of deepening in section 4.33. There I argued that citing a drug's "dormitive virtue" does not provide a causal explanation of the drug taker's deep sleep, because the property of dormitivity does not point to any particular sleep-producing causal process. In the same way, citing only the value of a physical probability for an event does not explain the event's occurrence: a deep standalone explanation must spell out the properties of the fundamental-level laws in virtue of which the explanandum has the physical probability it does. Even a simple probability—a probability that is itself in some sense metaphysically fundamental—must be derived from the relevant parts of the fundamental laws, rather than merely having its value stated.

In the remainder of this section, I ask two questions about my description of the construction of probabilistic explanations: First, what does it mean to say that the entailment of a physical probability for $e$ (or the entailment of $e$ with a certain inductive probability) mirrors the real-world causal production of $e$? That is, what is it for such an entailment to be a *probabilistic causal entailment*? Second, what complications are brought into the theory of explanatory relevance by the introduction of probabilistic causal models?

### 9.72 Probabilistic Causal Entailment

Just as a set of factors may entail the occurrence of an event without being causal producers of the event, so they may entail a physical probability for an event, or entail an event with a certain inductive probability, without being among its causal producers. That an event is reported in a newspaper of record may entail a high probability for the event, for example, but it plays no role in causing, hence no role in explaining, the event.

The notion of causal entailment was introduced in chapter three to distinguish the causal influences from other entailers in deterministic explanation. A similar notion, probabilistic causal entailment, does the same for probabilistic explanation. Let me say right away that the full story in the case of complex probabilistic and quasiprobabilistic explanation will have to wait until later chapters; here I confine myself to a few remarks, focused on simple probabilities, intended to give the gist of the idea.

I will consider explicitly only models employing deductive probabilistic entailment, that is, models that deductively entail a physical probability for the explanandum event, as opposed to inductively entailing the event itself. The extension to the inductive case is uncomplicated and uninteresting when it is a simple probabilistic process that is to be modeled; when the process involves complex probabilities, however, the choice between deductive and inductive modeling repays consideration (section 10.23).

There are two ways that a factor might causally influence a probabilistically produced event. First, it might be part of what some philosophers would call the supervenience basis for the probability. To put things another way, the factor might be one of the physical properties of the system quantified by the probability. Examples of such factors include the size of the potential barrier in the tunneling example discussed in the previous section and the physical asymmetry of a loaded die. Others are the biochemical structure of penicillin and the streptococcus bacteria in the swift-recovery explanation, the structure of the radium atom in the half-life and tunneling explanations, the physiology of finches in the finch sex ratio explanation, and the size of the population of elephant seals at its minimum in the homozygosity explanation.

Second, a factor might influence a probabilistically produced event by influencing factors of the first sort, as do the knob and button that control the potential in the previous section's examples. There is nothing special to say about influence of this second sort; it can be broken down into steps that are either deterministic or constitute influence of the first sort.

The interesting question, then, concerns the nature of probabilistic causal entailment between causal influences of the first sort—influences that constitute or in some other sense provide a metaphysical basis for the relevant probability—and the events that they influence. Like causal entailment, probabilistic causal entailment should mirror a dependence relation between the event to be explained and the causal influences that explain it.

What is the nature of the dependence relation? There are different relations for different varieties of probability. The nature of dependence for complex probabilities and quasiprobabilities will, as I have said, be examined in chapter ten; for simple probabilities, the dependence is determined by whatever is the correct theory of causal influence in simple probabilistic causation. Several theories of influence were discussed in section 1.4. They are tailored more to the deterministic case, but they could easily be adapted, I would guess, to the simple probabilistic case.

I would further guess that each such adaptation will yield an account of simple probabilistic causal dependence on which an event $e$ depends on a causal factor $c$ just when the laws of nature specify that the simple probability of $e$ depends on $c$. The laws of quantum mechanics, for example, say that the probability of a particle's escaping a potential barrier is determined in part by the size of the potential; thus, the escape causally depends, the story goes, on the size of the potential.

For an entailment in a probabilistic model to represent this sort of causal influence, the corresponding derivation must, as in the deterministic case, go by way of the dependences stated by the laws. For example, if a law specifies that the probability of $e$ depends on $c$ in certain conditions, then in the corresponding model, $c$ must not only entail a physical probability for $e$, it must do so by way of the law and conditions, with no tricks. In other words, the follow-through must cite $c$, the law, and the conditions, and it must derive the physical probability of $e$ from these factors using modus ponens in the usual, straightforward way (section 3.23). The entailment of $e$'s probability then mirrors its dependence on $c$ and therefore qualifies as a probabilistic causal entailment.

Why should an entailment that reflects the way in which a simple probability for $e$ depends on various causal factors also reflect the way in which $e$ itself depends on those factors? That is a question that cannot be answered without a metaphysical theory of simple probability. If simple probabilities are like dispositions, then the answer is relatively straightforward: it is the simple probability of $e$, or at least the causal complex on which the probability depends, that causally produces $e$. Otherwise, the answer is not so clear. But this is not my topic; I will stay in the shallows. In section 10.23, when probabilistic causal entailment in deterministic systems is discussed, there will be no such difficulties.

### 9.73 Probability and Explanatory Relevance

In probabilistic explanation, as in deterministic explanation, it is the optimizing procedure that picks out from among the causal influences on the explanandum those that are explanatorily relevant. In the deterministic case, the explanatorily relevant factors are identified by their playing an essential role in entailing the explanandum, but in the probabilistic case, this cannot be the test for explanatory relevance, as it is the physical probability of the explanandum that is entailed, not the explanandum itself.

What ought to be the test, then? There are two obvious suggestions:

1. The explanatorily relevant factors are those that play an essential role in entailing the probability; they cannot be removed from the model without either changing the probability of the explanandum or invalidating the entailment altogether, so that the model assigns no probability to the explanandum.

2. The explanatorily relevant factors are those that play an essential role in *increasing* the probability of the explanandum; they cannot be removed from the model without either *decreasing* the probability or invalidating the entailment altogether.

(An analogous choice arises for inductive causal models.)

To choose between these two possibilities is to take a stand on the elitism/egalitarianism debate, since on the first suggestion, probability-decreasers are explanatorily relevant, while on the second suggestion, they are not.

I will make the choice indirectly, as follows. I define the accuracy of a probabilistic model to be proportional to, among the other factors specified in section 5.1, the probability that the model assigns to the explanandum.

The explanatorily relevant factors are then characterized as before: they are factors that survive the application of the optimizing procedure to at least one probabilistic model for the explanandum. Now, the optimizing procedure seeks, roughly, to remove as much detail from a model as possible without lowering its accuracy. Thus, it will discard details that either make no difference to the probability of the explanandum or that lower the probability of the explanandum. The relevant factors, then, will be those that satisfy condition (2) above—with one important class of exceptions (see section 11.3).

The optimizing procedure removes everything from a probabilistic model but the probability-increasers. It will turn out that the kairetic apparatus does much more than this: it can change a deterministic model for an explanandum into a probabilistic model. It does not merely prune probabilistic models, then; it creates them.

# — 10 —

## Kairetic Explanation of Frequencies

### 10.1 Probabilistic Explanation in Deterministic Systems

The best explanation of a deterministically produced event or set of events is, I will argue, sometimes probabilistic.

There are two reasons for the explanatory superiority of a probabilistic model. First, the descriptive apparatus of probability theory allows for an especially abstract yet cohesive characterization of the relevant mechanism, hence a model that is better able than any nonprobabilistic model to capture just difference-making causal factors, omitting all explanatorily irrelevant detail. Second, a probability distribution over such a mechanism's initial conditions provides a far more general, hence explanatorily preferable, basing generalization than any deterministic alternative. You will see in section 10.27 that only the second and less important of these sources of explanatory power contributes to the indeterminism of a probabilistic model, an observation that will lead me in the same section to repudiate the received view that indeterminism is at the root of probability's explanatory role in science.

A probabilistic explanation of a deterministically produced explanandum implies a probability attached to the explanandum, either a complex probability or a quasiprobability: you cannot explain your getting about one-half heads on a series of coin tosses probabilistically unless the event of obtaining about one-half heads has a certain probability.

Rather than begin with these probabilities, however, I will avoid them and the metaphysical questions they raise until the final section of this chapter. The main goal of the chapter is to show that, for certain explananda, a formally probabilistic model is explanatorily superior to any deterministic model. I say *formally* precisely in order to bracket, for a time, the question of whether the high-level probabilities that the models assign to the explananda are real. Section 10.52 will provide a metaphysical basis for the probabilities parallel to that provided for high-level laws in

chapter seven. By that point, I hope, the explanatory power of the probabilistic models will be sufficiently clear that the question whether the causal
factors cited by the models are genuinely probabilistic will in any case seem
secondary.

A few remarks on organization. In this chapter, I consider the explanation of frequencies of outcomes within a particular sample population, such
as the frequency of alpha decay in a given sample of radium or the preponderance of large over small Galápagos finches after a particular drought.
Explanation using complex probability and explanation using quasiprobability will be discussed separately in sections 10.2 and 10.3. In the next
chapter, I consider the explanation of single outcomes, such as a particular
alpha decay or John Jones' swift recovery. Regularity explanation, including
both the explanation of probabilistic laws and the statistical explanation of
robust patterns, such as the fact that gases almost always occupy an available vacuum or the fact that Galápagos droughts almost always result in a
preponderance of large over small finches, is discussed in section 10.51.

I have organized the explanation of frequencies and single outcomes
as two separate topics not because there is any deep metaphysical difference between the explananda—both are singular states of affairs—but
rather for expository reasons: some issues are more easily discussed with
frequencies as explananda, some with single events. This, the frequency
chapter, will be concerned with the fundamental reasons that certain deterministically produced explananda are best understood probabilistically.
The single-outcome chapter (chapter eleven) will be concerned with subtle questions about difference-making raised by probabilistic explanation,
and in particular, with the observation that some probability-raisers and
some critical events—events without which the explanandum would not
have occurred—are not explainers.

The central argument of this chapter, I should note, presupposes material
covered in part three, specifically, the explanatory role of basing generalizations and the part they play in the explanation of singular events (section 7.3, especially section 7.35).

## 10.2   Explanation with Complex Probability

### 10.21  Probabilistic Patterns

This and the next section will discuss two classes of explananda, each the
product of a distinctive kind of deterministic process. I will show that

in both cases, a probabilistic model is the explanatorily best representation of the process in question and that such models correspond to, in the one case, explanation with complex probability (section 10.2), and in the other, explanation with quasiprobability (section 10.3). I do not claim that the processes to be discussed afford the sole opportunities for complex probabilistic and quasiprobabilistic explanation in our world; they are sufficiently important and sufficiently common, however, to serve as paradigms.

The characteristic explananda of probabilistic explanations, and in a certain sense the only explananda of complex probabilistic explanations, are what I call *probabilistic patterns*. A set of events, such as the outcomes of a series of coin tosses, is probabilistically patterned just in case the events have the statistical profile typical of a probabilistic process. There are many kinds of probabilistic processes, for which reason this definition is rather open-ended, but let me fix on the particular example of Bernoulli processes.

Coin tosses, die rolls, and roulette games are all Bernoulli processes. The pattern typical of a Bernoulli process's outcomes has two facets, a kind of short-term disorder and a kind of long-term order. The long-term order inheres in the tendency of outcomes of a Bernoulli process to occur, in the long run, with a given frequency. One-half of a long series of coin tosses will tend to be heads; one-sixth of a long series of die rolls will tend to be sixes, and so on. The short-term disorder lies in a lack of any further correlation between the events in the series: if you know the long-run frequency of sixes in a series of die rolls, knowing the result of some particular die roll will be of no additional help in predicting the outcome of the next (or any later) die roll. Aside from the long-run frequency, a series of die rolls looks totally disorganized.

A Bernoulli probabilistic pattern, then, is a pattern that has this sort of long-term order and short-term disorder. It is, if you like, a pattern that will pass a statistical test for the existence of an underlying Bernoulli process. Other probabilistic processes, such as Poisson processes and the various kinds of random walks, have their own characteristic patterns.

In the next section, I introduce a certain kind of deterministic process, which I call a microconstant process, that has a tendency to produce Bernoulli patterns, and I ask how patterns produced by such a process are to be explained. My focus is on the explanation of the ordered aspect of the patterns, that is, on the explanation of long-run frequencies.

## 10.22  Microconstant Processes

### The Wheel of Fortune

Many real-world Bernoulli patterns are produced by what I call a microconstant process. A simple example of a microconstant process is provided by a wheel of fortune, a device consisting of a rotating disk, divided into many equally sized sections like pieces of pie, and a fixed pointer. The wheel is spun and allowed to come to rest. One particular section will be indicated by the pointer; the identity of this section determines the outcome of the process. A simple wheel might have its sections painted alternately red and black, in which case the outcome of the process is either *red* or *black*.

Such a wheel, as everyone knows, produces probabilistically patterned outcomes. A series of outcomes displaying the pattern in question has both long-run order, in the form of a stable frequency—about one-half *red* and one-half *black* outcomes—and short-term disorder. It is therefore a Bernoulli pattern, belonging to the same class as the patterns produced by other simple gambling devices such as tossed coins, rolled dice, and roulette wheels. This Bernoulli patterning of the wheel of fortune's outcomes can be explained by two features of the underlying causal process, shared with the other gambling devices just mentioned: a property of the wheel's mechanics, which I call *microconstancy*, and a probabilistic property of the relevant initial conditions, which I call *macroperiodicity*. Microconstant processes take their name, obviously, from the first of these. Once I have characterized microconstancy and macroperiodicity, I will show how together they explain the fact that the outcomes produced by a wheel of fortune are probabilistically patterned.

### Microconstancy

Suppose, for simplicity's sake, that the outcome of a spin on the wheel of fortune is determined by a single initial condition, say the wheel's initial speed, designated $v$. Consider the function of $v$ that is equal to zero for values of $v$ that produce the outcome *black*, and is equal to one for those that produce the outcome *red*. Call it the *evolution function* for the wheel. Provided that the wheel is symmetrical in the way that such wheels are supposed to be, the evolution function will have a form similar to that pictured in figure 10.1.

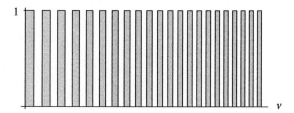

**Figure 10.1** Evolution function for a simple wheel of fortune. Areas where the function is equal to one, signifying a value of $v$ that produces *red*, are shaded gray.

The wheel's evolution function has two notable properties. First, it oscillates back and forth from zero to one very quickly. In other words, a small change in the initial speed of the wheel can change the outcome from *red* to *black* and vice versa. Second, there is a certain constancy to the oscillations: the areas of any two neighboring *red* and *black* regions (gray and white in figure 10.1) stand in roughly the same ratio—in the case of the wheel, a ratio of one to one.

I call an evolution function with these two properties *microconstant*. If a process has an evolution function for some outcome that is microconstant, the process, too, is called microconstant, relative to that outcome.

One more term is useful. I call the constant ratio in a microconstant evolution function the *strike ratio* of the function. This is usually expressed as a fraction; for example, the strike ratio for *red* on the wheel of fortune is 0.5, because the proportion of the function that is gray (signifying the outcome *red*) for any neighboring pair of gray and white sections is one-half.

### Macroperiodicity

Assume that there is a probability distribution over the initial conditions of the wheel of fortune, that is, over the wheel's initial spin speed. (The question as to the basis of such a distribution will be discussed in section 10.26.) Macroperiodicity may be thought of as a geometrical property of the distribution's probability density. Before I define it, let me briefly explain the nature of probability densities. The density for a distribution over a variable $v$ is a function defined over $v$ so that the probability that $v$ takes on a value greater than $x$ but less than $y$ is equal to the area under the graph between $x$ and $y$, as shown in figure 10.2.

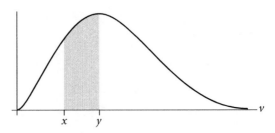

**Figure 10.2**  A density function over the initial condition $v$. The probability of $v$ taking on a value between $x$ and $y$ is equal to the area under the function between $x$ and $y$, shaded in the figure.

The density, then, is a convenient way of representing the probabilities for all the events of the form $v$ *is greater than* $x$ *but less than* $y$. Perhaps the most familiar probability density is the normal curve.

A probability distribution is *macroperiodic* if its density is approximately uniform over any small region. Macroperiodicity is, then, a kind of smoothness: if a distribution is macroperiodic, the density changes, if at all, only gradually, so that neighboring initial conditions are about equally likely. The density shown in figure 10.2 is, for example, macroperiodic, or at least it is close enough to macroperiodic for my purposes here.

What counts as a "small region"? As you will see shortly, for the purpose of understanding the microconstant production of Bernoulli patterns, what matters is that a density over an initial-condition variable be approximately uniform over the regions corresponding to neighboring pairs of gray and white areas in the relevant microconstant evolution function. The sort of macroperiodicity I am interested in, then, is defined relative to an evolution function. Since the identity of the evolution function will be obvious from the context, there will be no need to labor this relativity.

Alongside the macroperiodicity of initial-condition distributions, I will generally assume their probabilistic independence: I will suppose, for example, that the probability of obtaining a certain initial speed on a wheel of fortune spin is the same no matter what the speed of the previous spin. This allows the application of the law of large numbers to initial condition distributions, which has the crucial consequence that the actual initial conditions for a series of trials will tend to take on the macroperiodic shape of the distribution itself. For simplicity's sake, I will for the most part leave the independence assumption implicit: when I suppose that an initial condition is macroperiodically distributed, I will take it as read that the conditions for different trials are probabilistically independent.[1]

## Explaining the Patterns

The key to explaining the probabilistic patterns produced by a wheel of fortune—or rather, the key to explaining that aspect of the patterns on which I will focus, the long-run one-half frequency of the outcome *red*—is the following observation: a microconstant process with a macroperiodic initial-condition distribution will tend to produce an outcome *e* with a frequency approximately equal to the strike ratio for *e*. The frequency will be the same, then, whatever the initial-condition distribution, provided that it is smooth enough to qualify as macroperiodic.[2]

Figure 10.3 shows graphically, if informally, why this is the case. By the law of large numbers, the frequency of *red* will be (with high probability) approximately equal to the probability that a given value of $v$ produces the outcome *red*, which is equal to the shaded area under the densities in figure 10.3. When the evolution function for *e* is microconstant, you can

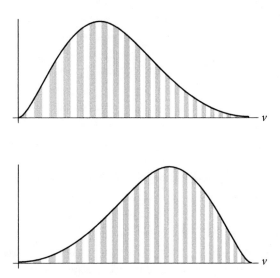

**Figure 10.3** The shape of the initial condition density, if smooth, makes no difference to the frequency with which an outcome on the wheel of fortune is produced: the shaded area of both densities is one-half of the total area.

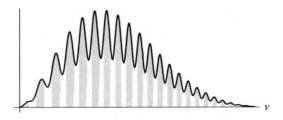

**Figure 10.4** A density that induces a probability for *red* other than one-half is not macroperiodic

see that this area is roughly the same no matter what the density, as long as the density is smooth.

Coming at the same fact from the other side, if you try to construct a probability density that induces a probability for *red* that departs significantly from the strike ratio of one-half, you will end up with a density that is clearly not macroperiodic, such as the density shown in figure 10.4.

The equality of frequency and strike ratio for *red* is an instance of the following theorem: if a process has a microconstant evolution function with strike ratio $p$ for an outcome $e$, and the probability distribution over the process's initial conditions is macroperiodic, then the probability distribution over the outcomes produced by the process is a Bernoulli distribution that assigns events of type $e$ a probability equal to $p$. Such a process will, then, tend to produce probabilistically patterned outcomes; more precisely, it will with a near one probability produce Bernoulli patterns with a frequency of $e$ events equal to $p$. The longer the series of outcomes, the more certain they are to be probabilistically patterned. (An equivalent result was sketched by Henri Poincaré and developed by Eberhard Hopf.[3] The form of the result stated here is worked out in detail in Strevens (2003b).)

To summarize: Because the wheel of fortune is microconstant and the distribution over initial spin speeds for the wheel is (or so I assume) macroperiodic, the wheel produces Bernoulli patterns of *red* and *black*. That is, outcomes are completely uncorrelated in the short run, but in the long run, *red* and *black* are each almost certain to appear with a particular frequency, equal to the strike ratio of one-half. The longer the run, the law of large numbers tells us, the closer to one is the probability that almost exactly one-half of the outcomes will be *red*, one-half *black*.

A few remarks. First, the fact that, say, one thousand trials on a wheel of fortune produced about one-half heads should be counted as a singular event, not a generalization, for the purpose of the study of explanation. We tend to say that the state of affairs of the frequency being such and such is realized by a series of events, but this does not, of course, preclude an aggregate property of the series as a whole from counting as a single event.

Second, microconstancy would be a mere curiosity if it were found solely in systems like the wheel of fortune. In Strevens (2003b) I make a case that ecosystems, the systems of statistical physics, and some other kinds of systems are microconstant with respect to many outcomes of interest; I give a few more details in section 10.25. Furthermore, although microconstant mechanisms produce only Bernoulli patterns, systems with microconstant mechanisms at their heart can produce Bernoulli, Gaussian, Markovian, and other patterns, the complex systems just mentioned being examples.

Third, the explanation of the probabilistic patterns assumes the existence of a macroperiodic probability distribution over the initial conditions. Why expect macroperiodicity? Why expect a probability distribution over initial conditions at all? I defer these questions to section 10.26, where I investigate possible sources of initial-condition distributions and sketch an argument of great generality that establishes a tendency of such distributions to be or to become macroperiodically distributed.

## 10.23 Microconstant Explanation

A wheel of fortune is spun 500 times. About one-half of the outcomes are *red*. How is this approximate frequency to be explained? How, in particular, would a microconstant explanation—a probabilistic explanation citing microconstancy and macroperiodicity—proceed? This section constructs a probabilistic causal model for the frequency that satisfies the requirements of the kairetic account. The model will be compared to its deterministic rivals in the next section.

What I will call a *microconstant model* for the one-half frequency cites two states of affairs:

1. The macroperiodicity of the probability distribution over the initial spin speeds.

2. The physical properties of the wheel's mechanics, paint scheme, and so on that make the evolution function for *red* microconstant with strike ratio one-half. Most important of these properties are the circular symmetry of the wheel's mechanics and the related symmetry of the red and black pattern of paint.

Together these facts entail a probability of near one that the frequency of *red* is approximately one-half. The microconstant model therefore has an accuracy of just less than one. (Note that the model is aggregative (section 5.5), as any model for a statistical property of independently generated events must be.)

My aim in what follows is to examine the way in which the parts of the microconstant model entail the probability, to determine the aspects of the world that are represented by the entailment, and to spell out the sense in which the model satisfies the requirement, laid down in section 9.72, that a probabilistic model's entailing of the explanandum with a certain probability should be a probabilistic causal entailment.

Begin with the probability distribution over initial spin speeds. My understanding of the explanatory power of the probabilistic model for the wheel of fortune hinges on one key premise concerning this distribution, namely, that it functions as a basing generalization, which is to say that it places the particular spin speeds that produced the outcomes whose frequency is to be explained—I will call these the actual initial conditions—in the context of a broader pattern of property entanglement. More exactly, it cites the macroperiodicity of the actual initial spin speeds as but one instance of a wide-ranging pattern of macroperiodicity in the spin speeds of wheels of fortune generally.

Two questions. First, in what sense can a set of initial conditions, such as the 500 spin speeds producing a one-half frequency of *red*, be regarded as macroperiodically distributed? After all, macroperiodicity was defined as a property of a probability density, but a finite set of initial conditions has no density. The solution: call such a set macroperiodic if the frequency with which conditions fall into any two small, equally sized, neighboring regions is approximately equal. This property is sufficient for a set of initial conditions to produce a frequency roughly equal to the relevant strike ratio (Strevens 2003b, §2.72). (For the case in which there are too few initial conditions to satisfy even this definition, see the treatment of single outcome explanation in section 11.1.)

Second, how is the spin-speed distribution a pattern of entanglement? What are entangled are two properties of a set of spin speeds, namely, the property of being a set of initial speeds of a wheel of fortune and the property of being macroperiodically distributed. The bidirectional robustness that constitutes entanglement therefore amounts to the following. On the one hand, under a range of counterfactual assumptions—the spins occurred at different times, there were a few more or a few less spins, and so on—the set of actual spin speeds would still have (very likely) been macroperiodic. On the other hand, if the spin speeds had not been initial speeds of a wheel of fortune, they might well not have been macroperiodic—as, for example, if they were the speeds with which my turntable plays the various LPs in my collection of classic vinyl (these all being a constant 33 RPM and so not macroperiodically distributed).

There are many further questions about the basing role of initial condition distributions to answer before I am done: Why is there an entanglement between the property of being a set of spins on a wheel of fortune and the property of macroperiodicity? In what sense does a probability distribution over initial conditions represent this pattern of entanglement? What kinds of facts can serve as initial condition distributions in this sense? These issues will be fully addressed in section 10.26.

Unlike the basing generalizations discussed in section 7.3, the probability distribution over initial spin speeds is a probabilistic generalization. This has parallel material and formal consequences.

The material consequence is that, by comparison with a nonstatistical pattern—such as a (fictional) pattern of exceptionless macroperiodicity in the initial speeds of wheel of fortune spins—the match between the pattern of *almost* exceptionless macroperiodicity in initial conditions generally and the macroperiodicity of the actual initial conditions is imperfect: because the rates of macroperiodicity are not exactly equal, the match is of less than 100% accuracy. Further, the macroperiodicity of the initial-condition distribution remains macroperiodic not under all perturbations but under *almost* all perturbations. Thus, the entanglement is less than absolute.

The formal consequence is that the basing generalization does not entail that the actual initial conditions that produce the explanandum exemplify the cited pattern of macroperiodicity; it entails that they do so with a high probability. (On some interpretations of the initial-condition distribution, it does not entail even the existence of the broader pattern but only that the pattern exists with high probability; see section 10.26.)

As a result, it is possible to conduct two distinct logical derivations of the explanandum using the model for the wheel of fortune and other microconstant probabilistic models. One derivation is purely deductive and the other is partially inductive, corresponding to the deductive and inductive versions of probabilistic causal entailment introduced in section 9.7. In the deductive version, the initial-condition distribution, together with the facts about the wheel's mechanism, deductively implies a high probability for a one-half frequency for *red*. In the inductive version, the initial-condition distribution *inductively* implies with high probability that the actual initial conditions for the series of trials in question are macroperiodically distributed. The macroperiodicity of the actual initial conditions together with the facts about the wheel's mechanism then deductively imply the explanandum, a one-half frequency for *red*; however, because the premise of this deduction—the macroperiodicity of the initial conditions—was derived only with high probability, the "uncertainty" is passed on to the conclusion, so that the net effect of combining the inductive and deductive steps is to imply the one-half frequency not with certainty but with high probability.

The advantage of the latter understanding of the model's entailment of the explanandum (using the term *entailment* loosely, as before, to include inductive implication) is that it divides the entailment into two steps representing distinct explanatory relations. The inductive step of the entailment represents relations of entanglement and pattern subsumption: first, the entanglement of the actual initial conditions' macroperiodicity with their being initial spin speeds on a wheel of fortune and, second, the subsumption of this entanglement under a broader pattern of initial condition macroperiodicity in wheels of fortune. The deductive step of the entailment represents a relation of causal difference-making, by which the macroperiodicity of the actual initial conditions, together with other facts about the wheel's mechanism, causally produced a one-half frequency for *red*.

Only the latter step represents a causal process; thus, only the latter step must satisfy a causal entailment requirement. Because this step is deductive, precisely the same requirement applies as in a purely deterministic case: a microconstant model's actual initial conditions and mechanism must causally entail the target, in just the sense of causal entailment characterized in section 3.23. (I leave it to you, the reader, to satisfy yourself that the macroperiodicity of the wheel of fortune's actual initial conditions, together with the relevant facts about its mechanism, causally entail an approximately one-half frequency for *red*.)[4]

This is all there is to probabilistic causal entailment: I say that the microconstant model as a whole "probabilistically causally entails" its target just in case the part of the model that represents a difference-making process causally entails its target. All that is new, then, is a way of talking.

Let me conclude by laying out the elements of the microconstant explanation of a frequency in a way that makes explicit the parallel with the form of a deterministic event explanation citing a basing generalization, such as the explanation of a particular raven's blackness held up as optimal in section 7.35. A particular wheel of fortune $x$ is spun 500 times; about one-half of the outcomes are *red*. The microconstant explanation of this approximate frequency cites a fact about $x$, a basing generalization, and a causal mechanism:

1. $x$ is a wheel of fortune.

2. There is a high probability that any large set of trials on a wheel of fortune is macroperiodically distributed (that is, there is a pattern of entanglement between being such a set and being macroperiodically distributed).

3. Wheels of fortune have such and such physical properties—namely, the physical properties in virtue of which their evolution function for *red* is microconstant with strike ratio one-half.

### 10.24 The Optimality of Microconstant Explanation

Now the pivotal moment: a comparison of the microconstant model with the deterministic alternatives, considered as explanations of the approximately one-half frequency of *red* outcomes on a long series of wheel of fortune spins. The microconstant explanation offers more explanatorily relevant information, I will argue, than any of its rivals.

## The Low-Level Deterministic Model

To evaluate these deterministic rivals, begin with what you might call a low-level deterministic causal model for the given frequency, by which I mean a model that causally entails the particular outcome of each spin, *red* or *black*, and thus entails the exact value of the frequency and so the fact that the frequency is approximately one-half. (The microconstant model, by contrast, inductively entails just the last of these facts, the approximate frequency.)

The most detailed low-level deterministic model contains a complete specification of the physics of every spin of the wheel, from the moment that the wheel is set in motion to the moment that it comes to rest. The description of each spin will specify (a) the initial speed of the wheel, (b) everything relevant to the spinning wheel's mechanics—among other things, the composition of the wheel, its bearings, and the local air density—and (c) everything relevant to determining which initial conditions produce which outcomes, in particular, the wheel's paint scheme and the pointer's position. Such a description causally entails the outcome of its particular spin; the concatenation of the however many descriptions—say, 500 descriptions for 500 spins—constitutes the setup of an aggregative causal model for the approximate one-half frequency of *red*.

Now apply the optimizing procedure to the model, but do not abstract to the point where you lose the entailment of the outcomes of individual spins. After optimization the model still contains, then, a separate, deterministic model for each spin. A considerable amount of abstraction is possible even within the bounds of this constraint. To describe any given spin, the initial speed need be stated only approximately, since an approximate speed is sufficient to determine whether the spin's outcome is *red* or *black*. For the same reason, the mechanics and paint scheme of the wheel need not be detailed down to the last molecule. When you are done discarding this irrelevant information, a spin description is just detailed enough to causally entail its outcome. (A further optimization of the low-level model will be considered at the end of this section.)

Is the low-level model as good or better an explanation of the approximate one-half frequency than the microconstant model? No, because it contains far more causal detail than is necessary to entail the frequency; it is therefore, unlike the microconstant model, bloated with causal irrelevancies. For example, whereas the low-level model must concern itself with the

magnitudes of and other parameters determining the frictional forces acting on the wheel, so as to predict correctly the outcomes of individual spins,
the microconstant model need state just the physical properties of the wheel
in virtue of which the forces have a circular symmetry (that is, in virtue of
which they are the same no matter what the position of the wheel). The
frictional details are therefore causally irrelevant to the frequency—only the
physical basis of the frictional symmetry matters—yet the low-level model
cites the details all the same.

The rationale for the low-level model's irrelevancies is its concern with
predicting individual outcomes. As the microconstant explanation shows,
in order to predict an approximate frequency, it is unnecessary to predict
the outcomes. You can therefore throw away causal detail that matters for
the outcomes considered singly, but not for their statistical properties taken
as a whole.

### The Statistical Deterministic Model

Suppose, then, that you fully optimize a low-level model, applying the
kairetic criterion for difference-making without regard for the prediction
of individual outcomes. Once all inessential details have been removed—
once all possible abstractions have been made, without compromising the
causal entailment of the approximate one-half frequency of *red*—you will
have a model that cites the following facts:

1. The macroperiodic distribution of the spins' actual initial conditions
2. The physical properties of the wheel of fortune in virtue of which its
   evolution function for *red* is microconstant with strike ratio one-half

This, then, is the optimal deterministic model for the frequency. As you can
see, it is identical to the causal part of the microconstant model—which is
to say, it is the microconstant model without its probabilistic basing generalization. Considered as an explanatory model in its own right, I call
the microconstant mechanism the *statistical deterministic model* for the frequency, *statistical* because, rather than modeling the causal production of
particular outcomes, it models the production of a certain statistical profile of outcomes given a certain statistical profile of initial conditions. To
put it another way, the statistical deterministic model, rather than specifying the physical properties of the wheel of fortune in virtue of which

causal trajectories connect particular initial conditions to particular outcomes, specifies more abstract physical properties in virtue of which kinds or sets of trajectories relate statistical properties of initial conditions to statistical properties of outcomes.

As an explanation of the one-half frequency of *red*, the statistical deterministic model is far preferable to an irrelevancy-packed low-level deterministic model. It is, therefore, the most serious competitor to the microconstant explanation. Which explanation of the frequency is better, the microconstant or the statistical deterministic model?

The two models are rather similar. They share the same causal mechanism, which is to say that they represent in exactly the same way the causal process by which the frequency of *red* is produced. The microconstant explanation differs from the statistical deterministic explanation in that it adds to this mechanism a basing generalization that subsumes the macroperiodicity of the actual initial conditions under a broad pattern of entanglement, namely, the entanglement between the property of being a set of initial spin speeds on a wheel of fortune and the property of being macroperiodically distributed. It is this explanatory supplement that makes the microconstant model probabilistic, in spite of its deterministic mechanism.[5]

The question as to which model furnishes the better explanation, then, is the question whether adding the basing generalization is explanatorily worthwhile. I argued in section 7.35 than an event explanation is always improved by subsuming its initial conditions under an appropriate pattern of entanglement, since the addition of a basing pattern to an explanation increases the quantity of explanatorily relevant information supplied. For example, I suggested, it is better to explain a particular raven *x*'s blackness by pointing to a pattern of entanglement between ravenhood and the blackness-producing properties *P* than by pointing simply to the fact that *x* has *P*.

The present case is no different. The statistical deterministic explanation of the frequency of *red* is good, but the microconstant explanation is better, because the microconstant explanation includes all the relevant information in the deterministic explanation and more besides. The best explanation of the frequency of *red* is therefore, as promised, probabilistic.

I should say that the difference in explanatory power between the probabilistic and the statistical deterministic model is qualitatively less significant than the difference between either the probabilistic or statistical deterministic model and the low-level deterministic model. The low-level model has the serious flaw of containing considerable quantities of explanatorily irrelevant information. The statistical deterministic model contains no irrelevancies; its explanatory transgression is merely the misdemeanor of failing to cite information that is relevant and available. (The difference between these two kinds of explanatory failing was laid out in section 7.34, pages 250.)

This is as it should be. The statistical deterministic explanation not only has the same mechanism as the probabilistic explanation; this shared mechanism cites what I will later argue are the principal constituents of the complex probability itself, the constituents that do the real explanatory work in a complex probabilistic explanation (sections 10.27 and 10.52). Though deterministic, the model is statistical in more than name.

### The Question of Accuracy

An important issue has, however, been elided in the comparison of the microconstant and the statistical deterministic models. Because the microconstant model is probabilistic, it entails the explanandum with a probability of less than one and thus has an accuracy of less than one (section 9.73). Does this affect its explanatory power? In the case at hand, the accuracy is so close to one it hardly seems worth worrying about. But explanatory accuracy, or rather inaccuracy, has important implications for the overall shape of the theory of probabilistic explanation, so I will not delay my treatment of the matter.

The inaccuracy of the microconstant model is due to the inaccuracy of its basing generalization. I have not yet formally characterized accuracy in a basing generalization; without going into great detail, let me say that the accuracy of a basing generalization with respect to a causal model is a measure of the fit between the basing pattern and the properties of the actual initial conditions subsumed under that pattern. Suppose that the model ascribes a property $P$ to the actual initial conditions on the grounds of their being $F$. If the basing generalization ascribes $P$ to $F$s with a probability of less than one, or implies a rate of occurrence of $P$ among $F$s of less than 100%, then the fit is not perfect. Equally, if the basing generalization assigns $F$s a property that is similar but not identical to $P$, the fit is not perfect. (Note that the fact of a basing generalization's being inaccurate for the purpose of explanatory pattern subsumption does not call into question the generalization's truth or the corresponding basing pattern's reality; see note 14 of chapter 7. Note also that accuracy in pattern subsumption is formally rather similar to accuracy in causal modeling; see section 5.1.)

In the case at hand, the lack of fit is due, as noted above, to the fact that the basing generalization ascribes the macroperiodicity of the actual initial conditions a probability less than one—the "rate of macroperiodicity" implied by the basing generalization is, as it were, slightly different from that found in the initial conditions (see section 10.26). I want to investigate the explanatory consequences of this looseness of fit; the question, then, is of how the accuracy of an explanation's basing generalization affects the quality of the explanation as a whole.

Let me consider two possible answers to this question. On the one hand, the explanatory contribution of an explanation's causal mechanism and of its basing generalization might be quite independent, in which case though inaccuracy degrades the explanatory contribution of a basing generalization, it cannot affect the contribution of a mechanism. It follows that the explanatory power of a mechanism/basing-generalization package is never less than the power of the mechanism alone, no matter how inaccurate the generalization—no matter how low, for example, the probability it ascribes to the initial conditions cited by the mechanism. On this view, adding even a rather inaccurate basing generalization to a mechanism will improve the resulting explanation or, at worst, leave it unsullied.

On the other hand, the quality of an explanation might be roughly proportional to the quality of its weakest link. An explanation that cites a bad basing generalization, then, is a bad explanation—though it may contain all the elements of a good explanation.

I have tended to this second way of treating the effects of defective explanatory supplements. Adding an irrelevant causal detail to a causal model makes the model worse than it was before. More pertinent to the case of basing generalizations, elongating a causal model by adding a bad explanation for one of its initial conditions makes it worse than it was without the elongation: we much prefer an unelongated model to a botched elongation, although the latter contains the former. The same is true, I suggest, for basing generalizations: citing an inaccurate basing generalization introduces an irrelevancy into the explanation; as in these other cases, in so doing it degrades the original explanation rather than merely failing to augment it.

Why do I say that an inaccurate basing generalization introduces an irrelevancy? Consider the following simple example of inaccuracy. Suppose that only 10% of ravens have the blackness-producing property $P$; the remainder are brown. You want to explain the blackness of some particular raven $x$. You cite the familiar mechanism, the aspects of the fundamental laws in virtue of which $P$ produces blackness, and the fact that $x$ has $P$. You could expand your explanatory model by adding a basing generalization that subsumes $x$'s $P$-hood under a wider pattern, namely, the generalization stating that 10% of ravens have $P$. The accuracy of the generalization is the degree to which it subsumes $x$'s $P$-hood, or in other words, the degree to which $x$ exemplifies the pattern. Obviously, $x$ does not exemplify the pattern very well at all; it would be a much better paradigm if it did *not* have $P$, since ravens without $P$ are the rule. (If it helps, think of the generalization as saying that 90% of ravens lack $P$.) Thus, relative to the explanatory work it is called upon to perform—the subsumption of $x$'s $P$-hood—the generalization is of low accuracy. Now let me show that this inaccuracy corresponds to an intuitive irrelevancy in the explanation. You are explaining $x$'s blackness in terms of its $P$-hood (no problems here) and then adding that $x$ is a raven and that a small minority of ravens have $P$. What seems to have gone wrong with your explanation is its citation of a property, ravenhood, that is of dubious relevance to the mechanism's initial conditions. It is simply not illuminating, and indeed is quite misleading, to cite $x$'s ravenhood as being, by way of $P$, a part of the explanation of its blackness. The technical property of inaccuracy, then, is a sign of an explanatory flaw in the basing generalization's antecedent property, namely, irrelevance. Like properties that are irrelevant in other ways—non-difference-making causal details and the faulty elements of bad elongations—the citation of this property undermines the model's explanatory power.

An explanation that subsumes the causally relevant initial conditions under a basing pattern for which they are a bad match should therefore be treated like any irrelevancy-citing model—it should be rejected. In particular, an explanation that cites a basing generalization ascribing a low probability to the causally relevant initial conditions is to be regarded as defective.

Let me apply this precept to microconstant explanation. The less than perfect accuracy of the microconstant model turns out, on the view I have endorsed, to be an explanatory liability. It points to a sense in which the antecedent property of the initial-condition distribution—the property of being a spin speed on the wheel of fortune—is less relevant to macroperiodicity than it might be. However, it is still highly, indeed almost completely, relevant, as reflected in the basing generalization's near-one accuracy, and so the microconstant explanation's citation of the basing generalization is a net explanatory good.

The use of microconstant models to explain low-probability frequencies will be explored in section 10.41.

Because accuracy, cohesion, and generality work in similar ways in determining both the optimality of causal models and the optimality of probabilistic basing generalizations, you can make a quick and dirty assessment of the quality of a probabilistic model by totaling these properties without regard to whether they come from the causal or the basing side of the model. In particular, you can judge probabilistic models by their accuracy without understanding whether the inaccuracy, when present, is due to the indeterministic causal production of the target by the actual initial conditions or to the initial condition distribution's assigning the actual initial conditions a probability of less than one. This heuristic will prove useful in later sections.

### Functionalization

Consider an objection to the claim that the microconstant and the statistical deterministic models have a mechanism that is strictly more abstract than that of the optimal low-level deterministic model. Looking back to the treatment of the ball in the basin in section 7.41, you might think that the low-level deterministic model is capable of further optimization, by characterizing the spins in terms of the functional relationship between their initial conditions and the parameters of the wheel. If you take this abstraction technique as far as possible, you will end up with two complementary functional descriptions: the one satisfied by all and only spins on the wheel yielding *red*; the other satisfied by all and only spins yielding *black*. Your low-level model will specify for each of the spins which of the two descriptions it satisfies, thus entailing its outcome.

Suppose that this fully functionalized model is the optimal low-level explanatory model for the frequency of *red*. Then it is false that the statistical deterministic model is an abstraction of the optimal low-level deterministic model, because the fully functionalized model does not entail the microconstancy of the evolution function for *red*, as it would have to if it were a concretization of the statistical deterministic model. The mechanisms of the statistical deterministic and the fully functionalized low-level models, then, would be two distinct, equally valid end points for the process of abstraction, reached by different decisions as to what to keep and what to throw away earlier in the process. It would follow that my earlier argument that the statistical deterministic model is superior to any low-level deterministic model rests on a faulty premise. Perhaps the conclusion, if not the argument, can be saved by holding, first, that the better explanation is given, all other things being equal, by the model of greater generality (as proposed in section 4.35) and, second, that the statistical deterministic mechanism has greater generality than the fully functionalized mechanism; whether this is the case is difficult to say without some characterization of degrees of generality more specific than any I have sketched so far.

There is, however, a quite different reason to explanatorily disdain the fully functionalized low-level model: it is not a causal model. Why not? The model ascribes to the initial spin speed of each trial one of two functional properties, the first of which is satisfied by any spin speed producing a *red* outcome, the second the same for *black*. These functional descriptions must depend on, among other things, the parameters of the wheel's paint scheme, in particular the boundaries of the red sections of the wheel. The descriptions do not specify values for the boundaries, of course; rather, they specify a certain functional relation that an initial spin speed must bear to the boundaries, however the boundaries are configured. Such a description, when predicated of a spin speed, ascribes to the speed a complex property constituted in part by the speed's bearing a certain relation to the boundaries and, more generally, to the paint scheme. It is the spin speed's having *this* property that will, in the fully functionalized model, entail that the speed produces a *red* outcome. Now, in order for the model to be a causal model, the entailment must be a causal entailment, which is to say that the properties figuring in the premises must play a part in the entailment that reflects their role in the causal production of the outcome. It is this condition that is not satisfied in the fully functionalized model. The course of the causal events is as follows: the spin speed, in virtue of its magnitude and various physical properties of the wheel, determines a final resting place for the wheel. The final resting place, in virtue of the position of the pointer and the wheel's paint scheme, determines the outcome, *red* or *black*. The paint scheme enters into the causal story only once the final resting place is determined, then, so it should not enter into the deduction of the outcome until the final resting place is deduced. In the fully functionalized model, however, it enters into the deduction right from the beginning, as a part of a complex property attributed to the initial spin speed, as though the causal influence of the spin speed depends on its having a certain relationship to the paint scheme. In fact, the causal influence of the spin speed depends on its magnitude alone, and thus the sole property that a causal model may attribute to the spin speed is the intrinsic property of having a certain magnitude.

To sum up, the properties that a causal model attributes to the initial conditions must answer the following question: Why did the initial condition have the causal influence that it did? Why did it affect the moment-to-moment unfolding of the causal process in the way that it did? The paint scheme played no part in spin speed's causal influence—we can see from the fundamental physical laws that changing the scheme would not have changed the influence—so properties involving the paint scheme are off limits in a causal characterization of spin speed.

I previously advocated a certain degree of functionalization in explanatory models, most notably in the case of the ball and the basin, where the relevant causal model specifies the existence of a certain "basin filigree" in functional terms (section 7.41). There, however, the functional property is specified in terms of variables—the initial position and velocity of the ball—whose values not only predate the causal contribution of the filigree but also themselves explain why that particular filigree is the one that makes the causal contribution. Consequently, the functional property that picks out the filigree is causally relevant to the filigree's causal contribution; it is therefore a legitimate part of the causal story. (An even better way to think about functionalization in the ball/basin model is advanced in section 11.1.)

## 10.25 The Range of Microconstant Explanation

I have argued that probabilistic explanation is not only permissible but obligatory wherever science investigates frequencies produced by microconstant processes. This is a very broad class of phenomena indeed, or so I argue in Strevens (2003b), where I suggest that all complex probability is based in microconstancy. Let me briefly survey some of the world's natural microconstancy.

The various macrolevel behaviors of gases, such as those laid down in the ideal gas law and laws of diffusion, are essentially frequency phenomena, because the macroscopic properties of gases are identical to or directly depend on the frequencies of various states of affairs, such as the frequency with which gas particles strike each other or strike container walls. For example, that a gas expands into a vacuum is a state of affairs that holds in virtue of the statistics, or frequencies, of gas molecules' positions.

If the behaviors of individual gas molecules are produced, as I claim in Strevens (2003b, §4.8), by microconstant processes, then the proper explanations of gas behavior are probabilistic explanations that cite the macroperiodicity of initial condition distributions and the factors responsible for the microconstancy and strike ratios of the relevant evolution functions. The best explanation of these phenomena is not deterministic, then, as Railton (1981), Glymour (2007), and some of the other writers cited in section 9.6 have argued, but probabilistic.

Not just the behavior of gases but all of the dynamics of heat undergirded by statistical mechanics is, I conjecture, produced by microconstant processes. Thus, all of the behavior that falls under the second law of thermodynamics—every approach to thermodynamic equilibrium, of which expansion into a vacuum is just one variety—is to be explained by probabilistic models that ignore vast amounts of deterministic detail concerning initial conditions, collisions, transmissions, and so on, and state just the physical facts underlying microconstancy and macroperiodicity.

The processes governing life, death, and reproduction are also, I have proposed, microconstant (Strevens 2003b, §4.9). Thus, any explanandum that is essentially the event of a certain frequency of deaths, births, and so on, having occurred in an ecosystem, ought to be explained as above.

One example is the preponderance of large over small finches in the aftermath of a drought in the Galápagos islands (section 9.2). What explains this statistic is not the collected life histories of the finch population but whatever factors are responsible for the fact that the strike ratio for survival and reproduction is higher in a drought for large birds than for small birds. In the literature on the finches, this is precisely what you find. Although the Grants and their collaborators keep track of every finch on the island of Daphne Major, where their studies take place, they explain larger birds' superior performance during a drought by citing just the one factor that affects the relative strike ratios: the prevalence of bigger, harder-to-crack specimens among the nuts available during the later stages of a drought (Grant 1986).[6]

The finch case is an example of natural selection: during a drought, larger birds are fitter than smaller birds, and they begin to replace the smaller birds in the population. Because the drought is temporary, and because other conditions favor smaller birds over larger birds, the trend in favor of large size is temporary. But when natural selection runs its course—when one variant of a species is at a fitness disadvantage for long enough that it is entirely replaced, that is, driven extinct, by another—the processes and the explanation are of the same sort. A fitter variant's replacing a less fit variant is to be explained, then, by citing the factors in virtue of which the strike ratios for survival and reproduction are higher for the victorious than for the vanquished variant. Any more detail degrades the explanation. Darwinian explanation is not probabilistic because of our laziness or ignorance, contrary to the arguments of Rosenberg (1994) and others. It will always be, and should always be, probabilistic.

Many other kinds of explananda are frequencies: the extinction of a great proportion of elephant seal alleles, the inordinate number of children from single-parent homes who turn to violent crime, and so on. Wherever a microconstant process produces the outcomes that collectively determine these frequencies, their best explanation is probabilistic—as you would infer from reading the science—not deterministic, as so often philosophers have insisted.

## 10.26  Initial-Condition Distributions

Microconstant explanation's use of initial-condition distributions as basing generalizations raises three questions. First, how does a probability distribution represent a pattern of actual and counterfactual initial conditions? Second, what kinds of things can play the role of initial condition distributions? Must initial-condition distributions represent physical probabilities? Third, how does macroperiodicity become entangled with other properties?

### Probabilistic Representations of Patterns of Entanglement

The explanatory role of a basing generalization is to contribute to an explanatory model a pattern of property entanglement. In the case of the microconstant explanation of a frequency produced by a wheel of fortune, the pattern in question is roughly that captured by the generalization *Almost all long series of spins on a wheel of fortune robustly have macroperiodically distributed initial conditions*. How does a macroperiodic probability distribution—which says, roughly *Probably, a long series of spins on a*

*wheel of fortune will have macroperiodically distributed initial conditions—*
represent such a pattern? The challenge is to get from the probability distribution's *probably* to the basing pattern's *almost all*.

There are some interpretations of probability, such as the view that probabilities are frequencies, on which the existence of a distribution that probabilifies macroperiodicity in a wheel of fortune's initial conditions deductively entails that most sets of initial conditions are macroperiodic. A frequentist in effect defines *probably* as meaning *almost all*. On other views,
however, a probability distribution can at best inductively imply the existence of a pattern of macroperiodicity.

My simple proposal is that it is by way of this inductive implication that a
nonfrequentist probability distribution represents the pattern. There is no
difference, then, between the basing pattern represented by a frequentist
distribution and the basing pattern represented by a nonfrequentist distribution: in both cases, the pattern contributed to the explanation is one of
pervasive but not exceptionless macroperiodicity. The only difference is in
the means of representation. A frequentist distribution states the existence
of the pattern directly, whereas a nonfrequentist distribution states its existence by inductive implication.

A nonfrequentist probability distribution will of course also imply something over and above the pattern's holding, namely, the existence of certain
physical probabilities. To represent these facts is not, however, a part of such
a distribution's explanatory function, which is nothing more than to contribute the pattern itself. You will recall from section 7.32 that it is quite normal for a basing generalization's content to extend beyond its explanatory
contribution. A causal basing generalization, for example, states or implies
the existence of an underlying mechanism, but only the pattern produced
by the mechanism finds its way into the explanation. So it is with probabilities and frequencies: a probabilistic basing generalization may have much
to say about what probabilities do or do not exist, but its function in an
explanation is limited to stating the existence of whatever pattern of robust
property coinstantiation the probabilities inductively imply.

### Interpreting the Initial Condition Distribution

In order to make its explanatory contribution, a basing generalization must
be true (or so I suppose). If a probabilistic claim about initial conditions is
to serve as a basing generalization in a microconstant model, then, there

must exist some sort of probabilistic distribution over initial conditions to give it a basis in fact. For example, there must exist facts that are in some appropriate sense probabilistic about the distributions of wheel-of-fortune spin speeds, molecular velocities, Galápagos finch locations, and so on.

What physical foundation might such distributions have? I will consider three possibilities: the distributions assert facts about either simple probabilities, complex probabilities, or frequencies.

First, simple probability. If the relevant initial conditions fall under a simple probability distribution, any worry about the foundations of the probabilistic model is immediately assuaged. There is, however, little reason to expect quantum probability distributions over many of the initial conditions of microconstant processes, such as the properties of finches relevant to their surviving a drought.[7]

To complex probability, then. The initial conditions of a microconstant process in a complex system—conditions such as the velocity of a given gas molecule or the satiety of a given finch—are often produced by earlier microconstant processes of the same sort. This suggests that the same complex probability distributions induced over the outcomes of such a process already exist over the initial conditions. For this and other reasons, I believe that many initial-condition distributions in microconstant models are indeed complex probability distributions (unless they are quasiprobability distributions, a possibility that I ignore for now).

This merely pushes back, however, the question of the probabilistic foundation of microconstant models. For each complex probability distribution over initial conditions, there must exist a microconstant mechanism to generate the conditions with its own initial condition distribution. Barring infinite regresses or circles of dependence, the plethora of complex probability distributions must be based, ultimately, on some other kind of distribution. (Networks of probabilistic dependence are discussed in more detail in Strevens (2003b, §2.4).) For the reasons given above, I do not want to rely on a simple probabilistic basis, so I turn to frequencies, arguing that frequency-based distributions provide everything that is needed in the way of a foundation for microconstant explanation.

An actualist frequency-based distribution summarizes the frequencies (or perhaps the limiting frequencies) with which actual initial conditions take on different values. When only countable numbers of conditions are represented, such a distribution will have no density, but an appropriate definition of macroperiodicity can be constructed along the lines proposed in section 10.23.

On the actualist interpretation, there is a macroperiodic frequency-based distribution over sets of wheel-of-fortune spin speeds just in case most such sets are themselves macroperiodically distributed; the frequency-based distribution simply represents the predominance of actual macroperiodicity.[8]

In order to represent patterns of entanglement, I will need a frequency-based distribution with a greater scope than an actualist distribution, one that is capable of representing outcomes produced in the sort of counterfactual circumstances that figure in the definition of entanglement. For example, that the property of being a set of initial spin speeds on a wheel of fortune is entangled with the property of macroperiodicity implies that, had some particular set of trials on a wheel of fortune been carried out under slightly different circumstances, the initial spin speeds would likely still have been macroperiodically distributed. If the *likely* is interpreted in frequentist terms, this robustness property amounts to the fact that in almost all the possible worlds you look to in evaluating such counterfactuals, the sets of spins are macroperiodic. What is wanted, then, is a pattern of pervasive, if not exceptionless, macroperiodicity in both the actual world and a certain set of nearby possible worlds. In what follows, I understand my frequency-based initial condition distributions in this way. The question as to what actual facts undergird the macroperiodicity of the possible but nonactual sets of trials will be answered at the end of this section.

### Objections to Explanatory Frequentism

The advantage of a frequentist interpretation of microconstant models' initial-condition distributions is that it promises to provide such models with an entirely nonprobabilistic foundation, thus allowing for probabilistic explanation in a deterministic world.

The potential disadvantages are as numerous as the objections that have been leveled at frequentist interpretations of probability over the years. Many of these arguments, I will allow, constitute potent reasons to reject a frequentist metaphysics of probability. This does not in itself, however, constitute a fatal flaw in my proposal to understand explanatory initial-condition distributions as frequency based. The role of a probabilistic basing generalization is to contribute a basing pattern to an explanation— nothing more. To provide a foundation for a microconstant explanation, then, an initial condition distribution need not be a probability distribution in anything but the mathematical sense. Its explanatory role is to imply the existence of the right sort of pattern, namely, a prevalence of macroperiodicity in the relevant initial conditions. And this is something that a frequency-based distribution does even more surely than its metaphysically more refined nonfrequentist counterparts.

You might think, nevertheless, that some of the reasons to reject actual frequentism as a metaphysics of probability are also reasons, independently of any properly metaphysical concerns, to reject frequency-based distributions as contributors of basing patterns. Let me consider several objections to the explanatory use of frequency-based distributions motivated to various degrees by well-known arguments against metaphysical frequentism.

First, probabilities have (it is usually said) the mathematical property of countable additivity, whereas frequencies do not. You do not need countable additivity to derive a basing pattern of prevalent macroperiodicity from a probabilistic basing generalization, however, so this complaint is beside the point.

Second, some writers who prefer the causal to the pattern-subsumption approach to explanation have thought that frequentist probabilities are incapable of explaining the outcomes to which they are attached, since those outcomes are constitutive of, rather than somehow being produced by, the frequencies. The causal-explanatory impotence of frequency-based distributions would be a catastrophe if the kairetic account called upon such distributions to provide a causal explanation of the events over which they are defined—to causally explain, in other words, properties of a set of trials' initial conditions. But this is not, of course, how the kairetic account employs initial-condition distributions. Rather, it uses the distributions to subsume facts about initial conditions; the causal work is done elsewhere. For the purpose of subsumption, the initial-condition distributions more or less have to be—or more exactly, have to represent—patterns of property instantiation, that is, frequencies with which initial conditions instantiate certain properties. If the kairetic account of basing generalizations' explanatory role is correct, then, it is hard to see how anything *but* frequencies could play the basing role.

The third and final objection to interpreting initial-condition distributions as frequency based is the problem of the reference class. A frequency-based initial-condition distribution represents statistics about actual initial conditions—but which initial conditions, exactly? If you are building a distribution to represent actual finch locations, do you restrict yourself to the locations of finches on Daphne Major? In the Galápagos? To *Geospiza fortis*, or to other species as well? In the 1970s? In the twentieth century? It is the hopelessness of any attempt to give a determinate, principled answer to this question, recall, that causes Fetzer to reject the possibility of probabilistic explanation in deterministic systems (section 9.6).

Within the context of microconstant explanation, however, this problem simply does not arise. In order to construct the best possible explanatory model of a microconstant process, what you need from your facts about frequencies is a cohesive pattern of (entangled) macroperiodicity that is as wide as possible in scope and of which the macroperiodicity of the relevant actual initial conditions is an instance. Even if (which I think will be rare) the optimality criterion for basing patterns does not determine a unique choice from among the possibilities, there is no cause for concern, since macroperiodicity prevails in all. What you will have is a number of equally explanatory models for your explanandum, each citing a different macroperiodic basing generalization based on a different, equally good reference class—a perfectly tolerable situation.

Before concluding, I should take note of a point well known to reference-class mavens: it is always possible to construct a reference class by hand-picking the initial conditions that go into it, in such a way that the distribution determined by the class has any property you like. You might use this power to create a difficulty for frequency-based microconstant explanation as follows.

Consider a microconstant device whose initial conditions are, for some systematic reason, usually not macroperiodically distributed—call it the *wheel of ill-fortune*. Take some series of trials on the wheel of ill-fortune that has, by a fluke, a macroperiodic set of actual initial conditions. It seems that the best explanation of the resulting frequency will make no appeal to a basing generalization but will simply say that, as it happened, the initial conditions were for once macroperiodically distributed. But you can construct some reference class by hand that gathers together the initial conditions for actual sets of trials on the wheel of ill-fortune on just those few occasions where they are macroperiodic, by finding a property $X$ gerrymandered so that it is shared by just these experiments and no others. Or you can achieve a similar effect by finding an $X$ that picks out the experiment producing the frequency to be explained together with all experiments on some other device—say the wheel of fortune—for which macroperiodicity is the rule. Either way, you can truthfully say that the initial conditions of type $X$ experiments are typically macroperiodically distributed. Citing such a generalization does not, however, appear to be more explanatory than saying, "As it happened . . . "—on the contrary, it is rather misleading. But is not the gerrymandered initial-condition distribution a far more general pattern and therefore explanatorily preferable?

The kairetic account in fact forbids the explanatory use of such a generalization in the basing role, because the entanglement, if any, represented by the generalization is absent in the actual initial conditions, in contravention of the requirement laid down in section 7.35. Why is it absent? Although the actual initial conditions are macroperiodic, they are not robustly macroperiodic: if the trials had taken place under slightly different circumstances (while still satisfying $X$), they would very probably have been nonmacroperiodic, like most sets of trials on the wheel of ill-fortune. (More exactly: almost all $X$-preserving perturbations of the circumstances would have resulted in nonmacroperiodic initial conditions.)

On top of this, the basing patterns in question in any case lack cohesion, because the property $X$ that circumscribes the reference class will be some disjunctive monstrosity. To put it more intuitively, the macroperiodicity of just the sets of initial conditions picked out by $X$ does not constitute a real pattern of entangled macroperiodicity—or, invoking the characterization of basing-pattern cohesion suggested in section 7.34, there is no single, systematic reason for the robust connection between $X$-hood and macroperiodicity that applies to all the $X$s.

### The Robustness of Macroperiodicity

In the course of understanding macroperiodic initial-condition distributions as basing generalizations, I have assumed almost without comment that there is a good deal of macroperiodicity around, and further, that it is around robustly: macroperiodically distributed series of trials, had they been conducted under somewhat different circumstances, would still have been, for the most part, macroperiodic.

What reason is there to accept this assumption? Elsewhere (Strevens 2003b, §2.53) I present an argument for expecting almost any variable you might take seriously to become macroperiodically distributed over time, both in actuality and under the usual range of counterfactual suppositions. (The variable must be what I call a standard variable; this restriction rules out "grueish" methods for describing initial conditions.)

The idea, roughly, is that given the prevailing fundamental laws of nature, macroperiodic distributions of a standard variable are the distributions with the highest entropy, in the sense that a perturbation of the instances of the variable—I am thinking of the disturbance due to the more or less random low-level disruption of any system by extraneous "noise"—will be likely to make a distribution more rather than less macroperiodic, given some weak assumptions about the distribution of the perturbations themselves.

This is not an a priori argument or a deduction from the laws of fundamental physics: the tendency to macroperiodicity is neither a metaphysical nor a physical necessity, because it depends on the physically contingent fact that the distribution of perturbations in the actual world has certain properties. (At least, I suppose that it is a fact, and I suppose that it is physically contingent.)

How can a tendency to macroperiodicity deduced from a contingent fact explain not only the macroperiodicity of actual initial condition distributions but also that of certain counterfactual distributions, as is required for robustness, hence for entanglement? The answer is foreshadowed in the discussion of counterfactual facts about ravens in section 7.32: when evaluating a counterfactual of the form *If I had conducted this series of 500 trials on the wheel of fortune a few minutes later . . .* , you do so against a background that includes the exact history of the actual world up until the moment when some sort of deviation from actuality becomes necessary in order that the counterfactual antecedent occurs. Thus, you will hold on to the actual distribution of perturbations in your workaday counterfactual reasoning, and so macroperiodicity will be the (statistical) rule for the kinds of counterfactual antecedents relevant to determining entanglement.

This argument for macroperiodicity, if correct, establishes the truth of the following generalization, which you might call the *law of macroperiodicity*:

> Almost all sets of standard initial conditions are macroperiodically distributed, except in cases where the initial conditions are produced by a mechanism that has the effect of transforming macroperiodically distributed inputs into nonmacroperiodically distributed outputs.

The scope of the law of macroperiodicity is wide open in two senses. First, it applies to the initial conditions, whatever they are, of any system or class of systems, with the one exception spelled out in its proviso. Second, it applies not only to actual sequences of trials but also to counterfactually generated sequences of trials, provided that the counterfactual assumptions do not depart too far from actuality.

If the law of macroperiodicity is true, it can be used as a basing generalization in any microconstant explanation in which its proviso is discharged. Being wider in scope than other generalizations of the same sort, while not notably less accurate, it is perhaps the preferred basing generalization for all such explanations—depending on the question whether the standard initial conditions have enough in common that the law states the existence of a cohesive pattern.

Can such a broad pattern—namely, the entanglement of the property of being a series of values of a standard variable (not generated in a certain way) and the property of being macroperiodically distributed—possibly be cohesive? Yes, according to the characterization of cohesion advanced in section 7.34, on which a pattern of entanglement is cohesive provided that the entanglement occurs in each instance of the pattern for the same reason: despite the many differences between different standard variables, perturbations tend to push any standard variable into a macroperiodic distribution in much the same way, and so for much the same reason.[9]

Here you can see, perhaps, the ultimate rationale for the indeterministic aspect of microconstant explanation. A part of event explanation is the subsumption of an entanglement under a more general pattern of entanglements that exist for the same reason. In the case of macroperiodicity, that "reason"—the process by which perturbations promote macroperiodicity—admits of exceptions. Thus, any generalization that sums up the pattern in such a way as to include all cases in which the process is operative is a generalization that itself has exceptions. The basing generalizations in microconstant explanation are therefore indeterministic; microconstant explanation itself inherits this indeterminism.

### 10.27 Indeterminism and Explanation

The indeterministic aspect of a microconstant explanation is, I have shown, entirely due to its citing a probabilistic basing generalization, which is to say that it is entirely due to the subsumption of the initial conditions that actually produce the outcomes whose frequency is to be explained under a pattern of macroperiodicity that is pervasive but not entirely exceptionless.

Even if you concede that the best explanation of frequencies on the wheel of fortune and so on is provided by a probabilistic model, you might nevertheless argue that such an explanation is probabilistic more in name than in nature, on the grounds that the indeterministic aspect of the model plays an explanatory role that is far from central—an aspect that, as the existence of the statistical deterministic model shows, can be removed from the explanation without doing great damage (though not without some decrease in explanatory power).

Such a worry allows that everything I have said in this chapter so far is correct, while denying that it provides much of a vindication for my claim that probabilistic explanation is invaluable even in a deterministic world, since almost all of what is invaluable in the explanations in question is not probabilistic. Before leaving the topic of microconstant explanation, let me address this complaint.

The objection is, I believe, based on a common but mistaken assumption about physical probability, that a probabilistic process has as its sole essence some kind of indeterminism. I accept that a part of what it is to be probabilistic is to be indeterministic; what I deny, drawing on arguments from Strevens (2000a), is that indeterminism is the most important or characteristic property of a probabilistic process. In what follows, I give my reasons for thinking that most of the properties that make a probabilistic process essentially probabilistic can exist in a deterministic system, and that microconstant explanation, in particular, though only peripherally indeterministic, is profoundly probabilistic.

Consider a process that produces the outcomes *red* and *black* in an entirely indeterministic way—not probabilistically, but in a way that is free from the influence of any natural law. Ask yourself: what would a sequence of outcomes generated by such a process look like? Presumably, the typical sequence of *red* and *black* would be quite disordered; it is difficult to say more. A probabilistically produced sequence of outcomes, by contrast, exhibits the kinds of order that define the probabilistic patterns. A Bernoulli process gives you a stable long-run frequency, for example, and a definite distribution of shorter-term frequencies as well (for example, about one-eighth of all sequences of three coin tosses contain no tails). The essence of a probabilistic process is far more, then, than mere absence of nomological constraint: it is whatever is required, in addition, to give you the order properties of its characteristic probabilistic pattern.

Furthermore, because probabilistic processes are almost always invoked to explain order in patterns of outcomes, it is this positive element of probability's essence that presumably does the greater part of the explaining.

When probability is called upon to explain the changing demographics of a Galápagos finch population, for example, probabilistic facts such as the higher chance of survival for large-beaked birds during a drought are used to explain the higher post-drought survival rate of larger birds—that is, they are used to explain a frequency. Indeterminism alone cannot even begin to explain why you get one frequency rather than another; indeed, it appears that it plays almost no part in such explanations at all.

Even when indeterminism looks to be important, as when explaining genetic drift, it has a far lesser role than you might think. What is important in a drift-based explanation such as the account of elephant seal homozygosity is a relation between population size and the average rate of genetic extinction, specifically, that the extinction rate is high in small populations. This is simply a higher-order kind of frequency, comparable to the one-eighth frequency with which sequences of three coin tosses all land heads. What does the explaining in the case of the elephant seals, then, is as elsewhere the part of the probabilistic process that produces frequencies. This positive aspect of the process is certainly not inherent in its indeterminism, which seems only ever to get in the way.

It may be, of course, that what you might call the positive part of a probabilistic process, the part that produces and explains the long-run frequencies, is in some cases inextricably entwined with indeterminism, so that, explanatorily empty though the latter may be in itself, it cannot be eliminated without also throwing away the part of physical probability that is explanatorily worthwhile. Perhaps; but this is a long way from putting indeterminism at the core of physical probability's explanatory power.

To return to microconstant explanation, then, it would be a great mistake to believe that, because the part of a microconstant model that introduces the indeterminism does not contribute a large part of the model's explanatory power, the resulting explanation is not a probabilistic explanation in the fullest sense.[10]

Here is a corrective proposal. A complex probabilistic explanation has two parts, a basing pattern and a microconstant mechanism. One of these parts is indeterministic, the other deterministic. Both are essential to complex probability, so both are probabilistic. In particular, the part that does most of the explaining when it comes to frequency—the microconstant mechanism—is probabilistic. An explanation that cites microconstancy, then, is to a great extent a probabilistic explanation.

But microconstancy is a deterministic property. How, you might ask, can it be probabilistic? Perhaps some of the perplexity motivating the question results from a lingering conflation of the probabilistic and the indeterministic. I argued above that probability is more than just indeterminism and, in particular, that the part of probability that explains frequencies goes beyond indeterminism. You should therefore expect to find a component of probability—an explanatory component—that is something other than, or above and beyond, indeterminism.

This establishes the possibility that a deterministic property such as microconstancy might be probabilistic; let me return to a familiar theme to show that it is indeed so. The power of probability to provide a satisfying explanation of a microconstancy-produced frequency is due above all to the potential for a certain kind of abstraction inherent in the descriptive framework of probability mathematics. By drawing on this potential in the right way, you can create a statistical description of a microconstant process that leaves out just the elements of physical reality that do not, according to the kairetic criterion, make a difference to the explanation of the frequency, or in other words, you can fashion a model that captures just the difference-makers for the frequency.

Both the statistical deterministic and the microconstant probabilistic models of frequency production take advantage of the mathematics of probability in this way. The former does so without departing from the deterministic regime. The latter discovers an additional source of explanatory goodness in its subsumption of the microconstant process's initial conditions under a wider pattern of entanglement, again making use of the mathematical apparatus of probability but in a somewhat different way.

What is captured at the level of abstraction provided by the tools of probability theory are all and only the explanatorily relevant elements of the microconstant process that produced the frequency to be explained. We call these elements, considered as a unified whole, the probability for the outcome in question (section 10.5). But although that name connotes indeterminism—and although indeterminism of a sort is indeed present in the optimal explanatory model—the core of the probabilistic explanation lies elsewhere, in the causal facts about difference-making, in microconstancy.

## 10.3   Explanation with Quasiprobability

### 10.31 Quasiprobability

*Quasiprobability* is my own term—and perhaps, my own notion. I have characterized quasiprobability using two examples—the probability of

John Jones's swift recovery from his strep infection, and the probability that a child growing up in a single-parent home turns to violent crime—and I have said that quasiprobabilities do not have exact values, that they are imperfectly formed complex probabilities, and that they are statistical amalgams.

Let me now provide a deeper characterization of quasiprobability (to be transformed into a definition in section 10.52). Whereas a complex probability explains probabilistic patterns of events, a quasiprobability explains *approximately* probabilistic patterns. Quasiprobability, then, is complex probability's not-so-elegant sibling.

An approximately probabilistic pattern is what you would think: a pattern that resembles imperfectly a true probabilistic pattern. An approximate Bernoulli pattern, for example, may have a long-run frequency that is not entirely stable, in the sense that it varies within a certain range without ever settling down, or short-term disorder that does not quite amount to a perfect lack of correlation between outcomes.[11] I will take imperfect Bernoulli patterns as my paradigm.

A quasiprobabilistic explanation explains such a pattern or an aspect of such a pattern, most often an approximate frequency. For example, if the frequency of a certain outcome varies between 85% and 95%, a quasiprobabilistic explanation may explain why the frequency hovers around 90%.

Typically, the probabilistic model used in such an explanation will not specify an exact value for the probability. The frequency of around 90% will be explained, not by a 90% probability, but by a probability of "about 90%." This is a quasiprobability, and the model is a quasiprobabilistic model. The inexactness might in some cases be considerable: the fact that some outcome is the exception rather than the rule might be explained by the fact that it has a "very low probability." There are more quasiprobabilistic models than you might think: sometimes a model that specifies an exact probability for an explanandum is best interpreted as quasiprobabilistic, the exactness being a kind of technical window dressing.


## 10.32  Imperfectly Microconstant Processes

There are many more ways to be imperfect than perfect. Thus, there are many kinds of imperfect probabilistic patterns, and correspondingly many kinds of mechanism that might produce such patterns. Whereas I ventured

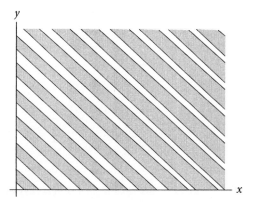

**Figure 10.5** Evolution function with imperfect microconstancy. Shaded areas correspond to pairs of values of $x$ and $y$ for which the process produces the explanandum event $e$.

the suggestion that all complex probabilities have their root in microconstancy (section 10.25), I will identify no universal basis for quasiprobability.

In the example examined in this section, the imperfection in the relevant probabilistic pattern will be due to a kind of imperfect microconstancy. Wherever there is microconstancy there is complex probability, but imperfect microconstancy does not always mean quasiprobability: for reasons to be explained in section 10.33, it depends on the context whether the imperfect patterns produced by imperfect microconstancy will be best explained by a probabilistic model.

Consider a process that has the evolution function for an event $e$ shown in figure 10.5. You will see that the process has two initial conditions, $x$ and $y$; shaded areas of the graph correspond to pairs of values of $x$ and $y$ for which $e$ is produced. Assume that there is a joint probability distribution over $x$ and $y$, and that it is macroperiodic. Assume also that the shape of this distribution is subject to change. In particular, sometimes higher values of $x$ are more probable, while at other times lower values are more probable.

What pattern of outcomes will the mechanism produce? The evolution function looks rather like a microconstant evolution function, but it does not have a constant strike ratio for $e$. Rather, the strike ratio increases as $x$ increases, from .5 for low values of $x$ to .75 for high values of $x$. Because the initial condition distribution is unstable, sometimes favoring lower, sometimes higher values of $x$, the frequency of $e$ outcomes produced by the mechanism is also unstable, varying from .5 to .75. Otherwise, though, the patterns will have the Bernoulli aspect.

To explain these approximately Bernoulli patterns, then, and in particular, to explain why *e* occurs with a frequency between .5 and .75, you can cite the following factors:

1. The persistent macroperiodicity of the initial-condition distribution, that is, the fact that the distribution, though its shape may change, is always macroperiodic

2. The physical properties of the mechanism that give the evolution function for *e* its approximately microconstant aspect

3. The physical properties of the mechanism determining that the strike ratio for *e* is always between .5 and .75

If this turns out to be the best explanation of the patterns, then *e* has a quasiprobability of "around .5 to .75."

Let me now give the model a physical interpretation. The interpretation is rather fanciful, but it will give you a feel for the explanatory use of quasiprobability in real science.

I will take as my outcome of interest the quick recovery of strep patients treated with penicillin. For the sake of the argument, I suppose that the evolution function for a quick recovery is as shown in figure 10.5. Whereas in Hempel's original example, the probability of recovery is near one, in my example it is between 50% and 75% (no doubt because of the evolution, since the 1940s, of resistance to antibiotics), and whereas in the original example the explanandum is a single quick recovery, in my example the explanandum is a large number of quick recoveries—between 50% and 75% of some large group of patients treated with penicillin.

The actual evolution function for recovery from a strep infection presumably has many more than two initial conditions, but never mind. What is important is that at least one variable does, and at least one does not, affect the strike ratio for recovery. In figure 10.5, it is *x* that affects the strike ratio: the higher the value of *x*, the more likely a swift recovery. Perhaps for any strain of bacteria, *x* quantifies some fact about the strain that affects its resistance to penicillin. In the example, then, there are many different strains with many different values for $x$, hence with many different degrees of penicillin resistance.

I will give initial conditions that, like $x$, affect the strike ratio of an imperfectly microconstant process a name: they are the *irregular parameters* of the process. Imperfect microconstancy implies the existence of at least one irregular parameter.

Quasiprobability is a scientifically useful notion when the probability distribution over one or more irregular parameters is liable to change. In the case of the strep infection, change is likely because different strains of strep, or different mixes of strains, will predominate in different areas. When explaining a trend across areas and thus across strains, there is no such thing as *the* probability of a swift recovery; there may, however, be such a thing as the quasiprobability of a swift recovery.

Let me now comment on some of my earlier remarks about the nature of quasiprobability, for the case of quasiprobabilities founded in imperfect microconstancy. *Quasiprobabilities have inexact values* because the probability distribution over the irregular parameters is not stable. *Quasiprobabilities are statistical amalgams* because they are amalgams of those exact probabilities yielded either by conditionalizing on particular values of the irregular parameters or by putting exact probability distributions over the irregular parameters. And they are *imperfectly formed complex probabilities* because they are built from an imperfect form of microconstancy.

In chapter nine, I also suggested that quasiprobabilities may deployed out of ignorance—as you can now see, that would be ignorance of the values of the relevant irregular parameters. I do not cite an exact probability for Jones's swift recovery because I do not know which strain of strep infects him. I will argue, however, that although quasiprobabilities may be especially useful in adverse epistemic circumstances, in some situations they provide the best explanation of a pattern regardless of the explainer's ignorance. My ignorance of Jones's strep strain obliges me to turn to the quasiprobability of recovery, but to explain a global pattern of between 50% and 75% quick recoveries, I must use quasiprobability even if I know the details of which strains were rife where and when. (This is true for explanation only; for prediction I will of course use all the information available.)

By the same token, if I use a quasiprobabilistic explanation out of ignorance, I explain successfully just in case my explanation is objectively the best explanation. (Contrast this with Hempel's is account of explanation, on which an explanation can never fail just because the explainer is ignorant of some probabilistically relevant factor.) To some extent, then, I must be lucky: I must give the optimal explanation even though I do not know enough to be sure that it is optimal.

### 10.33  Quasiprobabilistic Explanation

In what circumstances, then, is a quasiprobabilistic model the best explanation of an approximate frequency? Suppose that among 5,000 strep patients treated with penicillin, 66% enjoyed a speedy recovery. Your task is to explain the approximate recovery rate, or more exactly, why the recovery rate was between 50% and 75%.

Begin with a low level deterministic model, that is, an aggregative causal model that correctly predicts the outcome of interest—either a swift recovery or not—for each patient among the 5,000. The information that such a model must specify, in order to determine whether a particular patient recovers quickly or not, can be divided into two parts: the relevant initial conditions, such as the identity of the strain causing the infection, the state of the patient's immune system, and so on, and the mechanism by which these initial conditions either lead to a swift recovery or not, in this case an extremely complex process involving specifics of the biology of both streptococcus bacteria and humans. The deterministic model puts together the information about each of the 5,000 cases to deduce an exact rate of speedy recovery and, a fortiori, the explanandum, that the exact rate falls between 50% and 75%.

As in the microconstant case, the low-level model provides far more information than is needed to determine the fact that the explanandum occurred. The kairetic account enjoins you to remove this detail, abstracting the model as far as is possible without invalidating the causal entailment of its target, the fact of the frequency's falling within the given range. You might think of the different strains of streptococcus as wheels of fortune with different strike ratios for *red*. What the optimal explanatory model must specify is just enough information to determine the range of strike ratios for the wheels; as I showed in section 10.24, this is far less information than is needed to determine the outcomes of particular spins.

When you are done with abstraction, you will be left, I suggest, with a causal model stating the following facts about the recovery process:

1. The actual initial conditions pertinent to the effect of the penicillin in the 5,000 cases in question were macroperiodically distributed. In the toy case whose evolution function is shown in figure 10.5, what is cited is a macroperiodic distribution of the 5,000 actual pairs of values of $x$ and $y$.[12]

2. The biological properties of patient/bacterium/penicillin interaction are such and such, so that the evolution function for swift recovery is imperfectly microconstant with a strike ratio between .5 and .75.

This is a deterministic causal model, the counterpart of the statistical deterministic model described in section 10.24; I give it the same name.

(I remark in passing that the statistical deterministic model, though abstract in many respects, must cite the biological properties responsible for imperfect microconstancy. Even today, we lack much of the knowledge required to describe these properties explicitly; we may however cite them implicitly, and without ourselves grasping their precise nature, by using covering laws or other lawlike generalizations in the explanation, as described in section 4.33.)

The quasiprobabilistic model for the approximate frequency is obtained by adding a basing generalization to the statistical deterministic model, namely, a probability distribution over the initial conditions that ascribes a high probability to the macroperiodicity of the actual initial conditions cited by the deterministic model. The basing generalization is as accurate as the probability is high; in the case at hand, I suppose, the probability is very high, and so the relevance of the basing generalization is not undermined by an accuracy deficit. The addition of the basing generalization, then, not only makes the explanation probabilistic, it makes it better.

The three explanatory models for the approximate frequency may, in short, be ranked as follows. The low-level deterministic model should not be considered a serious explanatory candidate, because of its many irrelevancies. The statistical deterministic and quasiprobabilistic models, by contrast, cite only causally relevant properties of the process producing the explanandum; indeed, they cite precisely the same causally relevant properties. The quasiprobabilistic model is nevertheless to be preferred, because it supplements this causal information with additional information that is also explanatorily relevant. A quasiprobabilistic explanation of the approximate recovery rate is, then, best of all.

A fourth explanatory model for the recovery rate should also be mentioned. Suppose that in the region where the 5,000 cases of strep are treated there is a single, determinate probability distribution over the irregular parameters of the recovery process. Then a model that cites this probability distribution along with the facts about macroperiodicity and microconstancy can determine an exact probability of recovery and so, with high probability, something close to the exact recovery rate. Call this the *exact probabilistic model*.

Is the exact probabilistic model a better explanation than the quasiprobabilistic model for the recovery rate's falling between 50% and 75%? No. The exact model contains all the facts cited by the quasiprobabilistic model and two more as well:

1. The probability distribution over the irregular parameters

2. The facts determining the exact strike ratio for each set of values of the irregular parameters (in the toy example, the exact strike ratio for each value of $x$)

Apply the optimizing procedure to the exact probabilistic model, and you will find that both facts can be removed without invalidating the entailment of the explanandum; the facts are therefore explanatorily irrelevant, and the model that cites them explanatorily flawed.[13]

The redundancy of the exact probabilistic facts is due, of course, to the inexactness of the explanandum. A more tightly specified explanandum may merit explanation by an exact probabilistic model. Suppose, for example, that you want to explain why the recovery rate was between 65% and 70%. (The exact rate, you will recall, was 66%.) The quasiprobabilistic model can provide only a low-accuracy explanation of this state of affairs (section 10.41). The exact probabilistic model, though it must cite some additional causal detail to do so, provides an explanation of very high accuracy. Invoking the heuristic advocated in section 10.24—that the best explanatory model maximizes combined accuracy and generality—I conclude that the exact probabilistic explanation of the narrow band frequency should be preferred.

As the prevailing explanatory demands vary, then, even where they concern a single statistic such as the rate of swift recovery, the most explanatory model can go from being a quasiprobabilistic to an exact probabilistic model, or even—if, for example, the exact value of a frequency is to be explained—to a low-level deterministic model.

### 10.34 The Range of Quasiprobabilistic Explanation

#### Prevalence of Imperfect Microconstancy

Wherever imperfect microconstancy produces imperfect probabilistic patterns, quasiprobabilistic explanation is possible. How common is imperfect microconstancy? Since anything that affects the strike ratio of a microconstant evolution function has the makings of an irregular parameter, and there are always factors that affect strike ratios, there is imperfect microconstancy wherever there is microconstancy.

For example, if the evolution function determining finch survival over the course of a year is microconstant, but the strike ratio depends on an island's average rainfall in that year, then the explanation of the approximate finch survival rate over the Galápagos archipelago as a whole will invoke imperfect microconstancy.

Suppose that the following kind of imperfect microconstancy is found: the strike ratio for the relevant outcome varies between .5 and .75 for almost all values of the irregular parameters, but for one set of values—say, extremely high values—the strike ratio tends to zero. Is there any scope for quasiprobabilistic explanation? Yes, easily. The relevant explanation will cite not only the macroperiodicity of the initial condition distribution but also the fact that the distribution assigns a low probability to the event of the irregular parameters having extremely high values.

#### Channeling Processes

However pervasive microconstancy may be, it will be illuminating to sketch one other kind of process that produces imperfect probabilistic patterns and that can provide a basis for quasiprobabilistic explanation—a process especially important to understanding the explanation of single outcomes.

Consider a probabilistic device that has the following properties:

1. Channeling: Almost all initial conditions cause the device to produce an outcome of type $e$.

2. Nonclumping: The initial condition distribution assigns a very low probability to the event of the initial conditions for a long series of trials being clustered in any given small set.

A process of this sort—a channeling process—will tend to produce a high frequency of $e$ outcomes. (The only way for it not to do so is for the actual initial conditions producing the frequency to be concentrated on the set causing $\neg e$. By the channeling property, this is a small set, and so by the nonclumping property, the initial conditions will almost certainly not be concentrated on the set.) Note that channeling does not entail microconstancy or imperfect microconstancy, and that nonclumping does not entail macroperiodicity.

The fact that a channeling process almost always produces $e$ outcomes can be explained, I propose, by a model that cites a "very high" probability for an $e$ outcome and specifies as the basis for the probability the fact of nonclumping and the physical facts that underlie channeling. The indeterminately high probability cited by the model is a quasiprobability.

You could also explain the near-ubiquity of $e$ outcomes by using a low-level deterministic model that specifies the initial conditions for each outcome and shows how the mechanism converts those initial conditions into $e$ outcomes; by using an exact probabilistic model that specifies a precise and presumably high probability for an $e$ outcome (if there is a precise initial-condition distribution to be had); or by using a statistical deterministic model. But for the same reasons as in the case of imperfect microconstancy, a quasiprobabilistic model that cites channeling and nonclumping provides a better explanation than these alternatives. (The next best explanation is the statistical deterministic model, followed by the exact probabilistic model.)

Consider in particular a channeling model's statistical deterministic rival, a model citing the nonclumping of the actual initial conditions (not of the probability distribution over the actual initial conditions) and the channeling property of the evolution function. The quasiprobabilistic model consists of the statistical deterministic model supplemented with further explanatorily relevant information: it subsumes the nonclumping of the actual initial conditions under a broader pattern of entanglement. The ensuing explanatory advantage of the quasiprobabilistic over the statistical deterministic model is easy to appreciate. Whereas the deterministic model says only that the initial conditions just happened to belong (mostly) to a large set that all cause the explanandum, the quasiprobabilistic model illuminates the belonging by pointing to a robust connection between, on the one hand, being a set of initial conditions for the kind of device in question, and on the other hand, being unclumped. By appreciating this robustness you better understand the nonclumping.

Models based on channeling have a more restricted range of applicability than models based on imperfect microconstancy, insofar as they are limited to explaining frequencies near one, but their range is less restricted insofar as channeling and nonclumping are rather weaker conditions on the evolution function and the initial-condition distribution than imperfect microconstancy and macroperiodicity. One interesting possibility is that a channeling model might cite a *quasiprobabilistic* initial-condition distribution, that is, a distribution that assigns quasiprobabilities rather than simple or complex probabilities to events. Such a distribution can be nonclumping, by imposing an upper limit on the probability of any clumping event, and so can help to explain the pattern of events produced by a channeling process.[14] Quasiprobabilities can in this way beget more quasiprobabilities.

### Comparative Explanations with Quasiprobability

The quasiprobabilistic explananda I have discussed so far are semiquantitative, in that they consist in the relative frequency's falling within a broad range. Perhaps more often, quasiprobabilistic explananda are not explicitly quantitative at all, as when explaining, say, the fact that "many" strep victims treated with penicillin recover quickly.

Particularly interesting are qualitative comparisons: patients treated with penicillin recover far more quickly, on average, than the rest; more traffic accidents occur during rain showers than during dry spells; many more large than small finches survive a drought in the Galápagos islands; more children of single-parent families than of two-parent families turn to violent crime, and so on. In each case, the explanation comes from an appreciation of a certain role played by the specified causal agent—penicillin, drought, having a single parent, and so on. The nature of this role depends on the kind of quasiprobability involved:

1. When the process is imperfectly microconstant, the role of the causal agent is to provide an across-the-board increase in the strike ratio for

the event in question, that is, to increase the strike ratio for all values of the irregular parameters.

2. When the process is channeling, the role of the causal agent is to alter a nonchanneling evolution function so it becomes channeling. That is, the agent alters the effect of sufficiently many of the process's initial conditions so that a vast majority produce the event in question, where before they did not.

Because the comparative explananda in question are qualitative, details that are only quantitatively relevant, such as the details determining the exact value of a strike ratio, are omitted from the explanation. The value of this omission is not merely freedom from irrelevant detail. Since there is, in many of these cases, no exact probability to attach to the events of interest, probabilistic explanation would be impossible if quantitative details sufficient to entail a definite probability were required.

## 10.4   Elitism versus Egalitarianism the Kairetic Way

The formal framework for kairetic probabilistic explanation underwrites, as I showed in section 9.73, a moderate elitism in both the size and change debates: as to the size debate, all probabilities explain, but larger probabilities explain better; as to the change debate, all probability-increasers explain, but the larger the increase the better the explanation. In this and the next chapter, I will examine various complications, both apparent and real, in understanding complex probabilistic explanation as moderately elitist.

A prolegomenon: The discussion of elitism/egalitarianism will of necessity invoke a measure of the quality of an explanation. Such a measure need not impose a total ordering, but it must at least allow the comparison of different possible explanations of the same type of explanandum in different circumstances. In section 4.35, I suggested setting the quality of an explanatory model equal, for comparative purposes, to its combined accuracy, generality, and cohesion. I later introduced basing generalizations to the explanatory mix; since they are also evaluated according to their accuracy, generality, and cohesion (though these are somewhat different properties when it is subsumption under a pattern of entanglement that is to be assessed), the measure of quality can fruitfully be generalized, or so I proposed at the end of section 10.24.

## *10.41  The Size Debate*

According to moderate size elitism, models that entail their targets with high probability explain them better, ceteris paribus, than models that entail them with low probability. To what extent is this claim borne out by the account of the explanatory virtue of microconstant models presented earlier in this chapter?

The question is a perplexing one, because microconstant explanations paradigmatically confer a high probability on their targets: they cite macroperiodicity and microconstancy to explain a match between frequency and strike ratio, citing the high probability of the same. The complementary low-probability event—a mismatch between frequency and strike ratio—cannot be explained by citing macroperiodicity and microconstancy in any capacity. As far as I can see, it must be given a low-level deterministic explanation.

A typical deterministic model for a low-probability frequency does, it is true, score less well for combined generality and accuracy than a typical microconstant model for a high-probability frequency, because of the deterministic model's considerably lesser generality. It is thus an inferior explanation of its target. But moderate elitism says that models that cite low probabilities explain less well than models that cite high probabilities. The deterministic model does not cite any probability, thus it lies outside the jurisdiction of the moderate elitist principle.

It can at least be said that moderate elitism is, with respect to complex probabilistic explanation, superior to moderate egalitarianism. Of two microconstant models that assign high probabilities to their explananda, the one that assigns the higher probability provides a better combination of generality and accuracy, all other things being equal, and so explains its target better—ultimately because of the closer fit between the relevant initial conditions and the subsuming basing pattern, and perhaps also because of the greater degree of entanglement between the relevant properties of the initial conditions.

But why prefer moderate elitism to extreme elitism? The choice between the two hinges on the question of whether a well-formed complex probabilistic model that cites a low probability is genuinely explanatory. But there are no such models, and thus there are no test cases to decide the question. Or are there? Let me investigate two kinds of complex probabilistic explanation that may cite a low (or at least, not high) complex probability. What follows should be regarded as exploratory; it is certainly not central to the kairetic account of complex probabilistic explanation.

First, there is a way to use a microconstant model to explain a deviant frequency—a frequency that differs from the strike ratio—provided that it is not too deviant. Suppose that a microconstant model for the wheel of fortune entails with high probability that the frequency of *red* outcomes on a series of 500 spins will be between 45% and 55%. One particular 500 spin series results in an actual frequency of 40%. This is outside the limits allowed by the microconstant model: in effect, the only way to get a frequency that deviates from the strike ratio to this degree is to have a set of initial conditions that is clearly outside the bounds of any reasonable characterization of macroperiodicity.

As I proposed in section 5.2, however, if accuracy/generality tradeoffs are allowed, it is possible to have an explanatory model whose target is not the explanandum, provided that the target and the explanandum are close. For example, a model of Mars' orbit that gets the orbit approximately right has high, though not maximal, accuracy. If any increase in accuracy would come at a disproportionate cost in generality, the slightly inaccurate model may nevertheless be the best explanation of the phenomenon. In the astronomical case, you might doubt that the accuracy/generality tradeoff is worthwhile, but in the probabilistic case, a microconstant model that entails something near but not identical to the observed 40% frequency, though inaccurate, may be so much more general than the corresponding deterministic model that it is a superior explanation of the frequency.

Unfortunately, this case is not technically a vindication of moderate elitism. What the moderate elitist wants is an explanatory model that cites a low complex probability. But although the model cited to explain the 40% frequency is probabilistic, and the explanandum has a low complex probability, the model does not, strictly speaking, cite this low probability in the course of the explanation. Rather, it cites the high probability of a frequency between 45% and 55%, and then (as it were) points out that a 40% frequency is not too far off the mark.

The other situation in which a microconstant model may explain a low-probability frequency is a case in which the frequency matches the strike ratio but the explanandum puts very narrow bounds on the fact about the frequency that is to be explained. Suppose, for example, that you want to explain why the frequency of *red* in 500 spins on the wheel of fortune was between 49% and 51%. (The probability of such an event is about .38.)

A density is defined as macroperiodic if it is *approximately* constant over any two small neighboring regions. Given a microconstant evolution function, initial conditions that are macroperiodically distributed give rise to a frequency for an outcome *approximately* equal to the strike ratio of the outcome. The two *approximately*'s vary in proportion to one another: the tighter the constraint on the macroperiodicity of the actual initial conditions, the more exact the frequency you derive.

Thus, it is possible to construct a microconstant model for the 49%–51% frequency containing the following two steps:

1. From a macroperiodic initial spin distribution, inductively derive the macroperiodicity of the actual initial conditions according to a stringent standard of macroperiodicity.
2. From the stringent macroperiodicity of the actual initial conditions and microconstancy, deductively derive a frequency for *red* between 49% and 51%.

The initial spin-speed distribution that serves as the basing generalization is not, I assume, itself macroperiodic in the stringent sense. Thus, the stringent macroperiodicity of the actual initial conditions is derived from the distribution only with a relatively low probability—about 38% or so (if the degree of stringency is tuned just so). You have a microconstant model of the frequency that cites the frequency's rather low probability. If the microconstant model has greater combined generality and accuracy than its deterministic rivals (the statistical deterministic model is especially dangerous), then the low-probability explanation is the best explanation of the frequency.

I conclude, very provisionally, that low complex probabilities may occasionally explain. Thus, although complex probabilistic explanation is almost always high-probability explanation, it is moderate, not extreme, elitism that correctly characterizes the relation between probability magnitude and explanatory power.

## 10.42  The Change Debate

The change debate concerns the relation between a factor's effect on the probability of the explanandum and the factor's explanatory relevance. In the case of complex probabilistic explanation, the typical probabilistically relevant factor alters the strike ratio of the relevant evolution function. Though the probability cited in complex probabilistic explanation is, as a rule, high, the factors that affect the probability may do so to any degree. In the change debate about complex probabilistic explanation, then, in contrast to the size debate, there is no shortage of material to use in assessing the different positions.

I will confine myself, however, to certain specific objections to moderate elitism. Some of these arise in the context of the explanation of single outcomes; they will be discussed in the next chapter. In this section, I will discuss an argument that can be leveled when the explanandum is a frequency, in favor of the extreme egalitarian doctrine that probability-decreasers explain. The major premise of the argument is the kairetic account's commitment to transitivity.

Why think that, in the case of microconstant explanation, the kairetic account attributes explanatory power to probability-decreasers? The factors that make up the basis of a frequency's probability, in particular the strike ratio for the outcome whose frequency is to be explained, are uncontroversially difference-makers for the explanandum. The kairetic difference-making relation is transitive (sections 4.2 and 6.5). Thus, anything that makes a difference to the strike ratio is also a difference-maker. It follows that anything that makes a difference to the probability is a difference-maker, whether the probability is increased or decreased.

The reasoning is not quite correct, however. A difference-maker in a kairetic explanation is never a thing or a quantity, like a probability or a causal factor, but a state of affairs, a fact about a thing or quantity. As I showed in the discussion of misconnection (section 6.51), to become a difference-maker in virtue of transitivity, a factor must make a difference to the fact that this state of affairs obtains, that is, it must play a role in the state of affairs' having held rather than not held.

Let me illustrate with a quantitative but nonprobabilistic example. Take the ropes that bound Rasputin's hands and feet. They were difference-makers for his death. But it does not follow from the transitivity of difference-making that anything that makes a difference to the ropes thereby makes a difference to the death. The anointing of the ropes with holy oil is not a difference-maker, for example, unless it makes a difference to the fact about the ropes in virtue of which they were difference-makers for death. Suppose that this difference-making fact is the ropes' having such and such a minimum tensile strength, that is, having a strength greater than some strength $x$. For the oil to have made a difference, it must have contributed to the fact that this state of affairs held.

If the oil had no effect on strength, it is clearly not a difference-maker. But to count as a difference-maker for the strength's being greater than $x$, it is not enough for the oil to have affected the strength; the effect must be positive, that is, it must result in an increase of strength. Why? If the oil decreased the ropes' strength, it could be removed from a model without invalidating the entailment of the fact that the ropes' strength was greater than $x$.

Now apply this lesson to microconstant explanation. Suppose that what is to be explained is the fact that the frequency of $e$ outcomes produced by a microconstant process was approximately $r$. Suppose also that the frequency and the strike ratio for $e$ are not quite equal; they differ by a small amount $\epsilon$. Finally, assume that before the frequency was produced, the strike ratio was equal to the (future) frequency; some factor $c$, however, reduced the strike ratio by $\epsilon$ at the last moment. The factor $c$, then, decreased the probability of the explanandum. Is it a difference-maker for the frequency?

No. It is not the strike ratio per se that makes a difference to the frequency's being approximately $r$, it is a fact about the strike ratio, namely, its being within $\delta$ of $r$ (for some $\delta$ that must be greater than $\epsilon$, if microconstant explanation is to be possible in this case at all). A factor that makes a difference to the strike ratio therefore makes a difference to the frequency's being $r$ by way of transitivity only if it makes a difference to the state of affairs of the strike ratio's being within $\delta$ of $r$. The factor $c$ did not do so: the strike ratio is within $\delta$ of $r$ before and after the removal of $c$ from any relevant model. More generally, a factor that has the effect of taking the strike ratio further from the frequency to be explained does not make a difference to the microconstant production of a frequency. On the kairetic account of complex probabilistic explanation, then, probability-decreasers are explanatorily irrelevant after all. Moderate elitism stands.

## 10.5    Regularity Explanation and Probabilistic Metaphysics

### *10.51  Explaining Generalities with Probabilities*

The kairetic account of frequency explanation is easily extended to broader and more theoretical explananda, of which I will consider three varieties:

1. *Statistical regularities*, such as the fact that gases almost always expand to fill a vacuum or the fact that male finches tend to preponderate after any Galápagos drought

2. *Probabilistic laws*, that is, generalizations imposing probability distributions over certain classes of phenomena, such as the Maxwell-Boltzmann distribution over the positions and velocities of gases in equilibrium, the generalizations found in the theory of genetic drift that relate the expected rate of drift to the size of the population (unless these are understood as purely mathematical theorems), or the claim that single parenthood increases the probability of children's engaging in violent crime

3. *Single-case probabilities*, the probabilities assigned to singular outcomes of particular, or token, probabilistic processes, such as the one-half probability that the next toss of this very coin will land heads

As the fundamental theorems of explanation suggest, the explanation form for each of these three kinds of explananda is immanent in the explanation form for token frequencies.

Let me illustrate this claim using the case of the wheel of fortune. As before, take as the state of affairs of interest the event that 500 trials on a wheel of fortune produce an approximately one-half frequency for *red*. Since I will be talking about particular probability values, it will be useful to precisify. Assume that what is meant by "approximately one-half" is a frequency between 45% and 55%. Then the Bernoulli distribution assigns the event of 500 trials showing an "approximately one-half frequency" a probability of .975.

In section 10.2, my paradigmatic explanandum was a token frequency, that is, a frequency found in a particular set of trials on a particular wheel of fortune. There is a corresponding statistical regularity, probabilistic law, and single-case probability. The single-case probability is the .975 probability that a particular series of trials produces the frequency. The probabilistic law (in the liberal sense of "law") is captured by the claim that the probability of obtaining the one-half frequency from any 500 trials on any wheel of fortune is .975.[15] The statistical regularity is captured by the claim that about 97.5% of all 500-trial experiments on wheels of fortune show a one-half frequency for *red*. These latter two generalizations should be understood as having a certain modal extent: they range over possible as well as actual sets of 500 trials.

How to explain this array of explananda? My proposal is straightforward. You have already seen that the explanation of a token one-half frequency obtained on a particular wheel of fortune $x$ is given by a microconstant model citing the following facts:

1. The device $x$ is a wheel of fortune.

2. The initial-condition distribution over spin speeds for wheels of fortune ascribes a high probability to the event that any large set of spin speeds is macroperiodically distributed.

3. The evolution function for *red* on wheels of fortune is, in virtue of certain of their physical properties and certain aspects of the fundamental physical laws, microconstant with strike ratio one-half.

I suggest that the explanation of the single-case probability is identical to the explanation of the token frequency. The model above explains, then, not only why the frequency in question was one-half, but why the single case probability of the frequency was very high (indeed, why it was .975; more on this exact value below).

An explanation for both the statistical regularity and the statistical law is contained in the explanation of the token frequency: remove element (1) from the microconstant model above, and you have a type-level model that cites only the macroperiodicity of the initial-condition distribution and the microconstancy of the mechanism for wheels of fortune generally. It is this model that explains the law and the regularity. The situation exactly parallels the deterministic case: remove the particulars from a (single-mechanism) explanation of an instance and you have an explanation for the law (section 7.35); as a consequence of this parallel, the second fundamental theorem of explanation holds true for probabilistic explanation.

There is more to be said about the correspondence between deterministic and probabilistic explanation. It is worth examining, for example, the relation between the explanation of single-case probabilities and the explanation of deterministic dispositions; the sense in which statistical laws function in the same way as deterministic covering laws; and the fact that both deterministic and statistical laws are explained by exhibiting their constitutive facts. I leave the reader to investigate these connections further.

You might wonder about the explanation of another triple of single-case probability, statistical law, and statistical regularity associated with the wheel of fortune:

1. The single-case Bernoulli probability of one-half that a particular spin on the wheel of fortune yields *red*

2. The statistical law to the effect that there is a one-half Bernoulli probability that any wheel of fortune spin yields *red*

3. The statistical regularity that about one-half of all spins on wheels of fortune yield *red*

(Calling the one-half probability a Bernoulli probability implies the probabilistic independence of the outcomes.)

These facts are to be explained in exactly the same way as the corresponding explananda above; the law, for example, is explained by the macroperiodicity of the wheel of fortune initial-condition distribution and the microconstancy of the mechanism. There is no real distinction, then, between explaining on the one hand why the probability of *red* on a single spin is a Bernoulli probability of one-half and on the other hand why the probability of an approximately one-half frequency over 500 spins is .975. This is as it should be, since the one follows mathematically from the other.

## 10.52 Metaphysics of Complex Probability and Quasiprobability

A statistical law, such as the Maxwell-Boltzmann distribution for gas molecules, can be understood metaphysically in the same way as a deterministic law: it is constituted by the basing patterns and mechanisms by which it is explained. As in the deterministic case, then, there is a threefold harmony of the higher-level law governing, the causal process producing, and the explanation making sense of any pattern of events in the world.

The sole function of a statistical law is to assign a probability distribution over a certain range of outcomes. It is, then, natural (though of course not compulsory) to identify the probability distribution with the law: what it is for the law to hold and what it is for the probability distribution assigned by the law to exist are one and the same thing. The result is a ready-made metaphysics for complex probabilities and quasiprobabilities: a quasi- or complex probability distribution is constituted by the basing patterns and mechanisms that constitute the corresponding law. The Bernoulli distribution over spins on a wheel of fortune, for example, is made up of (a) a pattern of entanglement between the initial conditions' being wheel-of-fortune spin speeds and their being macroperiodically distributed, (b) a pattern of entanglement between the apparatuses' being wheels of fortune and their having certain physical properties, such as certain paint schemes (see note 4; you may think of these entanglements as existing in virtue of the very definition of a wheel of fortune), and (c) those aspects of the fundamental laws in virtue of which the physical properties cited in (b) imply that the relevant evolution function is microconstant with strike ratio one-half.

Is there a corresponding metaphysics for single-case probabilities? You might identify a single-case probability for *red* on some particular spin or series of spins with, first, the same macroperiodicity-involving pattern that goes into the law and, second, the instantiation of the causally relevant facts in the trials in question, for example, the fact that this particular wheel has a certain paint scheme at this particular time. On such a view, one part of the single-case probability—the causal or mechanical part—is intrinsic to the apparatus, but the other part, the pattern of macroperiodicity entanglement, is not.[16]

As in the case of deterministic laws, my doctrine about constitution falls short of providing a criterion for demarcation. More particularly, my metaphysical thesis about quasi- and complex probabilities—that they are constituted by basing pattern/mechanism bundles—does not settle the question of which such bundles constitute probabilities.

I am sure that I will not surprise you by proposing the following explanation-driven demarcation thesis: a complex probability distribution exists over a set of possible outcomes produced by a given type of system just in case (a) the outcomes are produced deterministically, (b) the outcomes tend to be probabilistically patterned, and (c) the tendency to probabilistic patterning is best explained by a single, formally probabilistic causal model. A causal model is "formally probabilistic" if it has the form characterized in section 9.7.

Two remarks. First, the demarcation criterion makes room in principle for complex probabilities that are not based in microconstancy.[17] Second, there are at least some deterministically produced probabilistic patterns that are best explained nonprobabilistically, such as a pattern of ones and zeroes carefully constructed by hand to pass the appropriate statistical tests. The explanatory part of the demarcation criterion, then, has some bite: a probabilistic pattern does not always signify a complex probability distribution.

Quasiprobability can be demarcated in a similar way. A quasiprobabilistic distribution (using the term *distribution* loosely) exists over a set of possible outcomes produced by a given type of system just in case (a) the outcomes are produced deterministically, (b) the outcomes tend to be imperfectly probabilistically patterned, and (c) the tendency to probabilistic patterning is best explained by a single formally quasiprobabilistic model (that is, a formally probabilistic model that assigns inexact probabilities). This criterion allows for any number of different physical bases for quasiprobability. I tacitly relied on the criterion in my earlier claim that there are quasiprobabilities only where quasiprobabilistic explanation succeeds—that is, only where a quasiprobabilistic model supplies a better mix of accuracy and generality than its rival deterministic and exact probabilistic models.

Let me conclude by remarking on a surprising consequence of my proposed metaphysics of complex probability: the probabilities attached to a complex probabilistic device's initial conditions are not, unless they are frequency based, constituents of the complex probability itself. The probability distribution over wheel-of-fortune spin speed, for example, if simple or complex, is in no sense a constituent of, or part of the supervenience basis of, the one-half probability for *red*. It is rather the pattern of entanglement inductively entailed by the probability distribution that is a constituent of the probability. This pattern is a kind of modal frequency: it is a pattern of the presence and absence of macroperiodicity in actual and certain possible sets of initial conditions.

I assured you in section 10.26 that you could accept a frequentist basis for initial-condition distributions without acceding to a frequentist metaphysics of probability. You may feel misled: I now tell you that patterns of initial conditions (albeit modal patterns) are a constituent of every complex probability, even those whose initial conditions fall under nonfrequentist probability distributions. Further, it is in virtue of these patterns—these frequencies—alone that complex probability has its indeterministic aspect, since its only other constituents are a deterministic mechanism and nonstatistical basing patterns and other initial conditions. Where does high-level probability come from? In the end, you might think, I have no answer but—*frequencies*.

This line of reasoning makes the mistake, deplored in section 10.27, of supposing that there is nothing more to being probabilistic than being indeterministic, and so that the source of complex probability's indeterminism must be its quintessence. The heart and soul of complex probability is not, however, macroperiodic frequencies but microconstant mechanisms. The basing patterns that make complex probability indeterministic are one of its necessary constituents, but they play only an auxiliary role in explaining its signature behavior, the production of probabilistic patterns.

Why only auxiliary? The frequencies that serve as the basing patterns of a complex probabilistic model constitute a kind of pattern, but they need not constitute a probabilistic pattern. A microconstant mechanism is able to take a very wide range of nonprobabilistic patterns and transform them into probabilistic patterns, by creating the right sort of short-term disorder and long-term order, as explained above and in Strevens (2003b, 2005). The mechanism therefore creates something probabilistic, a probabilistic pattern, from something nonprobabilistic. Frequencies provide the base, nonprobabilistic material; microconstancy transmutes this material into something that has the mark of probability.

So the line of the argument returns to explanation: it is precisely because microconstancy provides such a satisfying explanation of the probabilistic patterns that it ought to be regarded as, in great measure, the creator of the patterns; in this creative act, it earns, I submit, the right to be treated as the core of a variety of genuine—though complex—physical probability.

# — 11 —

## Kairetic Explanation of Single Outcomes

Microconstancy, imperfect microconstancy, and channeling are natural explainers of medium- and long-run frequencies. Can they explain single outcomes? I will suggest an approach to single-outcome explanation using complex probability and quasiprobability that treats a single outcome as a (maximally!) short-run frequency that is explained by what I have called the *channeling* property of the underlying mechanism. The official business of this chapter completed, I investigate the explanatory value of robustness, then use single-outcome explanation to investigate the relationship between probability-raising and difference-making in the kairetic account. The story is interestingly, exasperatingly complicated.

### 11.1  Single-Outcome Explanation

Consider the explanation of a single outcome produced by a microconstant process, a wheel of fortune with ninety red and ten black sections. The wheel is spun; the outcome is *red*. How ought this to be explained?

Formally, the single *red* outcome can be treated as a kind of degenerate frequency, that is, as a frequency of 100% *red* outcomes from a "series" of trials consisting of just one spin. The explanatory apparatus of complex probability, and in particular the microconstant model, is applied as before. That the outcome is *red*, then, is explained like any other frequency produced by a microconstant device, that is, by citing the facts underlying the wheel's 90% strike ratio for *red*, principally the rotational symmetry of the mechanism and certain facts about the paint scheme, and the macroperiodicity of the initial spin-speed distribution.

There is an upper limit on the accuracy of such an explanatory model. Accuracy is, you will recall, proportional to the probability ascribed to the frequency. When the "frequency" is the occurrence of a single outcome, accuracy is therefore proportional to the probability ascribed to the outcome itself. The accuracy of an explanation of a single *red* outcome on the

90/10 wheel of fortune is .9; the same model explains a single *black* outcome with an accuracy of an only .1. The higher the strike ratio for an outcome, then, the better its explanation by the corresponding microconstant model. (Contrast Jeffrey's view, discussed in section 9.54.)

So far, so good. A closer inspection of the workings of causal entailment in a microconstant model for a single outcome shows, however, that the analogy between the microconstant explanation of long-run frequencies and the microconstant explanation of single outcomes at a certain point breaks down. Although single-outcome explanation bears a strong structural resemblance to frequency explanation, and can safely be treated as such for the purposes of constructing explanatory microconstant models, when a microconstant mechanism explains a single outcome it functions more like a channeling mechanism (section 10.34) than a microconstant explainer of long-run frequencies (section 10.23).

Let me explain. When the explanandum is a long-run frequency, macroperiodicity and microconstancy play a role in the explanation captured by the following two facts:

1. The basing generalization that is the macroperiodic initial-condition distribution implies (with high probability) that the series of trials producing the frequency has a distribution of actual initial conditions that is macroperiodic.

2. A microconstant mechanism for an event *e* will, given a macroperiodic distribution of actual initial conditions, produce type *e* outcomes with a frequency roughly equal to the strike ratio for *e*.

The same story cannot be told if the explanandum is a single outcome (or a short-run frequency), because the initial conditions in such a case are not numerous enough to define an actual initial-condition distribution, or if they are, such a distribution could not be macroperiodic—it would consist of a few isolated humps.

An alternative causal story fits single-outcome explanation far better (assuming a high strike ratio for the explanandum):

1. In a microconstant mechanism with a high strike ratio for the explanandum *e*, almost all possible initial conditions bring about *e* (channeling).

2. For any set containing almost all possible initial conditions, a macro-periodic initial-condition distribution implies that, with high probability, the initial condition of any single trial will lie in that set (non-clumping).

Thus, any particular initial condition will, with high probability, lie in the *e*-producing set. This is more or less the causal schema for a channeling process. The microconstant explanation of a single outcome should be understood, then, as a kind of channeling explanation of a degenerate frequency.


When does a microconstant model supply the best explanation of a single occurrence of *red* on the 90/10 wheel of fortune, and when is the same outcome better explained deterministically?

When considering the same question with long-run frequencies as explananda, I made a distinction between a low-level deterministic model, that is, a deterministic model that causally entails the outcome of each trial in the series whose frequency is to be explained, and a statistical deterministic model, which causally entails the frequency but not individual outcomes. In the single-outcome case, no such distinction can be made; there is therefore only one deterministic model to be considered.

The optimal deterministic model will specify whatever physical features of the wheel of fortune are necessary to circumscribe the set of *red*-producing initial spin speeds, and it will assert that the actual initial conditions for the trial in question fell into this set. That is, it will state that the speed fell within one of a certain set of intervals (without identifying the interval in question), and it will then state the properties of the wheel of fortune in virtue of which any speed in any of the intervals would produce a *red* outcome.

The probabilistic model has two advantages over the deterministic model. First, as in the frequency case, it adds additional explanatorily relevant information in the form of a basing generalization stating a moderate degree of entanglement between, on the one hand, being a trial on a wheel of fortune, and on the other hand, falling into the set of intervals in question. The robustness required for entanglement is a consequence of the non-clumping property of the initial-condition distribution, in virtue of which most trials, including counterfactual variants of the very trial whose outcome is to be explained, will have initial conditions falling into the set. (The property of the set in virtue of which the entanglement exists is simply its size—there is otherwise nothing special about this set in particular.) The accuracy, and thus the explanatory value of the basing generalization, is therefore in proportion to the size of the set, hence to the strike ratio and probability for *red*. In the case at hand, the probability is high, so the basing generalization adds explanatory value.

The second way in which the probabilistic model is superior to the deterministic model is that its causal element is more abstract; the deterministic model is thus exposed as a purveyor of causal irrelevancies. How can this be? The deterministic model contains enough causal detail to pick out a particular large set of initial spin speeds as the *red*-producing speeds on the wheel of fortune in question; it then identifies the relevant initial spin speed as belonging to this particular large set. The probabilistic model contains just enough causal detail to imply that the evolution function for the wheel of fortune is microconstant and has a high strike ratio, and so to imply that the set of *red*-producing initial spin speeds is large and thus that the actual initial condition was likely to fall within its boundaries. But it does not identify the set. It thus describes strictly less of the dynamics than the deterministic model.

What causal details are in the deterministic model but not the probabilistic model? To draw accurately the boundaries of the *red*-producing set, the deterministic model must involve itself with the details of the frictional forces operating on the wheel. To imply microconstancy, the probabilistic model by contrast need only spell out the facts underlying the frictional forces' circular symmetry. (I used the same example in the discussion of long run frequency explanation in section 10.24.) In this and other ways, the causal component of the probabilistic model is an abstraction of the deterministic model, and so the probabilistic model ought to be preferred.

There is something quite puzzling about the claim that the optimal deterministic model is strictly less abstract than the causal part of the microconstant model, since the latter is, considered in isolation, itself a deterministic model for the occurrence of the *red* outcome to be explained. If there is a deterministic model for *red* that is more abstract than the putatively optimal deterministic model, then is it not the true optimal deterministic model?

Surprisingly, it turns out that the microconstant model's causal component cannot survive as such when detached from its probabilistic whole. To serve as a self-standing deterministic model, it must attribute to its initial condition, the spin speed, a property that guarantees that it is a member of whatever the *red*-producing set turns out to be. The identity of the set depends on various parameters of the wheel's operation, such as its paint scheme. The only way for the model to pick out the appropriate set, then, without importing additional causal detail over and above what is needed to imply microconstancy with a certain strike ratio, is by what I have called functionalization: the set will be specified in terms of its relation to the paint scheme and other factors. In attributing membership of the set to the initial spin speed, then, the model will attribute a relational property to the speed. Such a property, however, cannot appear in the setup of a causal model for a *red* outcome, because it is not a property in virtue of which the spin speed is a causal influence on the outcome. (This argument was developed in the final part of section 10.24.)

How does the probabilistic model get around this problem? It does not need to specify the *red*-producing property (that is, the property of a spin speed's falling into such and such a set of intervals). Rather, it shows—using only bona fide causal properties of the wheel—that the *red*-producing set, whichever one it is, is large, and it points to the high probability that the initial spin speed will fall into any large set in virtue of the set's size along. In other words, rather than picking out the actual *red*-producing set by invoking a definite, though abstract, *red*-producing property possessed by that set, it quantifies over such properties: rather than saying that the actual initial conditions had property $P$, and $P$ causes *red*, it says that whatever causal property plays the *red*-producing role, it has a high probability of being instantiated by the actual initial conditions. What is key here is that even when using this quantificational technique to reach an extremely high level of abstraction, it is possible to give a quite satisfactory causal story as to how the initial speed's having the property, whatever it was, led to *red*: it turned the wheel through just such an arc that the pointer indicated a *red* section.

In a purely causal model, quantification cannot be used as an abstracting technique, because a purely causal model's only means of attributing the relevant causal property to the initial conditions is to mention that property explicitly. A model that invokes a basing generalization can, by contrast, imply the presence of the property without, as it were, naming it. This is true for exceptionless as well as probabilistic basing generalizations: in the case of the ball and the basin (section 7.41), the existence of an appropriate basin filigree is implied by the basin basing generalization, without any need to give a functional characterization of the filigree. (Thus, although for reasons given in section 10.24 there is no problem with citing such a characterization explicitly, it is not necessary to do so.)

The microconstant model does not gain its causal generality entirely free of charge: it must cite a basing generalization that is considerably stronger than it could get away with citing if its causal component were identical to the deterministic model. To see this, suppose you were to add a basing generalization to the deterministic model. The deterministic model states that the actual initial spin speed had a certain property $P$, and it shows that any speed with $P$ produces a *red* outcome. The local entanglement to be subsumed under the basing generalization is therefore an entanglement between the property of being a wheel of fortune initial spin speed and the property of falling into the (large) set of speeds with $P$.

The microconstant model's basing generalization is, by contrast, something much stronger: it implies a pattern of entanglement between the property of being a wheel of fortune initial spin speed and the property of falling into *any* large set of initial spin speeds. The microconstant model therefore gains generality (a kind of logical weakness) for its causal model by increasing the strength of its basing generalization. An even trade? Not at all! Whereas weakness is an asset in a causal model, it is not at all to be preferred in a basing generalization: the sort of generality desired in a basing generalization is a kind of strength. The probabilistic model, by exchanging strength in its causal component for strength in its basing component, therefore makes an excellent explanatory bargain.

I have argued so far for the superiority of probabilistic to deterministic explanation of microconstantly produced outcomes with a high strike ratio and thus a high probability. What about lower probability outcomes?

As the strike ratio for an outcome decreases, the size of the region of initial conditions producing that outcome decreases, and the accuracy of the basing generalization decreases along with it. At some point the basing generalization's accuracy sinks so low as to begin to become a net explanatory liability (section 10.24). At the level of accuracy immediately before this point, the basing generalization is explanatorily neutral, but the probabilistic explanation is still superior to the deterministic explanation, because its causal component has greater generality than the deterministic model. Eventually, the basing generalization becomes so inaccurate as to erase the generality advantage, and the deterministic model edges its way into optimality.

You will see that the moment when the deterministic model overtakes the probabilistic model as explanatory champion depends on the generality advantage that the causal component of the probabilistic model holds over the deterministic model. The greater this advantage, the longer the probabilistic model can hold on in the face of decreasing accuracy.

To get a firmer grip on the sources of the generality advantage, divide the causal factors cited by the deterministic model for *red* into three sets. The factors in the first set either make a difference to the fact that the evolution function for *red* is microconstant, or they make a difference to the magnitude of the strike ratio for *red*. Call them *strike factors*. The factors in the second set make a difference to which initial conditions produce a *red* outcome, but they do not affect the evolution function's microconstancy or its strike ratio for *red*. As such factors are added, taken away, or have their magnitudes varied, then, the evolution function for *red* varies too, but it is always microconstant and always has the same strike ratio. Call these factors *permutators*, since they rearrange the gray and white patches that make up the evolution function in a figure such as figure 10.1 without changing its overall aspect. The circular symmetry of the frictional forces acting on the wheel, for example, is a strike factor; additional details about the forces are mere permutators. The factors in the third set are the initial conditions. When there is more than one initial condition, it is often the case that each condition will function as a permutator: fix its value and you get an evolution function that is microconstant with the same strike ratio as the unrestricted evolution function (Strevens 2003b, §2.2). I will, for simplicity's sake, include the initial conditions among the permutators in what follows; although there is in some cases a distinction, it makes no difference here.

The probabilistic model for *red* cites only the wheel of fortune's strike factors. The deterministic model cites the strike factors and also the permutators. The probabilistic model is more general than the deterministic model, then, to the extent that the *red*-producing process has many more permutators than strike factors. More generally, a certain degree of inaccuracy can be tolerated in the basing generalizations of—which is to say that an otherwise dangerously low probability is allowable in—a probabilistic explanation of an outcome produced by a process with a relative abundance of permutators. In other words, when the occurrence of the explanandum depends on myriad causal factors, but the overall outlines of the dynamics, in particular its microconstancy and a value for its strike ratio, depend on only a few high-level properties of the producing system, a probabilistic explanation may be apt even if the explanandum was not especially likely to occur.

To see how this might work out in practice, take a famous example of single-outcome low-probability explanation, the case of paresis (Scriven 1959; previously mentioned in section 9.52). Paresis is a progressive degeneration of the central nervous system caused by tertiary syphilis. Tertiary syphilis may develop if a secondary infection is left untreated; only a small minority of untreated patients develop paresis, however.

Can a patient's paresis be explained by citing only untreated syphilis and whatever probabilistic laws or other generalizations link syphilis to paresis? As far as I know, the difference-makers for paresis are not well understood; I am free to concoct an exemplary story. Assume that the process by which paresis develops is deterministic, so that a probabilistic model for paresis cites quasi- or complex probabilities. The question is whether such a model, when compared to a deterministic model of the process by which syphilis causes paresis, makes up for in the generality of its causal model what it sacrifices in the accuracy of its basing generalization.

Consider three different possible stories about the etiology of paresis.

1. The causal process by which syphilis causes paresis has just a few strike factors: a small number of gross biological facts determine that the process is microconstant with a certain strike ratio for the incidence of paresis. Whether or not any particular patient acquires paresis is determined by a single further initial condition $x$.

2. As in the first case, there are very few strike factors for the paresis-producing process; there are, however, many permutators and initial conditions.

3. There are many strike factors for paresis. To get to the point where you have a settled evolution function for paresis with a fixed strike ratio, you must take into account many parameters of the process, parameters that have different values for different syphilis patients. The strike ratio therefore varies with the details of the case.

Only in case (2), I suggest, is there any prospect that the optimal explanation for a case of paresis is a probabilistic model citing a low probability of contracting paresis given untreated syphilis.

In case (1), the accuracy penalty for citing such a low-probability basing generalization far outweighs the advantage in generality gained by the probabilistic model's not needing to cite the single additional factor $x$. The best explanation of paresis in case (1) is therefore a deterministic explanation that specifies the value of $x$.

In case (3), the probabilistic model's generality advantage is also not that great: the addition of whatever facts are needed to determine for sure that paresis occurs do not dramatically increase the explanation's causal specificity; it is therefore worth adding these facts to avoid the accuracy penalty, unless the strike ratio for paresis in the particular case at hand is high.

Even in case (2), it is not obvious that the probabilistic model is preferable; after all, the inaccuracy of the basing generalization is quite severe—so much so, perhaps, that its presence in a model renders the model explanatorily worthless. In that case, Hempel is correct in his claim that an understanding of the causal role of syphilis does not on its own constitute an explanation of paresis.

The ultimate resolution of the paresis case is not so important, however. What I want to stress here is that the cut-off point for the probabilistic explanation of a single outcome—the point at which the probability of the outcome is so low that citing the factors that determine the probability is not explanatory—depends on the causal workings of the process that produced the outcome. In particular, when a few broad, abstract properties of the process are sufficient to determine the relevant probability (by determining microconstancy with a certain strike ratio), the threshold for probabilistic explanation is relatively low.

Three concluding remarks. First, when a microconstant explanation of a single outcome is optimal, the permutators, though their values may have in some sense made a difference to whether or not the explanandum occurred, are determined by the kairetic account to be explanatorily irrelevant. Some ramifications will be explored in section 11.4.

Second, what I have said above about the microconstant explanation of single outcomes is also true, more or less, for quasiprobabilistic explanation, whether the quasiprobabilities are founded in imperfect microconstancy, channeling, or something else. You might even think that when explaining an occurrence of *red* on the 90/10 wheel of fortune, what you cite should not be the exact 90% probability of *red*, but a "very high" quasiprobability for *red*.

Third, a concluding worry: in many high strike ratio microconstant processes, it is possible that, although almost every initial condition for some mechanism produces the same outcome $e$, the set of $e$-producing initial conditions is not contiguous. In effect, the few non-$e$-producing initial conditions manage between them to slice the set of $e$-producing initial conditions into two or more pieces. A model that displays the microconstancy of the process is a model abstract enough to be realized by any of the $e$-producing processes. But since these form a noncontiguous set, the process lacks dynamic contiguity and so the model lacks cohesion. (The same issue may arise with other channeling processes as well, of course.) The problem may be resolved either by understanding the standards for cohesion in such a way as to allow such noncontiguity (recalling that dynamic contiguity is a heuristic, not the final word on cohesion), or by acknowledging a small degree of incohesion and understanding the microconstant model as making a cohesion/generality tradeoff (section 5.43). Both strategies put great weight on the fact that the different $e$-producing subsets lead to $e$ in very similar ways.

## 11.2   Robustness

What is the explanatory significance of robustness? The treatment of probabilistic single-outcome explanation in the previous section puts the last pieces of the kairetic answer to this question in place.

A connection between properties or complexes of properties is robust if it holds under a wide range of circumstances, actual and counterfactual. The kairetic account associates two different kinds of robustness with explanatory virtue, namely, causal robustness and the robustness that constitutes entanglement. I will discuss them in turn.

Causal robustness is the tendency of a causal process to produce an outcome consistently under a wide range of circumstances, that is, given a wide range of initial conditions and parameters.

There is something of a consensus on the explanatory virtues of causal robustness:

> The stability of an outcome of a causal process in spite of significant variation in initial conditions can be informative . . . in the same way that it is informative to learn, regarding a given causal explanation of the First World War, that a world war would have come about . . . even if no bomb had exploded in Sarajevo. This sort of robustness or resilience of a process is important to grasp in coming to know explanations based upon it. (Railton 1981, 251)

But why is stability, or causal robustness, a good thing?[1]

Causal accounts of explanation seem unable to account for robustness's explanatory importance. To say that a process is robust is to make a claim about other ways that the explanandum might have been caused but was not. On the standard causal approach to explanation, however, only information about how an event was actually caused is explanatorily relevant. Citing robustness would appear, on the causal approach, to add nothing to an explanation. (Strevens (2000a) develops this point with special attention to Railton's treatment of explanation in statistical mechanics.)

A number of philosophers have probed the explanatory virtues of robustness, including Wimsatt (1981), Jackson and Pettit (1992a), and Batterman (2002). Jackson and Pettit develop a view of explanation that is causal but on which explaining an event involves, sometimes if not always, the description of a range of nonactual causal processes. The point of such an exercise, Jackson and Pettit propose, is to appreciate the similarities between the actual causal process and other causal processes by which the explanandum might have been caused; they consider such an appreciation to be an explanatory end in itself.

Both Wimsatt and Batterman, by contrast, understand causal robustness as a practical virtue in explanation. On their views, a model that shows that the process producing a phenomenon is robust is not an explanatorily more valuable model, but it is more valuable in other ways, epistemic and utilitarian. For these reasons, you will find robust models everywhere in science; the explanatory enterprise is no exception.[2]

These two approaches to robustness both implicitly concede that the recognition of robustness has no role to play in that part of the explanatory enterprise concerned with describing the actual causal process leading to the explanandum.

The kairetic conception of difference-making supplies a very different perspective. When a process is robust relative to an outcome $e$, various of its initial conditions and parameters are not difference-makers: had they taken different values, $e$ would have been produced all the same. To grasp what actually makes a difference to a phenomenon, then—to see which are the essential parts of the causal process actually producing the phenomenon— you must grasp in what respects the process is and is not robust.

In order to explain, for example, why a ball released on the lip of a basin ends up at the basin's lowest point, you need not, and should not, take into account the particular release point. The key to your explanation is your appreciating the high-level causal factors that would have taken the ball to the bottom of the basin no matter what, that is, the high-level factors in virtue of which the process is robust—not because of their role in possible but nonactual histories, but because of their difference-making role in the actual history (section 7.41).

The ball's journey to the bottom of the basin is, of course, an extremely robust process, but any causal process that has a kairetic model (relative to some explanandum) that is even slightly abstract is, to the same degree, slightly robust: there is *some* detail, the tweaking of which would not have made a difference to the occurrence of the explanandum. The difference-making aspect of the kairetic account, then, is all about robustness; indeed, the kairetic account's optimizing procedure is essentially an algorithm for discovering in what respects the causal process that produced an event was robust.

It is trivial, then, for the kaireticist to account for the significance of robustness in building an explanatory model of the actual causal process producing an explanandum. What of a more presumptuous question: why do we understand events produced by very robust processes better than we understand mere flukes or coincidences? If the world is a deterministic place, then even the flukes have causal models of maximal accuracy. They differ from the models for robustly produced explananda only in their generality. But generality, I have suggested, brings its own kind of explanatory virtue, quite apart from its role in the optimizing procedure: all other things being equal, we should prefer more general to less general explanatory models, even when choosing among explanations that are locally optimal (section 4.35), because more general explanations are explanations of greater depth, in the second sense of depth (section 4.36). Which is to say: an event produced by a robust causal process can be given a deeper explanation than an event that is a mere "coincidence."

A qualification: the explanatory reach of robustness extends, on the kairetic account, only as far as the standards for cohesion allow. Consider the origins of World War One. This is, according to Railton, a classic case of causal-explanatory robustness: by appreciating that certain sociopolitical trends—say, the system of European alliances, the growth of nationalism, and the arms race—together made war almost inevitable (if indeed they did), you understand the war's outbreak far better than if you appreciate only the particular sequence of historical events, beginning with the assassination of the Archduke, by which the process was actually initiated. To put the claim in the kairetic idiom: the optimal explanatory model for the

war's outbreak will abstract away from all causal details apart from the sociopolitical factors that made war inevitable. (The assassination itself may
vanish altogether; see section 11.4.) But the claim is correct—and thus the
robustness of the onset of war is explanatorily relevant—only if a model at
this level of abstraction is causally cohesive. The cohesion requirement may
well be satisfied in the case of the guns of August, but it can never be taken
for granted.

Along with causal robustness, the kairetic account places value on the robustness involved in entanglement. I have little new to say about the explanatory contribution of this sort of robustness; I will simply remind you
of the three related ways in which the robustness of the connection between
a basing generalization's antecedent and consequent properties (the $F$ and
$P$ in *All Fs are P*) is explanatorily important:

1. The facts about entanglement are constituted by facts about robustness; there can be no basing patterns without robustness.

2. The greater the degree of entanglement between the antecedent and
   consequent properties—the more robust the connection between the
   properties—the better an explanation that cites the entanglement. (I
   advanced this suggestion tentatively and without argument in section 7.35; I include it here for completeness.)

3. The more widespread the entanglement between the antecedent and
   consequent properties—the more general the pattern of robustness—
   the better an explanation that cites the pattern.

The intensive and extensive flavors of robustness figuring respectively in (2)
and (3) are closely connected.

There is a supplementary explanatory benefit that accrues to an explanation that joins the right kinds of robustness in basing pattern and causal
process. I refer to the advantage that a probabilistic model has over a deterministic model when explaining a single outcome or a short-run frequency
produced by a microconstant process with a high strike ratio. As I showed
in section 11.1, the probabilistic model is able to cite a rather abstract, hence
robust, causal model for the outcome only because of the availability of
a wide-ranging basing generalization connecting the property of being an
initial condition for the mechanism in question and the property of falling

into a large set of initial conditions. The robustness in mechanism and basing pattern work together, then, to create a probabilistic explanatory model of greater causal abstraction than is possible using strictly deterministic resources.

To sum up, the kairetic approach to explanation connects robustness to explanatory virtue in four ways. First, the causal model that best exhibits a process's causal robustness also shows what makes a difference to the causal production of the target and what does not. Second, the more robust a causal process, the greater the generality of the explanatorily optimal causal model and so the deeper the explanation. Third, entanglement is a kind of robustness, and so an explanatorily desirable basing generalization picks out patterns of robust coinstantiation—the more robust, the better. Fourth, there is a remarkable synergy between causal robustness and basing robustness in the case of high-probability single-outcome explanation.

Is it a coincidence that robustness turns up as an explanatory virtue in more than one guise? Perhaps not if, as suggested in section 7.36, our explanatory practice is shaped by a concern with prediction and control.

## 11.3   Nonexplanatory Probability-Raisers

So far, I have treated probability-raising as a sufficient condition for explanatory relevance: in the explanation of both long-run frequencies and single outcomes, a causal factor is relevant if it raises the probability of the explanandum. This cannot be correct, however; the doctrine of moderate elitism in its simple form must be amended.

### 11.31  Probabilistic Difference-Making

Difference-making in probabilistic explanation is in an important respect quite different from deterministic difference-making. You will recall that all difference-makers in an explanatory model, probabilistic and deterministic, have an explanatory weight that is proportional to their contribution to the explanatory model's accuracy. The weight of deterministic difference-makers (and some probabilistic difference-makers) quantifies the "amount of difference made," in a certain sense, to the explanandum (section 5.1). But the weight of many probabilistic difference-makers quantifies not the amount of difference made but the probability that a difference is made at all.

To see this, consider the case of the exploding chair described in section 2.3. Rasputin's would-be assassins tie him to a chair, place a bomb under the chair, and activate the bomb's trigger. The trigger is somewhat unreliable: it detonates the bomb with a 75% probability. By activating the trigger, the conspirators have raised the probability of Rasputin's death from around zero to 75%, which gives it an explanatory weight of 75% (a factor's explanatory weight being its contribution to the probability of the explanandum). Now suppose that the bomb does not, in fact, go off. The conspirators then throw Rasputin into the river, where he drowns. Does the activation of the trigger make a difference to Rasputin's death? If explanatory weight is a measure of difference-making, the kairetic account says *yes*. But this is the wrong answer, since activating the trigger clearly made no difference in the case where the bomb fails to explode. Further, if the bomb does explode, the difference made is surely 100%, not 75%.

How to understand difference-making in this example? There is some probability that the causal factor cited makes a real difference—there is some probability that the bomb explodes—but also some probability that it makes no difference. It is striking that the 75% probability of making a difference is equal to the explanatory weight, also 75%. Let me make the natural suggestion that the explanatory weight of a probability-raising causal factor should be interpreted as the probability that the factor makes a difference, rather than the degree of difference made.[3]

What I will emphasize about this proposal is not the formula yielding the probability that a difference is made but simply the fact that difference-making is a probabilistic matter, and in particular, the fact that the factors cited in an apparently legitimate probabilistic model for an event might turn out not to have made a difference. When the difference-making of a causal factor in a model has this property, call it *probabilistic difference-making*.

There are three questions raised by the phenomenon of probabilistic difference-making.

1. For a given probabilistic model, how to tell which difference-making relations are probabilistic and which are not?

2. For a given explanandum and model, how to tell which probabilistic difference-makers in the model actually did make a difference to the explanandum?

3. When a probabilistic difference-maker does not make a difference, is it nevertheless explanatorily relevant?

Question (2) is answered at length below. I take it to be obvious that the answer to (3) is *no:* if a probabilistic difference-maker turns out to have made no difference to a particular event, it does not belong in the explanation of that event. A method for detecting difference-making when it happens is, then, an essential part of the probabilistic explainer's toolkit.

As for question (1), the answer is determined by the answer to question (2). Once there is a procedure for determining whether a difference-maker in a probabilistic model actually makes a difference to the model's target, you can ask of a given factor: Are there any realizations of the model's setup where the factor would not make a difference? If the answer is *yes*, the difference-making is probabilistic, otherwise not.

Much difference-making in probabilistic models is, intuitively, probabilistic. Even the microconstancy of a microconstant process's evolution function sometimes fails to make a difference to a long-run frequency, for reasons discussed in section 11.33. The one exception I know of is the property of the evolution function cited in a channeling explanation, that a great majority of initial conditions cause the explanandum. This property always makes a difference. By extension, the microconstancy and high strike ratio of a microconstant evolution function always make a difference when the explanandum is a single outcome, since as proposed above, the mode of difference-making in single-outcome explanations is the same for microconstant and imperfectly microconstant processes as for channeling processes.

### 11.32  The Expanded Model Test: Simple Probability

I will advocate what I call the expanded model test for determining explanatory difference-making. (For somewhat different approaches, see Menzies (1996) and Schaffer (2001).) Begin with a simple probabilistic process: suppose that the bomb placed under Rasputin's chair is triggered by some sort of quantum probabilistic device. The trigger causes the bomb to detonate with a simple probability of 75%; when it fails, the bomb becomes useless. If the bomb does not explode, Rasputin is killed in some other way.

Activating the bomb's trigger is a probabilistic difference-maker for death, but when does it actually make a difference? Obviously, triggering

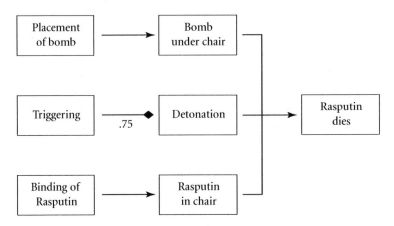

**Figure 11.1** A probabilistic explanation of Rasputin's death citing the triggering of the bomb placed under his chair. Some background conditions and all laws are omitted.


the bomb makes a difference just in case the trigger functions and the bomb explodes. But what general principle do you invoke to make this judgment?[4]

The example suggests the following line of thought. A probabilistic difference-maker stands to make a difference by probabilifying some particular outcome (such as the bomb's exploding) that in turn makes its own difference to the explanandum. The probabilistic difference-maker makes an actual difference just in case this outcome does in fact occur. What is needed, then, is a test that identifies these tell-tale outcomes and links their occurrence to the difference-maker's difference-making.

Consider the model for Rasputin's death by bomb shown in figure 11.1. Suppose that the bomb fails to detonate, but that Rasputin is killed in some other way. Can the model explain his death? No, because it is not veridical: it specifies that the bomb detonates. This nonveridicality is a sign of the triggering's failure to make a difference.

What is noteworthy about the model in figure 11.1 is that it spells out every step by which the activation of the trigger probabilifies Rasputin's death. I propose that the nonveridicality of such a model is a sure sign that some probabilistic difference-maker in the model failed to make an actual difference (more exactly, that it failed to make a difference in the way specified by the model, as explained below).

Given a candidate standalone explanation for an event *e* including prob-abilistic difference-makers, then, a test for the probabilistic factors' differ-ence-making—the *expanded-model test*—can be formulated as follows. There are two steps. First, construct an expanded model, which is to say, add to your model whatever intermediate setups are necessary to make explicit all probabilistic steps in the inductive derivation of the explana-tory model's target. The immediate outcome of every simple probabilistic process will therefore be spelled out in the expanded model. Second, test the expanded model for veridicality. If it is not veridical, then the proba-bilistic difference-makers in the model failed to make a difference to the explanandum.

Observe that the test has its bite because the addition of intermediate setups to—the intensification of—a probabilistic model, unlike a determin-istic model (section 4.32), logically strengthens the model, by specifying the occurrence of events that in the original model were only probabilified. In-tensifying a probabilistic model, then, does not have a merely pragmatic role; it adds explanatory information and so improves the model—and of course it serves an entirely novel function in determining probabilistic difference-makers.

The expanded-model test may strike you as too stringent. If the expanded model is not veridical, *all* probabilistic difference-makers in the model are declared not to make a difference. How can this be? Consider the placing of the bomb under the chair. Although the path from this event to the explanandum, Rasputin's death, does not traverse any probabilistic links (see figure 11.1), it is nevertheless a probabilistic difference-maker, because to make its difference, it requires a certain condition—the detonation of the bomb—that is stochastically produced. The failure of the detonation is just as much a sign that the bomb-placing has failed to make a difference, as it is a sign that the trigger activation has failed to make a difference.

A qualification: when a difference-maker fails the expanded-model test, the proper conclusion from a failed test is not that the putative difference-maker fails to make a difference at all, but that it fails to make a difference with respect to the model in question, which is to say that it fails to make a difference by way of the mechanism that the model describes. The same causal factor may make a difference relative to a different model, in which case it qualifies as a difference-maker for the explanandum by a different causal route described by the alternative model. Suppose, for example, that

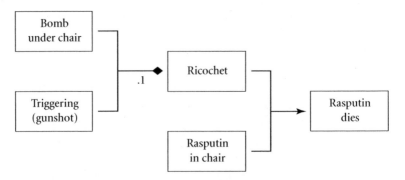

**Figure 11.2** An alternative model for Rasputin's bomb-related death: the gun that is supposed to trigger the bomb kills Rasputin by an alternative causal pathway (in a case where the bomb is not detonated).

the triggering apparatus for the bomb is activated by a gunshot, and that the bullet fails to cause a detonation but ricochets upward and kills Rasputin. Firing the gun is a difference-maker for death because it makes a difference in a certain model, namely, the ricochet model shown in figure 11.2. The nonveridicality of the bomb model in figure 11.1, then, does not rule out the gun-firing's making a probabilistic difference by way of the ricochet model. Alternatively, a causal factor in a model that fails the test because some probabilistic process falls through may, in the case where it contributes to the probability of the explanandum by way of a submechanism that is independent of the process that falls through, qualify as making a difference to the explanandum relative to a submodel of the original model.

Why is it useful to know relative to which model a probabilistic difference-maker makes its difference? When you ask whether a probabilistic difference-maker $c$ makes a difference, it is because you want to explain an event using a model containing $c$. Given this need, it is not enough to know that $c$ makes a difference; you must know that it makes a difference in the way specified by the model. In the case at hand, for example, knowing that the bullet made a difference is not enough to determine the correct explanation of Rasputin's death; you must know relative to which model—figure 11.1 or figure 11.2—the difference was made. The expanded-model test provides this knowledge: if the bomb is detonated, only the first model is veridical and so the first model explains the death; if the bullet ricochets, only the second model is veridical and so the second model explains the death.[5]

Observe that the expanded-model test cannot be applied when a simple probabilistic process directly probabilifies the explanandum. Suppose, for example, that I lower the potential in a potential well and a particle quantum-tunnels its way out of the well (as described in section 9.71). Did my lowering of the potential make a difference to the tunneling? The relevant probabilistic model cannot be expanded any further, so there are no tell-tale events that can be used to determine difference-making. What to say about the causal-explanatory relevance of my potential-lowering in such a case has been much discussed in the literature on probabilistic explanation and causation. Some writers hold that the probability-increaser is always explanatorily relevant (Humphreys 1989, 36–37). Some writers hold that it sometimes is and sometimes is not, depending on certain basic metaphysical facts about causal influence that we are not in a position to discern (Armstrong 1997, §14.2, following Tooley). I have nothing to add to the debate since, as best I can determine, there are no techniques to resolve such questions in our explanatory practice.

### 11.33  The Expanded-Model Test: Complex Probability

You conduct 100 trials on a normal wheel of fortune with a strike ratio for *red* of one-half, obtaining 50 *red* outcomes and 50 *black* outcomes. Strangely, however, every one of the *red* outcomes is the result of the pointer indicating the same red section, and every one of the *black* outcomes is the result of the pointer indicating the same black section. Does macroperiodicity explain the frequency?

If the interpretation of microconstant explanation given in chapter ten is correct, then the answer is *no*: the macroperiodicity of an initial-condition distribution is relevant to a microconstant mechanism's producing probabilistic patterns of outcomes only when the distribution of actual initial conditions is itself macroperiodic. In the case just described, the actual initial conditions are not macroperiodic at all, so macroperiodicity and consequently microconstancy have no explanatory bearing on the frequency (which must therefore be given a deterministic explanation).

As in the case of the bomb, it is clear when macroperiodicity does and does not count as a difference-maker for a 50% frequency of *red*: it counts

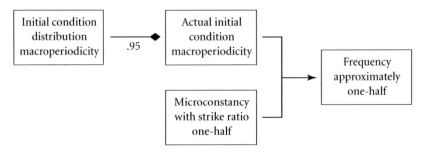

**Figure 11.3**  A typical microconstant explanation of a long-run frequency expanded to show the probabilistic derivation's route through the macroperiodicity of the actual initial-condition distribution.

when the actual initial-condition distribution is roughly macroperiodic, not when it is not. The ground for this judgment is, I will suggest, the expanded model test.

Take the microconstant model for the 50% frequency and make explicit the initial conditions for its causal component, that is, the macroperiodicity of the actual initial conditions. Such a model, shown in figure 11.3, has two parts, a probabilistic, acausal part whereby a macroperiodic distribution of actual initial conditions is subsumed under the basing pattern represented by the initial-condition distribution, and a deterministic, causal part whereby a one-half frequency for *red* is shown to be caused by the macroperiodicity of the actual spin speeds and the mechanism's microconstancy and one-half strike ratio for *red*.

Since the expanded model specifies the macroperiodicity of the actual initial-condition distribution, it is nonveridical just when macroperiodicity and microconstancy do not, intuitively, make a difference, as desired. The difference-making status of a causal factor that affects the probability of the explanandum by affecting the strike ratio of the evolution function is dealt with in the same way. It makes a difference when the evolution function's microconstancy makes a difference, that is, when the relevant initial conditions are macroperiodically distributed. Otherwise it does not (or at least, not by way of the causal pathway represented by a microconstant model). Even though the factor may affect the strike ratio deterministically, then, it is a probabilistic difference-maker because it depends for its ultimate effect on other factors that are probabilistic difference-makers (just as in the case of the bomb-placing in the previous section). Its difference-making is therefore to be determined by the expanded model test.

### 11.34  Overview—and a Problem

Let me sum up. In the simple probabilistic case involving Rasputin, the difference-making is probabilistic because it involves a stochastic causal process, the quantum triggering of the bomb. In the wheel-of-fortune case, the difference-making is probabilistic because the initial conditions are subsumed under a probabilistic basing generalization. Despite the difference in the nature of the underlying explanatory relations, the veridicality of an expanded model—a model that makes explicit all inductive steps in the relevant probabilistic causal entailment—appears to be necessary and sufficient for probabilistic difference-making, at least in those cases where we can determine difference-making at all.

My characterization of the procedure for expanding a model has been rather informal; you might desire some more systematic theory of expansion. I am not so sure that it is worth the effort; as far as I can see, there are only two occasions for expansion, namely, those specified in the previous paragraph: stating the occurrence of an outcome of an irreducibly stochastic process, and stating the instantiation, in the actual initial conditions pertinent to some complex or quasiprobabilistic mechanism, of a property that is probabilified by the initial-condition distribution. With this enumeration, the theory of expansion is for all practical purposes complete.

Consider an objection to the adequacy of the expanded-model test in the case where complex probabilities are used to explain single outcomes. Suppose that I take a wheel of fortune with 50 red and 50 black sections, repaint 40 of the black sections red, and spin the wheel once, obtaining *red*. Did my repainting make a difference to the outcome?

To answer this question, you might think that you require more information. If the red section indicated by the pointer at the end of the spin was one of the repainted ones, then the repainting did make a difference. But if not, not. How can the expanded-model test reproduce this intuitive judgment?

The test, it seems, must expand the microconstant model to make explicit certain facts about the actual initial conditions of the spin (just as in the case above where it was a frequency that was to be explained). Suppose that the set of initial conditions that would have led to *red* before the repainting is $X$, and the much larger set that would lead to *red* after the repainting is $X'$. We want to say that the repainting makes a difference just in case the initial spin speed for the trial in question falls into $X'$ but not into $X$. Thus, the expanded model whose veridicality is necessary and sufficient for the repainting to make a difference ought to say of the initial spin that it does not fall into $X$.

Now we have a problem: the explanatory advantage of the microconstant model in a high-probability single-outcome explanation is derived in part from its demurring to specify directly any properties of the relevant actual initial conditions (section 11.1). But the expanded-model test, it seems, will force the model to do exactly this, rendering it defective (because it will attribute a causally irrelevant property to the actual initial conditions). Must a special exception be made so that we can, for the purposes of testing difference-making, turn a blind eye to the defect?

More embarrassing still, the purely deterministic model for the *red* outcome has no difficulty whatsoever determining the difference-making status of the repainting. When the initial spin speed belongs to $X$, removing the fact of the repainting from the deterministic model—that is, failing to specify whether the sections in question were repainted or not—will make no difference to the entailment of *red*; the repainting, then, will be judged not to make a difference to the outcome. By contrast, when the initial spin speed belongs to $X'$ but not $X$, removing the fact of the repainting will invalidate the entailment, and so the repainting will be classified as a difference-maker, as desired.

What to do? The problem is, I will argue, misconceived. Examine more closely the question whether the repainting made a difference to the outcome. Suppose that the section indicated by the pointer is indeed one of the 40 repainted sections. Did my repainting the other 39 make a difference? Intuitively, no: only painting the very section that was indicated made a difference. Although the repainting increased the strike ratio for *red* from 50% to 90%, then, that fact about the repainting is not, in fact, adjudged to be a difference-maker; what *really* made a difference was the repainting of a single section, an act that in itself made a negligible difference to the strike ratio. The microconstant model, you will observe, represents both the repainting and the wheel of fortune itself at a level of abstraction that dispenses with physical properties of particular sections: it does not even specify how many sections there are, only that 90% of them are red. Thus, the model is incapable of pointing to the fact that is judged to be a difference-maker, the repainting of a single section. It simply does not represent the causal process at the necessary level of detail.

What this shows, I propose, is that when we think of the repainting as making or not making a difference, we are not asking whether the repainting, by raising the probability of *red* from 50% to 90%, made a difference. We are not thinking probabilistically at all. Rather, we are asking whether the deterministic model judges the repainting as a difference-maker. Thus, the probabilistic model cannot be burdened with delivering this judgment, and so there is no onus on the expanded-model test to vindicate the difference-making intuition.

What, then, to say about the question whether repainting's raising the probability of *red* makes a difference? And why do we have meaningful intuitions about difference-making in the deterministic model, if as I argued at the beginning of this chapter, the deterministic model is full of causal irrelevancies? Let me attempt to explain. I suggest that there is no determinate fact as to whether the repainting makes a difference to the *red* outcome at the probabilistic level, precisely because the expanded-model test cannot, for the reasons given immediately above, be applied to single-outcome complex probabilistic explanation. (Or at least: the facts about difference-making, if any, are in principle indiscernible, as in the case of direct simple probabilification discussed at the end of section 11.32.) For this reason, when we are asked about the repainting's difference-making, we apply an interpretive principle of charity and understand the question as concerning ceteris similibus difference-making (section 6.25). That is, we understand the question as follows: in a model in which everything except the repainting, including the actual spin speed, is held fixed at its actual value, does the repainting make a difference? To ascertain the answer, we quite correctly use a deterministic model.

## 11.4 Nonexplanatory Critical Events

Probabilistic relevance may not be sufficient for explanatory relevance, but it is necessary (in those cases where probabilistic explanation is apt at all). This much is a consequence of both the formal (section 9.7) and the material (chapters ten and eleven) aspects of the kairetic treatment of probabilistic explanation. The purpose of the present section is to further explore and defend the claim of necessity.

There are a number of nonprobabilistic tests for explanatory relevance, suggested both by the kairetic account and by other conceptions of explanation in the literature, that give us prima facie warrant for thinking that one event helps to explain another. For example, we have some reason to think that an event $c$ is explanatorily relevant to an event $e$ if the occurrence of $e$ counterfactually depends on the occurrence of $c$ (that is, had $c$ not occurred then $e$ would not have occurred), or if $c$ satisfies the manipulationist criterion for making a difference to $e$, or if $c$ is a ceteris similibus difference-maker for $e$, or if $c$ appears in a kairetically optimized deterministic model for $e$. No doubt there are other tests as well; there is no need to enumerate them here. Call an event that passes one or more such tests a *critical event* for $e$.

Inherent in the kairetic treatment of probabilistic explanation is the thesis that, in cases where an event $e$ is best explained probabilistically, a critical event for $e$ is explanatorily relevant to $e$ only if it makes a positive contribution to the probabilification of $e$—only if, when the event is removed from the appropriate model, the probability that the model assigns to $e$ either falls or becomes wholly indeterminate. I aim to vindicate this thesis. It is true, I will contend, even when $e$ is deterministically produced; the thesis is therefore in direct opposition to both the counterfactual and manipulation approaches to causal explanation.

As an example, consider an event $c$ that acts as a *permutator* for a quasi- or complex probabilistic process producing an event $e$ (section 11.1): it makes a difference to which sets of (other) initial conditions produce $e$, but it does not alter the strike ratio for $e$. Consider, in particular, a case where without $c$, the actual initial conditions would not have led to $e$; it is only because $c$ is present that $e$ occurs, then. Such a $c$ is a ceteris similibus difference-maker for $e$, and quite likely a difference-maker by the lights of both the counterfactual and manipulationist accounts as well. But it has no effect on the probability of $e$, and so if $e$ is best explained probabilistically, the kairetic account maintains that $c$ is irrelevant to the explanation of $e$— appreciating the role of $c$ in the causal production of $e$ in no way helps us to understand why $e$ happened.[6]

Before I leave the party, I stop to thank the host. I then get into my car and drive home. Rounding a blind corner, I hit an oncoming unicyclist. How to explain the accident? If I had not come around the corner at exactly the moment I did, I would have encountered the unicycle on some other stretch of road and been able to avoid it. If I had not left the party at exactly the time I did, I would not have come around the corner at exactly the moment I did. If I had not stopped to thank the host, I would not have left the party at exactly the time I did. Therefore, if I had not stopped to thank the host, the accident would not have occurred.

My act of thanking, then, is a critical event for the accident; indeed, it passes all the prima facie tests for relevance mentioned above. But the act does not increase the probability of the accident: it could just as well have prevented the accident, if the unicyclist's own timing had been slightly different.

The thanking is a critical event that is not a probability-raiser. This is not enough for you to assess its explanatory importance, however. You need to know whether the proper explanation of my accident is probabilistic or deterministic. To this end I provide two different contexts for the accident. In one, the accident is best explained deterministically; in the other, probabilistically.

First context: the probability of the accident was rather low. It was just an unfortunate coincidence that I encountered the unicycle on a blind corner.

Second context: the accident's probability was high. The road home has many blind corners. I had too much too drink, and I am in any case a bad driver who often corners in the wrong lane. A convention of unicyclists— as everyone knows a reckless breed—was taking place in the neighborhood. A storm had reduced visibility to a few feet. And so on.

In the first context, the probabilistic model has low accuracy, so the deterministic model will likely prevail as optimal. Among the factors appearing in a deterministic model will be critical events; thus, my thanking is, in virtue of such a model, a difference-maker and is explanatorily relevant to the accident—along with everything else that affected the timing of my departure.

In the second context, a probabilistic—or more likely, quasiprobabilistic—model of substantial accuracy is available. Such a model is considerably more general than the deterministic model because no detailed trajectories need be mentioned, simply the many different ways, broadly speaking, that an accident of the relevant sort could happen in the circumstances. Quite possibly the probabilistic explanation will be optimal; assume that it is. Then the thanking is not explanatorily relevant, since it does not increase the probability of the explanandum. (It is important that what is being explained here is a high-level event such as my colliding with a unicycle on the way home, not my colliding with a particular unicycle at a particular corner at a particular time. The deterministic model will almost certainly supply the best explanation of details such as these.)

I want to defend the view that in the second context, knowing how my stopping to thank the host helped to causally produce the accident does not enhance my understanding of the accident.

Let me begin by saying that this doctrine accords with practice. It would be strange to explain the accident by noting that I stopped to thank my host. It would remain strange even if I cited in addition all the probability-raising factors—the bad road, the unicyclists' convention, and so on—and then said: "and of course, I stopped to thank my host." Or at least it sounds strange to someone in full possession of the accident's causal history. To someone who does not know the details, it does not sound strange, but even more tellingly, it implies that the act of thanking somehow increased the probability of the accident. Was there something about the conversation with my host that distracted me as I drove home?

In the case where there are no probability-raising factors, by contrast, it is not strange to cite my stopping to thank the host, provided that it is not implied that this act was any more important to determining the exact timing of my journey than various other events at the party. The explanation goes as follows: it was just a matter of unfortunate timing, the unlucky combination of events such as my stopping to thank the host, my getting temporarily trapped in the guest bathroom, and so on. What makes the citation of these events relevant is the truth of the preamble: it was *just* a matter of unfortunate timing. When this claim is false—when there are significant probability-raisers such as the unicyclists' convention—the little matters of timing are no longer a legitimate part of the explanation.[7]

Now consider some objections to this claim. First, it might be argued that to dismiss the role of the thanking out of hand is to miss something important. The thanking played a role in the accident that some causal factors, such as the color of the shirt I was wearing as I drove, did not. True, but the kairetic account already recognizes this role, by deeming the thanking, but not the shirt color, a ceteris similibus difference-maker.

Second, it might be argued that events such as the thanking are not mentioned in explanations for utilitarian reasons, rather than because they are not genuinely explanatory. There is good practical reason to pay more attention to factors that raise the probability of undesirable events than to factors that sometimes play a critical role but that are not probability-raisers.

In reply, it is true that there is not much practical reason to worry about factors that do not increase the probability of dire events, but it is false that they are not psychologically salient for us. We humans thrill to the story about the passenger who for some trivial reason missed the plane that went on to crash, and so on. And we often rue the fact that we made the fateful choices that we did, even when the choices in no way probabilified the fates. Why did I have to visit the dentist the very day that the blackout disabled all the elevators in the building?

Third, perhaps what I am calling complex probabilistic and quasiprobabilistic explanations are merely explanation sketches (Hempel's term) rather than full-fledged explanations. That a factor, such as my host-thanking, does not appear in a sketch does not imply its nonappearance in the complete explanation.

Maybe, but that a factor *never* appears in a sketch does cast serious doubt on its explanatory potential. I might add that it is odd, if my explanations are indeed mere sketches, that no one shows any interest, ever, in filling them in.

Fourth, following Kitcher (1989, 449), you might argue that factors that confer larger increases on the probability of an explanandum are preferentially cited in explanations for decision-theoretic reasons. Given our limited time, knowledge, and attention span, we cannot test every causal factor for explanatory relevance. Which should we choose? Those that are most likely to have in fact made a difference to the explanandum. As I have shown, these are just the factors that confer the greatest probability increases on the explanandum (section 11.31). Now consider a factor, like my thanking my host, that does not increase the probability of the explanandum at all. Such a factor is, for the reasons given above, just as likely to prevent the explanandum as to cause it. To cite such a factor in an explanation is extremely risky; thus, such factors are seldom cited.[8]

What is wrong with this argument is that we are often in a position to know which factors did make a difference, but still we do not cite them if they do not increase the explanandum's probability. My act of gratitude is a case in point. I could never have predicted, in advance, that my thanking my host would cause, rather than prevent, the collision. But that is not my epistemic position. I know that the collision occurred; I know that it would not have occurred had I rounded the corner five seconds earlier or five seconds later; I know that thanking my host delayed my departure by at least five seconds. Thus, I know that the thanking was a difference-maker for the collision. There is no epistemic risk whatsoever in my citing it. Yet I decline to do so.

## 11.5   Elitism and Egalitarianism Revisited

If there is a simple answer to the elitism/egalitarianism question, then it is moderate elitism (section 9.73). But probabilistic explanation is a complex, multifaceted, environmentally sensitive practice; as I showed in section 11.3, the simple answer is simplistic. In what follows, I consider putative counterexamples drawn from single-outcome explanation to the two elements of moderate "change debate" elitism, that is, first to the doctrine that only probability-increasers explain, and second to the doctrine that the greater the increase in probability, the greater the contribution to understanding. Interesting questions are raised, but moderate change elitism survives more or less intact.

### Explanatory Probability-Decreasers

In the following case, a factor that lowers the probability of a certain event helps to explain the event.

I am trying to hit a beer bottle with a bullet. But because I do not have a clear line of sight to the bottle, I must get the bullet to execute a complicated series of ricochets. Nothing is certain, but some directions of fire are more promising than others. Firing at the trash can will result in my hitting the bottle about 80% of the time, whereas firing at the drainpipe will result in a hit only 20% of the time. Seeking to maximize my chances of breaking the bottle, I point my gun at the trash can and pull the trigger. As it happens, I am pointing at a spot where my bullet will miss the bottle. At the moment I pull the trigger, however, you deliberately bump my arm so I fire at the drainpipe. The bullet hits the bottle. Your bumping my arm lowered the probability of the bottle's breaking. But arguably, it also explains why the bottle did in fact break (Suppes 1970, 41).

The same sort of case, closer to the principal example of the previous section: Before leaving the party, I check my tires. This slightly decreases the probability of an accident, but as it happens, I collide with a unicyclist on a blind corner. Had I not checked my tires, I would have arrived a little earlier at the corner, and the collision would not have occurred.

Do these explanatorily relevant probability-decreasers refute moderate elitism? As I emphasized in section 10.41, elitism's doctrines apply only within the context of probabilistic explanation; moderate elitism therefore does not rule out the possibility that a factor that decreases the probability of an event might be a part of a deterministic explanation of that event.

And indeed, the explanation of the bottle's breaking that cites your bumping my arm, and the explanation of the collision that cites my checking my tires, are deterministic, or so I maintain, since both probability-decreasers are paradigms of the sort of critical event that, according to the previous section, is explanatory only in a deterministic context. The fact of their making an explanatory contribution, then, is quite compatible with moderate elitism.

What is potentially misleading about these cases is that the optimal explanation in question can go from being deterministic to probabilistic, and so the probability-decreasing factor from relevant to irrelevant, in virtue of a change in the surrounding environment—in particular, the presence of important probability-increasers, such as the bad road and the unicyclists' convention—that does not affect the causal role played by the probability-decreaser itself. If you fail to attend to the question whether the relevant optimal explanation is deterministic or probabilistic, then, you can easily find yourself thinking mistakenly that some probabilistic explanation cites a probability-decreaser for explanatory purposes.

### Explanatory Probability-Increasers

The second objection to moderate elitism challenges the claim that the greater the increase in probability due to a causal factor, the greater the factor's contribution to understanding. Of course, I have shown already that this elitist doctrine is false: if a probability-increaser fails the expanded model test in all relevant models, it makes no contribution at all to understanding (section 11.3). But the objection considered in what follows is quite different; it assumes that the factors in question pass the test for probabilistic difference-making.

Consider two possible deaths for Rasputin. Both involve bombs with probabilistic triggers placed under chairs. In one, the probability that the trigger detonates the bomb is 90%; in the other, the probability is 10%.

Suppose that in both cases the bombs explode. Would one death be better explained than the other? Does the model that cites the 90% probability of detonation provide a better explanation of its target than the model that cites the 10% probability?

On the one hand, the kairetic account's moderate elitism appears to answer in the affirmative: we understand the first death better than the second, because the explanatory models for the two deaths are of equal generality and cohesion but the first is far more accurate than the second (I am putting to use the heuristic that sets an explanatory model's power equal to its combined generality, accuracy, and cohesion; see section 10.24).

On the other hand, the account of probabilistic difference-making presented in section 11.3 suggests an argument for the contrary view. Accuracy in the two models for explosive death quantifies the probability that the triggering makes a difference to the death. As it happens, triggering makes a difference in both deaths. Indeed, it makes the very same difference. Why not consider the explanations equally enlightening, then? True, the more accurate model was antecedently more likely to pass the expanded-model test, but given that both models do in fact pass the test, why prefer one over the other? Better, perhaps, to endorse a kind of moderate egalitarianism: a causal factor's degree of probabilistic relevance is a measure of its chance of making a difference, but (even in the event that it does make a difference) not a measure of its contribution to understanding.

I believe that the former, elitist understanding of the connection between probabilistic difference-making and explanatory quality is correct. It is intuitively clear that we find the explanation citing the higher probability more satisfying, even when we are in no doubt that difference-making occurred in both models and to the same degree.

Yet egalitarians have, as I reported in section 9.53, happily denied this claim. Let me give a more subtle and less introspective argument, then, that in this matter our explanatory practice conforms to the elitist, not the egalitarian, doctrine. Suppose that a range of different causal factors are capable of triggering the bomb under Rasputin's chair. Consider two such factors. When they do trigger the bomb, they make similar, decisive contributions to the ensuing explosion, so that the sole reason to distinguish between them is on the grounds of the probability of difference-making, not on the difference actually made, when it is made. Suppose also that one factor raises the probability of detonation just slightly and the other does not affect the probability at all—in some circumstances it detonates the bomb, but in other equally probable circumstances, it hinders the detonation (compare the host-thanking in section 11.4). Then the latter factor is, in virtue of its probabilistic neutrality, explanatorily irrelevant, whereas the former, probability-increasing factor is a major explainer, if a causal factor's contribution to understanding is independent of its probability of making a difference.

This fits badly with our explanatory practice. If a factor's explanatory status were to depend entirely on such small differences in probability—on the difference between zero and something close to zero—we would be very careful about the values of probability increases when they were near zero. Being off in our estimates of these increases by even the smallest amounts could make the difference between, on the one hand, including important factors and excluding irrelevant factors, and on the other hand, doing the reverse. But instead, we pay little attention to factors that bring small probabilistic increases. The difference, to us, between a factor's conferring no increase in probability and its conferring a minute increase in probability is barely worth investigating. It seems that a factor that confers a small increase in probability thereby carries only a small degree of explanatory importance.

Why should this be? The underlying case for egalitarianism rests on the strength of the link between detonation and death. Because the triggering causes the detonation, it inherits—so the egalitarian says—the explanatory weight of the detonation. The elitist correctly counters that the link between triggering and detonation also matters. An explanation is no better than its weakest link (see the discussion of accuracy in section 10.24); in those cases where the triggering is not a good explanation of the detonation, because it probabilifies the detonation only a little, the explanation of death in which it is embedded suffers accordingly.

To summarize this and the previous section, then: moderate elitism in the change debate is correct with the following italicized qualifications. A factor is explanatorily relevant *in the context of a probabilistic explanation* just in case it raises the probability of the explanandum *and passes the expanded-model test*; if so, its explanatory contribution is proportional to the probability boost.

# — V —

## Valediction

# — 12 —

## Looking Outward

Many long- and short-standing philosophical problems concerning the nature of explanation in almost every branch of the sciences can, I think, be resolved by the kairetic account. This study has proceeded philosophically, organizing aspects of scientific understanding by their underlying explanatory structure rather than by their subject matter. In the present chapter, I will give you a taste of the way in which problems of explanation proper to particular sciences may be resolved using the resources developed above, in the hope that you philosophers of biology, psychology, economics, and so on, will be inspired to apply these resources intensively and systematically in your own work.

### 12.1   Biology: Probabilistic Explanation

Not only is Nature red in tooth and claw; she is irrepressibly stochastic in her violence. Of two equally well-adapted variants, it is more the rule than the exception that one will do better than the other, at any given time, because of chance fluctuations. As a consequence, the explanatory models of evolutionary biology will, not infrequently, have a probabilistic element.

Many philosophers have written on the question of how to understand this statistical aspect of evolutionary modeling and explanation (Sober 1984; Rosenberg 1994; Horan 1994; Glymour 2001; Walsh et al. 2002). I can hardly do justice to this literature here. But I can do justice to the problem: I can make sense of the role of probability in evolutionary explanation.

To do so, I appeal to the thesis that the population dynamics of an ecosystem has the same microconstant structure as the evolution function for a wheel of fortune—though of course, in many more dimensions (Strevens 2003b; see also section 10.25). From this claim, which I cannot defend here, it follows that evolutionarily relevant frequencies such as birth rates, death rates, and so on, can be given microconstant explanations of the sort discussed in section 10.2. Thus, the usual evolutionary explananda, such as

459

a particular allele or trait's becoming fixed in the population, are best explained using probabilistic models.

This is true whether the fixation is by selection or drift—that is, regardless of whether the trait that went to fixation had a systematic advantage over the trait that went to extinction—since the underlying processes of birth, foraging, reproduction, and death are the same, and are microconstant, in both cases. (However, as discussed below, in many cases of explanation by selection, the probabilistic aspect of the explanation will be obscured by idealization.)

Probabilistic models yield the best understanding of evolution by both selection and drift because they allow you to abstract away from many irrelevant causal details, most importantly biological facts that are mere permutators and thus that make no difference to the strike ratios, and to put certain other causally relevant facts, most importantly the macroperiodicity of distributions of actual initial conditions, in the context of a wider pattern of property entanglement.

For example, to understand why one variant went to fixation at the expense of an inferior rival, you do not need to follow the complex causal history of the two groups of organisms as their members live, love, and die over the course of the selection process. You need only see why one trait's strike ratio for some advantageous outcome—long life or reproduction—is higher than the other's.[1] Compare: what is important in understanding why a wheel of fortune with more red than black sections yields a higher frequency of *red* than a regular half-and-half wheel of fortune are the factors that make a difference to the strike ratios—in this case, the fact that one paint scheme has a greater proportion of red. The details of particular trials, or even the details of the paint scheme above and beyond the relative proportions of red, do not matter.

Because of the relation between strike ratios and probability, when you comprehend the wheel of fortune case, you paraphrase your understanding as follows: to see why the one wheel produces *red* more often than the other, you need simply grasp why the probability of *red* on the one is greater than the probability of *red* on the other. Similarly, in the case of the natural selection of one variant at the expense of the other, you take yourself to understand why the one outdid the other when you grasp why the relevant probabilities—of reproduction, death, and so on—differed, or as it is often said, why the mathematical fitness of the successful variant was greater than that of the other.

What about explanations that appeal to drift? In the case of selection, it is possible to use a microconstant model to explain why some particular trait or allele rather than another went to fixation. In the case of drift, by contrast, all that can be explained probabilistically is why traits or alleles went to fixation (or equivalently, why their rivals went extinct) at a certain rate. With the elephant seals, for example, we can explain why many alleles went to extinction—why there was a high rate of extinction—but not why those particular alleles, and not their counterparts, disappeared during the population bottleneck (sections 8.4 and 9.2).[2]

Such explanations unfold as follows. A trait drifts to extinction when it suffers what you might call a run of bad luck. Explaining extinction rates is, then, rather like explaining, in the case of the wheel of fortune, why every so often—though not extremely often—there is a long run of *red* outcomes.[3] (Within a population bottleneck, the run of bad luck required for extinction is much shorter than when the population is large.) Think of such a run as a single event, that is, the event of getting *n red* outcomes in a row. Then what is explained is why this event occurs with a certain frequency, approximately equal to the corresponding strike ratio.

The kairetic account of probabilistic explanation in evolutionary biology turns on the claim that the vast majority of facts about the life and death of competing organisms are irrelevant to understanding facts about fixation and extinction. This proposition has not gone unchallenged in the philosophy of biology literature. Rosenberg (1994), for example, argues that because small causal details about the lives of individual organisms, such as their foraging choices on any particular day, can make a decisive difference to whether they mate or when they die, and because the facts about fixation and extinction are nothing more than an aggregate of the facts about individuals' matings and dyings, the small causal details are explanatorily relevant to fixation and extinction.

The small causal details are indeed difference-makers for evolutionary explananda, in the sense that they are what I called in chapter eleven *critical events*: you can find, for an evolutionary explanandum such as an extinction, a set of small details on which the extinction counterfactually depends. To concede this point does not, however, give Rosenberg what he needs, for as I argued in section 11.4, some critical events for an explanandum may be irrelevant to its explanation. More specifically, a critical event will be explanatorily irrelevant when the proper explanation of the explanandum is probabilistic and the critical event does not appear in the explanatory model as a probability-raiser for the target. Rosenberg's small causal details fit this description exactly: an animal's taking one path rather than another to its foraging ground may have led to its death, but it did not probabilify death. A complete justification for this claim requires an account of the "ecological probabilities" in question, in the context of which it can be shown that such decisions are probabilistically neutral; this is accomplished in Strevens (2003b), some of the principal elements of which are summarized in Strevens (2005).

If the best explanatory models of trait fixation by natural selection are probabilistic, why are so many models proffered in the literature deterministic? The deterministic models make the idealizing assumption that the populations whose behavior they describe are infinite. In this extreme case, the fluctuations due to the stochastic nature of ecological processes effectively disappear; the model consequently takes on a deterministic aspect.

Let me describe the equivalent case on a wheel of fortune. Suppose you are to explain why, of 500 spins on the wheel, approximately one-half yield the outcome *red*. Rather than calculate the probability of the one-half frequency using the actual number of trials, you might assume that there were infinitely many trials, calculating the probability that *red* occurs in such a sequence with a limiting frequency of one-half. Using the law of large numbers, you conclude that the probability is equal to one and therefore deduce the occurrence of the explanandum with something functionally equivalent to certainty. In effect, you cite, as the explanation of the one-half frequency, a deterministic model in which the wheel of fortune determinately produces *red* outcomes with a limiting frequency of one-half—on the manifestly false assumption that there are infinitely many trials.

How to understand this explanatory falsehood? In chapter eight, I proposed that false idealizations should be understood as making, in an indirect way, true claims about what does not make an explanatory difference. In the case of the wheel of fortune, the precise number of trials does not make an explanatory difference to the fact that about one-half were *red*: change the specification that there were 500 trials to the specification of a range—say, that there were between 450 and 600 trials—and nothing that is important about the explanatory model is lost. You still have your derivation of the strike ratio for *red* from the physics of the wheel, of the macroperiodicity of the actual set of initial conditions (now of indeterminate number) from the initial-condition distribution, and the subsequent causal entailment of the one-half frequency. Clearly, the number of trials can be muddied further; in the end, what makes a difference is solely that there were a substantial number of trials, a condition that is satisfied even by the obviously fictitious model that posits an infinite number of trials. (A hiccup: the exact number of trials does make a difference to the exact probability of obtaining the approximate frequency, though when the number of trials is large, the difference is slight. Is the exact number of trials not therefore explanatorily relevant in a small way after all? It is possible that we are here trading off accuracy for generality. Or it may well be that the probability that figures in the evolutionary explanation of a nonquantitative explanandum such as trait fixation is in reality a quasiprobability, and thus has no exact value; altering the number of trials, while keeping it large, will make no difference to a quasiprobability, which has only a qualitative magnitude, such as "very high.")

The role of idealizations is to advertise particular facts about non-difference-making, by setting parameters that do not make a difference to zero or default values, and more generally by replacing aspects of the model that do not make a difference with especially simple or default structures. In the case of the number of trials, a zero value is of course ruled out. An infinite value is allowed and, furthermore, makes the derivation of the explanandum quite straightforward (provided that you have the law of large numbers in hand). An idealized model that assumes infinitely many spins on the wheel of fortune is therefore a natural choice to make if you wish to explain a one-half frequency of *red* in 500 spins in way that highlights the fact that the exact number of spins made no difference to the frequency.

In many explanations of trait or allele fixation by natural selection, the relevant actual population levels make no difference for much the same reason: had the levels been somewhat different, the trait would very likely have gone to fixation anyway. There are two exceptions. First, if the population levels are low, then there is a substantial chance that the fitter trait will not go to fixation in a given time frame; a run of bad luck might drive it to extinction or, less dramatically, preserve some organisms with the less fit trait. Second, if what is to be explained is not just the fact of fixation but the time taken to go to fixation, then the population levels will be difference-makers. When these exceptions do not apply, an idealizing explanation that assumes infinite populations, thereby emphasizing the explanatory unimportance of population levels, is apt.

Typically, models of natural selection in infinite populations have a structurally idealized form: they are mathematically deterministic. If my proposal concerning the role of the idealization is correct, however, a deterministic model of this sort represents a probabilistic model, in the sense that it communicates the content of a canonical explanatory model that is explicitly probabilistic—the probabilistic model that specifies only that the relevant populations are large and derives an equally large and indeterminate probability for the episode of trait fixation that is to be explained. In short, once you learn to see through the surface form of the idealized models to their explanatory content, you will appreciate that, despite their deterministic appearances, they are probabilistic models. There is far more probabilistic explanation in evolutionary biology than a shallow reading of the textbooks would suggest.

The same is true, I believe, in population ecology (which studies the dynamics of ecosystem populations, regardless of whether or not it leads to evolution). Deterministic models are the norm in population ecology, in explanation and elsewhere, but it would be a mistake to conclude that population ecologists believe that an ecosystem's population levels at one time completely determine its population levels at another, that is, that the fluctuations in population levels that constitute the very real phenomenon of genetic drift are nonexistent. Rather, you should conclude that with respect to many of the phenomena that population ecologists wish to model, the fluctuations make no difference: with or without the fluctuations there is a high probability that the phenomenon in question—say, the manifestation of a predator/prey population cycle—occurs. (The exceptions mentioned above, for low populations and more detailed explananda, of course apply here as well.)

In population ecology as in evolutionary biology, then, many deterministic models should be understood, for explanatory and perhaps other purposes, as standing in for probabilistic models. It is therefore not merely that a deterministic model is used to model a stochastic process—an unremarkable observation. A deterministic model is used to *represent a probabilistic model*, which in turn models the real-world process.

## 12.2   Psychology: Content and Explanation

The problem of the explanatory role of propositional attitudes in belief/desire explanations of reasoning and behavior is traditional and perhaps a little tired, but because it has been so much discussed, it serves as an excellent proxy for both the question of the explanatory role of "wide" properties and the question of the explanatory role of functional properties in the special sciences generally.

My belief that it is raining seems to play an important role in explaining my decision to pick up an umbrella as I leave my apartment. Further, the explanation in question appears to be causal: the belief sets in motion a train of thought leading to my umbrella-snagging in roughly the same way that the cue ball sets the eight ball in motion, or so I will assume. The belief is therefore causally relevant to the behavior to be explained. But is the property of its being that belief—the property of being a belief that it is raining—explanatorily relevant?

It may seem not, on the grounds that, first, relevance in such an explanation must be causal relevance, and second, the belief property itself cannot be causally relevant to the behavior. Though it is the former premise that the kaireticist will reject, I will organize my discussion around two arguments for the latter premise, beginning with the argument from wide content.

Some of the properties constitutive of being a belief that it is raining—in particular, some of the properties constitutive of the content of the belief—lie outside the head and thus are unavailable to do mental work. Part of what it is for a brain state to be a belief about rain, for example, is for it to stand in a certain causal relation to water, that is, to participate in a certain head-world relation (or so many philosophers suppose). This relationship cannot play a causal role in the train of thought leading from the belief to the decision to take the umbrella, it seems, because that train of thought occurs entirely in virtue of properties that lie within the skull (Stich 1978).

One attempt to restore to wide belief properties an explanatory role is Jackson and Pettit's (1990) notion of program explanation, discussed in section 7.34. The idea is that the instantiation of the belief property, though not itself directly causally relevant to the behavior, necessitates the instantiation of an underlying causally relevant property $P$. This is enough, on Jackson and Pettit's view, to confer explanatory relevance on the belief property itself. I cannot agree with this proposal, for the reasons given in my earlier discussion of program explanation, but it is a step toward the correct story.

Another attempt to find an explanatory role for belief properties looks to relations of counterfactual dependence between behaviors and the properties we suppose to explain them. Lepore and Loewer (1987) suggest that, had the mental state that is my belief that it is raining not had the property of being that belief, it would not have caused me to decide to pick up the umbrella (more exactly, the mental state that is my decision to pick up the umbrella would not have had the property of being that decision). This counterfactual dependence relation is similar enough to a causal relation, Lepore and Loewer contend, to confer a kind of weak causal relevance on the belief property.

The kairetic account of explanation is able to understand the explanatory relevance of a wide belief property in a way that, although it is independently motivated in chapter seven, might be seen as a hybrid of these two accounts: the belief property is noncausally but explanatorily relevant to the causation of the umbrella-taking because it is entangled with $P$, the underlying psychological or neural property in virtue of which the belief that it is raining causes the umbrella-taking. The belief property is relevant to the behavior, then, in the same way that ravenhood is relevant to blackness.

I will not attempt to defend here the claim that the belief property is entangled with the appropriate $P$. However, I remind you of two reasons that entanglement is easier to come by than you might think. First, entanglement requires only that my belief's $P$-hood survive local manipulations. Beliefs that it is raining need not have $P$ wherever they are found, or even wherever they are found in the human race—or even in me. Perhaps sometimes my belief that it is raining has $P$, sometimes $Q$. What matters for entanglement is that on this occasion it has $P$, and that small changes in my present situation will not undermine this $P$-hood.[4] Second, the entanglement requires only that, had the mental state that is my belief not had the belief property, then it *might very well* not have had $P$. It is not required that the removal of the belief property definitely remove $P$.

Entanglement is, as these remarks show and as I have remarked elsewhere, a rather weak relation; so weak, in fact, that it is quite possible that ineffable properties such as (on many views) moral properties could be entangled with physical, causally efficacious properties. If so, moral properties could appear in the antecedent of a legitimate basing generalization and so come to play a role in scientific explanation—even if their existence is entirely outside the realm of causality. Perhaps, for example, an action's property of being morally obligatory, or a desire's property of being reasonable, or a belief's property of being objectively compelling, is entangled, in some fortunate individuals, with physical properties that play a role in the causal explanation of the individuals' performance of the obligatory, their pursuit of the good, or their acting on sound reasons. Then these nonnatural properties (if such they are) would have an explanatory role to play in making sense of the operation of the human psyche.

An alternative strategy for understanding the explanatory relevance of propositional attitudes is motivated by a different argument for the causal irrelevance of the mental. Suppose (controversially, perhaps) that the propositional attitudes are defined in part by their inferential roles. Part of what it is for a mental state to be the desire to have another martini, for example, might be that state's ability, under certain circumstances, to cause an intention to have another martini. Uncontroversially, a person's desiring another martini is well able to explain their forming such an intention, and further, one state's having the property of being the desire is explanatorily relevant to the other state's having the property of being the intention. But how can a property defined in terms of its ability to cause the instantiation of another property contribute to a substantive explanation of that instantiation? Is this not the case of the dormitive virtue (section 4.33) all over again (Block 1990)?

In section 5.42, I proposed that functional properties in legitimate causal explanations play the role of black boxes, standing in for the genuinely causal properties of mechanisms that have been placed in the explanatory framework. The desire to have another martini figures in a psychological explanation of the corresponding intention legitimately, I suggest, just in case the causal process by which the desire causes the intention has been frameworked for the purpose of the explanation. Belief/desire explanation of this sort constitutes, in other words, a kind of functional analysis in which the physical implementation of the cognitive system in question is explanatorily parenthesized—placed in the explanatory framework—and then black-boxed. As a result, the physical properties of the desire in virtue of which it has the power to cause the intention need not (indeed cannot) figure in the explanation.

This understanding of the explanatory role of functional properties adheres to the conventional wisdom that such properties are not causally relevant. But it resists the conventional conclusion, that the desire property, or at least the functional aspect of the desire property, is out of place in the explanation of the intention. Though not explanatorily relevant in the narrow sense, it serves a quite legitimate explanatory function: it stands in for a causally relevant property that has been consigned to the framework. The same understanding, I should add, dissolves problems raised by the radical multiple realizability of functional properties (Kim 1992).

Two caveats on the suggestions made in this section. First, I have told two quite different stories as to how properties definitive of the propositional attitudes might be explanatory: they might be entangled with causally relevant properties, or they might stand in for causally relevant properties in the framework. Can both stories be correct? Perhaps: the first story might apply to the content, or propositional part, of the attitudes, the second to the attitudinal part (that is, the part that distinguishes your desire to drink another martini from your belief that you are drinking another martini). It is possible even that a propositional attitude property stands in for a frameworked property that is itself explanatorily relevant by way of entanglement. Not knowing what kinds of properties are in fact constitutive of beliefhood, desirehood, and so on, I will say no more.

Second, some philosophers of mind might disdain the explanatory relevance conferred on belief, desire, and other propositional attitude properties by way of either entanglement or a placeholder role. Noncausal explanatory relevance is not sufficient, they will protest, to rescue our pretheoretical intuitions about the importance of belief properties to behavior (Fodor 1989). That is a debate for philosophers of mind. It is enough for the philosophy of psychology that the practice of citing propositional attitude properties in the explanation of behavior is not scientifically flawed.

## 12.3   Economics: Abstraction

Strange that the social science concerned exclusively with the basest human motivations should have the most abstract, almost mathematical, conception of human nature. Some forms of naked desire are apparently in their aggregate effect closer to Newtonian mechanics than to Freudian hydraulics. Why is so much economics so abstract?

There are two respects, I think, in which economics seems to float free of its roots in human behavior. First, it appears to be apsychological: the most familiar economic model of the individual, the relentless maximizer of expected utility *Homo economicus*, lacks a great deal of the mental life that makes real human beings such interesting subjects for scientific research. Second, it can appear to be acausal: economic phenomena are not infrequently explained by citing their optimality without specifying the motive power that drives them to their optimal point. I should add that there is a recognizably "economic" approach in other social sciences that has some of the same features: a mathematical model of human action that dispenses with humanity itself, and in many cases, a concern with optimality that looks more teleological than causal.

The kairetic account provides the means to appreciate that economic explanations are quite causal and quite psychological. The appearance of acausality arises from an appeal to equilibrium explanation, in which what is cited are not particular causes but features of the laws and systemic structure in virtue of which any set of particular causes will lead to the same outcome. I defended this causal interpretation of equilibrium explanation against Sober's contrary view in section 7.41.

The appearance of independence from human psychology arises from the fact that most aspects of our psychology make no difference to the occurrence of economic explananda. The canonical explanation of such explananda will therefore abstract away from these non-difference-making psychological facets of humanity. A natural idealization then presents itself: rather than making no claim about the presence or importance of psychological elements that make no difference, construct an idealized model in which they are assumed not to exist (as suggested in section 8.32). Hence, the unattractive but explanatory economic automata of Microeconomics 101.

Why is the economically relevant facet of human psychology such a meager part of the whole? Is it because the salient economic processes are steered by the decisions of a highly professional class of decision makers, trained to focus on utility maximization—trained to emulate, as it were, *Homo economicus*? Is it because expected utility maximization is both *ceteris paribus* desirable and orthogonal to other cognitive pursuits, so that it runs its course with little or no interference from other and higher components of the mind's activity? Neither of these answers is adequate. The truth is more interesting: the human decisions on which economic processes depend are affected by many of the elements of human psychology absent in *H. economicus*. But the properties of these processes that we wish to explain depend on the existence of patterns in the decisions that exist also in the corresponding decisions of a simple expected utility maximizer (or perhaps a simple maximizer with one or two tics, such as risk aversion). That is, although a series of economic decisions made by *Homo sapiens* will be different in many ways from a series of economic decisions made by *Homo economicus*—although the decisions will in many ways be differently patterned—there is at least one pattern that they share, and it is this pattern, perhaps one of approximate or loosely implemented maximization, that drives and thus accounts for many of the economic phenomena that we wish to understand. To uncover the reasons for the importance of this pattern, and so the unimportance of many other aspects of our economic decision making, is a problem for philosophers of economics—perhaps *the* problem. I will leave it to them.

## 12.4   Explanatory Autonomy

Are the special or high-level sciences in some sense independent from physics? Are they, in particular, explanatorily autonomous? It depends what you mean by *independence* or *autonomy*.

In the strongest sense of the term, a high-level explanation is independent of physics if the understanding that it conveys cannot be captured in purely physical language. This kind of autonomy, then, precludes what you might call explanatory physicalism, the doctrine that everything that can be explained can be explained physically.

The kairetic account is consistent with and indeed vindicates explanatory physicalism, provided that two conditions hold:

1. All relations of causal influence relevant to the high-level sciences can be captured in physical terms.

2. All relations of property entanglement relevant to the high-level sciences can be captured in physical terms.

I have assumed throughout this study that relations of causal influence are invariably physical, and more particularly, that high-level causal relations are abstract relational properties of fundamental-level causal relations (sections 3.23 and 3.3, respectively). If I am right, the first condition holds. What of the second? It will hold if every property that is cited in the antecedent of a basing generalization, anywhere in the high-level sciences, can be defined physically.

I doubt that this is true: there is a real possibility that some properties deployed for explanatory purposes in the high-level sciences cannot be characterized in purely physical terms. More exactly, with respect to these properties, some variety of nonreductive physicalism holds: the instances of the properties are physical, but the shared feature in virtue of which the instances instantiate the property cannot be captured using the expressive power of physical language alone. It is my guess that species membership properties such as ravenhood are irreducible in this sense. Let me assume, for the sake of the argument, that the guess is correct. Then a claim such as *Ravenhood is entangled with P-hood* cannot be translated into the vocabulary of physics. Is the thesis of explanatory physicalism thereby disproved?

It is not. For explanatory physicalism to survive, there must be some way of capturing the pattern of entanglement between ravenhood and $P$ in physical terms. That is, there must be some way of making claims such as these:

1. Most or all actual ravens have $P$.

2. A certain range of counterfactual changes to those ravens will leave their $P$-hood undisturbed, except in the case where the change removes the bird's ravenhood.

3. A certain range of counterfactual changes to actual systems that bring nonactual ravens into existence (e.g., mating two ravens who in actuality never meet) will produce ravens with $P$.

In order to capture the truth conditions of such claims, it is not necessary to capture the essence of ravenhood (if there is such a thing) but only its "intension," that is, its extension in various possible worlds. Further, because the claims are restricted to ravens and would-be ravens in a narrow range of possible worlds similar to our own, what must be captured is not the extension of ravenhood in every possible world, but only its extension in these nearby "basing worlds." The physical ineffability of ravenhood does not rule out the existence of a physical expression picking out all and only the ravens in the basing worlds. Indeed, it seems to me that it would be relatively easy to construct such an expression, given that the basing worlds are so close to actuality that they share substantial portions of the actual world's evolutionary history and other biological detail. For a more careful statement of the case, including the argument that the import of the exception clause to condition (2) can be captured using any expression that is extensionally equivalent in the basing worlds to *ravenhood*, I refer you to Strevens (manuscript).

I conclude, then, that under some plausible assumptions (physicality of the causal; physical capture of all explanatory extensions in the basing worlds), the kairetic account entails explanatory physicalism. Does this leave any prospect for explanatory autonomy?

Characterize autonomy in the following rather loose way: a high-level explanation is autonomous if it has an unphysical aspect. There are as many varieties of autonomy as there are ways to be "unphysical." First, you might consider an explanatory model to be unphysical if it cites high-level properties that abstract away from low-level causal details (Kitcher 1984; Lange 2000, §8.7). The kairetic theory provides a good account of the fact that many high-level explanations are unphysical in this sense: low-level details tend not to make a difference to whether high-level explananda occur (section 4.4). Such details must therefore be omitted from the explanatory model—though of course, the model is in one important way no less physical for the omission, since it is a description of just those aspects of the physics of the situation in virtue of which the explanandum occurs.

Second, you might consider an explanatory model to be unphysical if it cites high-level properties that are physically irreducible. The kairetic theory can account for this kind of unphysicality too: a physically irreducible property is explanatorily relevant to a phenomenon if it is entangled with a property that is, with respect to the same phenomenon, causally relevant.

Third, you might consider an explanatory model to be unphysical if it hinges on mathematical, rather than physical, facts. The kairetic theory understands such explanations as examples of profound causal abstraction (section 8.4).

In sum, the kairetic theory of explanation accounts for, and in the case of causal abstraction requires, certain substantive and interesting varieties of explanatory autonomy in the high-level sciences—but not the extreme autonomy that refutes explanatory physicalism.

# — 13 —

## Looking Inward

There are, traditionally, three rewards for successful explanation. The first is metaphysical: insight into the inner workings of the universe. The second is more practical: with successful explanation comes, often enough, greater predictive power and control over nature. Philosophers have fixed their gaze on these first two rewards. In times when metaphysical insight has seemed unattainable, the practical virtues of the explanatory quest have necessarily been emphasized. Hempel and Oppenheim's assertion of the symmetry of explanation and prediction is, whatever its faults, a doctrine of great ideological purity.

What has been neglected is the third reward for successful explanation, the aesthetic reward. Some explanations are simply beautiful, an intrinsic virtue and an end in itself. But why a concern for beauty in an enterprise whose worldly image is a composition of white coats, exposed wiring, statistical analysis, and dubious haircuts?

Perhaps the beautiful in science is inseparable from the simple, and perhaps also, simple theories are better than complex theories—more likely to be true and easier to use. Then, in the same way that a taste for sweet things encourages the consumption of high-energy foods and a taste for clear skin encourages conjugation with healthy mates, a taste for beauty encourages the construction of simple explanations. Beauty's function is to catch the scientist's eye in such a way as to direct attention toward what is truly worth having.

In this final short chapter, I will propose a different, though similarly shaped, answer to the question of the role of beauty in explanation, suggested by the structure of the kairetic account. I begin by remarking on a similarity between the kairetic account and its principal rival.

In its conception of the explanatory relation, the kairetic account stands alongside other causal accounts. But in its form—I am thinking of the optimizing procedure for determining causal difference-making—it bears a surprising resemblance to the pattern-subsumption approach. (There is also, of course, an explicit subsumptionist element to the kairetic account, in its treatment of basing generalizations, but it is causal relevance that is my subject here.)

To appreciate the similarity, compare the standard form for a pattern-subsumption account laid out in section 1.32 with the optimizing procedure as presented in section 3.7. According to the optimizing procedure, those factors are explanatorily relevant that appear in a causal model best satisfying the following three criteria:

1. Accuracy, that is, the similarity between the model's target and the explanandum

2. Generality, that is, the abstractness of the model, and therefore, roughly, the number of possible physical systems that fit the model

3. Cohesion, that is, the extent to which the model represents a single kind of causal process and not a disjunction of several processes

According to the pattern-subsumption account, those factors are explanatorily relevant that appear in a model generating a pattern best satisfying the following three criteria:

1. Accuracy, that is, the degree of fit between the pattern and the explanandum[1]

2. Generality, that is, the number and perhaps variety of actual phenomena that fall under the pattern

3. Cohesion, that is, the extent to which the pattern is a single pattern and not a disjunction of more than one pattern

Why do these criteria for explanatory relevance have so much in common? It is to be expected that proponents of the pattern-subsumption account should, like any philosophers working on explanation, be drawn to criteria that capture our explanatory practice. Thus, there ought to be some convergence among the more sophisticated accounts of explanation, in form if not in fundamental approach.

Yet this cannot be the whole answer. The form I have given for the pattern-subsumption account is not the byproduct of many years of attempts to make the account fit the explanatory facts. It characterizes a conception of pattern that seems valid to us independently of and antecedently to any concern with explanation. What conception? The pattern picked out by the account as the explainer of a phenomenon is not always the one that most obviously subsumes the phenomenon; it is, however, the pattern that subsumes a phenomenon most strikingly. (As an example of nonobvious but dramatic subsumption, consider the effect of seeing that the parabolic motion of terrestrial projectiles and the elliptical motion of heavenly bodies are both instances of inverse-square-law behavior.) Let me suppose, then, that the criteria for explanatory pattern subsumption reflect our best account of *striking* pattern subsumption.

This provokes a new question: why should the difference-makers picked out by the optimizing procedure for some explanandum be the same causal factors that, when assembled into a model, generate the pattern of events that most strikingly subsumes the explanandum? Or to put it another way, why should a taste for striking subsumption lead you toward facts about difference-making? Perhaps this "strikingness" in a pattern is the phenomenological expression of a psychological tendency pulling us from explanandum to explainers. Perhaps, that is, our mind is built so that patterns of difference-making seem especially salient to us—when perceptible, they leap out at us, insisting on our attention—and this salience is what we are referring to when we describe a pattern as striking. Now take a further step, supposing that the sense of what is striking is at least in part an aesthetic sense, and a connection between beauty and explanation becomes clear: an eye for striking beauty of a certain sort is an eye for the explanatory.

There is hardly a perfect parallel between beauty, pattern subsumption, and difference-making. Some striking patterns have nothing to do with explanation. Humans and animals alike are struck by bilateral symmetry in part, it seems, because it is the characteristic symmetry of the face. And there are paisley, Pucci, and the pyramids. The Platonic thesis that love of beauty is just an unconscious urge to understand is, then, hardly credible. Let me conclude by advancing two less extreme possibilities.

Suppose that, by a stroke of luck, the pattern-subsumption criteria for a certain kind of beauty happened to resemble, perhaps only roughly, the criteria for difference-making. Those gifted with the right aesthetic sense would be able to pick out the difference-makers from the background better than the rest, like the color-sighted among the colorblind picking out red berries in the woods. For this reason, the aesthetic sense might have been hijacked and honed to the point where every one of us is able to recognize a profound explanation by its peculiar beauty.

Or suppose, as some have suggested (Simon 1996, 2), that the human aesthetic faculty is just our sense of pattern. (This would explain why beauty is connected to some of the senses—sight and hearing—and not others—taste and smell.) Any cognitive process that involves the detection of patterns will thereby count as engaging in the pursuit of beauty, in one of its many forms. Your search for difference-makers is a search for elements that figure in a certain kind of pattern. Thus, it involves the exercise of an aesthetic sense, an endeavor that takes a certain kind of beauty as its object. Should your search succeed, then, you will hold up your discovery as an object of beauty—and your pleasure in your success will be, in part, an aesthetic delight.

# Notes

## Chapter 1

1. *Kairetic* is my own coinage, loosely inspired by the ancient Greek *kairos*, meaning a crucial moment.

2. For this "erotetic" approach to explanation see Bromberger (1965, 1966), van Fraassen (1980), Achinstein (1983), and for a judicious assessment of the topic's place in the philosophy of explanation, Salmon (1990b, §2.2).

3. The relevance problem affects the expectability version, as well as the pattern-subsumption version, of the DN account. For attempts to deal with the problem that could be appropriated by a Hempelian, but which make no explicit appeal to pattern subsumption, see Salmon (1979) and Fetzer (1981).

4. You might measure accuracy either by the match between the pattern and the whole world, or by the match between the pattern and the parts of the world that are to be explained. Nothing too important turns on the choice; I note, however, that when the kairetic account invokes a notion of accuracy, it is of the latter variety.

5. For more on accuracy, generality, and other properties of models, see Weisberg (2003).

6. This problem was first noted by Hempel himself. He provides a purely syntactic solution for the case in which the explanandum is an event in the original DN paper (Hempel and Oppenheim 1948, §7). He is, however, unable to find a formal solution for the case in which the explanandum is a law (§7, n33); see section 7.1. The solution for events was later challenged, then amended to meet the challenge, and so on. See Salmon (1990b, §1.1) for a short history.

7. A somewhat different attempt by a proponent of the pattern-subsumption approach to say why the subsumption of a dissolution event under the salt/ravens law is not explanatory is Kitcher's introduction of a desideratum of *stringency* (Kitcher 1981, §8). The stringency of a model is a complex property; I will not try to define it here.

8. You might hold that the nature of the explanatory relation is a relative matter, but deny that it has changed over human history, on the grounds, for example, that the relation is relative to some set of facts fixed by human nature. This is

477

not what I mean here by *relativism*; indeed, everything I have to say about the kairetic account is consistent with this view.

9. The argument was urged in modern times by Sylvain Bromberger, though something similar can be found in Aristotle (*Posterior Analytics*, 78a). Aristotle might also be credited, no doubt with a few scholarly caveats, as an early causal theorist of explanation and as originating the view that causal explanations ought to be put in deductive form, with the logic of the derivation reflecting the causal order.

10. It is, in another sense, far less selective: as explained in section 6.32, it counts vast numbers of omissions as causes.

11. Recently, Lewis has defined a relation of causal influence much like the relation characterized here (the main difference being, as you might expect, that influence is a matter of chains of dependence) and has tried to give an account of causation between high-level events in terms of influence—in effect relinquishing the multilevel approach to causation and opting for a fundamental-level approach after all. See Lewis (2000), and for arguments against the account, Strevens (2003a) among others.

12. For a strictly correct treatment of the barometer case, a counterfactually defined notion of causal influence must, like Dowe's, admit of degrees, so that the influence of the barometer on the storm can be declared negligible. It is appropriate here to look to Lewis's own recent attempt to quantify influence (see note 11), which turns on the degree of change in the concrete realizer of the putative effect *e* that would be obtained by making small changes in the concrete realizer of the putative cause *c*.

13. In a review of Woodward's work (Strevens 2007a), I understood him as offering such a metaphysics himself, an interpretation that he has since, in my view rather tendentiously, repudiated.

14. Such a view should not be confused with the thesis that a certain fact about causation at the fundamental level, namely its direction, depends on statistical patterns that emerge only at a higher level of description and that do not exist in every physical system. Notions of causal influence that satisfy this latter thesis are quite sufficient for an explanatory causalist, and for the kairetic account in particular. Indeed, Dowe's view is among them.

15. David Lewis suggests that "making it happen" talk should be considered legitimate even in a Humean metaphysics, since such talk is nothing more than a nomological or causal idiom—an oblique way of talking about laws and causation. Realists disagree, holding by contrast that such talk captures an aspect of laws and causation absent in the Humean treatment. Many empiricists also disagree; they conclude that an empiricist metaphysics must sacrifice long-

held beliefs about the "event-making" power of causal processes—or perhaps even the notions of law and cause themselves (van Fraassen 1989).

## Chapter 2

1. For both Dowe and Lewis, causation is transitive by definition. On a manipulation view it is not, and transitivity fails for high-level causation, but I conjecture manipulation causation between concrete events—in other words, the manipulationist's version of causal influence—will always, or almost always, be transitive.

2. A suggestion made by Davidson (1967, 160–161).

3. An alternative response is to maintain that poison is irrelevant because it is screened off from Rasputin's death by his being thrown into the river (see section 1.47). This strategy will succeed only if influviation cannot fail to cause death—perhaps true in Rasputin's case, but obviously not true in any number of variant cases. An appeal to screening off will not do, then, as a general solution to the problem.

4. Hitchcock (1993) discusses the parallel problem for probabilistic accounts of causal, as opposed to explanatory, relevance.

5. For the complete account of event causation, see Woodward (2003, §2.7) and the work of Halpern, Pearl, and Hitchcock, on which Woodward's approach is based (Pearl 2000; Halpern and Pearl 2005; Hitchcock 2001a, 2001b).

   Although in what follows I treat only Woodward's "actual causes" as explanatorily relevant, Woodward himself at times appears to advocate a broader conception of the explanatory relation on which some events that were not actual causes of the explanandum nevertheless play a part in its explanation because they are potential causes—factors, knowledge of which would give you the power, in principle, to manipulate events like the explanandum. What implications this has for the explanatory relevance of, say, poisoning to the death of Rasputin, it is hard to say (Strevens 2007a).

6. Such graphs do not always provide the resources to evaluate counterfactuals in the Lewis manner, since they represent only one small part of any of the relevant closest possible worlds. In this case, however, the other regions of the relevant worlds may be safely ignored.

## Chapter 3

1. Strictly speaking, not every step in a causal entailment will represent a relation of causal influence. Using a typical system of natural deduction, for example, to get to $e$'s $Q$-hood from $c$'s $P$-hood by way of the causal law you will

first have to apply a rule of and-introduction to get from P($c$) and $Z$ to the antecedent of the law, the conjunction P($c$) $\wedge$ $Z$. Clearly the and-introduction does not represent a causal fact (or, I suppose, any nontrivial fact). It is groups of steps rather than individual steps, then, that must mirror a causal process in order for a derivation to constitute a causal entailment.

2. I am assuming that the negative condition is a part of any model that entails death, regardless of whether it mentions Mars. This might not be true of a model (which could never exist in practice) that specifies every gravitational influence in detail. In such a model, the removal of Mars will be a part of an abstraction operation that produces such a condition; see section 3.52.

3. Concerning the DN account of explanation and the problems arising from the appeal to essential roles in entailment, see Salmon (1990b, §1.1). For a discussion of similar difficulties for hypothetico-deductivism, see Glymour (1980, chap. 2), and for Mackie's account of causation, Kim (1971).

4. I assume here a metaphysics of causal influence that draws only on fundamental laws; any of the three theories discussed in chapter one would, I think, qualify.

5. The case of the indeterministic bomb under the chair (sections 2.3 and 11.3) shows that it is possible to see that something derailed a process even when, in a certain sense, there is no fact of the matter as to what went wrong.

6. The eliminative procedure does count the fact of the ball's being rather heavy as a difference-maker; simply start with a model that says no more about the ball's mass than that it is considerable. The problem, then, is not that the fact of rough mass is not counted as a difference-maker, but that the exact mass, too, is said to be a difference-maker.

7. Why is part (a) of the definition necessary? There are two senses in which $M$ might be more abstract than $M'$: it might say less about the causal process represented by $M'$ than $M'$ itself, or it might say less about the causal influences represented by $M'$ than $M'$ itself. It is the second, strictly stronger, notion that is wanted here. What is the difference? Suppose that $M'$ tells the complete story about the deterministic causal production of $e$ starting two minutes before $e$ occurred. A model that tells the complete causal story starting one minute before $e$ occurred is an abstraction of $M'$ in the first sense (because its entire setup is entailed by $M'$'s setup), but not the second.

8. There is one other principal ingredient of the high-level laws, and thus one other important determinant of high-level scientific structure: the basing patterns discussed in chapter seven.

9. To put it technically, contiguity requires for its foundation only a topology, not a metric; in practice, I would guess, the foundation for the topology is

likely to be a local metric, and judgments of long-distance similarity, though unnecessary, will not be unknown.

10. Or if they do—by way of a simultaneous poisoning/influviation where an infinitesimal adjustment makes the difference between death by poison and death by drowning—they touch only at a singularity. Let me declare this kind of "barely there" contiguity insufficient for cohesion.

## Chapter 4

1. This I take to be the primary notion of explanatory depth. Another notable notion of depth will be examined in section 4.36. Some of the extant philosophical literature on depth in explanation is best interpreted, I think, as attempting to capture this "second axis of depth"; see note 4.

2. For reasons that will be illustrated in section 8.32, the causal relationships represented by a causal model's follow-through ought to be regarded as a separate and substantial component of the causal facts picked out by the model, standing alongside the initial conditions and laws picked out by the model's setup as a part of the complete explanation in the ontological sense. These facts will also constitute a part of a covering law's "underlying mechanism" (see note 22 of chapter 7).

3. I identify the dormitive virtue, then, with the functional property of being sleep producing, rather than with the physical property in virtue of which the potion has the functional property. Only in this former sense is citing the dormitive virtue an example of black-boxing. However, citing the physical property as "the sleep-producing property" will also create the problem laid out in what follows, namely, that the logical derivation of sleep will not mirror the causal production of sleep.

4. The accounts of explanatory depth provided by Hempel (1965a, 345) and Hitchcock and Woodward (2003) might be read as alternative characterizations of depth along the second axis. Hempel connects depth to the generality and (more or less) the accuracy of an explanatory model, in the pattern subsumptionist's sense (section 1.32). Hitchcock and Woodward equate the depth of an explanatory causal model with the in-principle manipulative power it bestows on its user, meaning the range of changes in the "object or system that is the focus of explanation" that can be brought about by performing the sorts of manipulations whose effects the model describes (p. 182).

5. The maxims are from, respectively, Matthew 22:29 (and elsewhere) in the King James Version; Plato's *Phaedo*, 67e (as translated by Hugh Tredennick); Hunter S. Thompson, *Generation of Swine*.

## Chapter 5

1. There are a number of different ways to quantify weight in a probabilistic model; for some examples, see Pearl (2000, chap. 9).

2. In the probabilistic case (see below), the assumption is unlikely to hold, in which case weight will have to be relativized to a kernel. This is not a problem, since the question of a causal factor's weight is typically raised in the context of a particular explanatory model.

3. The time limit is imposed in order to forestall complications threatened by the possibly chaotic dynamics of the solar system.

4. Unless, of course, such events play a dual causal role, making a difference to other factors not in the framework. The complications arising are discussed at length in chapter six; see in particular sections 6.1 and 6.5.

5. The setup of a black box therefore contains one or more free variables. So far, I have dealt only with causal models that fully specify their initial conditions and thus that have setups containing no variables at all; such models capture particular chunks of the world's causal history. A black box is more naturally conceived of as a type-level model, representing a kind of causal process rather than any particular token process. Type-level models are introduced in section 7.2; the notion is intuitive enough, however, and I will proceed here on a provisional basis.

6. The relations between an explanatory model's various black boxes may be quite complex, if for example the inputs and outputs of a particular black box are themselves functional properties. Let me give two examples in which this complexity is less formidable than it may appear.

   A economics black box representing a process by which a central bank increases the money supply may relate levels of currency, itself a functional kind. In this case, I think, anything capable of serving as input or output of the black box in question will by that very token satisfy the functional definition of currency. The definition itself is therefore explanatorily otiose, and so adds nothing to the complexity of the model.

   A psychological black box representing an inferential process may have as its inputs and outputs propositional attitudes, which some philosophers define in terms of the inferential roles that they play in the mind. Here, the black box simply makes explicit the relevant elements of the functional definition of the propositional attitudes, without adding further complexity.

   I do not want to underestimate the potential difficulties in unraveling heavily functionalized explanations. Not every black box relating propositional attitudes, for example, is a mere unpacking of the functional role constituting those attitudes: think of the Davidsonian case in which the climber's fear of falling causes him to loosen his grip on the rope. Here, the functional role in virtue of which the culpable mental state qualifies as a fear of falling appears to be unrelated to the causal process. Perhaps it ought to be ignored altogether, rather than treated as an essential part of the explanation (though see section 12.2). In any case, I will not try to resolve these issues here; it is motivation enough for the ensuing discussion that certain black-boxing explanations provide a real challenge to the kairetic account.

7. There is a kinship between the pragmatic approach to black-boxing explanations and the pragmatic accounts of which difference-makers count as "the cause," and hence "the explanation," of an event in which contexts offered by Hanson (1958, 54), van Fraassen (1980, chap. 5), and Lewis (1986a, 215–216).

8. What is called the "hard-sphere dynamics," in which molecules bounce off one another like (classical) billiard balls, is a limiting case of powerful short-range repulsive forces—the range goes to zero and the force to infinity—thus, hard-sphere scattering is causally contiguous with scattering produced by short-range forces.

9. Lipton (2004) gives a good, if informal, treatment of the "aggregative" variety of contrastive explanation; he claims that the same account can in some sense be given of the pure variety, although he concedes that it is something of a stretch. He is certainly correct in thinking that there is considerable overlap in the way that the machinery of explanation works in the two cases. There would be some value to bringing out the commonalities, but I will leave that as an exercise to the reader.

10. Without the "relative plausibility" or "closeness" requirement, almost any difference-maker for death could qualify as a contrastive difference-maker by piggy-backing on the real switch. To make the reliability of influviation as a murder method into a switch, for example, take the contrastive dyad consisting of the veridical model for Rasputin's influviation and a fictional model for his incineration in which a volcano is nearby and influviation is unreliable because Rasputin can breathe underwater. Provided that the incineration model contains no other falsehoods, the dyad satisfies the first three conditions for being a contrastive explanation of Rasputin's being influviated rather than incinerated, with the switch having two parts: influviation's being reliable and a volcano's not being nearby. The explanation is not legitimate, however, because its incineration scenario requires the radical rewriting of Rasputin's biology, which entails a more profound departure from reality than the incineration scenario in which there happened to be a crater, but no river, nearby. The plausibility requirement makes contrastive explanation potentially a far subtler affair than regular explanation; I leave the details to some other investigator.

11. Technically, you could say that Rasputin's influviation-not-incineration is explained by a contrast, namely, the unwieldy fact that a-river-but-not-a-volcano-was-present-rather-than-a-volcano-but-not-a-river.

12. See, for example, van Fraassen (1980), Garfinkel (1981), Hitchcock (1996), and, writing about causal claims rather than explicitly about explanation, Schaffer (2005).

## Chapter 6

1. I could have said that *c was a cause of e* is true just in case *c* appears in a standalone explanation for *e*, a formulation that differs from the formulation in the main text in three ways. First, the alternative formulation would include among the causes of *e* events that are explanatorily relevant to *e* only by way of a basing generalization, that is, only by way of an entanglement relation—an element of the kairetic account to be introduced in section 7.3. Second, it would include among the causes of *e* events that are a part of the explanatory framework (since when not represented by black boxes, these are technically part of a standalone explanation even though they do not thereby qualify as difference-makers). Third, it would exclude as causes of *e* difference-makers deemed irrelevant as a result of an accuracy/generality tradeoff (section 5.2), if such tradeoffs are genuinely possible. The first and second consequences are at odds with the way we use causal claims; it is less obvious, however, that the third is mistaken. I remain agnostic while adopting the formulation in the main text as my official position.

2. The strategies I suggest for handling preemption were originally advocated in Strevens (2007b).

3. After publishing this treatment of late preemption on Mackie's behalf in Strevens (2007b), I found that Hempel had given the same solution to a similar problem raised by Scriven; see Hempel (1965a, 420).

4. This class of examples was suggested to me by John Pollock and Christopher Hitchcock. For a Rasputin variant, consider a poisoning model that derives Rasputin's death regardless of whether he is alive at the time that the poison would do its work, on the grounds that he is either already dead or is alive but the poison then kills him.

5. I might add that such models can never deem Sylvie's throw or Rasputin's poisoning a difference-maker simpliciter; rather, they declare the difference-maker to be some disjunction in which the throw or the poisoning feature as disjuncts.

6. Compare Bennett (1988, 140), who would attribute the vase's breaking to the fact of its being struck by *at least one* cannonball.

7. The cohesion requirement, you will observe, limits the cases to which the above treatment of overdetermination can be applied.

8. This is close to the treatment offered by Paul (2000). Hall (2000, 205) worries that, if the way that the chair's ducking is caused is sufficiently different with the bite than without, this approach will fail. Suppose that the provost contracts goat-bite fever and so must order the dean to throw the cannonball. Does the bite make a difference then? The effect of Hall's revision is to transform the example into a case of switching, discussed in section 6.53 below.

9. A separate question is whether the fact about the hurling that makes a difference to the chair's continued existence is the same fact that causes the ducking. It seems to me that the answer is no: the former fact is much more general than the latter (though not strictly more general—see the fake-out example in the next paragraph, where the chair ducks but is killed anyway). This provides an alternative strategy for resisting framework-independent forestalled threat counterexamples to transitivity, a strategy familiar from the discussion of misconnection above. Schaffer's (2005) treatment of forestalled threats is broadly along these lines.

10. Counterexamples to transitivity that take the form of switchings are developed and discussed at some length in Hall (2000).

11. There is a very loose parallel between these first two kinds of causal relations and the "two concepts of causation" mooted by Hall (2004) and others.

12. A fourth category of causal relations might also be distinguished, namely the causal-explanatory relations pertinent to complex structured forms of explanation such as aggregative and contrastive explanation. These are the relations asserted by claims that cite differences or contrasts as causes and effects; for example, *The difference in metabolic rate caused one strain of bacteria to replace the other* (section 5.5) or *My having grown up in New Zealand rather than France caused me to order the meat pie rather than the frisée aux lardons* (section 5.6; see also Schaffer 2005). As I noted in chapter five, the explanatory interpretation of causal claims relieves us of an embarrassing commitment to a raw metaphysical relation having such confections as relata.

## Chapter 7

1. This is perhaps an overstatement. For example, in *The Structure of Science*, published in 1960, Ernest Nagel can be seen grappling with something close to the conjunction problem (Nagel 1979, 36–37).

2. Craver's (2007, chap. 4) "constitutive mechanistic explanation" also, perhaps, exemplifies the metaphysical approach; unfortunately, Craver's book appeared too late to receive the consideration it deserves here.

3. Though see the end of section 7.62

4. A comment on atomic stability. Certain isotopes of sodium may be unstable—instability and reactivity being, note, quite different things—or, if the number of neutrons is allowed to be anything you like, physically impossible. The kairetic treatment of sodium's reactivity sketched in the main text assumes implicitly that the scope of the abstracted model is restricted to those isotopes sufficiently stable that an average sodium atom will exist long enough to participate in chemical reactions. Does this mean that the more general fact of sodium's having about the right number of neutrons counts, because of its contribution to stability, as explanatorily relevant to its reactivity? In other words, does sodium's stability explain its reactivity? It does not. To be sure, if sodium were not at least slightly stable, it would have no chance to react. But you would not say of an extremely unstable substance that, in virtue of its instability, it is not reactive. Talk of reactivity supposes that the substance stays around long enough either to react or not to react, in the same way that talk of Rasputin's survival implies a threat to his continued existence. When explaining reactivity, then, stability ought to be considered as a part of the explanatory framework, as explained in section 5.3. It follows that the scope of the explanatory model should be restricted to stable isotopes of sodium, but neither stability nor the explainers of stability—including neutron number—should qualify as explainers of reactivity.

5. An alternative is to restrict the scope of Newton's law to the early life of the universe and to invoke a basing generalization asserting that the universe's initial conditions are entropic, from which the entropic nature of later, but not too much later, conditions is usually supposed to follow.

6. Philosophers of science have not, of course, always acknowledged the modal dimension of the raven generalization; Hempel (1945) famously took it to assert only the blackness of actual ravens.

7. The requirement that basing generalizations specify intrinsic properties of the relevant system may be further narrowed by causal presuppositions of the explanandum itself. If, for example, *All ravens are black* means roughly "There is something about ravens that causes them to be black," then at least one explanatory basing generalization must attribute an intrinsic property not merely to the raven ecosystem as a whole but to ravens in particular. The nature and scope of such additional requirements lies outside the general theory of regularity explanation.

8. There is, then, an alternative counterfactual-dependence test that I am not endorsing but that also declares hexing to be irrelevant to the blackness of hexed ravens. Rather than requiring a basing generalization's antecedent property to

pass the dependence test as a single unit, even when it is a composite such as hexed ravenhood, the alternative test splits the antecedent into component properties—such as hexedness and ravenhood—and requires each such property to pass the test individually. If you adopt this test, explanatory relevance will depend in part on the facts as to how to divide an antecedent property into its proper parts, something that my official test avoids—much to my relief.

9. Two qualifications. First, the tyrosinase gene is perhaps an infelicitous choice, being a regular fixture in life on earth. But other parts of the mechanism for raven blackness are more particular to ravens, and so they are less likely to survive the loss of ravenhood.

   Second, it may be that counterfactuals involving such dramatic changes as a species switch are not evaluated by inspecting causal processes that lead in a relatively lawlike way to the transformation. Nevertheless, I believe that the explanation why the counterfactual nonraven may lack the gene, given in the following paragraph in the main text, is broadly correct.

10. The relation between the robustness of a generalization and the robustness of the basing pattern that is its ground is not entirely straightforward; see Strevens (2008b).

11. It is not true that there will always be, within the set of manipulations that create an $F$ where there was none before, a significant subset that in so doing create $P$-hood along with $F$-ness.

12. I happily concede that there is the bare possibility of a "demon" standing over a particular $F/P$ pair, determined and able to destroy its $P$-hood if the course of events deviates in any way at all from a certain fully specified schema that is uniquely satisfied by the actual world. Nothing in what follows is materially compromised by this observation.

13. Jackson and Pettit do not provide a precise definition of programming, but on any plausible interpretation of their work, the objections that follow will apply. I should note that if they were to apply the notion of programming to the raven case, they would perhaps not claim that ravenhood programs for $P$, but rather that it programs for a disjunction of properties including $P$, all causing blackness.

14. Accuracy, as you will see in section 10.24, should be understood for these purposes as measuring the fit between the subsuming pattern and the subsumed instances. Since basing patterns are understood as actual patterns of coinstantiation in the world, there is no sense in which they could fail to match the world as a whole.

15. It is less easy to construct a case in which there is no robust connection going the other way, that is, a case in which, had circumstances been even slightly

different, $x$ would not have had $P$. This is for the reason given in section 7.34: because of the conservatism of the rules for evaluating counterfactuals, whenever something has a property $P$, it has it robustly at least to a small extent (though see note 12).

16. One approach to regularity explanation that I particularly regret being unable to address is dimensional explanation (Lange forthcoming).

17. Of course this is not strictly correct, because of gravitational forces and so on—it is rather that the rest of the basin is not the right kind of causal influence. If you prefer, think, for the sake of the example, of a ball in a world with a stripped-down corpuscular physics in which the rest of the basin exerts absolutely no influence on the ball. The equilibrium explanation of the ball's ultimate fate is just as good in this world as in our world, I suggest.

18. In the unusual circumstances where there is a disposition but no such tendency, it is a more complex tendency that is to be explained (Lewis 1997).

19. What kind of causal influence is not, in our world, a Newtonian force? Two examples. First, Sober (1984) and other philosophers of biology have suggested that natural selection can be understood as a kind of non-Newtonian force. Second, if the stress-energy equation in general relativity is regarded as describing the causal influence of matter on the curvature of space, the influence in question is presumably not Newtonian force. I leave it to the causal metaphysicists to decide whether these are legitimate examples of causal influence. (I myself have higher hopes for the latter case than for the former.)

20. Overly simple principally because theoretical terms frequently lack definitions: their reference is, I think, fixed in more subtle ways.

21. What is explained is why integral spin particles cannot be restricted, unlike the fermions to which the principle principally applies, to antisymmetric states.

22. Although it will make no difference to what follows, I include as a part of the mechanism not only those initial conditions and facets of the fundamental laws described by an explanatory model's setup but also the specification, in the model's follow-through, of the way in which the setup causally entails the explanatory target, representing the mechanism's manner of operation. See note 2 of chapter 4.

23. Though the thesis is put forward as capturing the cognitive significance of any causal law, the arguments for the thesis are confined to laws associating biological taxa and chemical substances with their characteristic properties.

24. To "deploy a generalization as a covering law" to explain an instance is to cite both the generalization itself and certain appropriate initial conditions. For example, the covering-law explanation of a raven's blackness cites both the covering law itself—*All ravens are black*—and the ravenhood of the bird in

question. The law on its own, then, without the initial conditions, need not and does not explain its instances.

25. I say *perhaps* because it is unclear to me how the barometer generalization should or even could be deployed as a covering law; in particular, it is unclear to me what initial conditions should be added to the generalization to complete a covering law explanation of a particular storm/barometer drop coincidence.

## Chapter 8

1. McMullin (1985) surveys various kinds of idealization, causal and other. Barr (1974) is an early discussion of idealization from a DN perspective, drawing on Hempel's notion of approximative DN explanation (Hempel 1965a, 344–345). Some recent writers have been more concerned, as I am, not merely to excuse idealization, but to find a positive explanatory role for it to play (see the essays in Shanks 1998, e.g., Hartmann 1998).

   In this book, I can only touch on the rich literature on idealization that is not exclusively concerned, as I am here, with explanation. In addition to the work cited in what follows, see Giere (1988), Cartwright (1999), and Sklar (2000), among others.

2. Nowak does refer to the factors that are falsified in an idealizing explanation as "inessential," but in his theory, there seems to be no qualitative difference, for explanatory or any other purposes, between inessential and essential factors: "essentiality" is a matter of degree. The quality of an explanation, on Nowak's view, is proportional to the essentiality of the factors cited; however, since he holds that idealization implies a failure to cite some factors of nonzero essentiality, idealizing explanations can always be improved by removing the idealizations. Hence, his doctrine that the perfect explanation of a phenomenon will be idealization-free.

3. A logical empiricist would not say, of course, that the world is nonmathematical. That would be a category mistake. "Mathematical" is something that only a system of representation can be; thus, it is not the sort of property that reality either does or does not possess.

4. The sophisticated treatments more or less follow Clausius (1857), although Clausius's demonstration of A-2 is not entirely general.

5. Boyle's, Newton's, and Bernoulli's explanations are anthologized in Brush (2003).

6. At least, that is how I read Bernoulli, but he is quite vague. It is possible that he thought the assumption did not really matter; see section 8.34 below.

7. To do this, he need only examine, of course, the cells that lie next to the container walls. Pressure will be proportional to the number of impacts against the wall per cell multiplied by the number of cells per unit area of wall. The first is inversely proportional to the distance between the opposing walls of the cell, the second to the area of one wall of the cell. Multiplied together these give the volume of the cell.

8. Collisions might appear in an elongated explanation of Boyle's law that characterizes the process by which a gas reaches equilibrium. The explanations I consider in the main text assume that the gas is already at equilibrium.

9. Bernoulli gas molecules are uniformly distributed in space, but their positions are perhaps not stochastically independent of one another. Uniformity is sufficient for the textbook derivation of Boyle's law.

10. Or so it is thought; perhaps the causal order of things in general relativity is not as clear as I assume here.

## Chapter 9

1. However, Railton at one point writes of probabilities "bringing the world's explananda about" (1978, 223).

2. This is the standard way of talking probabilistically about radioactive decay. It is not entirely in accord with the standard way of talking about probability in quantum mechanics, the "collapse interpretation," on which atoms cannot be said to have decayed until the decay is measured. On the collapse interpretation, you can nevertheless say that, at the end of 1620 years, there is a high probability that a measurement of a radium sample will show that almost exactly half of the sample has decayed, which is sufficient for my purposes here.

   The same cautionary remark about probability and measurement applies to the description of quantum tunneling, to follow.

3. I have given an explanation of the gas's behavior in the Boltzmannian vein; an explanation in the Gibbsian vein directs attention away from probability distributions over the positions of individual particles and toward probability distributions over the possible configurations of the gas as a whole. The two explanations have in common the attribution of a high probability to the event of the gas's filling the vacuum. For a philosophical perspective on these and many other issues in the foundations of statistical mechanics, see Sklar (1993).

4. Here I read Darwinian arguments as involving a kind of informal probabilistic reasoning (Strevens 1998, 2003b).

## Chapter 10

1. The independence assumption makes for a simple and intuitive exposition, but for reasons given in Strevens (2003b), a far weaker assumption about a microconstant process's initial conditions will suffice to explain its production of a Bernoulli pattern, namely, the assumption that the relevant joint initial condition distribution is macroperiodic. (A joint distribution represents probabilities of initial conditions not for individual trials but for sets of trials. The joint distribution for a group of ten spins on the wheel of fortune, for example, will give the probability that any particular set of ten initial speeds serves as the initial conditions for the ten spins.) The weaker assumption allows a certain degree of correlation between trials; it is consistent, for example, with a fast spin speed's being more likely when the immediately preceding spin was also fast.

2. And provided that the initial conditions are probabilistically independent, or at least jointly macroperiodic—assumptions for simplicity's sake subsumed under the term *macroperiodic*, as specified in the previous subsection; see also note 1.

3. See von Plato (1983) and Strevens (2003b, §2.A) for the mathematical and philosophical history, respectively.

4. Why is the paint scheme a causal influence on the frequency? Because it figures as a background condition in fundamental physics' causal story as to why an outcome is *red*. It is therefore a causal influence in the wide, boundary condition–including sense defined in section 1.42.

   You might worry that only the color of the paint at the very points indicated by the wheel of fortune's arrow plays a part in the causal story. There is something to this; the full paint scheme enters into the explanation of a particular outcome not as a part of a singular causal story but in a basing generalization, in the same way as the complete basin, and not just a basin filigree, enters into the explanation of a ball's coming to rest at its bottom, as explained in section 7.41.

5. Either model may contain other, nonprobabilistic basing generalizations as well; see note 4.

6. Some further, albeit brief, comments on the way in which this fact affects the strike ratio are made in Strevens (1998).

7. There is more reason to expect a simplex probability distribution, that is, a distribution that combines both simple and complex aspects (section 9.3). Such a distribution would be the result of the upward "percolation" of quantum probabilities; for further discussion, see Strevens (2003b, 318–319).

8. In the main text, I write as though the outcomes over which the frequency-based distribution is defined are sets of trials; it would be more elegant to think of the distribution as either a macroperiodic joint distribution or an IID distribution over individual trials. Any of these distributions is equally able to represent macroperiodicity's prevalence.

9. This cohesion with respect to entanglement is quite likely not, I should point out, a variety of causal cohesion: the "pushing around" of different kinds of standard quantities by perturbations will take many different causal forms.

10. Even the short-term disorder in a microconstancy-produced sequence of outcomes is due, I might add, more to features of the deterministic mechanism than to the nonuniversal aspect of the basing generalization.

11. These properties are linked: the first entails the second.

12. What really matters is that the joint distribution is macroperiodic in the direction of $y$.

13. It is possible that the facts determining that the swift-recovery strike ratio varies from .5 to .75 are also sufficient to determine the exact strike ratios cited in (2); in this case, (2) specifies nothing that is not already specified in the quasiprobabilistic model, and so the exact probabilistic model's only flaw is its specification of the probability distribution in (1).

14. By contrast, there is no macroperiodicity-like property that a quasiprobability distribution might possess, that is, no property that implies, in conjunction with microconstancy, a frequency equal to the relevant strike ratio (unless the quasiprobabilities are very close to exact probabilities).

15. The law, and perhaps the statistical regularity, should have the same proviso as the law of macroperiodicity, stated at the end of section 10.26.

16. There are of course entanglement instances as well as patterns of entanglement. If you can think of a way to identify the initial-condition component of a single-case probability with a macroperiodicity-involving entanglement instance rather than a broader pattern of macroperiodicity entanglement, thereby making the entire probability intrinsic, more or less, to the probabilistic setup, I will buy you a drink. Good luck!

17. For a more sophisticated account than I have offered here of what it is for a probability to be "based in microconstancy," see the notion of *true probability* in Strevens (2003b, §2.44).

## Chapter 11

1. The passage from Railton might appear to suggest that a process is robust just in case variation in initial conditions *never* causes the outcome to change. If

this were true, channeling processes would not be robust. But Railton does not mean to require exceptionlessness: he introduces robustness in the discussion of the systems of classical statistical mechanics, which are robust only in the sense that *almost* all variations leave the typical explanandum unchanged.

2. Although this is Batterman's official view on the importance of robustness (see especially Batterman 2002, pp. 57–59), he favors an approach to explanation similar in spirit to my own, and so perhaps would agree with the observations about the importance of robustness that I am about to present.

3. Better, explanatory weight should be equal to the probability of making a difference multiplied by the amount of difference made, when a difference is made; such a measure of weight will follow from an appropriate definition of accuracy. The examples in the main text are all cases where the degree of the difference made is 100%, simplifying the issue for expository purposes.

4. In this particular example, if the trigger fails, there is no causal connection between placing the bomb and the eventual death. But it is easy to devise a similar case where such a connection exists; thus, causal influence is not a reliable sign of difference-making.

5. I assume that detonation and ricochet are mutually exclusive. But what if they are not? In a case where both models are veridical—the bullet both sets off the bomb and ricochets, striking Rasputin—which explanation is correct? If the explosion and bullet wound cause death simultaneously, you have a case of overdetermination (section 6.24). If not, you have preemption, so one of the models cannot be veridical (section 6.2). For the bomb to kill Rasputin, he must be alive, a background condition not shown in figure 11.1. If the bullet kills him first, this condition is violated and so the model in which the explosion kills him is not veridical. Parallel considerations apply to the ricochet.

6. For microconstant processes, then, there is a rough correspondence between non-probability-raising critical events and permutators, on the one hand, and probability-raising critical events and strike factors, on the other—rough because the notion of a critical event is itself rough.

7. There is some appeal to the view that even when the overall probability of the accident is very low, probability-raising factors such as my bad driving are explanatorily more relevant than probabilistically neutral factors such as my thanking my host. I suggest that this is so just in case the explanation is conducted relative to a framework within which the probability of the accident is high and so a probabilistic explanation is appropriate. In other words, what is explained is the fact that I collided with the unicyclist *given that* through sheer

bad luck, our timing determined that we would have a dangerously close encounter.

8. Kitcher cites Isaac Levi and David Papineau as inspiration for this argument.

## Chapter 12

1. It is, of course, a complex matter, in some cases, to see how different probabilities for survival and reproduction add up to an overall advantage or lack thereof.

2. I exaggerate somewhat; it is possible to explain why some alleles were more likely candidates for extinction than others, in the case where there are fitness differences between alleles.

3. In the case of drift what matters is not so much getting the equivalent of a long run of *red* but rather the equivalent of a long run of outcomes with a sufficiently high proportion of *red*.

4. The extent of $P$ among my and others' beliefs that it is raining will affect the generality of the corresponding basing generalization and thus the degree of the belief property's relevance, but not the fact that there exists such a generalization and thus not the bare fact of relevance itself.

## Chapter 13

1. On this way of characterizing accuracy, see note 4 of chapter 1.

# References

Achinstein, P. (1983). *The Nature of Explanation*. Oxford University Press, Oxford.

———. (1985). The pragmatic character of explanation. In P. D. Asquith and P. Kitcher (eds.), *Proceedings of the 1984 Biennial Meeting of the Philosophy of Science Association*, volume 2, pp. 275–292. Philosophy of Science Association, East Lansing, MI.

Anderson, J. (1962). The problem of causality. In *Studies in Empirical Philosophy*. Angus & Robertson, Sydney.

Armstrong, D. M. (1997). *A World of States of Affairs*. Cambridge University Press, Cambridge.

Atran, S. (1995). Classifying nature across cultures. In E. E. Smith and D. N. Osherson (eds.), *An Invitation to Cognitive Science: Thinking*. MIT Press, Cambridge, MA.

Barr, W. F. (1974). A pragmatic analysis of idealizations in physics. *Philosophy of Science* 41:48–64.

Batterman, R. W. (2002). *The Devil in the Details: Asymptotic Reasoning in Explanation, Reduction, and Emergence*. Oxford University Press, Oxford.

Beatty, J. (1995). The evolutionary contingency thesis. In G. Wolters, J. G. Lennox, and P. McLaughlin (eds.), *Concepts, Theories, and Rationality in the Biological Sciences*, pp. 45–81. University of Pittsburgh Press, Pittsburgh.

Bennett, J. (1988). *Events and Their Names*. Hackett, Indianapolis, IN.

———. (2003). *A Philosophical Guide to Conditionals*. Oxford University Press, Oxford.

Block, N. (1990). Can the mind change the world? In G. Boolos (ed.), *Meaning and Method: Essays in Honor of Hilary Putnam*. Cambridge University Press, Cambridge.

Bromberger, S. (1965). An approach to explanation. In R. J. Butler (ed.), *Analytical Philosophy*, volume 2, pp. 72–105. Oxford University Press, Oxford.

———. (1966). Why-questions. In R. G. Colodny (ed.), *Mind and Cosmos*. University of Pittsburgh Press, Pittsburgh.

Brush, S. (2003). *The Kinetic Theory of Gases: An Anthology of Classic Papers with Historical Commentary*. Imperial College Press, London.

Campbell, J. K., M. O'Rourke, and H. S. Silverstein (eds.). (2007). *Causation and Explanation*, volume 4 of *Topics in Contemporary Philosophy*. MIT Press, Cambridge, MA.

Cartwright, N. (1983). The simulacrum account of explanation. In *How the Laws of Physics Lie*. Oxford University Press, Oxford.

———. (1999). *The Dappled World: A Study of the Boundaries of Science*. Cambridge University Press, Cambridge.

Clausius, R. (1857). Ueber die Art der Bewegung, welch wir Wärme nennen. *Annalen der Physik* 100:353–380. English translation reprinted in Brush (2003).

Coffa, A. (1974). Hempel's ambiguity. *Synthese* 28:141–163.

Craver, C. F. (2007). *Explaining the Brain: Mechanisms and the Mosaic Unity of Neuroscience*. Oxford University Press, Oxford.

Cummins, R. (1975). Functional analysis. *Journal of Philosophy* 72:741–764.

———. (1983). *The Nature of Psychological Explanation*. MIT Press, Cambridge, MA.

Davidson, D. (1967). Causal relations. *Journal of Philosophy* 64:691–703. Reprinted in Davidson (1980).

———. (1969). The individuation of events. In Rescher (1969), pp. 216–234. Reprinted in Davidson (1980).

———. (1980). *Essays on Actions and Events*. Oxford University Press, Oxford.

Dennett, D. (1987). *The Intentional Stance*. MIT Press, Cambridge, MA.

Dowe, P. (2000). *Physical Causation*. Cambridge University Press, Cambridge.

Duhem, P. (1954). *The Aim and Structure of Physical Theory*. Translated by P. P. Wiener. Princeton University Press, Princeton, NJ.

Dupré, J. (1993). *The Disorder of Things*. Harvard University Press, Cambridge, MA.

Ebbing, D. D. (1987). *General Chemistry*. Second edition. Houghton Mifflin, Boston.

Elga, A. (2007). Isolation and folk physics. In H. Price and R. Corry (eds.), *Causation, Physics and the Constitution of Reality: Russell's Republic Revisited*, pp. 106–119. Oxford University Press, Oxford.

Fair, D. (1979). Causation and the flow of energy. *Erkenntnis* 14:219–250.

Fetzer, J. (1971). Dispositional probabilities. *Boston Studies in the Philosophy of Science* 8:473–482.

———. (1974). A single case propensity theory of explanation. *Synthese* 28:171–198.

———. (1981). *Scientific Knowledge: Causation, Explanation, and Corroboration*. D. Reidel, Dordrecht.

Field, H. (2003). Causation in a physical world. In M. Loux and D. Zimmerman (eds.), *Oxford Handbook of Metaphysics*. Oxford University Press, Oxford.

Fodor, J. A. (1974). Special sciences. *Synthese* 28:97–115.

———. (1989). Making mind matter more. *Philosophical Topics* 17:59–79. Reprinted in *A Theory of Content and Other Essays*, chap. 5, pp. 137–159. MIT Press, Cambridge, MA, 1990.

van Fraassen, B. C. (1980). *The Scientific Image*. Oxford University Press, Oxford.

———. (1989). *Laws and Symmetry*. Oxford University Press, Oxford.

Friedman, M. (1974). Explanation and scientific understanding. *Journal of Philosophy* 71:5–19.

Garfinkel, A. (1981). *Forms of Explanation*. Yale University Press, New Haven, CT.

Gasking, D. (1955). Causation and recipes. *Mind* 64:479–487.

Gelman, S. A. and K. E. Kremer. (1991). Understanding natural cause: Children's explanations of how objects and their properties originate. *Child Development* 62:396–414.

Giere, R. N. (1988). *Explaining Science: A Cognitive Approach*. University of Chicago Press, Chicago.

Gluck, S. and S. Gimbel. (1997). An intervening cause counterexample to Railton's DNP model of explanation. *Philosophy of Science* 64:692–697.

Glymour, B. (2001). Selection, indeterminism, and evolutionary theory. *Philosophy of Science* 68:518–535.

———. (2007). In defense of explanatory deductivism. In Campbell et al. (2007).

Glymour, C. (1980). *Theory and Evidence*. Princeton University Press, Princeton, NJ.

Goodman, N. (1971). Seven strictures on similarity. In L. Foster and J. W. Swanson (eds.), *Experience and Theory*, pp. 19–29. Duckworth, London.

Gopnik, A. (2000). Explanation as orgasm and the drive for causal knowledge: The function, evolution, and phenomenology of the theory formation system. In Keil and Wilson (2000).

Grant, P. R. (1986). *Ecology and Evolution of Darwin's Finches*. Princeton University Press, Princeton, NJ.

Hall, N. (2000). Causation and the price of transitivity. *Journal of Philosophy* 97:198–222.

———. (2004). Two concepts of causation. In J. Collins, N. Hall, and L. A. Paul (eds.), *Causation and Counterfactuals*. MIT Press, Cambridge, MA.

———. (2007). Structural equations and causation. *Philosophical Studies* 132:109–136.

Halpern, J. Y. and J. Pearl. (2005). Causes and explanations: A structural-model approach. Part 1: Causes. *British Journal for the Philosophy of Science* 56:843–887.

Hanson, N. R. (1958). *Patterns of Discovery*. Cambridge University Press, Cambridge.

Hartmann, S. (1998). Idealization in quantum field theory. In Shanks (1998).

Hempel, C. G. (1945). Studies in the logic of confirmation. *Mind* 54:1–26, 97–121. Reprinted in Hempel (1965b), chap. 1.

———. (1965a). Aspects of scientific explanation. In Hempel (1965b), chap. 12, pp. 331–496.

———. (1965b). *Aspects of Scientific Explanation*. Free Press, New York.

Hempel, C. G. and P. Oppenheim. (1948). Studies in the logic of explanation. *Philosophy of Science* 15:135–175. Reprinted in Hempel (1965b), chap. 10.

Hitchcock, C. R. (1993). A generalized probabilistic theory of causal relevance. *Synthese* 97:335–364.

———. (1995). Salmon on explanatory relevance. *Philosophy of Science* 62:304–320.

———. (1996). The role of contrast in causal and explanatory claims. *Synthese* 107:395–419.

———. (1999). Contrastive explanation and the demons of determinism. *British Journal for the Philosophy of Science* 50:585–612.

———. (2001a). The intransitivity of causation revealed in equations and graphs. *Journal of Philosophy* 98:273–299.

———. (2001b). A tale of two effects. *Philosophical Review* 110:361–396.

Hitchcock, C. R. and J. Woodward. (2003). Explanatory generalizations, part II: Plumbing explanatory depth. *Noûs* 37:181–199.

Horan, B. (1994). The statistical character of evolutionary theory. *Philosophy of Science* 61:76–95.

Humphreys, P. (1981). Aleatory explanations. *Synthese* 48:225–232.

———. (1989). *The Chances of Explanation*. Princeton University Press, Princeton, NJ.

Jackson, F. and P. Pettit. (1988). Functionalism and broad content. *Mind* 97:381–400.

———. (1990). Program explanation: A general perspective. *Analysis* 50:107–117.

———. (1992a). In defense of explanatory ecumenism. *Economics and Philosophy* 8:1–21.

———. (1992b). Structural explanation in social theory. In D. Charles and K. Lennon (eds.), *Reduction, Explanation, and Realism*, pp. 97–131. Oxford University Press, Oxford.

Jeffrey, R. C. (1969). Statistical explanation vs. statistical inference. In Rescher (1969), pp. 104–113. Reprinted in Salmon et al. (1971).

Keil, F. C. (2006). Explanation and understanding. *Annual Review of Psychology* 57:227–254.

Keil, F. C. and R. A. Wilson (eds.). (2000). *Explanation and Cognition*. MIT Press, Cambridge, MA.

Kim, J. (1971). Causes and events: Mackie on causation. *Journal of Philosophy* 68:426–441.

———. (1973). Causation, nomic subsumption, and the concept of event. *Journal of Philosophy* 70:217–236.

———. (1992). Multiple realization and the metaphysics of reduction. *Philosophy and Phenomenological Research* 52:1–26.

Kitcher, P. (1981). Explanatory unification. *Philosophy of Science* 48:507–531.

———. (1984). 1953 and all that: A tale of two sciences. *Philosophical Review* 93:335–373.

———. (1989). Explanatory unification and the causal structure of the world. In P. Kitcher and W. C. Salmon (eds.), *Scientific Explanation*, volume 13 of *Minnesota Studies in the Philosophy of Science*, pp. 410–505. University of Minnesota Press, Minneapolis.

Kitcher, P. and W. C. Salmon. (1987). Van Fraassen on explanation. *Journal of Philosophy* 84:315–330.

Kyburg, H. E. (1965). Comment. *Philosophy of Science* 32:147–151.

Lange, M. (2000). *Natural Laws in Scientific Practice*. Oxford University Press, Oxford.

———. (forthcoming). Dimensional explanations. *Noûs*.

Lepore, E. and B. Loewer. (1987). Mind matters. *Journal of Philosophy* 84:630–642.

Levine, I. N. (2002). *Physical Chemistry*. Fifth edition. McGraw-Hill, New York.

Lewis, D. (1973a). Causation. *Journal of Philosophy* 70:556–567. Reprinted in Lewis (1986b).

———. (1973b). *Counterfactuals*. Harvard University Press, Cambridge, MA.

———. (1986a). Causal explanation. In Lewis (1986b), pp. 214–240.

———. (1986b). *Philosophical Papers*, volume 2. Oxford University Press, Oxford.

———. (1986c). Postscript to "Causation." In Lewis (1986b), pp. 172–213.

———. (1997). Finkish dispositions. *Philosophical Quarterly* 47:143–158.

———. (2000). Causation as influence. *Journal of Philosophy* 97:182–197.

Lipton, P. (2004). *Inference to the Best Explanation*. Second edition. Routledge, London.

Lombrozo, T. (2006). The structure and function of explanations. *Trends in Cognitive Sciences* 10:464–470.

Lombrozo, T. and S. Carey. (2006). Functional explanation and the function of explanation. *Cognition* 99:167–204.

Machamer, P., L. Darden, and C. F. Craver. (2000). Thinking about mechanisms. *Philosophy of Science* 67:1–25.

Mackie, J. (1974). *The Cement of the Universe*. Oxford University Press, Oxford.

Maudlin, T. (1994). *Quantum Non-Locality and Relativity*. Blackwell, Oxford.

———. (2007). *The Metaphysics within Physics*. Oxford University Press, Oxford.

McDermott, M. (1995). Redundant causation. *British Journal for the Philosophy of Science* 46:523–544.

McGrath, S. (2005). Causation by omission: A dilemma. *Philosophical Studies* 123:125–148.

McMullin, E. (1985). Galilean idealization. *Studies in History and Philosophy of Science* 16:247–273.

McQuarrie, D. A. and J. D. Simon. (1997). *Physical Chemistry: A Molecular Approach*. University Science Books, Sausalito, CA.

Menzies, P. (1996). Probabilistic causation and the preemption problem. *Mind* 105:85–117.

Menzies, P. and H. Price. (1993). Causation as a secondary quality. *British Journal for the Philosophy of Science* 44:187–203.

Mill, J. S. (1973). *A System of Logic*. 8th edition. Routledge, London.

Mitchell, S. (2002). Dimensions of scientific law. *Philosophy of Science* 67:242–265.

Nagel, E. (1979). *The Structure of Science*. Hackett, Indianapolis, IN.

Nowak, L. (1992). The idealizational approach to science: A survey. In J. Brzezinski and L. Nowak (eds.), *Idealization III: Approximation and Truth*, volume 25 of *Poznań Studies in the Philosophy of the Sciences and the Humanities*, pp. 9–63. Rodopi, Amsterdam and Atlanta, GA.

Paul, L. A. (2000). Aspect causation. *Journal of Philosophy* 97:235–256.

Pearl, J. (2000). *Causality: Models, Reasoning, and Inference*. Cambridge University Press, Cambridge.

von Plato, J. (1983). The method of arbitrary functions. *British Journal for the Philosophy of Science* 34:37–47.

Putnam, H. (1975). Philosophy and our mental life. In *Mind, Language and Reality: Philosophical Papers*, volume 2. Cambridge University Press, Cambridge.

Quine, W. V. O. (1960). *Word and Object*. MIT Press, Cambridge, MA.

Railton, P. (1978). A deductive-nomological model of probabilistic explanation. *Philosophy of Science* 45:206–226.

———. (1981). Probability, explanation, and information. *Synthese* 48:233–256.

Reichenbach, H. (1956). *The Direction of Time*. University of California Press, Berkeley, CA.

Rescher, N. (ed.). (1969). *Essays in Honor of Carl G. Hempel*. D. Reidel, Dordrecht.

Rosenberg, A. (1992). *Economics—Mathematical Politics or Science of Diminishing Returns?* University of Chicago Press, Chicago.

———. (1994). *Instrumental Biology or The Disunity of Science*. University of Chicago Press, Chicago.

Salmon, W. C. (1970). Statistical explanation. In R. G. Colodny (ed.), *The Nature and Function of Scientific Theories*, pp. 173–231. University of Pittsburgh Press, Pittsburgh. Reprinted in Salmon et al. (1971).

———. (1979). Postscript: Laws in deductive-nomological explanation. In W. C. Salmon (ed.), *Hans Reichenbach: Logical Empiricist*, pp. 691–694. D. Reidel, Dordrecht.

———. (1984). *Explanation and the Causal Structure of the World*. Princeton University Press, Princeton, NJ.

———. (1990a). Causal propensities: Statistical causality versus aleatory causality. *Topoi* 9:95–100.

———. (1990b). *Four Decades of Scientific Explanation*. University of Minnesota Press, Minneapolis.

———. (1997). Causality and explanation: A reply to two critiques. *Philosophy of Science* 64:461–477.

Salmon, W. C., R. Jeffrey, and J. Greeno. (1971). *Statistical Explanation and Statistical Relevance*. University of Pittsburgh Press, Pittsburgh.

Schaffer, J. (1999). Causation by disconnection. *Philosophy of Science* 67:285–300.

———. (2001). Causes as probability raisers of processes. *Journal of Philosophy* 98:75–92.

———. (2003). Overdetermining causes. *Philosophical Studies* 114:23–45.

———. (2005). Contrastive causation. *Philosophical Review* 114:327–358.

Scriven, M. (1959). Explanation and prediction in evolutionary theory. *Science* 30:477–482.

Shanks, N. (ed.). (1998). *Idealization IX: Idealization in Contemporary Physics*, volume 63 of *Poznań Studies in the Philosophy of the Sciences and the Humanities*. Rodopi, Amsterdam and Atlanta, GA.

Simon, H. A. (1996). *The Sciences of the Artificial*. Third edition. MIT Press, Cambridge, MA.

Sklar, L. (1993). *Physics and Chance*. Cambridge University Press, Cambridge.

———. (2000). *Theory and Truth: Philosophical Critique within Foundational Science*. Oxford University Press, Oxford.

Sober, E. (1983). Equilibrium explanation. *Philosophical Studies* 43:201–210.

———. (1984). *The Nature of Selection*. MIT Press, Cambridge, MA.

Stich, S. P. (1978). Autonomous psychology and the belief-desire thesis. *The Monist* 61:573–591.

Strevens, M. (1998). Inferring probabilities from symmetries. *Noûs* 32:231–246.

———. (2000a). Do large probabilities explain better? *Philosophy of Science* 67:366–390.

———. (2000b). The essentialist aspect of naive theories. *Cognition* 74:149–175.

———. (2003a). Against Lewis's new theory of causation. *Pacific Philosophical Quarterly* 84:398–412.

———. (2003b). *Bigger than Chaos: Understanding Complexity through Probability*. Harvard University Press, Cambridge, MA.

———. (2004). The causal and unification accounts of explanation unified – causally. *Noûs* 38:154–176.

———. (2005). How are the sciences of complex systems possible? *Philosophy of Science* 72:531–556.

———. (2006). Scientific explanation. In D. M. Borchert (ed.), *Encyclopedia of Philosophy*, second edition. Macmillan Reference USA, Detroit.

———. (2007a). Essay review of Woodward, *Making Things Happen*. *Philosophy and Phenomenological Research* 74:233–249.

———. (2007b). Mackie remixed. In Campbell et al. (2007).

———. (2007c). Why represent causal relations? In A. Gopnik and L. Schulz (eds.), *Causal Learning: Psychology, Philosophy, Computation*. Oxford University Press, New York.

———. (2008a). Comments on Woodward, *Making Things Happen*. *Philosophy and Phenomenological Research* 77:171–192.

———. (2008b). Physically contingent laws and counterfactual support. *Philosopher's Imprint*, 8(8).

———. (forthcoming). Probabilistic explanation. In L. Sklar (ed.), *Handbook of Philosophy of Science*. Oxford University Press, Oxford.

———. (manuscript). The explanatory role of irreducible properties. Available at http://www.strevens.org/research/onlinepapers.shtml

Suppes, P. (1970). *A Probabilistic Theory of Causality*. North-Holland, Amsterdam.

Thomson, J. J. (2003). Causation: Omissions. *Philosophy and Phenomenological Research* 66:81–103.

Volterra, V. (1926). Fluctuations in the abundance of a species considered mathematically. *Nature* 118:558–560.

Walsh, D. M., T. Lewens, and A. Ariew. (2002). The trials of life: Natural selection and random drift. *Philosophy of Science* 69:452–473.

Waters, C. K. (1998). Causal regularities in the biological world of contingent distributions. *Biology and Philosophy* 13:5–36.

Weinberg, S. (1995). *The Quantum Theory of Fields: Foundations*. Cambridge University Press, Cambridge.

Weisberg, M. (2003). *When Less is More: Tradeoffs and Idealization in Model Building*. Ph.D. thesis, Stanford University.

Wilson, J. Q. and J. Petersilia. (2002). *Crime: Public Policies for Crime Control*. ICS Press, San Francisco.

Wimsatt, W. (1981). Robustness, reliability, and overdetermination. In M. Brewer and B. Collins (eds.), *Scientific Inquiry and the Social Sciences*, pp. 124–163. Jossey-Bass, San Francisco.

Woodward, J. (2003). *Making Things Happen: A Theory of Causal Explanation*. Oxford University Press, Oxford.

# Index

Harvard University Press is a member of Green Press Initiative
(greenpressinitiative.org), a nonprofit organization working to
help publishers and printers increase their use of recycled paper
and decrease their use of fiber derived from endangered forests.
This book was printed on recycled paper containing 30%
post-consumer waste and processed chlorine free.